PHOTOGRAPHING CIVIL DISOBEDIENCE

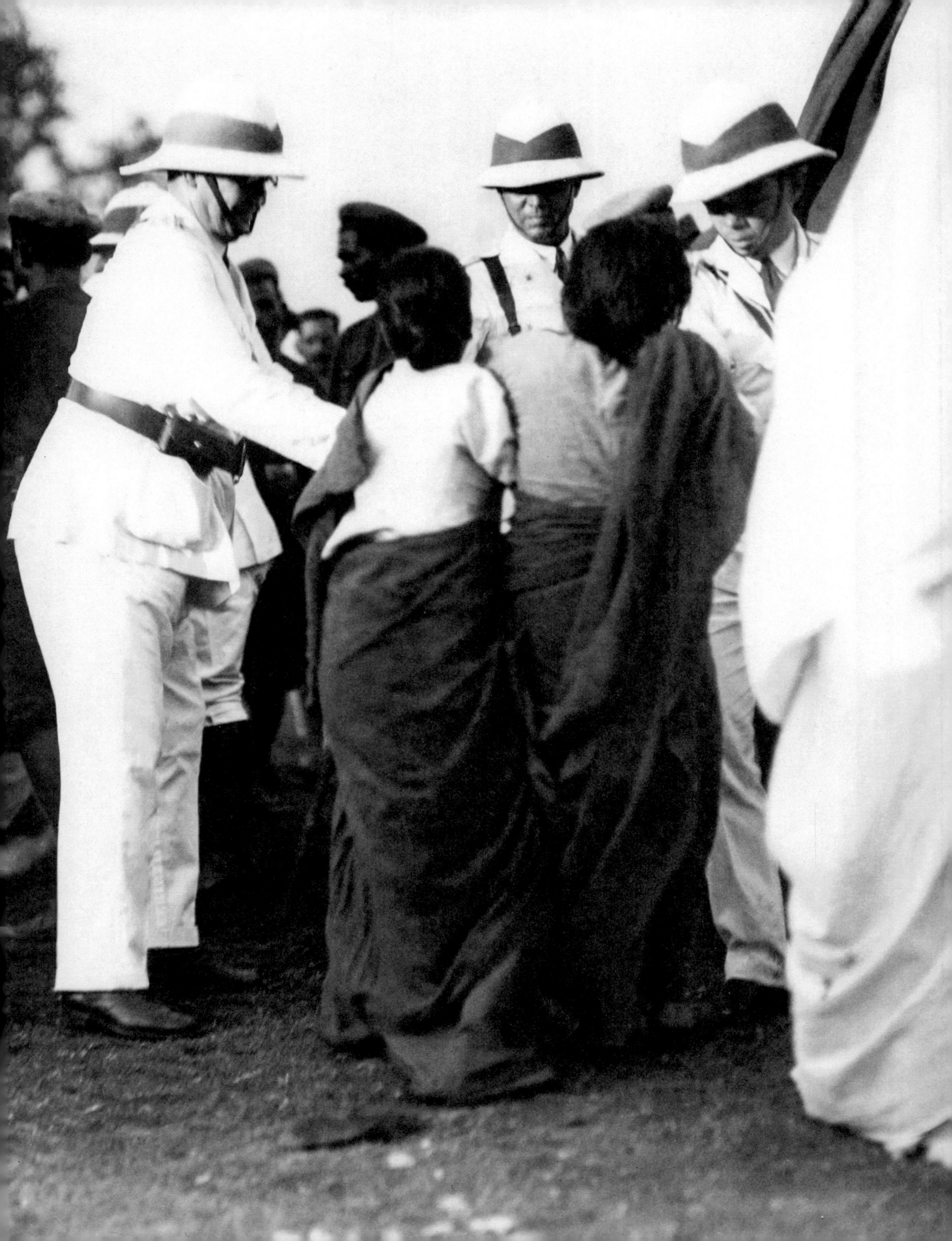

K.L. NURSEY'S OLD CONGRESS PARTY ALBUM

PHOTOGRAPHING CIVIL DISOBEDIENCE

Bombay 1930–1931

Edited by **Avrati Bhatnagar** and **Sumathi Ramaswamy**

Preface by **Rahaab Allana**

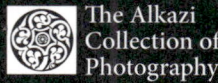
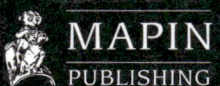

The Alkazi Collection of Photography in association with Mapin Publishing

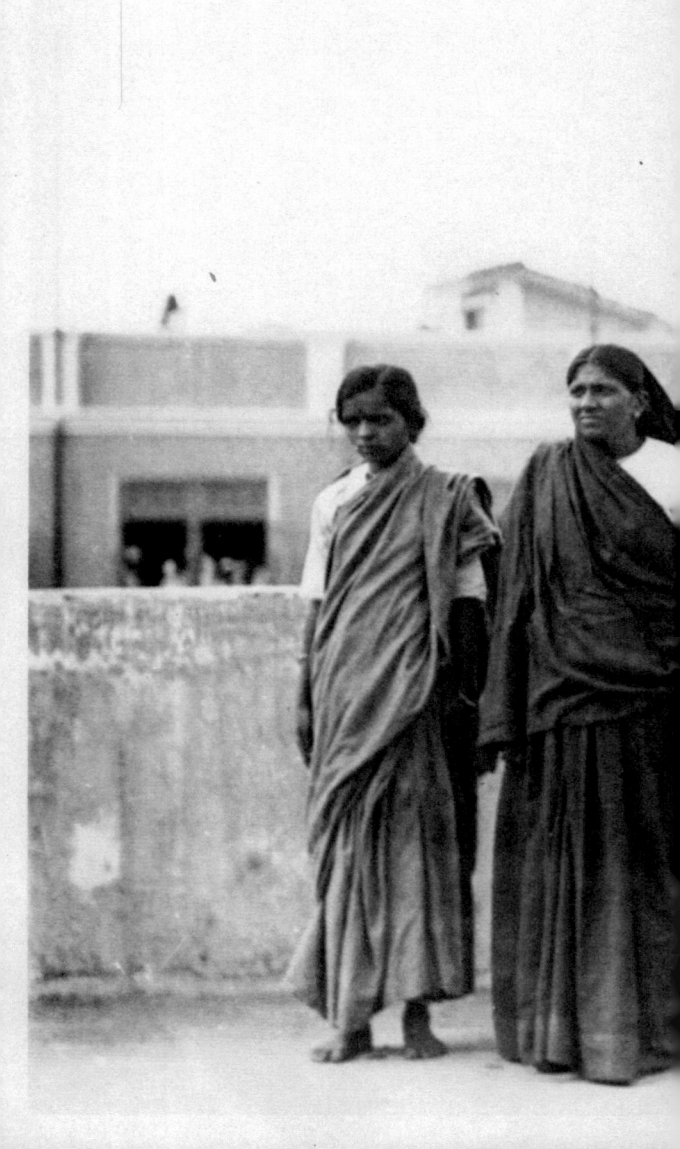

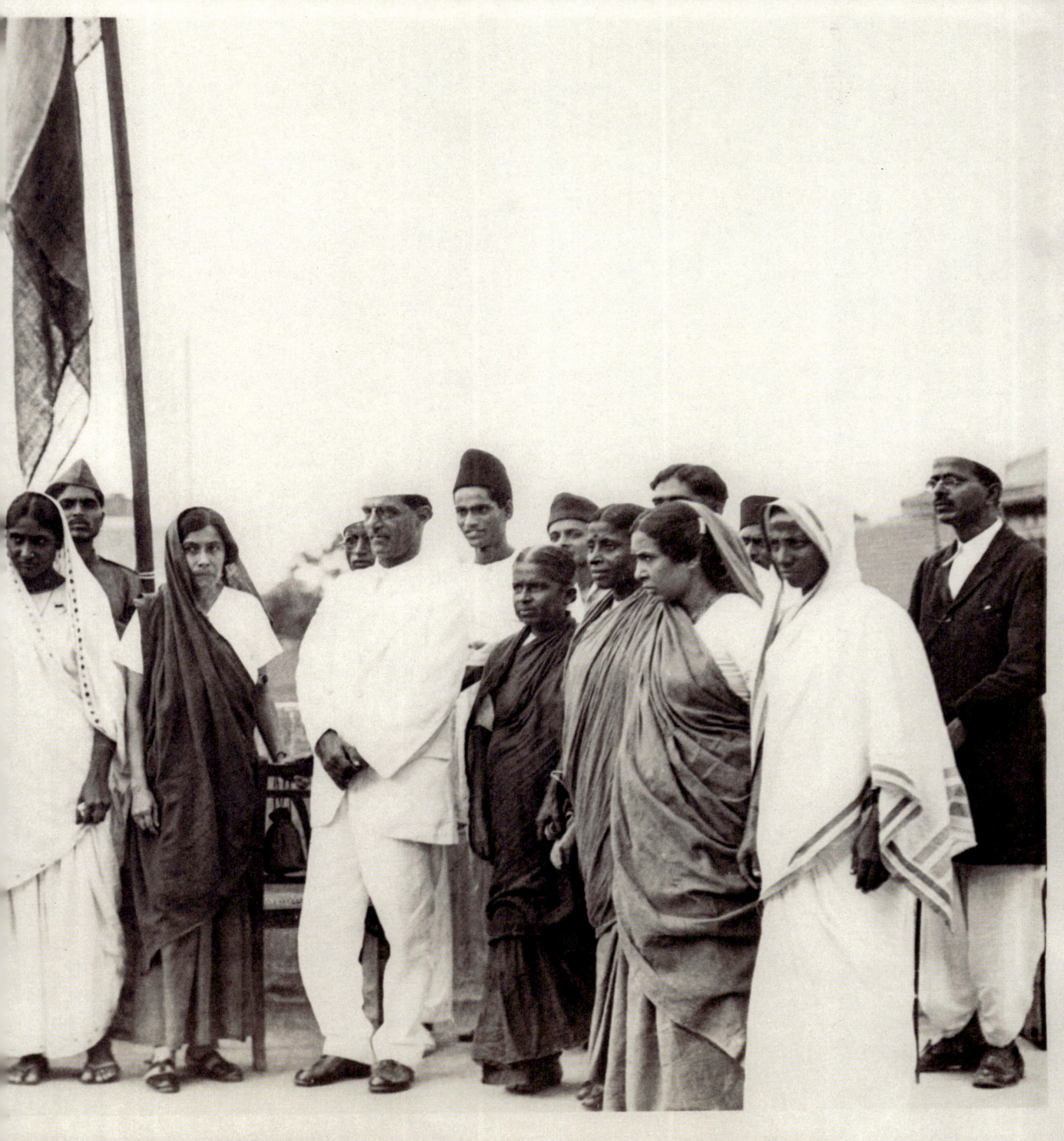

The Congress house was returned to the Congress after the Gandhi Irwin peace pact. Here is the flag hoisting ceremony.

First published in India in 2025 by

Mapin Publishing Pvt. Ltd
706 Kaivanna, Panchvati, Ellisbridge
Ahmedabad 380006 INDIA
T: +91 79 40 228 228
E: mapin@mapinpub.com
www.mapinpub.com

in association with

The Alkazi Collection of Photography
M 141 Greater Kailash-2,
New Delhi 110048 INDIA
T: +91 11 41437426/27
E: alkazifoundation01@gmail.com
www.alkazifoundation.org

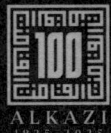

This book has been published in conjunction with the exhibition 'Disobedient Subjects: Bombay, 1930–1931' on view at the Chhatrapati Shivaji Maharaj Vastu Sangrahalaya, Mumbai, in partnership with The Alkazi Foundation for the Arts from 12 October 2025 to 14 April 2026. It is also a part of Ebrahim Alkazi's centenary celebration.

ISBN (SC): 978-93-94501-95-9
ISBN (HC): 978-93-94501-49-2

Copyediting: Smriti Vohra
Proofreading: Smriti Vohra, Marilyn Gore / Mapin Editorial
Editorial Management and Coordination: Hitanshi Chopra, Radhika Sharma and Jennifer Chowdhry / ACP Editorial
Editorial Support: Neha Manke / Mapin Editorial
Design: Nidhi Sah / Mapin Design Studio
Production: Mapin Design Studio
Printed in India by Thomson Press (India) Ltd.

Note: All images in this volume (unless otherwise mentioned) are from a rare album titled "Collections of Photographs of Old Congress Party", attributed to K.L. Nursey, now held in the Alkazi Collection of Photography (98.72.0002). The image captions reproduced in this volume are as in the original text, without corrections for punctuation, grammar, duplicated words, and typographical and/or spelling errors (with the proper usage/correct spelling given in square brackets).
All images from *The Bombay Chronicle* are courtesy of the Asiatic Society of Mumbai.

CAPTIONS

FRONT-COVER
"The Mandvi Congress dictator under arrest when he defied the police order by bringing our [out] a procession which was banned. Here the police are seen giving orders to disperse before making a lathi charge." (Detail, see p. 217)

PAGE 2
"A tug of war between police and Desh-Sewika's [desh sevikas] on the flag salutation day." (Detail, see p. 218)

PAGES 4—5
"The Congress house was returned to the Congress after the Gandhi Irwin peace pact. Here is the flag hoisting ceremony."
c. 1930
Gelatin Silver Print,
116 x 165 mm
ACP: 98.77.0002 (115b)

PAGE 8
"Police commissioner Wilson ordering the arrest of a Congress dictator [demonstrator]." c. 1930
Gelatin Silver Print,
117 x 165 mm
ACP: 98.77.0002 (39b)

PAGE 264
"Ladies meeting on the Esplanade maidan to condemn the Government, of its repressive policy." (Detail, see p. 238)

BACK-COVER
"The merchants of Bombay organised a a [sic] procession and a demonstration to condemn the Government of its repressive policy." (Detail, see pp. 54—55)

For Jim Masselos

(1940–2025)

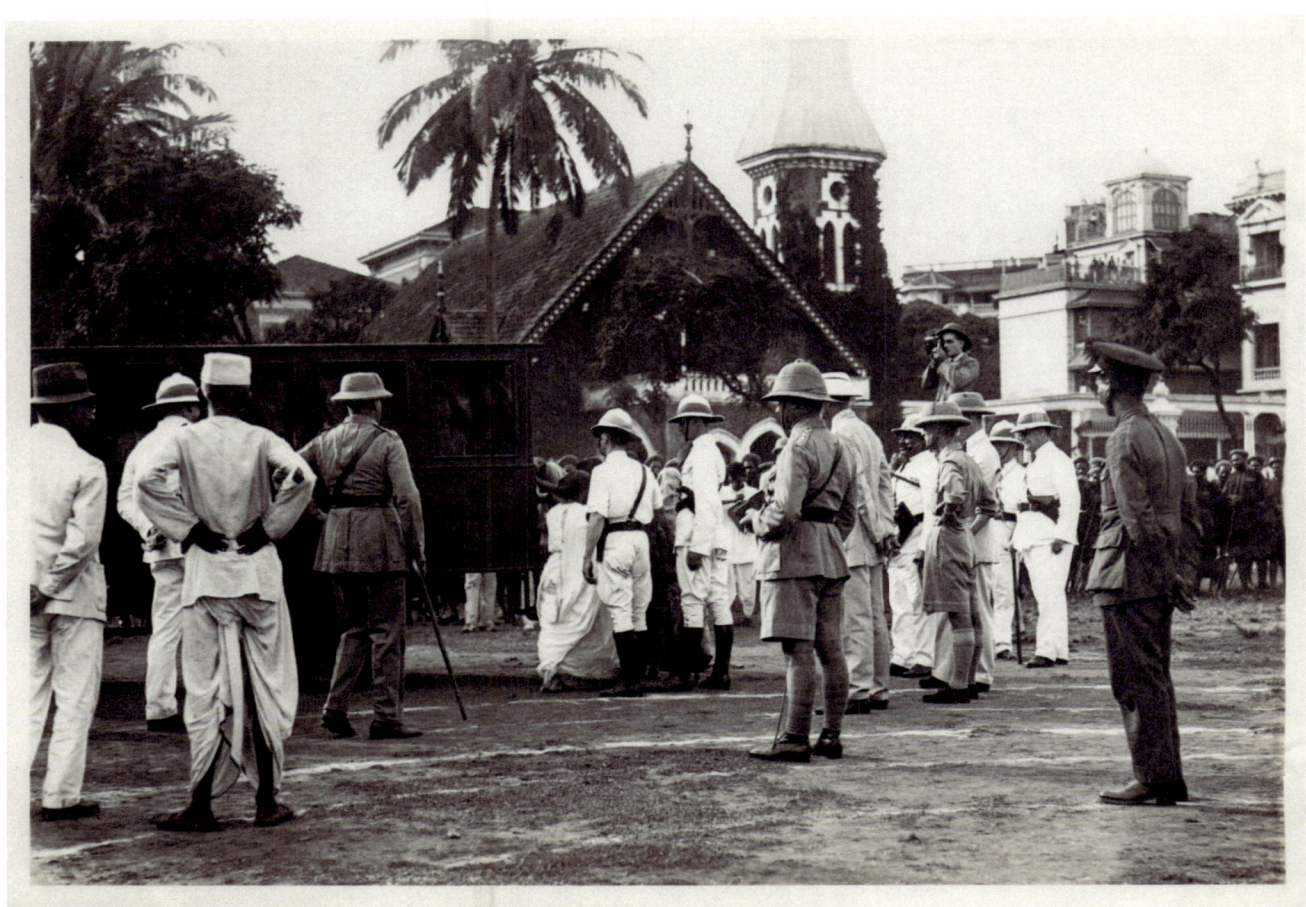

Police commissioner Wilson ordering the arrest of a Congress dictator.

CONTENTS

ACKNOWLEDGEMENTS AND DEDICATION

It takes more than a village to produce an interdisciplinary work such as this with contributions coming in from three different continents over a span of five years and more. Our first words of gratitude are to Rahaab Allana, the visionary curator of the Alkazi Foundation for the Arts (AFA) in New Delhi, India, who entrusted us with the precious archival object that is the focus of the extended meditations in the pages that follow. Although unremarkably titled *Collections of Photographs of Old Congress Party*, this rare album took us—two U.S.-based historians of colonial and modern South Asia—into the "disobedient streets" of the city of Bombay (now Mumbai) in 1930–1931, on which journey we were joined by six other talented and thoughtful scholars, each an authority on the subject they have written about for this volume. Our collective work on this project started at the height of a global pandemic which may well have confined us to our homes and our laptop computers, but which did not stop us from building camaraderie and community with each other that sustained us through some difficult and dark times. As we jointly worked our way through the pages of what we refer to as the "Nursey album," poring over the extraordinary photographs and pondering over their intent and effect, we debated and discussed. Along the way, an external reviewer gave us insightful feedback on the project, for which we are very grateful.

We only reached the final stage of sharing this work with you, our intended reader, because of the indefatigable and impeccable assistance of ACP's editorial staff, in particular Hitanshi Chopra and Jennifer Chowdhury Biswas. We thank them especially for their meticulous, rigorous and ever-cheerful help.

We are also immensely grateful to Smriti Vohra for her careful copyedits (and her infinite patience!). The Trustees of the Alkazi Foundation for the Arts (AFA) Amal Allana and Feisal Alkazi have our sincere appreciation, as do others on the AFA staff (Vijay Kumar, Ganesh Prasad, Santosh Udayan and Radhika Sharma) for their assistance. At Mapin Publishing in Ahmedabad, Gopal Limbad has been masterful in his creative design of this publication, a joy to behold, and we are immensely grateful to him, and to Neha Manke for her editorial assistance. For their enthusiasm and support for this project from the start, many thanks to Bipin Shah and Priyanka Raja at Mapin.

Not least, we are grateful to have each other—student and teacher, mentee and mentor, junior and senior colleague, but above all, friends—as our scholarly lives came to be enriched and deepened by our collaborative engagement with this striking testimonial compiled almost a hundred years ago but whose images continue to have relevance today to a world riven by conflict and hatred. Inspired as well by bearing witness to those who gathered on the streets of Bombay in solidarity and with remarkable courage took on the armed might of a global empire in the past century, we dedicate our endeavours here to all those who continue to come together to fight injustice, and help create an equitable and inclusive society across the world.

Avrati Bhatnagar and **Sumathi Ramaswamy**
Durham, NC (USA), 2025

PREFACE

Rahaab Allana

This very special constellation of images from the vintage album *Collections of Photographs of Old Congress Party (1930–31)* in the Alkazi Collection of Photography (ACP), New Delhi, is a rare example of anticolonial visual historiography and perhaps even feminist history in India. Known informally as the "Nursey" album, from the name "K.L. Nursey" stamped on the spine, it offers extensive documentation, possibly on Agfa film, of the Civil Disobedience Movement in Bombay during a year of dramatic nationalist dissent. It came to the ACP archive after being alerted to it by a revered landmark in South Bombay: *Phillips Antiques*, established in 1860 and today operated by Mr. Farooq Issa, located opposite the Prince of Wales Museum in the city's Kala Ghoda precinct.

This area, known as "Fort" (after Fort George, built by the British in 1769 as an extension of the fortified Bombay region), was a major site of political mobilization and "disobedient" protest marches, speeches, demonstrations, arrests, blockades and frequently brutal encounters with the baton-wielding white officers and native constables of the colonial police. Hence it was symbolically resonant and entirely fitting that our exhibition of Nursey images and the release of the concomitant scholarly volume take place at the Chhatrapati Shivaji Maharaj Vastu Sangrahalaya (CSMVS) as part of its Mumbai Gallery initiative.

The figure of "K.L. Nursey" is a curious enigma that warrants further research and investigation, for we know nothing of his identity. We attribute authorship to him, but it is hypothetical. Was he a resourceful patriot who commissioned or sponsored the work? Was he the compiler of the images? Was he the photographer, or both photographer and compiler? If so, did he work alone or with professional colleagues, united under one name? Did he belong to the cadre of nationalist photographers who aligned their work with their political ideals? Was he self-employed or with an individual or institution? Was he an official photographer for a local paper or a news agency? Was some part of his work voluntary? Were the images taken randomly and spontaneously when, camera in hand, "Nursey" chanced upon public protest action? Or were they planned and purposive, enabled by his prior knowledge of "disobedient" events, so that he was always in the right place at the right time to press the shutter?

How was "Nursey" able to cover often chaotic and widespread mass action from different and precise angles? Did he also type and paste the innumerable image captions? If this multitude of images was produced by someone else, how did he acquire them? How did some of his photographs find their way into the pro-British *The Times of India* and the pro-nationalist *The Bombay Chronicle*, prominent dailies of the time? And was "Nursey" inspired by the earlier work of Narayan Vinayak Virkar (1890–1968), a committed nationalist who documented the aftermath of the 1919 Jallianwala Bagh massacre in Amritsar, photographed many meetings of the Indian National Congress and portrayed famous nationalist leaders, including Gandhi, Chittaranjan Das, Subhas Chandra Bose and Bal Gangadhar Tilak?[1]

As a curator, the varied pleasures I experienced through immersion in our Nursey project included tracing how photographs that cohere around and concentrate on a central theme—civil disobedience—galvanise into a spectrum of linked trajectories, thus easily facilitating interdisciplinary explorations of a singular moment in modern Indian history, as exemplified in this volume. Crucially, such widening and deepening of the analytical field also enables us to connect with influential scholarship and critique from other political and social contexts, past and present; I list here just a handful of the many that struck me.

For instance, with its many images of spectators viewing nonviolent "disobedient" action, especially that which has provoked violent response from the colonial police, the Nursey album invites us to introspect upon our viewing experience— in the words of scholar Ariella Azoulay, to pay attention to the "duties of the civil spectator," and to "anchor spectatorship in civic duty" through a "civil contract" that shapes a new political relationship with the photographed subject. Can this album or photobook then transcend geographical and political boundaries, to connect with similar instances globally and make us aware of ongoing resistances in the present? Could we consider recent womens' marches in Afghanistan, bearing the slogan 'bread, work, freedom' that were mercilessly suppressed? Is its message embedded in the archive of Shaheen Bagh (as recorded in Prarthna Singh's *Har Shaam Shaheen Bagh*, 2022), which took place in Delhi in the aftermath of the controversial CAA amendment? Or, the work of Uzma Mohsin and the RTIs filed by the people to fight for their land/labour/personal rights? Or, the iconic feminist work of Sheba Chhachhi titled *Record/Resist* from the 1980s and '90s.

The Nursey images powerfully invoke what Hannah Arendt identifies as two crucial and interdependent aspects of the "public sphere" in her theorization of citizenship. As lucidly summarized by scholars Tatjana Tömmel and Maurizio d'Entreves:

> The first is "the space of appearance, a space of political freedom and equality which comes into being whenever citizens act in

concert through the medium of speech and persuasion. The second is the common world, a shared and public world of human artifacts, institutions and settings which separates us from nature and which provides a relatively permanent and durable context for our activities. Both dimensions are essential to the practice of citizenship, the former providing the spaces where it can flourish, the latter providing the stable background from which public spaces of action and deliberation can arise … individuals must be able to see and talk to one another in public, to meet in a public-political space, so that their differences as well as their commonalities can emerge and become the subject of democratic debate."[2]

The Nursey album is also an extraordinary inscription of "the crowd"—in this case, disenfranchised and dispossessed colonial subjects—as an empowered collective political actor/agent in the "disobedient" streets of Bombay in 1930–1931. The skilfully composed photographs of mass gatherings bring to mind Elias Canetti's classic philosophical delineation of the "four main attributes of the crowd": "*The crowd always wants to grow.* There are no natural boundaries to its growth." "*Within the crowd there is equality.* This is absolute and indisputable and never questioned by the crowd itself. . . one might even define a crowd as a state of absolute equality." / "*The crowd loves density.* Nothing must stand between its parts or divide them; everything must be the crowd itself [...]." / "*The crowd needs a direction.* It is in movement and it moves towards a goal. The direction, which is common to all its members, strengthens the feeling of equality..."[3]

The fervour of the disobedient crowd's political commitment and the intensity of its public "eruption" were regularly described in the press in India at the time, these accounts supported by photographs. For example, mass support for the nationalist cause was reported as due to "Not coercion but conversion by moral persuasion";[4] protesters openly declared their defiance, as many who were beaten and/or arrested unfailingly returned to disobedient action after being released.

Images in the Nursey album occasionally invite us into tangential meta-histories of nationalism entwined with visual culture and photography practice.[5] For instance, I was strongly drawn to the quiet image of a street vendor hawking *swadeshi* goods (Fig. 4.3), as it invokes the exhibition practices associated with the annual Congress Party meetings since the 1880s. These exhibitions, documented through photographs, re-conceptualized the organization and dissemination of "native" arts and crafts, including handloom weaving, and thus supported the formal merchandising of *swadeshi* as focused political action—the production of *khadi* and other *swadeshi* textiles seen both as a form of resistance and a means of funding the Civil Disobedience Movement through patriotic, economically sound and sustainable commerce.

Scholar Atreyee Gupta notes that first large-scale Congress Industrial Exhibition was strategically timed to coincide with the Delhi Durbar of 1903 (King Edward VII and Queen Alexandra did not attend and were represented by the Duke and Duchess of Connaught).[6] This spectacular imperial pageant organized by Viceroy Curzon was thoroughly documented both in the press and in visual terms: Bourne & Shepherd were the official photographers, along with Lala Deen Dayal; and other professionals were hired by participating maharajas, some themselves talented amateur lensmen, to record the Durbar events for their own private and state archives. Significantly, the Durbar included a "great Exhibition of Indian arts manufactures," with Curzon "confidently" assuring the public "that they would be greatly astonished at the range, the variety, and the beauty of this Exhibition ... artificers still exist in India, even in these days of commercial ideals and debauched taste, who are capable of satisfying the demand for the artistic and beautiful and rare."[7]

The 1903 Congress exhibition was naturally overshadowed by the Durbar's scale and spectacle, but the exhibitions that followed were ineffective for other reasons, such as internal party conflicts and fluctuating public interest. In their initial years the Congress exhibitions were heavily critiqued in the press, and labelled as "a glorified bazaar" with "no surprises;" later there was a shift in public opinion, with the exhibitions deemed "marvellous"; and they soon became a central focus of the Congress meetings, with a separate committee formed for curating them.[8] One image in particular caused tremors within the Congress exhibition of 1928: a hand-coloured photograph of Gandhi, wearing a *khadi* cap and *khadi* wrap, seated cross-legged on the floor against a backdrop of Victorian opulence.

This juxtaposition was so offensive to the leader that he allegedly stormed out of the room. A correspondent for the *Khadi Patrika,* a monthly supplement to Gandhi's *Young India,* wrote: "The Congress Exhibition last year was more of a tamasha [spectacle] than an exhibition in the real sense of the term."[9] Yet inexplicably, this very image was subsequently published as the frontispiece of Lala Lajpat Rai's *Unhappy India* (1929), a response to American journalist Katherine Mayo's racist polemic *Mother India* (1927). And Gandhi and other party members remained keenly aware of the power of photography and the need to deploy the printed image skilfully and continuously across the country to achieve nationalist goals, including *swadeshi* production and propagation in which "disobedient" women played a large and crucial role.[10]

As remarked by scholar Emilia Terracciano, "In the triangulated vision between those photographed, the photographer and the viewer, the image can and must be made to speak in the present."[11] Does our "watching" of the images of activist women—the intrepid *desh sevikas* on the protest frontlines, featured as central protagonists in the Nursey album—enable us to connect with depictions of women in resistance movements in other contexts, and with contemporary women artists whose lens-based work pivots around themes of justice, equality and human rights?[12]

We are indebted to this volume's contributors for their critical re-readings of organized nonviolent protest against imperial power, as depicted in the Nursey album—itself a "public sphere" into which we are thrust as witnesses to mass political dissent *in medias res*. It makes us consider other geopolitical changes taking place in the 1930s which are of interest from an art historical perspective: new political alignments were being sought with Communist Russia, and many photographers and artists were drawn to its egalitarian ideals, including Chittaprosad, Somnath Hore, Zainul Abedin and Quamrul Hasan.[13] As scholar Sanjukta Sunderason notes, images in the press actively illustrated these inclinations through images of child labour, displacement, and socialist internationalism. This leftist imagery could be found in the later works of Sunil Janah published in *People's War*. The work of the Nursey album also finds alignment through other arts initiatives—the All India Progressive Writers Association was established soon after in 1935, and the Indian People's Theatre Association in 1943. PC Joshi, Bishnu Dey, Faiz Ahmad Faiz and Sardar Jafri were central figures.[14]

The vintage photographs in the album urge us to exercise "civic skill" and to "watch," rather than to "look," as we immerse in the resilient script, theatre and choreography of civil disobedience in the streets of Bombay. The images also provoke us to reflect on what continued to unfold beyond these particular views—the broad arcs of nationalist struggle, the blood spilled, voices silenced, lives taken, sacrifices made.

And the intimate aura of the handmade, irregularly captioned, evidentiary frames of the Nursey album is especially haunting in the contemporary moment—embedded as we are, an abstract "crowd" of users and producers, within the borderless digital "space of appearance" and "common world", subject to the hegemonies of media and the algorithmic grand narrative that collapses time, space, action, image and text into the unperturbed rectangles of our large and small screens.

Notes

1. Trained by Shripad Damodar Satwalekar, a Lahore-based activist, Virkar operated a studio in Girgaum, Bombay, where he specialized in studio portraiture, photographing the local elites and their families. Two of his Jallianwala Bagh images were featured in the *Congress Punjab Inquiry* (1920), a report by a special sub-committee formed to investigate the atrocity; it was mainly drafted by Gandhi. See MAP Academy website, article on Narayan Virkar, published online, 21 April 2022. Also see Sean Wilcock, "Guilt in the Archive: Photography and the Amritsar Massacre of 1919", *History of Photography*, vol. 43, no. 1 (2019), pp. 47–59.

2. Tatjana Tömmel and Maurizio Passerin d'Entreves, "Hannah Arendt" [Section 5: Arendt's Concept of Citizenship; italics in original], Stanford Encyclopedia of Philosophy, revised 12 February 2024. Emilia Terracciano observes that "Congress-led agitation in the form of the Non-Cooperation Movement in the early 1920s, civil disobedience in the early 1930s, and the Quit India campaign of 1942 were all events in which processional marches, prayer meetings and public rallies became affective theatrical performances, fundamentally sabotaging the functioning of the colonial public sphere. Increasingly, confined meeting places were abandoned in favour of assemblies in public squares and parks." Consequently, the "formation of crowds" in the streets enabled people to experience themselves as an ideologically cohesive, politically purposive body, "supplanting earlier displays of a subservient, carefully selected audience mesmerized by the composed spectacle of the imperial pageant. Public space could either be strategically occupied or vacated by large crowds to sabotage colonial expectations." See Emilia Terracciano, "Beyond or in Emergency? The Emergence of Photography during the 1943 Bengal Famine: Sunil Janah," in Rahaab Allana (ed.), *Another Lens: Photography and the Emergence of Image Culture* [India Since the 90s series], Vol. 4 (New Delhi and Shanghai: Tulika Books and West Heavens, 2024), p. 31.

3. Elias Canetti, *Crowds and Power*, translated from the German by Carol Stewart (New York: Continuum, 1962), p. 29.

4. "Woman's Part in National Struggle," *The Bombay Chronicle*, 10 April 1930, p. 1.

5. The Alkazi Collection of Photography houses '*Les Ruines de Paris et de ses Environs*' / 'The Ruins of Paris and Its Surrounding Areas', an album in two volumes, each of 50 albumen prints, by French photographer Alphonse Justin Liébert (1826–1913). It contains images of the patriotic "nationalists" of the 1871 Paris Commune that were later used to identify and target the very same individuals as dangerous "anarchists." The photographs include architectural views of Paris and the surrounding areas after the insurrection.

6. Atreyee Gupta, "The Promise of the Modern: State, Culture, and Avant-gardism in India (ca. 1930–1960)", Ph.D. dissertation, University of Minnesota, Minneapolis, December 2011, pp. 40-41; Retrieved from the University Digital Conservancy.

7. See H. Caldwell Lipsett, *Lord Curzon in India, 1898-1903* (London: R.A. Everett & Co., 1903); the volume includes "an Appendix containing Lord Curzon's speech justifying the Delhi Durbar" to critics who alleged he was "going to throw away on senseless pomp and show a sum of two millions sterling" (pp. 127, 128, 129). Also see Julie F. Codell (ed.), *Power and Resistance: The Delhi Coronation Durbars* (New Delhi: The Alkazi Collection of Photography, 2012); and Julie Codell, "On the Delhi Coronation Durbars, 1877, 1903, 1911", *BRANCH: Britain, Representation and Nineteenth-century History*.

8. Atreyee Gupta, "The Promise of the Modern", p. 42.

9. ibid., pp. 61–62.

10. "Gandhi was probably the first political figure to self-consciously exploit photography for political purposes. Although the leader did not court photographers, he harnessed mechanical reproduction to affirm his iconic public persona, achieving the complete integration of private and public, as well as religious and secular realms, which he so crucially advocated both in his writings and incendiary speeches ... From the Johannesburg certificates bonfire of 1908, to the Dandi Salt March of 1930, to the numerous 'fasts unto death' that Gandhi endured, his actions were all means to this end: the choreography of politics for both Indian and imagined, faraway, international publics." See Emilia Terracciano, "Beyond or in Emergency?", p. 32.

11. See Emilia Terracciano, *Art and Emergency: Modernism in Twentieth-Century India*, London: Bloomsbury Publishing, 2017, p. 71.

12. Recent examples of such work by contemporary women artists include Prarthna Singh's *Har Shaam Shaheen Bagh* / 'Shaheen Bagh Each Evening' (2022), self-published and Uzma Mohsin's *Songkeepers* (2018). Also see Kamayani Sharma, "Prarthna Singh: One Hundred Days of Resistance" and Jyoti Dhar, "Uzma Mohsin: Songkeepers", in Rahaab Allana (ed.), "Delhi: Looking Out/Looking In" [Special Edition], *Aperture* 243 (Summer 2021). For a discussion of Sheba Chhachhi's iconic feminist work from the 1980s and 1990s, see Kumkum Sangari (ed.), *Arc Silt Dive: The Works of Sheba Chhachhi* (New Delhi: Tulika Books, 2016).

13. See Emilia Terracciano, "Beyond or in Emergency?", p. 41.

14. Sunderason, Sanjukta. "Freedom by Other Means: Art as Archives of Decolonisation." In *Third Text's Online Forum/Living Archives*, 2023.

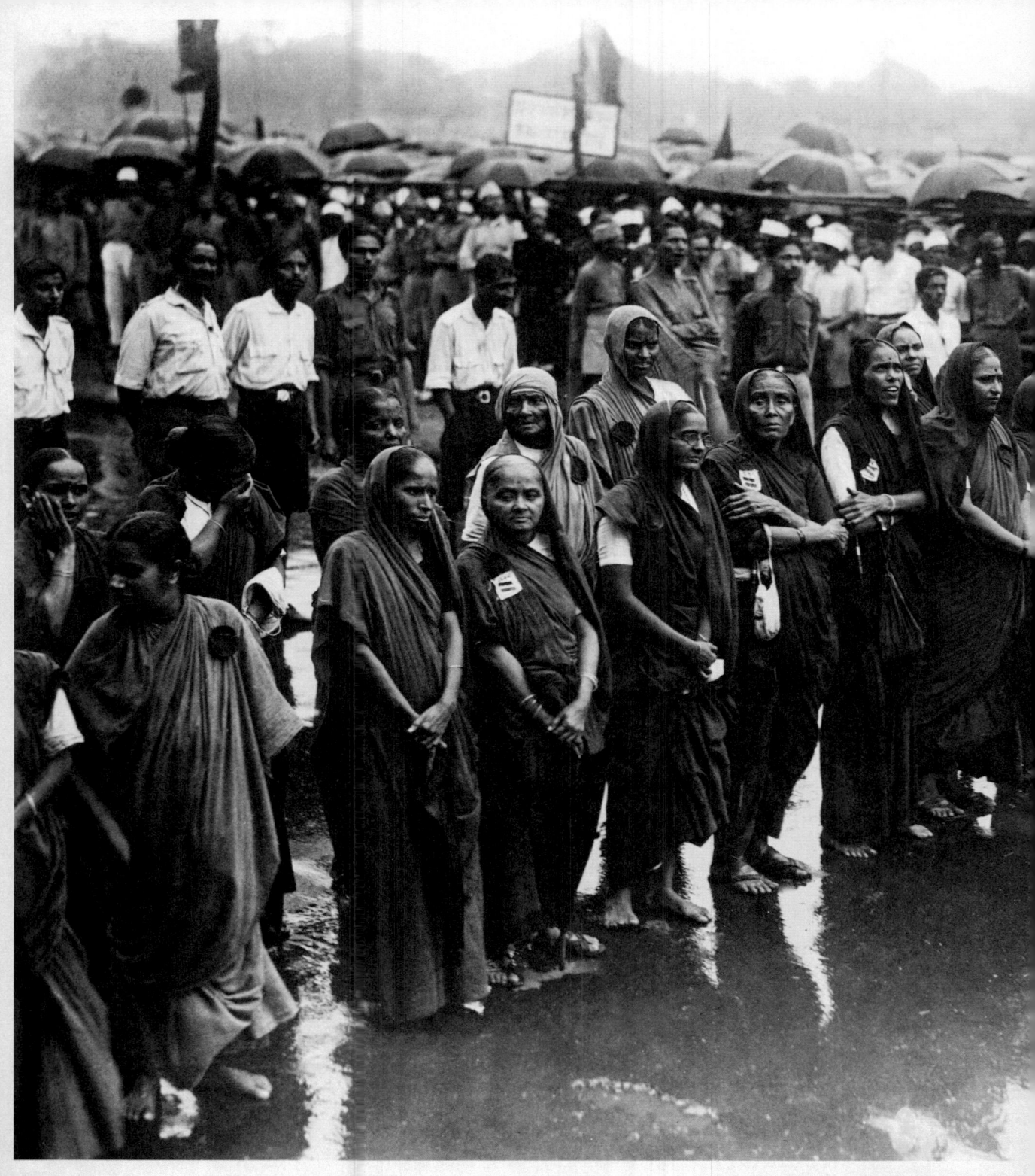

Desh sevikas waiting to greet mahatma their
loved leader, at Fallard Pier.

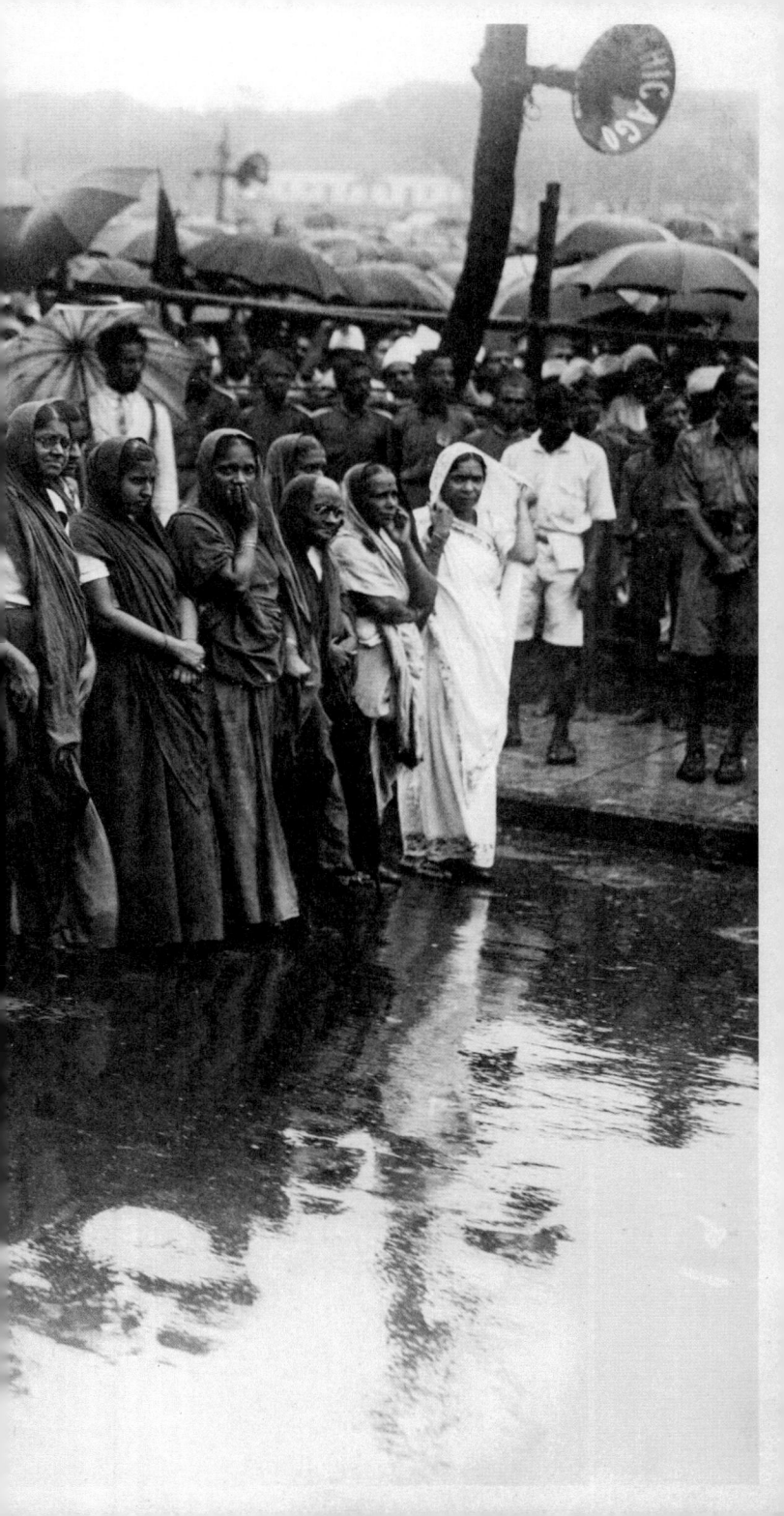

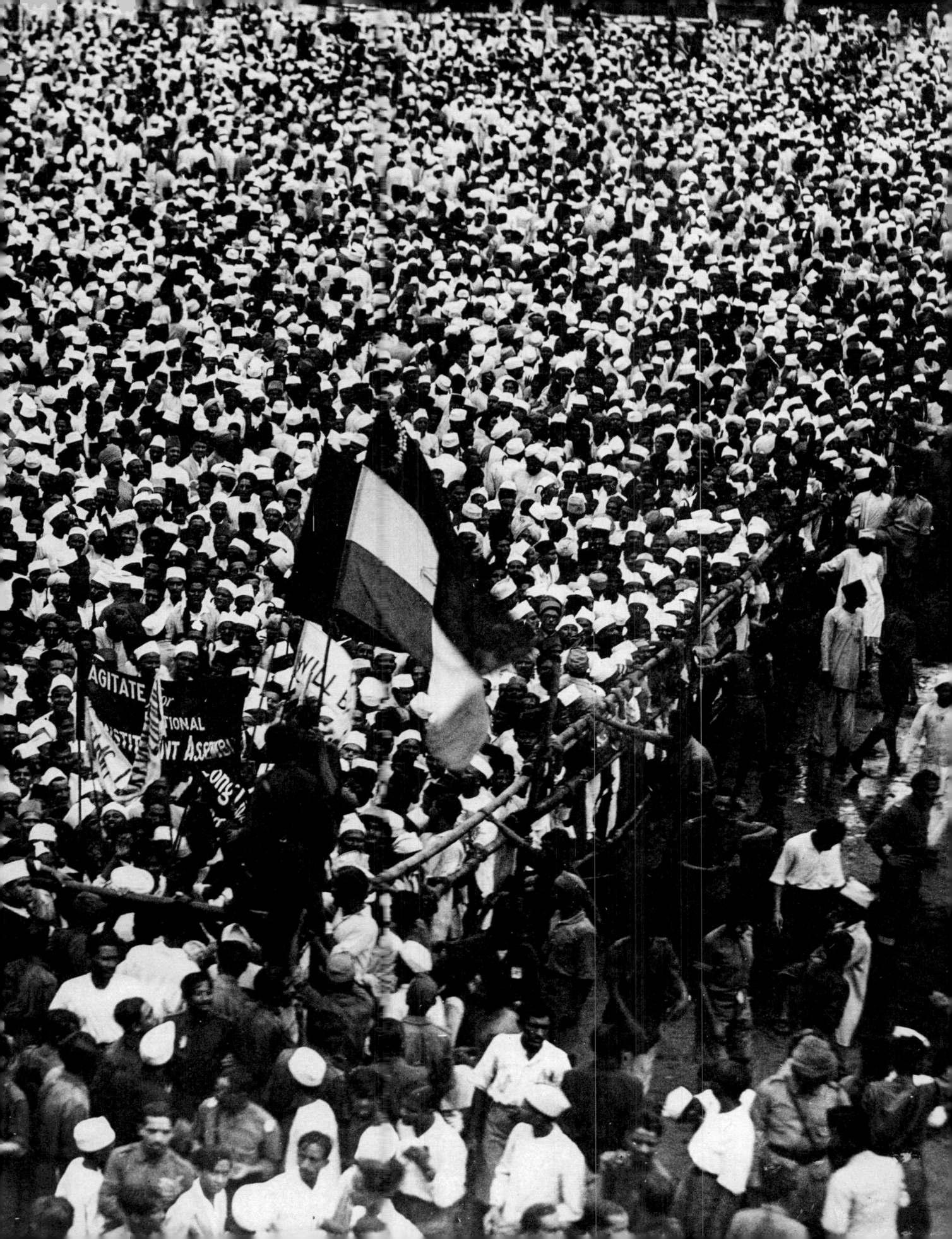

CHAPTER 1

INTRODUCTION
WORDS OF LIGHT IN DISOBEDIENT BOMBAY

Avrati Bhatnagar and Sumathi Ramaswamy

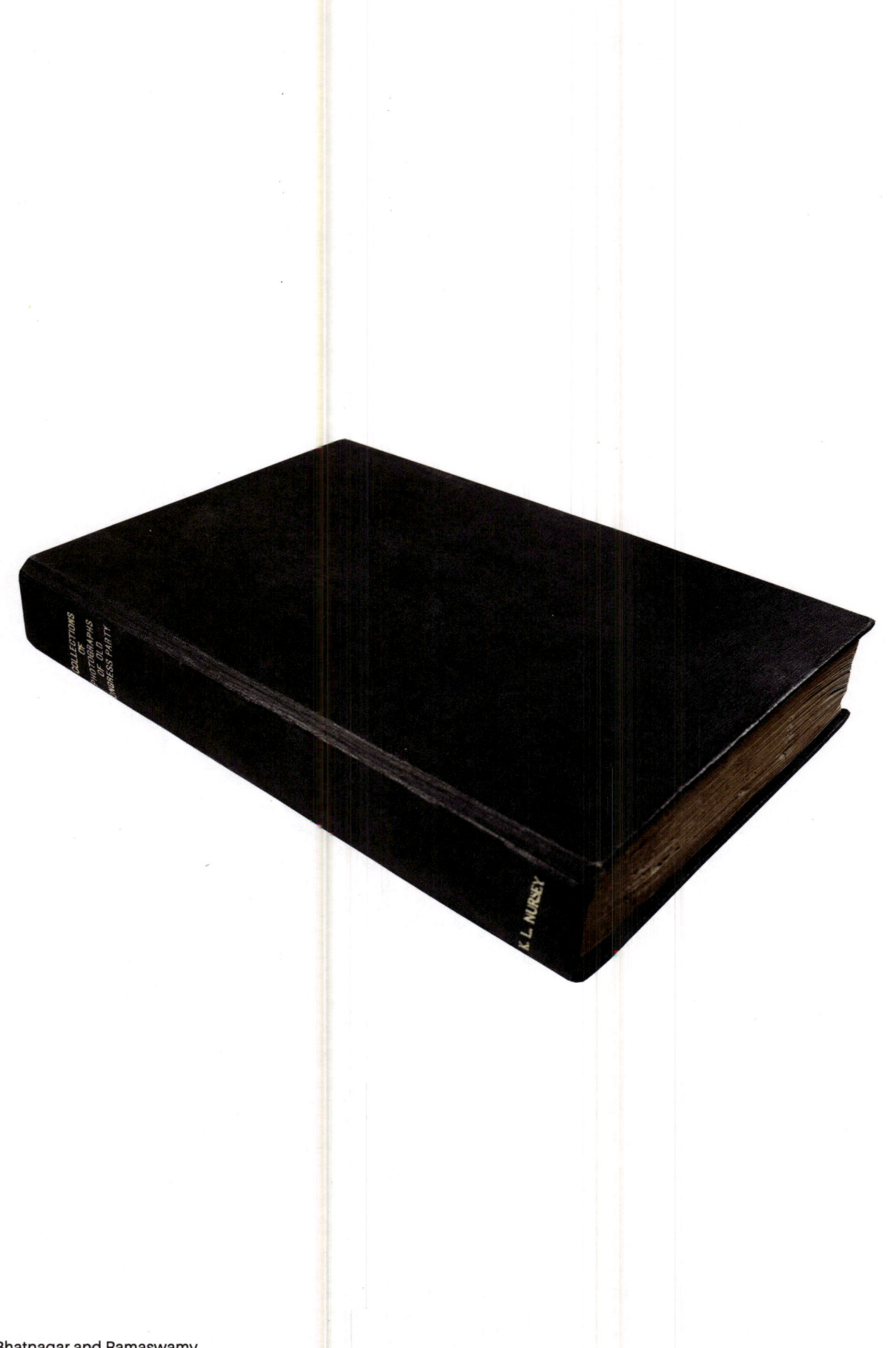

COLLECTIONS
OF
PHOTOGRAPHS
OF OLD
CONGRESS PARTY

K. L. NURSEY

A photograph does not provide a narrative, only its opening terms—
its stage, if you will.[1]

The Alkazi Collection of Photography's album titled *Collections of Photographs of Old Congress Party—K.L. Nursey* takes us on a visual journey around Bombay (now, Mumbai) so that we too can bear witness, almost a century later, to the unfolding of the Civil Disobedience Movement in British India's most important commercial city, and its financial capital. Soon after Mohandas K. Gandhi broke the infamous colonial salt laws on the Dandi seashore at the crack of dawn on 6 April 1930, he called upon his fellow citizens across India to join him in protesting the longstanding British monopoly on the production, distribution and sale of this most essential of life-sustaining commodities. The burden of this monopoly was particularly heavy on the most vulnerable sections of the Indian populace on whose behalf Gandhi led the charge. Among the first to heed his call were the "disobedient" men and women (and some children) of Bombay who took to the streets in large numbers in parades, protests, processions and, of course, illicit salt-making along the seashore.

The carefully preserved and meticulously captioned 245 photographs of the Nursey album take us into the heart of this revolutionary mass action, allowing us to get a feel for the energy and enthusiasm of disobedience from early April 1930, with the commencement of the Salt Satyagraha in the city, to 29 August 1931, when Gandhi set sail from Bombay to attend the Second Round Table Conference in London as the sole representative of the Indian National Congress. When we first encountered this bound-in-black album at the Alkazi Foundation for the Arts in New Delhi (Fig. 1.1), it underscored for us the power of the dissenting multitude: the anonymous patriotic residents of the city joined in solidarity with Congress Party volunteers and well-known nationalist leaders. Contained within the folios of this modest-looking image-object, we found an impressive visual archive of Bombay's remarkable transformation into a city of disobedience propelled by its ordinary residents, as we show and argue over the course of these pages. This led us to move our lens of analysis away from prominent leaders of the movement to focus on the sea of ordinary people participating in public events and turning the streets of Bombay into sites of

PAGES 18–19
"Desh sevikas waiting to greet mahatma [Mahatma] their loved leader, at Ballard Piar [Pier]."
c. 1930–1931
Gelatin Silver Print,
114 x 158 mm
ACP: 98.77.0002 (117a)

PAGE 20
"A great multitude that had assembled to wish Mahatma Gandhi success at the R.T.C as the representative of the congress [Congress]. Photo shows the crowd at the Azad maidan."
(Detail, see p. 25)

Fig. 1.1
K.L. Nursey album [Attributed]
Collections of Photographs of Old Congress Party,
n.d.
365 x 240 x 60 mm
ACP: 98.77.0002

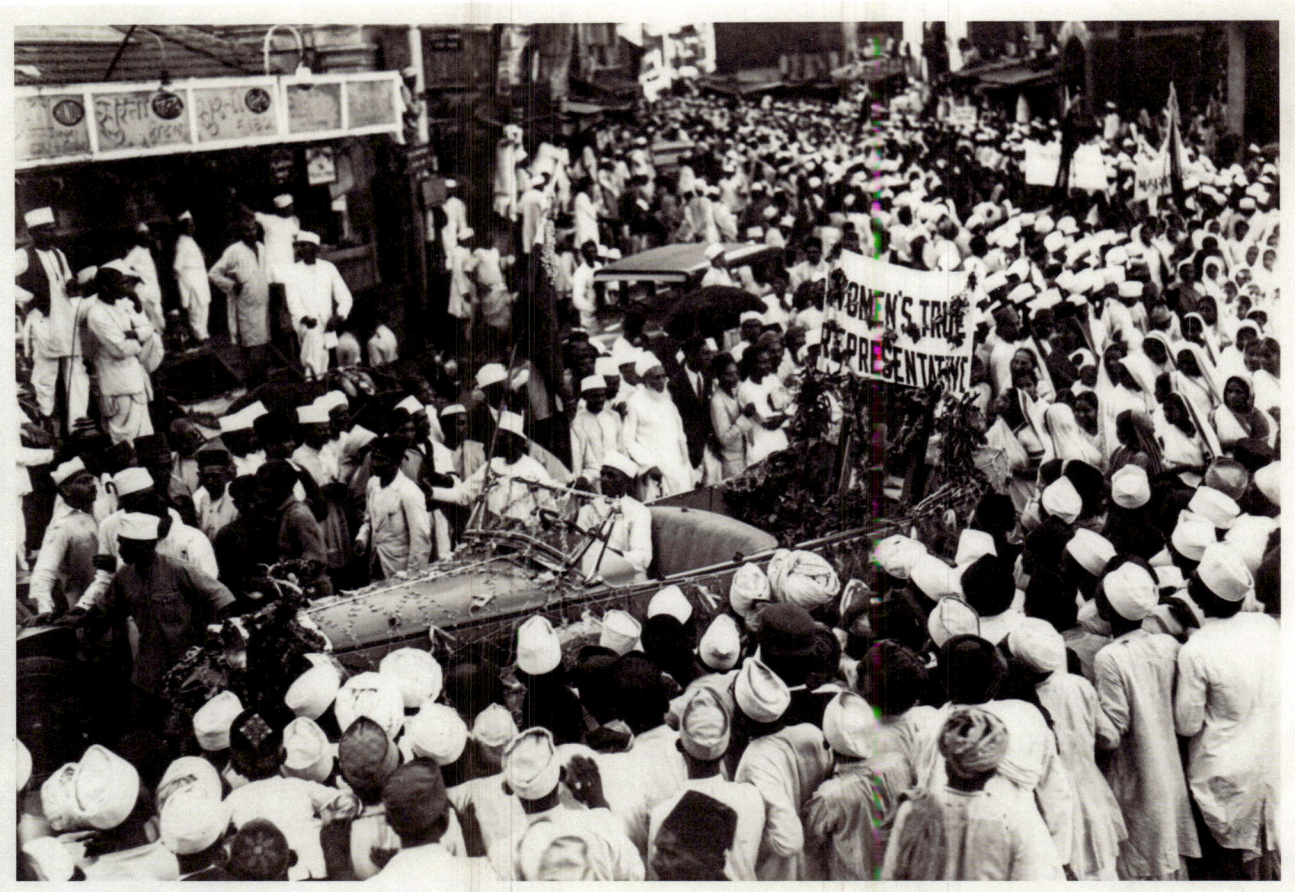

anticolonial and nationalist assertion. The photographs register key locations of the city where colonial power was confronted and challenged day after day in these heady months. As the streets virtually disappear under the ever-growing *khadi*-clad crowds who also succeeded in bringing traffic to a halt and in masking imperial edifices of power, we get a sense of how the colonial city was reclaimed by its anticolonial residents (Fig. 1.2, Fig. 1.3).

Among the rich and compelling images in this historical album are also those of the newly formed, albeit short-lived, cadres of *desh sevikas* (lit., "handmaids of the nation"), marching on the streets, speaking at mass gatherings, picketing shops selling foreign goods, and making and selling salt illicitly (for example, Fig. 7.12). Another set of powerfully composed images puts the exercise of colonial violence on full display as the ubiquitous baton of the Lathi Raj is turned on peaceful protesters practising the Gandhian gospel of non-violent civil action or *satyagraha* (Fig. 8.8).[2] Scattered through the album are revealing images of the man who is credited with starting it all, M.K. Gandhi (for example, Fig. 1.4, Fig. 1.5). But we would be mistaken if we were to think that he is the principal protagonist of the album. On the contrary, the photographs are a striking visual reminder of the role and power of the multitude in the constitution of the Mahatma.

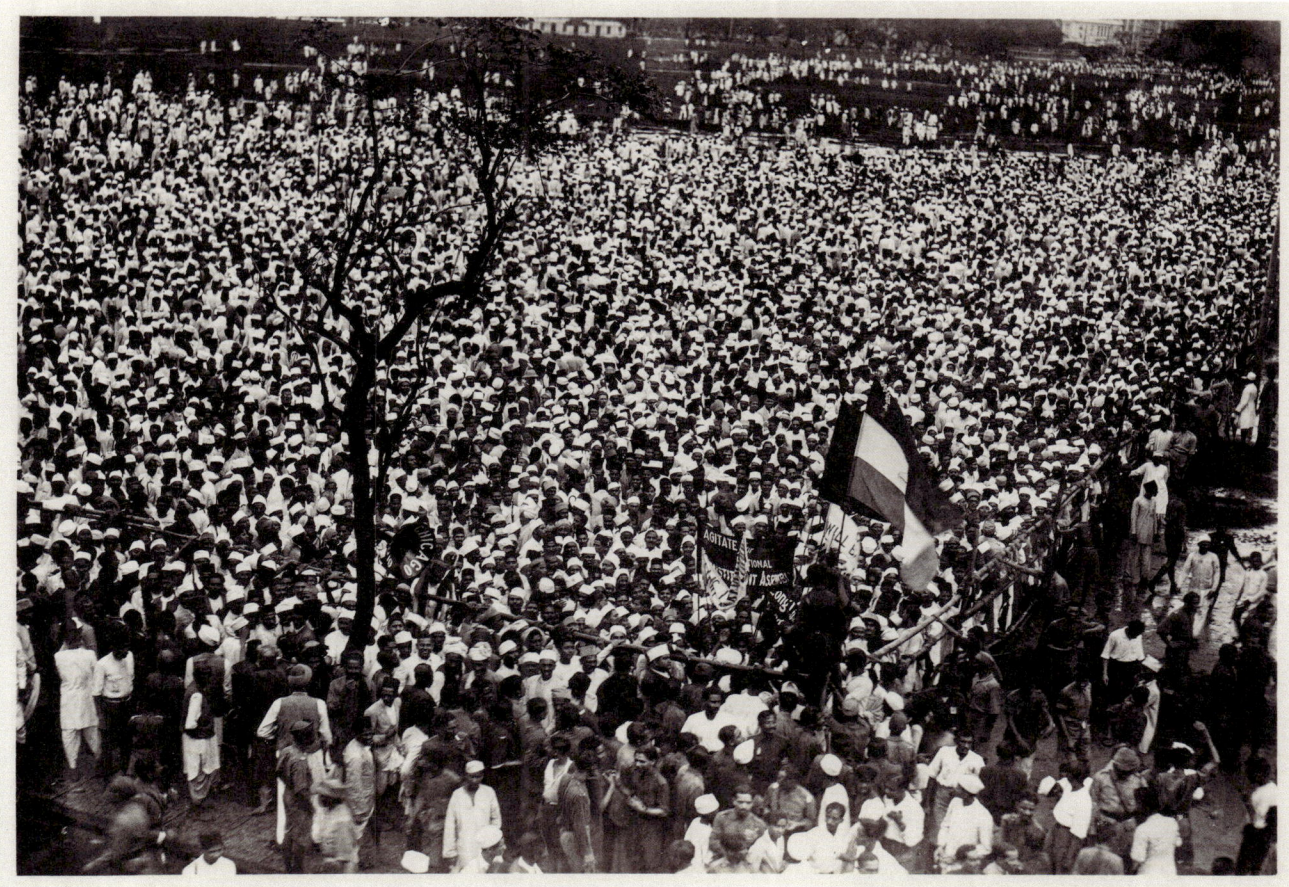

Writing in the immediate aftermath of the movement, the Congress leadership remarked, "The year nineteen thirty was the *annus mirabilis*, the year of great deeds and great sacrifices of the Indian people. ... The future historian may make a record in gold print of these heroic deeds."[3] Historians have indeed made a record of this critical moment in India's colonial history many times over (albeit not in gold print). This volume, however, and the accompanying exhibit for which it serves as a scholarly catalogue, bring to light for the first time a collection of images that have not been publicly seen or reckoned with by scholars of the city, or by historians of photography. Our essays are guided by an impulse to write new narratives and tell new stories powered by the force of the historical photograph. Even as we acknowledge with Georges Didi-Huberman that "we often ask too much or too little of the image,"[4] we bring into focus an alternate view of the Civil Disobedience Movement—hitherto largely documented through texts and discourse—as we take you back to the colonial streets of Bombay with the help of the camera.

Fig. 1.3
"A great multitude that had assembled to wish Mahatma Gandhi success at the R.T.C as the representative of the congress [Congress]. Photo shows the crowd at the Azad maidan." 1931 Gelatin Silver Print, 114 x 58 mm
ACP: 98.77.0002 (117b)

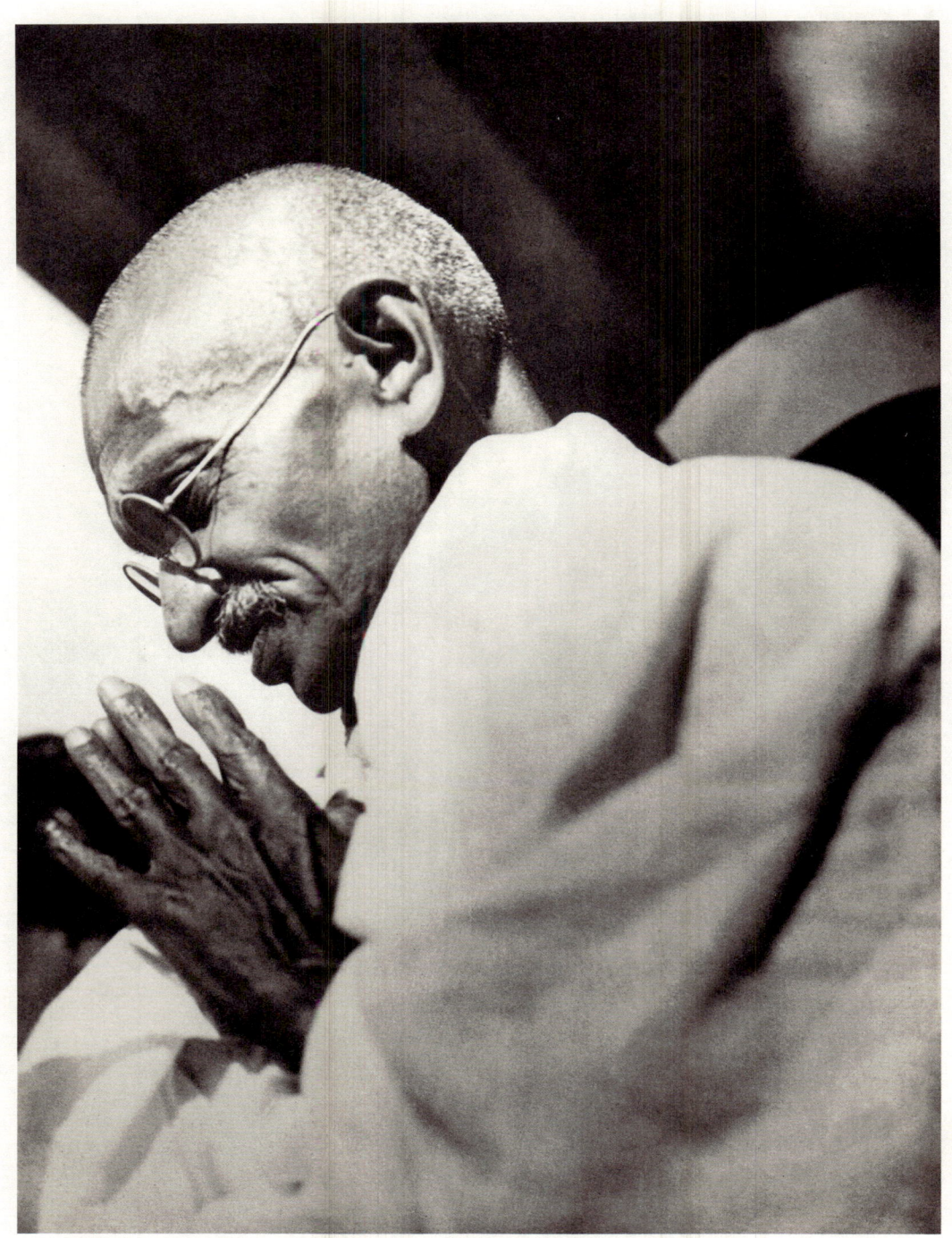

Fig. 1.4
"Mahatma Gandhi
making dharsan
[darshan] to his
admirers." 1931
Gelatin Silver Print,
156 x 115 mm
ACP: 98.77.0002 (01a)

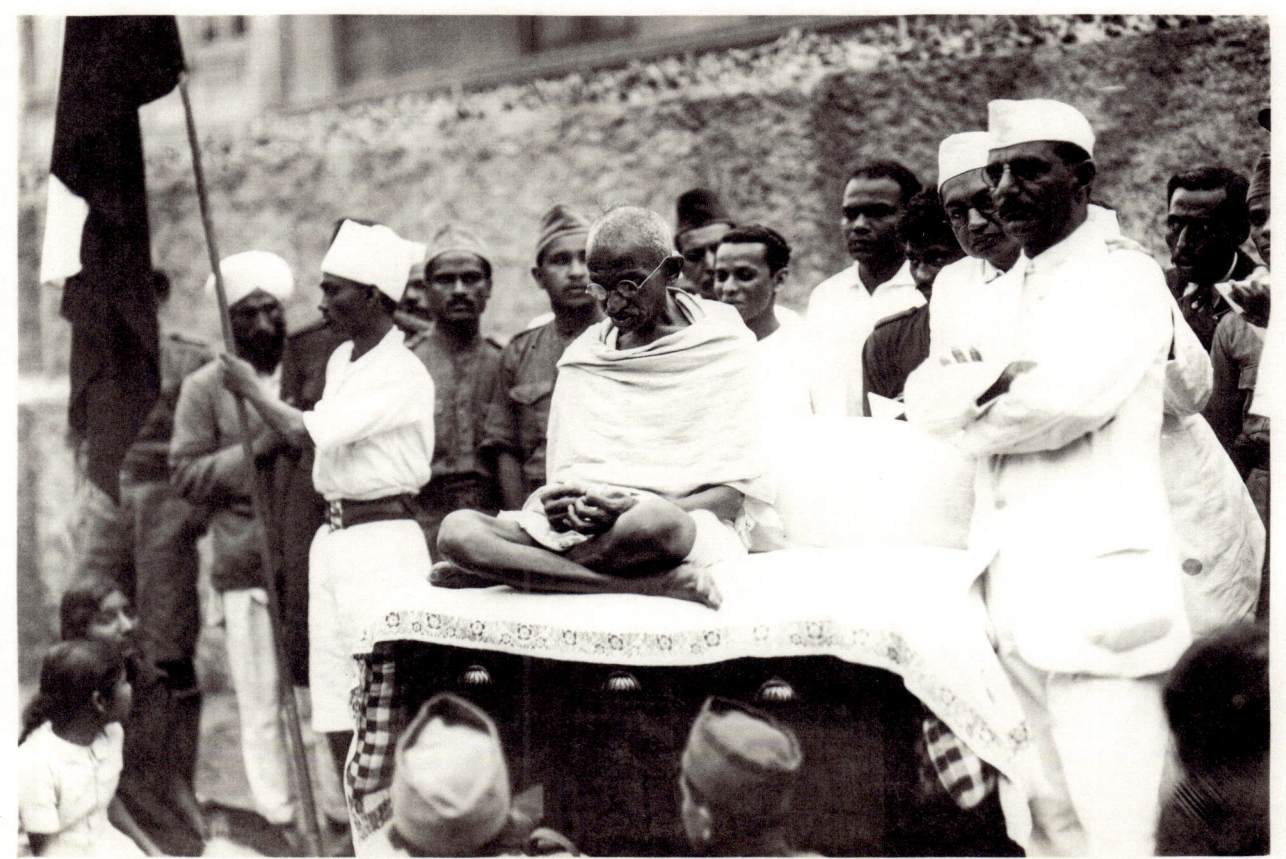

Fig. 1.5
"Mahatma Gandhi
having a chat with the
National volunteers
Bombay." 1931
Gelatin Silver Print,
111 x 158 mm
ACP: 98.77.0002 (116b)

Disobedient Bombay

On 2 April 1930, the nationalist newspaper *The Bombay Chronicle* outlined for its readers the plan for Bombay to turn "disobedient." The chroniclers of the city argued that this teeming metropolis had a penchant for defiance long before it was turned into "a citadel of the national movement."[5] For, colonial Bombay was made unlike any other city of its time in the subcontinent. In no small measure, the uniform appraisal of Bombay as a cosmopolitan haven of commerce turns around the critical role played by the city's merchant class in shaping its urban spaces, infrastructures and social relations. As art historian Preeti Chopra has shown, modern Bombay was essentially a "joint enterprise"

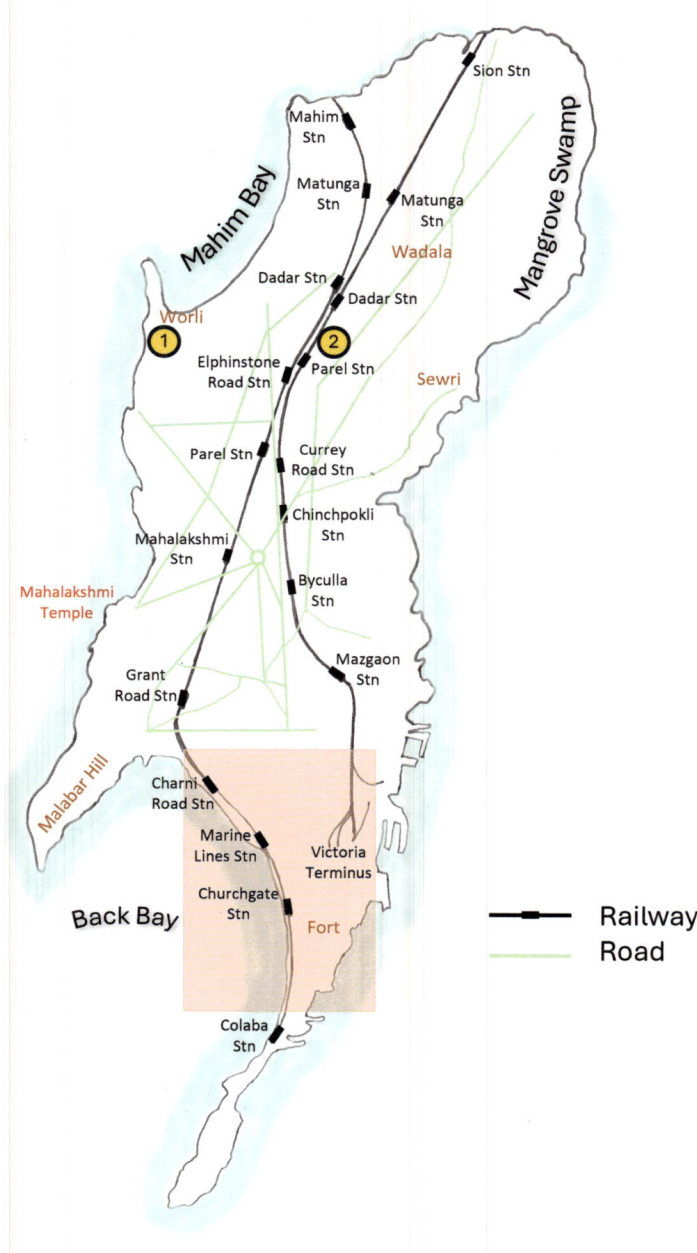

Fig. 1.6
Bombay Island:
A Bird's-Eye View.
Cartography by
Lakshmi Venkatesh,
2024
The highlighted
section on the map
shows the South Bombay
area.

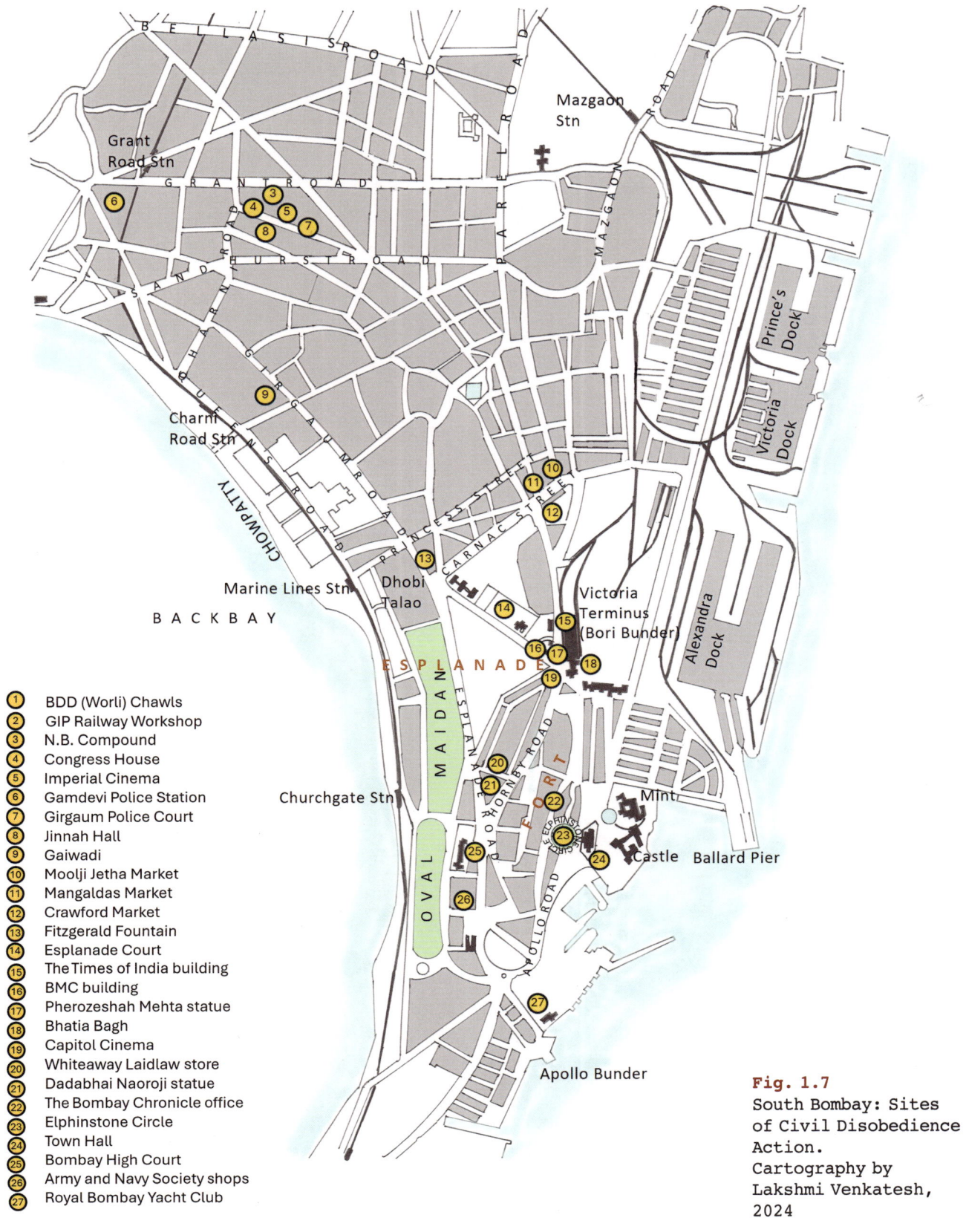

1. BDD (Worli) Chawls
2. GIP Railway Workshop
3. N.B. Compound
4. Congress House
5. Imperial Cinema
6. Gamdevi Police Station
7. Girgaum Police Court
8. Jinnah Hall
9. Gaiwadi
10. Moolji Jetha Market
11. Mangaldas Market
12. Crawford Market
13. Fitzgerald Fountain
14. Esplanade Court
15. The Times of India building
16. BMC building
17. Pherozeshah Mehta statue
18. Bhatia Bagh
19. Capitol Cinema
20. Whiteaway Laidlaw store
21. Dadabhai Naoroji statue
22. The Bombay Chronicle office
23. Elphinstone Circle
24. Town Hall
25. Bombay High Court
26. Army and Navy Society shops
27. Royal Bombay Yacht Club

Fig. 1.7
South Bombay: Sites of Civil Disobedience Action.
Cartography by Lakshmi Venkatesh, 2024

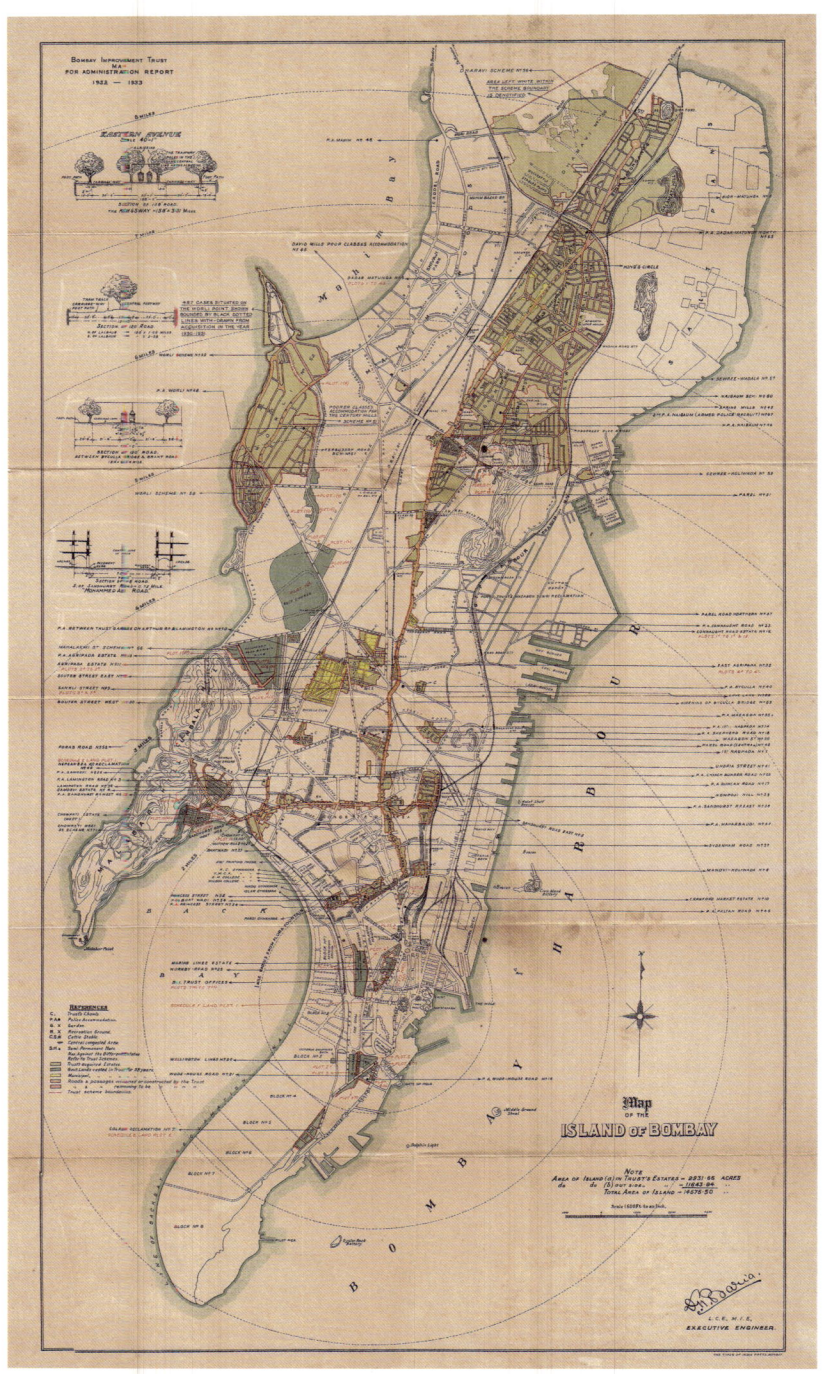

of British and Indian actors of many stripes and diverse communities.[6] Bolstered by the immense profits made by exporting opium to China, and diversifying into shipping, banking, and eventually, industrial enterprises, Bombay's mostly Parsi industrialists also took charge of urban governance and construction, leaving an indelible mark on the built geography of the contemporary city. Private commercial enterprise freed the fortunes of the city from sole dependence on the ebb and flow of British imperial trade and engendered a class of *swadeshi* capitalists who unsurprisingly remain some of the wealthiest business families in India today.[7]

Bursting at its seams to accommodate an ever-increasing population by the end of the 19th century, the city rebelled against authority even in its urban development. As leading Bombay historian Jim Masselos succinctly put it, "The city defie[d] the intentions of its masters to impose an orderly planned pattern upon it."[8] Extending its limbs, Bombay flourished by reclaiming the sea as land, appropriating idyllic fishing villages and building extensively networked yet spectacularly disparate neighbourhoods for its equally eclectic citizenry. In proportion to its size, the city's reputation continued to grow in the 20th century to such an extent that *The Times of India* declared on 24 May 1911, "It is to Bombay that the Government look[s] for the reflection of the best Indian opinion on the politics of the day, and for a lead in currency and finance."[9]

So, what did the colonial rulers see in 1930 vis-à-vis "Indian opinion" and "the politics of the day" when they "looked" to Bombay during the turbulent months of the Civil Disobedience Movement? As the photographs of this album showcase, they saw that "India's most materialistic city" had "[found] in itself to start dressing in coarse homespun, give up liquor and repeatedly brave police lathis."[10] They also found that this imperial city was readily and quite visibly donning the colours of anticolonial nationalism, with the message to boycott foreign goods and embrace *swadeshi* loudly broadcasted across its teeming marketplaces and bazaars (Fig. 1.9).

It is fitting that such a city, groomed to be a hub of trans-oceanic business, would embrace a form of nationalist politics that hinged upon the regulation of trade, commerce and consumption. As Dinyar Patel reminds us in his essay in this volume, the idea of *swadeshi*, after all, was not new to Bombay, which boasted its own brand of *swadeshi* politics long before it was adapted for mass nationalism. Bombay was thus primed to embrace a Gandhian style of politics, which it went on to reconfigure and make it its own. Others as well have noted this "symbiotic relationship" between Bombay and the Mahatma's nationalist project, recalling that "if Gandhi's leadership was magnetic, the city's response was overwhelming."[11]

Indeed, while the Indian village was the ideal of Gandhian thought, it was in the urban centres of colonial India that Gandhian-style activism, especially in the course of the Civil Disobedience Movement, unfolded in its most spectacular form.[12] Bombay, the *Urbs Prima* of India, fittingly led the charge, offering thousands of volunteers—men, women and children—who collectively sustained a year-long campaign against British rule, to the fury and exasperation of local colonial authorities. As the nationalist volunteers sought to challenge the colonial

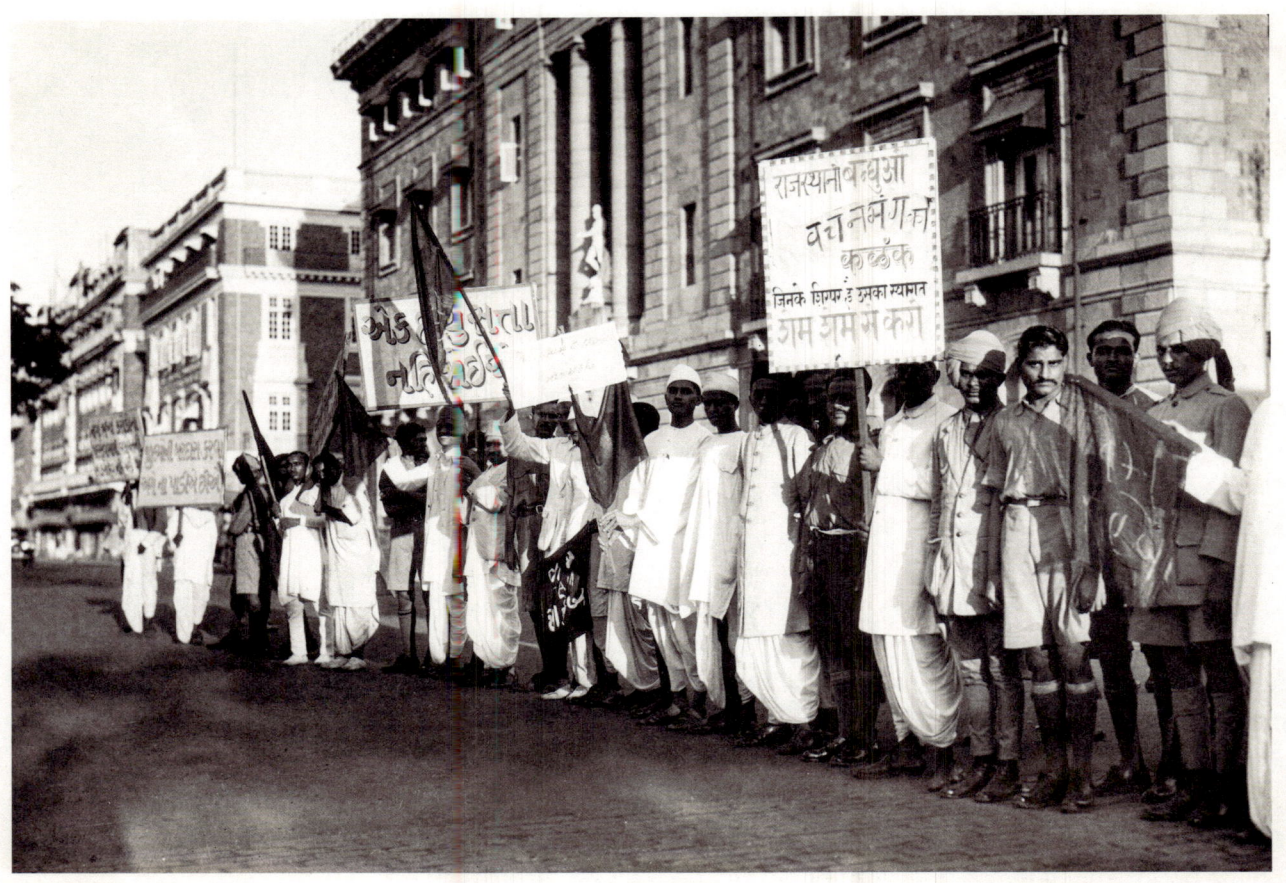

state by disobeying unjust colonial laws, they also catered to the Bombay public at large, putting up a show for the city crowds at its thoroughfares and creating an audience for their anticolonial action, as theorized by Debashree Mukherjee in her essay. The streets, obscured frequently in the photographs by a sea of Gandhi caps and *khadi* saris, gained a disobedient character themselves as theatres of anticolonial drama, offering the gathered spectators reasons for halting traffic, climbing atop buses and trams and up trees, and non-violently confronting the blows of the *lathi*-bearing policemen who often made no distinction between the protesting volunteers and their streetside admirers.

The black-and-white photographs of the Nursey album also take us back to familiar scenes of British Bombay, featuring its Victoria Terminus (now known as the Chhatrapati Shivaji Maharaj Terminus), Chowpatty Beach, and even the BEST buses and iconic department stores, as shown in Abigail McGowan's essay. Time and again, volunteers and city residents collected for public meetings and commemorations at the Esplanade Maidan. This open space, a British creation initially meant to separate the White and "native" parts of the city (and to strategically distance the fortified colonial section), was ironically but appropriately renamed Azad Maidan (lit. "Freedom Field"). Reclaimed by the newly disobedient public, Azad Maidan became the focal point of nationalist political action in the city (Fig. 5.16), as much as *swadeshi* and boycott became the rallying cry of the urban nationalist worker, energetically led by the determined women of Bombay.

But the work of the camera conceals as much as it reveals, and this remains true for the street politics captured in the folios of this album. Bombay's brand of a politics of disobedience was layered with many textures, and not just limited to a Gandhian style of nationalist action. As Naresh Fernandes reminds us, "Two of the Mahatma's most spirited political opponents were Bombay men, who had honed their ideas and oratorical skills in the city's conference halls and at the rallies of its maidans."[13] On one hand, B.R. Ambedkar remained a critical opponent of Gandhian nationalism and attendant rural fantasies to offer a robust critique and framework for Dalit liberation, located firmly in the city.[14] On the other, Muhammad Ali Jinnah began his formidable legal career in Bombay, from where he negotiated and debated British India's postcolonial destiny with Gandhi, most famously during the 1944 Gandhi-Jinnah meetings.[15] Meanwhile, the growing working class in Bombay, politicized over its own set of concerns, remained wary of the nationalist project which was intent on assimilating the moral cause of workers' rights into that of the nation writ large.

Though the photographs in the Nursey album fail to capture these alternative histories of anticolonial resistance, they do offer an opportunity to be read against the grain. As visual testimonies of an "Old Congress" history of the city, they serve as windows into this specific past, capturing as only a camera can the spectacular ways in which a Gandhian nationalist ethic came to dominate the urban imagination of disobedience.

"Drawing with Light" in Disobedient Bombay

Almost a century before the camera went to work on the streets of disobedient Bombay from April 1930 to August 1931, it had fallen in love with the city, the "eye of history"[16] repeatedly drawn to a place that contemporaries referred to as "the eye of India."[17] The historian of photography Susan Hapgood writes, "Long before the invention of moving pictures, and long before Bollywood, Bombay was the first Indian city where the photographic needs of the public, including more affluent indigenous Indians as well as the British, were catered to."[18] Within months of the invention of the daguerreotype in Europe, the new process was being discussed in Bombay's English-language newspapers. It is likely that the earliest photograph taken in India was in Bombay around 1840. By 1844, we are told that "any wealthy person could have his or her portrait taken" in some of the city's more affluent neighbourhoods.[19] A year later, the directors of the East India Company—still the formal ruling power in much of the subcontinent—were encouraging the Bombay government to establish "the study of this useful art of photography" in the scientific and educational institutions under its control, a recommendation that they repeated in December 1854.[20] By that time, the first photographic society of India had met in the city in October 1854, and in September 1855, the first photography class was convened at the Elphinstone Institution, several of its graduates going on to produce some of the earliest works in the new medium by Indians.

From the 1860s, the imperial edifices, the colonial streets, the new schoolrooms and the native bazaar became a favourite subject of what historian of photography Christopher Lee names as "the colonizing camera": a tool of conquest, command and control, of the lionizing of the white rulers and their accomplishments, and of the corresponding exoticizing or dehumanizing of the native body.[21] At the same time, in the hands of enthusiastic Bombay photographers whose work is now being recovered by scholars—"native" lensmen such as Narayan Daji, Hurrichund Chintamon, Shivashanker Narayen and Shapoor N. Bhedwar—an alternate corpus of views of the city and its residents and their lives and livelihoods was also beginning to take shape by the closing decades of the 19th century as photo studios became, if not ubiquitous, a standard feature of the built environment.[22]

As the nationalist movement began to gain momentum in the early decades of the 20th century, the camera was increasingly drawn into chronicling anticolonial politics, the panacea of the colonial state turning into the poison directed against it.[23] A striking demonstration of the subversive use of this imperial technology is available in the work of N.V. Virkar, a young photographer who had set up shop on Girgaum Road in Bombay and whose incendiary photographs of the infamous Jallianwala Bagh massacre in Amritsar in April 1919 "document the scene of a crime," even as they "witness and preserve an event."[24] Virkar's images of this moment are also symptomatic of the consequential movement of the camera out of the confines of the studio and onto the crowded streets of the subcontinent, as is also evidenced by the photographs which liberally began to pepper various reports and publications of the Congress party from around this time.[25] In the words of Christopher Pinney, "a mobile photographic technology was more easily able to document increasingly chaotic public spaces in which colonial hegemony appeared increasingly fragile."[26]

We place the Nursey album's images from 1930–1931 in the wake of such critical transformations in the work of photography in British India. The camera that yielded these images stays resolutely outside, with few if any attempts to take us indoors where scenes of disobedience, in ways big and small, also undoubtedly unfolded. Much has been written on the genres of public and street photography, largely a 20th-century phenomenon, including expressions of concern over "the representation of individuals without their knowledge or consent."[27] The album might well be guilty of the likely charge of "the predatory, possessive, and aggressive aspects of the photographic act," especially important to flag at a time when colonial censorship measures were in place.[28] And yet it is also worth noting that the patriotic residents of Bombay paused amidst their actions, repeatedly, to look directly at the photographer(s) wielding the camera and posed (Fig. 4.2, Fig. 7.8)—likely aware that they were leaving traces of their disobedience for the colonial state to act upon. This, after all, was the key ethical charge of Gandhian-style politics and is what makes this collection historically significant as it indexes the political charge of widespread nationalist action.

To date, we cannot name with certainty the creator(s) of these photographs, although historian Kama Maclean hazards in her essay that Navin Khandwala, a Congress activist and "keen photographer," might be a likely candidate. Nor can we say with certainty if the images are the work of a single photographer or multiple; local, expatriate or foreign; man or woman. As Murali Ranganathan notes in his contribution to this volume, the focus of a vast majority of the images suggests a familiarity and comfort with the city proper rather than its growing suburbs to the north (where also there was considerable disobedient action during these months). Several photographs from the album found their way into contemporary newspapers, especially the English-language dailies of the Times of India group; one of them—the stunning panorama reproduced as Figure 2.5—was even published in *The Illustrated London News* on 14 June 1930. This suggests that the photographer(s) may have contracted with stock photography agencies that may have licensed the work for commercial use. Used though some of these images might have been by pro-government publications, the camera repeatedly bears witness to the heroic actions of the disobedient residents of the city even while exposing the brutality of the colonial state's proxies in the form of the cross-racial Bombay police, whose white officers are almost the only Europeans visible in the album's pages. It is also striking that a vast majority of those who posed for the camera signal by their attire or by banners they carry that they were Congress volunteers or associated with that nationalist party. As far as these images are concerned, disobedient Bombay was in essence a Congress city. The lack of the presence of nationalists or activists of other stripes is almost as remarkable as the absence of white civilians who also, after all, populated this most cosmopolitan of British India's cities.

Undaunted by all such uncertainties and unknowns, we engage with this album, taking heart from theorist of photography Ariella Azoulay who has invited us to shift our attention from questions of authorship or provenance and attend instead to what she calls "the event of photography." In her words, "The photograph is evidence of an event—the taking of a photograph, the event of photography— which the photographic image could never exhaust on its own. This event is an invitation for yet another event—the viewing of the photograph, its reading, taking part in the production of meaning. The photograph cannot determine the limits of this event."[29]

"The event of photography" thus includes past, present, and future viewers. One past viewer—who may well have been seeing these photographs in the aftermath, their future—was undoubtedly the collator of the *Collections of Photographs of Old Congress Party*: a rather banal title, we admit, for an object that has within its covers such fascinating images that provide a rich afterlife to a historic event. Whether K.L. Nursey—whose name appears on the spine of the album—was the name of the collator is not clear, nor is it apparent who wrote some of the copious captions to the images. Occasionally including erroneous dates and spelling errors, frequently not naming well-known figures of the Bombay political and social scene, and often replete with details that suggest a lack of immediate knowledge, these captions—which guide us as post-facto witnesses to the events captured by the photographs—were obviously added later, perhaps around the time of collation (several images are reproduced in the volume with the captions attached to give a flavour of these). Such lacks notwithstanding, the album is nevertheless imbued with a spirit of historical curiosity and is an object that lends itself to historical inquiry, even deserving of it. This particularly comes through when one pauses over the strategic and conscious inclusion of a few anachronistic photographs, such as one of Bombay's favourite sons—and the Grand Old Man of India—Dadabhai Naoroji, seated with a group of women, invoking the longer tradition of the city's *swadeshi* and nationalist aspirations, as flagged by Dinyar Patel in his essay (Fig. 4.12)

The album, however, is not chronologically arranged, nor is there an apparent logic to the sequence of photographs, although it begins with portraits of key political figures—men and women, and all associated with the Congress—who either visited the city or were its leading lights. One of its last pages includes a dramatic panorama focused on a large crowd facing off against the mounted police (Fig. 2.5). This is an appropriate manner with which to close an album which has elevated the faceless crowd to the status of historical protagonist, as we have noted.

Lacking though it may be in many of the traits of a formal album—many such were created and circulated in British India since the advent of photography —we choose to treat and mine it as an archive of disobedience which visually counters photographs published in the dominant pro-imperial news media, such as *The Times of India* or *The Illustrated London News*.[30] It may be even seen as a counter-archive, the product of the "disobedient" camera that sought out anticolonial subjects in action, offering resistance, challenging the might of the world's biggest imperial power. As such, each photograph in the album is an inscription of sheer presence on the streets of Bombay, possibly of a terrifying moment experienced when confronting the might of empire, but also, for sure, performances of disobedience.[31] At the same time, every photograph is also a "first draft of history... holding open the potential tensions of the draft."[32] As such, we dwell over the course of these pages on the many ambiguities and recalcitrances, the silences and absences, that inevitably accompany "first drafts."

Not least, we present the photographs of the Nursey album as "civil" images in the very basic sense of being primarily focused on civilians engaged in acts of disobedience, which befits the non-violent movement that they capture within their frame.[33] Indeed, many of the men, women and children of these times are guaranteed a historical existence only because of these photographs that offer material and visual evidence of their acts of disobedience. Even though we may never ever know their names or apprehend anything else about them, their faces gaze out at us with a presence and liveliness with which we are able to connect almost a century later.

As such, the Nursey album is patriotic patrimony that arrives in our midst with all the complications that inevitably accompanies such an inheritance. As we have been reminded, "When photographs come out of storage, it is as if energy is released."[34] It is precisely this energy that we tap in this scholarly catalogue, putting it to good use to offer fresh perspectives and new arguments about a critical moment of our past that we think we know all too well, only to discover—when we are offered visual reminders—of how much more there is to know and learn.

Writing with Words of Light

Seized thus by a sense of shared commitment to pay appropriate tribute to such a rich inheritance, the authors of this volume draw on these photographs to make visible the differing historical processes that animated and informed disobedient action and nationalist politics in colonial Bombay in the 1930s. In the words of Jim Masselos, "Whatever techniques one uses to study this city there is still more to study."[35] In the spirit of this statement by one of the city's most memorable chroniclers, we draw upon tools and techniques derived from and driven by visual materials to contextualize the diverse narratives revealed in the folios of this image-object. These compelling photographs allow us to focus on Gandhian anticolonial action as it played out on the cosmopolitan and crowded streets of colonial Bombay. The historical and visual themes captured in this hitherto unexplored photo archive go well beyond engaging a nationalist/anticolonial historiography by mobilizing the insights of recent scholarship on swadeshi nationalism, gender and women's studies, urban studies, film, photography and visual studies, consumer history, as well as material history and the history of colonial institutions, such as the cross-racial colonial police in India.

What happens when Bombay's mighty colonial public buildings become part of the background of a photograph, sometimes presenting fragmented views, at other times completely occluded by the disobedient actions of its residents?

This is the principal question explored by art historian Preeti Chopra in the essay that follows this Introduction. Chopra dwells as well on what she calls "street furniture"—a fountain or statue here, a tram there—and other building elements that came to be used as props by the protesters. Even as her chapter pays attention to the gap between what the album makes us believe and what the historical record tells us about matters such as participation, violence and non-violence, its photographs reveal new centres of power, such as Congress House, that challenged the might of the colonial state. Her essay contends that with its curated images and captions, the Nursey album is a distinct staging of the Civil Disobedience Movement.

Film and media studies scholar Debashree Mukherjee moves our attention in the next essay to the people who thronged the streets and obscured the grand edifices of colonial Bombay discussed by Chopra. Alongside "agitators," "volunteers" and "party workers," the Nursey album's photographs bring to light a new group: urban spectators who watched, witnessed and perhaps were even moved by what they witnessed across the city in these disobedient months. In particular, Mukherjee sets up a dialogue between the album and the histories of cinemagoing in 1930s Bombay in order to situate mass spectatorship as a central catalyst for mass politics in the modern city, be it in movie theatres or on the streets. By connecting acts of disobedience and film viewership in the city, she frames "cinema" as a mass perceptual machinery that attunes the individual to a collective gaze and extends into the street as political spectatorship.

The remaining essays are by historians, as befits the historical project on hand. In his essay "From Profits and Patriotism to Gandhian Austerity," Dinyar Patel introduces us to a longer history of *swadeshi* in Bombay, identifying significant changes and continuities from the mid-19th century through the Civil Disobedience Movement. As a hub of modern textile manufacturing, Bombay had, long before Gandhi's rise to power, established a close connection between cloth and *swadeshi* activism. Business people, industrialists and political elites pioneered a distinct "profits and patriotism" model of *swadeshi*. However, this model suffered a grave crisis in the early 1910s, helping usher in significant Gandhian innovations in methods of economic self-reliance and popular attitudes towards big business. Photographs in the Nursey album attest to several of these innovations: women's mass participation and the tactics of boycott and bonfires. While such action dramatically changed the street politics of *swadeshi*, Patel argues that they were undergirded by a strong sense of historical memory of earlier *swadeshi* activity in the city.

Among the most innovative of activities and performances inaugurated in the city during the Civil Disobedience Movement was the illicit making of salt and its vending on its streets and in marketplaces. This is the subject of Sumathi

Ramaswamy's essay "Salt of the City," which makes a case for Bombay's vital role in transforming Gandhi's singular act of disobedience on the Dandi seashore, when he broke the colonial salt law, into a mass urban phenomenon. The photographs of the Nursey album demonstrate how British India's premier hub of commerce and capital was transformed into a "contraband city" in the summer of 1930, with its patriotic men and especially women (several with children in tow) making their way to the sea to extract the mundane but magical mineral. The camera follows them to reveal the everyday but effective material infrastructure—pots and pans, clay stoves and earthen hearths—with which the citizenry conducted their elementary act of disobedience against the world's mightiest empire.

If the Civil Disobedience Movement was innovative in its methods of anticolonial resistance, the people who participated in it were equally remarkable. Women's participation in this movement, especially in Bombay, was unprecedented, as they took over the city—and several photographs of the album—in large numbers. Murali Ranganathan engages with these photographs to contend with the anonymity of the average Congresswoman. In doing so, he leads us to the suburbs of colonial Bombay, spaces of intense disobedient action which regrettably were left just slightly outside the frame of our unknown photographer(s). With the help of the few photographs taken in these locales, Ranganathan shows us how the identity of suburban Congresswomen was rendered doubly elusive: first, on account of their gender; and second, because of the suburban nature of their protest sites. The images in the album open ways to understand the motivations and aspirations of these women and how suburban sites of protest offered them an arena which the city perhaps could not.

Back in the heart of colonial Bombay, women filed through the city's busiest market areas in boycott processions, stationed themselves outside shops and led stand-offs with the police in front of European-owned stores. In women's hands, the boycott movement became more than just diverting demand from foreign to Indian goods. Instead, boycott efforts deployed women on the streets as well-dressed agents of unrest to moralize consumption. In her essay "Boycotting Women," Abigail McGowan engages with such new aspects of "the street politics of consumption" under Gandhian nationalism as archived in the photographs of the album. Through McGowan's critical lens on the bustling world of the Bombay bazaar, we understand how processions, pickets and speeches in European business districts and Indian markets staged boycott as "women's work," even as women claimed authority over consumer practices in the marketplace.

Indeed, the cadres of sari-clad female nationalist volunteers are the prominent protagonists of the visual narrative of disobedience assembled in the Nursey album. However, in her essay "Patrolling the Streets of Disobedience in Bombay,"

Avrati Bhatnagar draws our attention to the photographs of the low-ranked, *lathi*-wielding police constable of native origin. Although colonial ideology sanctioned the use of authoritarian violence as a manly act, the constable's ruthless assault on his disobedient compatriots was widely perceived as brutal and inhumane by observers and critics of the colonial regime. The policeman's violent manhood also contrasted with Gandhian nationalism's prescriptive ideals that valorized self-sacrifice as an essential trait among Indian women. But such careful constructions of gendered public and political behaviour were repeatedly troubled in the course of the Civil Disobedience Movement in the city. The Bombay police constable embodied colonial authority, and yet he remained in a fraught position as a split colonized subject, simultaneously victim and perpetrator. The selection of photographs in this essay captures this layered crisis of social and gender relations that came to converge on this feared and reviled figure.

Concluding this volume, Kama Maclean examines a number of photographs that feature speeches being delivered by Congress leaders to large crowds at key public spaces in Bombay, such as Chowpatty Beach and the Esplanade/Azad Maidan. Her essay takes up the images' invitation to think of how urban space was politicized and utilized in sonic terms. Indeed, these busy photographs are also *noisy*, illuminating how Congress leaders sought to vocally project their messages to increasingly larger crowds, aided by rhetoric, gesture and performance, and eventually, through the use of microphone and loudspeaker technologies that enabled more expansive publics. The images also provide a window on concepts of power as indexed by the revolving possession of the microphone, indicating a diffused leadership of Congress workers who rotated through the movement as arrests removed them from the field of action.

Through this volume's diverse essays—each with a singular theme, yet woven into meta-textual dialogue with all the others—we invite you into a remarkable visual history of radical collective disobedience, resistance and revolution centred on the power of the photograph as well as on its elisions and slippages. We also invite you to reflect upon the valuable role played by archives such as the Alkazi Collection of Photography in recovering and housing works from the past to hand down into the present for a future to come.

Notes

1. Zahid Chaudhary, *Afterimage of Empire: Photography in Nineteenth-Century India* (Minneapolis: University of Minnesota Press, 2012), p. 186.

2. Avrati Bhatnagar and Sumathi Ramaswamy, "Light Writing on the Lathi Raj: Bombay, 1930–31", *History of Photography*, vol. 45, no. 4 (2021), pp. 304–19.

3. File no. G-2/1931, All India Congress Committee [AICC] Files, Nehru Memorial Museum and Library [NMML], New Delhi.
4. Georges Didi-Huberman, *Images in Spite*

of All: Four Photographs from Auschwitz, trans. Shane B. Lillis (Chicago: University of Chicago Press, 2003), pp. 32-33.

5. Usha Thakkar and Sandhya Mehta, *Gandhi in Bombay: Towards Swaraj* (Oxford: Oxford University Press, 2017), p. 159.

6. Preeti Chopra, *A Joint Enterprise: Indian Elites and the Making of British Bombay* (Minneapolis: University of Minnesota Press, 2011).

7. On the emergence of *swadeshi* capitalism in the interwar period of colonial India, see Aashish Velkar, "Swadeshi Capitalism in Colonial Bombay", *The Historical Journal*, vol. 64, no. 4 (2021), pp. 1009-34.

8. Quoted in Prashant Kidambi, Manjiri Kamat and Rachel Dwyer (eds.), *Bombay Before Mumbai: Essays in Honour of Jim Masselos* (New York: Oxford University Press, 2019), p. 5.

9. Quoted in R.P. Karkaria, *The Charm of Bombay: An Anthology of Writings in Praise of the First City in India* (Bombay: D.B. Taraporevala, 1915), p. 170.

10. Quoted in Naresh Fernandes, *City Adrift: A Short Biography of Bombay* (New Delhi: Aleph Book Company, 2013), p. 72.

11. Thakkar and Mehta, *Gandhi in Bombay*, xxiii.

12. Prashant Kidambi, "Nationalism and the City in Colonial India: Bombay, c. 1890-1940", *Journal of Urban History*, vol. 38, no. 5 (2012), pp. 950-67.

13. Fernandes, *City Adrift*, p. 77.

14. Jesús Francisco Cháirez-Garza, "Touching Space: Ambedkar on the Spatial Features of Untouchability", *Contemporary South Asia*, vol. 22, no. 1 (January 2014), pp. 37-50.

15. Thakkar and Mehta, *Gandhi in Bombay*, xxxvii.

16. Georges Didi-Huberman, *The Eye of History: When Images Take Positions*, trans. Shane B. Lillis (Toronto: RIC Books, 2018).

17. Quoted in Avrati Bhatnagar, "Disobedient Women in a Consumer City: Picturing Swadeshi Politics in Interwar Bombay", unpublished Ph.D dissertation, Department of History, Duke University (2024).

18. Susan Hapgood, *Early Bombay Photography* (Ahmedabad: Mapin Publishing, 2015), p. 11.

19. ibid., p. 13.

20. G. Thomas, "Photography and the Elphinstone Institution of Bombay", *History of* Photography, vol. 5, no. 3 (1981), pp. 245-47, at p. 245.

21. Christopher Lee, "The Decolonising Camera: Street Photography and the Bandung Myth", *Kronos*, vol. 46, no. 1 (2020), pp. 195-220. For two recent analyses of imaging the "native Other" within frameworks of colonialism and "internal colonialism", see David Odo, "Anthropological Boundaries / Photographic Frontiers: The Visual 'Language of Salvage'", in Rahaab Allana (ed.), *Unframed: Discovering Image Practices in South Asia* (New Delhi: HarperDesign, 2023), pp. 129-40; and Parul Dave Mukherjee, "Mimicking Anthropologists: Re-Membering a Photo Archive via *Pata* Paintings, Performative Mimesis and Photo-Performance", in Rahaab Allana (ed.), *Another Lens: Photography and the Emergence of Image Culture*, Volume 4 [India Since the 90s series] (2024), pp. 178-99.

22. Hapgood, *Early Bombay Photography*. See also Rahaab Allana (ed.), *The Artful Pose: Early Studio Photography in Mumbai, 1855-1940* [exhibition catalogue] (Ahmedabad: Mapin Publishing in association with The Alkazi Collection of Photography and Dr Bhau Daji Lad Mumbai City Museum, 2010).

23. Christopher Pinney, *The Coming of Photography in India* (London: The British Library, 2008).

24. Christopher Pinney, "The Prosthetic Eye: Photography as Cure and Poison", in Matthew Engelke (ed.), *The Objects of Evidence: Anthropological Approaches to the Production of Knowledge* (Oxford: Wiley-Blackwell, 2009), pp. 31-42, at p. 34.

25. Christopher Pinney, "Civil Contract of Photography in India", *Comparative Studies of South Asia, Africa and the Middle East*, vol. 35, no. 1 (2015), pp. 21-33, at pp. 24-29.

26. Pinney, *Coming of Photography*, p. 83. In an influential essay, the author advocates a "world-system photography" to counter the dominant Euro-American paradigm of photographic history, and points to the medium's latent "propensities and potentialities," noting that "a technology dependent on a colonial *habitus* initially found itself reproducing that *habitus*'s 'structuring determinations.' As this protean technical practice found itself freely roaming the streets, it located new subjects through which to create new publics. A protean photography proved itself capable of generating several directly opposed outcomes. From cure to poison, and all the while the same." See Christopher Pinney, "Seven Theses on Photography", *Thesis Eleven*, vol. 113, no. 1 (2012), pp. 141-56, at p. 155.

27. Abigail Solomon-Godeau, *Photography after Photography: Gender, Genre, and History* (Durham: Duke University Press, 2017), p. 81.

28. ibid.

29. Ariella Azoulay, "Potential History: Thinking through Violence", *Critical Inquiry*, vol. 39, no. 3 (2013), pp. 548-74, at p. 556.

30. Elisa DeCourcy and Miles Taylor, "Salt and the National Imaginary: The Photojournalism of the Dandi Satyagraha", *South Asia: Journal of South Asian Studies*, vol. 46, no. 4 (2023), pp. 820-33.

31. Elizabeth Edwards, "Anthropology and Photography: A Long History of Knowledge and Affect", *Photographies*, vol. 8, no. 3 (2015), pp. 235-52.

32. Patricia Hayes and Gary Minkley, "Introduction: Africa and the Ambivalence of Seeing", in Patricia Hayes and Gary Minkley (eds.), *Ambivalent: Photography and Visibility in African History* (Columbus: Ohio University Press, 2019), pp. 1-34, at p. 4. The authors draw on Siegfried Kracauer's meditations on the photograph to make this assertion.

33. In so suggesting, we are also inspired by the critique in Ariella Azoulay's *Civil Imagination: The Political Ontology of Photography* (London: Verso, 2012).

34. Lee, "Decolonising Camera", p. 201.

35. Jim Masselos, "Remembering Bombay: Present Memories and Past Histories", in Kidambi et al (eds.), *Bombay Before Mumbai*, p. 314.

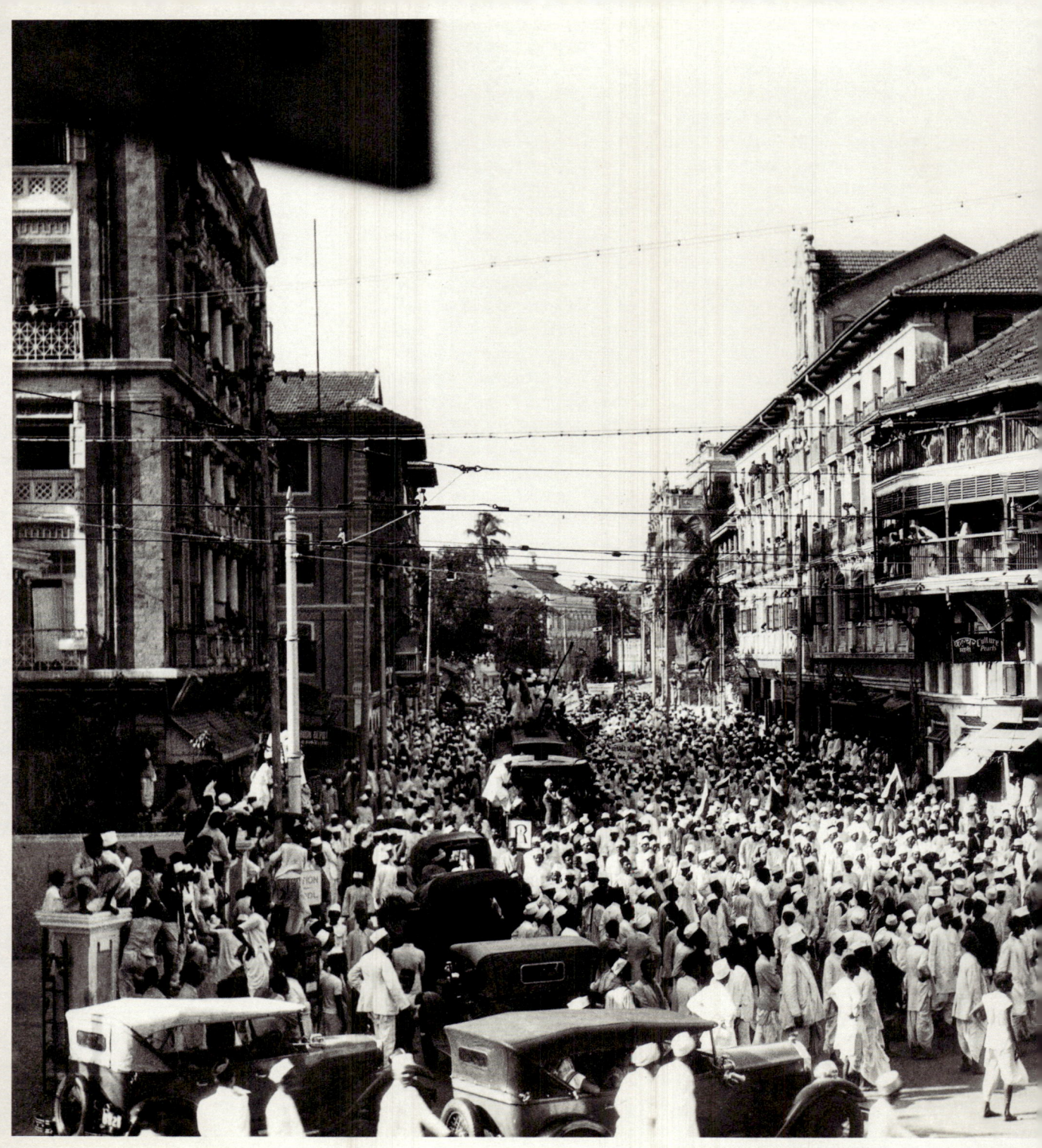

The Mohomedans of Bombay in sympathy with
their Hindu brothern organised a procession
which started from Dongri and terminated
on the Esplanade maidan. The procession start-
ting from the Dongri maidan.

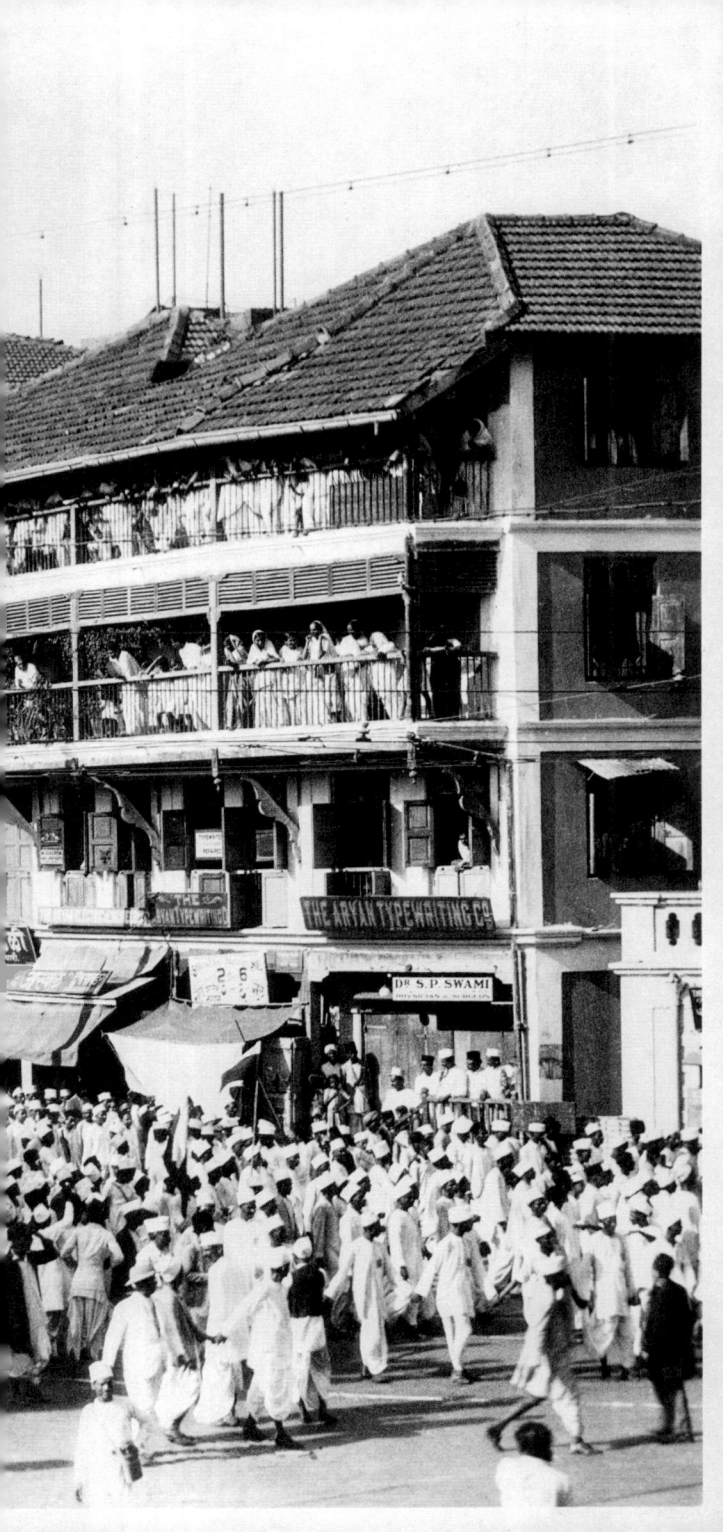

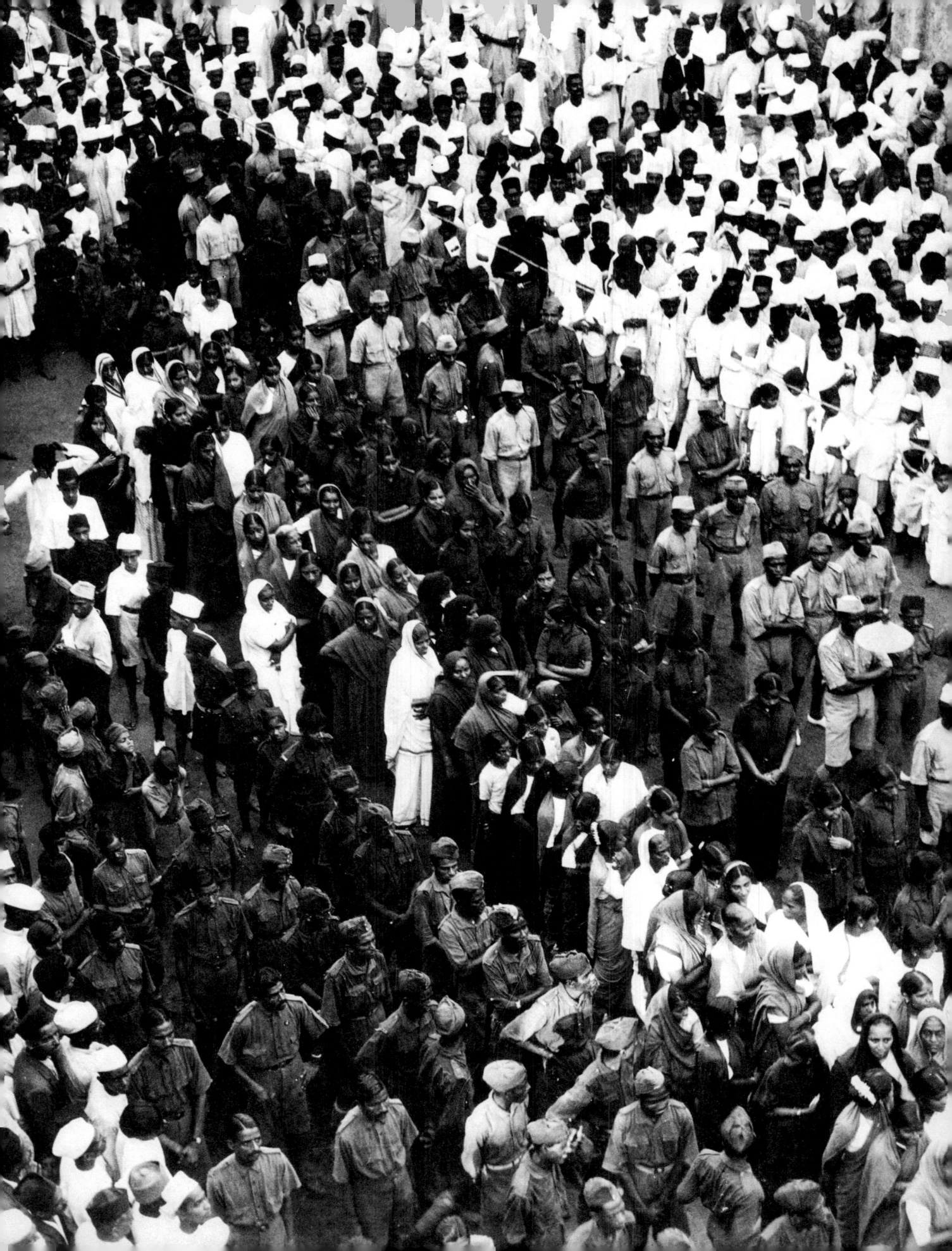

CHAPTER 2

THE STAGES OF
A DISOBEDIENT BOMBAY

Preeti Chopra

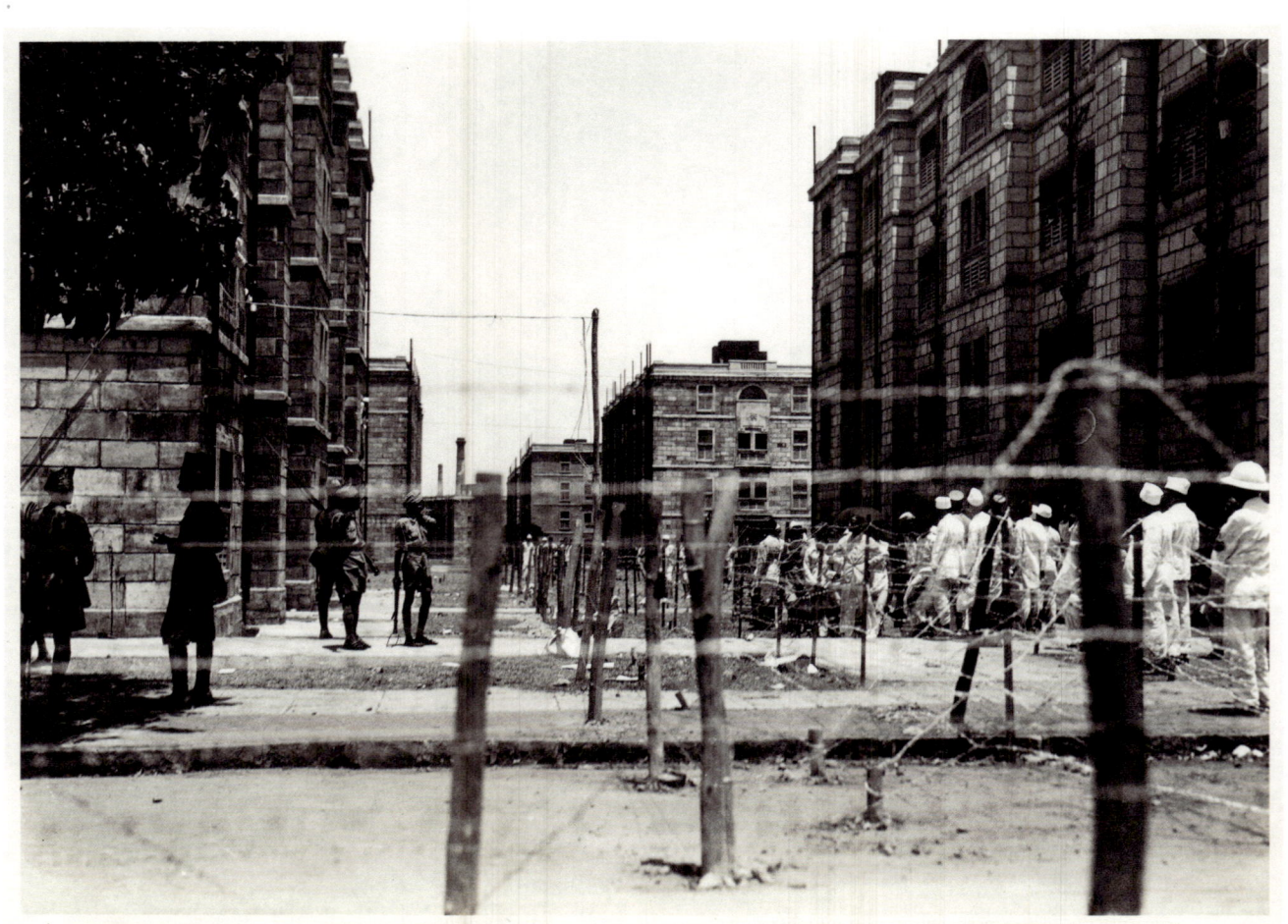

The Worli chawls used as temporary prisons for the civil disobedience prisoners.

The iconic colonial buildings and public spaces in south Bombay highlighted in K.L. Nursey's historical album serve as—what may be read as—crucial backdrops, stages, sets, props and repositories of civil disobedience protest activity in the city. Together with the participants, these buildings and areas are the focus of this chapter. I discuss the album's depiction of the architecture, public spaces and "street furniture" (objects and equipment installed as amenities that provide functional services for the public and are generally maintained by municipal authorities). They are utilized and navigated in this mode of political theatre by diverse native and European "actors"—protesters, native constables, colonial police officers and administrators, Congress leaders, crowds, satyagrahis, spectators, bystanders, picketers, processions, rallies, observers who became participants, etc. I also identify those who were excluded from the civil disobedience agenda by the nationalist leadership, and those who, for multiple reasons, chose not to participate in protest activity.

The varied urban spaces and built forms used by heterogenous protagonists to enact satyagraha and other modes of nationalist activism may conform to what is defined as constituting a stage, i.e., "The platform in a theatre upon which spectacles, plays, etc., are exhibited; esp. a raised platform with its scenery and other apparatus upon which a theatrical performance takes place."[1] The Nursey album offers remarkable views of what might be called "stages of disobedience" in what I have elsewhere described as the city's "joint public realm" that includes the seashore, public buildings, maidans and other open spaces, roads, trams/ tram tracks, steps, as well as bazaar shops, department stores and the array of what David Arnold has called "subaltern streets."[2] These stages hosted choreographed satyagraha, individual protests, mass gatherings and spectacles of dissent such as bonfires of foreign-made cloth.

One of the few photographs in the Nursey album where built forms, rather than political "actors," are the subject is Fig. 2.1, an image of the punitive "stage" of the Worli chawls (tenements), "used as temporary prisons for the civil disobedience prisoners."[3] In the foreground and out of focus are the requisite "props" of upright posts and barbed-wire boundaries that very literally remind us that this was a place of imprisonment. With three kinds of actors—white

PAGES 42–43
"The Mohomedans [Mohamedans] of Bombay in sympathy with their Hindu brothren [brethren] organised a procession which started from Dongri and terminated on the Esplanade maidan. The procession starting from the Dongri maidan." c. 1930–1931 Gelatin Silver Print, 115 x 160 mm ACP: 98.77.0002 (44a)

PAGE 44
"A flag hoisted [hoisting] ceremony resently [recently] held in the premises of Congress House by Sarojini Naidu. All CoNgress [Congress] volunteers saluting the flag."
(Detail, see p. 58)

Fig. 2.1
"The Worli chawls used as temporary prisons for the civil disobedience movement prisoners."
c. 1930–1931 Gelatin Silver Print, 115 x 156 mm ACP: 98.77.0002 (37b) View through barbed wire fence of two lines of chawls facing each other across a lane, with native constables (left), a white officer in a pith helmet (lower right), and a group of prisoners (centre right).

police, native constables/"guards" and detained protesters—this was a space of confinement and intimidation. An awareness of the political context, which is conveyed to us through the album and the individual image captions, allows us to understand the intent of this photograph. As with albums in general, the Nursey album is a curated collection of captioned images which help us to identify particular subjects, events and spaces, set up relationships between images, build meta-narratives through image trajectories, and persuasively offer a specific perspective: in this case, a distinctive and dramatic staging of the Civil Disobedience Movement in Bombay.

Many images depict the outright use of brute force by the police against non-violent *satyagrahis* (see Chapter Eight in this volume); however, the story of colonial domination/subjugation is far more complicated and ambivalent, and images of counter-violence by nationalist protesters is not presented at all. My account pays attention to the gap between what the album as ideological testimony would have us believe, and what is actually documented in the historical record. The album shows us a different view of many colonial buildings, so prominent in histories of the city. It also reveals new centres of power, such as Congress House, that challenged the might of the colonial state. Thus, I also raise a particular question vis-à-vis our viewing experience of the material "stages" and collective "performances" by civil disobedience "actors" within highly politicized/mobilized urban spaces: Do we respond to the prevalent political script differently when Bombay's mighty colonial public buildings are framed only in segments or fragments on the nationalist-colonial "sets"?

Buildings as Backdrops and as Fragmented Views

The visual historiography of the Nursey album shows us mass-mobilized civil disobedience participants, groups of *satyagrahis* and individual demonstrators filling up and moving through urban streets and maidans, the seashore and salt pans, engaged in mostly orderly and peaceful processions and activities. Some of Bombay's splendid colonial architecture features as stage, as set, as backdrop, as prop, as well as an immutable signifier of imperial force and, simultaneously, as a mute witness to the unfolding public actions of civil disobedience. For instance, the famous Great Indian Peninsular Railway Victoria Terminus and Administrative Offices at Bori Bunder (designed by British architectural engineer Frederick Williams Stevens and built in stages from 1878 to 1887; henceforth, VT), is often shown as merely the backdrop to ongoing paradigmatic events. In Fig. 3.1, VT looms behind a crowd of spectators viewing a procession from inside and on top of a tram; and in Fig. 9.16, a depiction of nationalist leader Vithalbhai Patel addressing a large crowd at Esplanade Maidan, the top of VT's spires and pediment and the domed Municipal Corporation (also designed by Williams and completed in 1893) are an intrusive lurking presence. Throughout the album, images that feature colonial buildings, shot from varied angles and

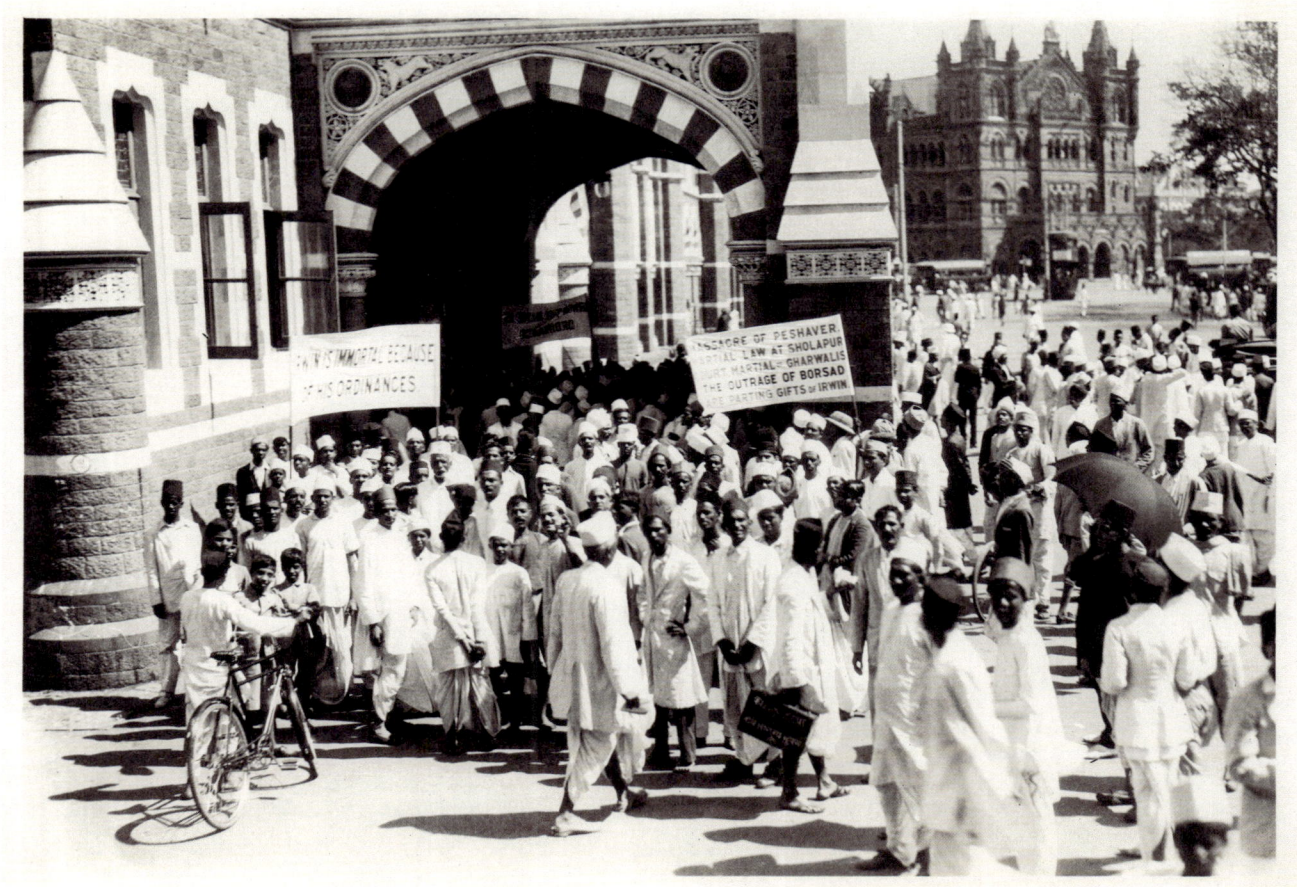

perspectives, reiterate the same theme: the validity, necessity and urgency of civil disobedience action.

These iconic buildings, shown in image after image, help us identify the sites of protest and contextualize the nationalist agenda as it unfolded through individual and collective protest. Historians of Bombay, such as Jim Masselos and Prashant Kidambi, discuss how the nationalists used mass action to temporarily appropriate, disrupt and occupy the city's public spaces, including the administrative and commercial areas of the colonial elite.[4] Kidambi notes that "Gandhian nationalism in Bombay produced an impressive array of political spectacles … that reinscribed the city's public arenas as nationalist space."[5] In the protests against the Rowlatt Act of 1919 and during the Non-Cooperation Movement of 1920–1922, the arenas for protest were usually restricted to areas occupied by Gujaratis and Maharashtrians in the so-called "native town," with massive nationalist rallies at the Chowpatty beach on Back Bay, the western foreshore of the city.[6] However, it was the city's workers who first infiltrated the spaces of the colonial elite, with nationalists following in their wake during the Civil Disobedience era. As Robert Rahman Raman has shown, workers had used some of these spaces as protest sites as early as 1915; and a few months

Fig. 2.2
"Demonstration at the Bombay Municipal office when the body proposed to give a farewell address to Lord Irwin." 1931
Gelatin Silver Print, 114 x 159 mm
ACP: 98.77.0002 (84b)
View of protesting crowds with banners at the arcuated *porte-cochère* of the Bombay Municipal Corporation Building. The Victoria Terminus is partly visible in the background.

prior to the Civil Disobedience Movement, workers had already claimed as protest sites the Esplanade Maidan, Elphinstone Circle Garden, Bhatia Bagh and other areas central to the British administrative, commercial and political establishments.[7] Similarly, Arnold has described how nationalists from the 1919 Rowlatt Satyagraha onwards had incorporated "subaltern streets" for anticolonial protest and nationalist parades.[8] Images of grand colonial buildings, such as VT and the Bombay Municipal Corporation that serve as backdrops of the nationalist stage in the Nursey album, reveal that the Civil Disobedience Movement had made territorial gains for the nationalist movement by systematically moving through, disturbing and occupying the spaces generally inhabited and controlled by the city's colonial elite, as earlier mentioned. Accepting that "the Esplanade Maidan in South Bombay, a vast open space … was the physical and symbolic center of the British and political establishment within the city,"[9] the presence there of prominent nationalist speakers such as Vithalbhai Patel and of huge crowds would have threatened the sense of privilege and security of those in power.

Colonial buildings framed in the album as backdrops to nationalist action compel us to view the events and their material contexts—the building itself and the specific institution it housed—in new ways. This is seen, for instance, in an image of demonstrators outside the Bombay Municipal Corporation, protesting the civic body's proposal to give a farewell address to Lord Irwin, the departing Viceroy (Fig. 2.2). Support for the Civil Disobedience Movement and attitudes towards the colonial government among native communities were hardly unanimous, and the Municipal Corporation, responsible for local self-government, was itself a site of political struggle.[10] Overall, the Corporation was in the hands of colonial administrators and wealthy European and Indian business elites. The less privileged sections of society, such as workers, lower castes and the middle class, were excluded from municipal politics (see Chapters Seven and Eight in this volume).[11]

Ongoing political theatre is perfectly summarized in Fig. 2.3, which presents the civil disobedience "stage"—the impressive steps and columns of Bombay's neoclassical Town Hall—and the "actors" performing prescribed "roles" within the "script" of nationalist dissent/colonial suppression of dissent (picketers, native constables, a white officer). Since the main focus is on the protesting actors, we are offered only a fragment or segment of the building in this view of the Town Hall. The women's banner carries the Marathi message *dāru pinyāmuleṅ hindustānchi shakti haran jhāli āhe* ("Liquor has ruined India").[12] In all likelihood this duo is from the Desh Sevika Sangh (the volunteer women's auxiliary of the Congress; henceforth, DSS) that had taken over the task of organizing and overseeing the picketing campaign in Bombay. Women over the age of 18 were eligible for DSS membership, and the leadership only recruited women from "good classes," rejecting "undesirable women" (i.e., prostitutes) and "leftists,"

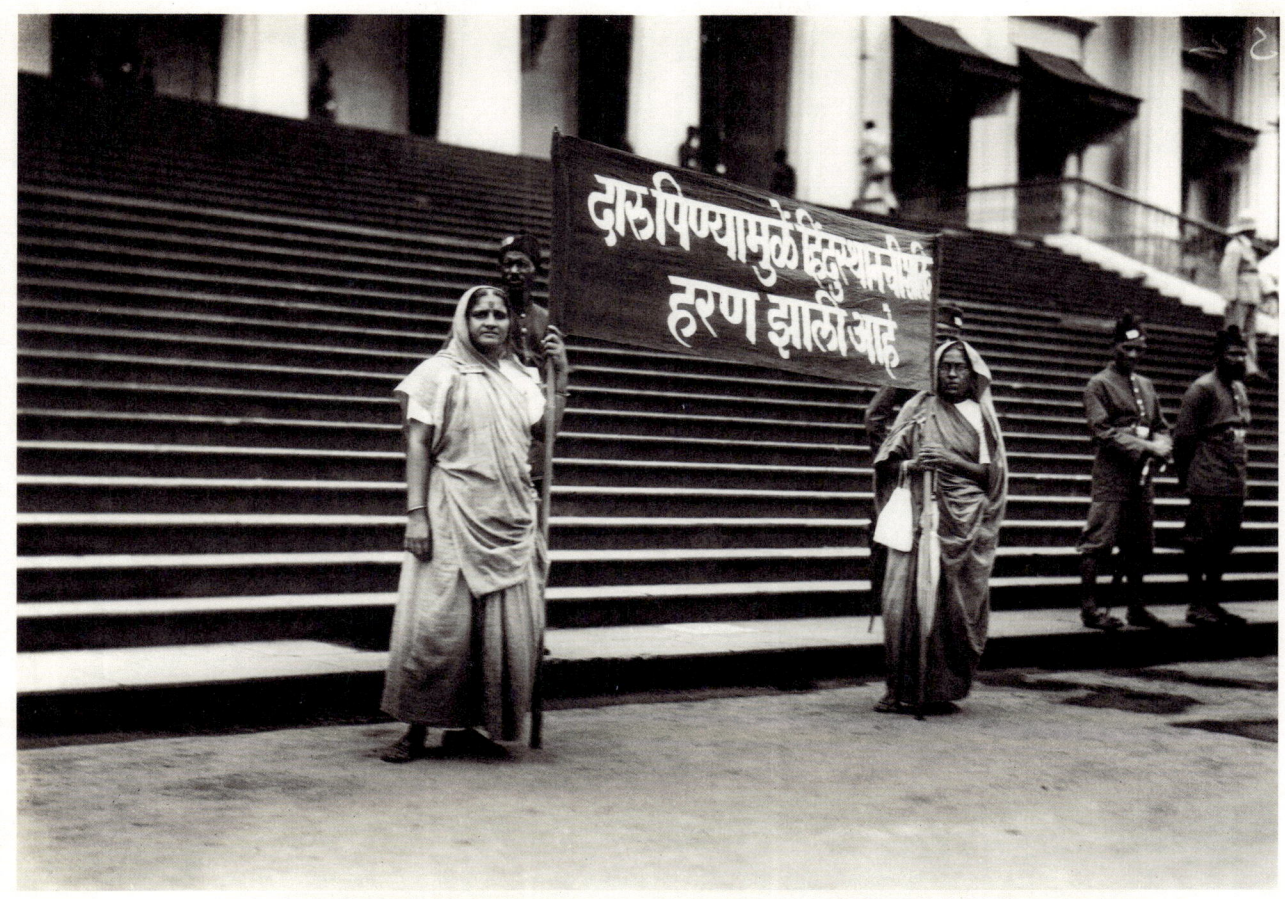

whose more radical protest methods were considered inappropriate (i.e., incompatible with Gandhi's prescriptive ideal of Indian womanhood as modest, chaste, compassionate, patient and nurturing). The initial DSS membership was over 500, but dropped to a steady 300 as a number of uncommitted "ornamental sevikas" subsequently drifted away.[13] Active members chose to be included in one of four categories: "A"/prepared to picket toddy shops, face public insult and go to jail; "B"/prepared to picket cloth shops and to be arrested but unwilling to face assault or go to jail; "C"/prepared to go from house to house to preach *swadeshi* (this work was considered suitable and safe for women with young children); and "D"/willing to go from house to house to preach the Gandhian ideal of spinning, a core aspect of *swadeshi* philosophy.

In Fig. 2.3, Fig. 2.12 and Fig. 8.14, we see category "A"—*desh sevikas* picketing and being arrested outside the Town Hall, designed by Colonel Thomas Cowper, a military engineer, and built in stages from 1811 to 1833. Architectural historian Sten Nilsson rightly observes that "Cowper's building conveys an impression of might and *mass* ... and the long façade has room for three porticos. The one in the middle, above the flight of steps and the main entrance, is like the whole Doric

Fig. 2.3
"Posters Bearing 'Liquor has ruined India' were displayed at the entrance to the Town hall Bombay."
c. 1930–1931
Gelatin Silver Print, 115 x 156 mm
ACP: 98.77.0002 (80a)
View of *desh sevikas* holding up a banner with a slogan in Marathi, overseen closely by four native constables; a white officer is visible on the right. The impressive steps leading up to the main entrance of the Town Hall entirely fill the middle section of this beautifully balanced composition.

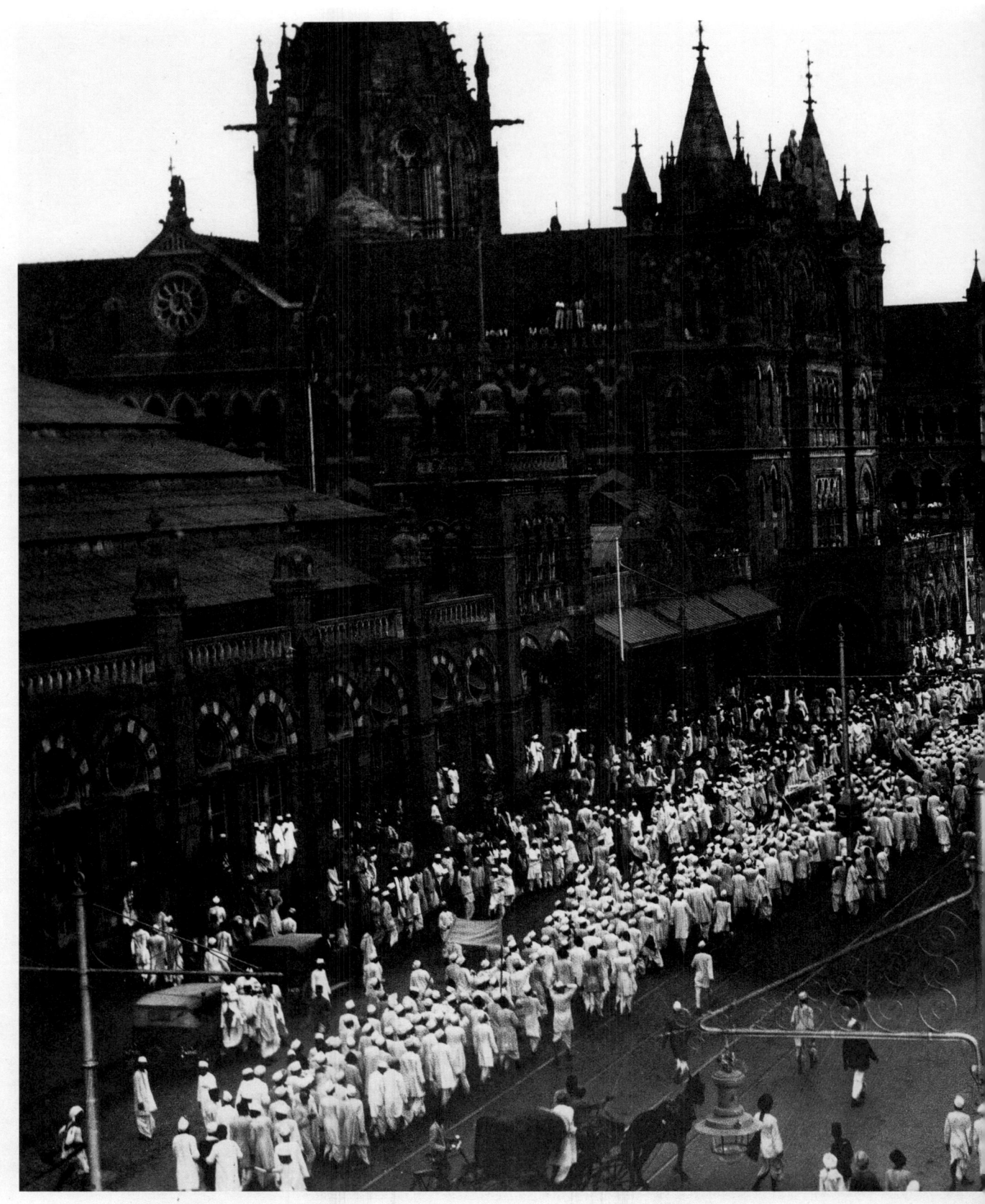

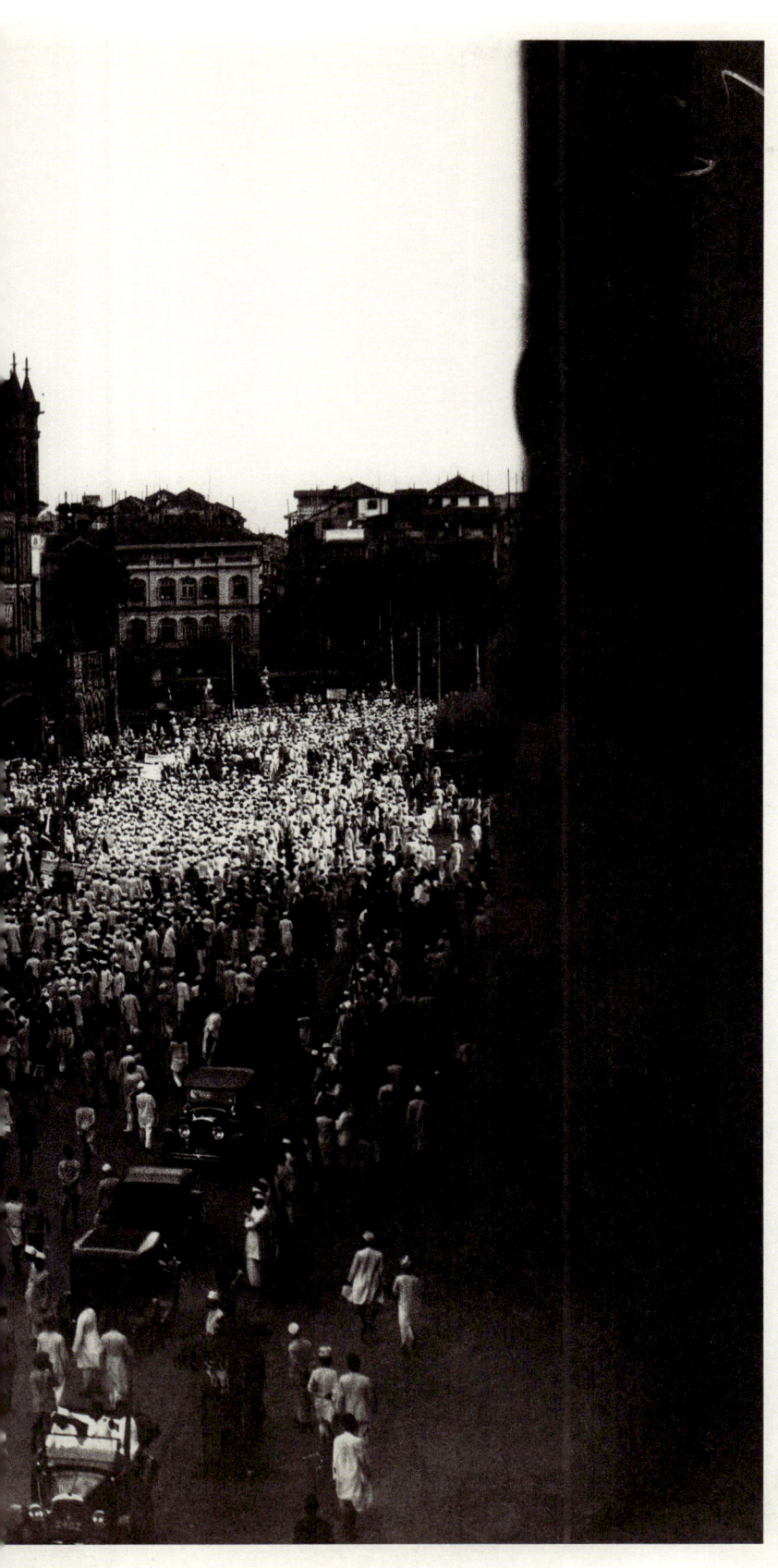

Fig. 2.4
"A procession
organised by the
Bullion market
Bombay to condemn the
repressive policy.
The procession
passing the Victoria
Terminus."
c. 1930—1931
Gelatin Silver Print,
113 x 156 mm
ACP: 98.77.0002 (110b)
The photographer
likely took the
photograph from an
upper storey of a
building opposite the
terminus to capture
an extensive view
of the length of the
procession.

Fig. 2.5

"The merchants of Bombay organised a a [sic] procession and a demonstration to condemn the Government of its repressive policy. The procession as it reached the Capitol cinema was stopped by a cordon of police about 300 strong. The mile long procession squatted on the road till about 8 p.m. The police withdrew to save an ugly situation. This joint picture gives a part view of the procession. Remove the photo to have a full view. Date of incident [sic]." 1930 Gelatin Silver Print, 110 x 386 mm ACP: 98.77.0002 (122) The central background is occupied by the facade of the Victoria Terminus with a dense crowd in front of it.

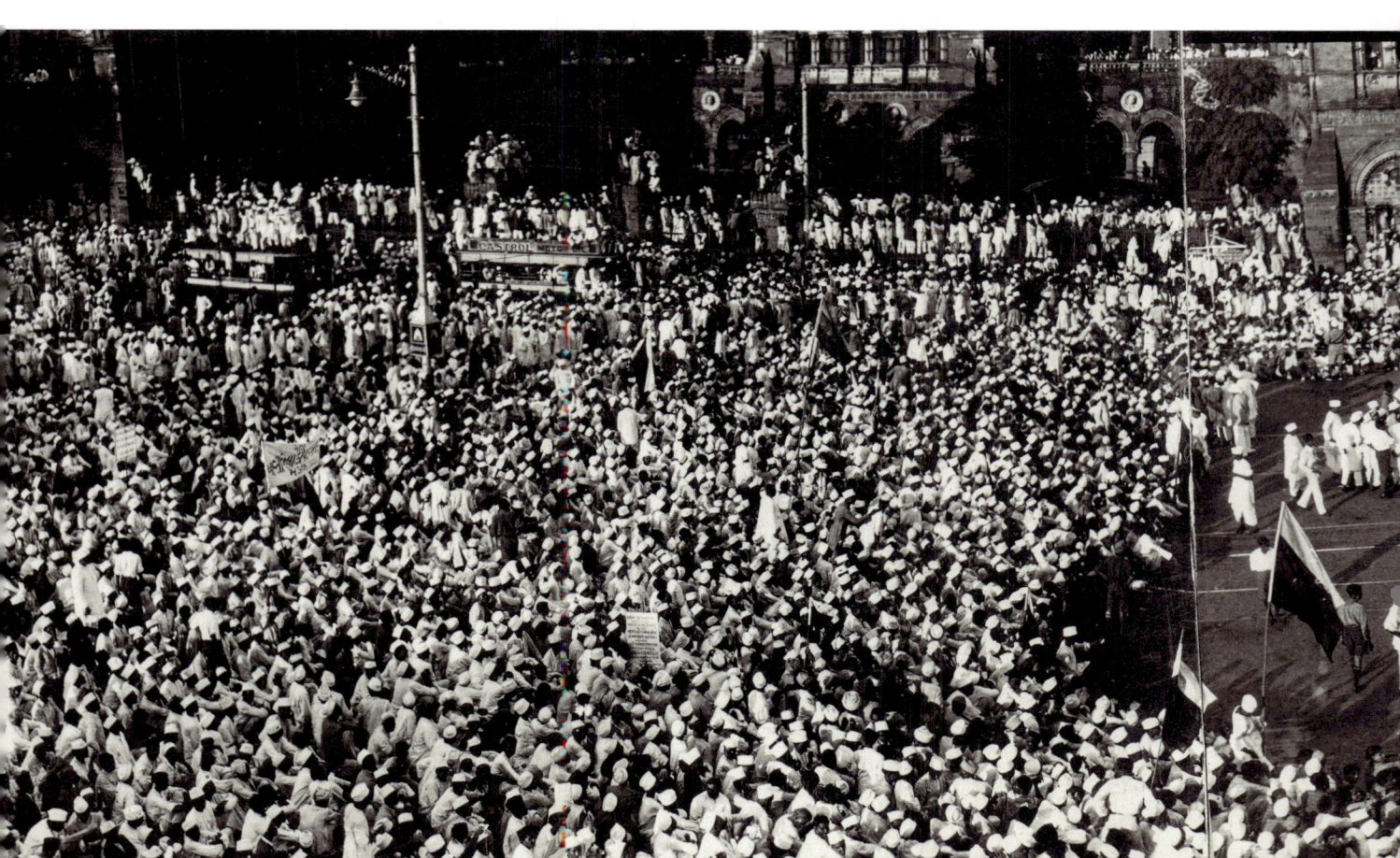

order borrowed from the Parthenon in Athens."[14] However, in the Nursey album the architectural beauty, power, and magnificence of Bombay's colonial public buildings, including the Town Hall, are usually hidden or diminished through the composition of the photograph or a focus on events and human activity— sometimes to the point where the building can be identified only via a caption.

In order to maximize visibility while protesting outside edifices of colonial power such as the Municipal Corporation and the Town Hall, protesters took up positions at the entrance or just beyond (Fig. 2.2, Fig. 2.3, Fig. 2.12). Such positioning makes us aware of the building's threshold, a place of crossing from one realm to the other, reminding us of two ever antagonistic realms—the imperial and the nationalist—intimately bound in ferocious incompatibility. The women protesters holding up a banner at the Town Hall are careful to stand below the first step, while protesters at the Municipal Corporation pass under the *porte cochère* where cars and other modes of transportation would have halted to pick up and drop municipal councillors, officials and visitors. A different perspective is offered in Fig. 2.4, this image likely taken from a building across the road from VT, showing a vast orderly procession organized "by the Bullion market [of] Bombay to condemn the repressive policy."[15] The extended diagonal of the white-clad participants is paralleled and accentuated by the dark diagonal of the station's facade stretching to the horizon; and yet, while setting the context, the dense mass of imperial architecture somehow does not visually subjugate

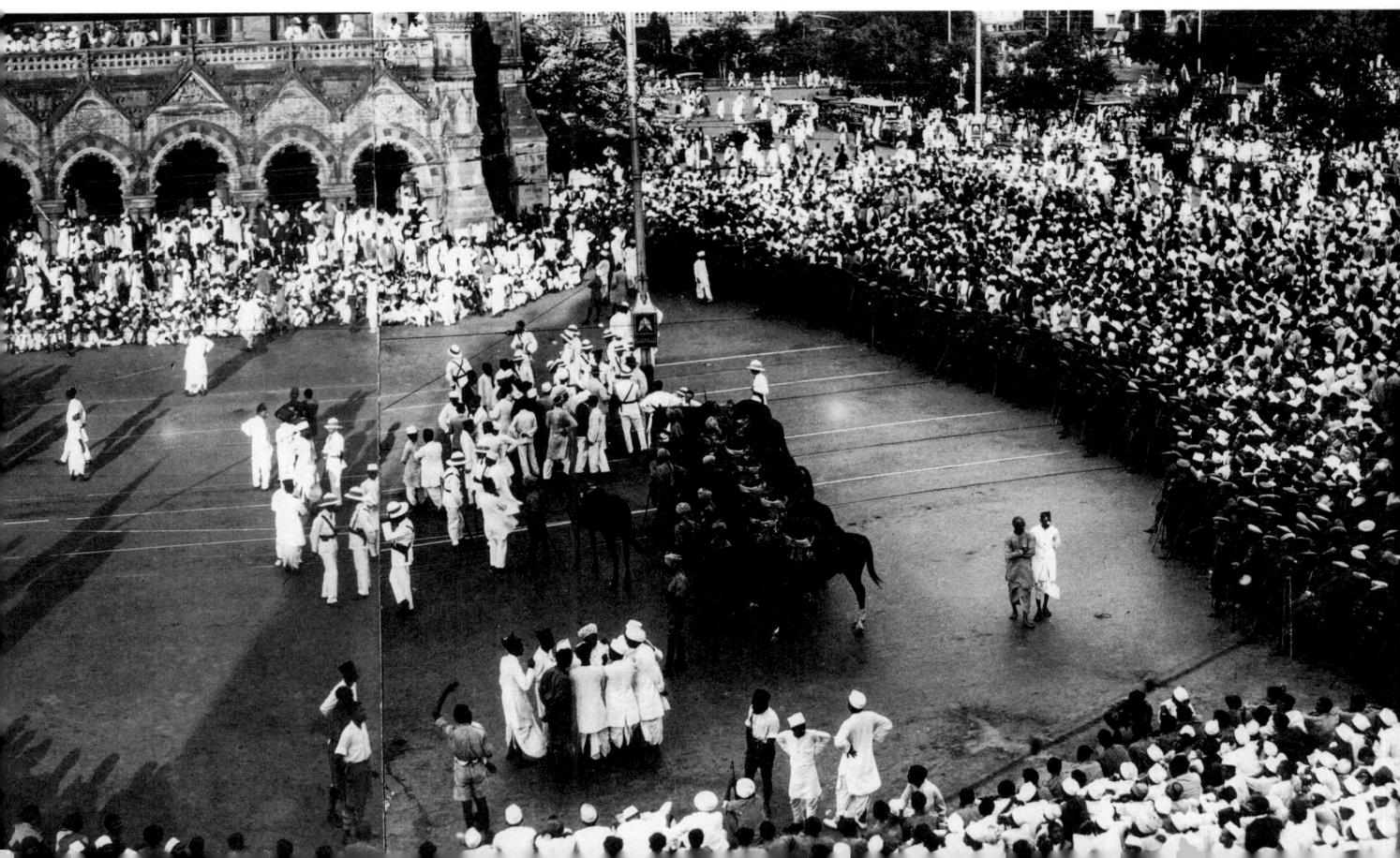

or overwhelm the enactment of nationalism on the street. Davies remarks that if one were to criticize VT, it would be for its proportions—its height being overwhelmed by the massive foreground and the train shed to the left—that give it an enormous horizontality.[16] In this photograph, the horizontality of the building serves to starkly accentuate the length of the procession.

Masselos has pointed out that both Bori Bunder and the Fort precinct "had thus become an objective as well as a battleground" in the Civil Disobedience Movement, with the expansive space at Bori Bunder, framed by important buildings, at the junction of six main roads: "one from Crawford Market, another from Dhobi Talao, two from the dockyards and two more from the European business areas."[17] A crucial site of mass gatherings, the Esplanade Maidan, renamed Azad ("Freedom") Maidan by the nationalists, is adjacent to the road from Dhobi Talao. At one corner of this extensive space at Bori Bunder is Capitol cinema; another corner is occupied by the notable Municipal Corporation Building with its prominent statue of the famous politician-lawyer and four-time Municipal Commissioner Sir Pherozeshah Mehta; VT station stands at the corner opposite the Corporation building. This was the broad arena for the mass action featured in many Nursey images, and the site where the police halted many nationalist processions (Fig 2.2, Fig. 2.4, Fig. 2.5, Fig. 2.14, Fig. 2.15, Fig. 2.16, Fig. 2.17, Fig. 3.1, Fig. 4.11).[18]

It is obvious that the colonial state understood and participated in the tactical use and reimagining of urban space. The administration had noted how the Congress party strategically used the judicial system to benefit their cause during the Non-Cooperation Movement of the 1920s. Drawing upon this realization, provincial governments found new ways of managing mass-mobilized non-violent protesters in Bombay's public spaces, thus avoiding the use of prisons and regular courts. Two compelling images from the Nursey album are evidence of the state's new strategies of crowd control.[19] In Fig. 2.5, we are given an astonishing "part view" of a "mile long procession and a demonstration" organized by Bombay merchants "to condemn the Government of its repressive policy"—this may well be the procession of 23 May 1930 identified by Masselos as one of several such processions that started entering the Fort area from 6 May onwards, going all the way to Apollo Bunder and the Yacht Club, a European preserve.[20] The procession was blocked in front of Capitol cinema by "a cordon of police about 300 strong," and the demonstrators "squatted on the road until about 8 pm," till the drama was resolved by the police withdrawing "to save an ugly situation."[21] Here, we see the state deploying the public space as a kind of temporary open-air jail. Our gaze is drawn to the broad open arc, formed by the crowd, at the centre of the image—an apparent "stage" for the theatre of negotiations, or at least some form of direct communication, between white officers and protesters; police horses are lined up ready for mounted assault should the need arise, while the dark wall of massed native constables on the right leads the eye towards VT's Gothic Revival facade, its entryway occupied by the crowd.

The second "part view" (Fig. 4.11) was taken during a massive procession organized by the Bombay Provincial Congress Committee to observe the 10th death anniversary of the nationalist leader Bal Gangadhar Tilak (the movement had a new calendar, and this anniversary celebration was one of the events commemorated). The procession was "banned from entering into the Fort area"[22] and the public space in front of VT was cordoned off by a force of 400 policemen. Here we see a closed "stage" of negotiations, shaped through the crowd solidly encircling a group of white officers in dialogue with a group of protesters at the centre of the image; as in Fig. 2.5, the densely packed multitude sat on the road until 8 pm, essentially in open-air detention.

An Alternative Centre: Congress House

In contrast to the iconic public buildings of British Bombay that stood as the elegant backdrop to much civil disobedience upheaval, Congress House and its compound at 414 Girgaum Back Road[23] pulsed with the activity of strategizing, planning and implementing the Gandhian vision of nationhood through mass mobilization. It could even be stated with confidence that such activity and the public support it gathered, along with the "virtual collapse of government control" in Bombay, re-centred the city, making Congress House its definitive political hub.[24] This is also suggested by many images in the Nursey album that showcase the activities in the public space of the building's compound, a sanctuary from colonial rule. In an extraordinary image of a flag salutation ceremony within the compound, the frame is filled from end to end with a mass of people, the central diagonal of women volunteers mirrored on the top right by the small diagonal of the compound wall, beyond which a fragment of road and of an automobile are visible—the only evidence of the city beyond (Fig. 2.6).

Support for the nationalist cause was also found in close proximity to Congress House. In the 1930s, some of the city's most well-known courtesans, who were skilled dancers and singers, set up their establishments in the N.B. Compound opposite the building. Geeta Thatra has argued that "Congress House (the hub of the nationalist movement) and the Compound (the centre of *mujra* [a courtesan's performance that combines poetry, gestures, music and dance] and entertainment in Bombay) evolved simultaneously in evidently mutual and harmonious coexistence."[25] Courtesans had previously supported the nationalist movement in various ways, for example by donating to the Tilak Swaraj Fund, which was used by the Congress to sustain various political activities and to buy Congress House.[26] Mahatma Gandhi attracted many women across class, community and region to the nationalist movement: not just "'respectable' women" but also "women marginalized by middle-class society," such as

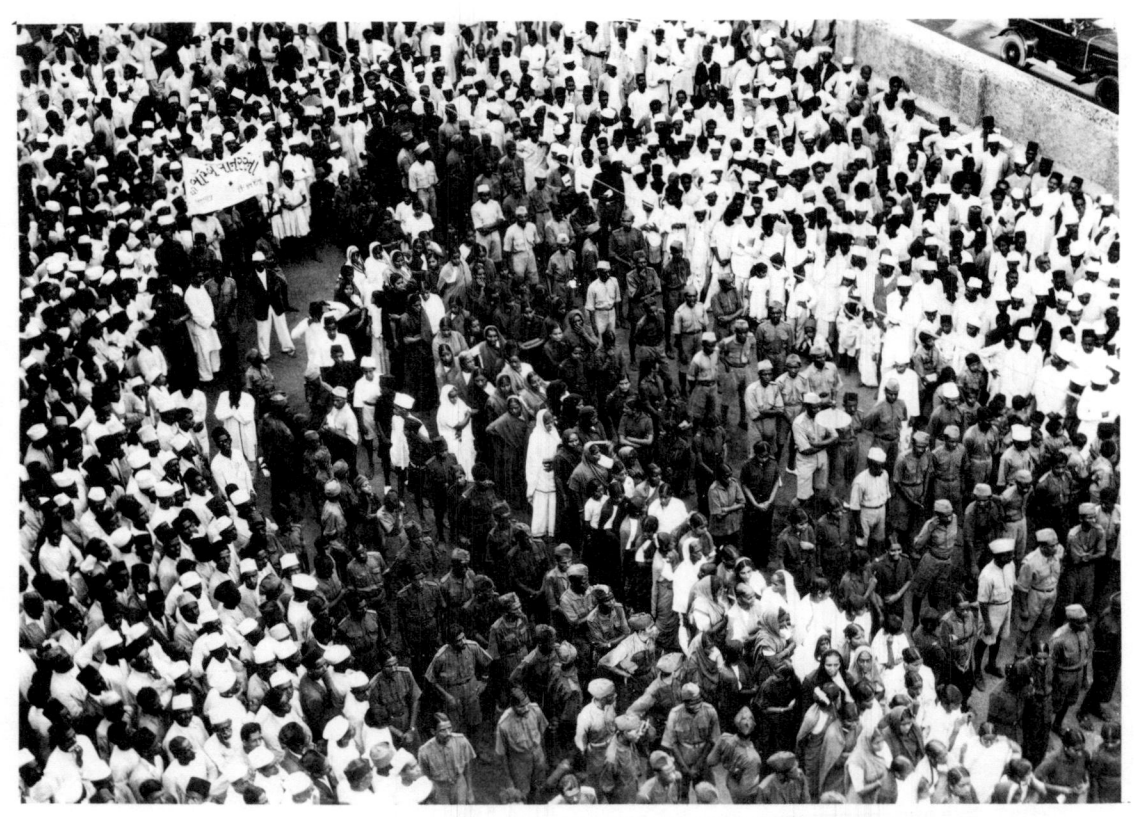

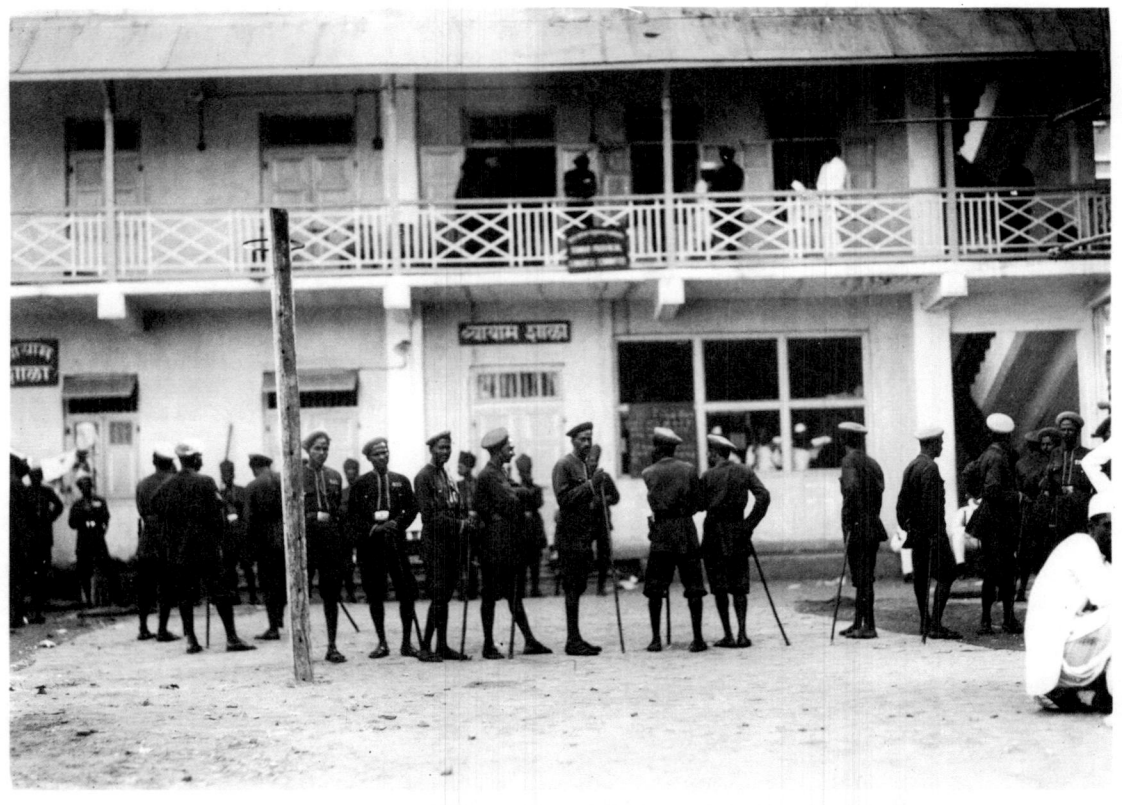

*devadasi*s (girls and women trained in dance, lifelong servitors of the main deity of an important temple), courtesans and prostitutes.[27] However, women's organizations were quick to distance themselves from a sisterhood considered disreputable and immoral, and did not consider prostitutes to be worthy "partners in struggle"; and neither Gandhi nor women's organizations viewed prostitutes as "legitimate nationalist actors."[28]

There are no Nursey photographs of the interior of the Congress House, but this space was of course crucial to the planning and organization of "disobedient" mass actions. Government controls made it difficult for the Congress to broadcast and disseminate nationalist content through printed leaflets, bulletins or news-sheets from a central node at an all-India level, hence provincial Congress offices had to take up this work. In historian Judith Brown's estimation, "Probably the best organized and best equipped of the local Congresses was that in Bombay City, where the hub was Congress House." The government raided both Congress House and Jinnah Hall (in the compound) and found "two cyclostyle machines and other materials for issuing cyclostyled bulletins," which they would have most likely confiscated (Fig. 2.7).[29] Despite these raids, the Bombay Congress managed to evade the authorities and continued to publish its bulletin.

In Figure 5.10, we see groups of women and children within the compound of Congress House, and thus safe from police surveillance and intervention, making salt from seawater as part of Gandhi's Salt Satyagraha. The static tenor of this remarkable composition—the seated women and girls, the wall of standing men behind them—is accentuated by the huddle of *sigri*s, *kadhai*s and *matka*s. The diagonal of the gunny sack in the foreground directs the eye towards this set of disciplined actors in the often highly gendered local/national drama of civil disobedience. The photographer has skilfully crafted an aura of collective anticipation and resolve in a tightly cropped image that gives no clue as to the physical setting, which is identified in the caption. Through the Nursey album's astonishing photographs of salt-making, we witness how this radical act spread through Bombay, carried out both in the private space of the home and in the public space of the city's maidans[30] in open defiance of and in the face of state violence.[31] Gujaratis—no particular Gujarati communities are specified in the image captions—are highlighted as particularly enthusiastic participants as "the salt preparing craze spread over the city."[32] Bombay's maidans, homes and the seashore itself were transformed into "stages" of ongoing nationalist theatre. And while Congress House introduced new itineraries of mass disobedience in the city by planning and directing a variety of protest activities in different areas,[33] it remained the ideological, tactical and material centre of these itineraries and activities. For instance, groups of salt *satyagrahi*s would arrive at the compound of Congress House every day after collecting seawater from the ocean and proceed to make salt on the grounds.

Fig. 2.6
"A flag hoisted [hoisting] ceremony resently [recently] held in the premises of Congress House by Sarojini Naidu. All CoNgress [Congress] volunteers saluting the flag."
c. 1930—1931
Gelatin Silver Print, 115 x 156 mm
ACP: 98.77.0002 (102a)
The massed volunteers in the frame underscore the large size of the compound, a fragment of its boundary wall angled at top right, beyond which a road and part of an automobile can be glimpsed.

Fig. 2.7
"Police raid on the Congress house Bombay." c. 1930—1931
Gelatin Silver Print, 117 x 158 mm
ACP: 98.77.0002 (81b)
This rare view of the Congress House building, is a beautifully composed grid of horizontals, verticals and diagonals, including the *lathi*s of the native constables.

A majority of the women participating in civil disobedience activities did not belong to the female intelligentsia or to elite families, but were what historian Gail Pearson calls "the women of the extended female space" who "had simply a few years learning in a formal educational institution, or training in a less-structured women's association, and were still essentially of the separate female world."[34] These women had been committed to the nationalist ideal from the Non-Cooperation Movement onwards, but had largely remained politically dormant. This changed dramatically during the Civil Disobedience Movement.[35] The "extended female space" was further stretched to meld with the concentrated "national" political space of Congress House, the public spaces of mass protest, and the activist spaces of women's groups such as the Desh Sevika Sangh. However, as mentioned earlier, this "extended female space" was not uniformly hospitable, since "undesirable" women, such as prostitutes who violated prescriptive codes of social and, particularly, Gandhian morality, were excluded from participation in *satyagraha*.

The Topography of Dissent: Street Furniture and Reimagining Parts of Buildings

Civil disobedience participants—the general public and state agents (colonial officials and the police)—are the main protagonists in the Nursey album. However, the many images of street furniture and sections of buildings, temporarily repurposed or assimilated within the staging of events, indicate that these are as essential within the theatre of mass protest. People who transformed a tram-shed into a viewing gallery and platform to watch a merchants' procession are crowded together like the spectators in the street (Fig. 2.8). Public transport was essential for mass movement, but it was also often brought to a halt through *hartal*s (labour strikes), newly minted nationalist days, occupation of roads by demonstrators and spectators, and the use of stones and other obstacles to block tram routes, as evident in Fig. 8.12. Here we see a white officer in a sola *topi* holding a chain in one hand and his *lathi* in another. He appears to be directing a native constable, who is bent over in the path of an approaching tram, as they attempt to remove chains laid across the tracks. The complex weave of the colonizer-colonized relationship may be read in this image of white officer and native policeman working together against civil disobedience action. The wide rambling loops of the chains offset the purposive diagonals of the tram tracks.

In one striking composition, we see an "excited crowd" inside and atop an immobilized BEST tram transformed into a viewing platform, craning their necks to view the "Gharwal [Garhwal] day procession," the crowd leading the viewer's gaze towards the right, to the procession that itself is offstage (Fig. 3.1). The angle of the shot elevates the crowd towards the level of VT's dome and spires that make for an impressive backdrop. Victoria Terminus was named after the reigning British monarch/Empress of India on Jubilee Day, 20 June

1887, marking the 50th anniversary of her accession to the throne. The central dome is surmounted by a statue of Progress, and below the clock on the facade, sheltered by a gable, is a statue of a seated Queen Victoria; neither is visible in Fig. 3.1, but the monarch can be seen in Fig. 2.9 (not from the Nursey album).[36] Davies has characterized the Gothic Revival terminus as "an architectural sensation both in perspective and in detail."[37] However, in Fig. 3.1, the mass of native bodies, inside and atop the tram that extends beyond both sides of the frame, effectively occludes and overwhelms the mass of the magnificent building—in symbolic terms, a simultaneous repudiation of the colonial regime in Bombay and the coercive reach of empire.

The Nursey album offers a few images of specific street furniture—a statue of the eminent Parsi leader Dadabhai Naoroji—being incorporated into public rituals, as seen in a depiction of a Parsi nationalist procession: a young girl, helped by two men, garlands "the gra[n]d old man of India" who is almost obscured by the three figures, with the Oriental Building dominating the background (Fig. 2.10). We are also shown spectators perched on the Fitzgerald Fountain at Dhobi

Fig. 2.8
"Another view of the crowd watching Merchents [merchants] procession standing on Tram-shed."
c. 1930–1931
Gelatin Silver Print, 114 x 156 mm
ACP: 98.77.0002 (30b)
The overwhelming horizontality of the composition is adeptly countered by the vertical electric pole, and the slight arc of the wire extending beyond the frame.

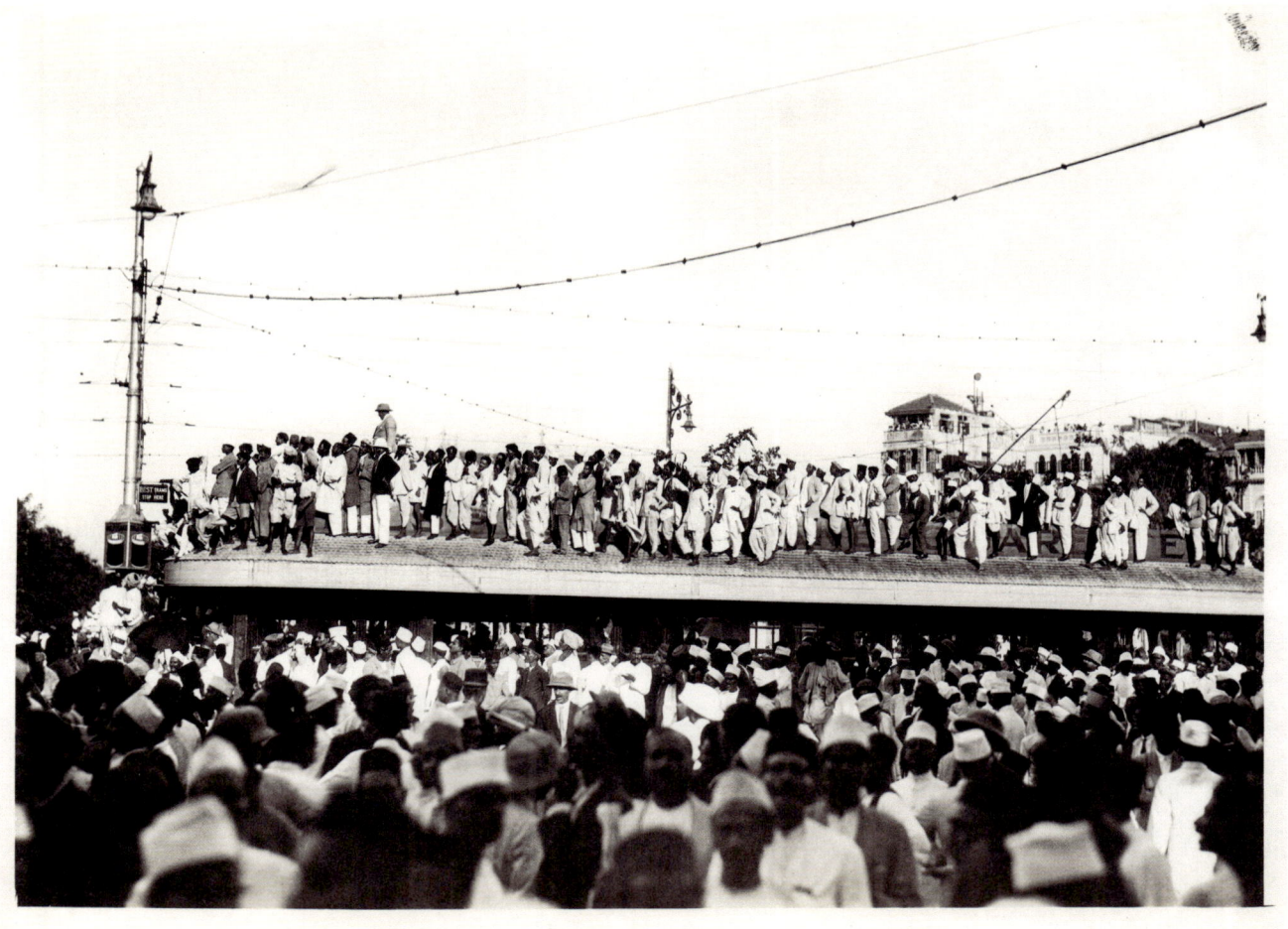

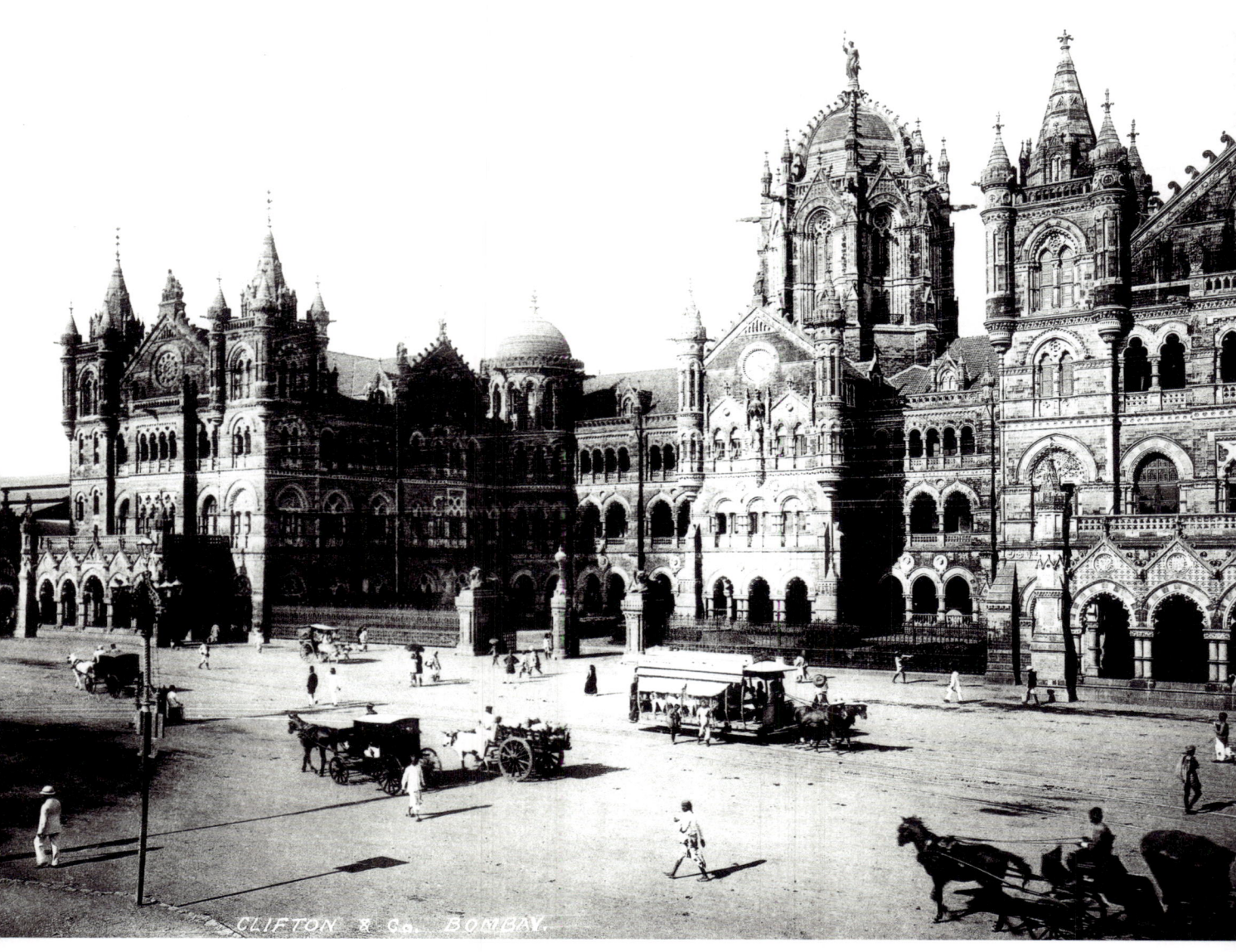

Fig. 2.9

View of the western facade, Great Indian Peninsular Railway Victoria Terminus and Administrative Offices, Bombay. Photograph by Clifton & Co., c. 1880s. Image courtesy: Phillips Antiques, Bombay. A canopied marble statue of Queen Victoria is visible under the clock on the elaborate Gothic Revival exterior. It was removed during a post-Independence campaign to take down statues of prominent British figures from government buildings and public spaces, and with other colonial statues was left out in the open in Victoria Gardens, Bombay's oldest public park, in Byculla for the next three decades; it has since mysteriously disappeared. In 2017 Victoria Terminus was renamed Chhatrapati Shivaji Maharaj Terminus after the famous warrior-king and founder of the Maratha empire.

Talao watching a procession from an elevated position (Fig. 2.11).[38] This was not the only example of Parsi support expressed in public. For example, on 22 May 1930, the *Bombay Congress Bulletin* reported on "the spontaneous rally of the Parsi youths [a]round the Congress Flag"—an articulation and affiliation seen as positive and noteworthy as the community had previously distanced itself from political activities.[39] On 29 May 1930, the Parsi Rajkiya Sabha organized a procession of approximately 2,000 Parsis, including about 600 women. The public presence and participation of Parsis, a highly influential minority community, was critical in terms of the nationalists' refuting the government's assertion that the Congress "was a Hindu organization."[40] This claim was not without merit. Despite efforts by the "Congress Muslim party," which I take to mean Muslims in the Congress party, Muslim involvement in the movement was low. At a meeting chaired by Mohammed Ali and attended by about 5,000 on 23 April 1930, it was decided that Muslims should not take part in civil disobedience as the movement "was aimed at establishing Hindu raj."[41] Perhaps as an attempt to counter this view, the Nursey album includes a photograph of a procession organized by the "Mohomedans of Bombay" to commiserate with "their Hindu brothern" [brethren]; however, the caption does not state why or when this supportive public act was undertaken.[42] The album thus offers some evidence that Congress supporters belonged to different faiths.

Of all the colonial buildings in Bombay, the Town Hall—a frequently occupied site of disciplined disobedience as well as of violent clashes with state forces —was best adapted for the political theatre of *satyagraha*, especially in the form of picketing, staged individually, in pairs, or in larger groups. The building was a meeting ground for both European and Indian elites, who congregated there to discuss salient issues and take important decisions, within the prescribed protocols of colonial civic engagement. The Town Hall's impressive flight of steps was easily transformed into a stage with a varied "cast" of colonial "characters," the scripted action often catalysed by picketers en masse.

In Fig. 2.12, we see two bold *desh sevikas* who "picketed the auction of toddy licenses at the Town Hall and ensured it was a complete failure," their banner in Marathi declaring *dāru manushyālā pashu banavite* ("Liquor makes a man turn into an animal" or "Alcohol dehumanizes man").[43] In this remarkable composition, state authority unfolds in a graduated sequence. Three native constables stand on the steps behind the *desh sevikas*; a group of three British officers dominates the foreground, flanked by a native constable, a native official and a barely glimpsed third figure slightly behind them. Uniformed white officers and possibly high-ranking British administrators are centrally positioned further up the steps; a little higher we see a pair of native constables; at the top, on the right, is a pair of men: one white, one native; and in the deep shadow of magnificent pillars we see native constables apparently on guard duty at the entrance. The sloganeering

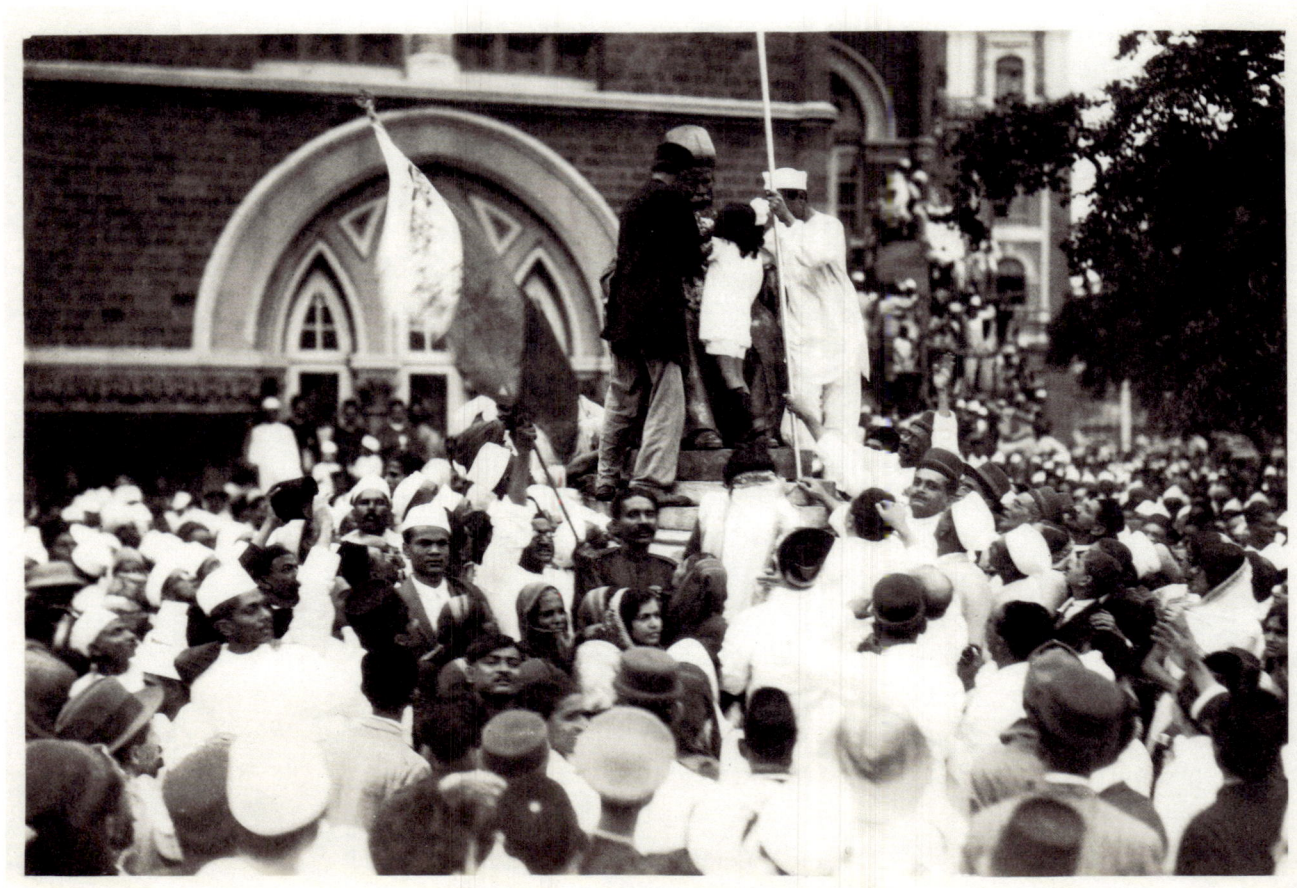

Fig. 2.10

"The Parsis of Bombay organised a procession to support the civil disobedience movement. The procession started from the fort area and on its way halted to garland the statue of Dadabhai Nowrojee [Naoroji] the grad [grand] old man of India. Here [is] a little girl seen garlanding the statue." c. 1930–1931 Gelatin Silver Print, 114 x 161 mm ACP: 98.77.0002 (100a) Prominent in the background is the Oriental Building, a fusion of Gothic and Indian architecture, built in 1885.

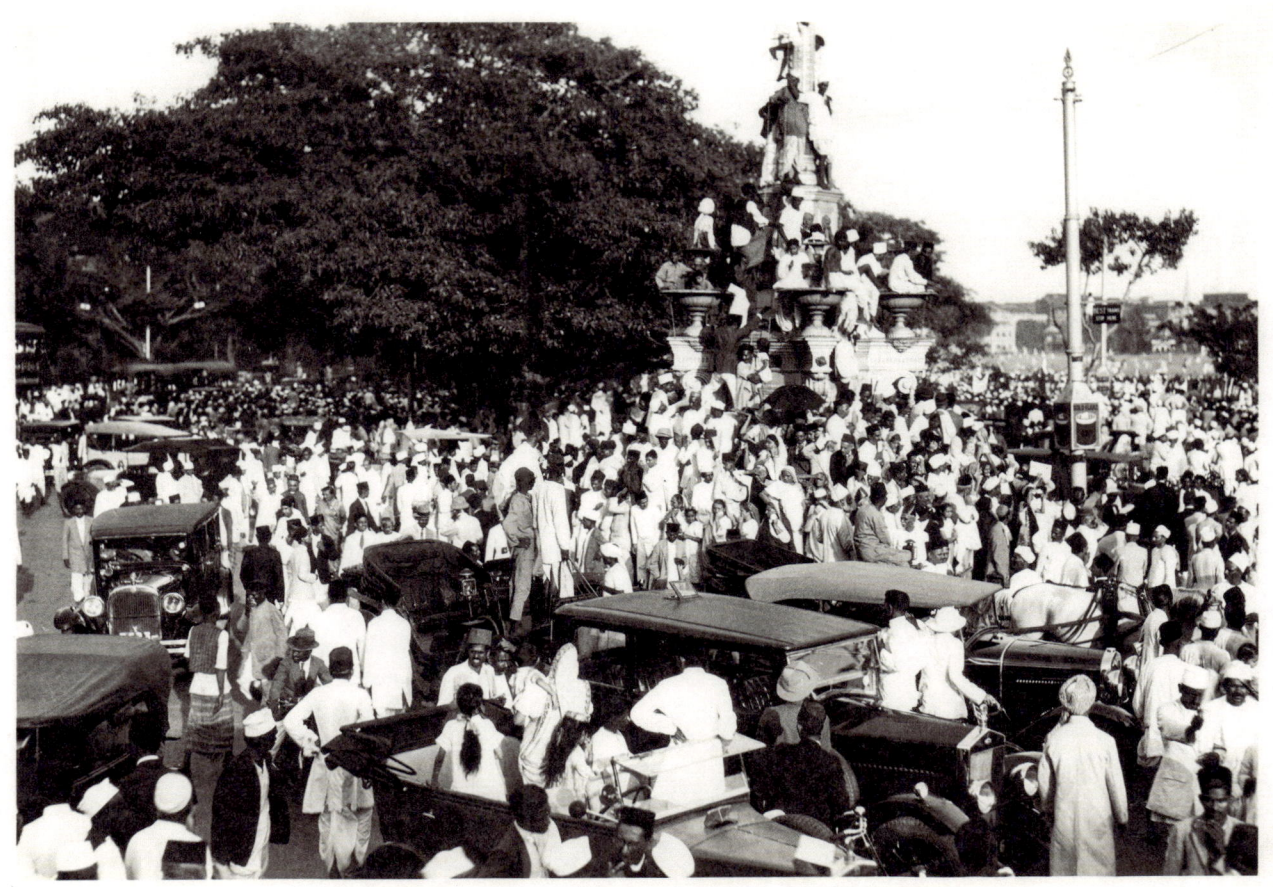

women and other "actors" here face an "audience" that we cannot see. The banner emphasizes the ill-effects of alcohol on individuals and communities, whereas the Marathi banner in Fig. 2.3, that reads *dāru pinyāmuleṅ hindustānchi shakti haran jhāli āhe* ("Liquor has ruined India"), raised by *desh sevikas* at this same location, condemns alcohol's ruinous effects on the nation as a whole.

We catch a rare glimpse of a section of the Greek Revival facade of the Town Hall in an image taken from across the street (Fig. 2.13). It captures a scene during the Legislative Council elections when Congress volunteers, including *desh sevikas*, picketed the Town Hall, completely taking over its steps.[44] "The Congress was assisted by large crowds as seen in the picture," states the caption; these energized "crowds" occupy the street, and seem ready to block the tram tracks being used as a path by the convoy of automobiles moving diagonally across the frame.[45] In these symbolically resonant images, the protesters, particularly women—whether general volunteers, *desh sevikas* or picketers from diverse communities politicized/mobilized by the nationalists—have literally turned their backs on the intimidating, hierarchical, exclusionary edifice of colonial privilege, power and oppression; instead, addressing mass audiences in public space, they are scripting and conducting a radically different mode of participatory dissent (see Chapter Seven in this volume).[46]

Fig. 2.11
"A view at Dhobi Talao of Parsi Nationalist Procession."
c. 1930–1931
Gelatin Silver Print,
116 x 159 mm
ACP: 98.77.0002 (82a)
Spectators from the surging crowd have climbed up onto Fitzgerald Fountain for a better view. The structure was erected in 1867 in honour of Sir Seymour Fitzgerald, the governor of Bombay from 1867–72.

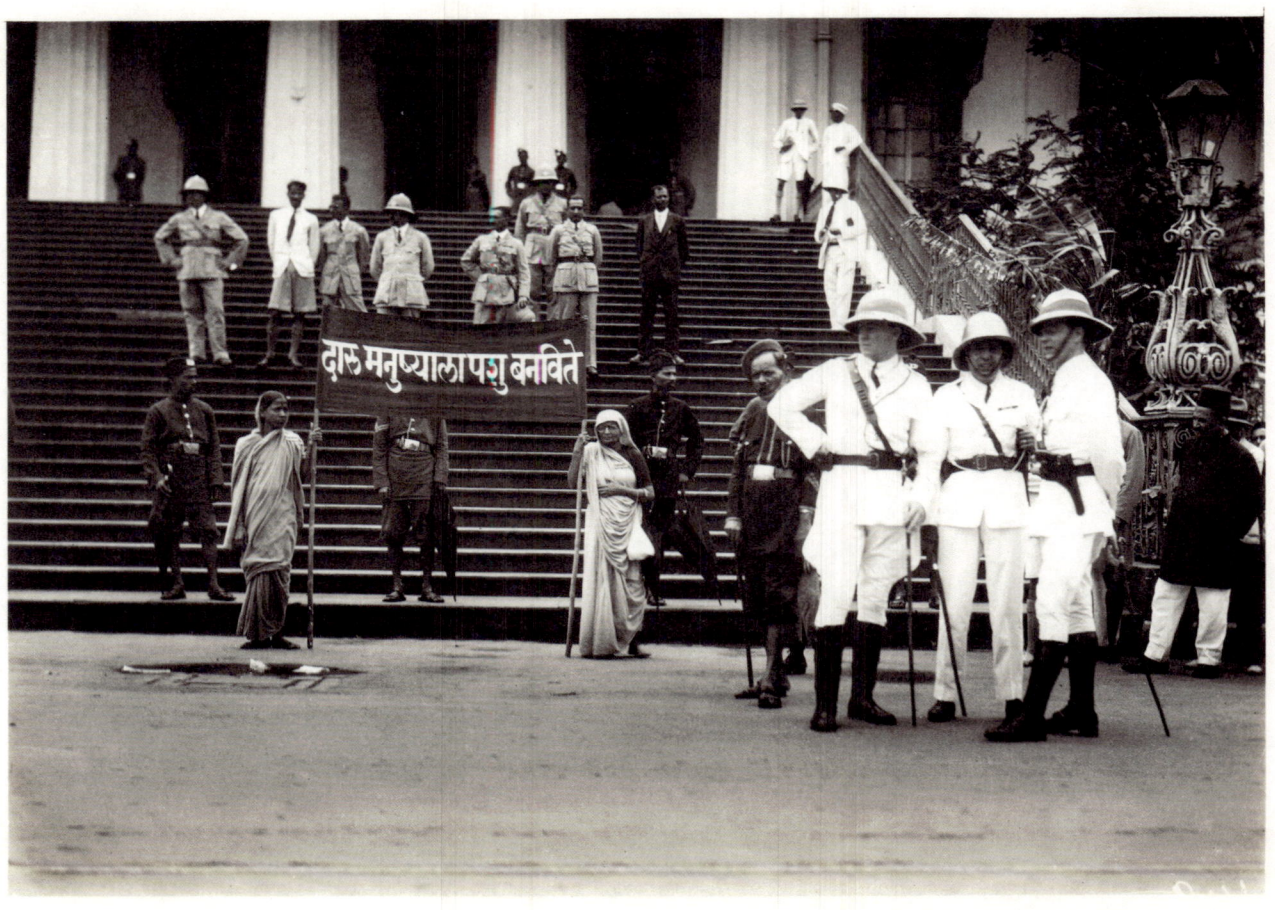

Fig. 2.12
"Women pickting [picketing] the entrance to the Town [Hall] with poster when the sale of Toddy license was held."
c. 1930—1931
Gelatin Silver Print, 112 x 156 mm
ACP: 98.77.0002 (69b)
The Marathi slogan on the banner translates as "Liquor makes a man turn into an animal" or "Alcohol dehumanizes Man." The group of *lathi*-bearing white officers in the foreground starkly contrasts with the two resolute *desh sevika*s, behind whom stand native policemen and white officials framed against the steps and pillars of the Town Hall, the embodiment of institutionalized colonial power.

FACING PAGE
Fig. 2.13
"When the Bombay Legislative [Council elections] were held the Congress organised large bands of picketers to Picket the Town hall. The congress [Congress] was assisted by large crowds as seen in the picture."
c. 1930—1931
Gelatin Silver Print, 115 x 156 mm
ACP: 98.77.0002 (72b)
This view includes on the right a rare glimpse of part of the Town Hall facade, including a section of the triangular pediment. The composition is beautifully balanced via the strong diagonal of the tram tracks.

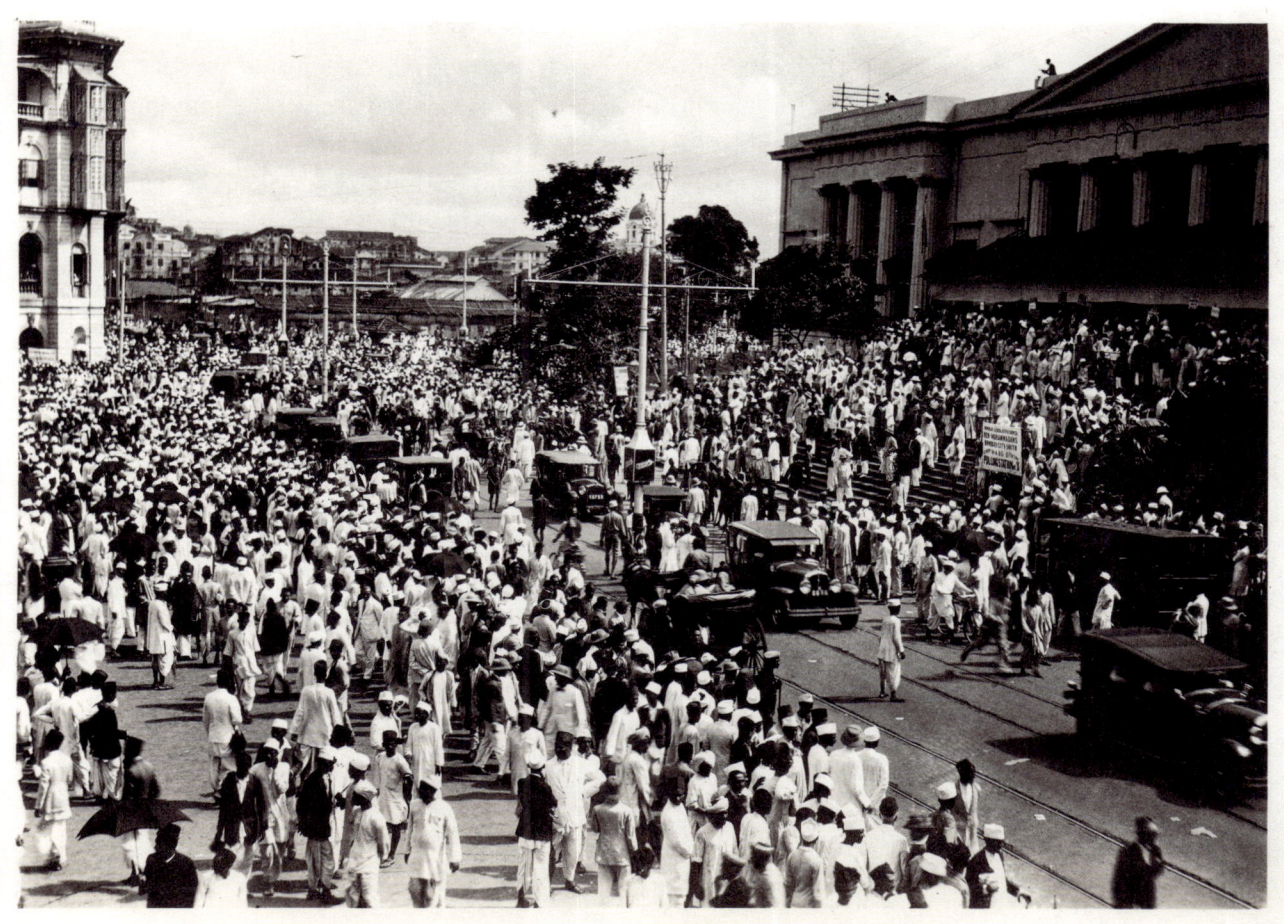

Systematic Violence / Strategic Non-violence

The threat of violence and the theatre of non-violence were both of crucial importance to the success and failure, progress and retardation of civil disobedience action played out on different "stages" in Bombay's public spaces. The Nursey album persuasively highlights the nationalist agenda by focusing on violence perpetrated by agents of the colonial regime, with many images showing unresisting *satyagrahi*s submitting to state force; crowds scattering in the presence of *lathi*-wielding native police; white officers on foot or horseback, ready to charge or in mid-assault; and demonstrators boldly facing down their armed opponents.[47]

Taylor Sherman has pointed out that one tactic deployed by the police as a substitute for arrest and detention in the Civil Disobedience Movement was to physically remove *satyagrahi*s from protest areas (see Chapter Six in this volume). Force was often used, resulting in a massive escalation in the confrontations between police and protesters, and in the gravity of bodily conflicts.[48] For instance, the Nursey album documents an unarmed "Sikh batch" by the tram tracks being hit with *lathi*s, with the VT facade and a crowd of onlookers in the background

(Fig. 2.14). The caption to another image of this event informs us that despite the assault—two white officers, one with a raised *lathi*, are visible amidst the seated group, while a squad of native constables stands passively to one side—the "brave Sikhs" in this "Gharwal Day" protest did not leave and had to be "lifted from the spot."[49] Others, including the huge crowds taking part in or watching a "Gharwal Day" procession organized by the Congress" to sympathize with the suffers [sufferers] of Garwali [Garhwal] regiment," fled police *lathi* charges in which hundreds were injured (Fig. 2.15). Without providing specific details, the caption here invokes the reason for this procession and the defiance it commemorated.[50] Soldiers of the Royal Garhwal Rifles, an infantry regiment, had disobeyed direct orders of their British officers and refused to shoot native protesters, an act of rebellion that drew severe military punishment, presumably the cause of the suffering mentioned in the caption.[51]

However, the Nursey album also affirms Congress anticipation of and preparation for state violence, as in Fig. 2.16 where in the foreground we see Congress ambulance volunteers with stretchers lined up to carry away demonstrators wounded at the "disturbance outside the ... Victoria Terminus ... on the Garwali [Garhwal] day." In the middle ground, a large group of native constables waits on the left, three mounted policemen close by. Further up, cars and Victoria carriages ferry passengers, and a mass of spectators fills the top of the frame. In Fig. 2.17, we see "Congress Ambulance Volunteers" carrying the injured

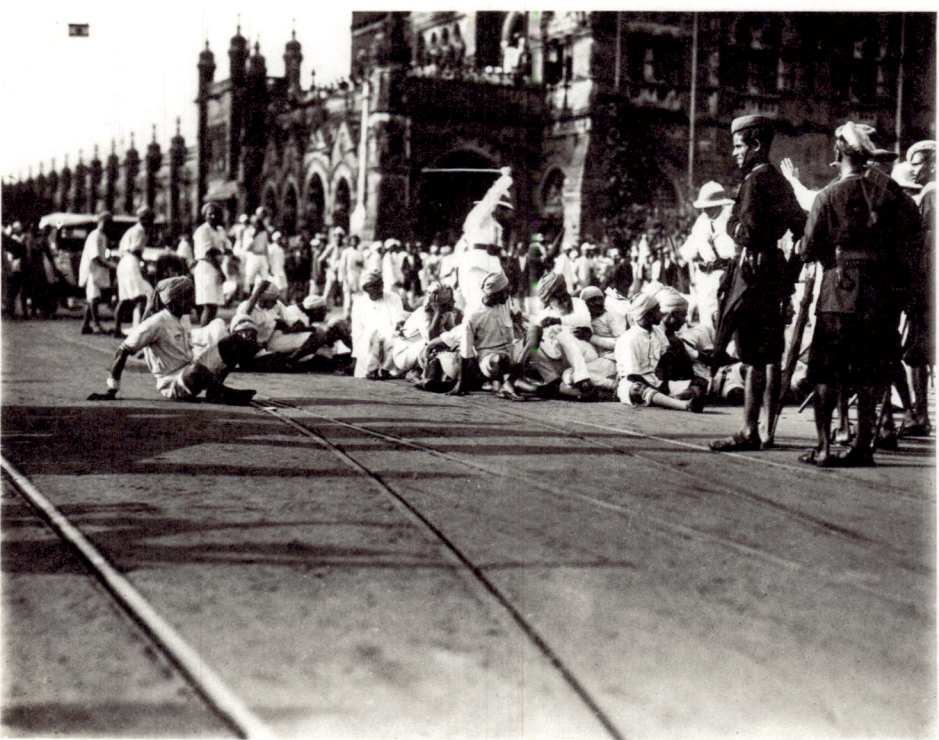

Fig. 2.14
"'Gharwal Day' Lathi in action on Sikh batch." c. 1930–1931 Gelatin Silver Print, 116 x 157 mm
ACP: 98.77.0002 (64a)
The Victoria Terminus is a grand backdrop to active and passive police violence—the white officers beating the protesters while the *lathi*-bearing native constables look on.

to ambulance vans not visible within the frame. At the centre of the image, an injured protester has been lifted onto a volunteer's shoulder, and volunteers on the lower left huddle around what we can assume to be an injured protester laid on a partly visible stretcher, while a semi-circle of white officers and *lathi*-bearing native constables look on. Stretchers are clearly visible in the chaotic scene depicted in Fig. 8.8, likely unfolding outside the Town Hall or Victoria Terminus where we see the "Ambulance attending to the Wounded," at this or another disturbance. In Fig. 2.18, which documents the "Swastic League Ambulance Corps in action on one of [the] Flag Salutation Day[s],"[52] the bent knees of a wounded figure on a stretcher are visible as he is loaded into an ambulance van through its wide open doors.

A beautifully balanced composition captioned "Police arresting the women pickets at the Town Hall"[53] shows us a very different kind of van—a menacing police truck into which two sari-clad *desh sevikas* are about to climb under the supervision of a white-uniformed British officer, the downward angle of his *lathi* mirrored by the upward angle of the ascending picketer's arm, upon which are hooked an umbrella and a small pouch (presumably containing items for use during long hours of outdoor protest); a white-clad native bystander looks on (Fig. 8.14). As earlier mentioned, women participants were highly visible, and highly disciplined, in both picketing and processions, and were prepared to be injured, arrested and imprisoned for breaking the law and disturbing the peace.[54] Sherman has pointed out that, as part of the Civil Disobedience Movement's propaganda, nationalist publications repeatedly drew attention to violence directed by the state towards women, especially respectable women of various ages, and young girls. For nationalists, women—only "respectable" women—personified the nation, and thus state violence against women could easily be translated to denote India's subjugation under British colonial rule. It also implied that native women could not protect themselves against colonial force, and that native men were helpless in terms of shielding women from the direct violence of the state.[55]

The caption to Fig. 3.1, "People done too much damage to Tram by standing on it,"[56] is a rare critical comment on the violence of local communities participating in mass mobilization, indicating the belief of the movement's leaders that the ideology of non-violence should extend from living entities to all material domains, including property. Violence in any form and from any source was to be unequivocally abjured and condemned; and neither state nor private assets were to be destroyed, even unintentionally, as is the case in this image of people crammed into and on top of a tram to view a "Gharwal day" procession. The caption to Fig. 2.19, "Mrs Kamladavi [Kamaladevi Chattopadhyay] trying to pacify a wild crowd of people at the Girgaum police court," is similarly critical, in this case an atypical warning in the Nursey album against the ever-present potential for mob violence.[57]

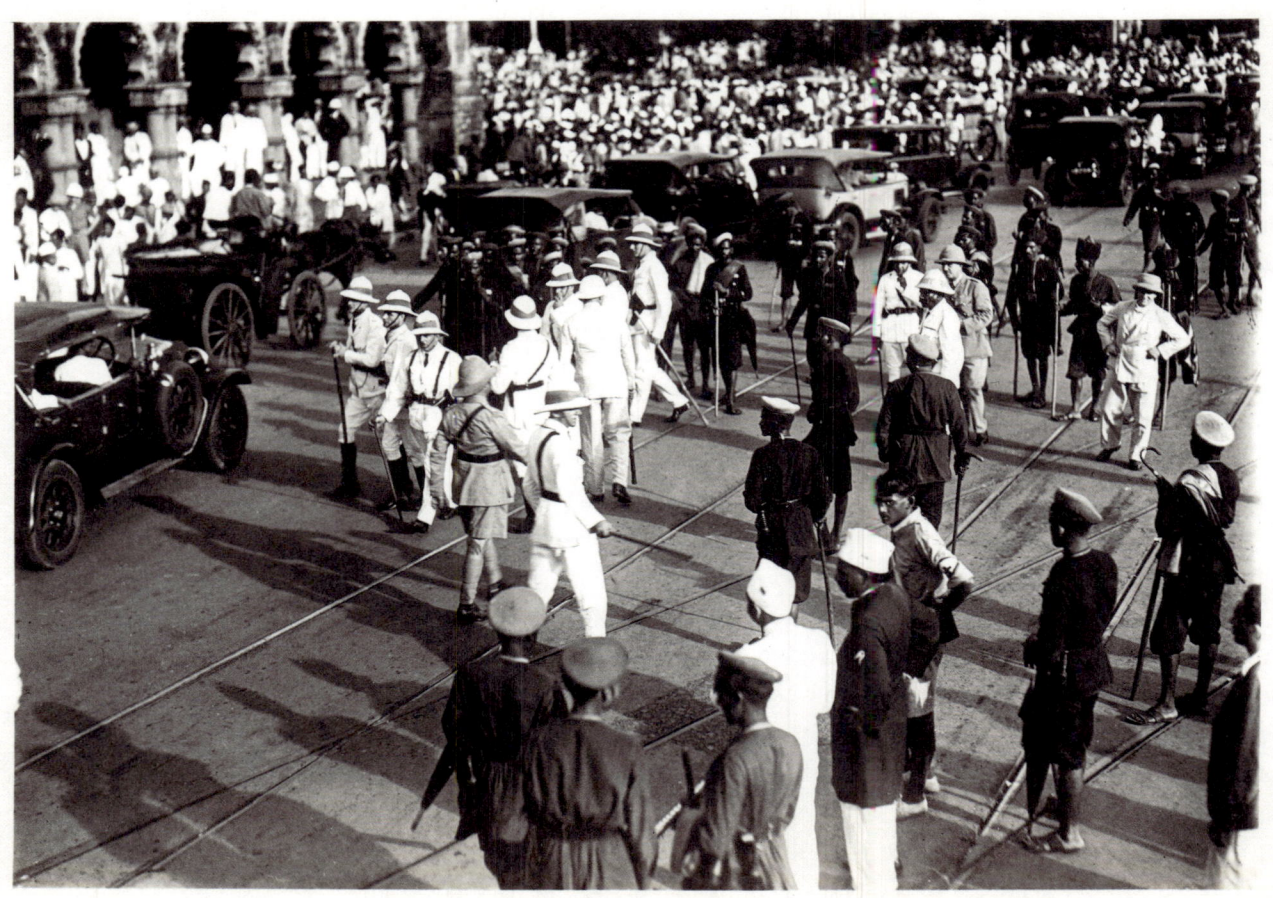

Fig. 2.15
"Garwali day procession. The Congress organised a procession to sympathise with the suffers [sufferers] of the Garwali regiment. The procession when it reached Bori-Bunder station was ordered to disperse and on refusing to do so[.] A lathi charge was ordered from which nearly three hundred people were injured." c. 1930–1931
Gelatin Silver Print, 115 x 157 mm
ACP: 98.77.0002 (66b)

Lengthy captions, such as this, offer helpful contextualization for multiple photographs. As with many images in the album, the composition pivots around the active group of white officers at the centre, with *lathi*-bearing native constables standing by passively.

FACING PAGE, ABOVE
Fig. 2.16
"A disturbance outside the the [sic] Victoria Terminus Bombay on the Garwali day." c. 1930–1931
Gelatin Silver Print, 116 x 155 mm
ACP: 98.77.0002 (63a)
Both the police and Congress ambulance volunteers bearing stretchers wait to spring into action.

FACING PAGE, BELOW
Fig. 2.17
"Wounded been [being] carried by Congress Ambulance Volunteers to the Vans on Gharwal Day." c. 1930–1931
Gelatin Silver Print, 116 x 157 mm
ACP: 98.77.0002 (66a)
White officers and native police observe those injured by *lathi* blows being helped by fellow protesters. Neither the stretchers nor the ambulance vans mentioned in the caption are visible.

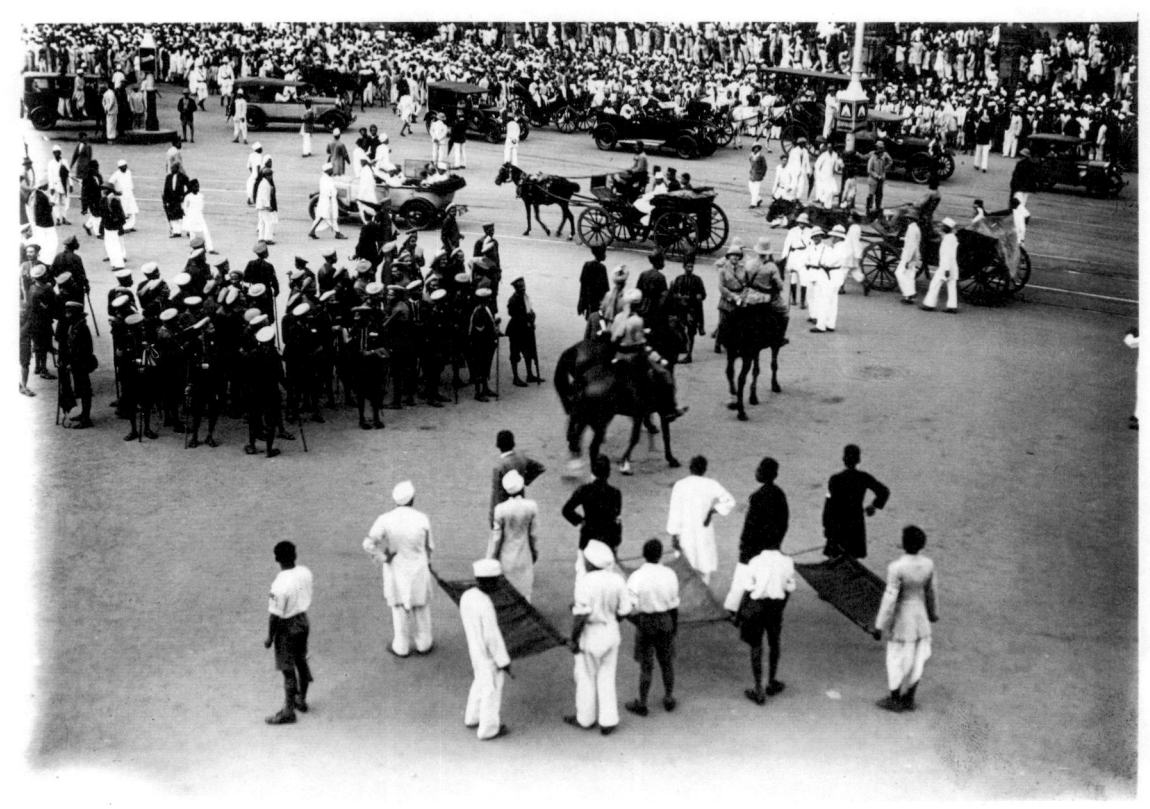

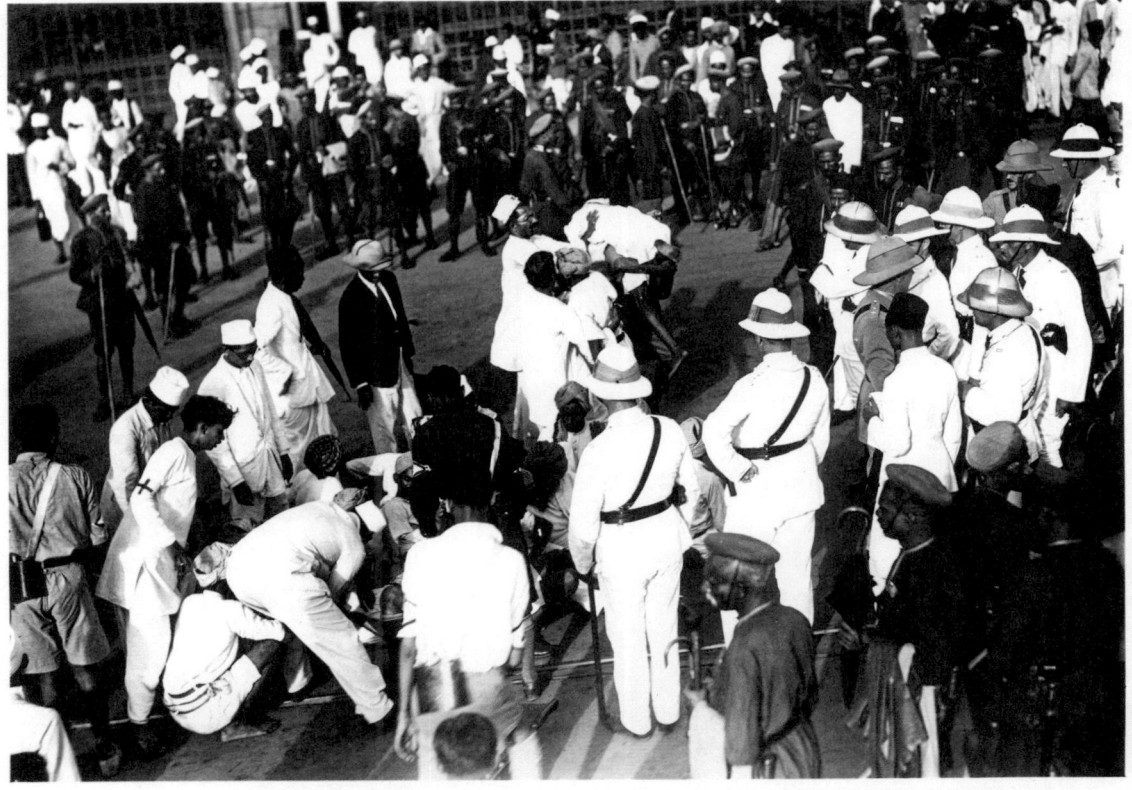

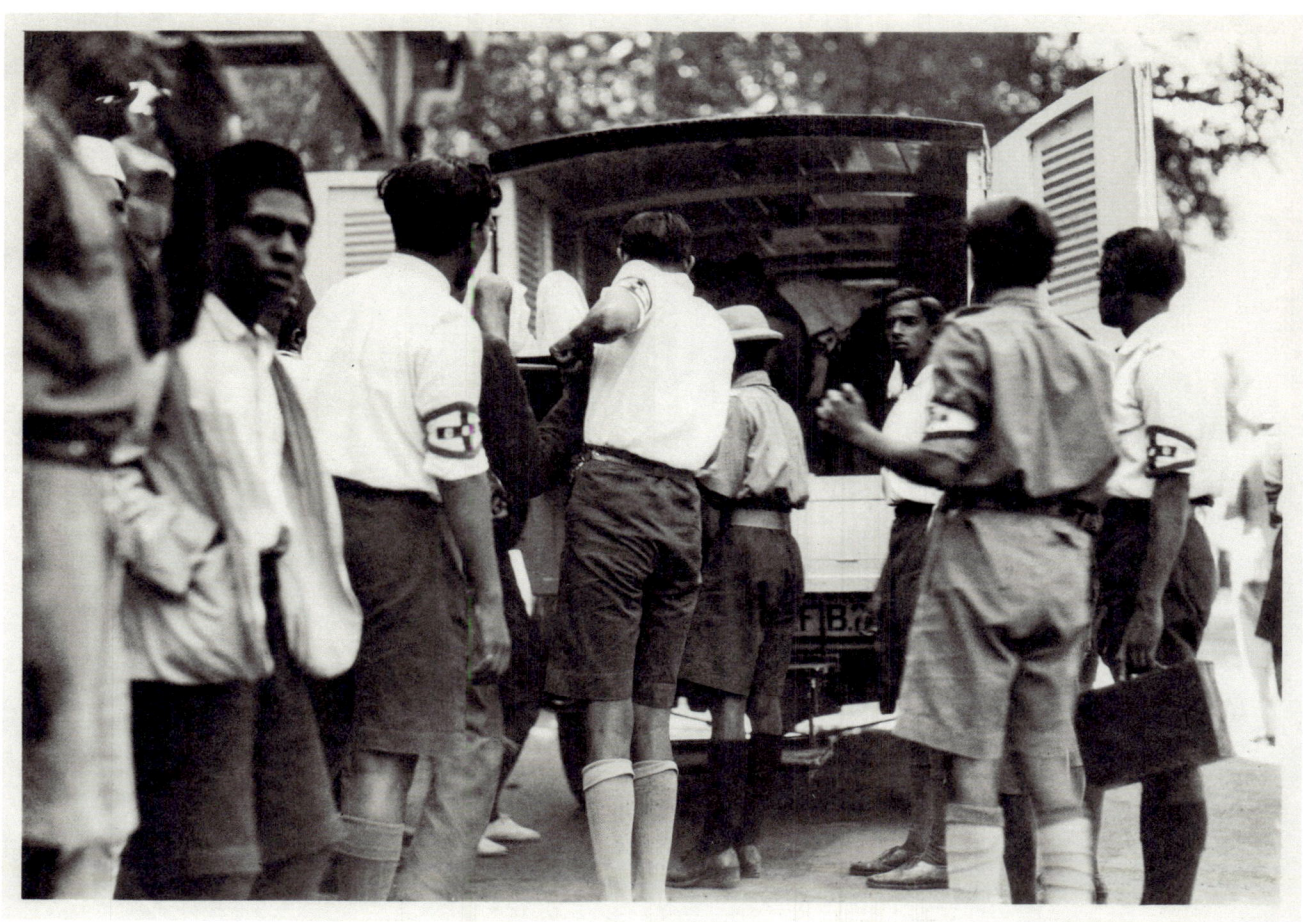

Fig. 2.18
"Swastic League
Ambulance Corps in
action on one of
[the] Flag Salutation
Day[s]." c. 1930–1931
Gelatin Silver Print,
117 x 158 mm
ACP: 98.77.0002 (120a)

Just one image in the album depicts state violence against workers. In Fig. 2.20, we see a group of employees of the Great Indian Peninsular Railway "offering *satyagraya* [sic] in front of the shops at Parel"; the *satyagrahi*s have positioned their arms to protect their heads from blows by the *lathi*-wielding white officer, blurred through being photographed in action. A native bystander looks on, as does a group squatting by the wall, while a native guard stands on duty at the open gate of this (work)shop for the repair and maintenance of trains.[58]

However, what the album leaves out is as important as what it includes. There are no images of the retaliatory violence by *satyagrahi*s that sometimes did occur despite the generally disciplined conduct of protesters, picketers, processions and crowds. In this context, let us briefly examine the relationship between Bombay's workers and the city's political leaders in order to understand the violence associated with the labour force in the context of *satyagraha*. In terms of leadership, Maharashtrians and the more left-affiliated local leaders had been far more successful than Congress centrists and conservative Gandhians in influencing the city's workers, as the former shared greater cultural and regional affinities with the workers, and were also more sympathetic to the "immediate aims of labour."[59] Workers often responded to their exploitative working conditions with repeated *hartal*s—a form of strike that involved short-term work stoppages and shop closures rather than the extended total shutdowns organized and controlled by union leaders. As a result of the Congress's inability to effectively lead the city's workers, and with the wrecking of both the Communists and the Girni Kamgar Union,[60] an economic depression was prevalent when civil disobedience was initiated in Bombay in 1930, with the city's labour force devoid of any significant political and union leadership. Workers' civil disobedience action was accompanied by escalating violence that included "stoning police and each other, breaking up meetings, and breaking into and destroying foreign cloth stores;" this was deeply embarrassing to the movement and blemished the "non-violent image" so fervently valorized and propagated by the Congress.[61] By July 1930, "it had become apparent that [the] Congress had not only failed to harness labour as a non-violent cadre in the struggle, but that the majority of the workers were, increasingly, rejecting it altogether."[62]

Fig. 2.19
"Mrs Kamladavi
[Kamaladevi
Chattopadhyay] trying
to pacify a wild
crowd of people at
the Girgaum police
court." c. 1930—1931
Gelatin Silver Print,
114 x 155 mm
ACP: 98.77.0002 (24b)
Here the arc of the
crowd straightens
into a diagonal
that bisects the
frame, dramatically
isolating the
Congress leader like
an actor on a stage.

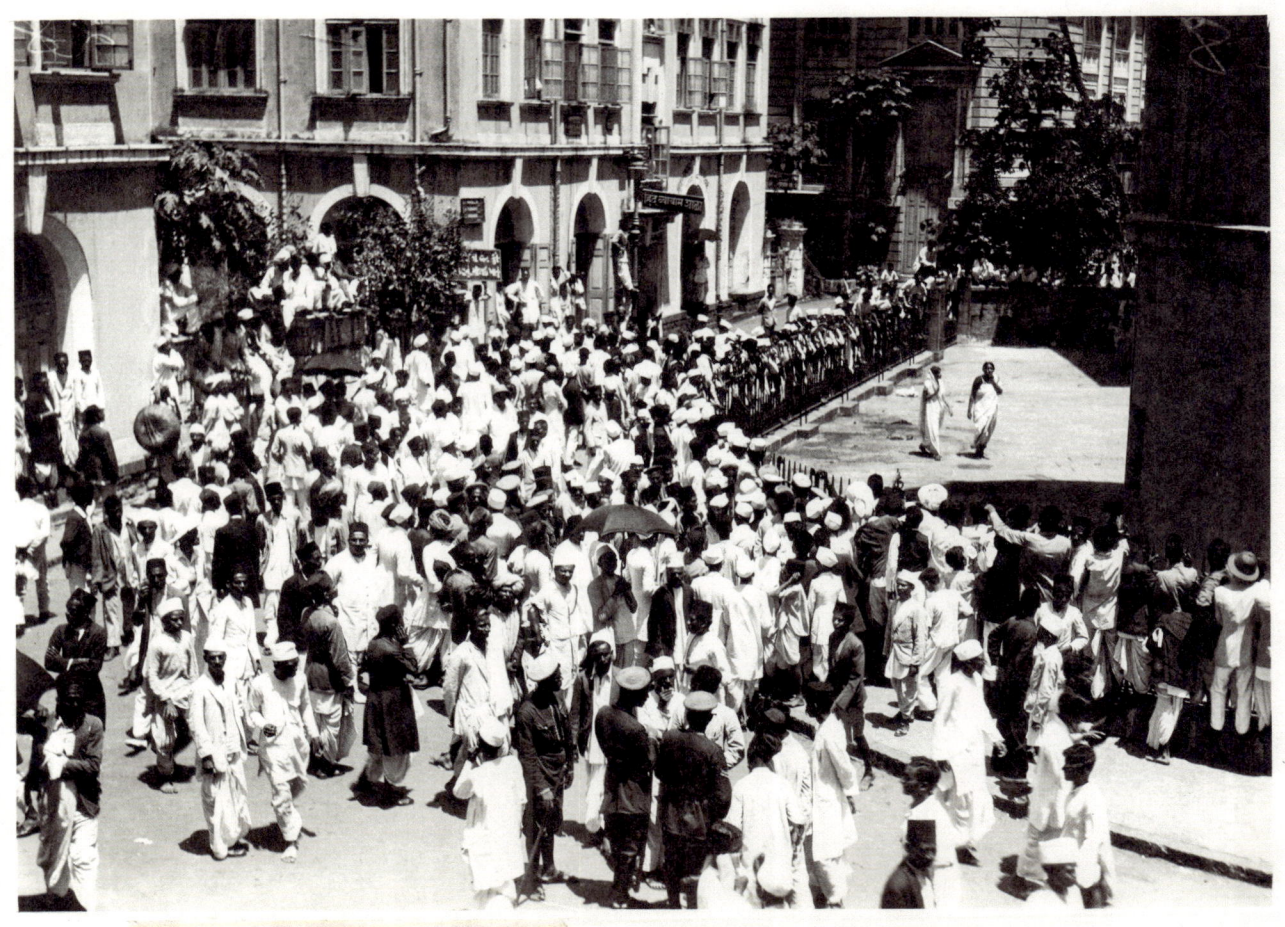

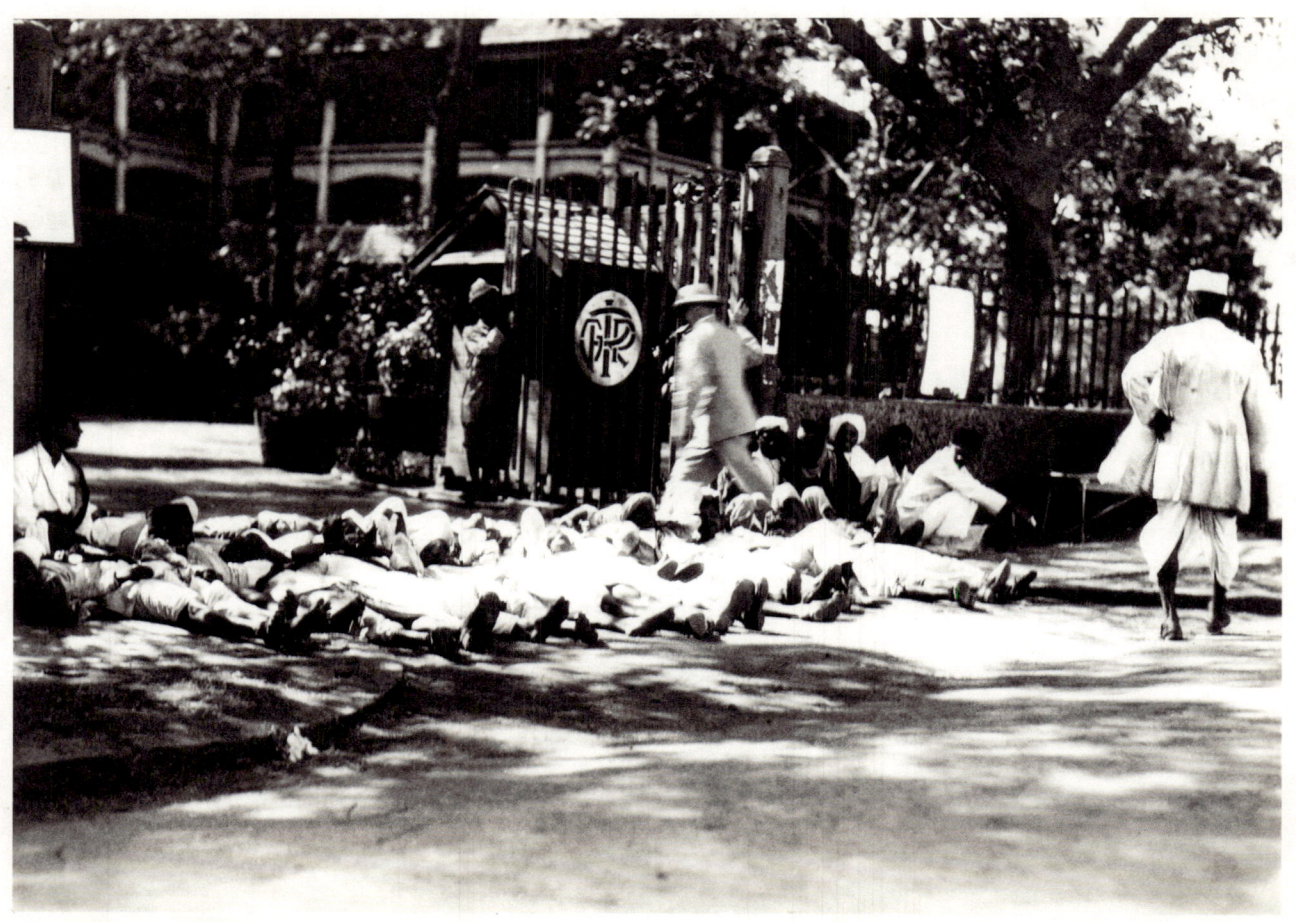

Fig. 2.20

"G.I.P.RLY WORKERS OFFERING SATYAGRAYA [satyagraha] IN FRONT OF THE SHOPS AT PAREL." c. 1930–1931 Gelatin Silver Print, 115 x 156 mm ACP: 98.77.0002 (27a) A white officer stands amid the prone protesters, arm raised to strike with a *lathi*. "Shops" here presumably means railway maintenance workshops. Congress leaders did not generally succeed in persuading the city's labour force to join the Civil Disobedience Movement in large numbers.

Conclusion

This essay has delineated the multiple ways in which participants in the Civil Disobedience Movement—volunteers, supporters, spectators, nationalist leaders and state agents—operating on multiple "stages" in Bombay are the main protagonists of photographs in the Nursey album. In many of these images, iconic colonial buildings in south Bombay serve as the backdrops to public political theatre: to the turbulence of choreographed *satyagraha*, speeches, rallies, processions, picketing and various other forms of protest action. The camera's prominent focus on the human subject frequently reduces magnificent colonial architecture to diminished, fragmented, partial and tangential views, signifying the inability of the state to control its mass-mobilized native subjects. Bombay's colonial buildings witnessed "disobedient" participants infiltrate and occupy city spaces dominated by the colonial elite. In contrast, Congress House emerged as a dynamic new centre of power and tactical node for planning and executing *satyagraha* and the mass takeovers of public spaces, as a stage of disobedient action, and as a space for the scripting of dissent and for imagining and projecting the sovereign nation of the future. The movement's participants and audience incorporated Bombay's street furniture into the collective action; and on its part, the colonial state too reimagined and repurposed urban topography for its own ends, as seen in many images. For example, the police attempted to prevent the deeper penetration of the movement into spaces dominated by the colonial elite by restricting processions from entering the Fort area and by halting them at Bori Bunder, which became an open-air prison, with the protesters encircled by a dense cordon of native constables. The steps of the Town Hall were regularly deployed for the nationalist drama of picketing, sloganeering, demonstrations and other modes of non-violent protest, under the hostile gaze of colonial administrators and the *lathi*s of native constables and their white officers.

The visual historiography we encounter in the Nursey album presents a disciplined and united protest movement, involving masses of ordinary people who courageously adhered to the ideology of non-violence in the face of brutal state force. However, the historical record indicates that the movement did not succeed in incorporating all groups of potential activists in Bombay. Some communities kept their distance; some were affiliated with the colonial regime; some were deliberately excluded; and the Congress leadership was sometimes unable to prevent participants from retaliating with violence when the state used force. As a rare archive of mass-mobilized public dissent, as a layered testimonial to a crucial phase of India's freedom struggle, and as an effective instrument of nationalist propaganda, this unique compilation of images above all astutely maps the transformation of Bombay's public spaces and iconic imperial buildings into multiple "stages" of disobedient action, frame by compelling frame.

Notes

I gratefully acknowledge the support provided for the initial stages of my research by the American Academy of Rome, the Office of the Vice Chancellor for Research and Graduate Education at the University of Wisconsin-Madison, with additional funding from the Wisconsin Alumni Research Foundation. I thank Sumathi Ramaswamy and Murali Ranganathan for their insightful comments on an earlier draft of this chapter, and also thank Murali for assistance with translating and transliterating the Marathi text on banners in the two images of women picketers featured in this chapter.

1. OED online: https://www.oed.com/dictionary/stage_n?tab=meaning_and_use#21137021. Accessed 1 March 2024.

2. See Preeti Chopra, *A Joint Enterprise: Indian Elites and the Making of British Bombay* (Minneapolis: University of Minnesota Press, 2011), xx-xxii; and David Arnold, "Subaltern Streets: India, 1870-1947", in Tariq Jazeel and Stephen Legg (eds.), *Subaltern Geographies* (Athens: University of Georgia Press, 2019), pp. 36-57.

3. Quote from image caption (37b), Nursey album.

4. See Jim Masselos, "Audiences, Actors and Congress Dramas: Crowd Events in Bombay City in 1930", *South Asia*, vol. 8, no. 1 (1985), pp. 71-86; and Prashant Kidambi, "Nationalism and the City in Colonial India: Bombay, c. 1890-1940", *Journal of Urban History*, vol. 38, no. 5 (2012), pp. 950-67.

5. Kidambi, "Nationalism and the City", p. 959.

6. ibid., p. 959.

7. Robert Rahman Raman, "Civil Disobedience and the City: Congress and the Working Classes in Bombay, c. 1930-32", in Prashant Kidambi, Manjiri Kamat and Rachel Dwyer (eds.), *Bombay before Mumbai: Essays in Honour of Jim Masselos* (Oxford: Oxford University Press, 2019), pp. 270-71.

8. Arnold, "Subaltern Streets", p. 52.

9. Kidambi, "Nationalism and the City", p. 959.

10. See K.K. Chaudhari, *History of Bombay: Modern Period* (Bombay: Gazetteers Department, Government of Maharashtra, 1987), pp. 324-25.

11. In short, it was seen by one critic as "representing less than half the population of the city." See Chaudhari, *History of Bombay*, pp. 106-07, at p. 107.

12. Translation from image caption (80a), Nursey album.

13. See the chapter "The Politics of Respectability: Indian Women and the Indian National Congress", in Geraldine Forbes, *Indian Women and the Freedom Movement: A Historian's Perspective* (Mumbai: Research Centre for Women's Studies, S.N.D.T. Women's University, 1997), pp. 67-68, at p. 68.

14. Sten Nilsson, *European Architecture in India 1750-1850* (London: Faber and Faber, 1968), p. 117.

15. Quote from image caption (110b), Nursey album.

16. Philip Davies, *Splendours of the Raj: British Architecture in India, 1660-1947* (Hammondsworth: Penguin Books, 1985), p. 173.

17. Masselos, "Audiences, Actors and Congress Dramas", p. 81.

18. ibid.

19. Taylor C. Sherman, *State Violence and Punishment in India* (London: Routledge, 2010), p. 58.

20. Masselos, "Audiences, Actors and Congress Dramas", pp. 79-80.

21. Quote from image caption (122), Nursey album.

22. Quote from image caption (61a), Nursey album.

23. For the address of Congress House, see Judith M. Brown, *Gandhi and Civil Disobedience: The Mahatma in Indian Politics 1928-34* (Cambridge: Cambridge University Press, 1977), p. 119.

24. ibid., p. 135.

25. See Geeta Thatra, "Contentious (Socio-spatial) Relations: *Tawaifs* and Congress House in Contemporary Bombay/Mumbai", *Indian Journal of Gender Studies*, vol. 23, no. 2 (2016), pp. 191-217, at p. 200. The word *mujra* has various other meanings, including "One who pays his respects." See *Atlantic's Urdu-English Dictionary: A Comprehensive Dictionary of Current Vocabulary*, Revised Edition (New Delhi: Atlantic Publishers, 1989), p. 676.

26. Thatra, "Contentious (Socio-spatial) Relations", p. 198.

27. Geraldine Forbes, *Women in Modern India* (Cambridge: Cambridge University Press, 1996), p. 127.

28. Ashwini Tambe, *Codes of Misconduct: Regulating Prostitution in Late Colonial Bombay* (Minneapolis: University of Minnesota Press, 2009), p. 105.

29. Brown, *Gandhi and Civil Disobedience*, p. 119.

30. For salt preparation on the Esplanade/Azad Maidan, see image caption (14a), Nursey album; and for salt preparation instruction, image caption (17a), ibid.

31. For salt preparation in the home, see image caption (12b), ibid.

32. See image and caption (17a), ibid.

33. Brown, *Gandhi and Civil Disobedience*, p. 135.

34. See Gail Pearson, "Nationalism, Universalization and the Extended Female Space", in Gail Minault (ed.), *The Extended Family: Women and Political Participation in India and Pakistan* (Delhi: Chanakya Publications,1981) pp. 174-91, at p. 177.

35. ibid., p. 182.

36. Chaudhari, *History of Bombay*, p. 61.

37. Davies, *Splendours of the Raj*, p. 175.

38. For information on the fountain, see Arita Sarkar, "Solving the Fitzgerald puzzle", Mid-Day, http://www.mid-day.com/sunday-mid-day/article/solving-the-fitzgerald-puzzle-20540161 (updated 10 March 2019), accessed 11 March 2023.

39. K.K. Chaudhary (ed.), *Source Material for the History of India's Freedom Movement*, vol. XI (Bombay: Maharashtra State Gazetteers Office, 1991), pp. 123-24, at p. 123. A similar sentiment is expressed in the image caption which notes that the Parsis "who were keeping aloof ... suddenly joined the movement whole heartdly [heartedly]," 101a, Nursey album.

40. ibid., p. 146, note 1.

41. Brown, *Gandhi and Civil Disobedience*, p. 137.

42. See image and caption (44), Nursey album. The caption in full reads: "The Mohomedans of Bombay in sympathy with their Hindu brothern [brethren] organised a procession which started from Dongri and terminated on the Esplanade maidan. The procession starting from the Dongri maidan."

43. Sandhya Rao Mehta and Usha Thakkar, *Gandhi in Bombay: Towards Swaraj* (New Delhi: Oxford University Press, 2017), p. 168. I thank Murali Ranganathan for the second option for translating the Marathi banner text to English.

44. Mehta and Thakkar, *Gandhi in Bombay*, pp. 168–69.

45. See image and caption (72a), Nursey album.

46. See Preeti Chopra, "The Colonial Bombay Town Hall: Engaging the Function and Quality of Public Space, 1811–1918", in Swati Chattopadhyay and Jeremy White (eds.), *City Halls and Civic Materialism: Towards a Global History of Urban Public Space* (London: Routledge, 2014), pp. 158–176.

47. See Avrati Bhatnagar and Sumathi Ramaswamy, "Light Writing on the Lathi Raj: Bombay, 1930–31", *History of Photography*, vol. 45, no. 3–4 (2021), pp. 1–16.

48. Sherman, *State Violence*, p. 58.

49. See image and caption (64a), Nursey album.

50. See also image and caption, p. 65, Nursey album.

51. See Chaudhary (ed.), *Source Material*, vol. XI, p. 70.

52. See image and caption (63), (Fig. 2.16) and p. 66 (Fig. 2.17), Nursey album. For a view of "Ambulance attending to the Wounded" and visible stretchers, most likely outside the Town Hall, see image and caption p. 74a (Fig. 8.8), Nursey album. For a view of a stretcher being loaded into the back of an ambulance van, see image and caption, p. 120, Nursey album.

53. ibid., (70a).

54. Brown, *Gandhi and Civil Disobedience*, p. 136.

55. Sherman, *State Violence*, p. 64. For more on nationalism as read through diverse tropes of nation-as-woman in visual culture, see Sumathi Ramaswamy, "Midnight's Line", in Rahaab Allana (ed.), *Another Lens: Photography and the Emergence of Image Culture*, Volume 4 [India Since the 90s series] (New Delhi: Tulika Books, 2024).

56. Quote from image caption (31a), Nursey album.

57. ibid., (24a).

58. ibid., (27).

59. A.D.D. Gordon, *Businessmen and Politics: Rising Nationalism and a Modernising Economy in Bombay, 1918–1933* (New Delhi: Manohar, 1978), p. 220.

60. ibid., pp. 219–21. The nationalists' involvement with labour went through various phases, beginning from about 1917, when they helped to found unions for Bombay's mill workers, led strikes and supported the demands of the labour force, represented by the Girni Kamdar Union (GKU) that was dominated by Communists. During the five-year-long Meerut Conspiracy Case initiated in 1928, wherein several trade union activists, including three Englishmen, were arrested and convicted for organizing a railway strike, the tenuous relationship between Congress and the labour force further deteriorated, and the GKU itself collapsed. However, within the party there had long been tensions between the left-wing ideologues and the hierarchy dominated by those from business backgrounds. In 1929, those on the left split from the Congress party and participated in the city's municipal elections as the Workers' and Peasants' Party, paralleling the split in the All India Trade Union Congress (AITUC) itself that same year. In the vacuum created by the sharp decline in Communist influence, in the mid-1930s Congress took control of GKU, now greatly diminished in terms of its membership and authority. This instigated growing criticism from the Workers' and Peasants' Party and the Young Workers' League, who opposed Gandhi.

61. ibid., p. 220.

62. ibid., p. 221.

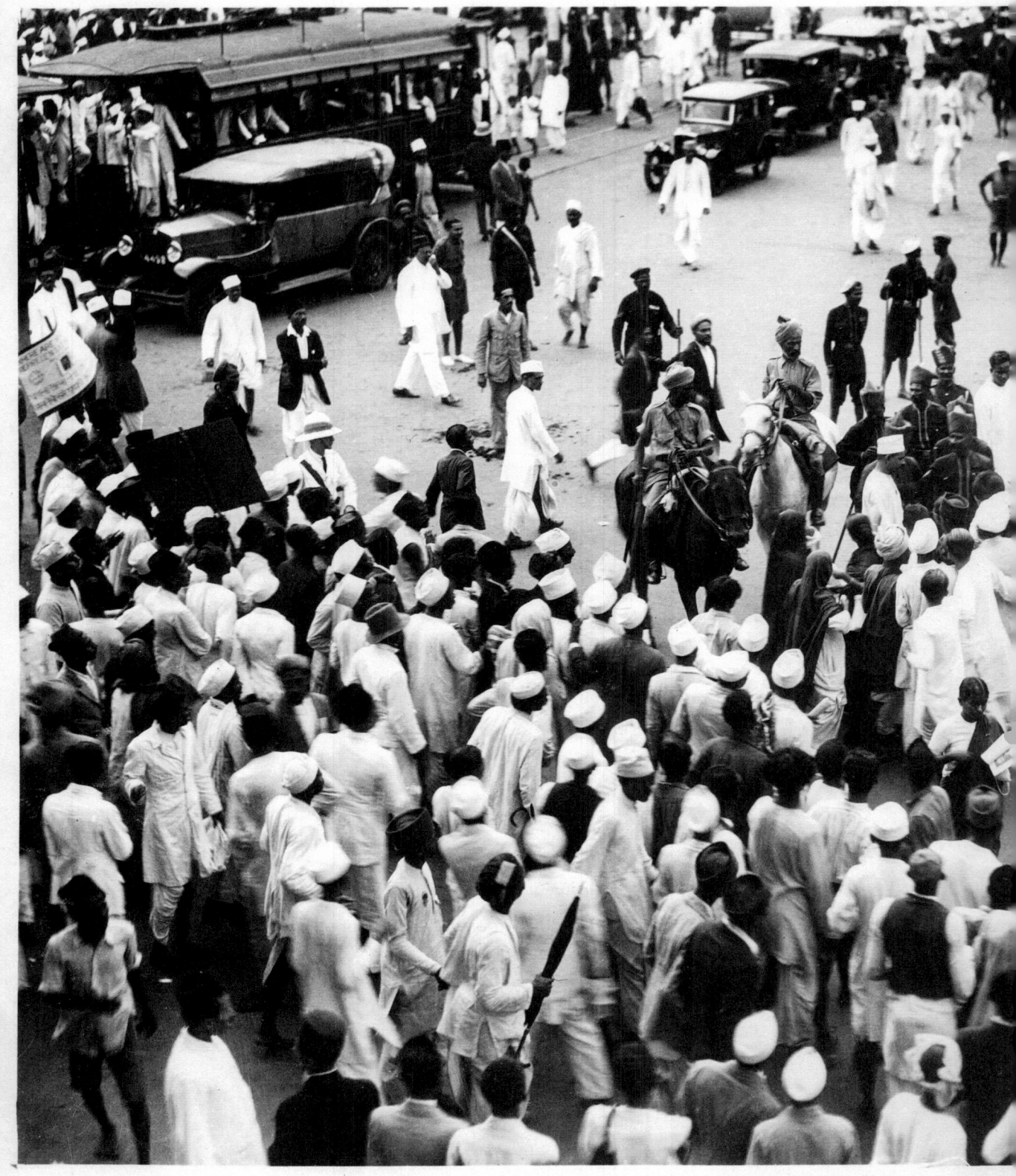
Picketers requesting the voters not to vote.

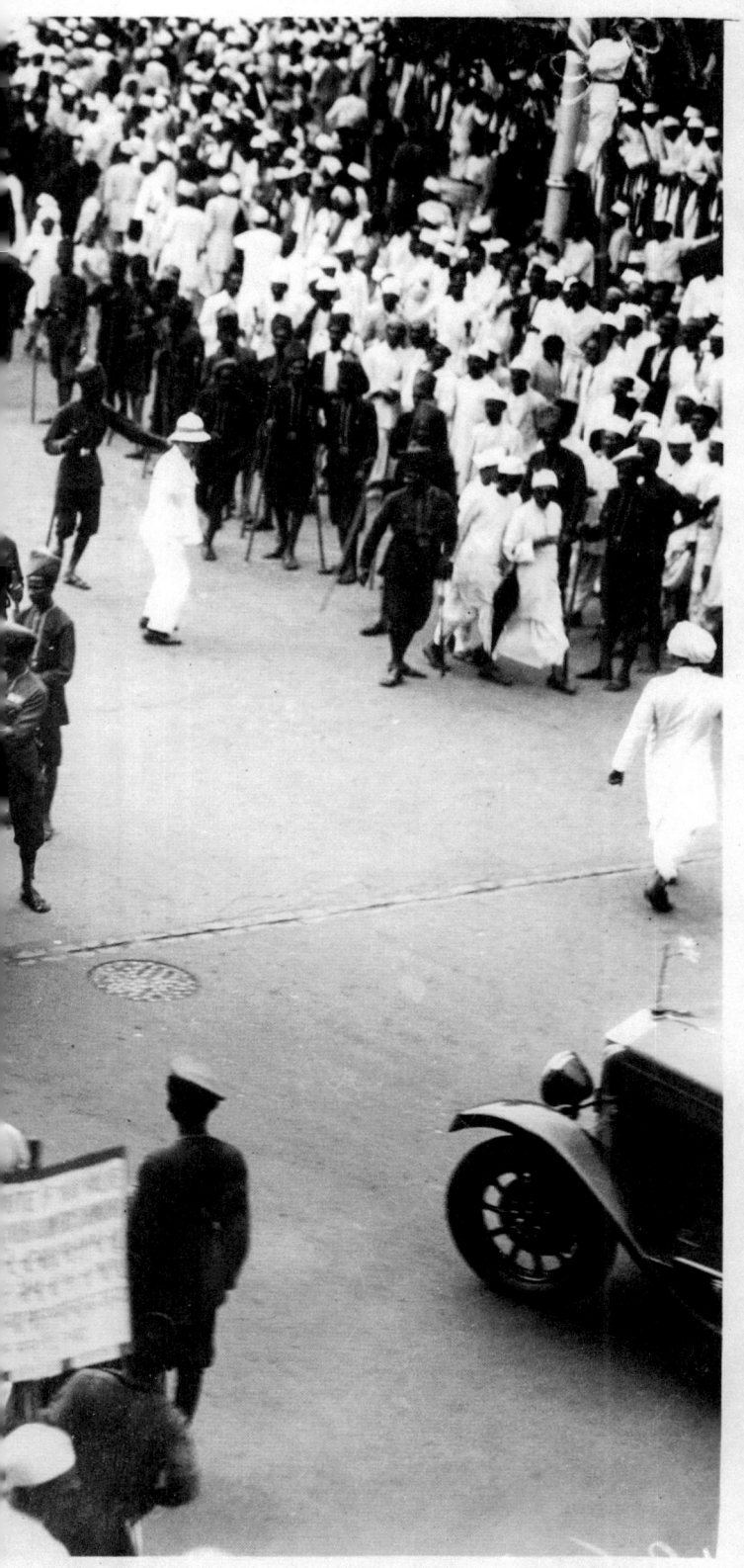

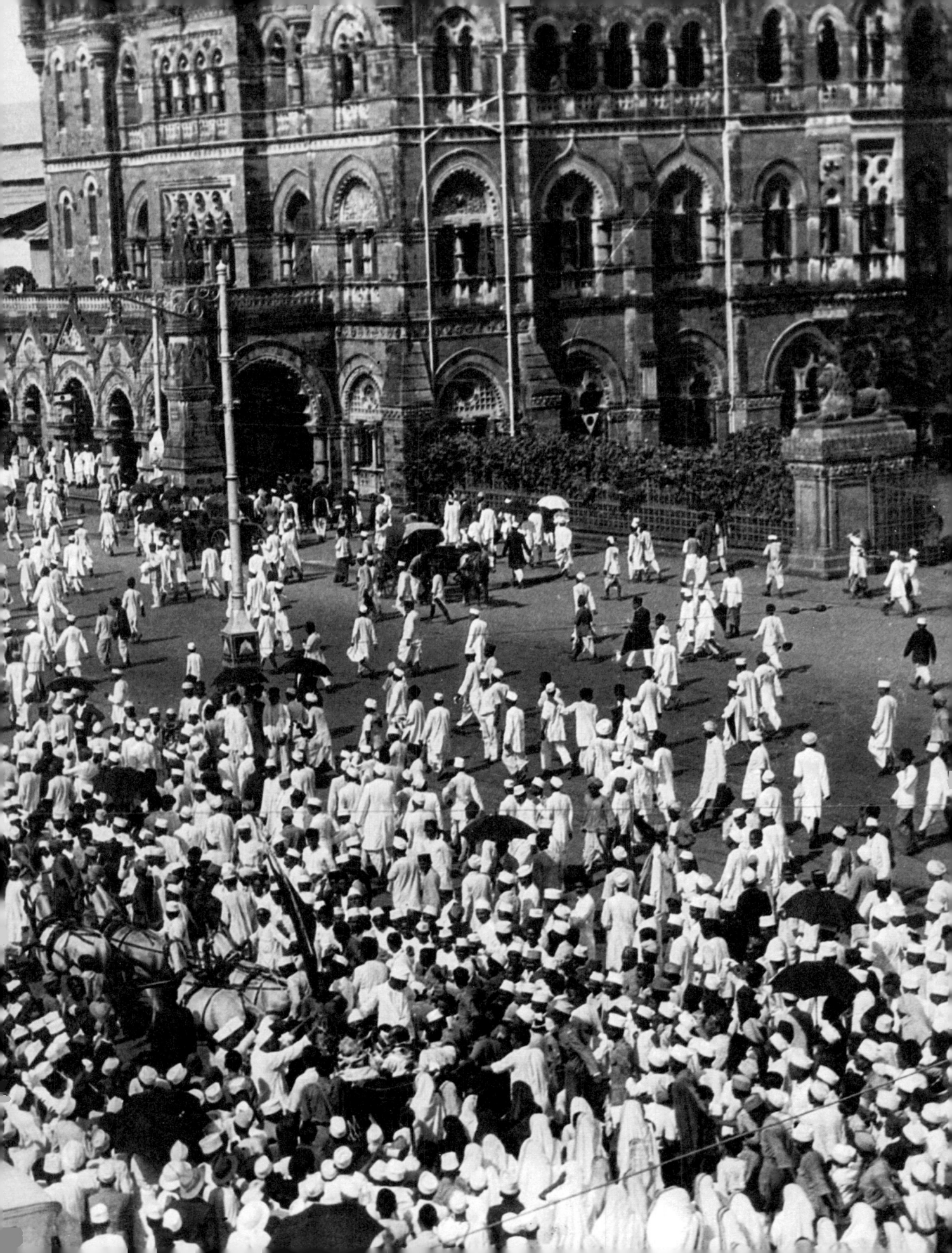

CHAPTER 3

VISUALIZING THE URBAN CROWD
POLITICAL SPECTATORSHIP
IN THE AGE OF CINEMA

Debashree Mukherjee

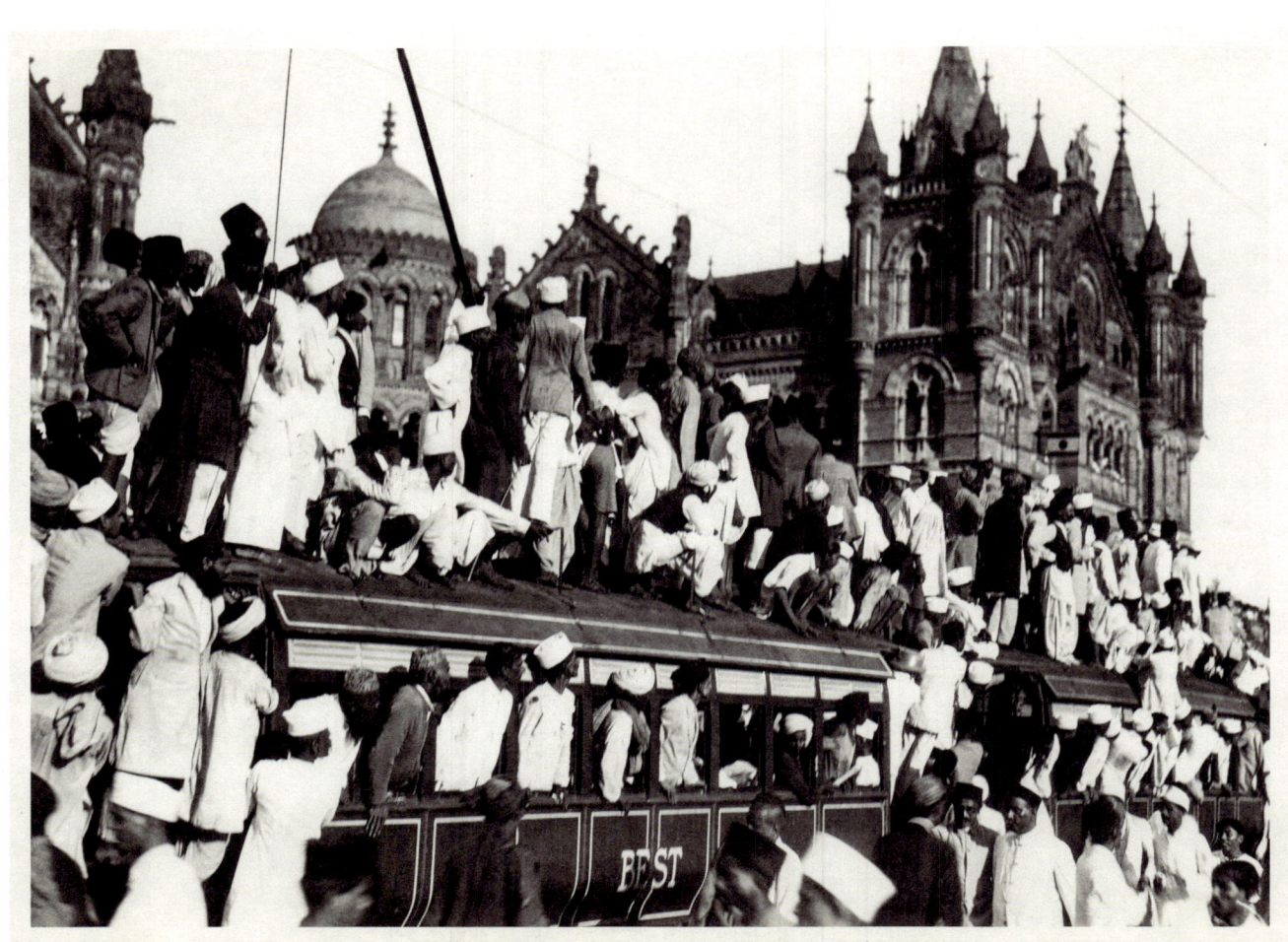

People done too much damage to Trams
by standing on it.Here is a picture
excited crowd watching the Gharwal
day proceession.

One of the key markers of Bombay's conspicuous modernity in the 1930s was the urban crowd, strategically and differentially named as "crowd," "mass," or "public" depending on who was doing the naming. These emerging urban collectivities signalled both promise and danger for a range of city elites. The colonial administration strictly surveilled anticolonial protests, while local Indian capitalists were unnerved by waves of labour mobilizations. At the same time, nationalist political parties pivoted towards new voter and supporter constituencies. Focused on the mass political mobilizations of the Civil Disobedience era, the Nursey album foregrounds and names some of the political protagonists of the time: new social and historical figures such as "agitators," "volunteers" and "party workers." To this mix I add a fourth term based on a recurring activity seen in the album—"spectating," done by "spectators"—i.e., those who watch, witness and are moved by what they see. These are not "political" actors in the usual sense of the word—many just happened to be there as disinterested bystanders, others were curious onlookers, and still others were sympathetic witnesses not yet ready to sign up as "party workers."

In this brief essay I set up a dialogue between the Nursey album and histories of cinemagoing in 1930s Bombay in order to situate mass spectatorship as a central catalyst for mass politics in the modern city, be it in movie theatres or in the streets.

Crowd Politics

The Nursey album is a testament to its immediate place of production—Bombay city—but also to a wider transformation in the visual public sphere across cities of the East and West. By the late 1920s, media forms such as the illustrated newspaper, weekly and monthly magazines (be they film magazines, science magazines or political publications) and cinema had entered headfirst into a vexed conjuncture of mass politics and agitational movements across the interwar world. We can say that the new media of the 20th century—shuttling between the heady pull of socialism in Eastern Europe, Russia and China; the capitalist euphoria of the United States' "Roaring Twenties" alongside factory strikes; and strident anticolonial movements across Asia, Africa and Latin America—were called forth by the actions of emerging political collectives, even

PAGES 78—79
"Picketers requesting the voters not to vote." c. 1930—1931
Gelatin Silver Print, 116 x 158 mm
ACP: 98.77.0002 (73a)

PAGE 80
"Dr Ansaria taken in procession on his arrival in Bombay. Photo shows the procession at V.T."
(Detail, see p. 86)

Fig. 3.1
"People done too much damage to Tram by standing on it. Here is a picture [of an] excited crowd watching the Gharwal day procession."
c. 1930—1931
Gelatin Silver Print, 117 x 156 mm
ACP: 98.77.0002 (31a)

as these new media were pressed into the urgent task of documenting the very same publics. To understand this better, we first have to understand the palpable sense of fear and excitement surrounding the emergence of the urban crowd, or what I wish to call the "collective."

Let us turn to the case of Weimar Germany, the field site for some of the most enduring theorizations of crowds and masses. Stefan Jonsson identifies an interwar German fixation with the masses, and locates this fixation in two main areas: politics, where there was an urgent need to imagine a post-imperial German nation amid tense oppositional currents; and culture, where the rapid growth of an urban proletariat paralleled the emergence of mass media. It was becoming increasing clear to observers that "power was from now on linked to mass mobilization" and that modern mass media like newspapers and cinema would be key vehicles for this mobilization.[1] The photographic image "was believed to possess unique and advantageous properties for instruction and propaganda, all the more so if one wanted to reach an audience with poor education and literacy."[2] Therefore, illustrated newspapers and magazines were the hot new media of the day. This is very similar to the situation in South Asia. Sumit Sarkar has argued that as early as the Swadeshi Movement in Bengal in 1905, "techniques of mass contact" such as "the press and the platform" broadened the scope and address of the nationalist movement, turning the tenor of anticolonial agitation away from the standard mode of petitioning the government, and instead orienting towards the public in "a new creed of radical nationalism."[3] Bombay's nationalist illustrated newspapers, such as *The Bombay Chronicle*, took up this line of politics, using photographs to document colonial violence as well as anticolonial protest, making a visceral appeal to the reader-viewer's emotions.

Fig. 3.2a
"A police officer thrashing a volunteers [volunteer] outside the high court."
c. 1930—1931
Gelatin Silver Print,
114 x 161 mm
ACP: 98.77.0002 (89b)

Fig. 3.2b
"Congress volunteers giving first aid to the wounded from lathi blows." c. 1930—1931
Gelatin Silver Print,
114 x 157 mm
ACP: 98.77.0002 (37a)

The Nursey album centres this mode of news photograph, one that visually chronicles both protest and punishment. Figures 3.2a and 3.2b are exemplars of what can be identified as an emerging genre of political news photography—the *lathi*-charge photo—in which the photographer documents police violence against a crowd of protesters, also chronicling the aftermath.[4] We see the *lathi*-charge photo feature repeatedly in *The Bombay Chronicle*, often in a documentary series, as a sequenced testimonial that starts from the site of attack, moves on to the administration of medical aid, and ends with photographs of injured volunteers proudly posing with their bandages as they might with medals for bravery.[5] Note that the *lathi* charge is a form of *crowd control*, albeit a violent one. It cannot be deployed against solitary individuals but needs a confrontational mass of bodies in order to be effective and justifiable. Ironically, the same *lathi*-charge photos that were read as patriotic protest in Indian newspapers were interpreted as laudable examples of British law and order in venues such as *The Illustrated London News*.[6] These

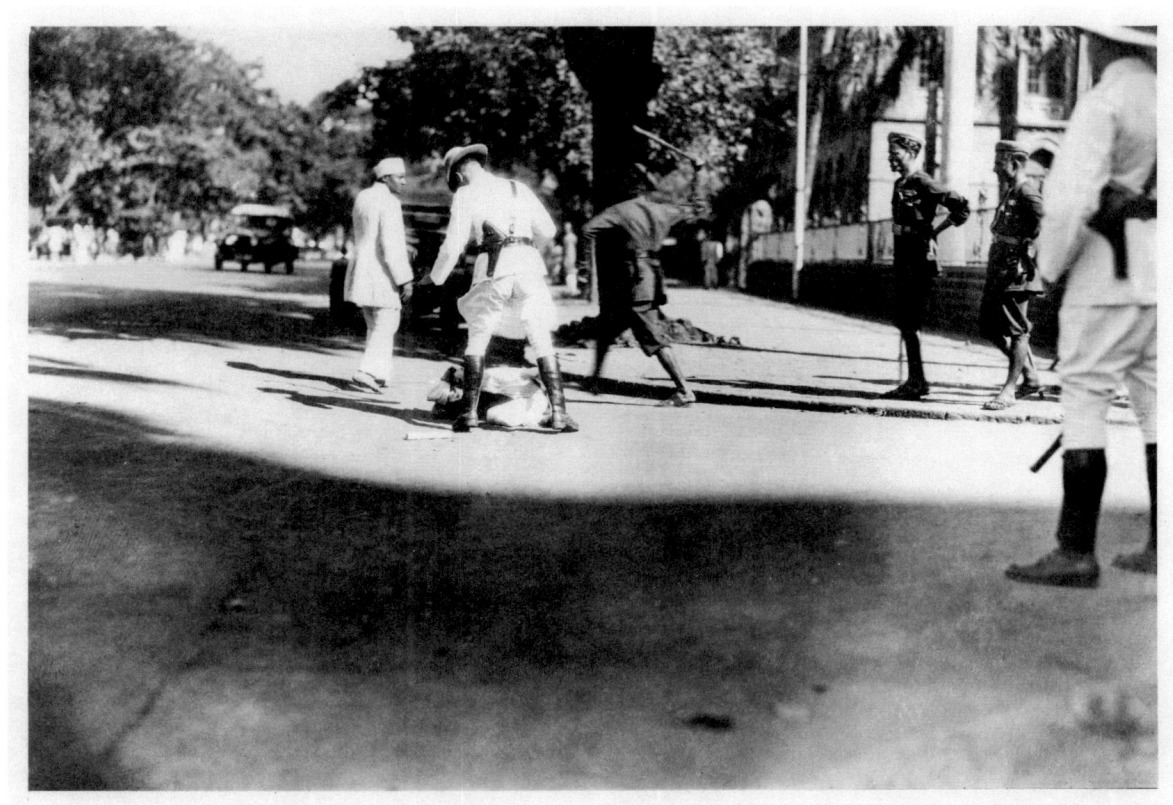

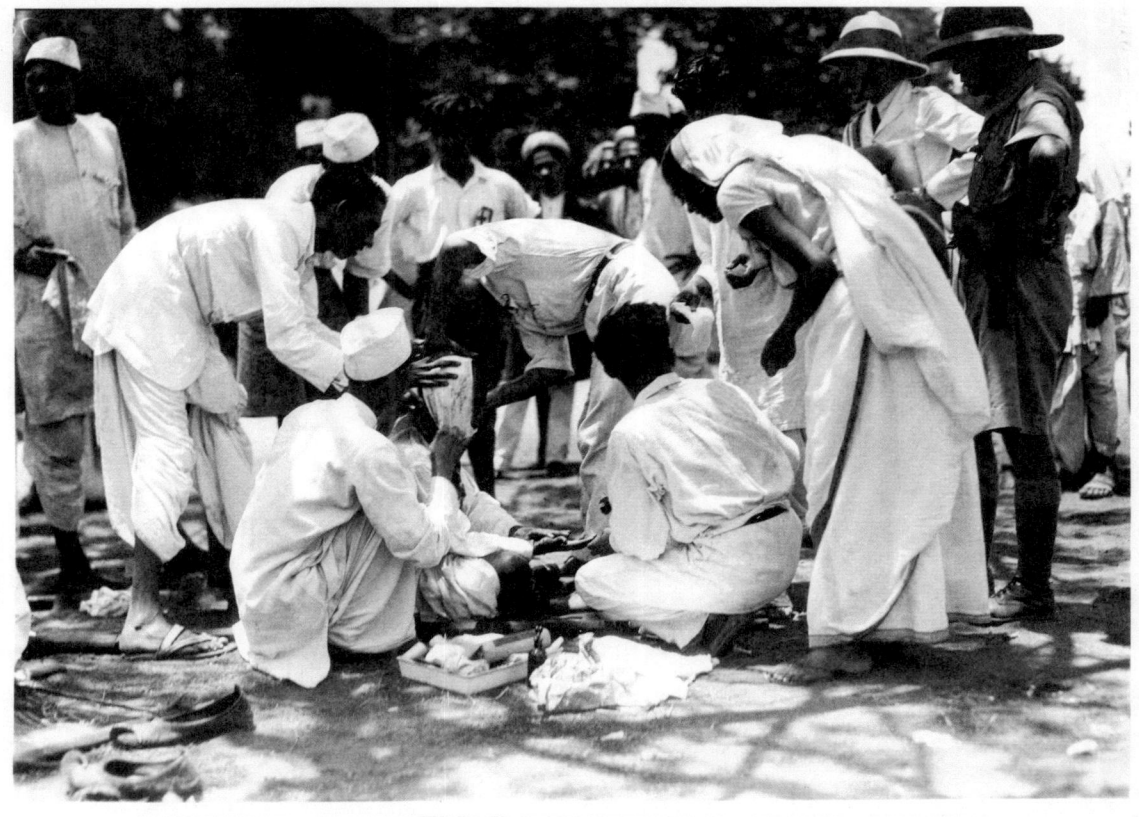

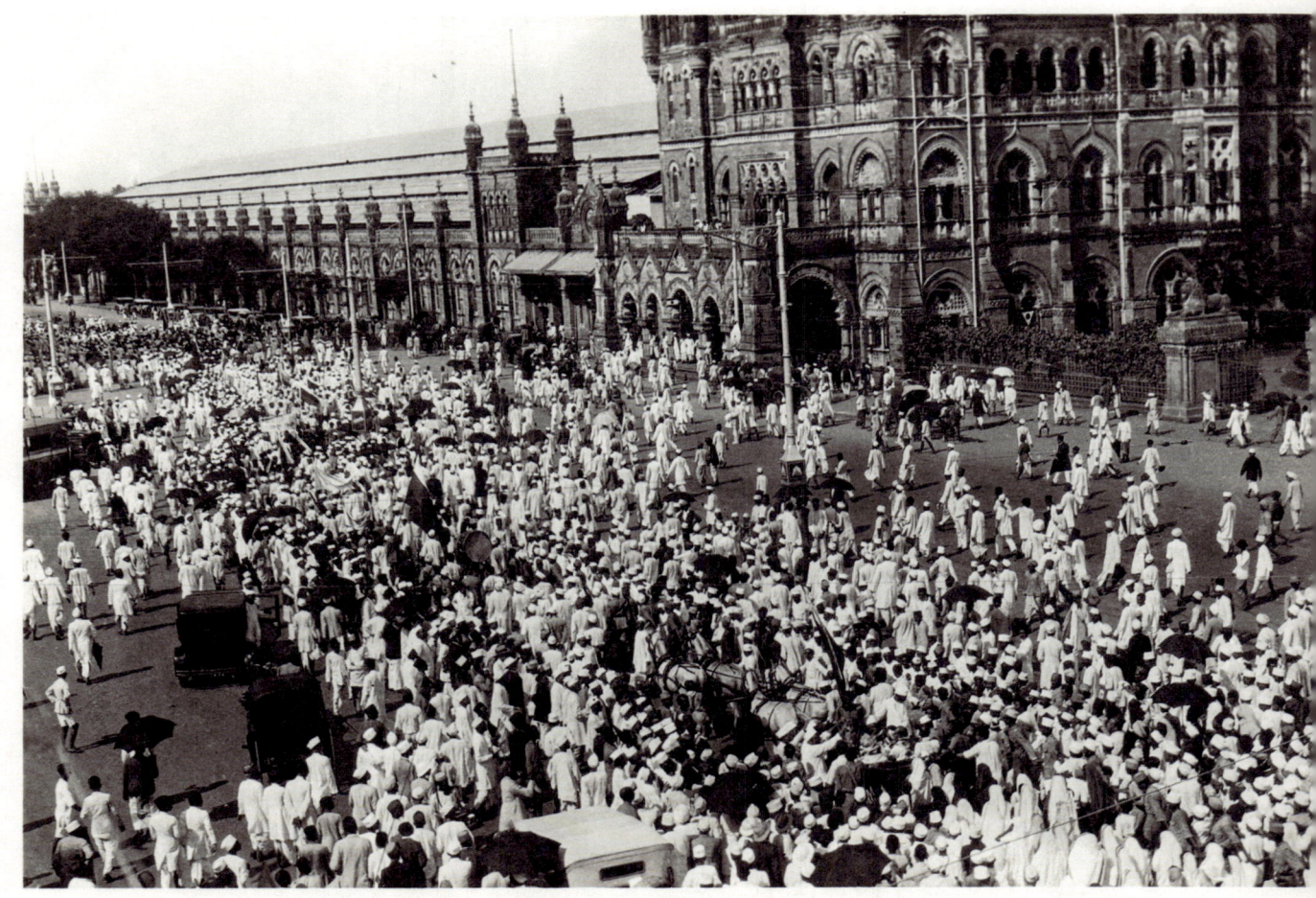

Fig. 3.3
"Dr Ansaria taken
in procession on his
arrival in Bombay.
Photo shows the
procession at V.T."
c. 1930–1931
Gelatin Silver Print,
114 x 165 mm
ACP: 98.77.0002 (28a)

contradictory uses point to the intense struggle over images that marked this period, as new forms of mass media joined with new forms of collective mobilization.

Jim Masselos has studied the forms and methods of the Civil Disobedience Movement in Bombay in 1930-31 in terms of techniques of crowd mobilization.[7] He points to the very controlled manner in which the Congress staged daily ritualized public performances—starting with the march to collect salt from the seashore in the morning, to the rousing speeches in the evening, all punctuated through the day by *prabhat pheris*, *lathi* charges and endless processions.[8] All of these tactical forms depended critically on the crowd, the large numbers of what Masselos calls "actors and audience"—where Congress workers and volunteers are the actors, while the "spectating" onlookers, both random and purposive, might be called the "audience."

This audience is interesting to me because it lends itself to many roles in the historical narrative and is not easily definable. The success of the Civil

Disobedience Movement depended on the ability of the Congress to mobilize supporters towards the political horizon of *purna swaraj* (total self-government). Each of the tactical political events produced and performed by the Congress depended on watchers and witnesses, those large numbers of people who showed up to observe, cheer or spontaneously join in the drama of nationalism. Masselos describes the "monster meetings" that took place every day in Bombay, and the Nursey album helps us visualize them (Fig. 3.3). What I wish to highlight is that such spectacular crowds are not simply a fallout of modern urban political events, but their very goal. These are "spectacles of presence,"to cite Nusrat Chowdhry,[9] and they evidence the political potentialities of the collective.

It has been argued that there were certain pre-existing particularities in Bombay city that were conducive to this form of public watching, gathering and walking. Masselos points to religious practices that utilized the cityscape as a venue, demonstrating the simultaneous private-public nature of religious festivals such as Ganpati or Muharram processions. Some of these, especially Muharram, were frequently marked by police presence and surveillance. There is a suggestion here that the crowd watching the religious procession is not only affectively mobilized by the spectacle, but also politically interpellated as oppositional to a governmental/colonial authority. What I would like to add to the list of the particular conditions that made Bombay city a prime venue for mass politics is the historical fact of cinema and the city as a cine-ecology.[10] As an art form and a social space, cinema was becoming a conspicuous presence in the city and was also being tested as a venue for political contestation.

Seeing like a Collective

For more than two decades, the India Office in London had been petitioned by angry film viewers, religious leaders, journalists and politicians who objected to sensitive content in both Indian and foreign films, and by those who sought the proscription of films that were racially or religiously offensive to Indians. By the late 1930s, a vibrant and heterogeneous film audience was in place, one that recognized the social effects of mass media and treated cinema as a site of political protest.[11] At the same time, bourgeois anxieties about unruly audiences who could be instigated by nationalist, anti-capitalist or anti-racist film messaging overlapped with anxieties about workers' unions, urban Muslim youth and the middle-class working woman. Let us consider an example from this decade as illustration.

In 1934, a highly anticipated film titled *The Mill* or *Mazdoor* (trans. Worker) was made in Bombay, scripted by the acclaimed Hindi novelist Premchand and directed by Mohan Bhavnani, a veteran filmmaker. *The Mill*'s plot was extremely topical: a love story between a millowner's daughter and a trade union leader, which presented a romantic solution to Bombay's decades-long labour agitations against the powerful textile industry. An added attraction of the film was the fact that it was shot on-location at Bombay's Hansraj textile mill and promised realistic footage of workers' rallies and strikes. However, *The Mill* was immediately proscribed and the filmmakers were subjected to a five-year-long battle with the censors. The main fear was that because it graphically depicted violent proletarian resistance to capitalist exploitation, the film would cause unrest in the city. The censor's paper trail reveals some locational specificities of Bombay city that caused these acute apprehensions—its changing demographics as the foremost centre of trade and industry in the region, its status as the centre for Communist Party activities, and its reputation as a city of strikes—all of which were only possible because of the emergence of a new historical figure with a reflexive class consciousness, the *girni kaamgaar*, or more broadly, the *mazdoor*.[12]

Statistics from this period show that Bombay audiences constituted a big chunk of who was watching Bombay films, with a 33–47% share in nationwide theatrical revenues.[13] This local film viewership depended heavily on working-class audiences solicited in theatres built in cotton-mill neighbourhoods. *The Mill*'s censors were therefore not simply speculating about an imagined working-class audience, they were also envisioning the actually existing proletarian film publics of Bombay who seemed ripe for radical socialist messaging. I suggest that the rise of Bombay's mills and the new-media context of rapid mass reproduction and dissemination historically converged to produce a "perceptual machinery of the collective"[14] wherein visual technologies such as photography and cinema

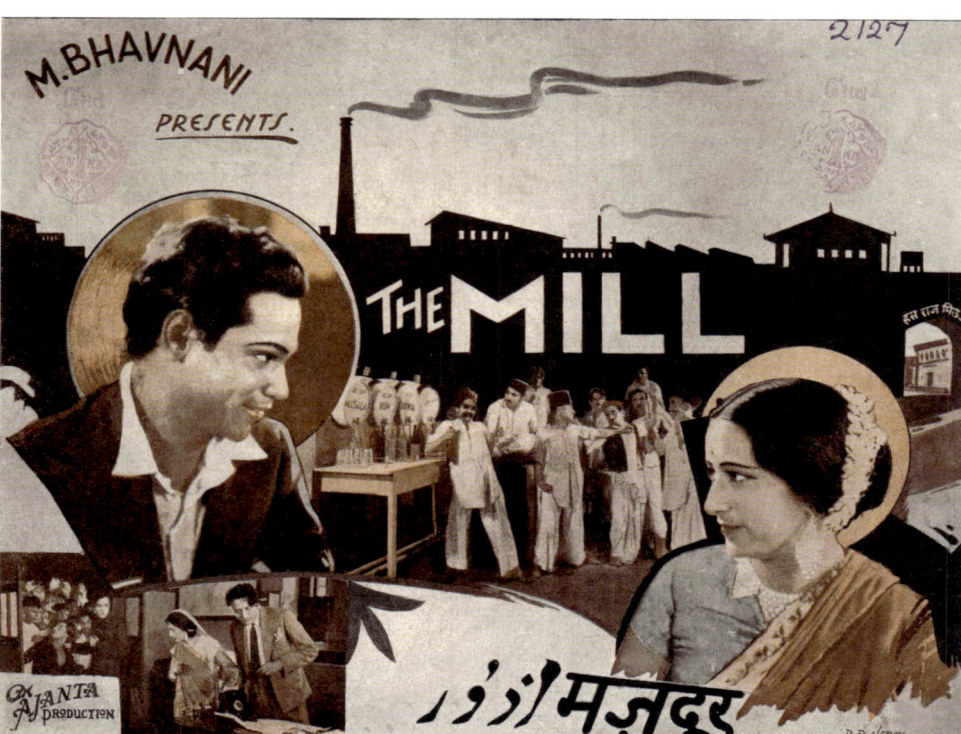

Fig. 3.4
Cover of a song booklet for *The Mill/ Mazdoor* (1934), directed by Mohan Bhavnani.
Image courtesy: National Film Archive of India, Pune

were rapidly enlisted to *address* the collective and, at the same time, *represent* the collective. Cinema in Bombay at this time thus rose to the occasion and visualized the new proletarian collective, romantically individualized into the icon of the *mazdoor*. But, and this is important, cinema also provided the perceptual training of *seeing like a collective*. As the urban masses gathered in the darkened anonymity of a movie hall, they were sensorially trained in the perceptual art of seeing like a collective—gasping, laughing, cheering, crying in a shared affective moment. This mass affect, produced by the movies, had the potential to incite as much as to educate, and elite interests recognized this ambivalent potential almost immediately.

My argument is that the spectating crowds we see in the Nursey album are oriented towards the compelling scenography of outdoor street rallies and political processions in a way that is similar to their orientation towards the filmic image inside the movie theatre. There is a direct overlap between the demographics that would throng a film screening and those who crowded the streets as loiterers, workers, vendors, shoppers or commuters. The screen calls a collective into being by addressing strangers and drawing them into a shared embodied experience. The political procession or other protest spectacles from the 1930s similarly craft a public out of the amorphous crowd. Like the rally-watcher, the moviegoer intuits, quite viscerally, that a group affect has been created by the spectacle, a kind of energetic pact that pulls the individual out of solipsism and into the collective.

The curious onlookers we see in the Nursey album further exemplify the cinematic mode of distracted viewing that was characteristic of the moviegoing experience at the time, and cyclically drew on the distracted gaze that marks the urban sensorium.[15] Whether in a built theatre in Grant Road or a temporary screening tent in a maidan, cinema was a noisy social space of distracted viewing with hawkers, film narrators and jokesters competing for attention. The screen, like the rally, gathers bodies into a shared space, but it cannot fully control the multiple meanings that will be made from the experience. In the streets of Bombay in 1930, the spectating crowds watched political protests with a mix of curiosity, thrill and indifference, or simply to pass the time. It is neither necessary nor possible for us to ascertain whether they "got the message" or not, or whether they were engaged, attentive viewers. The noteworthy point is that these bodies were physically drawn into an anticolonial geography that was temporarily produced in the triangulation of public space, crowds and political performance. The rally, like the movie, produced a social space, and this spatial production (or appropriation) is a "condition of possibility for the crowd's assumption of a political role ...."[16]

In Figure 3.5, we see an orderly procession of Congress workers—men, women and children—as they walk down a busy market area wearing their

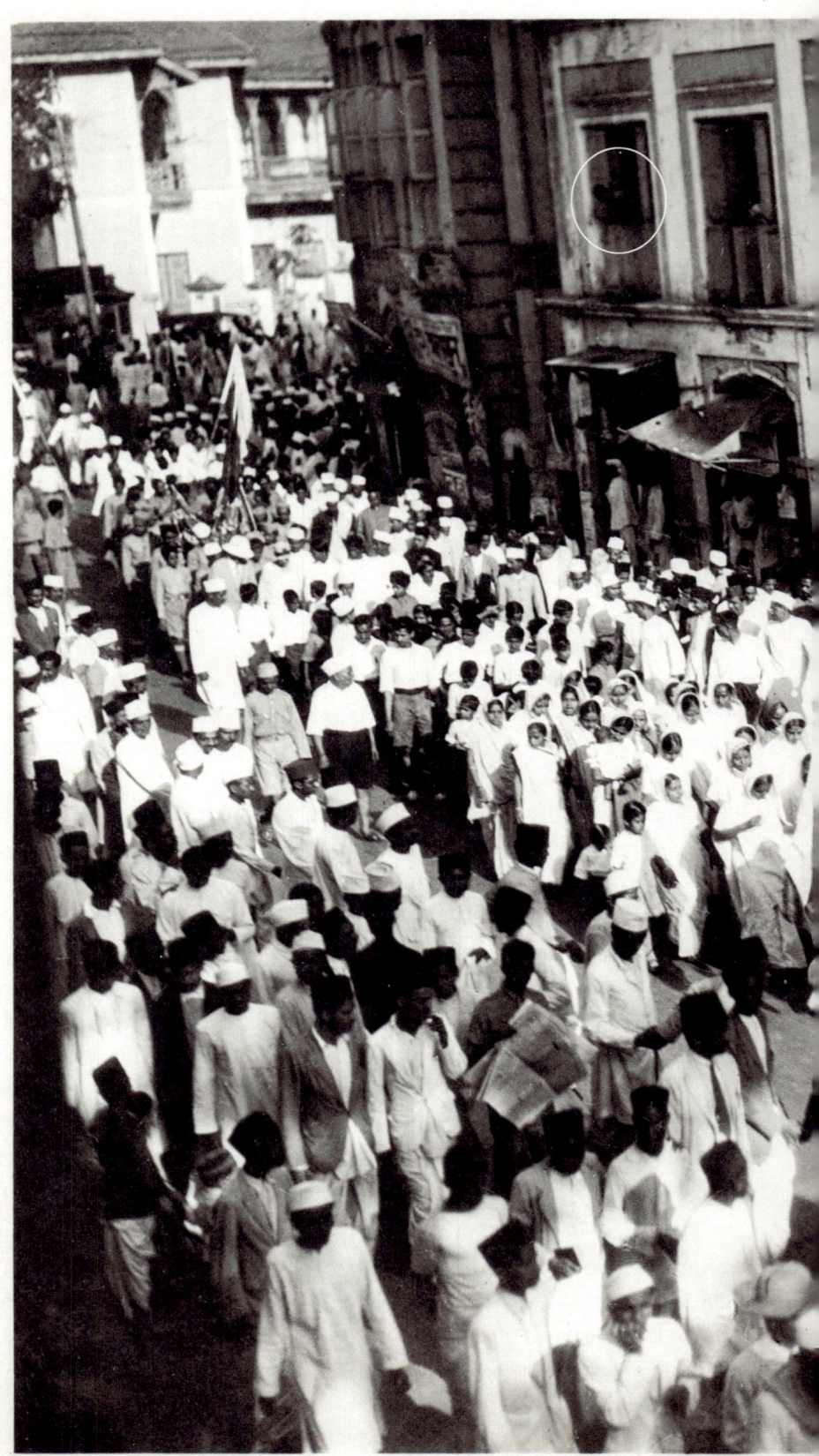

Fig. 3.5
"A boycott procession
in the market area."
c. 1930—1931
Gelatin Silver Print,
115 x 160 mm
ACP: 98.77.0002 (90b)
The circled sections
in the photograph
reveal shadowy figures
on the edges of the
rally, spectators
on the verge of
being swept into the
political space of the
procession.

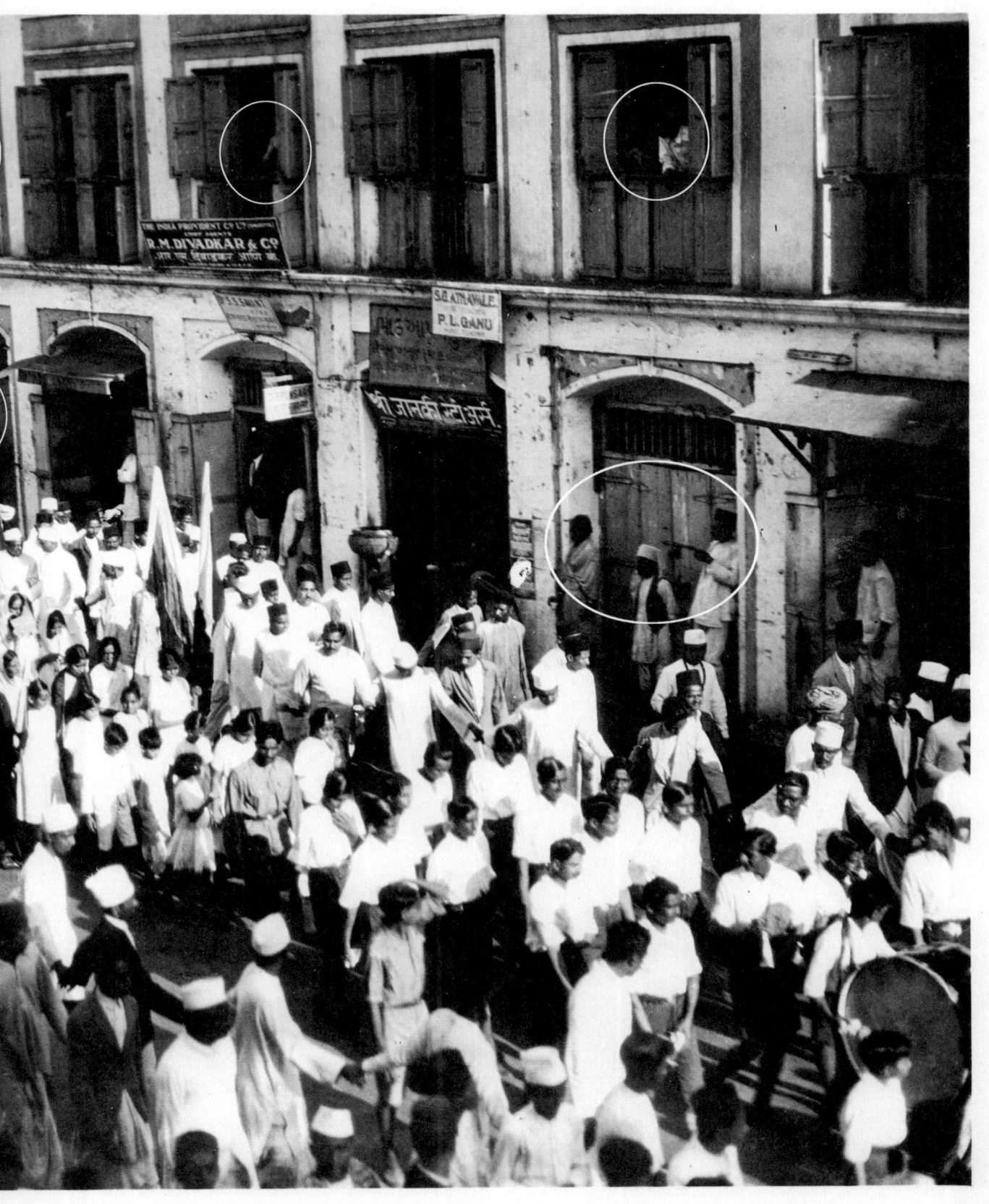

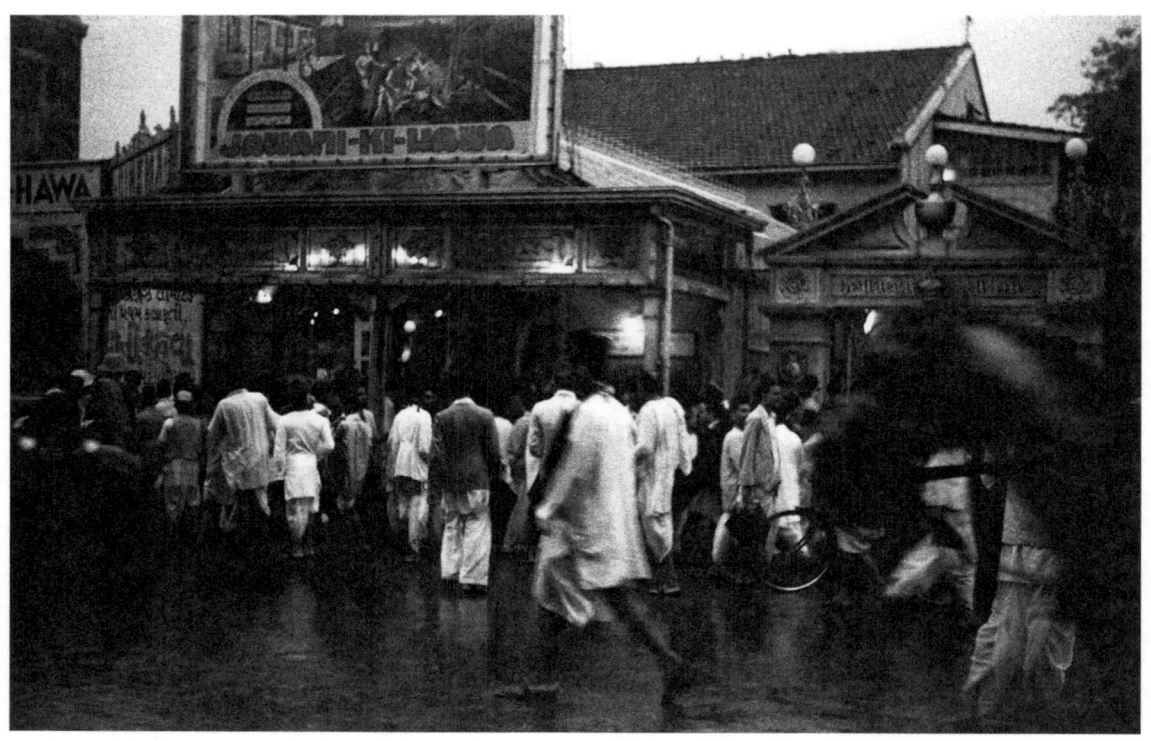

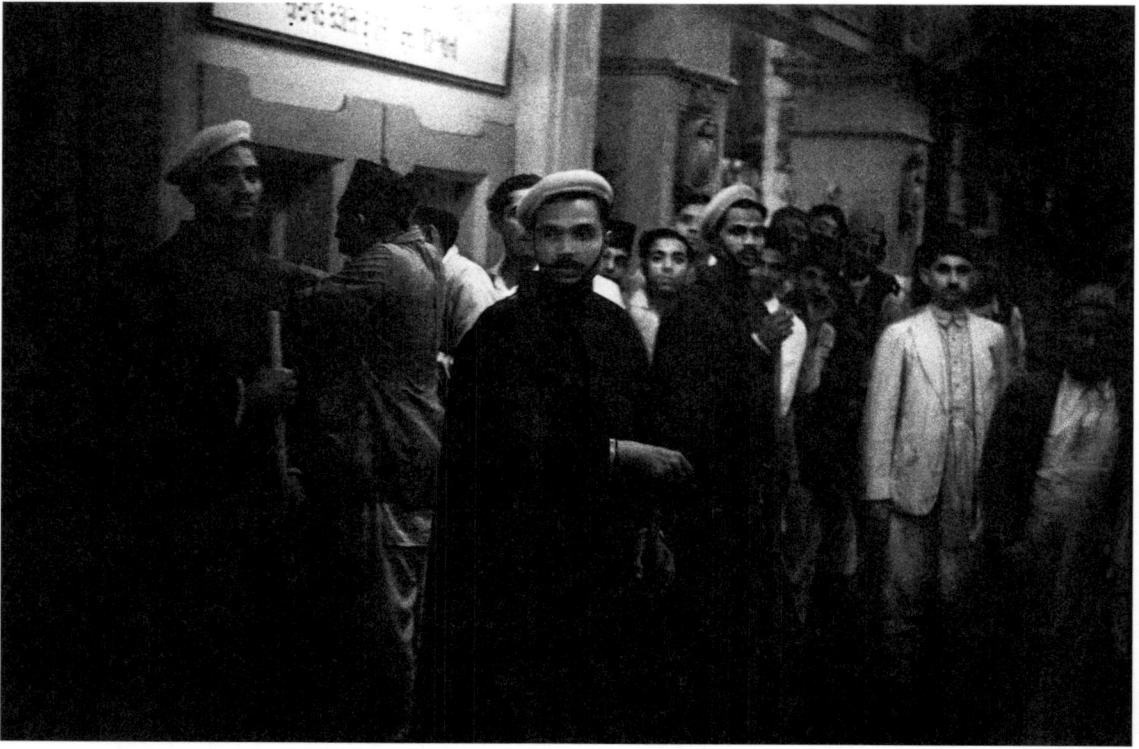

white caps and holding hands to redirect the traffic flow. The superimposed circles highlight the barely visible "audience" for this show, hidden in shadowy doorways and overhanging windows, quite like film spectators watching from stalls and balconies. Standing in the literal margins of this photograph and away from its central focus (the political procession), these bystanders are nevertheless a key part of the demonstration. Without their voluntary witnessing and accidental presence, the rally could not be deemed a success in scale. Moreover, an agitational charge is unleashed in a street that is taken over by chanting cadres, and this charge is its own form of political pedagogy. It sensorially introduces onlookers to the language of rights and demands, opens up an imagination that it is possible to enact public opposition to the regime.

Aesthetics and Politics

In a recent book, Francis Cody notes that "the popular phrase 'media event' points to the fact that we have long recognized conditions in which events are staged in anticipation of recording by news cameras and reporters."[17] Undoubtedly, many of the Nursey album photographs were designed to generate a media event through the combination of planned daily practices of mass civil disobedience and strategically placed cameras that documented these staged events. Representationally, these photos were intended to fulfil a political function: to document and disseminate political rallies, but also to intervene in the active erasure or misrepresentation of anticolonial activities in mainstream media, which was a visual mode of political suppression. In response, these images defiantly configure the public spaces of Bombay city as spaces of oppositional politics, framing the varied actors as visibly antagonistic: police versus public, colonial power versus people power, might versus right. But media don't simply represent events or publics—media such as photography and cinema can materially engineer significant orientations of social relations and attitudes.

It is in the early 1930s that cinema emerged as a conspicuous site for—and subject of—political debate, negotiation and contestation in colonial India. By the late 1930s, a robust anticolonial cultural movement had sprung up against foreign films that displayed a patently racist or imperialist agenda in their depictions of India.[18] Whether we examine the censor's control of films considered unsuitable in a factory town, or the nationalist Indian's outrage against racist representation, we are confronted by a widespread belief in the power of cinema to sway hearts and minds. This power was conceived to lie in cinema's sensory address, the visceral potential of *mise en scène* and spectacle to move audiences into action and agitation. The palpable quality of this power is clear in descriptions of the heavily-censored *The Mill* that was released in 1939. A young socialist Khwaja Ahmad Abbas excitedly wrote, at the time, "Whatever

Fig. 3.6a
Crowds outside the Imperial Cinema in Bombay being surveilled by a police *bundobast* (deployment). Photograph taken during the premiere of Bombay Talkies' debut Hindi feature film *Jawani ki Hawa* (1935). 35 mm Negative
Image courtesy: Josef Wirsching Archive/ The Alkazi Collection of Photography (2019.01.0049)

Fig. 3.6b
Crowds outside the Imperial Cinema in Bombay being surveilled by a police *bundobast* (deployment). Photograph taken during the premiere of Bombay Talkies' debut feature film *Jawani ki Hawa* (1935). 35 mm Negative
Image courtesy: Josef Wirsching Archive/ The Alkazi Collection of Photography (2019.01.0050)

dramatic vigour [*The Mill*] has is in the strike scenes ... A shot in which a worker is shown clenching his fist in indignation, by itself, has intense drama in it."[19] For the censor board, the dramatic intensity of a filmic fist clenched in anger threatened to translate into a thousand fists raised against the city's capitalist infrastructure. At the core of the censor's anxiety was trepidation about the mimetic power of cinema to induce action, to successfully instigate a collective uprising by an anonymous urban crowd that has turned political.

Lotte Hoek has written powerfully about the actual use of film projection screens in political processions in present-day Bangladesh. For her, the "screen in the crowd" is a "modular political form in the digitally enabled crowd of the 21st century," and is effective because it taps into the political potentials of a crowd that is immersed in the visual proliferations of a heavily mediatized contemporary world.[20] In this brief essay I have tried to shed light on the spatial and sensorial continuities between cinema-in-the-hall in 1930s Bombay and politics-in-the-streets. Here, the very specific crowds of Bombay city are attuned to an emerging visual imagination via the movies and are being trained in new techniques of seeing. The continuities between cinema hall and city street pulse along the axes of spectacle and address, the training of the gaze and the material interpellation of a collective. The Nursey album images, with their immediate appeal to the visual and the spatial, urge us to move beyond the content of speeches (which we cannot hear), to the material practices of civil disobedience, the physical choreography of collective resistance and the physical reconfiguration of city spaces into political theatre. The album offers an intermedial story that moves between architecture, photography, newspapers, urban design, public processions and policing. My goal has been to introduce the urban fact of cinema into the story as a mass perceptual machinery that attunes the individual to a collective gaze and extends into the street as political spectatorship.

Notes

Parts of this text draw on ideas first developed in the author's essay, "A Specter Haunts Bombay: Censored Itineraries of a Lost Communistic Film", *Film History*, vol. 31, no. 4 (2019), pp. 29-59.

1. Stefan Jonsson, *Crowds and Democracy: The Idea and Image of the Masses from Revolution to Fascism* (New York: Columbia University Press, 2013), p. 10. For more on crowds, see Elias Canetti, *Crowds and Power*, trans. Carol Stewart, 12th ed. (New York: Farrar, Straus and Giroux, 1980); and Christian Borch, *The Politics of Crowds: An Alternative History of Sociology* (Cambridge: Cambridge University Press, 2012).

2. Jonsson, *Crowds and Democracy*, p. 217.

3. Sumit Sarkar, *The Swadeshi Movement in Bengal, 1903-1908* (New Delhi: People's Publishing House, 1994), pp. 252-54.

4. See Avrati Bhatnagar and Sumathi Ramaswamy, "Light Writing on the Lathi Raj: Bombay, 1930-31", *History of Photography*, vol. 45, no. 4 (2021), pp. 304-19.

5. Photographers credited in *The Bombay Chronicle* in 1930 include P.K. Chowdhary, D. Misra and Khanchand.

6. Bhatnagar and Ramaswamy, "Light Writing", pp. 5-6.

7. Jim Masselos, "Audiences, Actors and Congress Dramas: Crowd Events in Bombay City in 1930", *South Asia*, vol. 8, no. 1 (1985), pp. 71-86. *Prabhat pheris* or morning processions were a popular political technique used by the Congress wherein small groups of (mostly) women cadres walked through residential neighbourhoods in the early hours of the morning, singing a mix of religious and patriotic songs.

8. ibid., p. 72.

9. Nusrat S. Chowdhury, *Paradoxes of the Popular: Crowd Politics in Bangladesh* (Stanford: Stanford University Press, 2019), p. 10.

10. For more on "cine-ecology," a spatial concept that brings together arenas of film exhibition, production and consumption with practices of urban work, leisure and politics, see Debashree Mukherjee, *Bombay Hustle: Making Movies in a Colonial City* (New York: Columbia University Press, 2020).

11. For detailed discussions on Indian reactions to colonialist and racist films, see Prem Chowdhry, *Colonial India and the Making of Empire Cinema: Image, Ideology and Identity* (Manchester: Manchester University Press, 2000); Babli Sinha, *Cinema, Transnationalism, and Colonial India: Entertaining the Raj* (New York: Routledge, 2013); and Poonam Arora, "'Imperilling the Prestige of the White Woman': Colonial Anxiety and Film Censorship in British India", *Visual Anthropology Review*, vol. 11, no. 2 (1995), pp. 36-50.

12. For a detailed study, see Mukherjee, "A Specter Haunts Bombay".

13. This large audience share was mainly due to the state of distribution and exhibition infrastructures in the 1930s, with film theatres concentrated in a few urban centres and a distribution network focused on building up a few "territories" and unable to expand much further due to a lack of reliable capital. See Valentina Vitali, *Hindi Action Cinema: Industries, Narratives, Bodies* (Bloomington and Indianapolis: Indiana University Press, 2008), pp. 75, 96.

14. Jonsson, *Crowds and Democracy*, p. 216.

15. Foundational theories of the relation between cinema and urban modernity build on this idea of "distracted" vision in an urban landscape of electric signs, shop windows and frenetic traffic. See, for example, Anne Friedberg, *Window Shopping: Cinema and the Postmodern* (Berkeley, Los Angeles and London: University of California Press, 1993).

16. Rosalind C. Morris, "Theses on the New Öffentlichkeit", *Grey Room*, vol. 51 (2013), pp. 94-111, at p. 103.

17. Francis Cody, *The News Event: Popular Sovereignty in the Age of Deep Mediatization* (Chicago and London: University of Chicago Press, 2023), p. 3.

18. Prem Chowdhry, "Propaganda and Protest: The Myth of the Muslim Menace in an Empire Film (The Drum, 1938)", *Studies in History*, vol. 16, no. 1 (2000), pp. 109-30, at p. 109.

19. Khwaja A. Abbas, "'The Mill'—But What About 'Mazdoor'?", *The Bombay Chronicle*, 14 June 1939, p. 10.

20. Lotte Hoek, "A Screen in the Crowd: Film Societies and Political Protest in Bangladesh", in Zhen Zhang, Sangjoon Lee, Debashree Mukherjee and Intan Paramditha (eds.), *Routledge Companion to Asian Cinemas* (New York: Routledge, 2024).

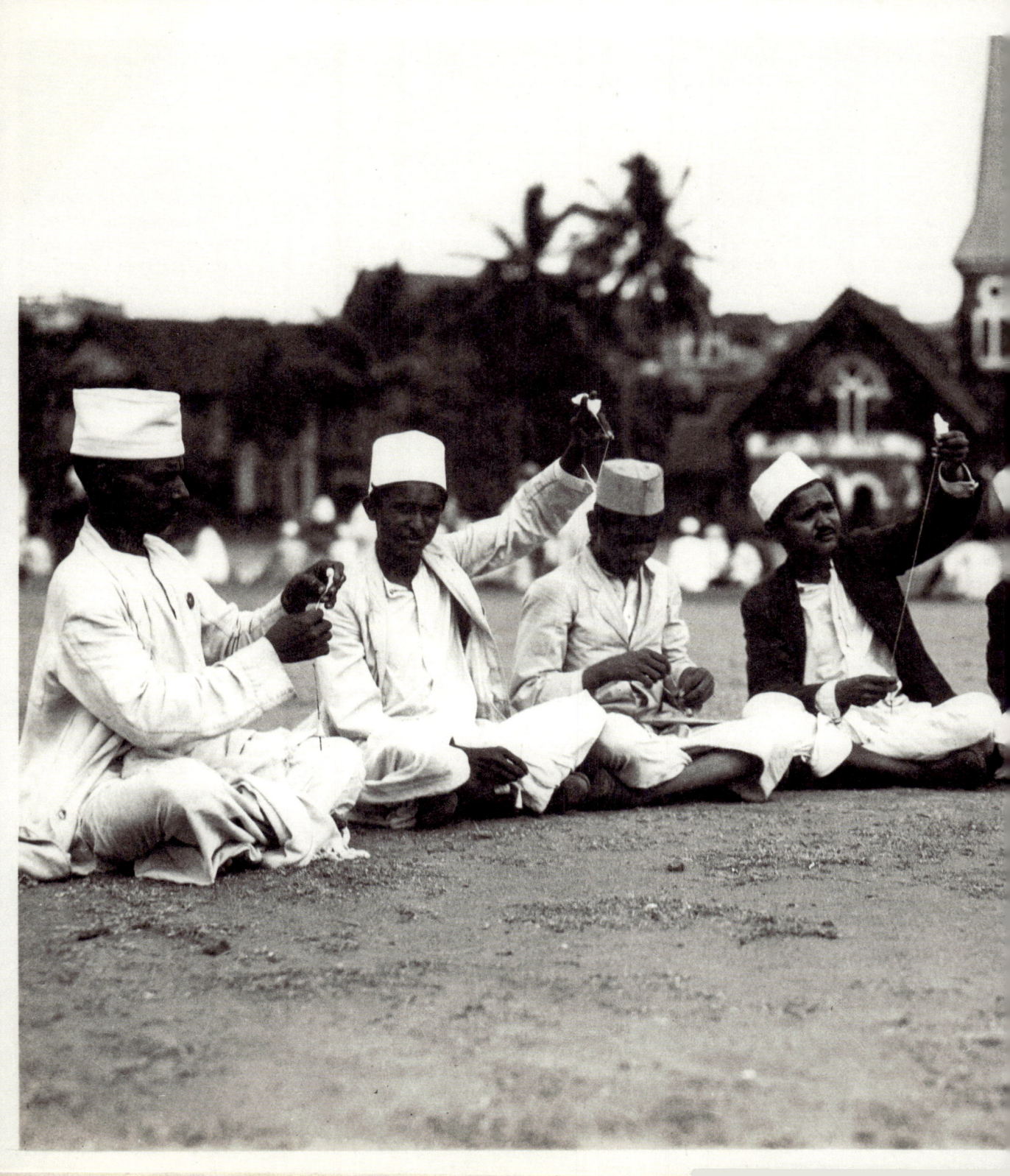

A group of men spinning the takli.

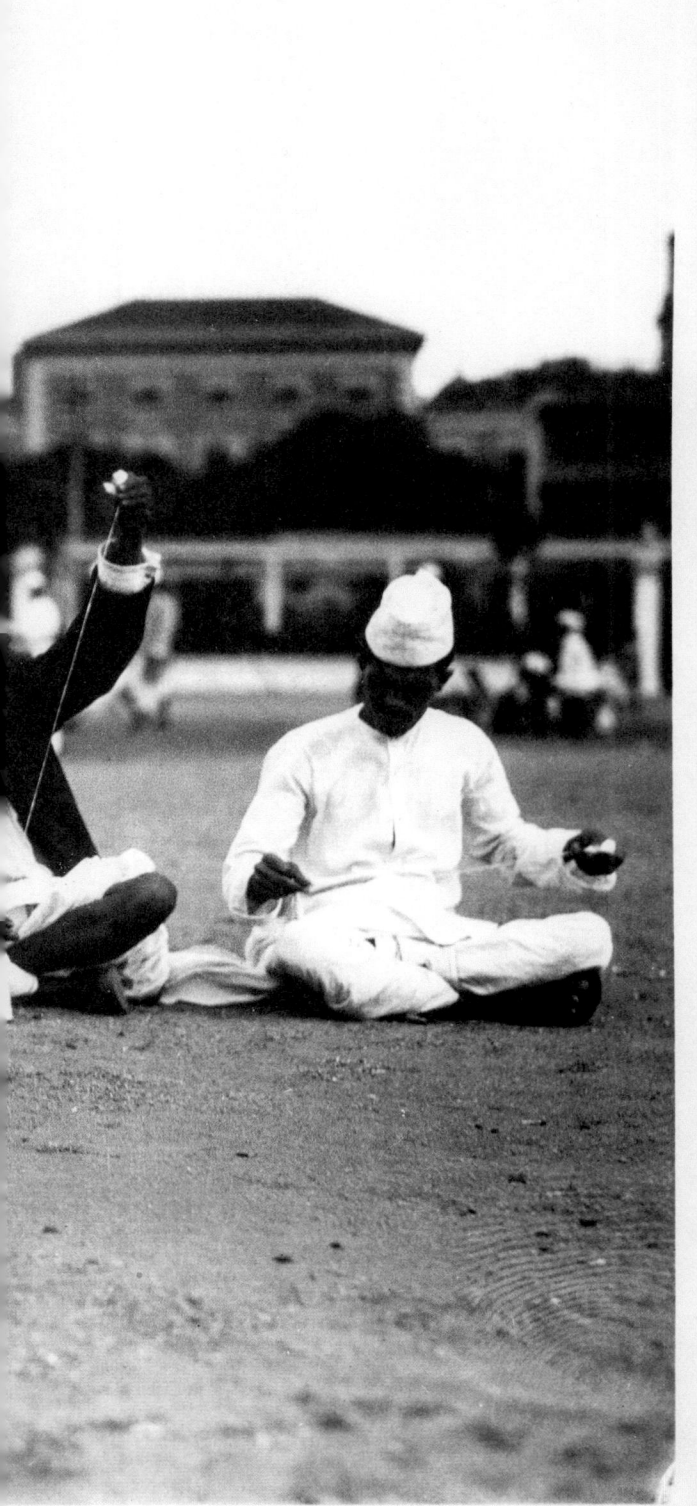

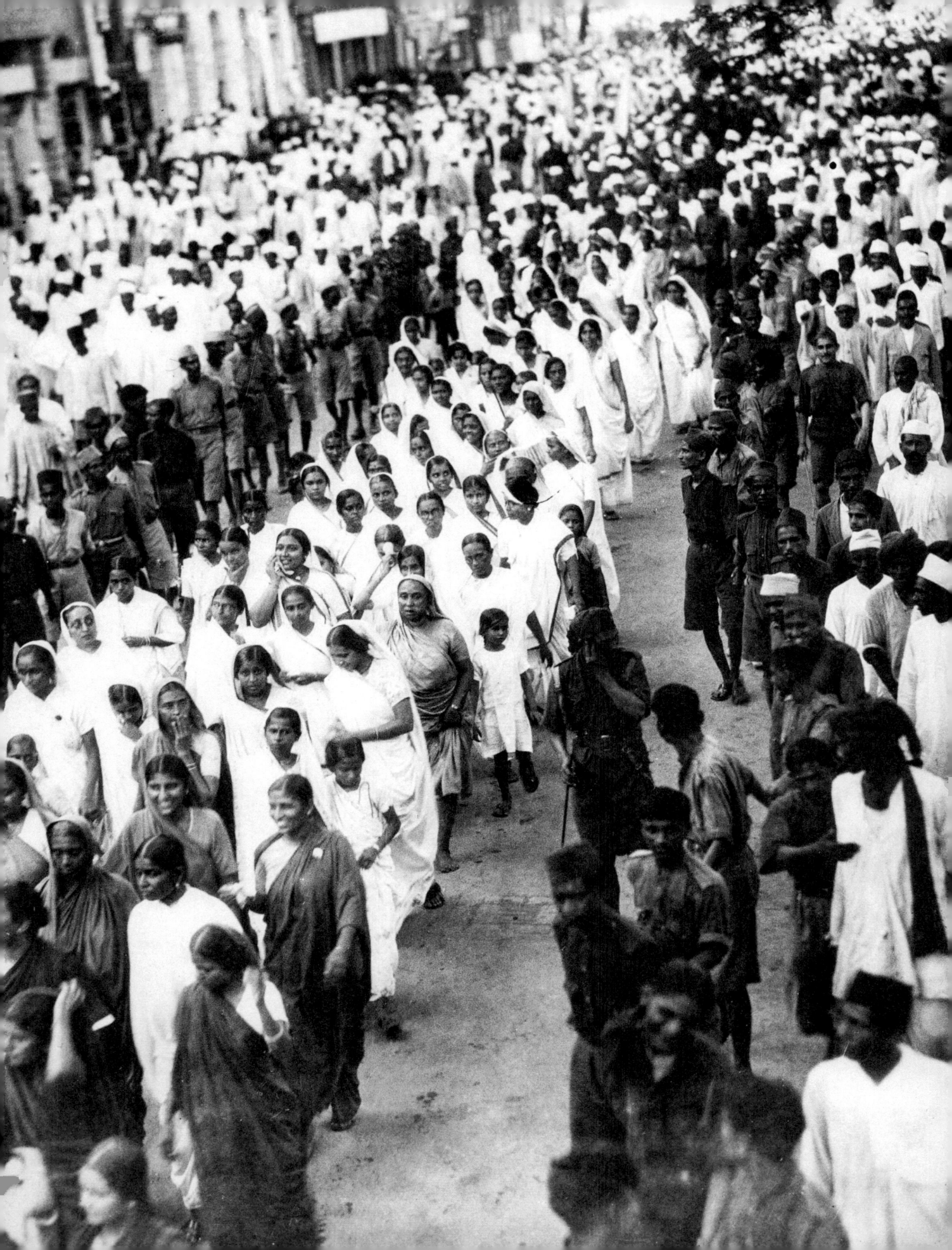

CHAPTER 4

FROM PROFITS AND PATRIOTISM TO GANDHIAN AUSTERITY

TRANSFORMATIONS IN BOMBAY'S SWADESHI LANDSCAPE

Dinyar Patel

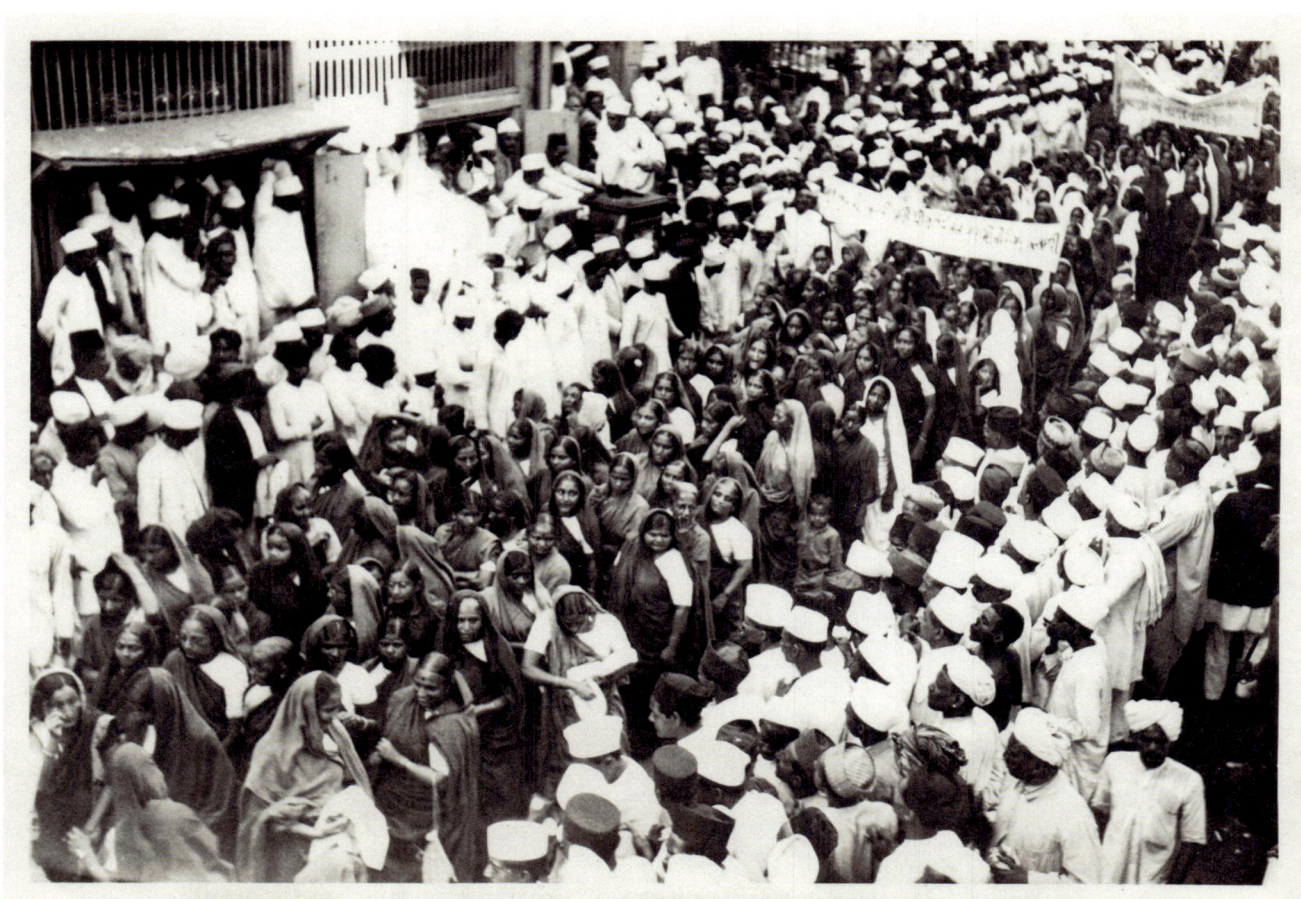

A takli procession organised by the congress
to encourage the art of hand spinning the
procession passed through many prominent street
in the city.Photo shows the procession in
progress.

When hundreds of women embarked upon a *takli* (spindle) procession through Bombay's streets in the thick of the Civil Disobedience Movement, they did much more than simply demonstrate their fervour for *khadi* cloth and other domestically produced goods (Fig. 4.1). Rather, they orchestrated a remarkable reversal of street politics in Bombay: one where women took centre stage and men were relegated to being mere onlookers, with many of them sequestered under the eaves of nearby houses. Within the Nursey album are several other examples of bold new directions in the propagation of *swadeshi*, the ethos of economic self-reliance which had been a pillar of Indian nationalist politics since the late 19th century. In Fig. 7.7, Lilavati Munshi, the wife of the Indian National Congress stalwart K.M. Munshi and a prominent political figure in her own right, strikes a pose of resolute defiance while picketing in front of the police posse placed right at the main entrance of cavernous shop windows of Whiteaway Laidlaw on Hornby Road. Elsewhere, three anonymous women stare defiantly into the camera while picketing outside a shop selling foreign cloth (Fig. 4.2).

Taken together, these three photographs reveal important tactical innovations in *swadeshi* activity during the Civil Disobedience Movement. They also demonstrate radical change in the longer history of *swadeshi* in Bombay, a city where ideas of economic self-reliance had been vigorously debated and contested by a wide range of actors.

Scholars of *swadeshi* have focused on the Swadeshi Movement in Bengal (1905–1908) and Gandhian activity from the Non-Cooperation Movement (1920–1922) onward. They have largely missed the rich history in western India of experiments in economic self-reliance during the 19th century.[1] In order to truly understand the significance of the *takli* procession or the picketing done by Lilavati Munshi and the three anonymous women, it is necessary to trace some of this history. Direct protest and confrontation—moreover, protest and confrontation orchestrated by women—represented novel departures in the evolution of Bombay *swadeshi*. But these tactics and methods also revealed certain historical continuities.

We can trace the origins of *swadeshi* sentiment to the tectonic economic convulsions which shook India in the early 19th century. In the first decades

PAGES 96–97
"A group of men spinning the takli."
c. 1930–1931
Gelatin Silver Print,
117 x 158 mm
ACP: 98.77.0002 (46b)

PAGE 98
"Boycott procession of women in the market area."
(Detail, see p. 111)

Fig. 4.1
"A takli procession organised by the congress [Congress] to encourage the art of hand spinning [.] the [The] procession passed through many prominent street[s] in the city. Photo shows the procession in progress."
c. 1930–1931
Gelatin Silver Print,
116 x 164 mm
ACP: 98.77.0002 (49a)
Taklis are traditional spindles used in hand spinning. This picture, in many ways, represents an inversion of gender dynamics in Bombay's streets, with women relegating men to the position of bystanders—and some men even pushed into local houses.

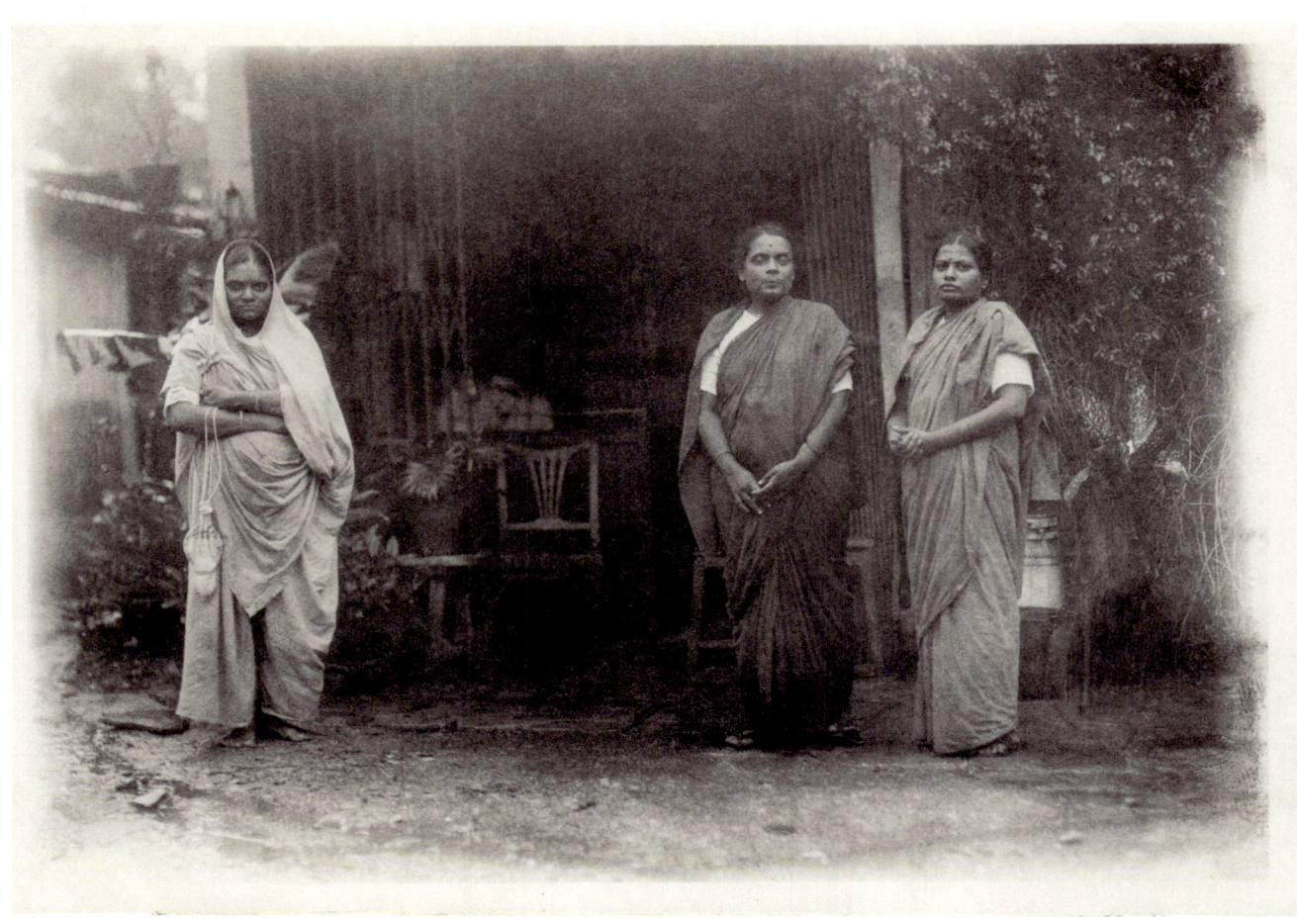

Fig. 4.2
"Picketing at the forengn [foreign] cloth shops in the Market." c. 1930—1931
Gelatin Silver Print, 114 x 163 mm
ACP: 98.77.0002 (45a)
Picketing—of both foreign cloth shops and liquor stores—became a topic of fierce contestation in the gender politics of the Civil Disobedience Movement. Gandhi initially believed that picketing was the most appropriate activity for female volunteers and expressed reluctance to further widen their scope of involvement.

of British imperial rule, Indians observed a process of deindustrialization—especially the destruction of the indigenous textile industry—and began articulating the idea of a colonial-induced drain of wealth from the subcontinent. These observations also had a constructive element: In western India, a band of intellectuals, educators and business entrepreneurs put forth ideas for industrial regeneration and economic self-reliance. As early as 1849, for example, the Maharashtrian writer and social reformer Gopal Hari Deshmukh, better known as Lokahitavadi, exhorted fellow Indians to forswear the purchase of foreign-made goods. He suggested a rudimentary form of import-substitution industrialization whereby Indians would master the production of goods such as glassware, machinery and clocks.[2] By the early 1850s, some of Bombay's most prominent citizens joined hands with sympathetic Britons to establish pioneer industrial outfits, such as a paper manufacturing company, and a dedicated school for training Indians in modern industrial and technological methods.[3]

Western Indians excelled at what the historian David Arnold terms "everyday technology": the production of simple household goods such as pencils, knives, ink and matches.[4] By the 1870s, inspired by the early economic writings of Mahadev Govind Ranade—one of the most innovative social, economic and political thinkers of early Indian nationalism—a diverse group of professionals, industrialists, educators and princely-state officials began organizing exhibits of such goods to popularize them among the general public. The Poona Exhibition of Native Arts and Manufactures, first held in 1875, helped galvanize *swadeshi* activity in western India, bringing together technological tinkerers from the mofussil and cotton mill magnates from Bombay. Not surprisingly, it was around this time that western Indian newspapers began widely employing the term "*swadeshi*" to describe home-made articles.[5]

Throughout the remainder of the Victorian era, cities and towns such as Bombay, Poona, Ahmedabad, Surat and Nagpur became hubs for a distinct "profits-and-patriotism" model of *swadeshi* activity. Political elites and professionals joined hands with businesspeople to subscribe capital and open joint-stock companies and stores. They relied on talented locals to fine-tune production of *swadeshi* goods and market them to the public. Some *swadeshi* products—such as the medicines of T.K. Gajjar, founder of Alembic Chemical Works—could be quite sophisticated, enjoying a measure of consumer trust which helped generate greater profits.

We can observe some early 20th-century continuities in Fig. 4.3, where a man sells a variety of *swadeshi* belts—most likely made from cotton cloth. By the time this photograph was taken, *swadeshi* hawkers such as this man had been a fixture in Bombay for at least two decades, serving as interlocutors between money-minded *swadeshi* businesses and a wide consumer base. In a 1909

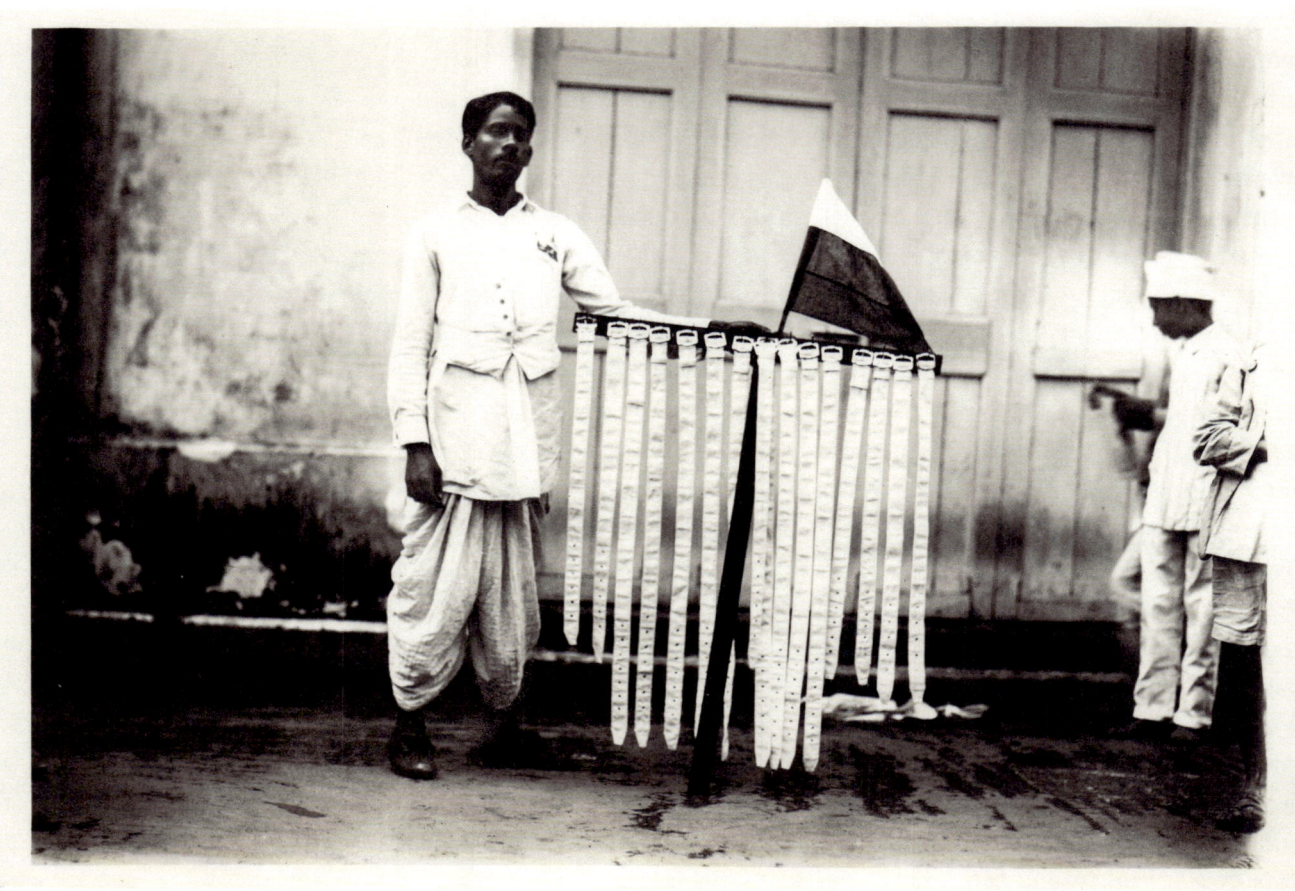

Fig. 4.3
"A Hawker selling shadeshi [*swadeshi*] articles."
c. 1930–1931
Gelatin Silver Print, 114 x 161 mm
ACP: 98.77.0002 (41b)
This *swadeshi* hawker appears to be selling white cloth belts, while a tricolour Congress flag flutters above his merchandise.

profile of *swadeshi* hawkers, *The Times of India* asserted that they were "a great deal more intelligent and open-minded than the ordinary hawker," eager to disclose precise details of manufacture and reluctant to bargain with customers. The hawkers' cries of "Swadeshi *Mha-a-l*" ("*swadeshi* goods"), the paper suggested, enjoyed greater popularity along Bombay's streets than the political slogan of "Vande Mataram." Their wares included soaps, hair oils, candles and cutlery—and, interestingly, a variety of Japanese manufactures, which somehow passed the test of qualifying as *swadeshi* goods. These items, like the *swadeshi* cloth belts in Fig. 4.3, helped propel what the historian Douglas Haynes has called "small-town capitalism" in western India from the 1870s onward. Indeed, *The Times of India* profile hinted at dense networks of *swadeshi* capitalism in Maharashtra and Gujarat, noting that *swadeshi* hawkers' goods could come from Bombay localities such as Girgaum and Mahim or from further afield such as Sholapur or "some village in Baroda [now, Vadodara] or in the Konkan."[6]

Apart from the continuity represented by *swadeshi* hawkers, much of this activity can seem strikingly different from the protests and confrontation of the Civil Disobedience Movement captured in the Nursey album. By the eve of the Swadeshi Movement, furthermore, Bombay *swadeshi* was also distinct from its counterparts elsewhere in the country. In Bengal, in the very first years of the 20th century, some commentators derided what they termed as an insufficiently nationalist "commercial *swadeshi*" and "industrial *swadeshi*," arguing that profits and patriotism were simply incompatible.[7] Bombay, in contrast, celebrated the marriage of these two impulses. Someone like the Congress leader Gopal Krishna Gokhale could extol the *swadeshi* potential of big capitalists.[8]

Dadabhai Naoroji encapsulated the spirit of the times when, in December 1906, he delivered a speech to mark the opening of the Bombay Swadeshi Co-operative Stores—whose founders included Bal Gangadhar Tilak and Ratanji Tata—in The Times of India building. What the *swadeshi* entrepreneurs "had to bear in mind," Naoroji counselled, "was not only patriotism, but also the laws of trade and industry." They needed "to be guided by business principles along with patriotism."[9] Naoroji was not alone in giving such advice. N.B. Wagle, a Maharashtrian *swadeshi* entrepreneur (whose training in glass manufacture in the United Kingdom had been partially funded by Naoroji), called for the maintenance of "sound economic principles" in all attempts at economic self-reliance. He urged Indians to only concentrate on goods where the country had a comparative advantage, dismissing attempts to mimic superior foreign goods. At the same time, he held out hope that *swadeshi* goods could be produced for export and encouraged Indians to "study the foreign markets."[10] Overall, western Indian advocates of *swadeshi* were far less hostile towards foreign influences and foreign trade (perhaps this is one reason why the *swadeshi* hawkers profiled by The Times of India had no qualms about selling Japanese goods). Gokhale even defended members of the Tata family for driving an imported automobile, telling an Allahabad audience that this in no way diminished their *swadeshi* credentials.[11]

How can we explain the apparently profound disjuncture between this longer history of Bombay *swadeshi* and the intense picketing, boycott processions, mass protests and bonfires of foreign goods depicted in the Nursey album? Simply put, the profits-and-patriotism model suffered a grievous setback across India at the end of the Swadeshi Movement. In Bombay, many *swadeshi* entrepreneurs did not, after all, heed advice about "sound economic principles"—they engaged in fraud and deceit, causing the dramatic collapse of many businesses. By 1909, Bombay newspaper columns already carried some titillating accounts of *swadeshi* fraudsters, such as the owner of a cap factory in Girgaum who slapped images of Shivaji on foreign headgear and declared them to be home-made. Tilak was hoodwinked by this ruse, issuing the factory owner with a certificate praising the caps' *swadeshi* bona fides (once the owner was hauled before the Bombay High Court, he was represented by none other than Muhammad Ali Jinnah).[12]

The denouement of the profits-and-patriotism model occurred in late 1913. A wave of *swadeshi* bank failures triggered a broader financial crisis, carrying under tow a number of *swadeshi* businesses. Some of these failures had almost Shakespearean qualities of drama and tragedy. On the morning of 29 November 1913, for example, Chunilal Dharamdas Saraiya, managing director of the Indian Specie Bank and a man celebrated as the "king of *swadeshi* banking," suddenly died. That same day, his assistant admitted to bank directors that Saraiya had created dummy accounts for fictitious holdings of silver—and that the bank was basically bereft of any real capital. Within a few hours, as Saraiya's body was hauled to the Bandra funerary ghats, the bank had shuttered, triggering mayhem in the city's bazaars. A subsequent audit ordered by the Bombay High Court pronounced the Indian Specie Bank to be "a miserable tale of the lowest form of fraud."[13]

Bombay, it is true, was not the only epicentre of this financial crisis. *Swadeshi* banks and businesses collapsed like so many houses of cards in Bengal, Punjab, Sindh and elsewhere through late 1913 and 1914. These failures animated political discussion in New Delhi and were minutely picked apart by members of the Indian Industrial Commission, which convened between 1916 and 1918. But the damage was particularly grievous in Bombay, where *swadeshi* proponents and opponents alike wrung their hands about Indians' "commercial morality" and how business interests took advantage of patriotic sentiment. Narayan Chandavarkar, the moderate Bombay Congress leader, rued "the utter collapse of Swadeshism" in a December 1913 speech which presaged Mohandas K. Gandhi in its moralizing tone and religious allusions. Chandavarkar condemned "industrial and commercial enthusiasts" for being "more anxious to produce swadeshi money than to produce *swadeshi*sm."[14]

The discrediting of the profits-and-patriotism model, in many ways, cleared the way for the Mahatma. During his meteoric rise to political power in the late 1910s, Gandhi helped bring about four critical transformations in Bombay *swadeshi*, all of which underwent their own processes of development and change in the years leading up to the Civil Disobedience Movement. These four transformations are clearly visible in the Nursey album's photographs.

First, beginning in the years before the Non-Cooperation Movement, Gandhi reoriented *swadeshi* away from profits and patriotism and towards the issue of Indian poverty. Cast in its new austere garb, *swadeshi* was a means for poverty reduction, with *khadi* goods symbolically tying together both rich and poor consumers. In June 1919, nearly 13 years after Naoroji opened the *swadeshi* store in The Times of India Building, the Mahatma inaugurated a *swadeshi* store in Kalbadevi and offered very different advice. The store, Gandhi declared, would ensure that "that the poor people would get Swadeshi goods at the cheapest rates." Its purpose was "not to make money," nor would it generate any "middle-man's profit."[15]

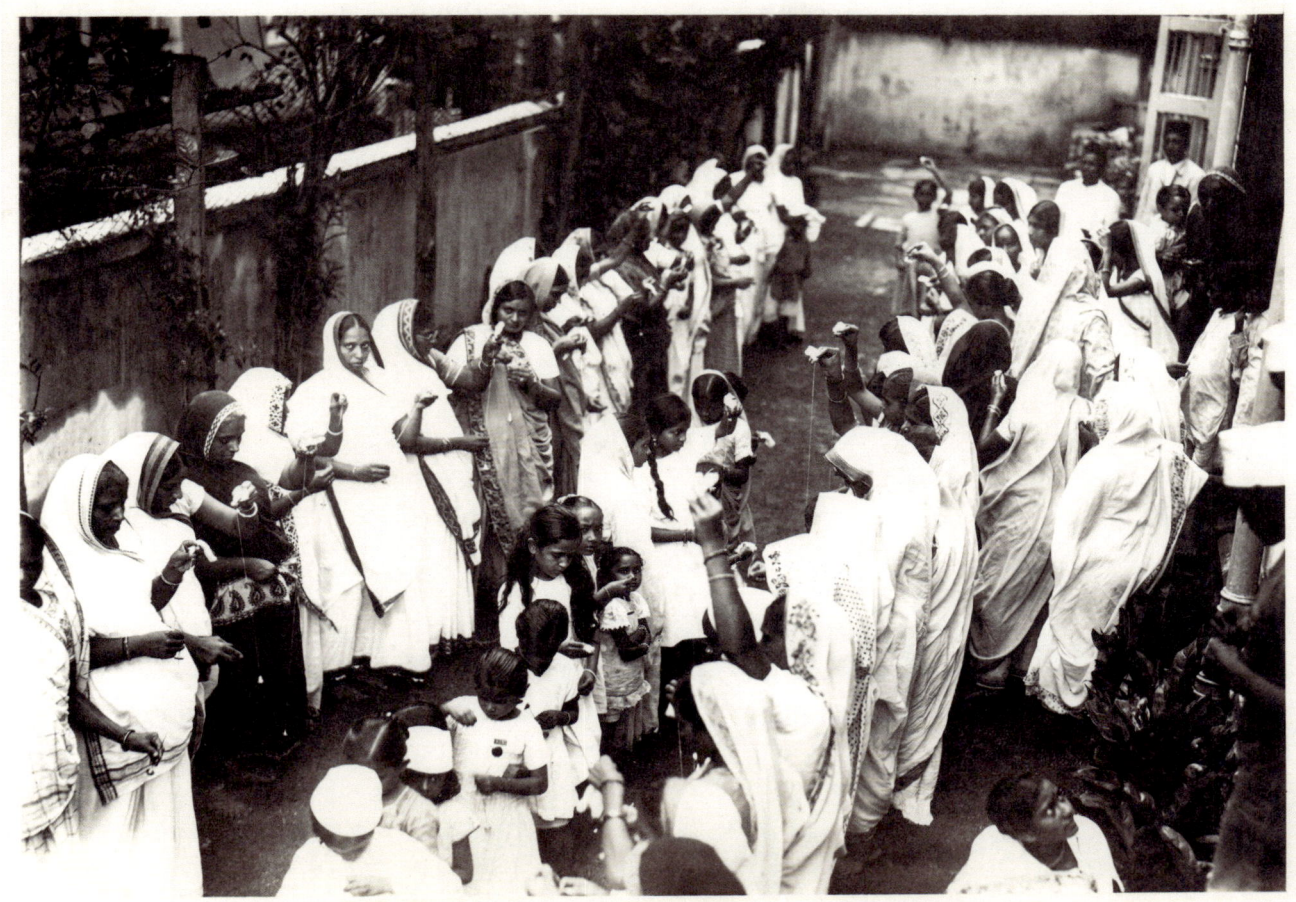

While Gandhi courted the political support of small merchants in Bombay's bazaars and markets, Gandhian activity in the city revealed a strong sense of suspicion towards the role of big capitalists and businesspeople in *swadeshi*. Speaking before a crowd at French Bridge in the pre-monsoon heat of 1919, for example, one Gandhian volunteer reminded his audience that the Swadeshi Movement "had cooled down owing to the mill-owners and the Indian traders having taken a mean advantage of the movement." He argued that Indians' "first duty" now was "to fight every kind of dishonesty on the part of their mill-owners and traders."[16] Demonstrations depicted in the Nursey album indicate how such attitudes continued to resonate in 1930. *Satyagrahi*s organized shows of strength both in small merchant-dominated market areas and at major commercial sites such as Hornby Road, lined with the offices of the Indian capitalists, industrialists, lawyers and bankers who had orchestrated the earlier avatars of *swadeshi*. It is even more significant that some of these demonstrations, like the *takli* processions depicted in Figs. 4.1 and 4.5, celebrated activities such as hand-spinning—activities which were associated with poverty reduction rather than profit generation, and with simple home production rather than the modern mills of Mahalakshmi and Parel.

Fig. 4.4
"A takli procession in progress at Pydownie [Pydhonie]."
c. 1930–1931
Gelatin Silver Print, 114 x 156 mm
ACP: 98.77.0002 (47a)
Notice the inclusion of girls—perhaps the daughters of the demonstrators—operating the *takli*s.

The *takli* processions, like Lilavati Munshi's resolute stand in front of Whiteaway Laidlaw and the anonymous women picketing a foreign cloth shop, demonstrate the second transformation in Gandhian *swadeshi*: women's mass participation.[17] This was truly revolutionary. Despite scattered references to female participation, earlier *swadeshi* activity in Bombay had been mostly the preserve of elite men. Not surprisingly, after his return to India from South Africa, Gandhi relied on many of these male elites' wives and female relatives for *khadi*-spinning, while broadening the appeal of *swadeshi* among the general population of women. Female participation became a hallmark of Gandhian *swadeshi* by the time of the Non-Cooperation Movement; women picketed in front of Bombay's liquor stores and collected foreign cloth for disposal. They took charge of household consumption decisions which favoured *swadeshi* goods. In November 1921, Bombay witnessed what was described as the city's first-ever women's procession for *swaraj*, with female *satyagrahi*s decked out in *swadeshi* attire while parading a portrait of the Mahatma.[18]

But women's participation in *swadeshi* activities during the Civil Disobedience Movement was of an entirely different order of magnitude. Only a few years earlier it would have been unimaginable to conceive of regular boycott and *takli* processions in Bombay which were dominated by women. Pictures in the Nursey album attest to the fact of female political empowerment—indeed, even dominance—on Bombay's streets. Women conducted processions without male accompaniment or, in the case of the *takli* procession mentioned at the beginning of this essay, relegated menfolk to the roles of passive observers and occupants of domestic spaces. It is even more significant to see a broad social spectrum of women participating in protests and meetings, rather than just political elites such as Sarojini Naidu, Kamaladevi Chattopadhyay and Lilavati Munshi. As Fig. 4.4 attests, some women felt confident enough to include girls—perhaps their own daughters—in overtly political demonstrations, helping along a process of politicization and *swadeshi* activism among the next generations of women.

Female leadership in *swadeshi* activities provides further insight into how, by the time the Civil Disobedience Movement took full shape, the relationship between women volunteers and Gandhi was rapidly evolving. As the historian Ramachandra Guha has noted, the Mahatma had been absolutely pivotal in moving women into leadership roles in social and political movements, beginning with his South African *satyagraha*s and continuing with the selective incorporation of women into boycotting and picketing activities during the Non-Cooperation Movement.[19] With Gandhi's support, women steadily rose to leadership positions within the Congress—once an almost exclusively male preserve. True, Gandhi's attitudes towards women's political participation could be patronizing and inconsistent. But, by the Civil Disobedience Movement, female *satyagrahi*s were increasingly comfortable with challenging his opinions, changing his views or simply taking matters into their own hands.[20] Some female *satyagrahis* protested the Mahatma's original exclusion of women from the Salt March, while thousands of other women basically forced Gandhi's hand after his arrival in Dandi by actively participating in the contraband manufacture of salt. Yet, even at its most fraught moments, the complex relationship between women volunteers and Gandhi remained an important cornerstone in *swadeshi* activism and nationalist politics in general. In Fig. 1.2, a procession of women follows a decorated car carrying a garlanded portrait of Gandhi with a banner anointing him as "Women's True Representative." This was not simply a sycophantic gesture: it is important to recognize how Gandhi *did* encourage a vast ambit of female participation after the Salt March, especially while more conservative, patriarchal leaders in the Congress dithered and prevaricated about women's politicization and public presence. At the same time, women could use Gandhi as a symbol of their own agency and increased political consciousness.

The women marching in Fig. 4.5 and Fig. 4.6 attest to the third major innovation in Gandhian *swadeshi*: boycott. Boycotting foreign goods was not a new idea in western India. Lokahitavadi, after all, had practically suggested the idea as early as 1849, and he was by no means the first to do so. In Bombay, the tactic of boycott (and its terminology[21]) steadily gained currency after its successful deployment by activists of the Irish National Land League in Ireland in 1880, an event widely covered in Indian broadsheets. But many in Bombay fiercely opposed the tactic. In 1905, the *swadeshi* industrialist Lalubhai Samaldas drew a careful distinction between boycott and *swadeshi*, labelling the former as a "negative movement" and pointing out that the boycott of foreign goods would devastate Indian merchants who sold them. "The leaders of the boycott movement have, perhaps unconsciously, done a great harm to their own countrymen," he concluded.[22] Moderate Congress leaders from Bombay and Poona, such as Gokhale, Pherozeshah Mehta and Dinsha Wacha, all roundly criticized the efficacy and appropriateness of boycotting.

Pictures in the Nursey album demonstrate how much the ground had shifted between the Swadeshi Movement and the Civil Disobedience Movement. Whereas earlier *swadeshi* enthusiasts had specifically targeted British products for non-consumption, the men and women marching through Bombay's market areas now made a sweeping condemnation of all "foreign goods." In Fig. 4.5, they even parade in front of a store whose Gujarati signboard declares: *Dhī Maṇekjī Pīṭīṭ Mīl tathā Kānpur Mīlnā Kāpaḍnī Dukān*, indicating that it sold cloth from the mills of the Petit family—one of Bombay's most established industrialist families—and perhaps from Kanpur, where many industries were in the hands of European owners. While pictorial evidence is insufficient to directly link the march with boycott of these specific goods, *swadeshi* activity during the Civil Disobedience Movement did convey an unambiguous message: indigenously produced cloth was not immune from the threat of boycott or other

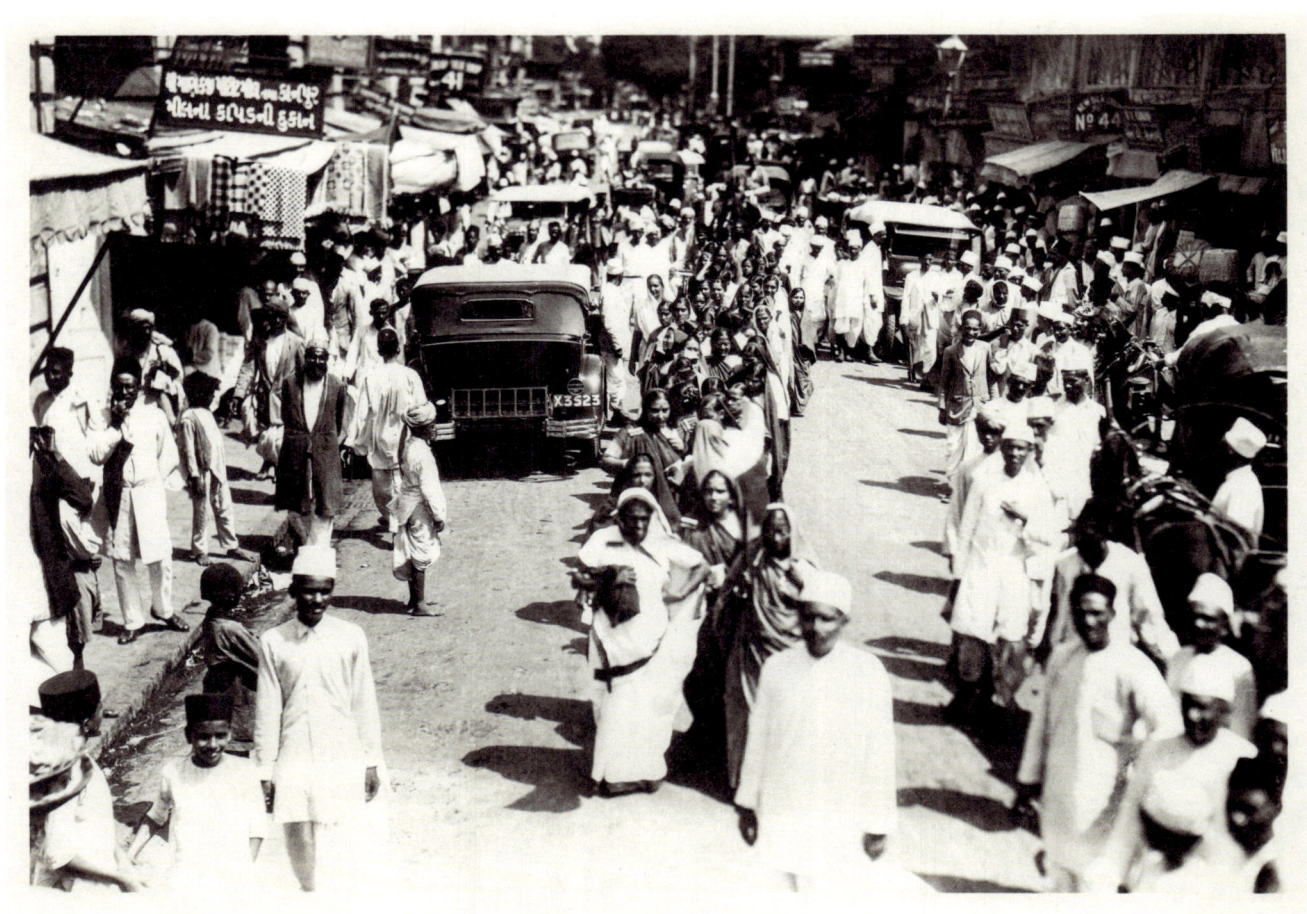

Fig. 4.5
"A Boycott procession
in the market area."
c. 1930—1931
Gelatin Silver Print,
114 x 159 mm
ACP: 98.77.0002 (47b)
Women march by cloth
shops, including
one advertising
merchandise from a
mill owned by the
industrialist Petit
family and perhaps a
mill in Kanpur.

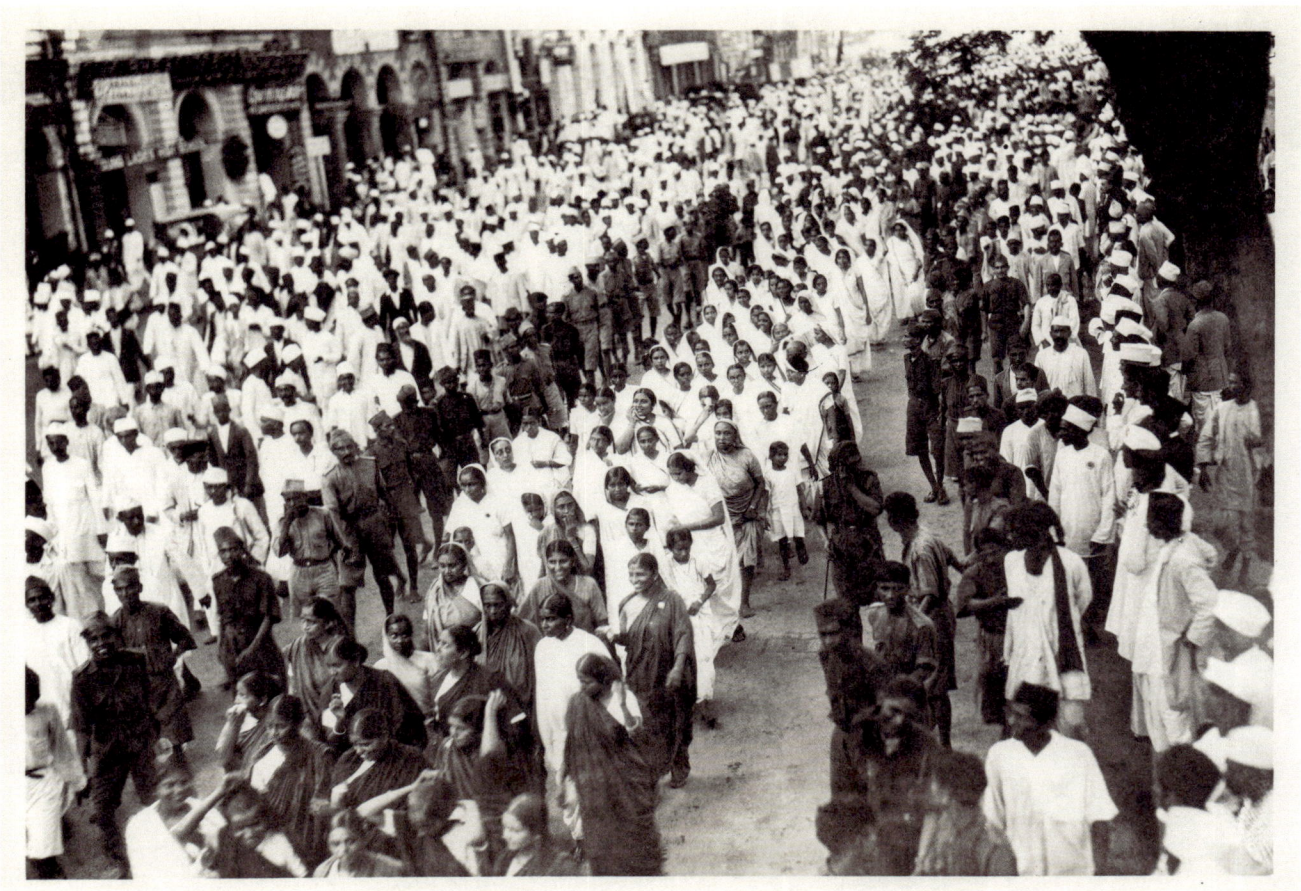

Fig. 4.6
"Boycott procession
of women in the market
area." c. 1930—1931
Gelatin Silver Print,
115 x 161 mm
ACP: 98.77.0002 (50a)
Notice the rigid
separation between
columns of male and
female procession
members, kept apart
by uniformed male
volunteers.

forms of politicized consumer activism. Tellingly, in 1930, the Bombay Millowners' Association succumbed to pressure from retailers and consumers to ensure that their textile products were authentically Indian. The Association agreed to discontinue the use of foreign yarn in its members' mills and affix labels to all products, printed in English and Hindi, providing an "unqualified guarantee" that goods were made "by an Indian company and by Indian labour."[23]

Lilavati Munshi and the anonymous women in Fig. 4.2 furthermore demonstrate that, by the time of the Civil Disobedience Movement, boycott had become a tactic of direct confrontation and disruption. This was another element which would have been frowned upon by earlier generations of Bombay *swadeshi* enthusiasts. In 1905, Samaldas had worried about how boycott would "embitter the feelings not only between the rulers and the ruled, but also between the non-official English community and the Indian"—a sentiment which sounded positively anachronistic by 1930.[24] In any case, the *satyagrahi*s pictured in the Nursey album made no racial distinctions: they targeted Indian patrons in the "market areas" as well as British customers of upmarket European department stores such as Whiteaway Laidlaw.

It was one thing to boycott foreign goods—it was quite another thing to burn them (Fig. 4.7). The fourth innovation of Gandhian *swadeshi* was the popularization of bonfires. Setting foreign cloth alight became commonplace during the Swadeshi Movement. Immediately after his return from South Africa to India, however, Gandhi had avoided burning foreign cloth, believing that it would, as Samaldas had earlier feared in relation to the act of boycotting, stoke anger towards Europeans. During the Non-Cooperation Movement, however, Gandhi reversed his position and adopted the technique, drawing sharp criticism from allies such as C.F. Andrews ("Destruction is the quickest method of stimulating production," the Mahatma retorted, proving that this Gujarati *bania*'s mercantile instincts were not entirely extinguished).[25] Bonfires carried about them the threat of violence. This became tragically apparent on 17 November 1921, during the visit of the future King Edward VIII to Bombay. Gandhi protested the visit by burning foreign cloth near Elphinstone Mills (Figs. 4.10 and 4.11). Soon, whole parts of the city went up in flames, with members of minority communities who had turned out in support of the visit attacked by Hindus and Muslims vehemently opposed to it. The citywide conflagration, known as the Prince of Wales Riots, left at least 58 people dead. The riots chastened the Mahatma and prompted significant soul-searching about majoritarianism and the propensity of non-violence to descend into violence.[26]

But it did not deter Gandhi from torching more foreign goods: the practice became entrenched during the Civil Disobedience Movement, undergoing certain innovations. First, as Fig. 4.7 suggests, bonfires became routine events, localized spectacles which drew medium-sized audiences. Second, bonfires

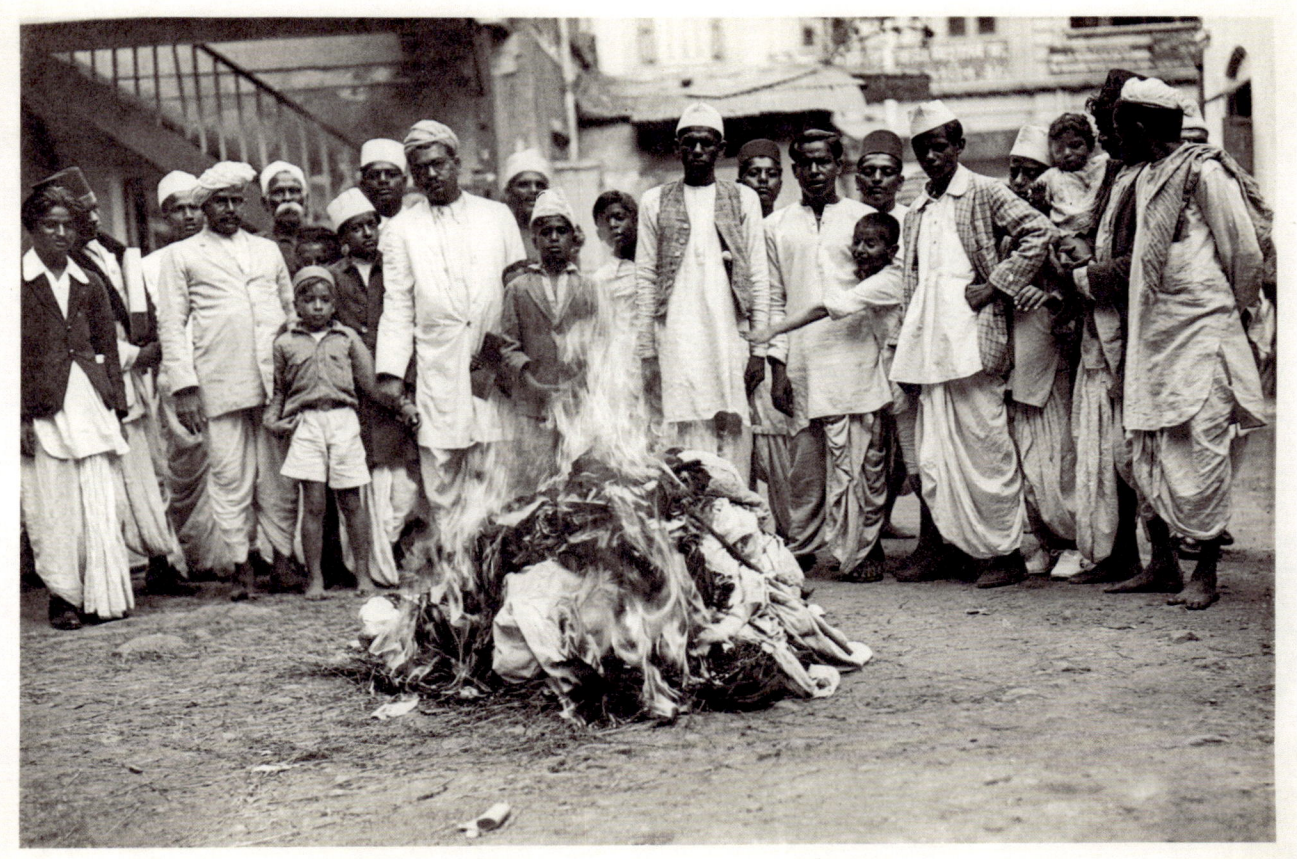

Fig. 4.7

"A bon-fire of foreign cloth" c. 1930—1931
Gelatin Silver Print, 115 x 165 mm
ACP: 98.77.0002 (56a)
By the time of the Civil Disobedience Movement, bonfires had evidently become very localized affairs, quite different from the mass bonfires which Gandhi organized during the Non-Cooperation Movement. While the crowd at this bonfire is exclusively composed of men, we have evidence of large numbers of women attending bonfires in places such as Ahmedabad.

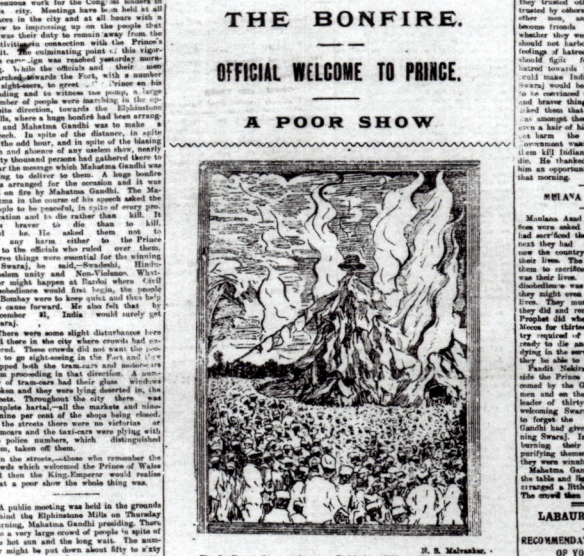

Fig. 4.8
An advertisement from
The Bombay Chronicle,
16 November 1921,
for a mass bonfire,
presided over by
Mohandas K. Gandhi,
at Elphinstone Mills.
Women and children,
as the advertisement
notes, were exempt
from purchasing
tickets.

Fig. 4.9
A report from *The
Bombay Chronicle*,
18 November 1921,
which includes an
image of the bonfire
of foreign cloth
held the previous
day at Elphinstone
Mills. By the time
this issue of the
Chronicle was being
distributed across
the city, Bombay was
already convulsed
by communitarian
violence in what
became known as the
Prince of Wales Riots.

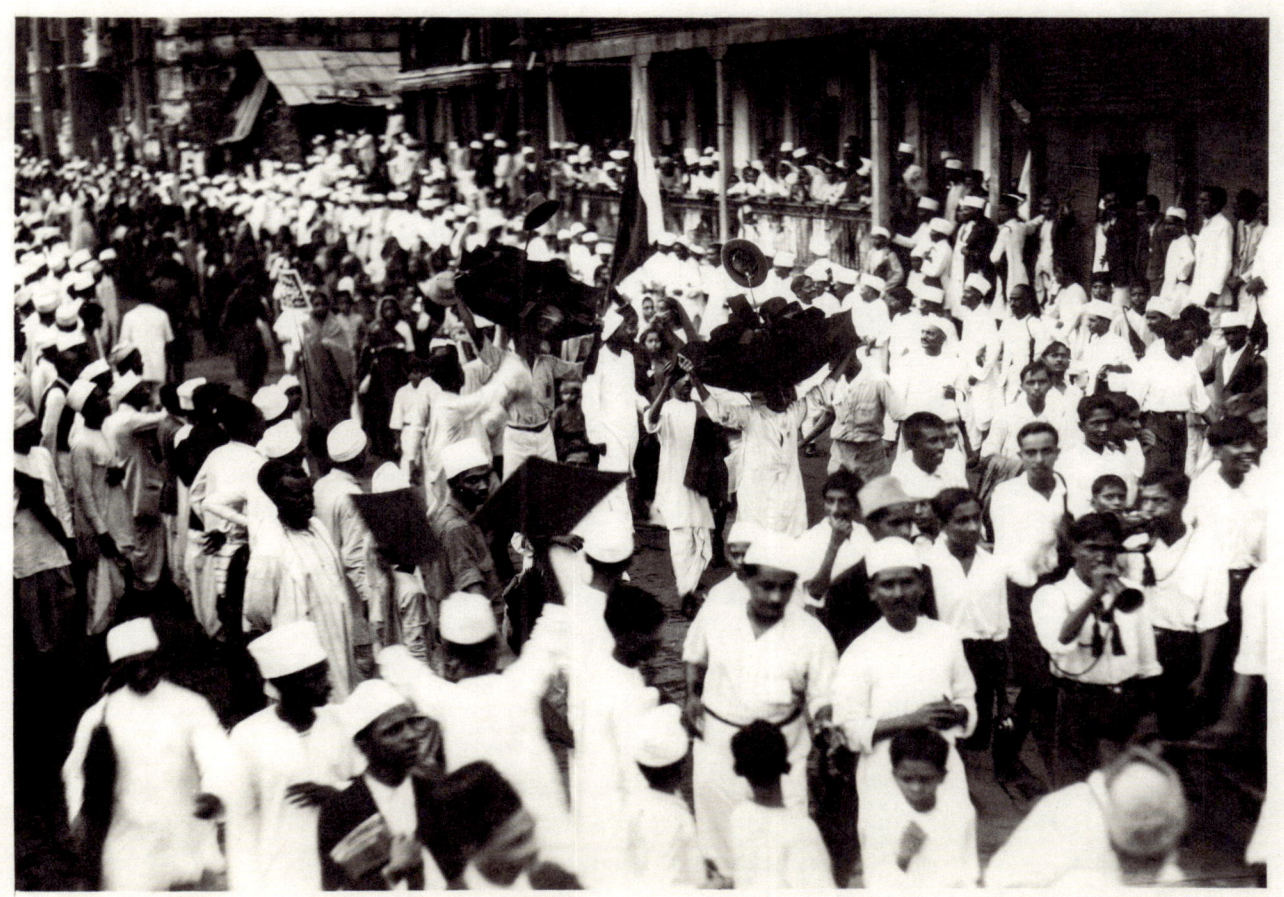

attracted female participation. During the bonfire which set off the Prince of Wales Riots in November 1921, the audience appeared to be overwhelmingly male, despite earnest efforts made to attract women participants (who were allowed to attend without special tickets distributed by Congress district committees). In contrast, by April 1930, newspaper reports indicated that, even in more conservative and parochial locales like Ahmedabad, women attended bonfires of foreign cloth "in large numbers."[27]

Figure 4.10, meanwhile, demonstrates that burning cloth was a multi-step process. Foreign cloth first had to be collected and transported to bonfire sites. We have some colourful accounts of this process from the Non-Cooperation Movement that help us understand key changes that had occurred by 1930. In one such account from 1921, just before the Prince of Wales's arrival in Bombay, *satyagrahi*s guide a hackney carriage—increasingly weighed down with donated non-Indian articles—pulled by a horse festooned with "foreign shirting, sarees and other articles of manufacture." As the carriage moves down Bombay's streets, sympathetic onlookers fling down silk saris from their balconies, with some of these items getting tangled along telegraph lines. All of the characters in this account are men: there is no indication of the presence of women even among the onlookers discarding foreign-made saris. Women only appear in a conversation between male *satyagrahis*, who express disgust that Indian girls were participating in welcoming ceremonies for the Prince of Wales, where they would "dance before all sorts of strangers."[28] In contrast, as seen in Fig. 4.10, women played a prominent and visible role in the collection of foreign goods during the Civil Disobedience Movement. Here, they parade just behind two men carrying aloft a sack of clothing and hats. Most men, as in the *takli* processions, are simply bystanders.

Despite evidence of significant innovations in *swadeshi* tactics, the Nursey album also reveals certain continuities in Bombay *swadeshi*. Bustling commercial activity forms an omnipresent backdrop in photographs: packed bazaars, multilingual store signs and advertisements for nationalist-aligned companies such as Chicago Radio. Although political elites set a tone of Gandhian austerity, *swadeshi* remained a potentially remunerative endeavour in 1930. The financial crisis of 1913–1914 might have inflicted a severe blow to the profits-and-patriotism model, but the blow was not fatal. *Swadeshi* capitalism roared back to life during the Civil Disobedience Movement, with big capitalists and industrialists playing an outsized role, although they were now more reluctant to maintain international mercantile and financial links. Once more, there were stories of fraud and deceit: for example, foreign firms passing off their products as *swadeshi*. As in the Swadeshi Movement, purists attacked *swadeshi* capitalists for their money-mindedness as well as their reliance on foreign capital and expertise. Indian capitalists were aided by the Congress, which coordinated boycott activities and authenticated and publicized certain *swadeshi* products.[29] The hawker in Fig. 4.3 provides eloquent testimony of this relationship: fluttering above his cotton belts is the tricolour national flag adopted by the Congress.

Photographs in the Nursey album also capture a collective memory of the history of *swadeshi* in Bombay. The sea of white *khadi topis* (caps) in Fig. 4.11, part of a procession to mark the 10th death anniversary of Tilak, was a fitting tribute to one of the most towering pioneers of *swadeshi* in western India. Naoroji's statue, at the foot of Hornby Road, was a rallying point for demonstrations. The album includes an image of an aged Naoroji (who died in 1917) with a women's delegation, perhaps one of the numerous groups of female educationists and social service volunteers who visited the nationalist leader during his retirement in a seaside bungalow in Versova (Fig. 4.12). This photograph is not a random addition: Naoroji's championship of Indian economic development and female emancipation would have been handy reference points in the visual tapestry on display during the Civil Disobedience Movement. For female *satyagrahis*, a picture of an earlier generation of women leaders with one of the founders of the Congress provided clinching evidence of their long-term stake in the nationalist project.

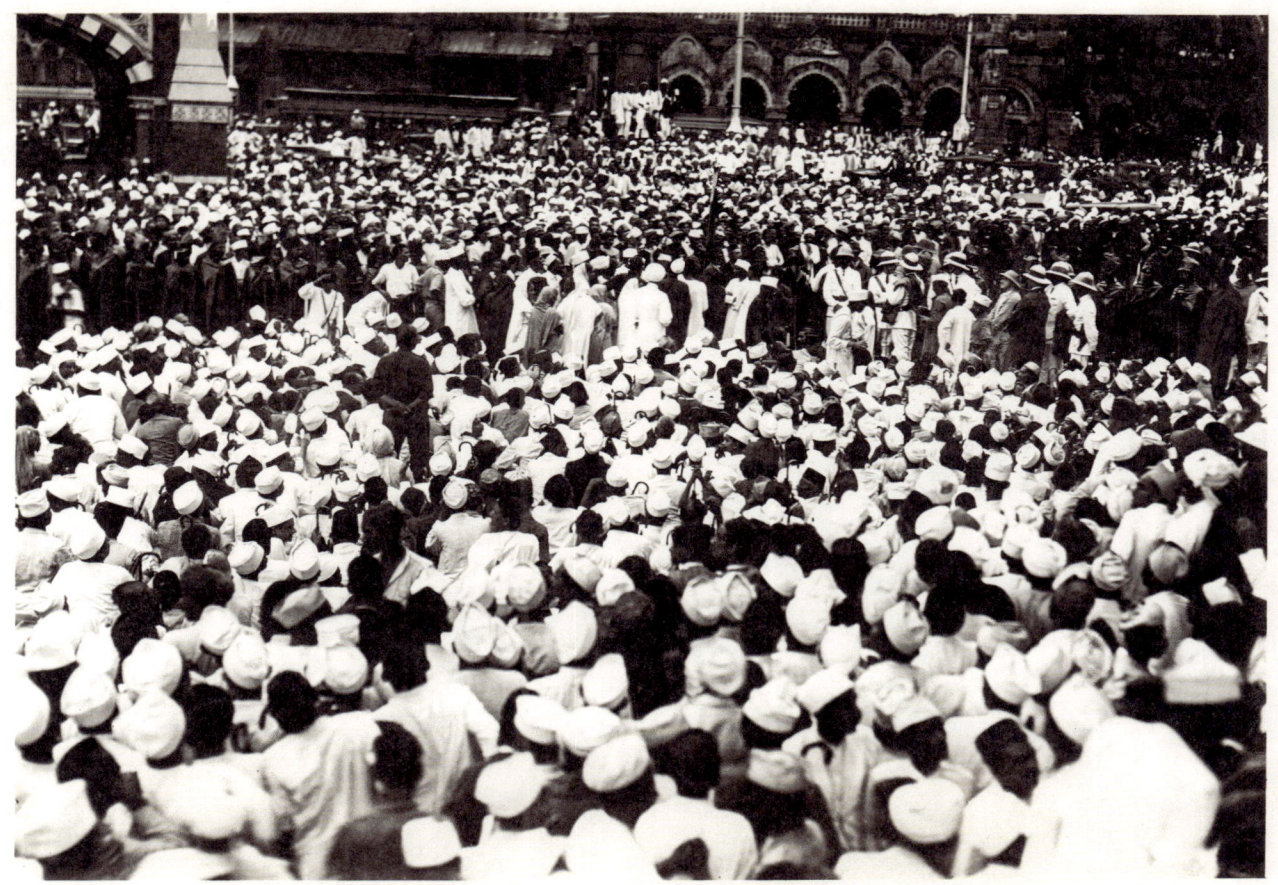

Fig. 4.11

"A procession was organised by the Bombay Provinci [Provincial] Congress Committe [Committee] to celebrate the 10th anniversary of Tilak,[.] The procession was banned into from entering the fort area, when the procession reached the Victoria Terminus a pose [posse] of police about 400 strong formed a cordon and immediately stopped the procession[.] the [The] processionist[s] squatted on the road till the next morning. In the morning after the arrest of the leaders a lathi charge was made where many were injured. Photo shows the procession halted at […],"
c. 1930—1931
Gelatin Silver Print, 115 x 159 mm
ACP: 98.77.0002 (61a)
Tilak Day—observing the 10th anniversary of Bal Gangadhar Tilak's death—was one of several special events observed by volunteers during the Civil Disobedience Movement, alongside Gandhi Day, Garhwal Day, Prohibition Week, Bhagat Singh Day and Flag Salutation Day, among others. Here, demonstrators converge at the wide intersection of Hornby Road and Cruickshank Road, in front of the offices of the Bombay Municipal Corporation and Victoria Terminus.

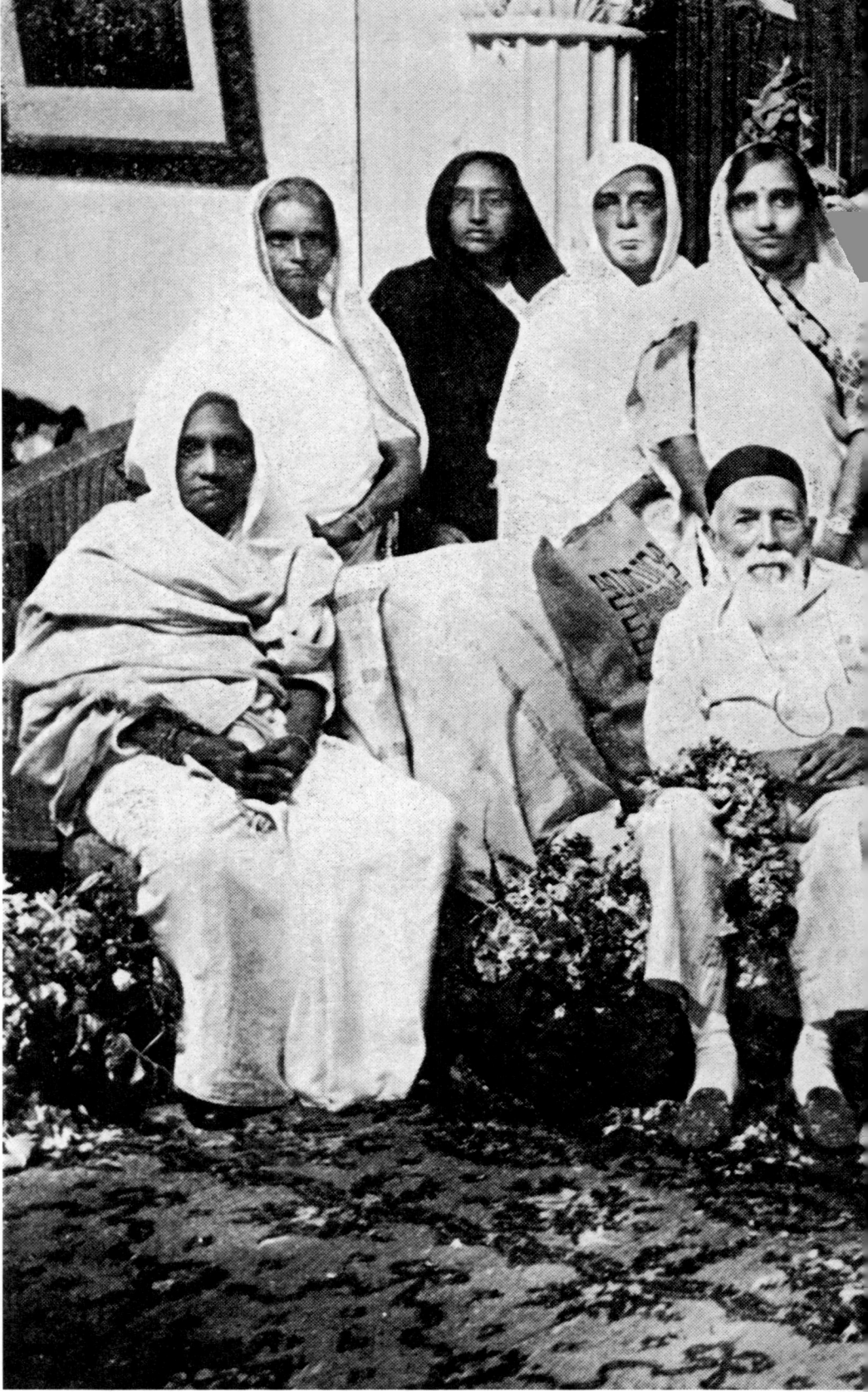

Fig. 4.12
An aged Dadabhai
Naoroji, probably
at his home in
Versova and most
likely meeting one
of the many women's
delegations which
visited him during his
retirement. Naoroji,
who passed away in
1917, was, like
Tilak, incorporated
into K.L. Nursey's
visual tableau of the
Civil Disobedience
Movement. He would
have been an instantly
recognizable figure
to viewers of this
album in the early
1930s: the compiler
did not even feel the
need to caption this
photograph.
n.d.
Gelatin Silver Print,
120 x 172 mm
ACP: 98.77.0002 (121b)

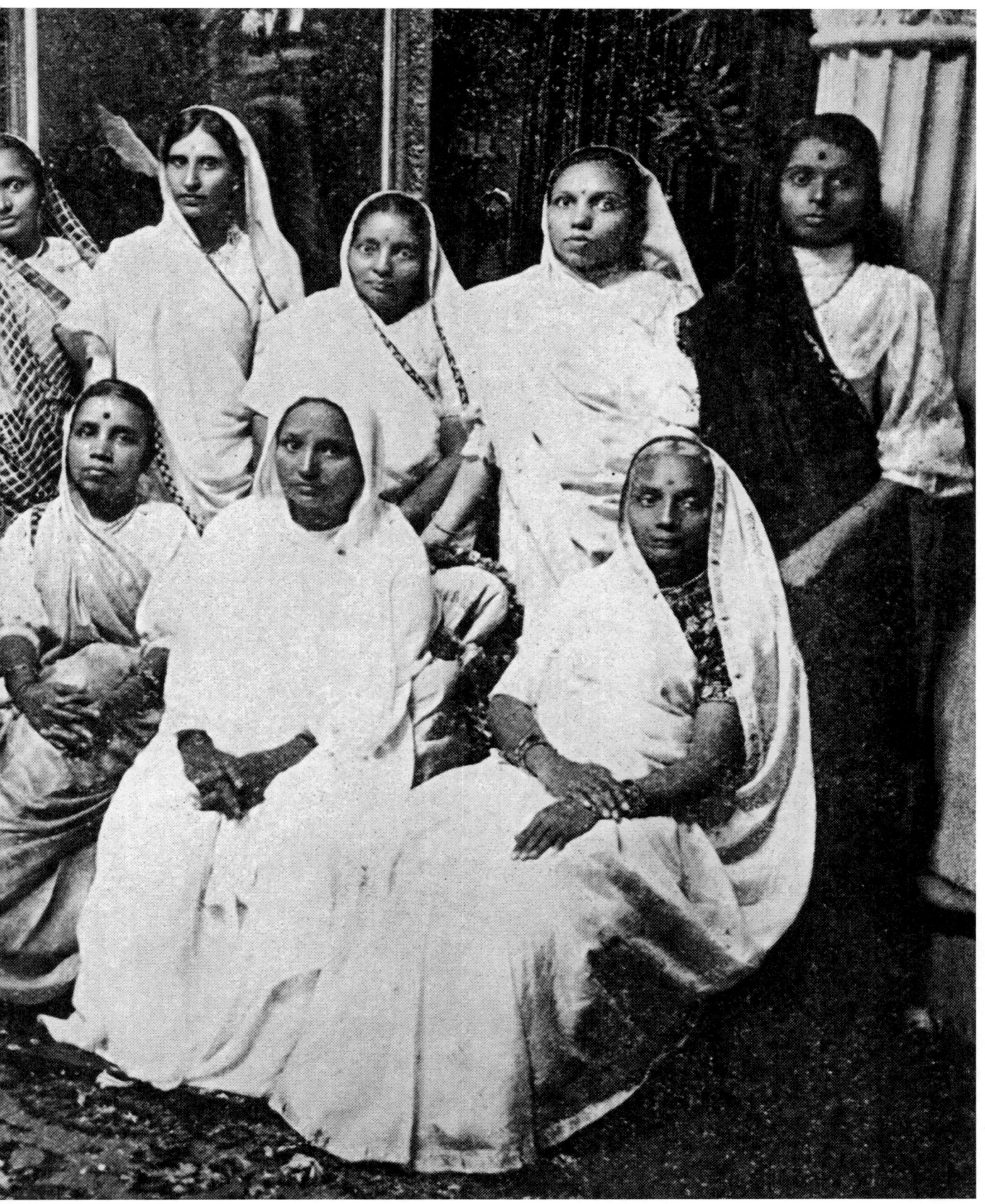

Naoroji's inclusion in a series of photographs of the Civil Disobedience Movement, furthermore, constitutes a unique historiographical intervention by the album's compiler. Historians have too frequently drawn a neat division between the Gandhian and pre-Gandhian phases of Indian nationalism—and have generally dismissed the long-term legacies of liberal leaders such as Naoroji after the Gandhian Congress adopted new tactics and objectives. Yet, Fig. 4.12 demonstrates that memories of early Indian nationalism remained strong in 1930, and that contemporary viewers would have understood a certain continuity between the ideas championed by a 19th-century nationalist—significantly, one who enunciated the relationship between *swadeshi* and *swaraj* by identifying the inherent interconnectedness of economic development and self-government—and the events unfolding on Bombay's streets during the Civil Disobedience Movement. The compiler of the album has not even found it necessary to identify Naoroji in a caption. A single image, in this case, goes against the grain of a dominant perspective in historical scholarship.

Tilak and Naoroji were reminders of the deep roots of *swadeshi* in Bombay. Lilavati Munshi, meanwhile, represented both the Gandhian political moment and India's future political and economic possibilities (she was a Congress MP in the Rajya Sabha in the 1950s before switching, along with her husband, to the economically conservative Swatantra Party). Along with the thousands of anonymous men and women depicted in the Nursey album, they demonstrate how, in India's financial and business capital, *swadeshi* was a constant work in progress—an ever-evolving movement with a widening ambit of techniques, symbols and participants. And these photographs point to two final innovations in Bombay *swadeshi* by 1930: the willingness of *swadeshi* activists to be photographed and the imperative of providing a visual record of their activities. One is struck by the utter dearth of images of *swadeshi* activism in Bombay prior to the Civil Disobedience Movement. We have few visuals of bonfires and demonstrations from the Non-Cooperation Movement and practically no pictorial or illustrated record from the Swadeshi Movement and the 19th century. The Nursey album therefore sits at the very juncture of continuity and change in Bombay *swadeshi*. It attests to a longer history of political protest, economic nationalism, female empowerment and *swadeshi* entrepreneurship in the *Urbs Prima in Indis*. At the same time, the album speaks to a relatively new era of mass media and mass politics, one where anonymous *swadeshi* activists were willing to stare straight into the camera and have their activities—the hawking of *swadeshi* goods, *takli* processions and bonfires of foreign cloth—visually documented for posterity.

Notes

I thank Avrati Bhatnagar, Abigail McGowan and Murali Ranganathan for reading and commenting on earlier drafts of this essay.

1. See Sumit Sarkar, *The Swadeshi Movement in Bengal, 1903-1908* (New Delhi: People's Publishing House, 1973), and Lisa Trivedi, *Clothing Gandhi's Nation: Homespun and Modern India* (Bloomington: Indiana University Press, 2007). For *swadeshi* in 19th-century western India, see my article, "To Revive India's Industries: The Global and Imperial Roots of Swadeshi in the Nineteenth Century," *Modern Asian Studies*, vol. 58, no. 3, May 2024, pp. 686-716.

2. Anant Kakba Priolkar, *Lokahitvādīkrut Nibandhsaṅgrah* (Collected Essays by Lokahitavadi) (Bombay: Popular Prakashan, 1967), pp. 143-44, 153. I thank Ajinkya Lele for providing translations from the original Marathi.

3. Patel, "To Revive India's Industries".

4. David Arnold, *Everyday Technology: Machines and the Making of India's Modernity* (Chicago: University of Chicago Press, 2013).

5. Patel, "To Revive India's Industries"; "*Puṇe Kauśalyaśikṣak Maṇḍḷī*" (Pune Technical Training Society), *Native Opinion*, 5 April 1874, p. 220.

6. "Behind the Indian Veil: Pedlars and Politicians", *The Times of India*, 25 May 1909, p. 7; Douglas E. Haynes, *Small Town Capitalism in Western India: Artisans, Merchants and the Making of the Informal Economy, 1870-1960* (New York: Cambridge University Press, 2012).

7. "The Strength of Indian Swadeshi and Its Present Weakness: Commercial Swadeshi vs. People's Swadeshi", *Dawn and Dawn Society's Magazine*, vol. 12, no. 3 (March 1909), pp. 9, 10.

8. "Mr. Gokhale's Tour: Indian Industries", *The Times of India*, 8 February 1907, p. 7.

9. The store survives today as the Bombay Store. "Bombay Swadeshi Stores: Opened by Mr. D. Naoroji", *The Times of India*, 18 December 1906, p. 5.

10. "Notes and Comments", *The Tribune*, 23 January 1904, p. 3.

11. "Mr. Gokhale's Tour: Indian Industries", p. 7.

12. "Alleged Cheating", *The Times of India*, 17 July 1909, p. 7; "The Swadeshi Cause: European Caps Sold", *The Times of India*, 16 October 1909, p. 7; "The Swadeshi Cause: Curious Business Ways", *The Times of India*, 18 October 1909, p. 8.

13. "Death of Chunilal: Specie Bank in Liquidation", *The Times of India*, 1 December 1913, p. 7; "The Financial Situation", *The Times of India*, 1 December 1913, p. 6; "Auditor's Report: 'Lowest Form of Fraud'", *The Times of India*, 20 December 1913, p. 9.

14. "Collapse of Swadeshism", *Indian Social Reformer*, 4 January 1914, pp. 209, 210.

15. "Swadeshi Movement: Cloth Stores Opened", *The Times of India*, 4 January 1919, p. 8.

16. "The Swadeshi Movement", *The Times of India*, 23 June 1919, p. 11.

17. For more on women's participation in activities during the Civil Disobedience Movement, see Chapters Five, Six, Seven and Eight in this volume.

18. "India's Painful Duty to Boycott the Prince's Visit", *The Bombay Chronicle*, 17 November 1921, p. 9.

19. Ramachandra Guha, *Gandhi: The Years That Changed the World, 1914-1948* (Gurgaon: Penguin Random House India, 2018), pp. 916-17.

20. For an analysis of how Gandhi's relationship with one particular female *satyagrahi* transformed over time, with the Civil Disobedience Movement as a critical juncture, see Dinyar Patel, "The Singing Satyagrahi: Khurshedben Naoroji and the Challenge of Indian Biography", in *A Functioning Anarchy? Essays for Ramachandra Guha* (Gurgaon: Penguin Random House India, 2021), pp. 105-25.

21. The word originates from a name: Charles Cunningham Boycott, a British land agent in County Mayo, whose oppression of local tenant farmers led to the community successfully punishing and ostracizing him in multiple ways.

22. Lalubhai Samaldas, "Swadeshism. A Native View", *The Times of India*, 20 October 1905, p. 6.

23. *Report of the Millowners' Association, Bombay for the Year 1930* (Bombay: G. Claridge & Co., 1931), pp. 39, 40.

24. Samaldas, "Swadeshism. A Native View", p. 6.

25. Guha, *Gandhi*, pp. 142, 143; *Collected Works of Mahatma Gandhi*, vol. 21 (New Delhi: Publications Division, Ministry of Information and Broadcasting, 1966), p. 44.

26. Dinyar Patel, "Beyond Hindu-Muslim Unity: Gandhi, the Parsis and the Prince of Wales Riots of 1921", *Indian Economic and Social History Review*, vol. 55, no. 2 (2018), pp. 221-47.

27. "When Women Refuse to Obey", *The Illustrated Weekly of India*, 27 April 1930, p. 21.

28. "Boycott the Visit: Campaign in the City", *The Bombay Chronicle*, 16 November 1921, p. 10.

29. Aashish Velkar, "Swadeshi Capitalism in Colonial Bombay", *Historical Journal*, vol. 64, no. 4 (2021), pp. 1009-34.

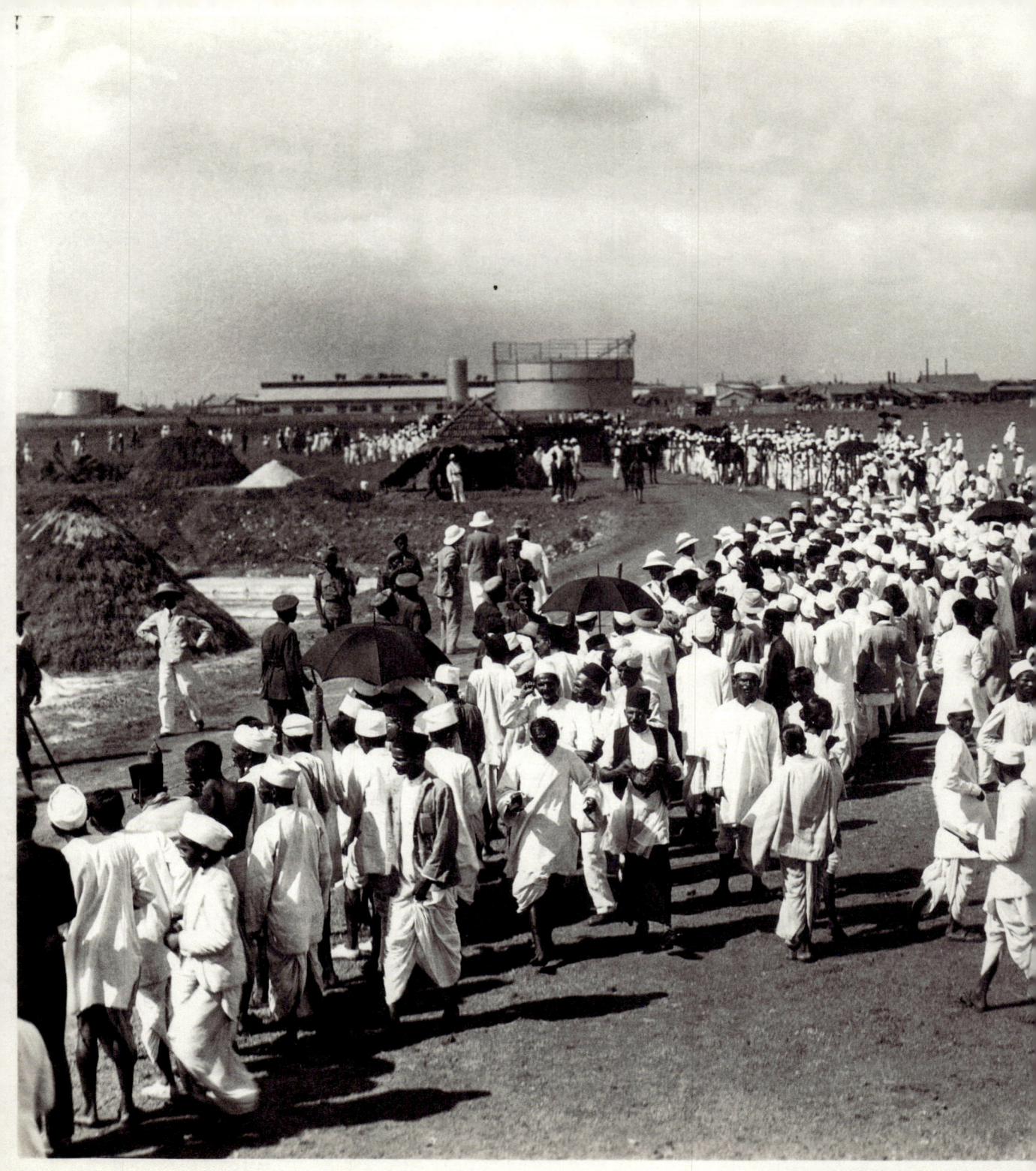

The public watching the raids conducted by the
Congress at Wadhala.

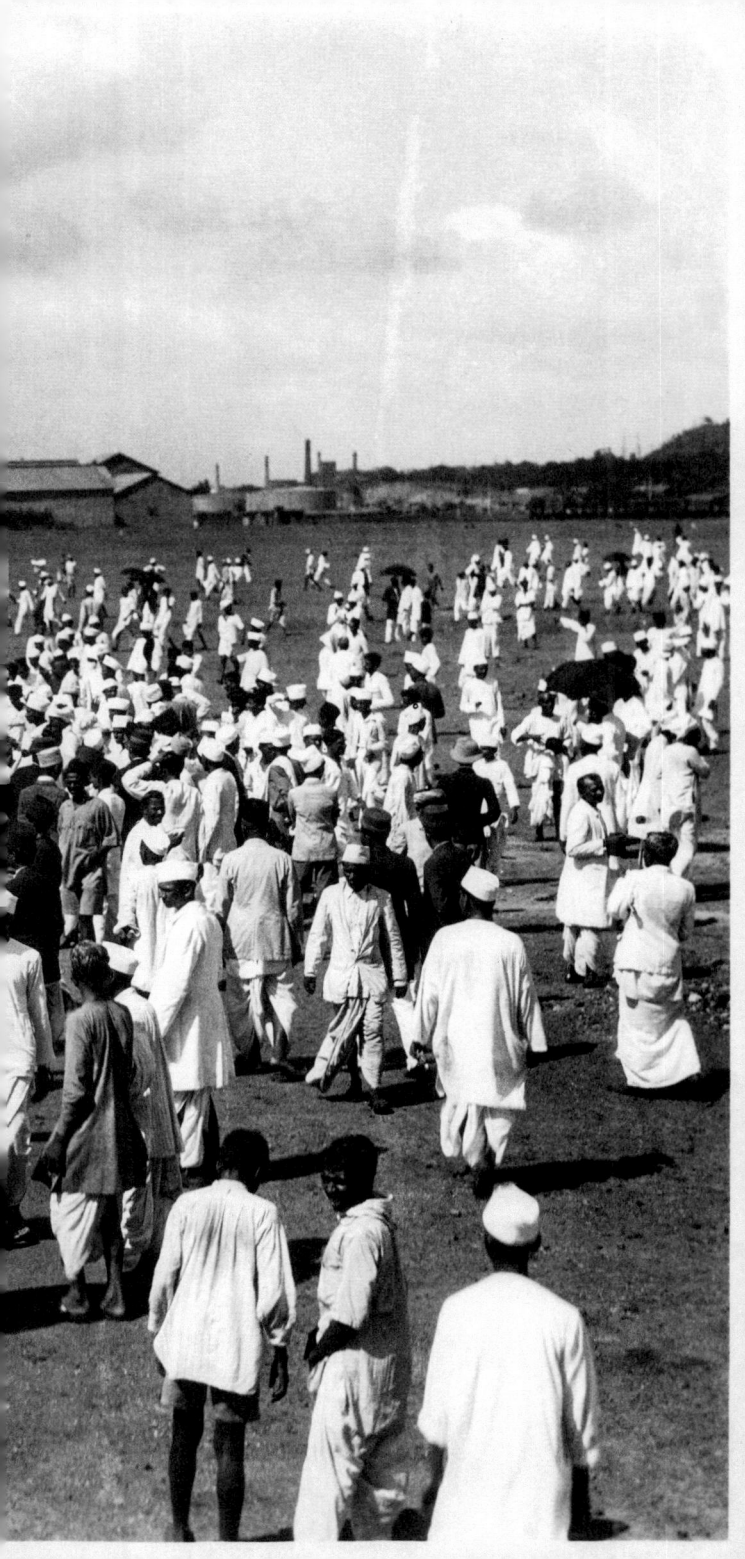

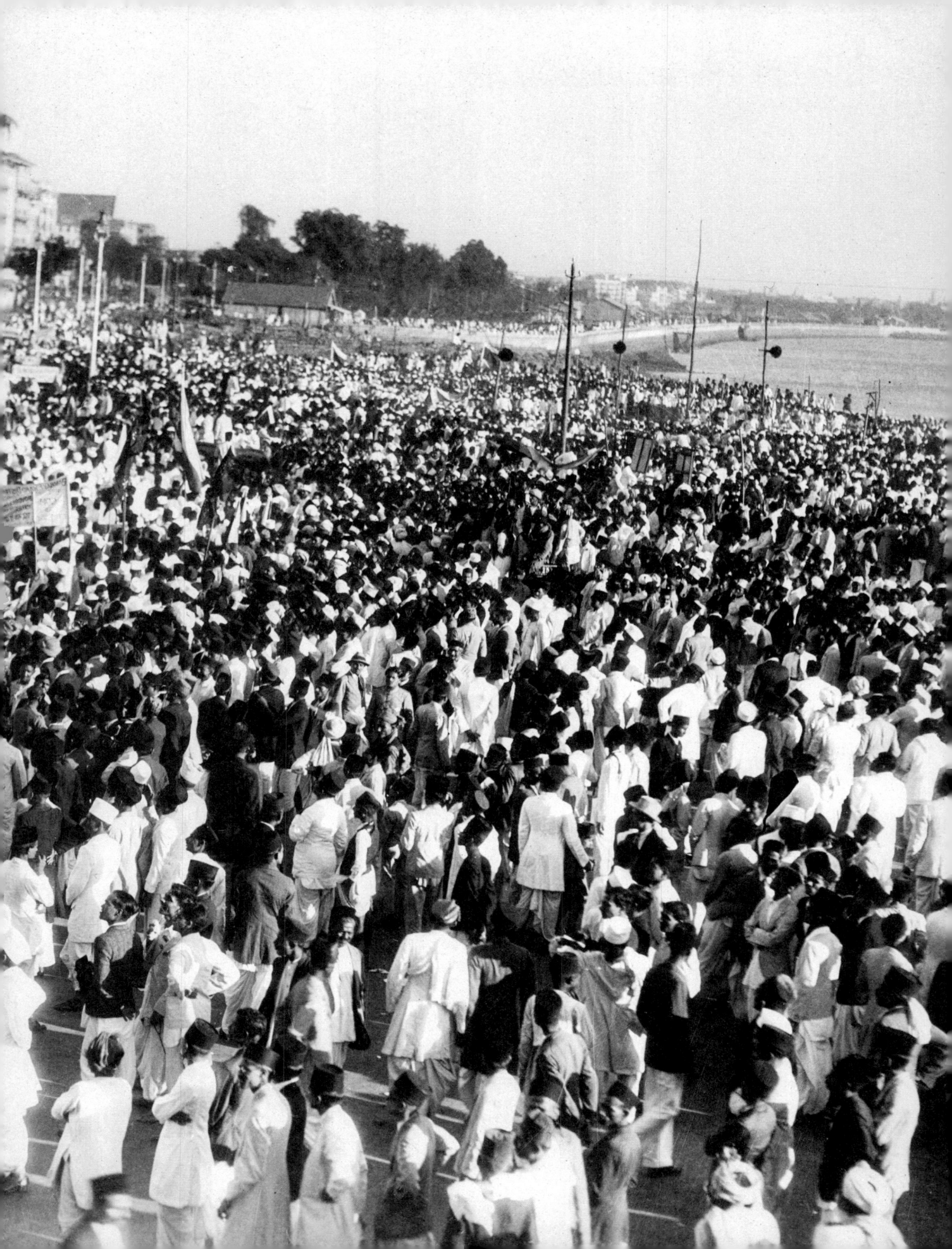

CHAPTER 5

SALT OF THE CITY

Sumathi Ramaswamy

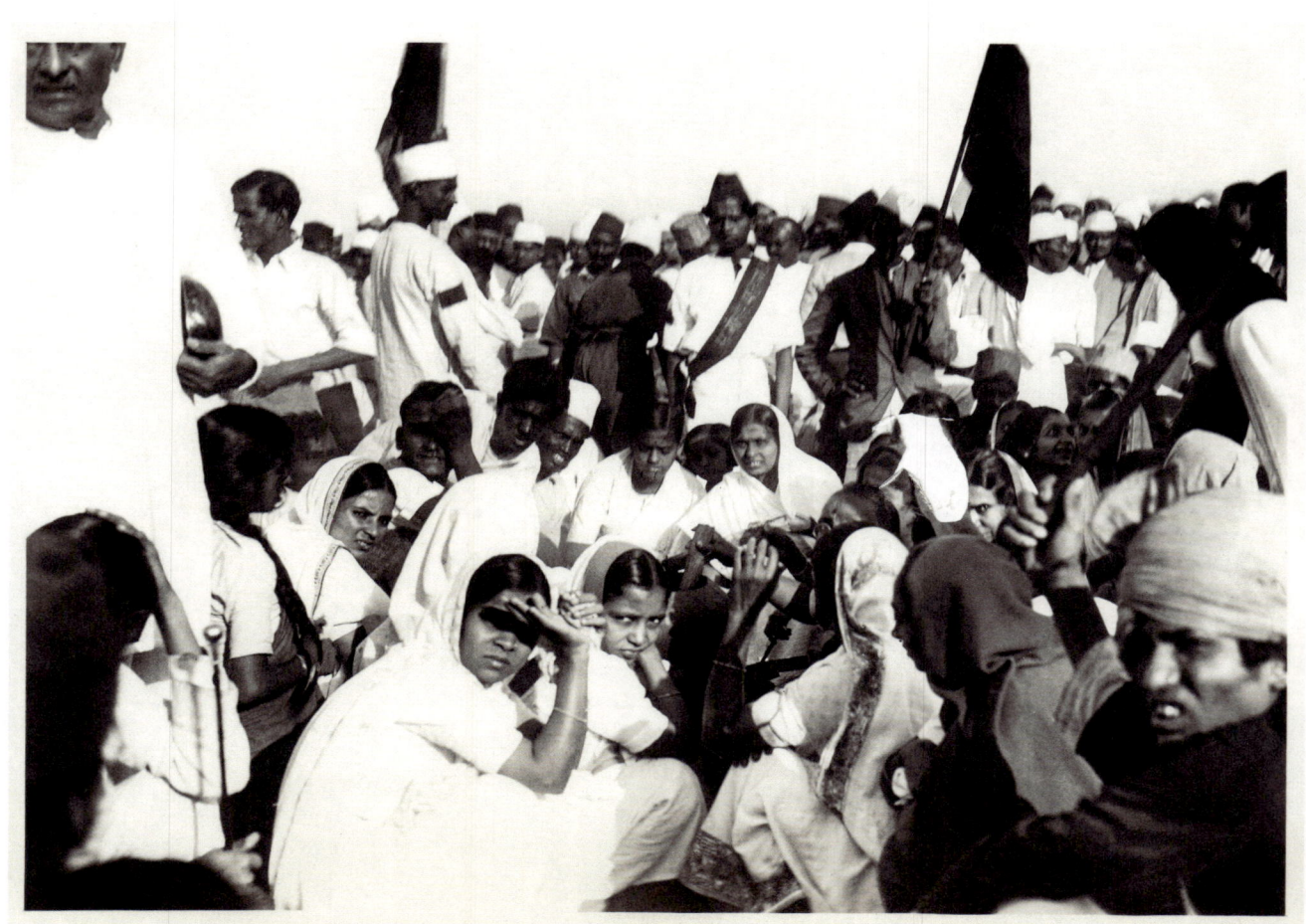

Soon the salt preparing craze spread over the
city and hundreds of Gujeratis went to the
chaupatty shore to fetch sea water which they
used to prepare salt. Photo taken on the
14th March 1930.

The remote hamlet of Dandi on the Gujarat coast is indelibly associated in the mythology of Indian nationalism with M.K. Gandhi and his ingenious campaign against the colonial monopoly on salt production, but it was the densely populated city of Bombay that scaled it up to a mass movement in a few heady weeks in the summer of 1930. As thousands of its patriotic residents obeyed the call of the sea,[1] they turned salt, the most mundane albeit essential of minerals, into a catalyst for their acts of disobedience. Correspondingly, British India's premier hub of commerce and capital was transformed into a "contraband" city from the moment the stringent colonial salt laws and salt monopoly began to be challenged: first in the northern suburb of Vile Parle soon after Gandhi's disobedient act in Dandi at dawn on 6 April and then, more spectacularly, in the heart of the metropolis at Mahalakshmi on the morning of 7 April.[2] As evidenced as well by numerous photos in the Nursey album, day after day in the months that followed, the city was witness to patriotic men, women, even children, making their way to the sea to collect water to make salt (Fig. 5.1, Fig. 5.2, Fig. 5.4; see also 6.4a). In doing so, they took on the mantle of the salt *satyagrahi*, a new and coveted status: mobile, patriotic and disobedient, forged around the making and selling of this prohibited mineral—publicly but peacefully.

There is little doubt that the non-violent violation of colonial regulations was a learned activity that the "law breaker" had to be scrupulously taught, even as the Nursey album makes visible the most modest of domestic devices—*lota*s (small metal water pots) and *sigri*s (portable clay stoves)—with which the citizenry conducted its small but momentous acts of mass disobedience against the world's largest imperial power. The album also captures nationalist leaders of the stature of Motilal and Jawaharlal Nehru, Khan Abdul Ghaffar Khan, as well as the Mahatma himself, who visited the city, undoubtedly drawn by its energy and enthusiasm for non-violent lawbreaking. The real heroes of the moment, however, are the disobedient residents, especially women carrying a humble pail or pot, who are rendered visible in the album's pages gathering up bits of the sea to bring to a boil, and proudly displaying and selling the extracted contraband salt. They are the true salt of the city, and it is their actions and activities that catch the attention of the camera, and hence also constitute the focus of this short essay.

PAGES 122–123
"The public watching the raids conducted by the Congress at Wadhala [Wadala]."
1930
Gelatin Silver Print,
116 x 160 mm
ACP: 98.77.0002 (32b)

PAGE 124
"A flag salutation ceremony on the chaupatty [Chowpatty] sands, Bombay."
(Detail, see p. 131)

Fig. 5.1
"Soon the salt preparing craze spread over the city and hundreds of Gujeratis [Gujaratis] went to the chaupatty [Chowpatty] shore to fetch sea water which they used to prepare salt. Photo taken on the 14th March 1930."
Gelatin Silver Print,
114 x 156 mm
ACP: 98.77.0002 (17b)

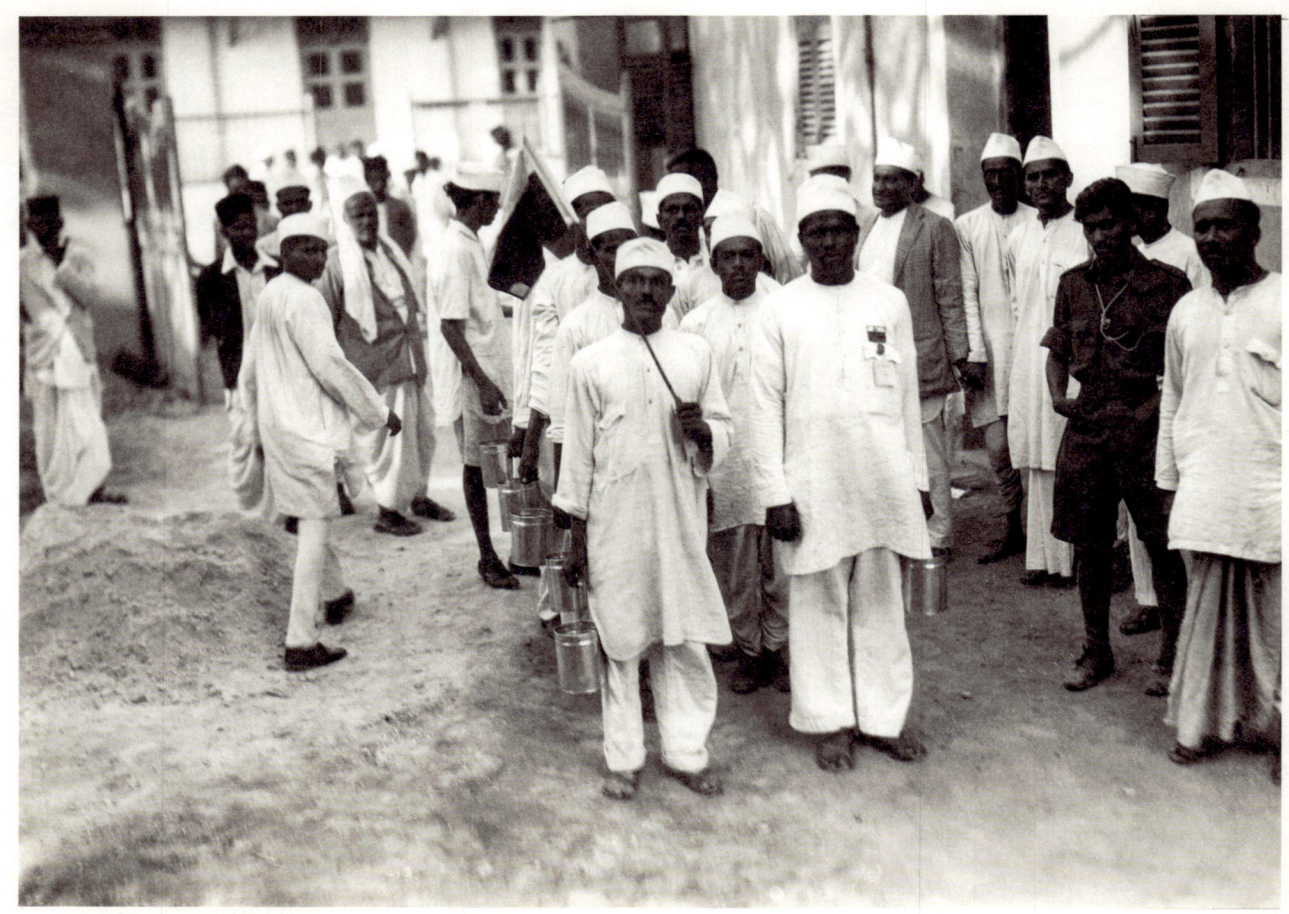

Fig. 5.2
"This is another batch
of salt satyagrahis."
1930
Gelatin Silver Print,
115 x 155 mm
ACP: 98.77.0002 (13b)
This photograph was
reproduced in *The
Illustrated Weekly of
India*, 20 April 1930,
with the caption:
"A batch of volunteers
going to Chowpatty to
collect saltwater for
contraband salt."

The Call of the Sea

On 11 March 1930, on the eve of Gandhi's departure from his ashram on the banks of the Sabarmati to walk to Dandi with a select band of (male) followers, a distance of over 350 kilometres that they covered in 24 days, the so-called "War Council" of the Bombay Provincial Congress Committee urged its constituents to "arise, awake and plunge into the struggle for independence," asking rhetorically, "How will Bombay hail him?" (Fig. 5.3).[3] In response to the exhortation to hail Gandhi, Bombay's patriotic residents turned to the sea, on whose shores the city sprawled, to use its waters to fuel their collective act of disobedience. Consider a photograph in the album with the caption "Women and children picking salt from the rocks at Mahalaxshimi [Mahalakshmi] shore" (Fig. 5.4). The foreground is taken up by large boulders close to which the photographer wielding the camera must have been standing to capture on film the handful of sari-clad women and frock-wearing girls as they gingerly attempt to get to the sea, their posture and footing suggesting that this was not necessarily an everyday—or easy—act for them. Three male figures clad in short pants, two of them sporting the trademark Gandhi cap, offer a helping hand. *Lota*s are visible in the hands of the four women, the only clue—other than the caption, likely added much later—of the group's intention, the camera

CITIZENS, ARISE, AWAKE!

AND

PLUNGE INTO THE STRUGGLE FOR INDEPENDENCE

To-morrow (Wednesday) at 6-30 a. m.

MAHATMA GANDHI BEGINS HIS MARCH

From Satyagrahashram, Sabarmati.

HOW WILL BOMBAY HAIL HIM?

The Bombay Provincial Congress War Council
expects every citizen to do his/her
duty by taking part in

TO-MORROW'S PROGRAMME
AND MAKING IT A COMPLETE SUCCESS

THE PROGRAMME:—

1. Volunteer parade at the Congress House at 6-30 a.m. (S.T.) (the time when Mahatma Gandhi commences his march from the Satyagraha Ashram, Sabarmati).
2. National Flag Salutation at 8 a.m. (S.T.) at the Congress House followed by public meetings after which the Volunteers will form a Procession and March through important streets.
3. Public meeting at the Esplanade Maidan at 6 p.m. (S.T.) Mr. K. F. Nariman will preside.
4. Public meeting at Dadar, Tilak Bridge, at 9 p.m.
5. Volunteers will enrol Congress Members and hawk Khadi.

ENROL AS VOLUNTEERS.

in any of the following three classes:—

1. Ironsiders: Those prepared for immediate Civil Resistance.
2. Reserves: Those who will take the places of Class I when they are removed from scene of action.
3. Irregular Territorials: Who will take part in demonstrative programme of the "War" Council.

LEFT
Fig. 5.3
"Citizens, Arise, Awake!" Bombay Provincial Congress pamphlet, reproduced in *The Bombay Chronicle*, 11 March 1930, page 1

BELOW
Fig. 5.4
"Women and children picking salt from the rocks at the Malaxshimi [Mahalakshmi] shore." 1930
Gelatin Silver Print, 115 x 155 mm
ACP: 98.77.0002 (13a)

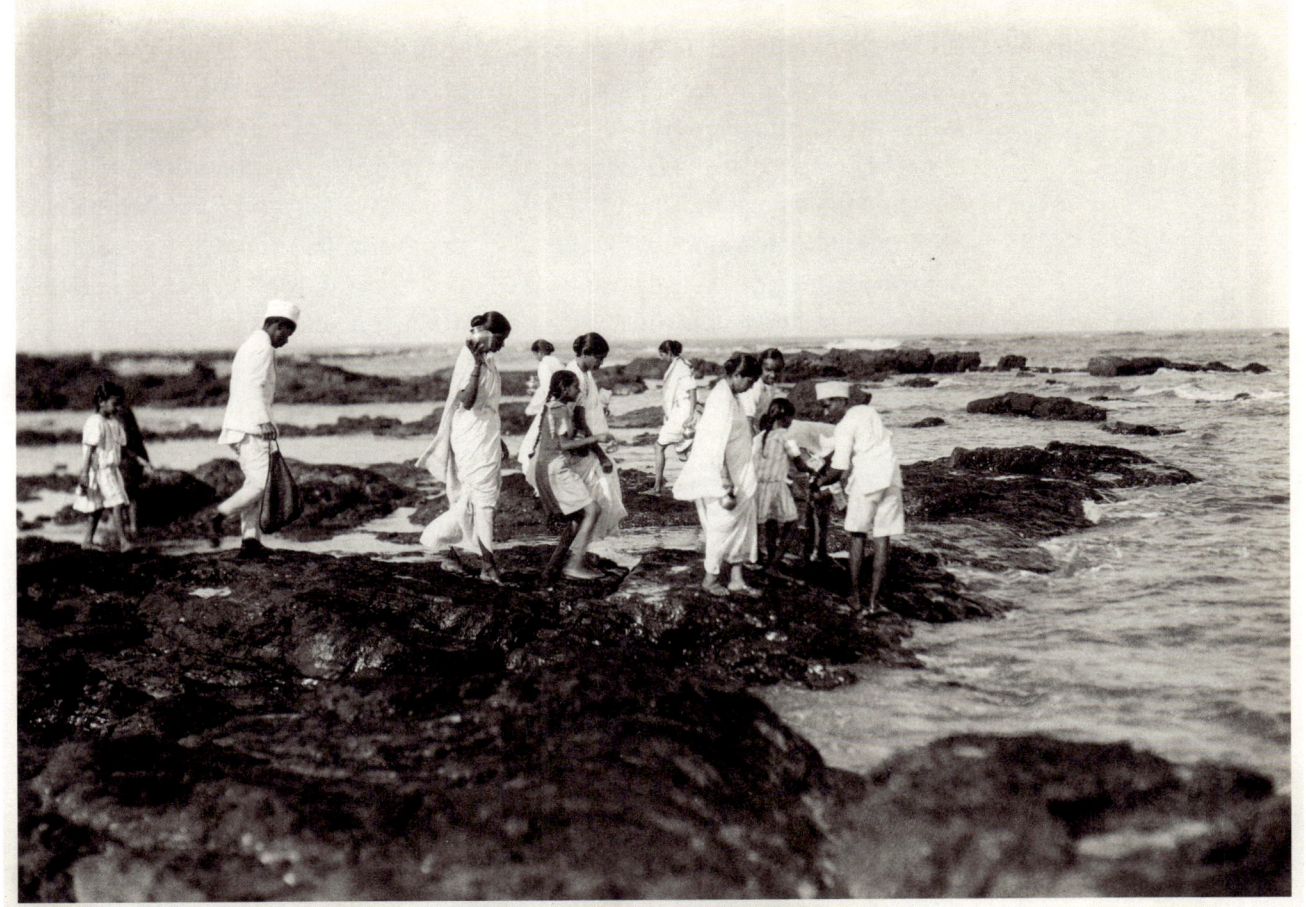

anticipating the act of disobedience to follow as these and numerous other women and children seek to forge a new relationship with the sea by wading into it, filling their utensils with it, and making off with the potentially incendiary contraband contents to be boiled down at home to extract the salt.

Rich as the photograph is in such details, it is a rare one in the album, the only image that specifically captures one of the numerous "salt dramas" enacted with the sea as a backdrop that police reports and contemporary newspapers recounted from around 6 April 1930 onwards.[4] In fact, this photo is the sole visual counterpart in the album to numerous confidential police transcripts such as that filed on 9 April which reported a large nationalist meeting attended by over 30,000 people on the ocean's edge in Chowpatty, including "200 ladies. About 30 or 40 ladies carried salt water in *lotas* to their houses from the meeting. This act was applauded by the audience."[5] Or that of 14 April, which similarly reported, "The mass meeting at Chaupatty [Chowpatty] was attended by about 50,000 people including about 1,000 ladies. Many people took sea water to their houses."[6] The sea thus literally and symbolically entered people's daily lives in these months, becoming an intimate part of homes and hearths transformed now into hotbeds of domestic disobedience.

In turn, the humble and ubiquitous commodity of salt—to which its daily partakers might not have hitherto given much thought—also came to be seen in a different manner, taking on a supernatural quality as the destroyer of mighty empires. In the fascinating words of one of the leaders of the movement, Kamaladevi Chattopadhyay (whose sari-clad figure is visible in some photographs of the album), "So universal was the desire to participate in this law-breaking campaign that sea water was carried from the coast to remote nooks and corners in the interior to enable people to manufacture salt. *This innocent life-sustaining grain of salt had become transformed into dynamite, threatening the powerful British rule so long thought to be invulnerable.*"[7]

As "the salt-preparing craze" took hold in the city (Fig. 5.1), ocean-side neighbourhoods and beaches in Mahalakshmi, Chowpatty, Worli, Juhu and elsewhere on the Bombay coastline became sites for the almost daily staging of this new secular ritual of gathering up the sea to boil it and extract the mundane mineral that had become the "dynamite, threatening the powerful British rule." Those who did not themselves wade into the ocean gathered instead on the shore on various occasions, "occupying all vantage points on trees, buildings, and other structures. They waited and watched the small groups who came to collect sea water."[8] As the sea became the site of daily disobedience that drew towards it the patriotic lawbreaker as well as the curious spectator, it also afforded other unusual acts, such as on the evening of 13 April 1930, the anniversary of British India's most calamitous massacre in Jallianwala Bagh in distant Punjab, when it was reported that 200,000 people ("on a modest estimate") had gathered on the Chowpatty sands and witnessed the drowning of an effigy of the salt tax, previously hoisted and displayed on a pole (an event not captured, alas, in the album).[9]

The sea was also recast as the source of contraband in contemporary media as in a photo spread published in *The Illustrated Weekly of India* on the very Sunday when the salt law was broken for the first time in Bombay Presidency. "Much of India's salt is derived from sea-water, and the *satyagrahi*s intend producing the most necessary commodity of life in this way, by the sea shore," the English-language pictorial magazine published by the British-owned *The Times of India*, informed its mostly elite colonial and Indian readership.[10] All the same, although the sea—and the seashore—was the scene of so much protest action in these days (Fig. 5.5, Fig. 5.6), including arrivals and departures, we barely get a glimpse of the wider ocean in the pages of the album.

For instance, the album includes several photographs of Gandhi in the city on his way to London to attend the Round Table Conference, departing on 29 August 1931 on the *S.S. Rajputana*. As the caption of one photo has it,

Fig. 5.5
"A flag salutation ceremony on the chaupatty [Chowpatty] sands, Bombay." 1930 Gelatin Silver Print, 113 x 161 mm
ACP: 98.77.0002 (108a)

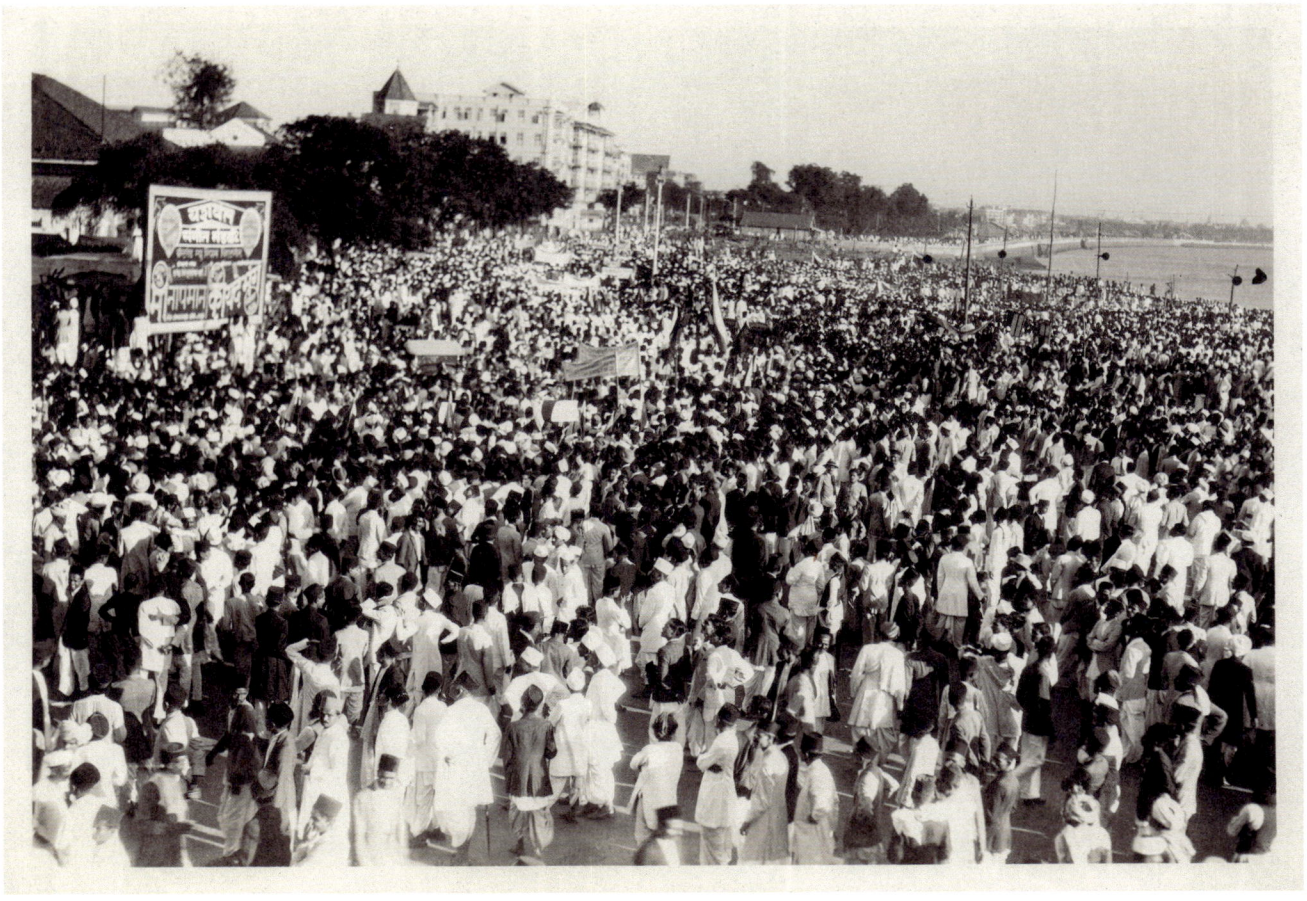

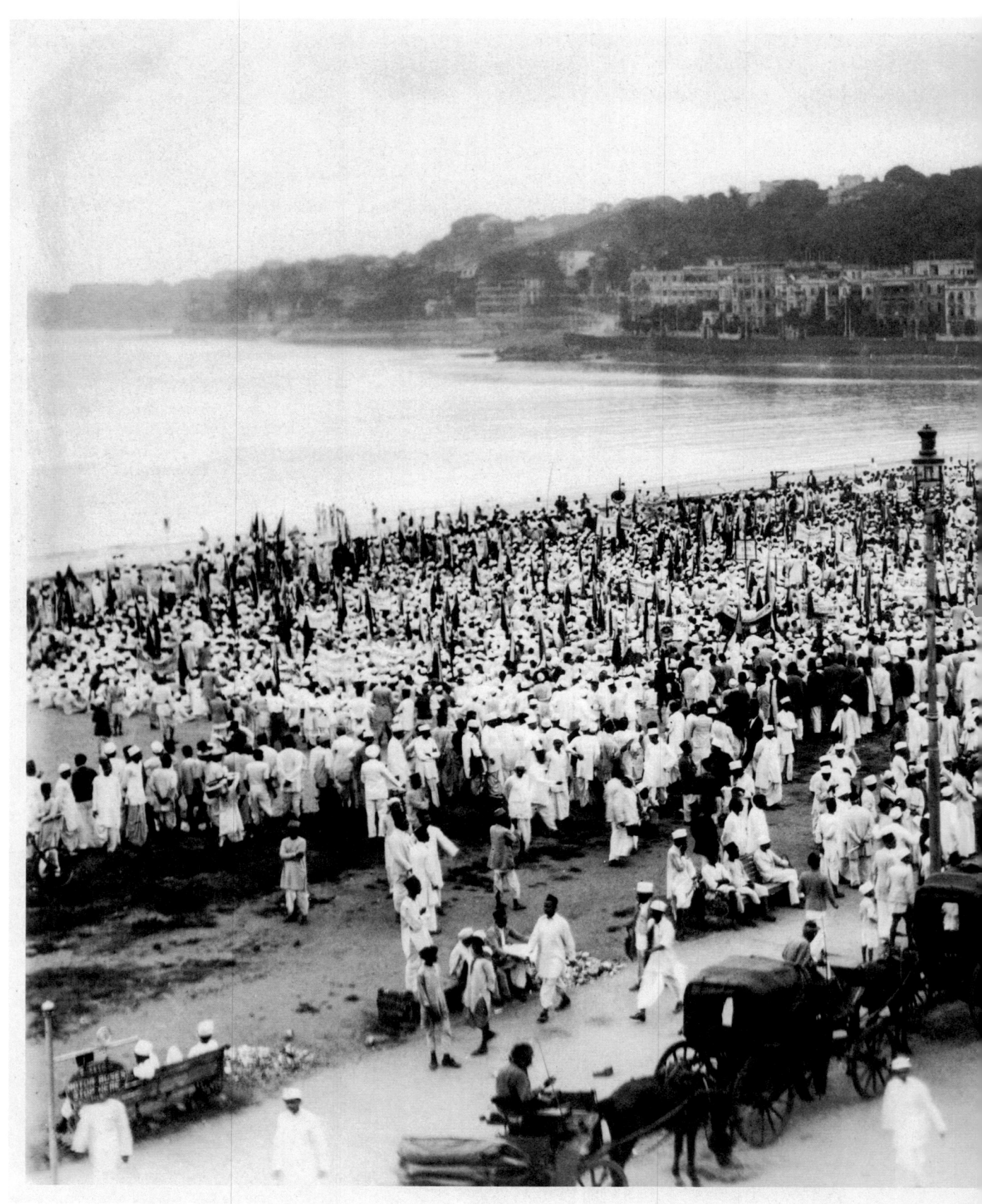

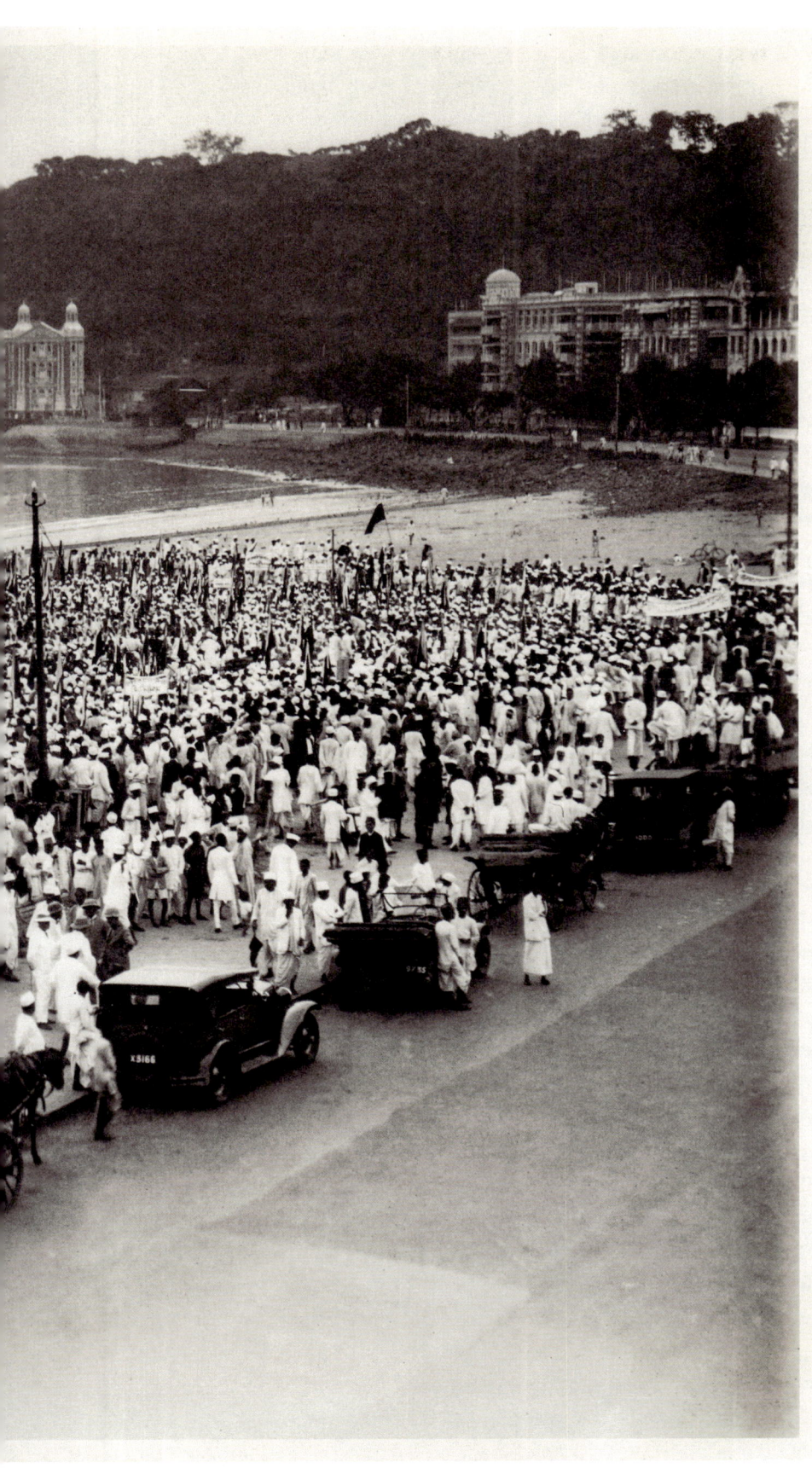

Fig. 5.6
"A flag salutation
ceremony on the
chaupatty [Chowpatty]
sands." c. 1930—1931
Gelatin Silver Print,
114 x 159 mm
ACP: 98.77.0002 (91b)

"Bombay went Gandhi mad" on the occasion, thick crowds lining the streets to bid him farewell. The camera also captured a group of *desh sevikas* (lit., "handmaids of the nation") waiting patiently at Ballard Pier to greet him before he boarded his ship on that rainy day. In another photo, we glimpse Gandhi's partly covered back as the British captain in his pristine white uniform meets with him on the crowded deck. But for the captions, however, we would not know that these scenes were unfolding on the seafront.[11]

In contrast, *The Illustrated Weekly of India* published a photograph with the caption "More Salt Law Breakers," which showed "women and girls filling their vessels at Chawpatty [Chowpatty] to make contraband salt."[12] The women are captured ankle deep in the sea, holding their saris up to the knees, while one young girl looks directly at the camera whose wielder too must have entered the ocean to catch the close-up (see also Fig. 6.4a). Such views of the sea, and of the disobedience being performed in and around it, are missing in the Nursey album from which we do not get a sense of the enabling part played by the ocean. Indeed, had this album been the sole source of images of the city, a viewer would entirely miss the fact that Bombay was a port, its contours and rhythms shaped by the waters surrounding it. Even as the disobedient dramas of these months served to re-forge the connection between the city and the sea with the patriotic salt-making resident now serving as a new conduit, what the geographer Stephen Legg refers to evocatively as "sea writing" seems to have evaded the "light writer(s)" whose photographs found their way into the album.[13]

Salt Lessons

The disobedient resident of Bombay had to not only learn how to forge a new relationship with the sea, but also had to be taught how to make it yield the precious mineral whose illicit extraction and possession enabled the salt *satyagrahi* to challenge the might of an empire. As historian David Arnold writes, salt-making was arduous, back-breaking work, seared through by "the drudgery of daily manual toil" and conventionally undertaken by workers (both women and men) far removed from the (mostly) middle-class urbanite who posed for the camera in the images of the album, or in those that were published in contemporary media.[14] Anticipating that salt lessons were valuable, indeed necessary, the salt-makers of Vile Parle, who first broke the law on the morning of 6 April 1930, released a bulletin on the eve of their act, specifying details of the necessary equipment and the processes to be adopted. They recommended pots and pans made of wood, glass, enamel or china, and declared as "undesirable" the use of copper, brass, zinc and aluminium. They also gave detailed instructions for boiling, filtering and evaporating the seawater that had been arduously collected.[15] By all accounts, the resulting salt was neither fine nor particularly clean, but no matter—it was sold or auctioned for "fabulous sums" and "fancy prices," the proceeds deployed for supporting the disobedient activities of the city under the leadership of the Bombay Provincial Congress.[16]

Several photographs in the Nursey album focus upon salt lessons being conducted in makeshift outdoor schools, the teacher typically an older man sporting a Gandhi cap, the eager students, adult men and women, and the occasional child (Fig. 5.7, Fig. 5.8, Fig. 5.9). The caption given to Fig. 5.7 is particularly interesting. On one hand, it (incorrectly) gives a date of 1 April, when such lessons were not yet being delivered openly or publicly. On the other hand, it misses identifying a key leader of these protests, likely Lilavati Munshi, a privileged upper-class activist (see Chapters Four, Six and Seven in this volume) being instructed on the art of stirring seawater in a pan on a *sigri*, typical of working-class kitchens. It is hard to miss the irony of middle-class men—who might have hardly entered the kitchen in their pre-disobedience days—offering lessons in boiling and cooking to those who habitually undertook such tasks! This was not the only reversal of the times. While schools typically teach obedience and compliance, these impromptu salt classes did the exact opposite as they taught their avid pupils to break the law, publicly and proudly on

Fig. 5.7
"There were regular salt preparing classes where the public were given instructions to prepare salt. Here are some Congress women boiling salt water on Sigris in the compound of the Congress house. Photo taken 1st April." 1930
Gelatin Silver Print, 114 x 158 mm
ACP: 98.77.0002 (15b)

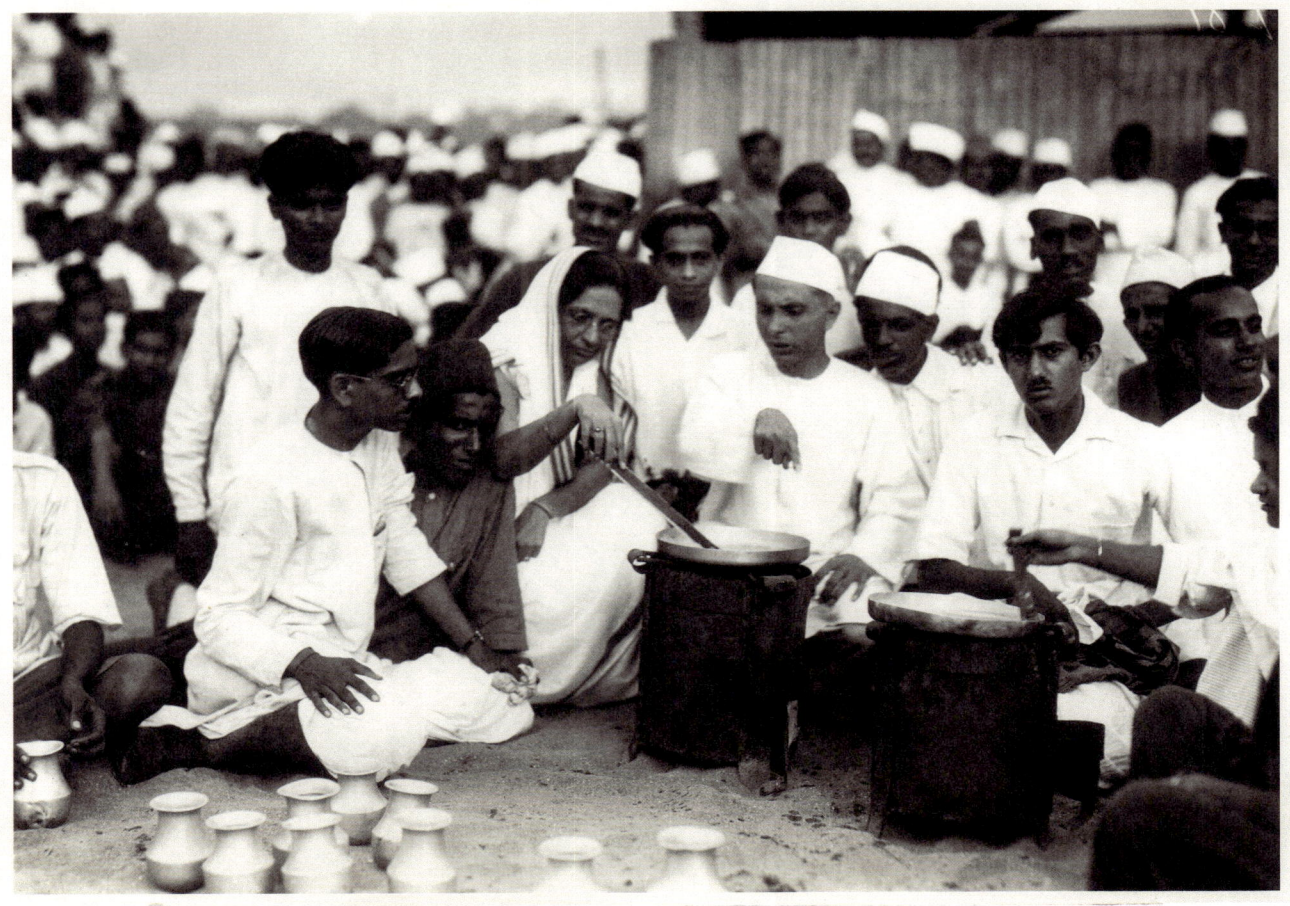

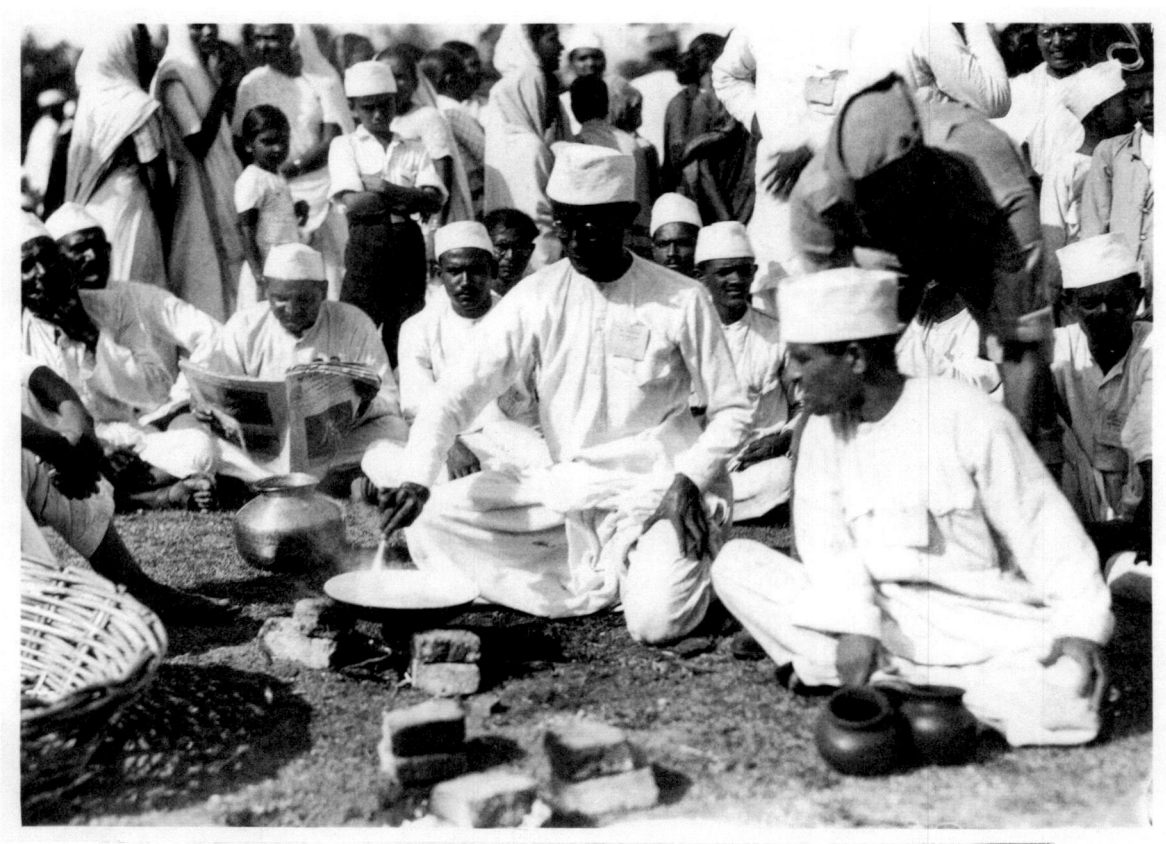

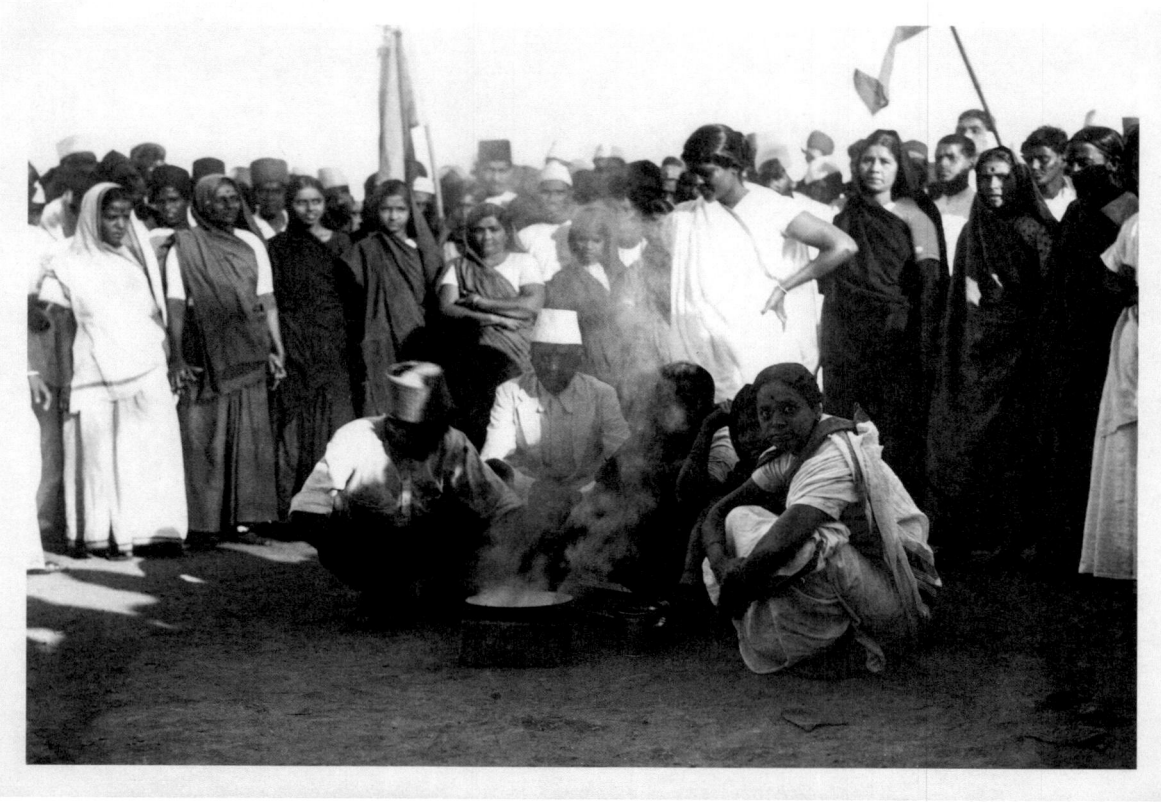

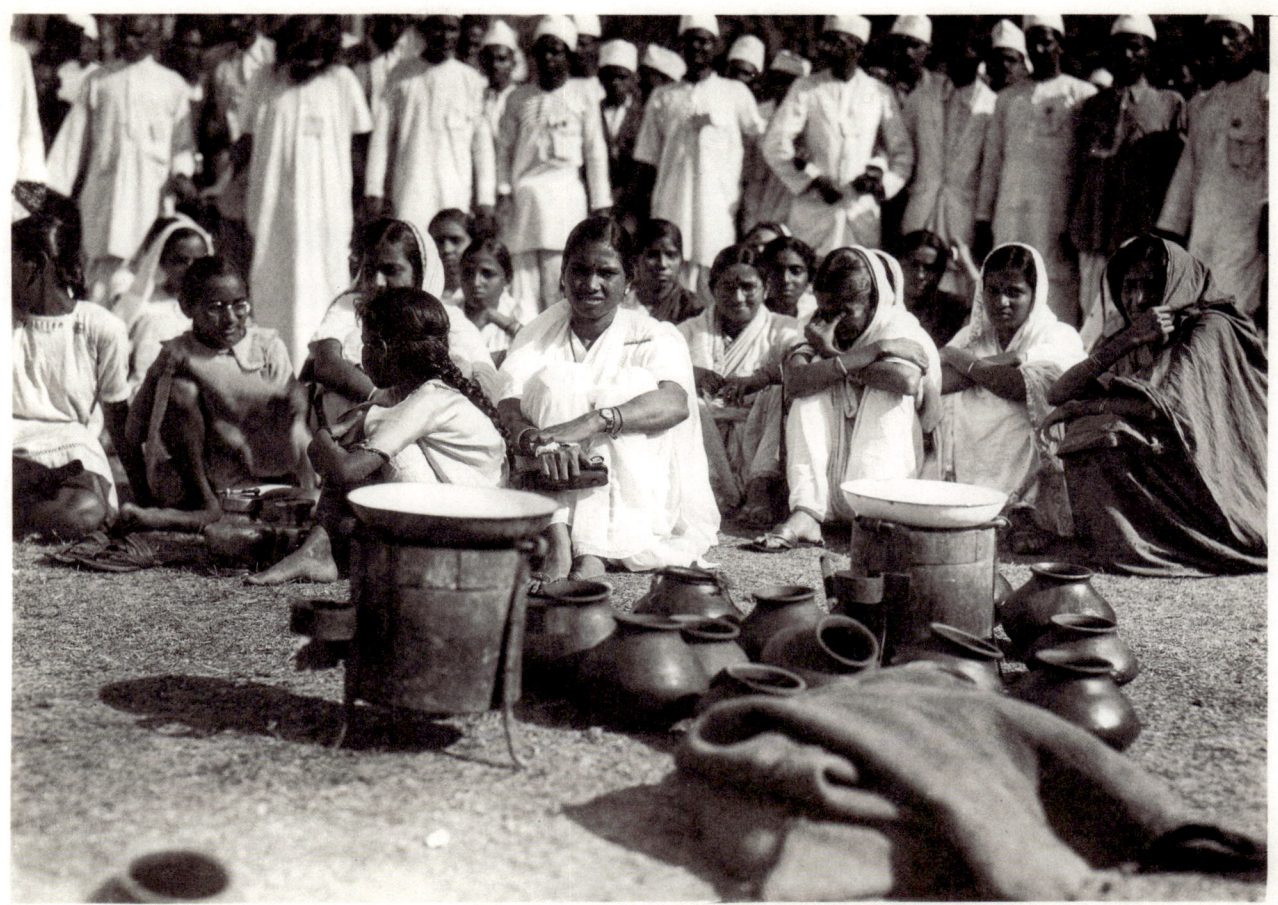

FACING PAGE, ABOVE
Fig. 5.8
"Here's another salt class in progress were [where] some Congress leaders are instructing the public how to manufacture salt."
1930
Gelatin Silver Print, 114 x 155 mm
ACP: 98.77.0002 (17a)

FACING PAGE, BELOW
Fig. 5.9
"Congress Women receiving instructions as to preparing salt." 1930
Gelatin Silver Print, 114 x 163 mm
ACP: 98.77.0002 (22b)

Fig. 5.10
"A group of women and children preparing salt from the sea water in the compound of the congres [Congress] house."
1930
Gelatin Silver Print, 113 x 155 mm
ACP: 98.77.0002 (18a)

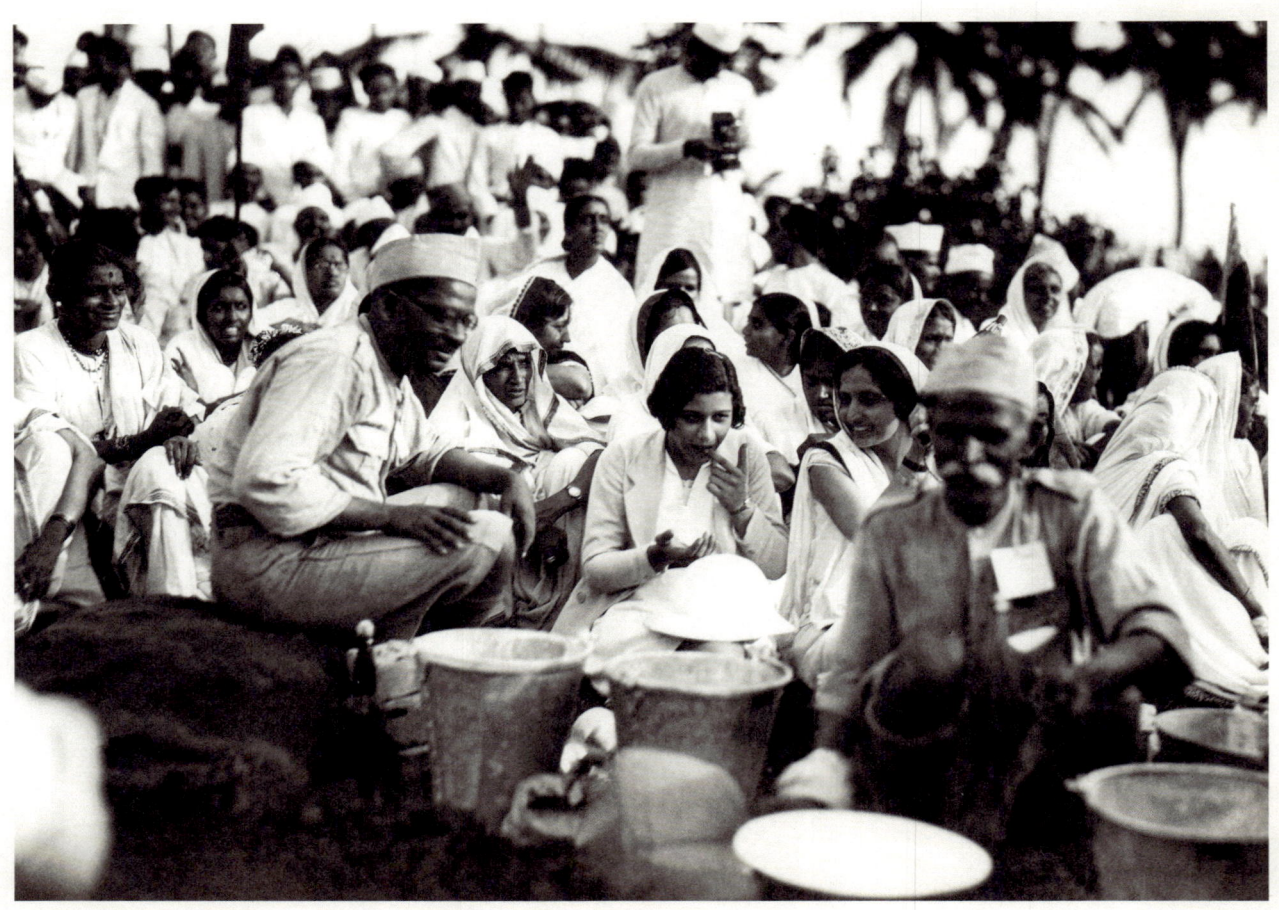

Fig. 5.11

"On 12th March 1930 Mahatma Gandhi started his historic march from the Subarmati Asharam [Sabarmati Ashram] with 79 of his followers across the river Sebarmati [Sabarmati] to lodge the civil disobedience movement in Gejerat [Gujarat], while his supporters broke the salt laws by preparing salt from the sea water at Worli. This was the first step in the movement in Bombay. Photo shows some prominent people people [sic] tasteing [tasting] the salt prepared." 1930 Gelatin Silver Print, 117 x 157 mm
ACP: 98.77.0002 (11b)

camera. Contemporary reports note that as the movement picked up momentum, such temporary sites of instruction-by-doing faced the wrath of the police who "attempted to stop salt manufacture in public by the use of lathis, by snatching away or breaking sigris and other utensils and by putting off the fire. *Satyagrahi* volunteers offered peaceful, yet heroic, resistance by forming cordons around the fire and the police used their lathis injuring many. On one occasion six times did they break the cordon, and six times did the *satyagrahi*s manufacture salt. From the next day, the police stopped coming even near the salt manufacture demonstration."[17] The album, alas, does not carry such images of explicit police action against these makeshift sites of instruction.

What its photographs do reveal is that the equipment deployed was rough and ready, clearly cobbled together from things at hand, an instance of *jugaad* (frugal innovation/improvisation). The portable *sigri* is in the foreground of some images (for example, Fig. 5.7, Fig. 5.10), others feature *chulha*s (makeshift hearths) fashioned from bricks (Fig. 5.8, Fig. 5.9). Despite the Vile Parle lawbreakers' admonition to not use copper, brass or aluminium utensils, most of the household buckets and pails, pots and pans, tumblers and *lota*s seen in the photographs of the Nursey album appear to be fashioned out of metal (for example, Fig. 5.2, Fig. 5.13); earthen pots appear in Fig. 5.10. The pedagogic impulse is obvious, with male and female learners intently looking to the teacher as he stirs the water boiling in the small *kadhai* (shallow wok), although in several photographs the pupils appear to be as curious about the (invisible) photographer for whom they readily pose without averting their gaze, possibly with an awareness that they are indeed participating in a moment worthy of being on camera (Fig. 5.8, Fig. 5.9). In a photograph of one such salt-manufacturing class in Worli, a standing figure in the background even holds a camera, presumably photographing the lesson in progress, possibly for subsequent documentation or circulation; the caption reads, "The photo shows some prominent people people [sic] tasteing [tasting] the salt" (Fig. 5.11). Manufacturing, selling *and* consuming contraband salt were all punishable offences under existing laws, but clearly these "prominent" women—one of them quite stylish in appearance—did not care. They posed for the camera, delicately tasting the fruit of their patriotic labours, however crude and unpalatable it might have been.

"When Women Refuse to Obey"

"Women of Bombay really and truly formed the vanguard of the law-breaking movement. They celebrated the occasion like a marriage festival. From the early afternoon, groups of them wended their way towards Chowpatty with 'lotas' and pots in their hands, waving the national flag amid joyous shouts of 'Vande Mataram' [Homage to Mother (India)] and 'Gandhiji ki Jai' [Long Live Gandhi]. Filling their pots with the sea water, they returned to their homes to manufacture salt."[18] Page after page in the Nursey album visually affirms this media account

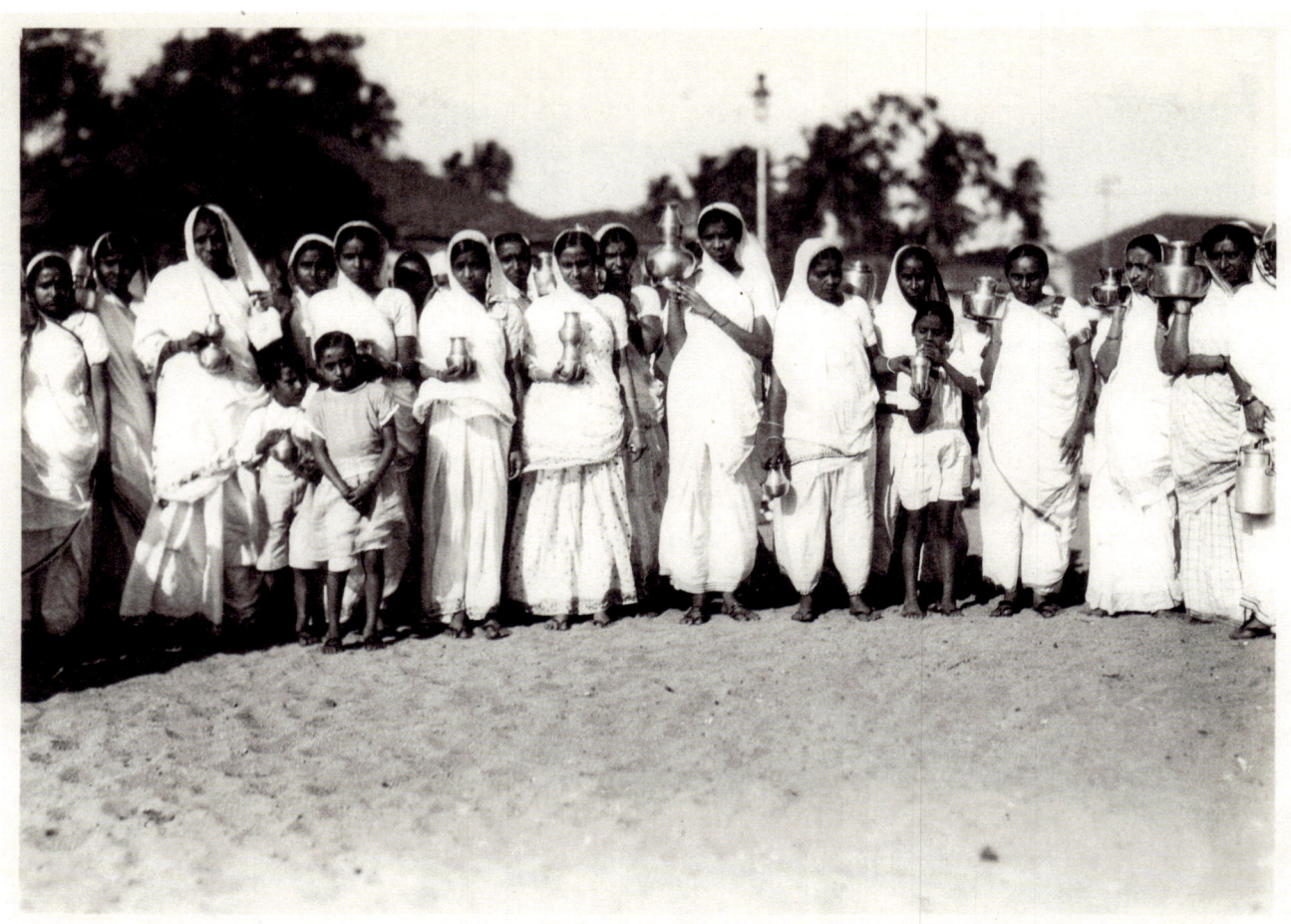

Fig. 5.12
"Young and old
women flocked to the
chaupatty [Chowpatty]
shore some with
brass utensils while
others had earthern
[earthen] pots. As
seen in the photo."
1930
Gelatin Silver Print,
114 x 155 mm
ACP: 98.77.0002 (15a)

in its focus on the disobedient woman of the city, her child(ren) frequently in tow, as she went about picketing shops selling foreign goods or liquor, raising the national flag, processing through streets with nationalist banners, delivering speeches and, of course, making salt illegally (Fig. 5.10, Fig. 5.12, see Fig. 6.5). Revealing as these black-and-white photographs are in providing a visual afterlife to women who would otherwise remain invisible, they nevertheless lack the punch of words uttered by Kamaladevi Chattopadhyay as she drew attention to the "thousands of women [who] strode down to the sea like proud warriors gracefully balancing their water pitchers. Some of scarlet red, others of somber grey earth, others of shimmering brass which scattered a thousand hues as the sun rays swept them."[19] All too often, pictures step in when words fail, but in this case, we are treated through the power of words to a moment that exceeded the capacity of the camera to capture the colours placed before it.

As is well known, when he first set out from Dandi, Gandhi was most reluctant to include women in his band of followers, even a few days into his march reportedly advising Kamaladevi, "If impatient sisters will be a little patient, they will find ample scope for their zeal and sacrifice in this national struggle for

Fig. 5.13

"The Gujeratis [Gujaratis] took special interests in the civil disobedience movement because Mahatma requested their support. Here's a group of young Gujeratis [Gujarati] women carring [carrying] sea water to their respective homes for the purpose of making salt. Photo taken 15th March 1930."

Gelatin Silver Print, 114 x 164 mm ACP: 98.77.0002 (12b) Republished in *The Illustrated Weekly of India*, 27 April 1930 with caption: "'Taking Home a Pinch of Salt': A few of the thousands of salt law breakers who took home vessels full of sea water from Chowpatty to be converted into salt. Youngs and boys freely joined in the game—Dwarkadas."

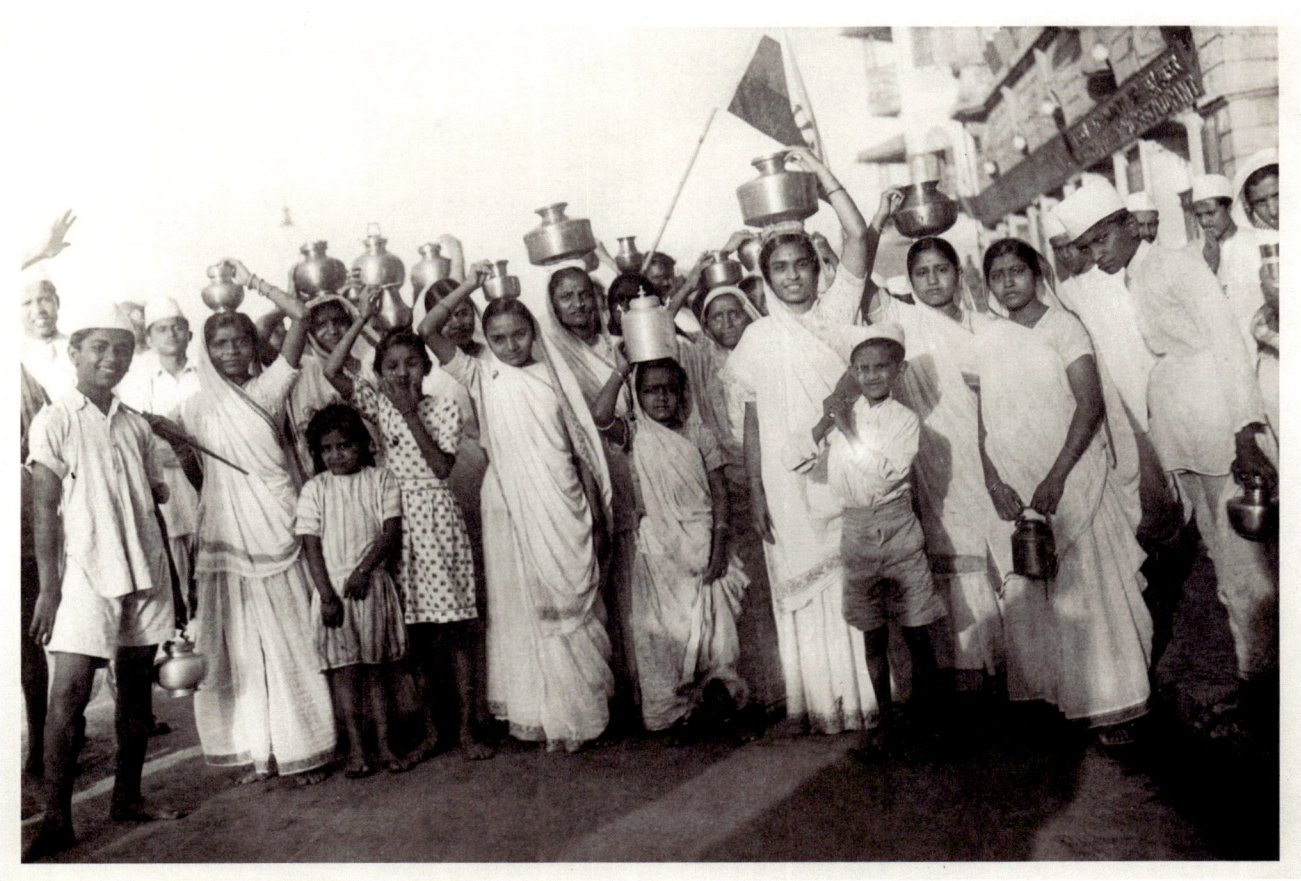

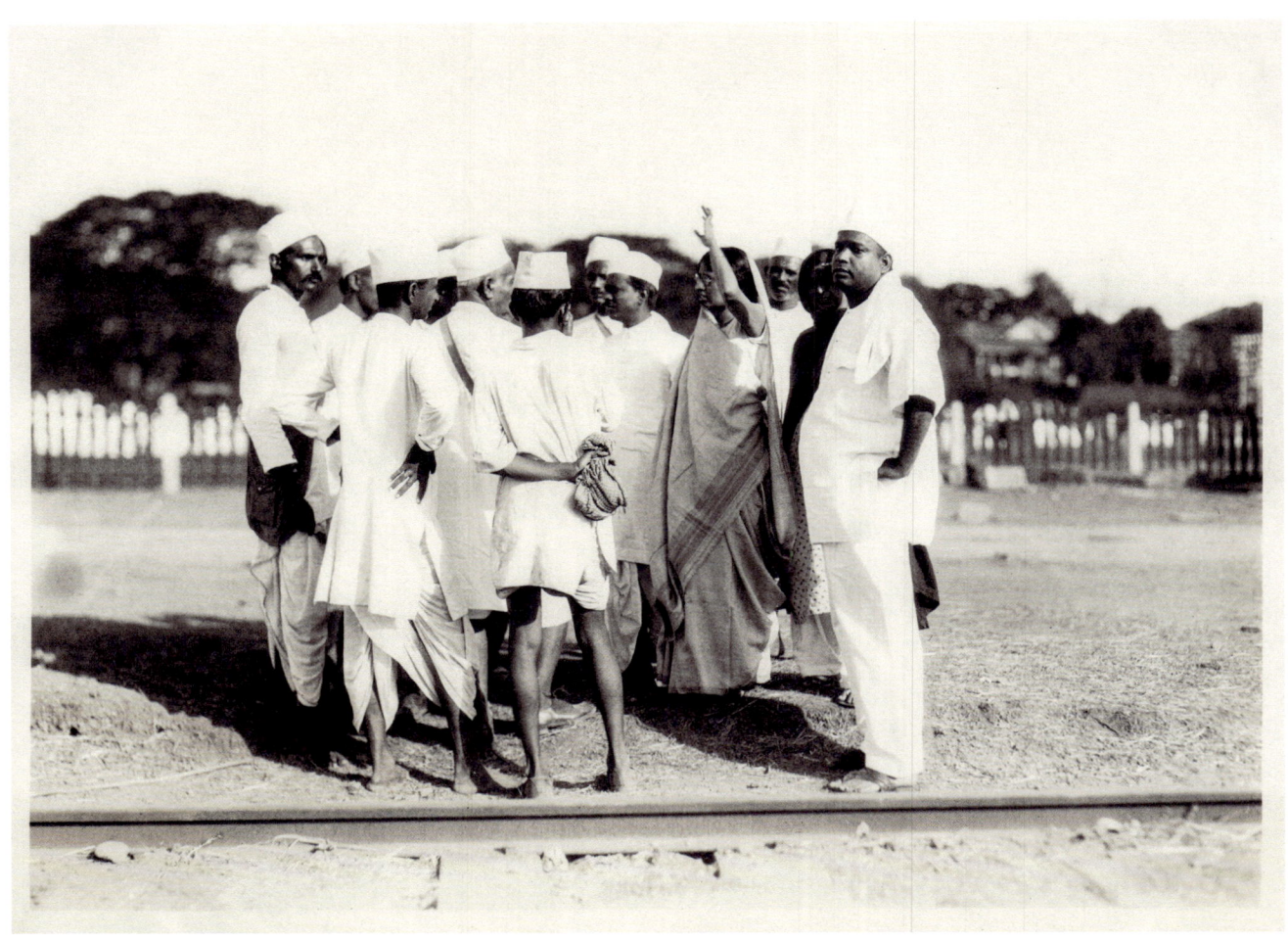

Fig. 5.14
"Mrs Lilavati Munshi
preaching the non-
violent gospel to the
Congress volunteers
at the Wadhala
[Wadala] salt pans
during the salt
raids." 1930
Gelatin Silver Print,
115 x 157 mm
ACP: 98.77.0002 (35a)

freedom."[20] But the "impatient sisters" of Bombay soon exceeded his expressed desire "to leave the salt issue to men"[21] and took the lead, becoming even "the vanguard of the law-breaking movement." The sari-clad woman of the city, carrying a *lota*, pot or pail, and with a child (or two) accompanying her, became a most visible collector of seawater, producer of salt and vendor of the contraband, not to mention a "raider" (a descriptor for *satyagrahi*s found in contemporary reports) of the government salt pans at Wadala on the northern edge of the city. Consider a photograph in the album which captures boys, girls, a few men, and several women wearing saris in the Gujarati style looking directly at the camera as they carry "sea water to their respective homes for the purpose of making salt" (Fig. 5.13). This same photo was also reproduced in *The Illustrated Weekly of India* on 27 April 1930 with the revealing caption "Taking Home a Pinch of Salt," part of a large photo spread with the provocative title "When Women Refuse to Obey." Many other photos in the Nursey album show women, sometimes on their own, at other times in the company of men, squatting in public spaces in front of the portable *sigri* with pots and pans meant to be used to boil seawater and extract salt scattered around (Fig. 5.10; see also Fig. 5.7 and Fig. 5.11).

Although so much about the Salt Satyagraha pivoted upon its consciously public enactments, the home too became a site for contraband production as a result of women's involvement, although no image in the album takes us into these intimate domestic spaces. Women leaders such as Lilavati Munshi also exhorted others, including men, to become salt manufacturers and raiders, as we learn from the caption of one of the photographs in the album (Fig. 5.14). Not least, the visible presence of children—boys, and especially girls—in these photographs is noteworthy, for clearly, these women overlooked Gandhi's expressed wish that mothers "should wait and bide their time."[22] Instead, these photographs suggest that patriotic mothers were eager to raise and nurture a generation of future *satyagrahi*s for the movement, teaching them by example on how to practise non-violent politics. At stake is the creation of the disobedient child, aiding the adult in the righteous breaking of a repressive and exploitative colonial law, *and* being caught on camera doing so.

So it is that the sari-clad patriotic woman of Bombay in these days fashioned for herself a new persona and subjectivity—that of boldly going out on the street, sometimes with her child(ren), making her way to the sea, producing a contraband substance in clear violation of colonial laws, and willing to be photographed and risking arrest for doing so (see also Chapter Eight in this volume). In a recent essay, David Arnold asks insightfully, "Is salt itself gendered? Does it have a particular value for the personal and public lives, the social roles and work regimes of women?" Noting that in most languages salt is a masculine noun, possibly reflecting the association of men with its production, he rightly points out that salt-making was traditionally women's work as well. The photographs of the Nursey album provide visual affirmation that the Civil Disobedience Movement gave an opportunity to urban and upper-caste middle-class women "far removed from the salt-caked grind of manual labour" to come to the fore, even allowing some among them, by virtue of their special relationship to this mineral as homemakers, to assert autonomy and leadership.[23]

Contraband City

As is apparent from the essays in this volume, the photographs of the Nursey album visually chart the transformation of the public spaces, iconic colonial buildings, streets, bazaars and shops of Bombay into sites of civil disobedience and non-violent action in the face, repeatedly, of police brutality and violence.[24] As the zeal for making contraband salt spread in the weeks and months after 6 April 1930, numerous neighbourhoods, many critical to the exercise of colonial administrative power and social life, were transformed into hotspots of contraband activity, including the seashore at Mahalakshmi and Chowpatty in the city proper, and Juhu and Vile Parle with their prosperous Gujarati and Marwari enclaves in the northern suburbs (see also Fig. 6.4a and 6.4b). The

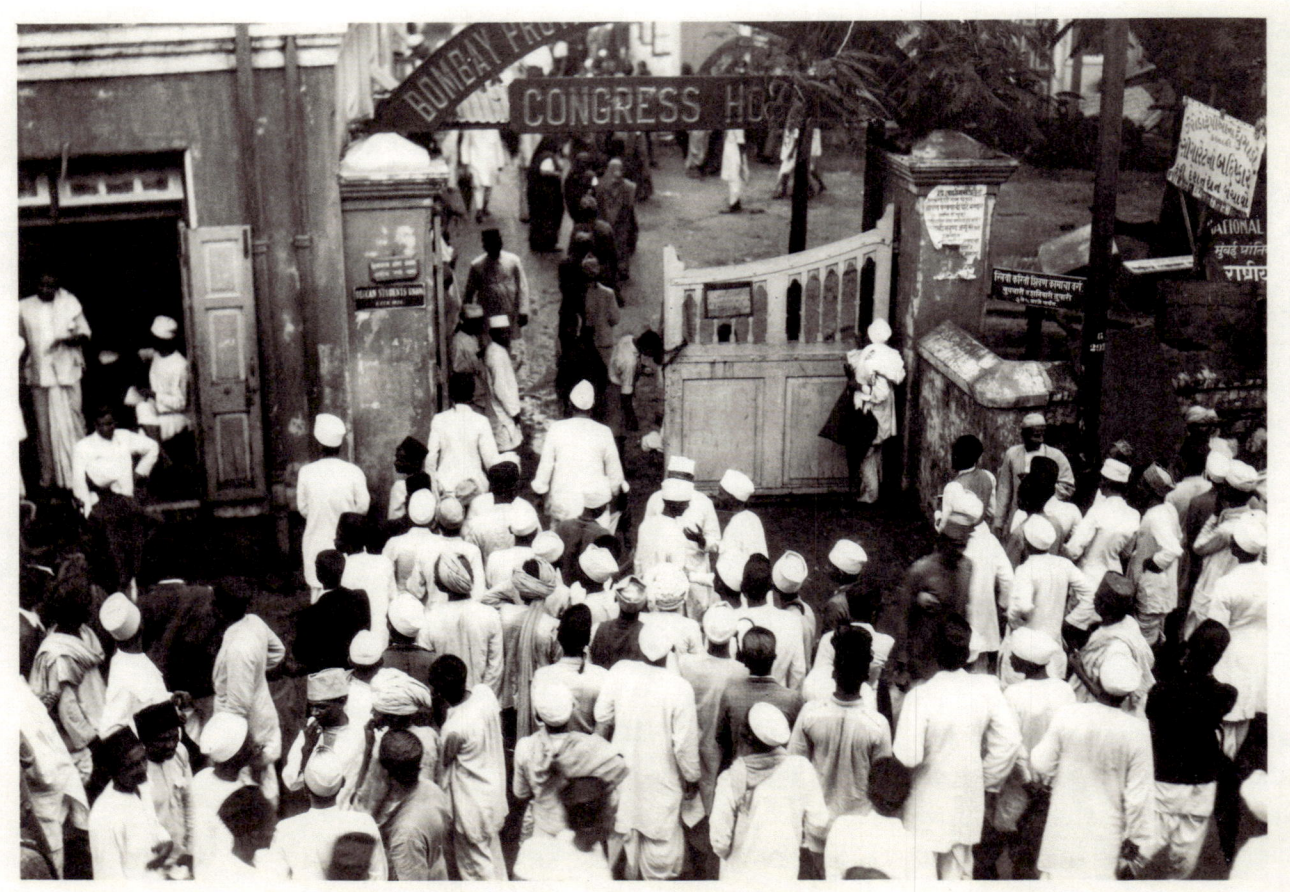

Fig. 5.15
"The Bombay Congress house." c. 1930–1931
Gelatin Silver Print,
115 x 160 mm
ACP: 98.77.0002 (107b)

ideological and material centre for the entire movement was Congress House in Girgaum (Fig. 5.15)—a quintessential middle-class Maharashtrian locality—which metamorphosed, almost overnight, into a miniature "salt factory," with makeshift cement pans constructed on its terrace, and pots and basins bubbling away in the compound (see also Chapter Two in this volume). It served as the meeting point from where volunteers proceeded to the shore, as also noted in a contemporary report which remarked on what a sight it was "to see thousands of ladies fetching sea water ... with pitchers on their heads and pouring it into the Congress House Salt Factory."[25] Impromptu salt classes were conducted on the premises (Fig. 5.7), drawing the wrath of the police, but to no avail, it seems, for as soon as they left the House reverted to a hub of disobedient activity.

Another hotspot was the Esplanade, renamed Azad Maidan ("Freedom Field"), as also evidenced by a photograph in the album which draws attention to "Congress volunteers preparing salt," the men all clad in white *khadi*, several wearing Gandhi caps, the national flag intensifying the aura of collective defiance (Fig. 5.16). The photographer has also partially caught a young man clad in dark shorts at the right edge of the frame, passively observing the scene of disobedience unfold before his eyes, reminding us that many Bombay residents

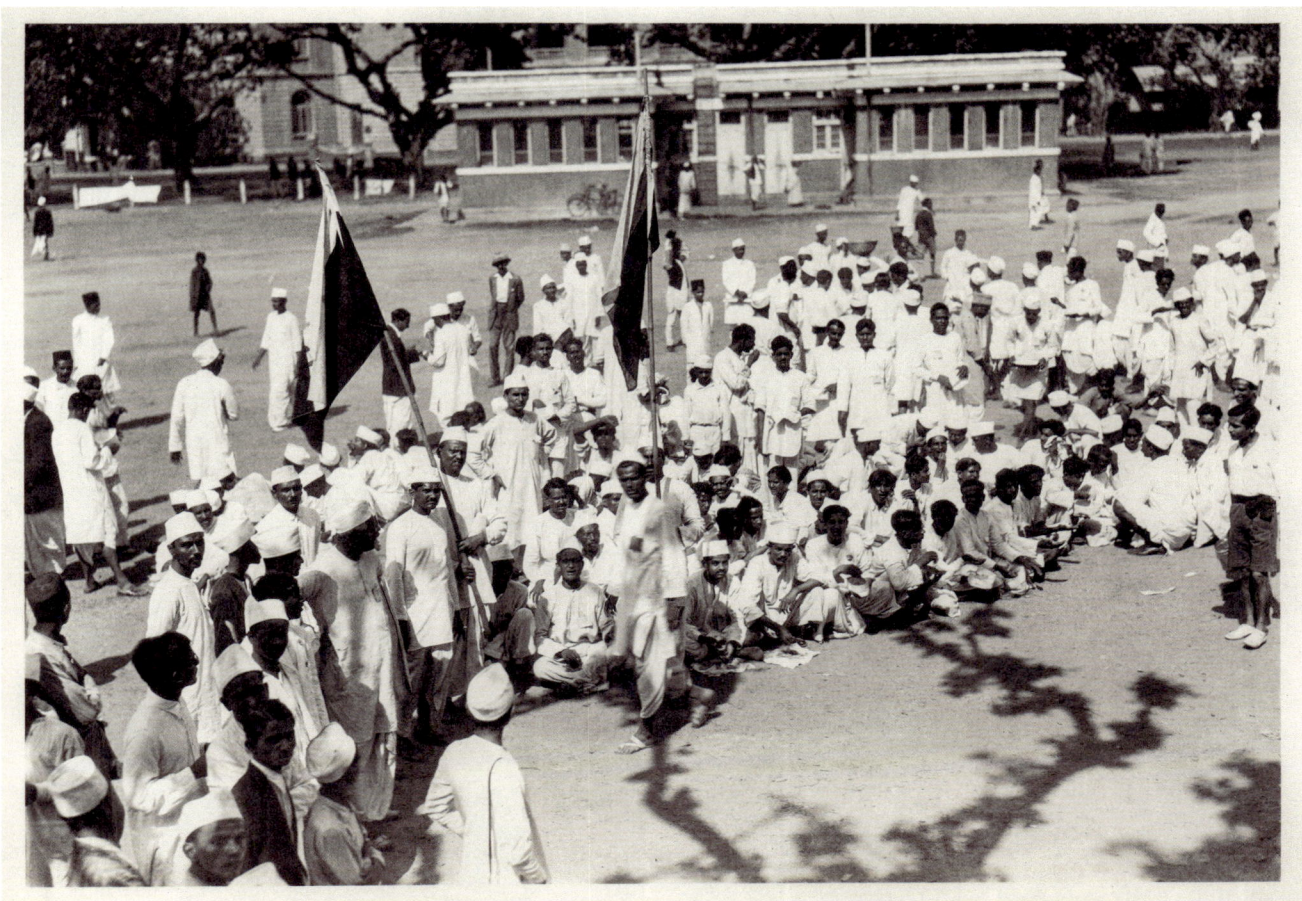

Fig. 5.16
"Congress volunteers
preparing salt on the
Azad maidan."
c. 1930—1931
Gelatin Silver Print,
115 x 160 mm
ACP: 98.77.0002 (42b)

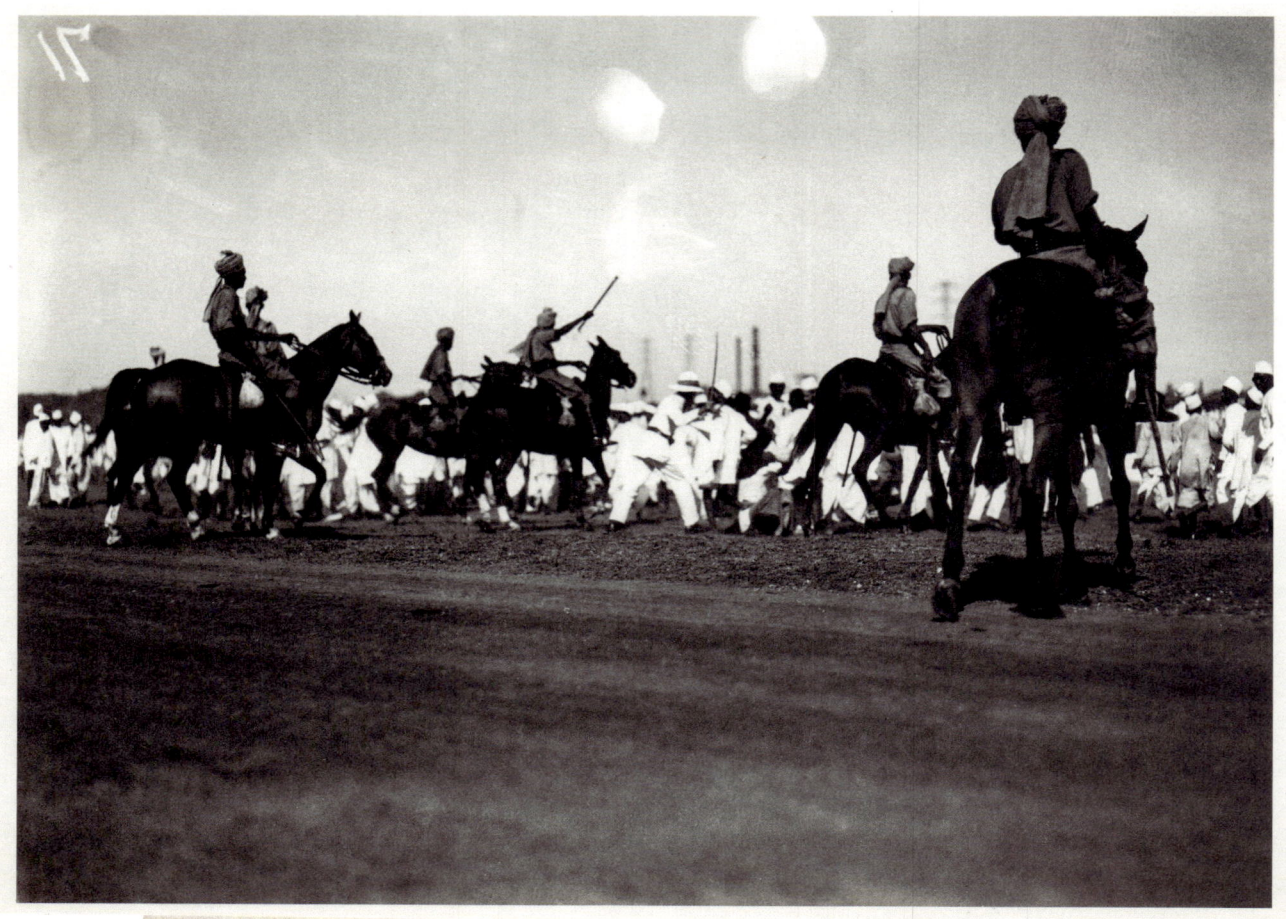

Fig. 5.17
"Many hundreds were injured from lathi blows during the recent Wadhala [Wadala] raids. Here the mounted police are seen deliverying [delivering] a lathi charge." 1930 Gelatin Silver Print, 115 x 158 mm
ACP: 98.77.0002 (36b)

did remain bystanders and spectators despite the numerous attempts by the Congress to persuade them to volunteer for the movement.[26]

The most visible in the album of such hotspots is Wadala to which, after an initial foray on 16 April, large numbers of salt *satyagrahi*s, also named "raiders" by the police, ventured, almost daily, from mid-May until early June, in order to "raid" the government salt pans and depot and make, or make off with, salt. The camera followed these sorties, albeit from a distance, offering visual evidence for something largely masked in contemporary police reports. The *lathi* was used— and frequently—both by brown and white policemen, many of whom showed up on the scene mounted on horses, as is visible in photo after photo (for example, Fig. 5.17).[27] Among these photographs of vicious brutality, however, is a wondrous image of almost lyrical beauty that reminds us that in the midst of the fiercest battles, moments of solitude, even peace and harmony, may be found, and also offering a valuable reminder that even the most "documentary" of images might carry an aesthetic charge. Titled "A Salt Raider on the Wadhala Salt Pans," the photograph captures not one but three raiders in the foreground clad in white, two others squatting in the far distance (Fig. 5.18). Dark clouds in

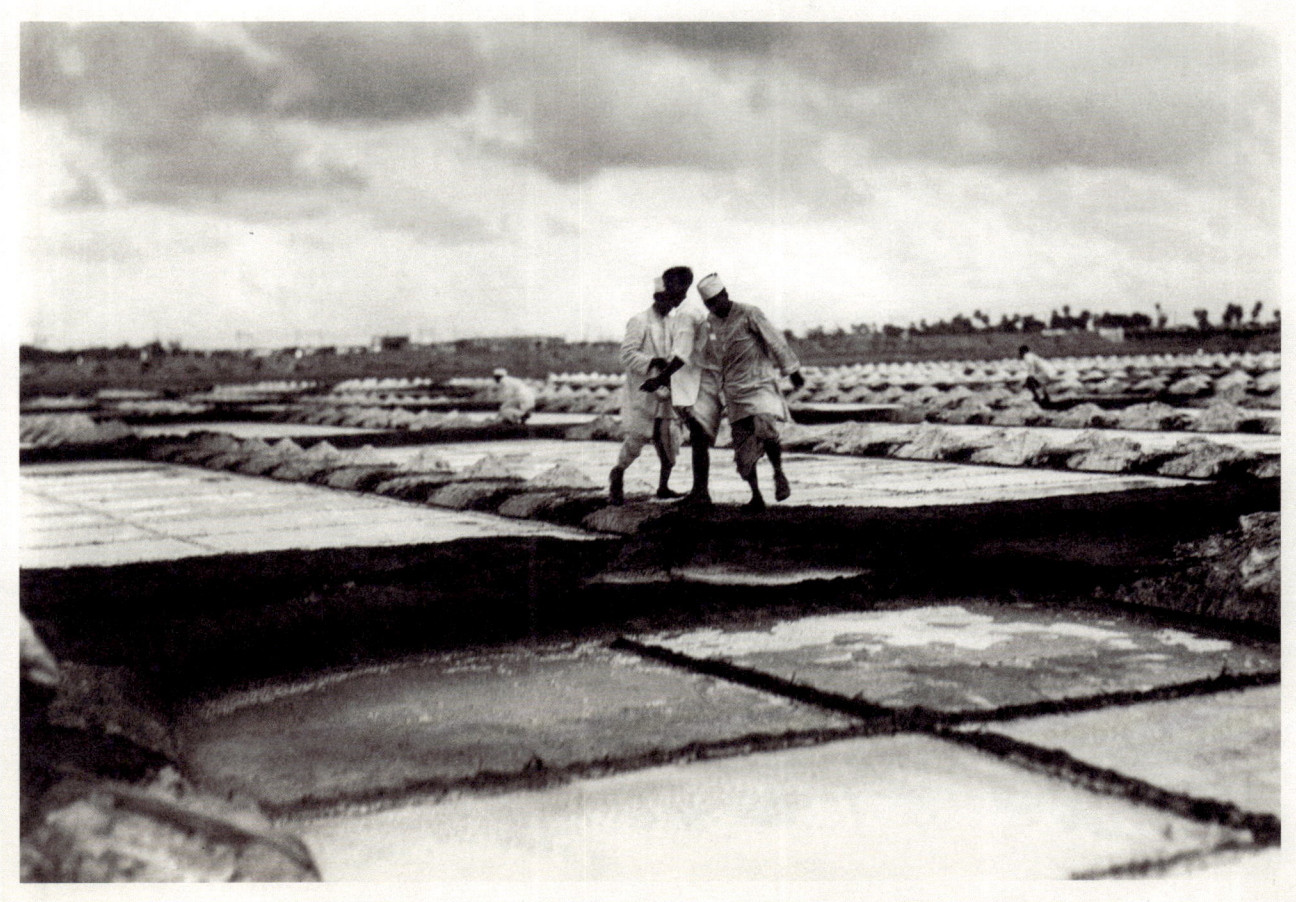

Fig. 5.18
"A salt raider on the
Wadhala [Wadala] salt
pans." 1930
Gelatin Silver Print,
115 x 161 mm
ACP: 98.77.0002 (34b)

the sky above suggest the imminence of the monsoon (which the contemporary records also note). Piled up behind the men—and into the distance as far as the eye can see—are heaps of the mundane mineral that had become magical during the Salt Satyagraha, for which the patriotic residents of Bombay were prepared to take on the might of a colonial empire, prepared to court arrest and grievous injury, and even to die.

Coda: Salt in the Aftermath

What memory remains of these potent months and moments in this most disobedient of British India's cities when so many came together to do something that was quite foreign and new to them, and yet which they embraced with a courage, passion and imagination that led the authorities to sit up and take stock—and bring the full force of the law and the *lathi* to bear down? Precious little, is what one can conclude. This is what makes the Nursey album such an important archival and historical object, for it can be viewed as an attempt by its maker(s) in the aftermath of the many-faceted Bombay *satyagraha* to visually recall, remember, caption and to hand down to posterity some images of these times which would otherwise have been lost. Over the decades, the Salt

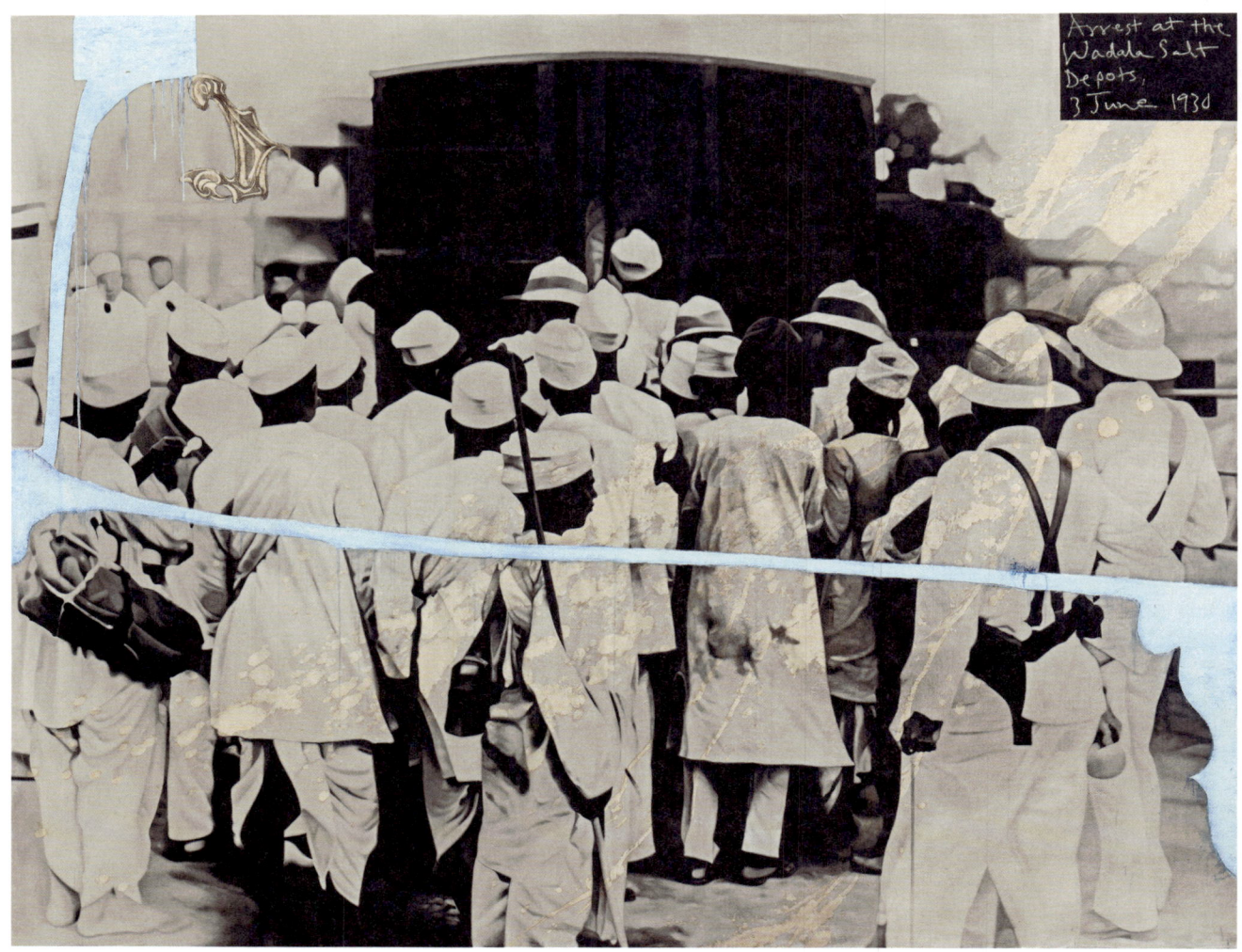

In the image, handwritten text reads: *Arrest at the Wadala Salt Depots, 3 June 1930*

Fig. 5.19
Atul Dodiya, *Arrest at the Wadala Salt Depots-3rd June 1930* Oil, acrylic with marble dust and oil-stick on canvas, 70 x 90 inches (1778 x 2286 mm), 2014 Image courtesy: The artist

Satyagraha of 1930 has indeed attracted the attention of the public, the politician and especially the artist, but typically the focus has been on Dandi where Gandhi first staged his dramatic disobedience.[28] Yet, as the Nursey album so powerfully reminds us, Bombay too mattered in turning what Viceroy Irwin first dismissed as Gandhi's "silly salt stunt" into an anticolonial movement of national, even global, consequence.[29] It took another resident of Mumbai (the erstwhile Bombay), the renowned artist Atul Dodiya (b. 1959), to conscientiously retrieve the memory of that moment and place it within the horizon of our times in a series completed in 2014 as "a project for the Republic of India," which includes a luminous work titled *Arrest at the Wadala Salt Depots—3rd June 1930* (Fig. 5.19). I give the last word to the artist himself: "Not many people know that during the Salt Satyagraha, thousands of people went to the Wadala salt pans to pick up salt... They were lathi-charged and then arrested by the police. Police lathi-charged so many people protesting against the unjust salt-tax at the V.T. station..."[30] The artist, however, "knows," and remembers, and so are we obliged to do so, as citizens and inheritors of such an important—and disobedient—past.

Notes

Acknowledgements: I thank all the contributors to this volume for their thoughtful engagement with the ideas in this essay. Special appreciation to Avrati Bhatnagar and Debashree Mukherjee for their astute comments on an earlier draft. I also owe deep gratitude to Avrati Bhatnagar for sharing some of the archival findings of her doctoral research which has enriched this essay.

1. *The Illustrated Weekly of India*, Late News Supplement, 20 April 1930, p. 69.

2. An early historian of the city—and former editor of the Bombay-based *Times of India*— even insisted that it was "Bombay researchers who … provided the moral, economic and political justification" for protesting the colonial monopoly on salt, "long before Gandhi evolved details of his Dandi March." See K. Gopalaswami, *Gandhi and Bombay* (Bombay: Bharatiya Vidya Bhavan, 1965), pp. 240–41. For a more recent account from a Gandhian perspective of the events that transpired in the city during these months, see Usha Thakkar and Sandhya Mehta, *Gandhi in Bombay: Towards Swaraj* (New Delhi: Oxford University Press, 2017), pp. 159–201.

3. *The Bombay Chronicle*, 11 March 1930, p. 1.

4. My concept of "salt drama" is indebted to Jim Masselos's influential essay "Audiences, Actors, and Congress Dramas: Crowd Events in Bombay City in 1930", *South Asia*, vol. 8, no. 1 (1985), pp. 71–86.

5. Quoted in K.K. Chaudhary (ed.), *Source Material for a History of India's Freedom Movement*, vol. XI (Bombay: Maharashtra State Gazetteers Office, 1991), p. 14.

6. ibid., p. 20.

7. File no. 95, Kamaladevi Chattopadhyay papers, Nehru Memorial Museum and Library, New Delhi, n.d., emphasis added. Many thanks to Avrati Bhatnagar for directing me to this wonderful comment from her archival research.

8. Masselos, "Audiences, Actors, and Congress Dramas", p. 74.

9. *The Bombay Chronicle*, 14 April 1930, p. 1.

10. *The Illustrated Weekly of India*, 6 April 1930, p. 25. The Bombay-based *Times of India* was consistently hostile to Gandhi's salt campaign, publishing a cartoon on 28 March 1930 in which civil disobedience was caricatured as "a Frankenstein of the East," as noted by Elisa DeCourcy and Miles Taylor in"Salt and the National Imaginary: The Photojournalism of the Dandi Satyagraha", *South Asia: Journal of South Asian Studies*, vol. 46, no. 4 (2023), pp. 820–33; see especially p. 824.

11. For a photo not in the album where we get a glimpse of the sea at this moment of departure, see Thakkar and Mehta, *Gandhi in Bombay*, p. 178.

12. *The Illustrated Weekly of India*, 27 April 1930, p. 21. See also a similar photograph with the caption "Women and children filling brass pots with sea water for manufacturing salt at home in defiance of the Salt Act", published in the same magazine on 20 April 1930. Similarly, *The Times of India* published the photograph in Fig. 6.5 with the caption, "A group of women returning with seawater in pails from which they propose to manufacture salt."

13. Stephen Legg, "Political Lives at Sea: Working and Socialising to and from the India Round Table Conference in London, 1930–1932", *Journal of Historical Geography*, vol. 68 (2020), pp. 21–32.

14. David Arnold, "Salt: An Afterword", *South Asia: Journal of South Asian Studies*, vol. 46, no. 4 (2023), pp. 886–94, at p. 888.

15. *The Bombay Chronicle*, 4 April 1930, p. 7.

16. K.K. Chaudhary (ed.), *Source Material*. See also *The Illustrated Weekly of India*, 27 April 1930, p. 21.

17. Report of the Bombay Provincial Committee, Bombay, 13 June 1930 (AICC G102 to G106 1930, Nehru Memorial Museum and Library Archives, New Delhi). I thank Avrati Bhatnagar for this reference.

18. *The Bombay Chronicle*, 14 April 1930, p. 1.

19. Quoted in Avrati Bhatnagar, "Disobedient Women in a Consumer City: Picturing Swadeshi Culture in Interwar Bombay", unpublished Ph.D. dissertation, Department of History, Duke University (2024).

20. *The Bombay Chronicle*, 24 March 1930, p. 1. For a slightly different take on this moment based on her memoir, see Nico Slate, *Kamaladevi Chattopadhyay: The Art of Freedom* (New Delhi: HarperCollins, 2024), p. 51. There is much written on Gandhi and the women of India during the Salt Satyagraha, but for a recent piece, see Rosalind Parr, "Self-Sacrifice, Suffrage, and Socialism: Gandhi and the Mobilisation of Women, 1930–1931", *South Asia: Journal of South Asian Studies*, vol. 46, no. 4 (2023), pp. 834–50.

21. Quoted in Bhatnagar, "Disobedient Women in a Consumer City".

22. *The Bombay Chronicle*, 24 March 1930, p. 1. I thank Avrati Bhatnagar for reminding me of this.

23. Arnold, "Salt", pp. 887–88.

24. For a discussion of the "spatial templates" of Bombay during the Salt Satyagraha, see Robert Rahman Raman, "Civil Disobedience and the City: Congress and the Working Classes in Bombay, c. 1930–1932", in Prashant Kidambi, Manjiri Kamat and Rachel Dwyer (eds.), *Bombay Before Mumbai: Essays in Honour of Jim Masselos* (New Delhi: Oxford University Press, 2019).

25. Report of the Bombay Provincial Committee, Bombay, 13 June 1930 (AICC G102 to G106 1930, Nehru Memorial Museum and Library, New Delhi). I thank Avrati Bhatnagar for sharing this reference.

26. Masselos, "Audiences, Actors and Congress Dramas".

27. Avrati Bhatnagar and Sumathi Ramaswamy, "Light Writing on the Lathi Raj: Bombay, 1930–31", *History of Photography*, vol. 45, no. 3–4 (2022), pp. 304–19.

28. Sumathi Ramaswamy, *Gandhi in the Gallery: The Art of Disobedience* (New Delhi: Roli Books, 2020), pp. 85–109.

29. ibid., p. 108.

30. Naushil Mehta, "An Artist's Jugalbandi with Art Viewers: Conversation with Atul Dodiya", in *7000 Museums: A Project for the Republic of India: Atul Dodiya* (Mumbai: Bhau Daji Lad Museum, 2015), pp. 17–50, at p. 37.

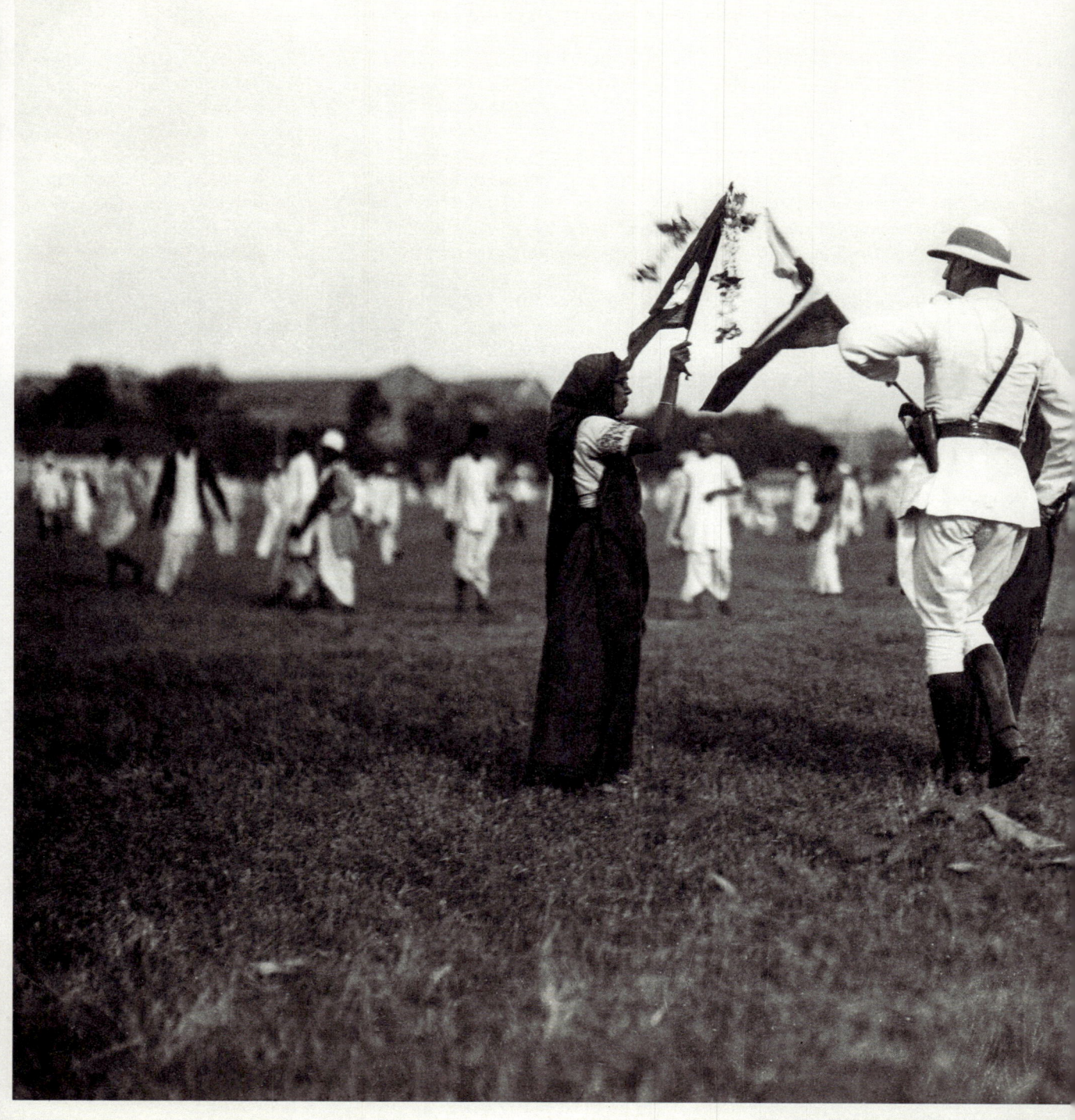

A police officer snatching away the flag from
a Desh Sevika during a meeting on the Esplanade
maidan Bombay.

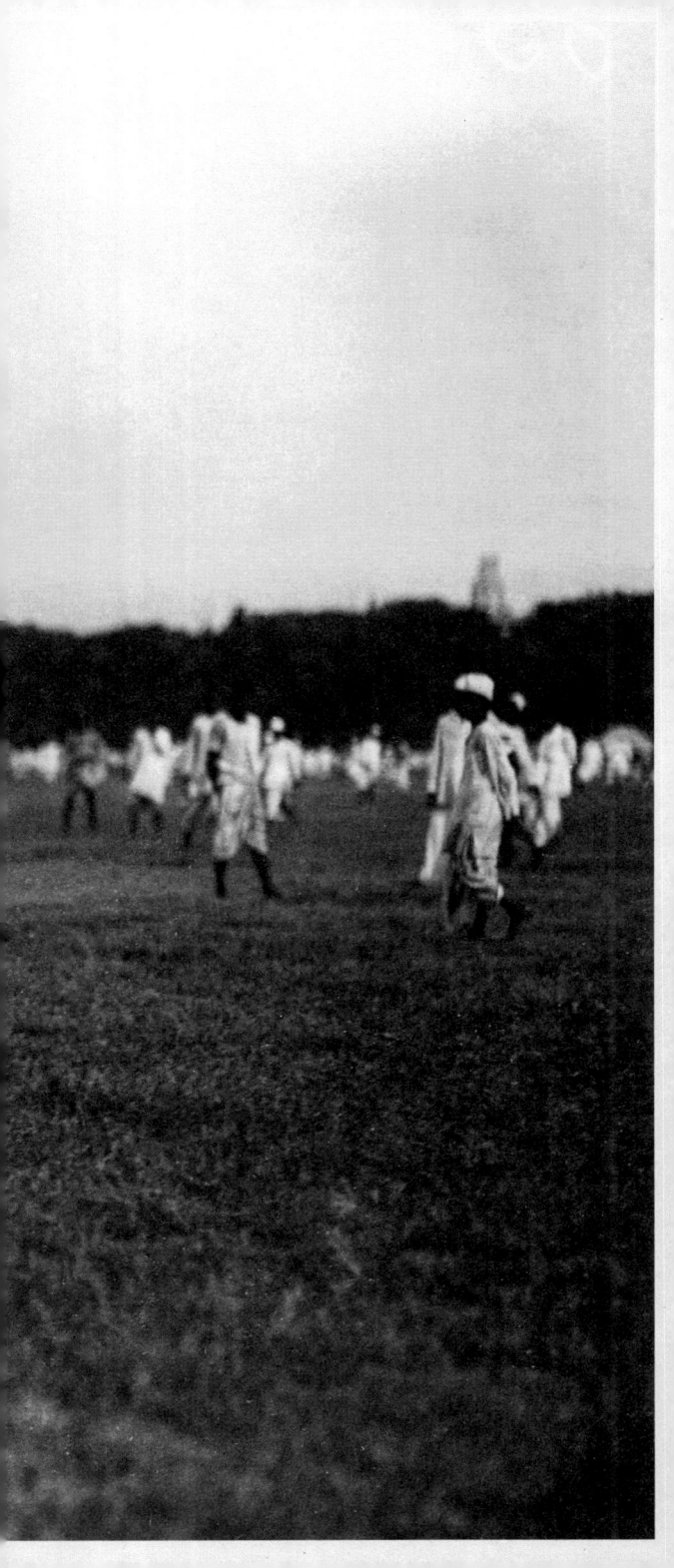

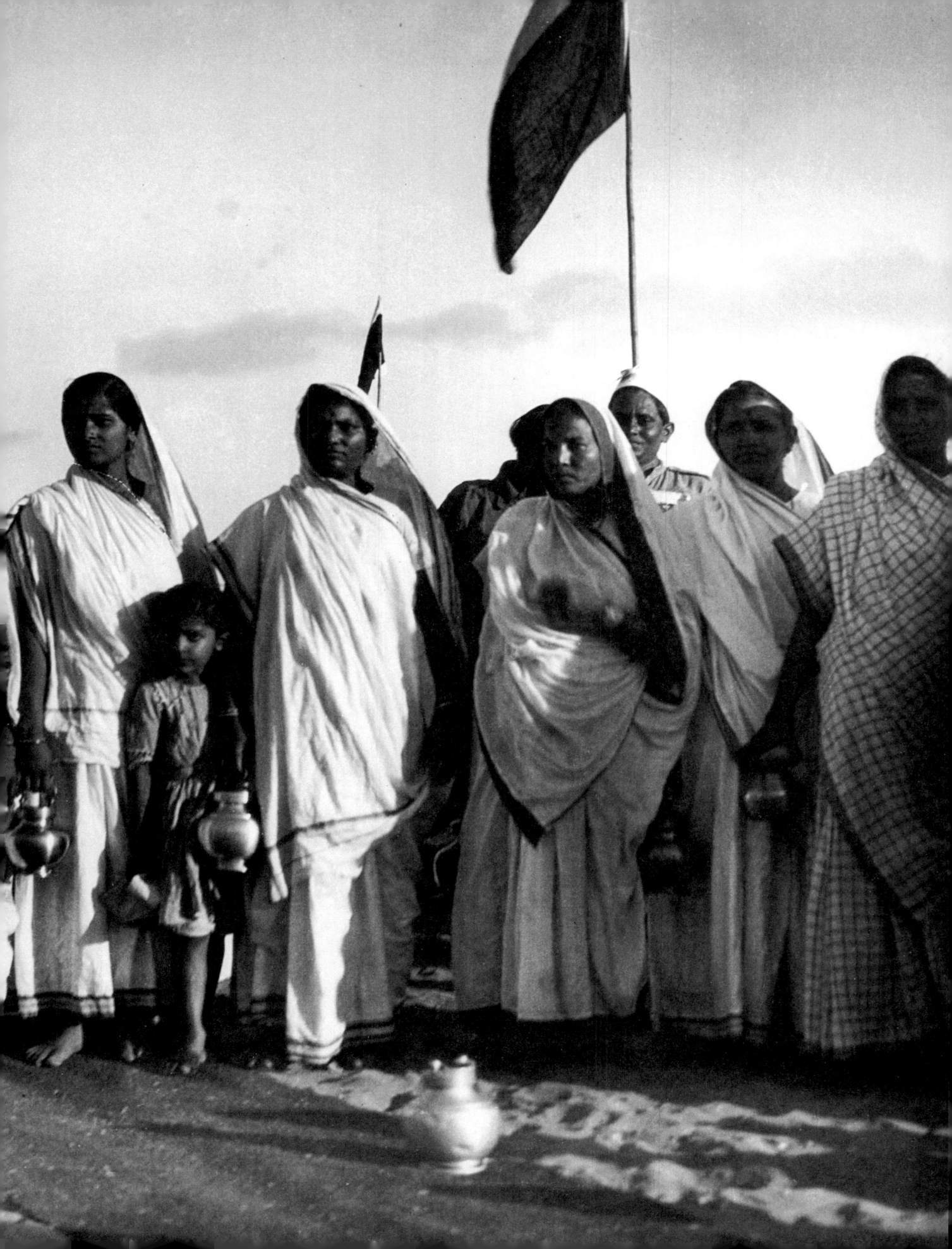

CHAPTER 6

THE SUBURBAN CONGRESSWOMAN

Murali Ranganathan

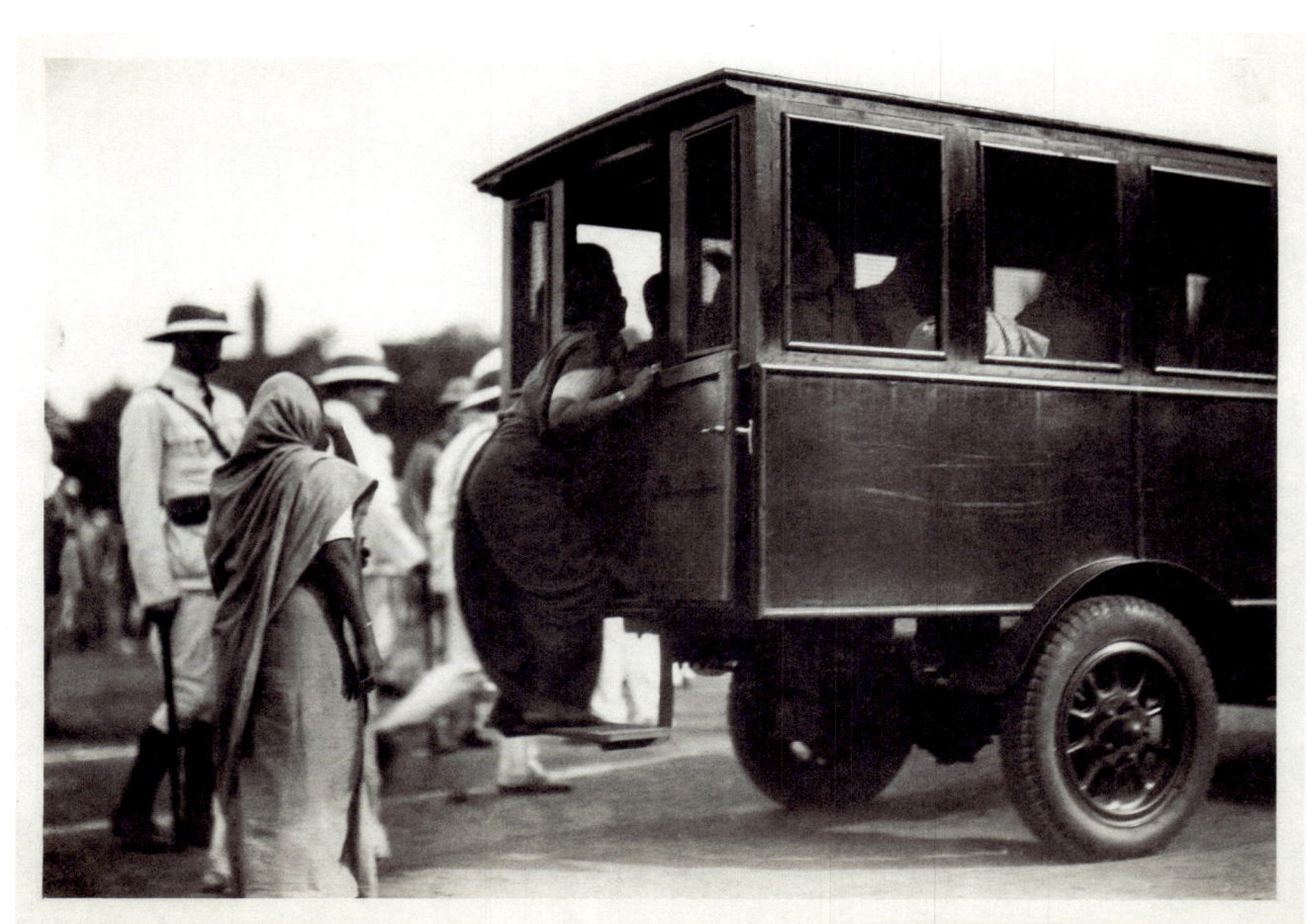

Women pickets arrested outside the Town hall when the picketing of Toddy shop license was held.

On 26 October 1930, when the Civil Disobedience Movement was at its crescendo, the Bombay War Council, the team of senior Congress leaders developing and implementing strategies for *satyagraha*, attempted to hold a flag salutation ceremony at the Azad ("Free") Maidan, formerly a part of the Esplanade of Bombay, renamed so by the nationalists. After a group of male demonstrators were arrested, a group of women activists from the Desh Sevika Sangh entered the fray. They resisted all attempts by the police to seize their flags and stood their ground in spite of a *lathi* charge (Fig. 8.15). A few women were arrested, but the rest were bundled into a police van (Fig. 6.1), and dropped off at Ghatkopar, about 15 miles (nearly 24 km) away, in the Bombay Suburban District.[1] Implicit in this action was the assumption that the suburbs of Bombay were unlikely sites of protest; the suburbs neither had the monumental setting which the city of Bombay could provide in plenty, nor could they command the audiences necessary to render protests meaningful. And by temporarily exiling women into the suburban wilderness, the colonial regime assumed that it could thus discourage their further participation in the protests. But were these assumptions borne out by the actual situation on the ground?

Of the 245 photographs in the Nursey album, just two are captioned with locations in the suburbs of Bombay. And both of them depict women picketing the auction of toddy shop licences at Bandra in the Bombay Suburban District in July 1930. In one photograph (Fig. 6.2), women with their backs to the camera are, as the caption suggests, "urging bidders not to bid for the auction," even as a posse of *lathi*-bearing policemen look on. Women were at the forefront of the agitation—leading processions, picketing foreign cloth shops, hoisting Congress flags, breaking the salt laws, protesting against the evils of alcohol—all through 1930-31. And the Nursey album features hundreds of women, many from the Bombay suburbs. On the other hand, though these areas were significant sites of nationalist protest, they do not seem to have caught the attention of photographers. The suburban Congresswomen and their suburban protest sites have both suffered varying degrees of erasure, not just in the Nursey album but also in the larger historical narrative. And, in most cases, they haven't merited a mention in the footnotes of history.

PAGES 150—151
"A police officer snatching away the flag from a Desh Sevika during a meeting on the Esplanade maidan Bombay." c. 1930—1931
Gelatin Silver Print, 117 x 159 mm
ACP: 98.77.0002 (51b)

PAGE 152
"Daily there were numerous batches of salt satyagrahis who fetch water from the sea shore to the Congress house to prepare salt[.] As seen in the photo." (Detail, see p. 160)

Fig. 6.1
"Women pickets arrested outside the Town hall when the picketing of Toddy shop license was held." c. 1930—1931
Gelatin Silver Print, 115 x 160 mm
ACP: 98.77.0002 (68b)
The arrested women were dropped off at Ghatkopar, about 15 miles away, in the Bombay Suburban District.

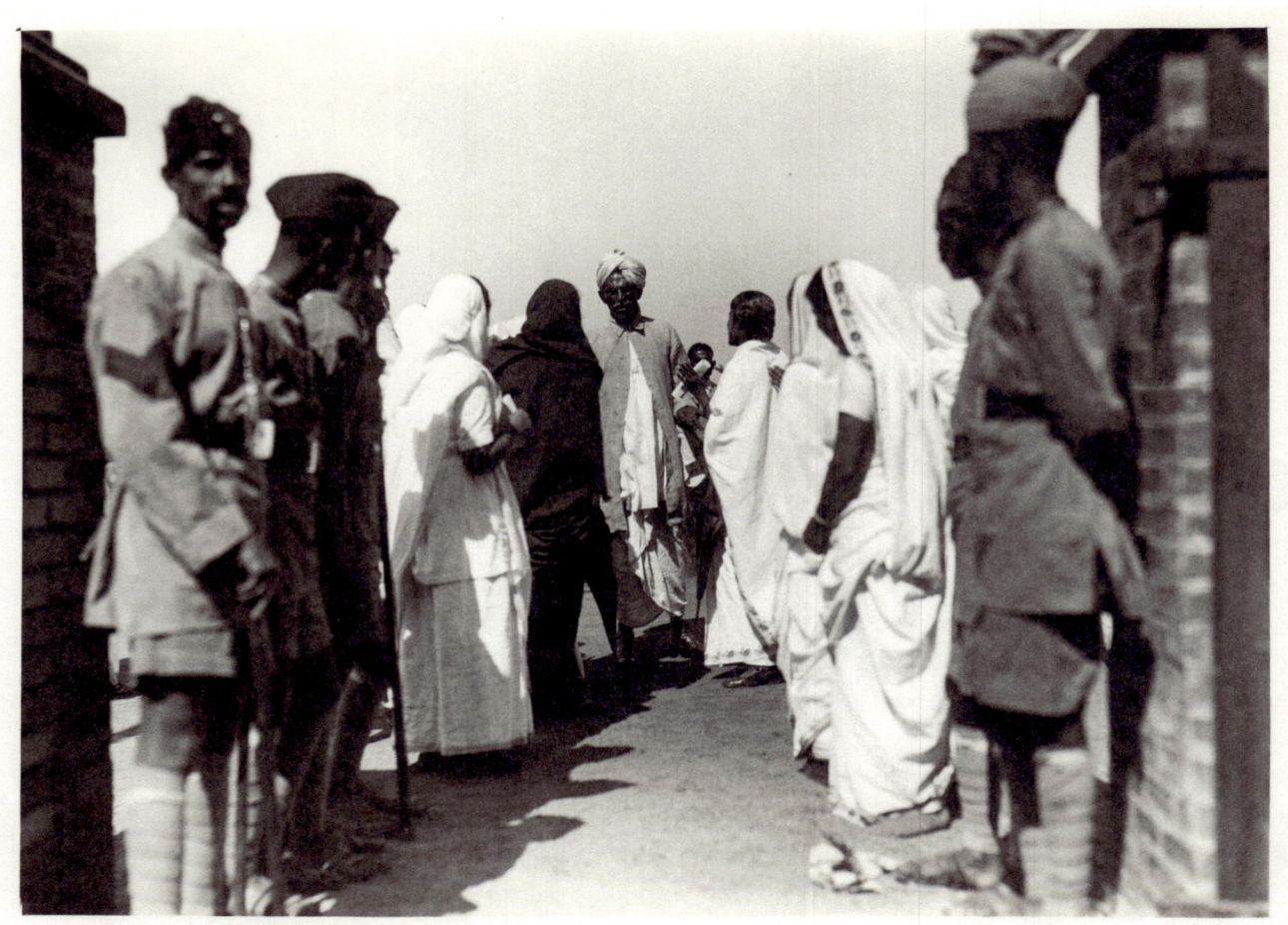

Fig. 6.2
"[B]andra toddy
shop auction day.
Picketing by ladies,
urging bidders not to
bid for auction."
Gelatin Silver Print,
116 x 158 mm
ACP: 98.77.0002 (111b)
This photograph was
taken in July 1930.

Is it possible to imagine a nationalist historiography where some of these suburban women and their sites of protest are foregrounded? Can we, a hundred years later, map those sites of resistance which were as important to the movement as any other? And is it possible to assess the significance of these women's contributions to a movement which was national in scale?

The Suburbs of Bombay

Even before the Mahim Causeway connecting the islands of Bombay and Salsette was built in the 1840s, Bandra was a suburb from where a few people, crossing the Mahim creek on boats, commuted daily to work in Bombay. The southern parts of Salsette gradually began to assume a suburban character in the second half of the 19th century. The plague epidemic which lasted nearly two decades from 1896 and the influenza pandemic of 1918–19 contributed to increased migration from Bombay to Salsette, especially by middle-class families. By the 1920s, quite a few urban agglomerations, planned and unplanned, had emerged in Salsette. This led to the South Salsette *taluka* of Thana district being designated as the Bombay Suburban District; its boundaries were largely coterminous with that of contemporary Greater Bombay.[2] While the municipalities of Bandra and

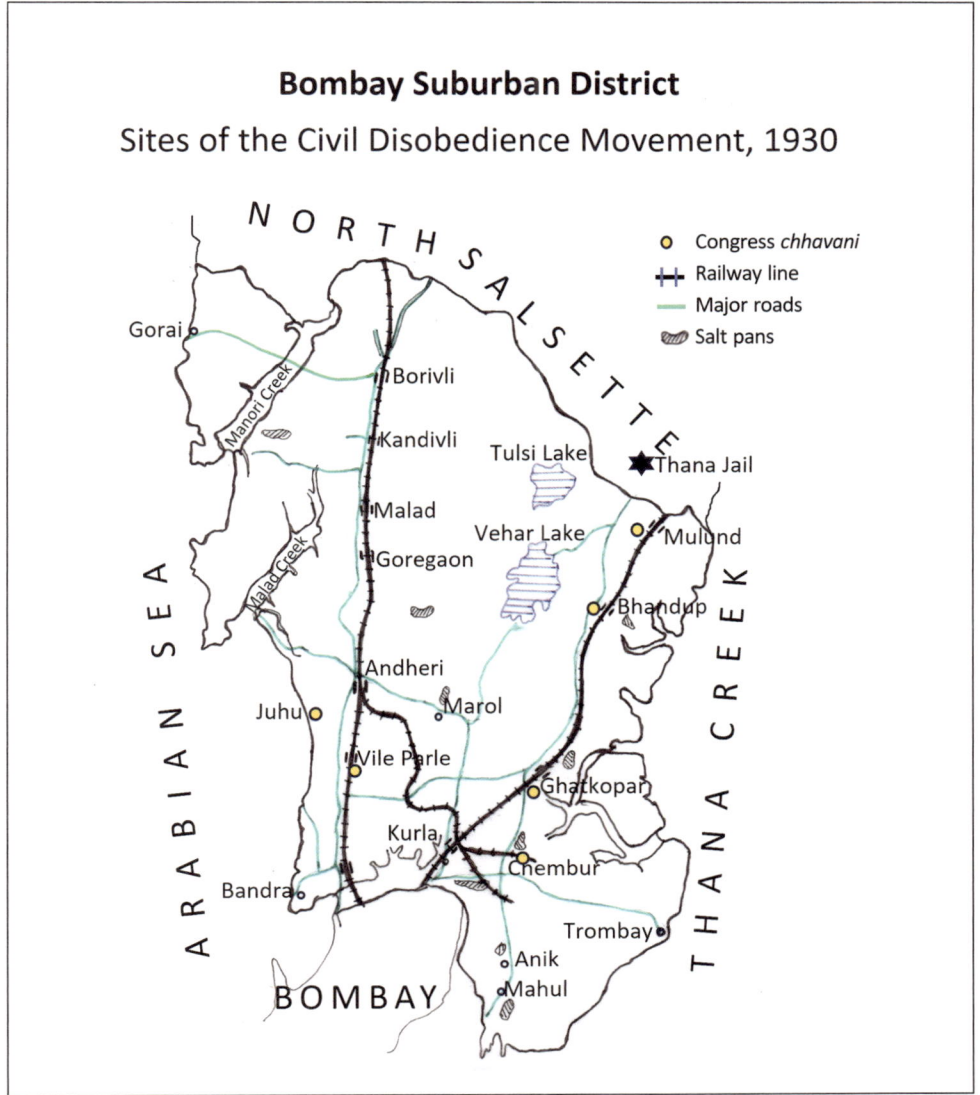

Bombay Suburban District
Sites of the Civil Disobedience Movement, 1930

Legend:
- Congress *chhavani*
- Railway line
- Major roads
- Salt pans

Labels on map: NORTH SALSETTE, Gorai, Borivli, Kandivli, Tulsi Lake, Thana Jail, Manori Creek, Malad, Vehar Lake, Mulund, Malad Creek, Goregaon, Bhandup, ARABIAN SEA, Andheri, Marol, THANA CREEK, Juhu, Vile Parle, Ghatkopar, Kurla, Chembur, Bandra, Trombay, Anik, Mahul, BOMBAY, THANA CREEK

Fig. 6.3
Bombay Suburban District: Sites of the Civil Disobedience Movement. Cartography by Lakshmi Venkatesh, 2024.

Kurla had been in existence from the 19th century, the ones for Vile Parle-Andheri and Ghatkopar-Kirol were more recent. Mulund and Chembur, modelled after the garden cities of Letchworth and Welwyn in the vicinity of London, were still at a nascent stage and housed a few thousand people each.[3] All these towns were connected to the city by the suburban railway network, and one could reach Victoria Terminus in less than an hour. Particularly relevant to the Civil Disobedience Movement were the salt pans which dotted the landscape of the Bombay Suburban District (Fig. 6.3).

During 1930–31, these suburban towns not only served as logistical bases for the Bombay campaigns of the Congress but also were the sites for breaking the salt laws, picketing toddy vendors and undertaking flag salutation marches and other forms of protest. Each of these suburban towns already had local Congress committees; they also formed *prabhat pheri* (lit., "dawn rounds") and *vanar sena*

Fig. 6.4a, Fig. 6.4b
Ladies and children
returning from sea
with pots full of
brine in Vile Parle,
1930
Image courtesy: Nehru
Memorial Collection,
New Delhi, Nos. 2169
and 2170.

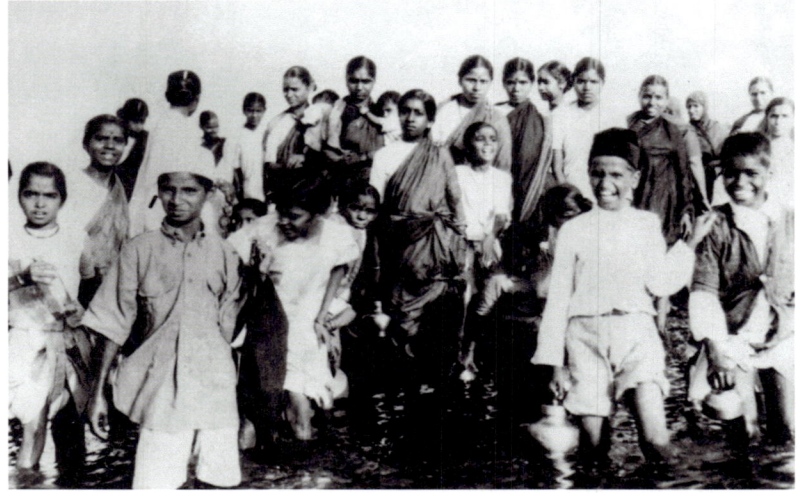

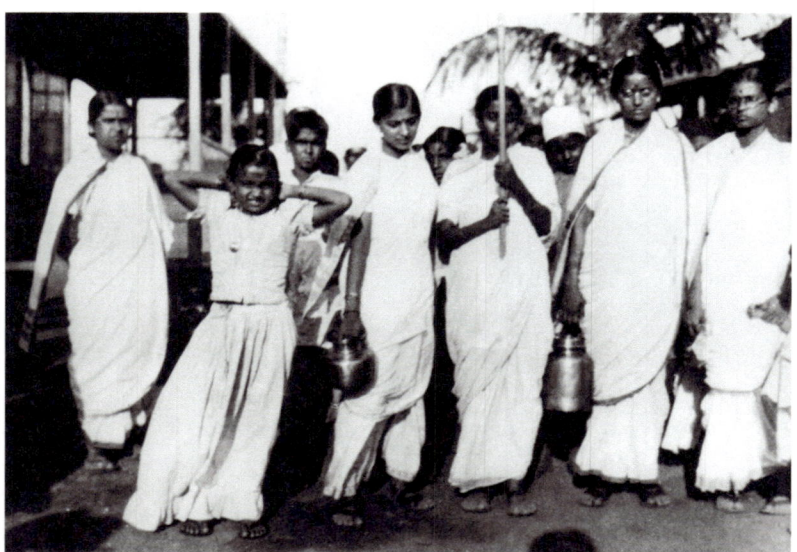

(lit., "monkey brigade") contingents. In line with the overtly military vocabulary used within the Congress to designate many aspects of the Civil Disobedience Movement, *chhavani*s (lit., "cantonments" or "camps") were established in these towns. These camps housed Congress volunteers from other parts of the Bombay Presidency who could be dispatched to Bombay at short notice for picketing and processions. The Maharashtra War Council chose Vile Parle in suburban Bombay as the site for the main *chhavani*; subsidiary *chhavani*s were set up at Ghatkopar, Bhandup, Mulund and Chembur. Each *chhavani* was headed by a *senapati* who daily conferred with the Congress House in Bombay to decide the protest strategy for the next day or week.

The first *senapati* of the Vile Parle *chhavani* was Jamnalal Bajaj,[4] who initiated the Civil Disobedience Movement in suburban Bombay on the morning of 6 April 1930, just when Gandhi was breaking the salt laws at Dandi. The venue was the seashore at Juhu, a small island municipality connected by a causeway to Vile Parle. Volunteers from Bombay, its suburbs and adjoining districts gathered in large numbers to prepare salt by boiling seawater (Fig. 6.4). As the protesters were constantly being arrested, the number of volunteers at the *chhavani* kept fluctuating. By the end of June 1930, the Vile Parle *chhavani* had registered 144 men and 164 women, of whom 57 stayed on the premises, including Jamnalal's wife Janakiben and Gandhi's wife Kasturba. The *chhavani* ran a hospital to treat volunteers who sustained injuries during protests, and also ran a *swadeshi* shop. The residents kept busy with classes on *takli* (spindle) and *charkha* spinning. By August 1930, the Vile Parle *chhavani* had been outlawed along with numerous other Congress institutions, and had to be dissolved. The residents set up another *chhavani* in the neighbourhood in a building owned by Bajaj. On 19 October 1930, this *chhavani*, known as Satyagraha Chhavani, was raided along with those at Chembur and Ghatkopar. Many of the residents were arrested.[5] Though constant efforts were made by the local police to disrupt these suburban institutions, local families, particularly through their women, continued to ensure that a Congress presence was maintained in the suburbs of Bombay. Many of these families—Chemburkar, Vileparlewala, Vandrekar—had surnames which were demonyms of Bombay suburban towns.

Women in the Nursey Album

From as early as the 1889 Bombay Congress, a women's contingent had been present in the annual meetings of the Indian National Congress. Many of these women were spouses of Congressmen while others were nationalists in their own right. In the following decades, women in ever increasing numbers stepped outside the domestic threshold and became members of the local *mahila mandal* or *stri sabha*. However, with the advent of Gandhi, their participation in public protests grew exponentially. After successful participation in the Non-Cooperation Movement of the early 1920s, women were at the forefront of the agitations connected with the Civil Disobedience Movement right from its inception. Be it breaking the salt laws (Fig. 6.5) or picketing shops selling foreign cloth (see Fig. 4.2), women took the lead. It was also one of the first Indian mass movements to be extensively chronicled by photographers using still and moving cameras. Not only did the colonial government and its nationalist adversaries have their own photographers, both the local and global press were well represented. The front pages of leading newspapers were frequently dominated by photographs of key moments in the Civil Disobedience Movement. Numerous newsreels were produced for global consumption.

While the Nursey album is not rigorously captioned, it is particularly negligent in identifying women. Leaders with a national cachet, such as Sarojini Naidu, who had been president of the Indian National Congress in 1925, are frequently noted (for example, Fig. 6.6). Kamaladevi Chattopadhyay, who would rise to

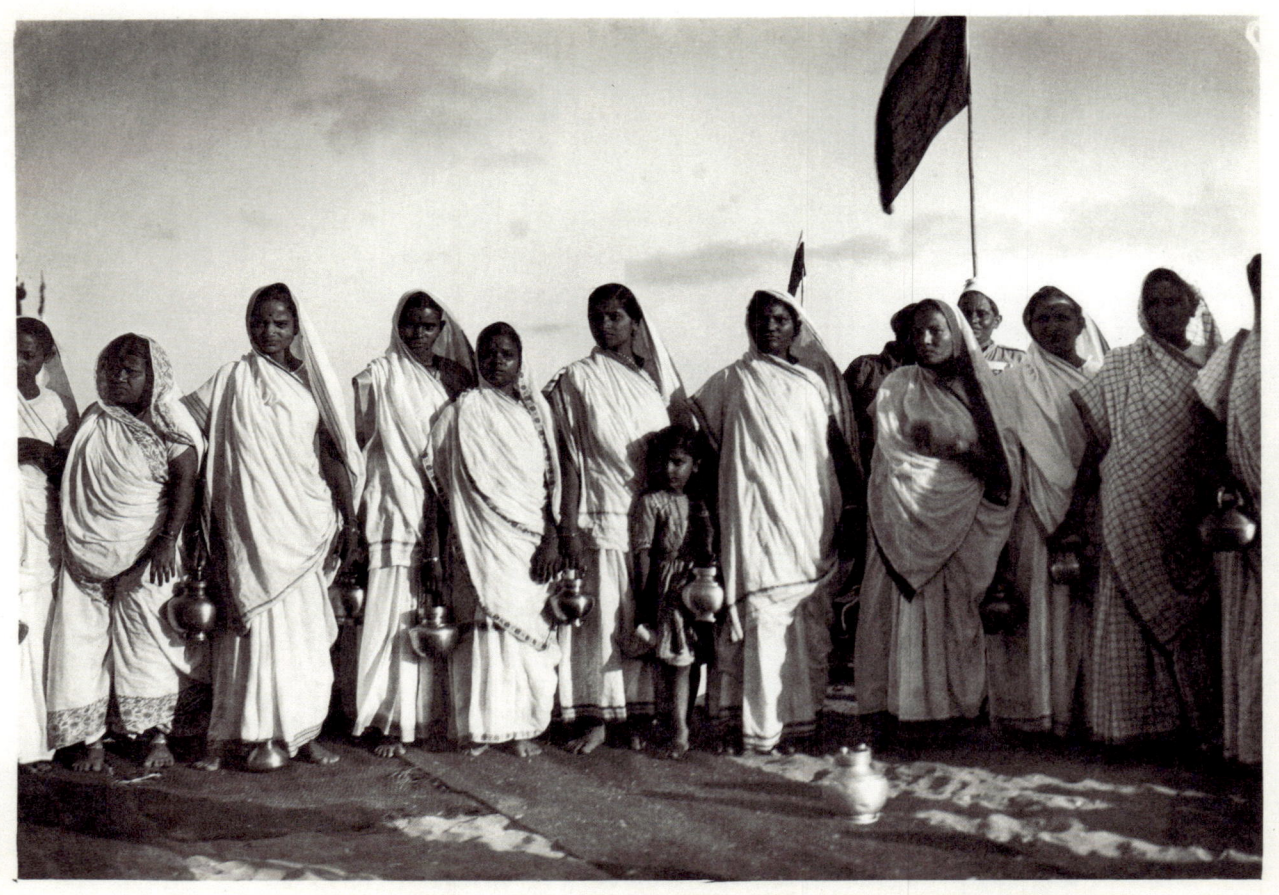

Fig. 6.5
"Daily there were
numerous batches
of salt satyagrahis
who fetch water from
the sea shore to the
Congress house to
prepare salt[.]
As seen in the photo."
1930
Gelatin Silver Print,
117 x 160 mm
ACP: 98.77.0002 (12a)
Also published in
The Times of India,
10 April 1930.

FACING PAGE, ABOVE
Fig. 6.6
"Mrs Sasojini
[Sarojini] Naidu
after her release from
the Central jail."
c. 1930—1931
Gelatin Silver Print,
116 x 161 mm
ACP: 98.77.0002 (6a)

FACING PAGE, BELOW
Fig. 6.7
"A young hindu
boy singing the
"Rastra Gita" the
National Anthem at
a meeting held in
chaupatty [Chowpatty]
during the civil
disobedience
movement. Seated on
the platform are Mrs
Kamladevi [Kamaladevi
Chattopadhyay] and
[Yusuf] Meherally."
c. 1930—1931
Gelatin Silver Print,
116 x 158 mm
ACP: 98.77.0002 (18b)

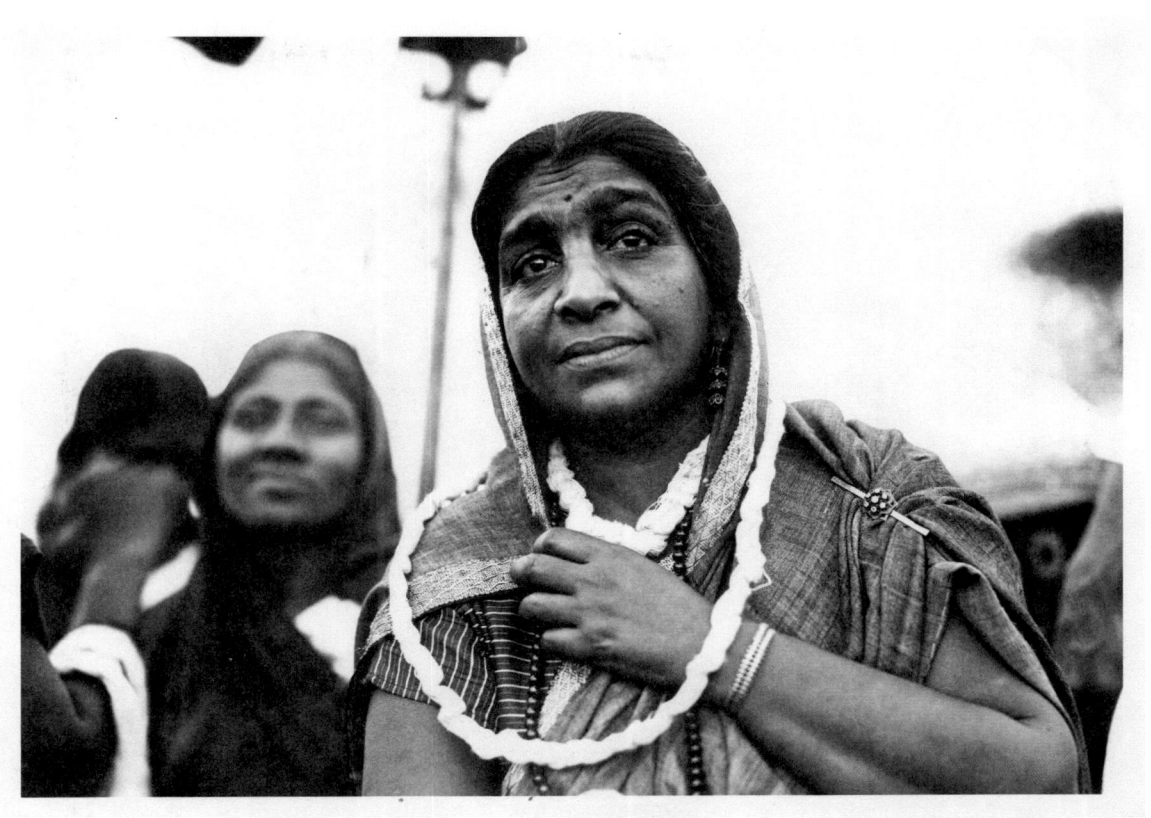

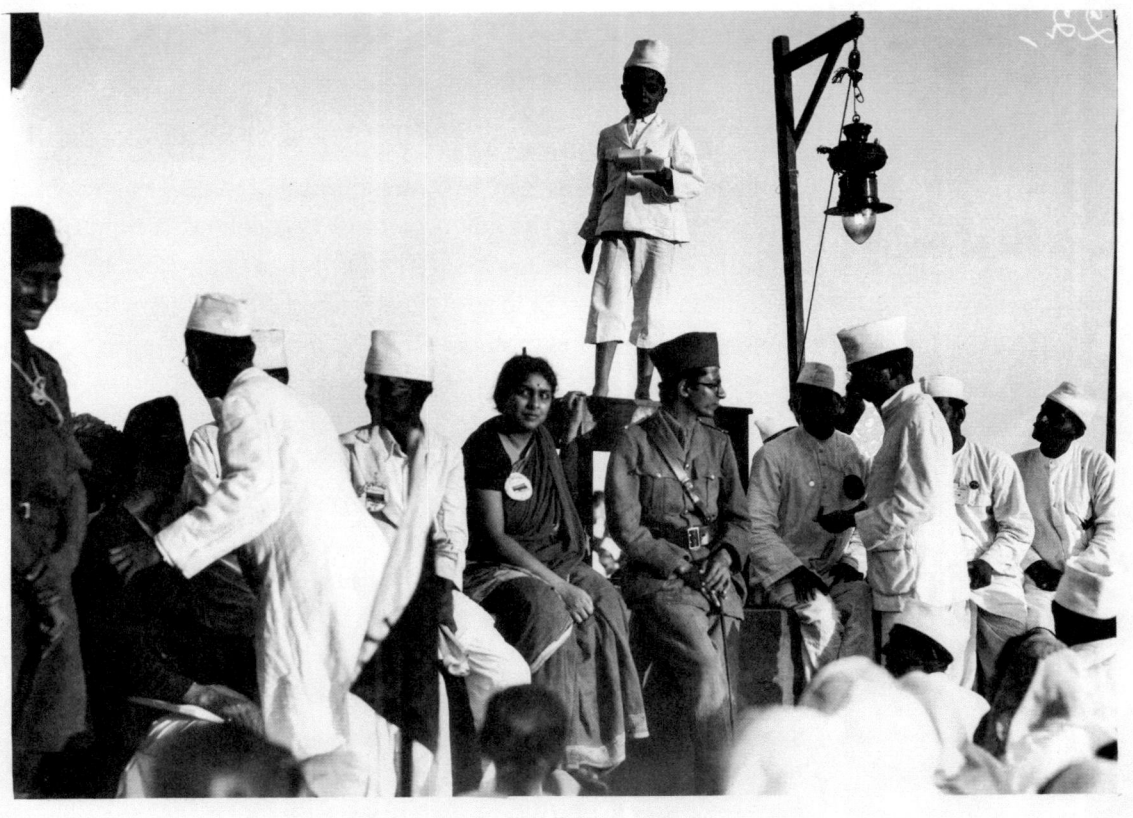

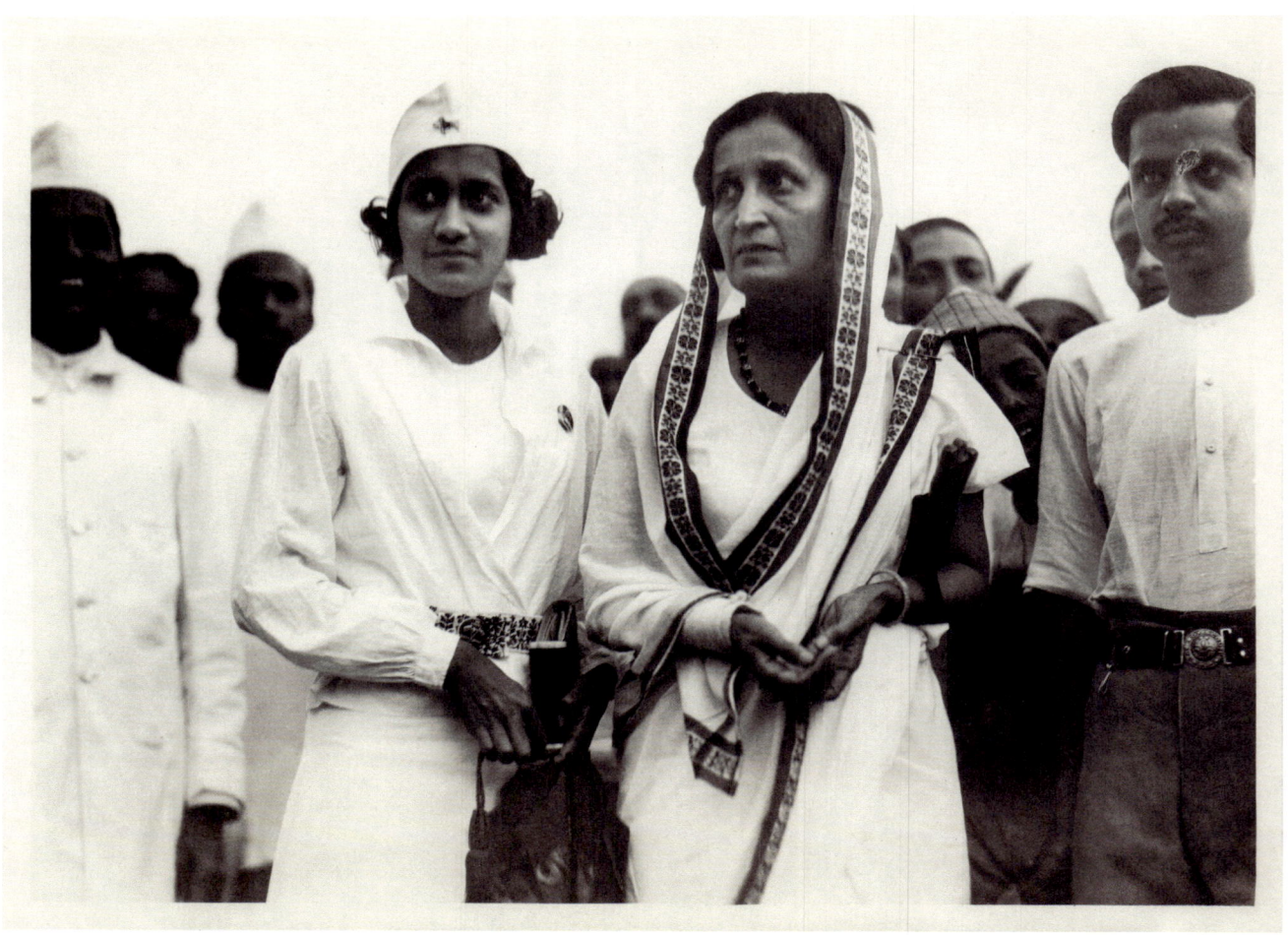

Fig. 6.8
"Miss Leila [Leela]
Row and her mother[,]
the Indian Tennis
stars." c. 1930—1931
Gelatin Silver Print,
116 x 157 mm
ACP: 98.77.0002 (115a)

prominence from the 1930s as the organizer of the Desh Sevika Dal (the women's wing of the Seva Dal, the main volunteer body of the Congress), is identified once (Fig. 6.7). The presence of a celebrity like Leela Row, the recently crowned national tennis champion, is duly registered (Fig. 6.8). But the vast majority of Congresswomen, the protagonists of so many photographs, remain anonymous.

In a posed photograph taken during the picketing of toddy shop auctions in Bandra on 23 July 1930 (Fig. 6.9), 10 faces can clearly be discerned but just two women are identified in the typewritten caption underneath. Centre stage is Lilavati Munshi (1899–1978), vice president of the Bombay Congress Committee and a ubiquitous figure in the Nursey album. Be it picketing the departmental store of Whiteaway Laidlaw on Hornby Road (Fig. 7.8) or posing with her husband, the writer and political activist K.M. Munshi, and friends (Fig. 6.10), Munshi ensures that the camera is focused on her. Though wearing a sari in the Gujarati style like the other women picketers, Munshi stands out with her confident pose, chic handbags and the daring cut of her short blouse sleeves. In all likelihood, she never stepped out for a Congress activity without a photographer in tow.

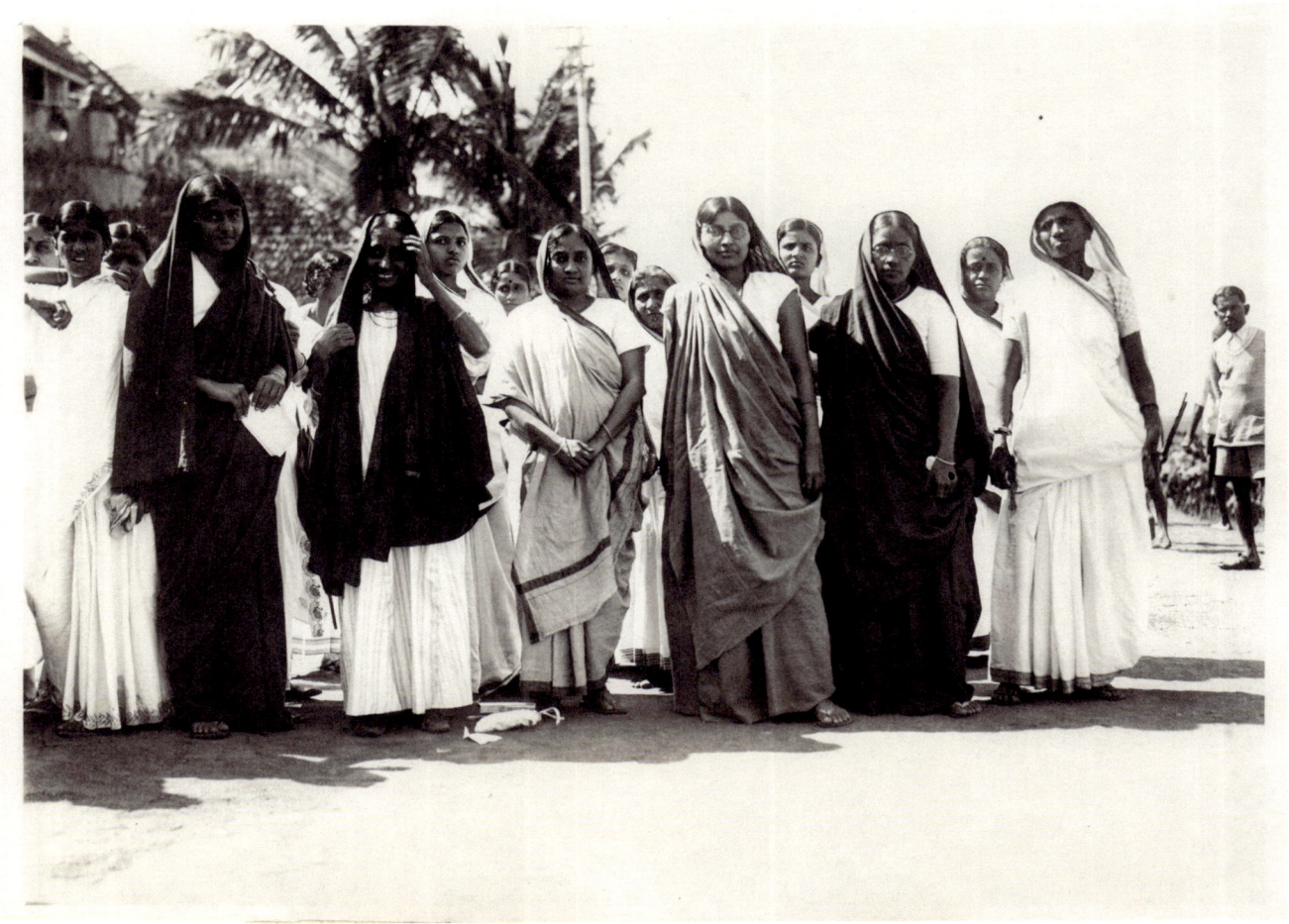

Fig. 6.9
"Miss. Sofia Somji
and Mrs. [Lilavati]
Munshi at Bandra Toddy
shops auction day."
Gelatin Silver Print,
114 x 156 mm
ACP: 98.77.0002 (112a)
This photograph was
taken on 23 July
1930. Somji can be
identified as standing
second from left (face
obscured by shadow)
while Munshi is fifth
from left.

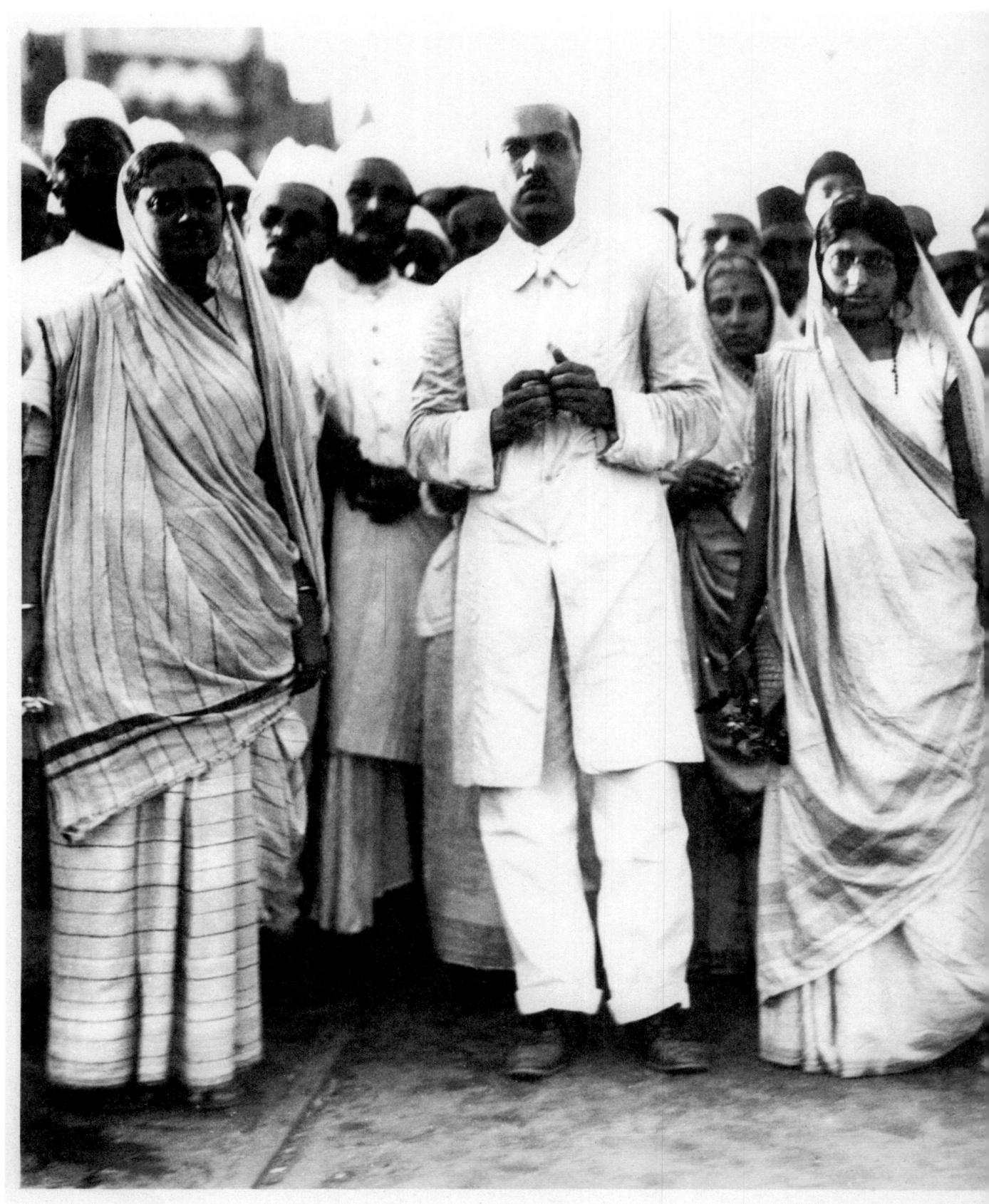

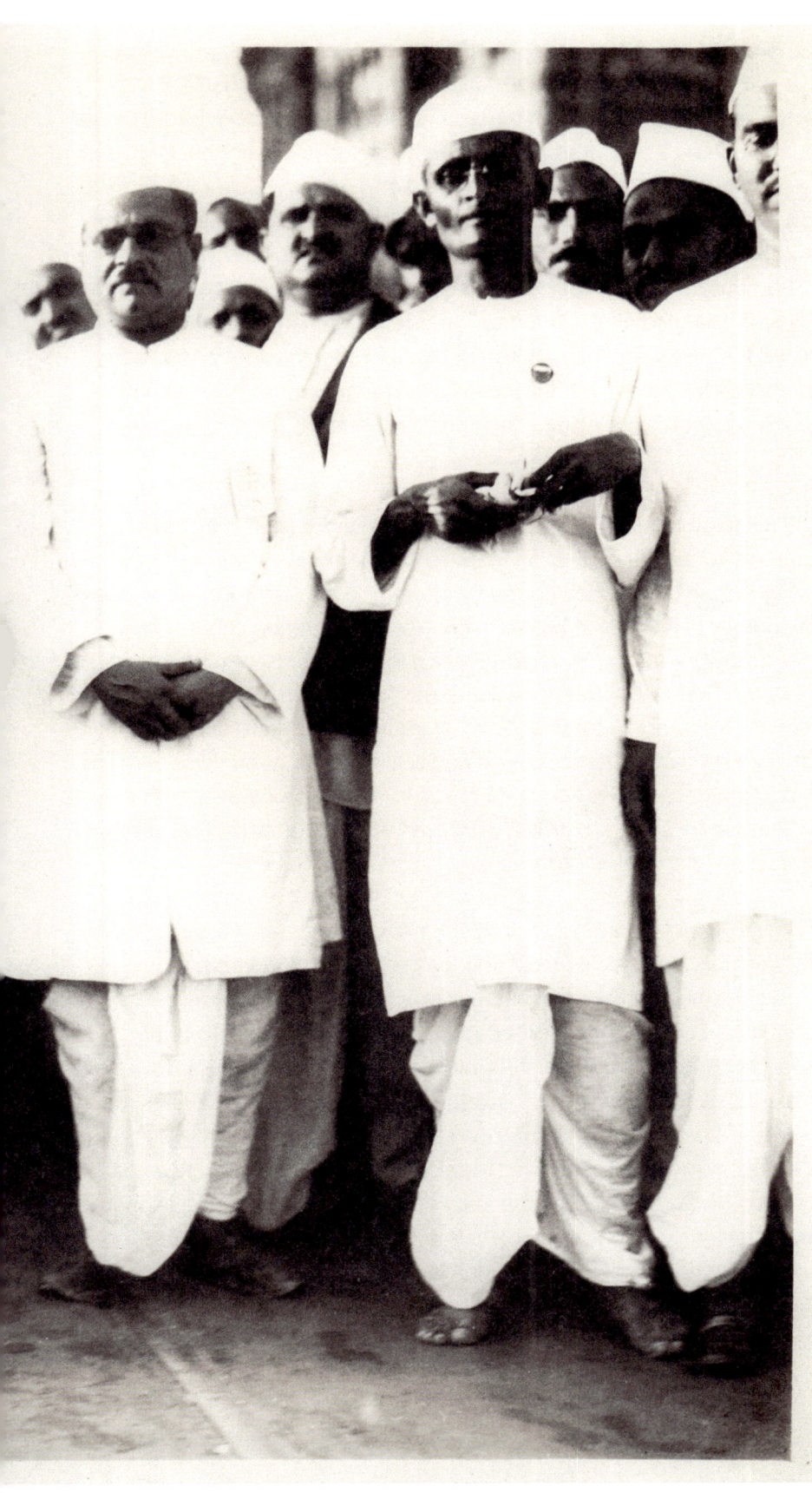

Fig. 6.10
"Mr [K.M.] and Mrs
[Lilavati] Munchi
[Munshi] with
friends."
c. 1930—1931
Gelatin Silver Print,
116 x 161 mm
ACP: 98.77.0002 (16a)

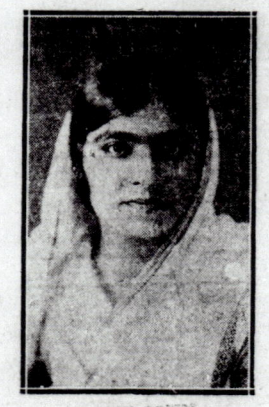

Fig. 6.11
"Safia Somji Engaged.
To Wed Sadullah
Khan, the 'Red Shirt'
Leader."
The Bombay Chronicle,
27 January 1935.

The only other name in the caption for Fig. 6.9 is that of Sofia Somji[6] who can be identified as standing second from left through another photograph (Fig. 6.11). Somji was not yet 18 when she joined the women picketing the toddy shop. Unlike many of her compeers, Somji does not seem to have had family connections with the Congress. Her father, Gulam Husain Ahmed Somji, was a solicitor while an uncle was a judge of the Bombay High Court. Hailing from a Khoja Muslim family in Bandra, Somji would have been able to walk over to the picketing site from her residence. Perhaps this spell of picketing at Bandra was her first experience as a Congress protester. A total of 31 women had participated in that action. They were detained for the day by the police and released after the auction for toddy vending licences had concluded. Besides Lilavati Munshi, who were the other women activists picketing alongside Sofia Somji at Bandra?

Congress Families

Perhaps the most remarkable of those suburban women obscured by the historical shroud is Ratnaben Meisheri (1892–1931). In the early 1920s, Ratnaben was a close associate of Burjorjee Bharucha, perhaps the most ardent advocate of *khadi* in Bombay in the period between the Non-Cooperation and the Civil Disobedience movements. When *khadi* stocks piled up after Gandhi's sudden withdrawal of the Non-Cooperation Movement in 1922, Bharucha and Ratnaben hit the streets of Bombay to liquidate them. Bharucha recalls that "at a time when it was particularly necessary to popularise and sell *khadi*, Ratnaben was perhaps the only Hindu woman who was equal to the task. Her services were better than the best."[7] She had herself worn only *khadi* from 1920 and gradually coaxed her family members to take the *swadeshi* vow.

The Meisheri family (Fig. 6.12)[8] belonging to the Kutchi Dasha Oswal Jain community were long-time residents of Mandvi in the heart of Bombay. At Mandvi, not only had Ratnaben been politically active with the Congress, she also established a *mahila mandal* to organize the local women.[9] In 1924, Ratnaben and her husband, Virji Meisheri, moved to Mulund, already famous for its sanatoriums established by numerous Gujarati communities, to recover her health after a prolonged illness. Soon after their arrival, they helped establish the Mulund Residents Association to deal with civic matters. Additionally, their long-standing association with the Congress led to the formation of the Mulund Village Congress Committee, with Virji elected president and Ratnaben a member. She was chosen as a delegate of Thana district in the Belgaum Congress of 1924. In a short period of five years, Ratnaben was instrumental in establishing the Mulund Gujarati Marathi Boys & Girls School, the Vanita Gyan Mandir for the education of women, and a medical dispensary; she also continued to work as a *khadi* evangelist.

The Meisheris found themselves in the thick of the Civil Disobedience Movement from the outset. One of the first persons to be arrested in Bombay was their

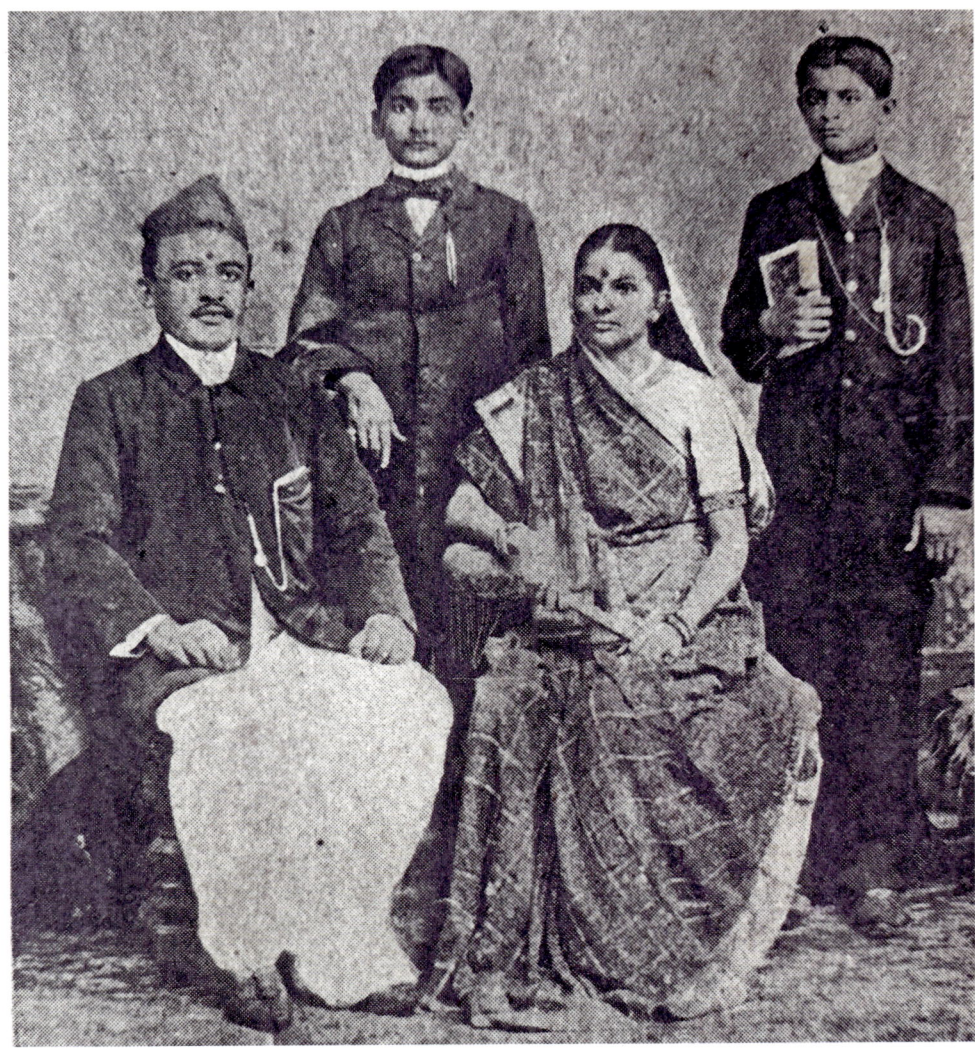

Fig. 6.12
The Meisheri family, c. 1910. Seated, Virji Gangajar Meisheri (aged 32) and his wife, Ratnaben (aged 18). Standing, Jethabhai Damji Meisheri (aged 16) and B.N. Meisheri (aged 15). N.V. Thakkar (ed.), *Mulundna Hindu Veer Mahila athva Ramaniratna Ratnadevi* (Vadodara, 1932). Image courtesy: Forbes Gujarati Sabha, Mumbai

nephew, B.N. Meisheri, a municipal councillor and the editor of the Gujarati weekly *Swadesh*. On 11 May 1930, Virji Meisheri was also arrested and sentenced to nine months of rigorous imprisonment by the Magistrate's Court in Kurla. Ratnaben was present at his trial and accorded him a proud send-off to the Thana jail.[10] Meanwhile, Jayantiben Jethabai, a 16-year-old grand-niece studying at a boarding school in Panchgani, was summoned and enrolled as a *desh sevika*. For many months, Jayantiben would travel by train everyday from Mulund to Bombay to take part in picketing and flag salutations.[11]

Though in delicate health, Ratnaben did not stay away from the political arena. Accompanied by Congresswomen from Mulund, she would regularly travel to Thana, Bhiwandi and Kalyan to protest the sale of alcohol (Fig. 6.13).[12] When toddy licences were being auctioned in Bandra (see Fig. 6.9), Ratnaben was part of the picketing party along with Sofia Somji and Lilavati Munshi.[13] She was famed for her long and articulate speeches; an admirer was particularly

Fig. 6.13
"Women Picketing Toddy Licence Auction Sales. A group of Desh Sevikas picketing at the Collector's office, Thana during the auction of the toddy booths."
The Bombay Chronicle, 10 July 1930.

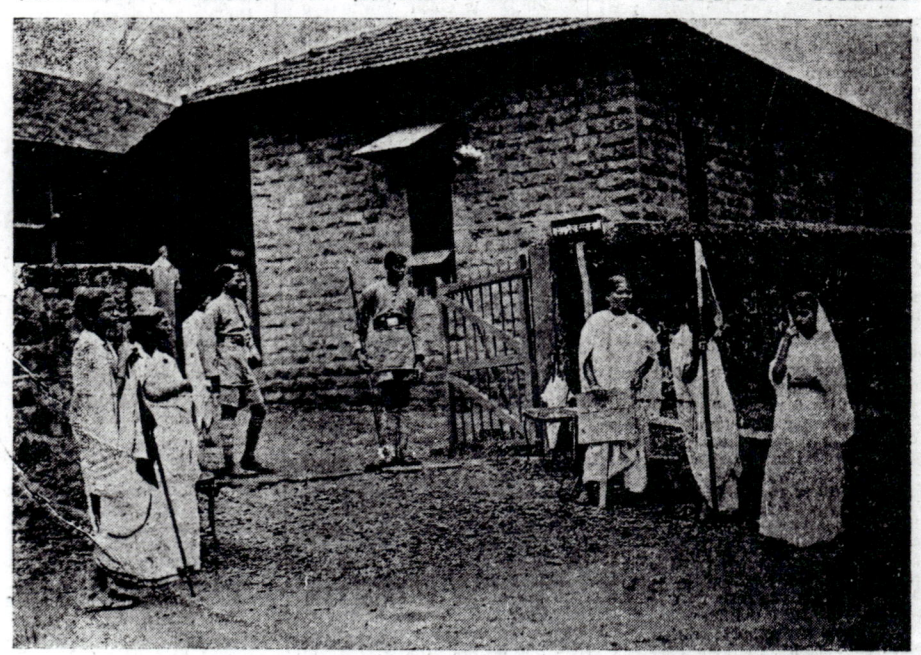

WOMEN PICKETING TODDY LICENCE AUCTION SALES.

A group of Desh Sevikas picketing at the Collector's office, Thana during the auction of the toddy booths.

Fig. 6.14
"Mrs. [Sakinabai] Lukmani, wife of Dr. Lukmani and daughter of the late Justice Budruddin Tyebji [Badruddin Tyabji] was sentenced to five months' rigorous imprisonment for picketing at Chembur. She is 65 (sic) years of age."
The Bombay Chronicle, 11 July 1930.

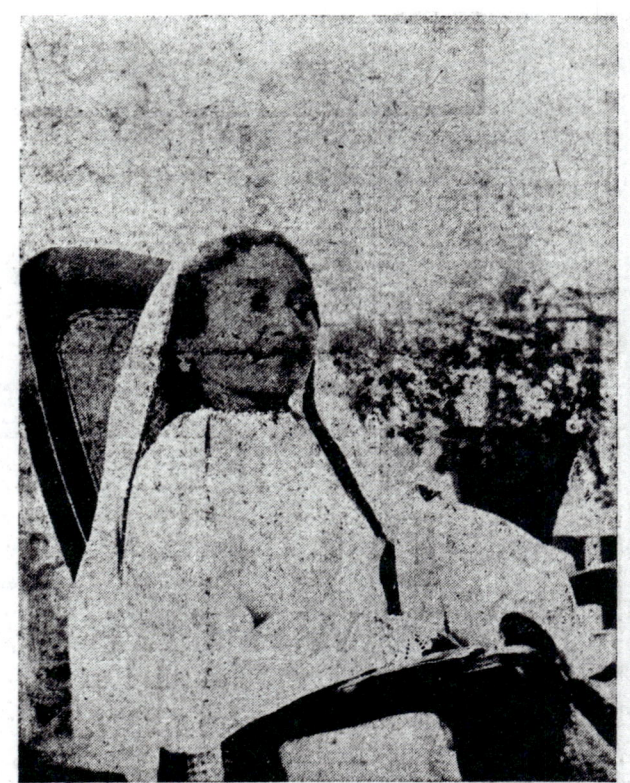

Mrs. Lukmani, wife of Dr. Lukmani and daughter of the late Jusice Budruddin Tyebji was sentenced to five months' rigorous imprisonment for picketing at Chembur. She is 65 years of age.

impressed by her oratorical skills: "I myself never heard such a vehement speech from a mere woman, even when I remember the speeches of [British suffragette leaders] Mrs. [Emmeline] and Miss [Christabel] Pankhurst on the rights of opinion in London."[14] Even more remarkable was Ratnaben's breaking the taboo of women singing on public platforms; she was a trained musician, and most of her songs were intended to popularize *khadi* and support the Swadeshi Movement.

Since no one came forward to take over the presidency of the Mulund Village Congress Committee after Virji Meisheri's arrest, Ratnaben volunteered to become its president. Besides helping manage the Mulund *chhavani,* she organized the local *vanar sena* and *prabhat pheri* activity. She continued as president until the Mulund Village Congress Committee was dissolved on 20 October 1930.[15] But she was not the only female president of a Congress Committee in suburban Bombay.

If there was one family in Bombay which could claim a Congress pedigree of the first order, it was the Tyabji family from the Sulaimani Bohra Muslim community.

Fig. 6.15
"A march of women through Bombay's streets to protest against the imprisonment of Mrs. Lukmani, during the ongoing demonstrations which called for the boycott of British goods, on 29 July 1930." Image courtesy: Getty Images

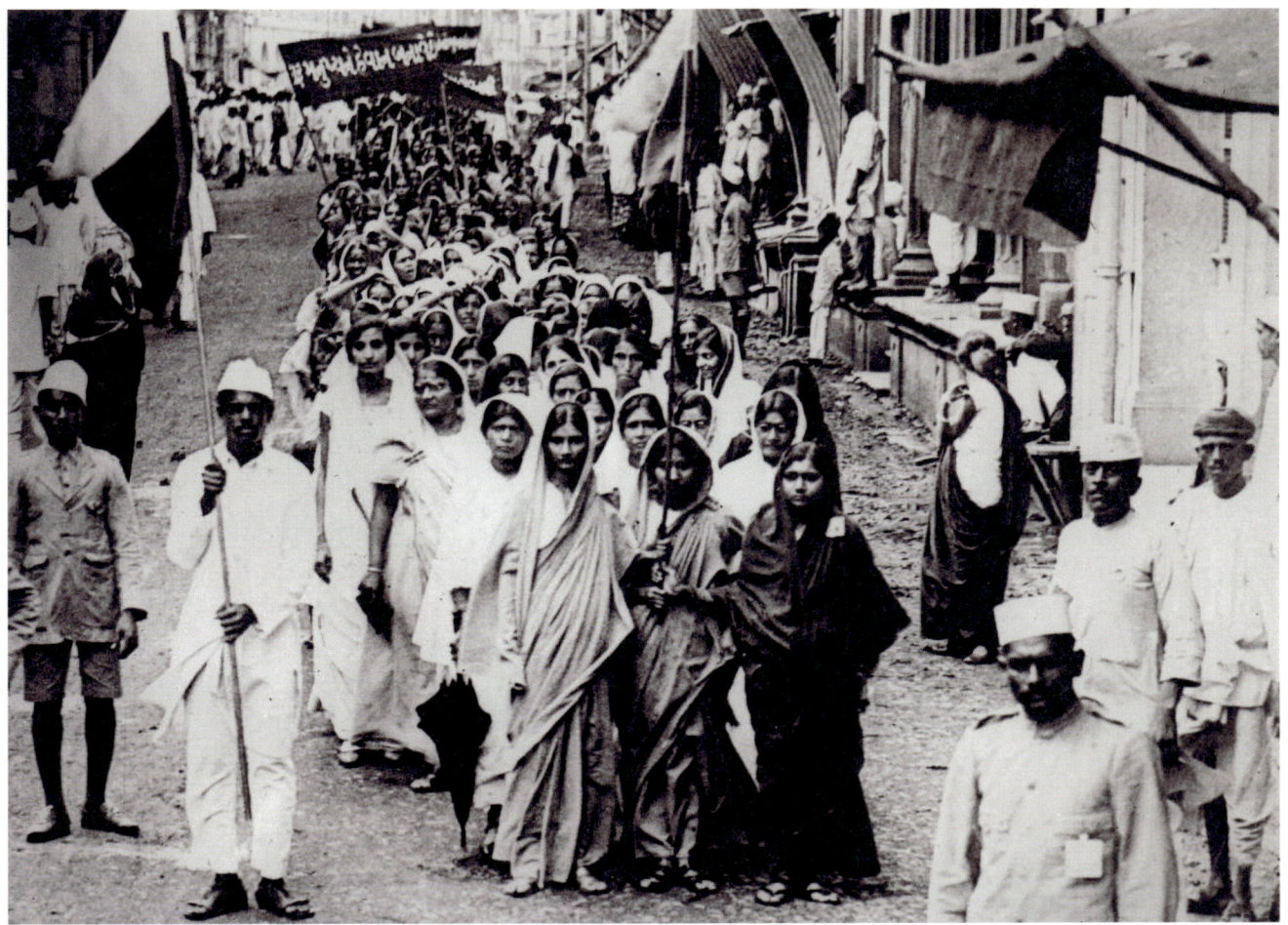

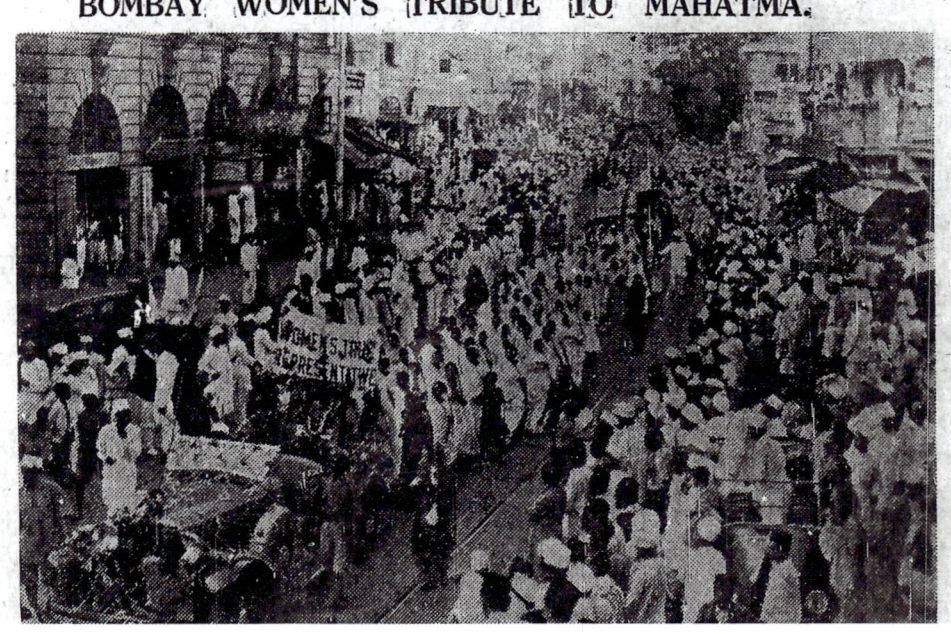

BOMBAY WOMEN'S TRIBUTE TO MAHATMA.

Beginning with Badruddin Tyabji, a judge of the Bombay High Court and the third president of the Indian National Congress (1887), many members of the family, including its women, had joined the Congress movement. However, those members who preferred a suburban arena of operations are largely ignored by the mainstream historical narrative. One such Tyabji scion was Sakinabai Lukmani (1871–1960), Badruddin Tyabji's second daughter. Sakinabai and her husband, Badruddin Lukmani, a doctor, had been social workers from the early days of their marriage. Sakinabai was the treasurer of the Bombay Ladies Branch of the National Indian Association while Badruddin Lukmani was appointed a Justice of the Peace in 1913.[16] After his retirement they moved to the newly laid-out garden city of Chembur in suburban Bombay in 1928.[17] Soon after their arrival the Chembur Village Congress Committee was established and Sakinabai became its president.

A long-time temperance activist, Sakinabai began picketing the local country liquor shops in Chembur during the Civil Disobedience Movement. Since her mere presence in the vicinity of the shop was enough to persuade tipplers to forego their drink, she was arrested on 7 July 1930 as "she loitered near the shop where [the shopkeeper] carried on the business of selling liquor."[18] When the Resident Magistrate, Kurla, sentenced Sakinabai to four months rigorous imprisonment and a fine of Rs 100, a wave of indignation swept through the city and its suburbs (Fig. 6.14). *The Bombay Chronicle* carried a headline which highlighted both her age and pedigree: "Muslim Lady of 65 given Hard Labour: Late Justice Badruddin Tyabji's Daughter Jailed."[19] Immediately, on 9 July 1930 a protest march of 300 *desh sevika*s and 200 other women wound its way from Jama Masjid to Azad

Maidan.[20] Within a week the Bombay government, unprepared for public outrage, commuted the sentence to simple imprisonment.[21] Sakinabai was granted parole for 15 days on 25 July 1930 as she was suffering from dysentery, but was back in jail mid-August.[22] Another protest march, led by Sakinabai's daughter Shamima Futehally, was held on 29 July 1930 to protest her arrest (Fig. 6.15). Since Sakinabai, like all Congresswomen, would not participate in the juridical process, the Sessions Judge at Thana referred the case to the High Court of Bombay. Even before the High Court ruled that the arrest was illegal and set aside the conviction on 29 September 1930,[23] Sakinabai was released on 17 September.[24] Her case became a cause célèbre and a rallying point for the Congress.

Sakinabai was back on the streets in early October to celebrate Gandhi Jayanti. On 3 October 1930, flanked by Lilavati Munshi and Perinben Captain, Sakinabai led a mile-long procession of Congresswomen across the streets of Bombay which culminated in a public meeting at Azad Maidan (Fig. 6.16).[25] In January 1931 Sakinabai became president of the Trombay Prohibition League, and later led a team of five volunteers to picket the auction of toddy vending licences in Thana.

Khadi Weddings

After a political compromise was effected between Gandhi and Viceroy Irwin at the Second Round Table Conference in London in March 1931, there was a lull in Congress activities. Protests and picketing ceased and most political prisoners were released. Ratnaben was waiting outside the Thana jail to receive her husband. They went to Deolali, near Nasik, to recuperate for a few days but Ratnaben did not miss out on welcoming the stalwarts of the Bombay Congress—S.A. Brelvi, K.F. Nariman and Jamnalal Bajaj—as they stepped out of the Nasik jail. They were accorded the standard Congress honour, a garland of hand-spun *khadi* yarn.[26]

It was also time to catch up with life. As her health continued to deteriorate, Ratnaben hoped to arrange the wedding of her grand-niece Jayantiben who was like an adopted daughter to her. Preparations were set afoot to conduct the marriage in a reformist style befitting a Congress family. The religious ceremonies would be kept to a minimum; all the vestments would be in *khadi*; even the marriage *shamiana* would be made of khaddar; and the guest list would be made up of Congress members. Though her family was worried about whether she would be able to handle the strain of arranging an event that was as political as it was personal, Ratnaben carried on, unconcerned.

This Congress wedding was perhaps inspired by the wedding of Gandhi's third son, Ramdas Gandhi, on 27 January 1928 at Sabarmati Ashram, Ahmedabad. The bride and groom were dressed in white *khadi* and wore no ornaments. All traditional rituals were dispensed with and the ceremony concluded in 90 minutes. There was no customary music or wedding feast. It was an altogether solemn occasion which culminated with Gandhi delivering a sermon.[27] Even the most ardent proponents of *khadi*, such as Ratnaben, could not match this austerity.

On 21 April 1931, a bevy of Congress leaders and activists arrived in Mulund to attend Jayantiben's wedding. With Sarojini Naidu heading the list, almost all the prominent Bombay Congress leaders—K.F. Nariman, K.M. Munshi, B.G. Kher, Jamnadas Dwarkadas, Abdurrehman Mitha, Shoorji Vallabhdas, and others—attended the event. The rituals, conducted in the Jain tradition, lasted a mere four hours and the guests were treated to a concert by the famed Hindustani classical vocalist Ganpatrao Dewaskar. The refreshments menu was designed to accommodate the ritual culinary scruples of the cosmopolitan crowd.[28]

A few years later another suburban Congresswoman also had a Congress wedding. On 26 January 1935—the fifth anniversary of the day the Indian National Congress proclaimed *purna swaraj*, or "complete independence"—Sofia Somji was engaged to be married to Saadullah Khan, the son of Khan Abdul Jabbar Khan (generally known as Dr. Khan Sahib).[29] The chief interlocutor was Jamnalal Bajaj, then the treasurer of the Congress and a mentor to Somji.[30] After the wedding the couple continued to stay in Bombay though their Congress work took them to all parts of India.

If a life-affirming occasion of joy, such as a wedding, could be used to celebrate the contemporary spirit of the Congress through its cherished symbology of *khadi*, *swadeshi* and communal fraternity, then death could be appropriated for the same purpose.

Afterlives

Not unlike Ratnaben Meisheri and Sakinabai Lukmani, most suburban Congresswomen preferred to work within their local areas. They used the organizing and fund-raising skills which they had honed in the city to launch new initiatives in the suburbs. They helped create civic infrastructure such as hospitals and schools in Mulund and Chembur, which, at that time, had no such facilities. These institutions not only improved the quality of life in those locations, but also effectively served as sites of Congress activity. For instance, in 1928, Ratnaben had invited Purushottamdas Thakurdas, a businessman with Congress leanings, to inaugurate a newly constructed school building which also housed the Town Hall of Mulund (Fig. 6.17).[31] In the late 1930s, Sakinabai invited B.G. Kher, then the premier of Bombay, to inaugurate a maternity hospital in Chembur. Many of these institutions survive to this day, nearly a hundred years later.[32]

After successfully conducting the Congress wedding of her grand-niece, Ratnaben Meisheri's health rapidly declined. As she lay on her deathbed in

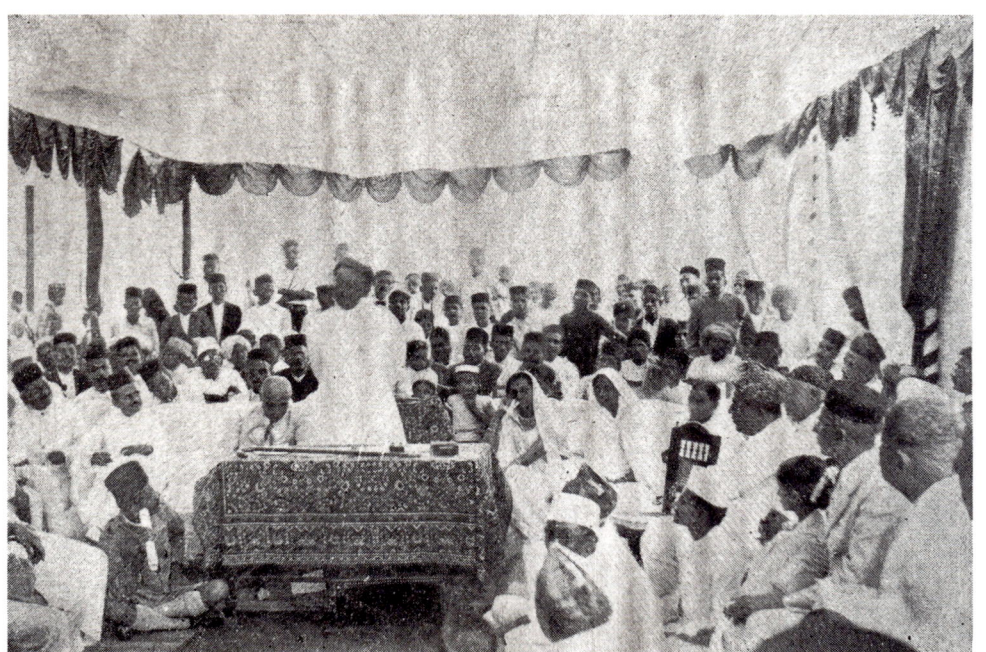

Fig. 6.17
Inauguration of
Mulund Gujarati
Marathi Boys & Girls
School in the presence
of Ratnaben Meisheri.
N.V. Thakkar (ed.),
*Mulundna Hindu
Veer Mahila athva
Ramaniratna Ratnadevi*
(Vadodara, 1932).
Image courtesy:
Forbes Gujarati
Sabha, Mumbai

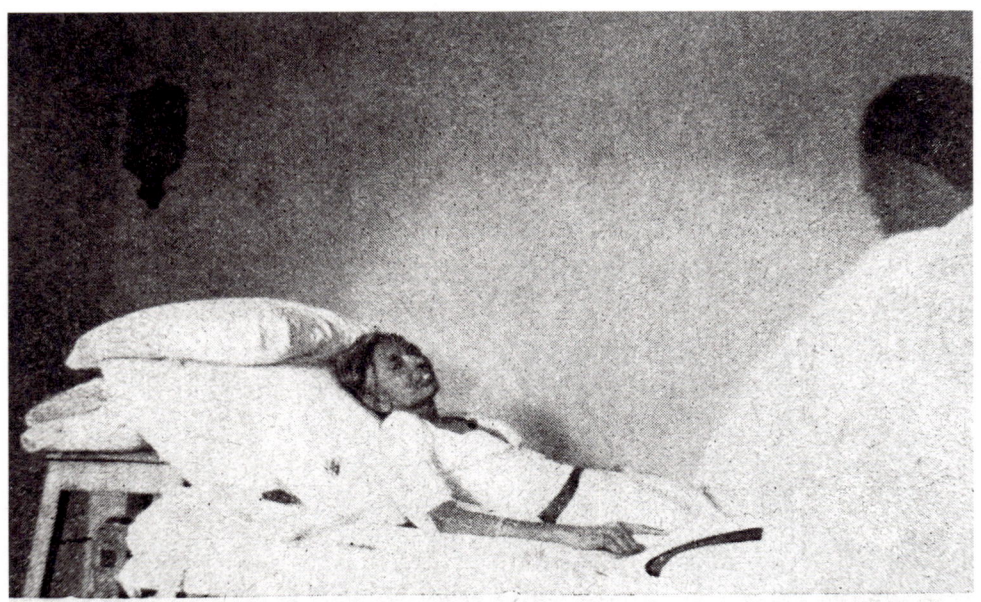

Fig. 6.18
Ratnaben Meisheri
(aged 39) receives
a visitor on her
deathbed, May 1931.
N.V. Thakkar (ed.),
*Mulundna Hindu
Veer Mahila athva
Ramaniratna Ratnadevi*
(Vadodara, 1932).
Image courtesy:
Forbes Gujarati
Sabha, Mumbai

અખંડ સૌ. શ્રી રતનબાઇ વીરજી ગંગાજર માહેશ્વરી; મૃત્યુશય્યામાં
(અંતિમ દર્શન) (વય વર્ષ ૩૯)

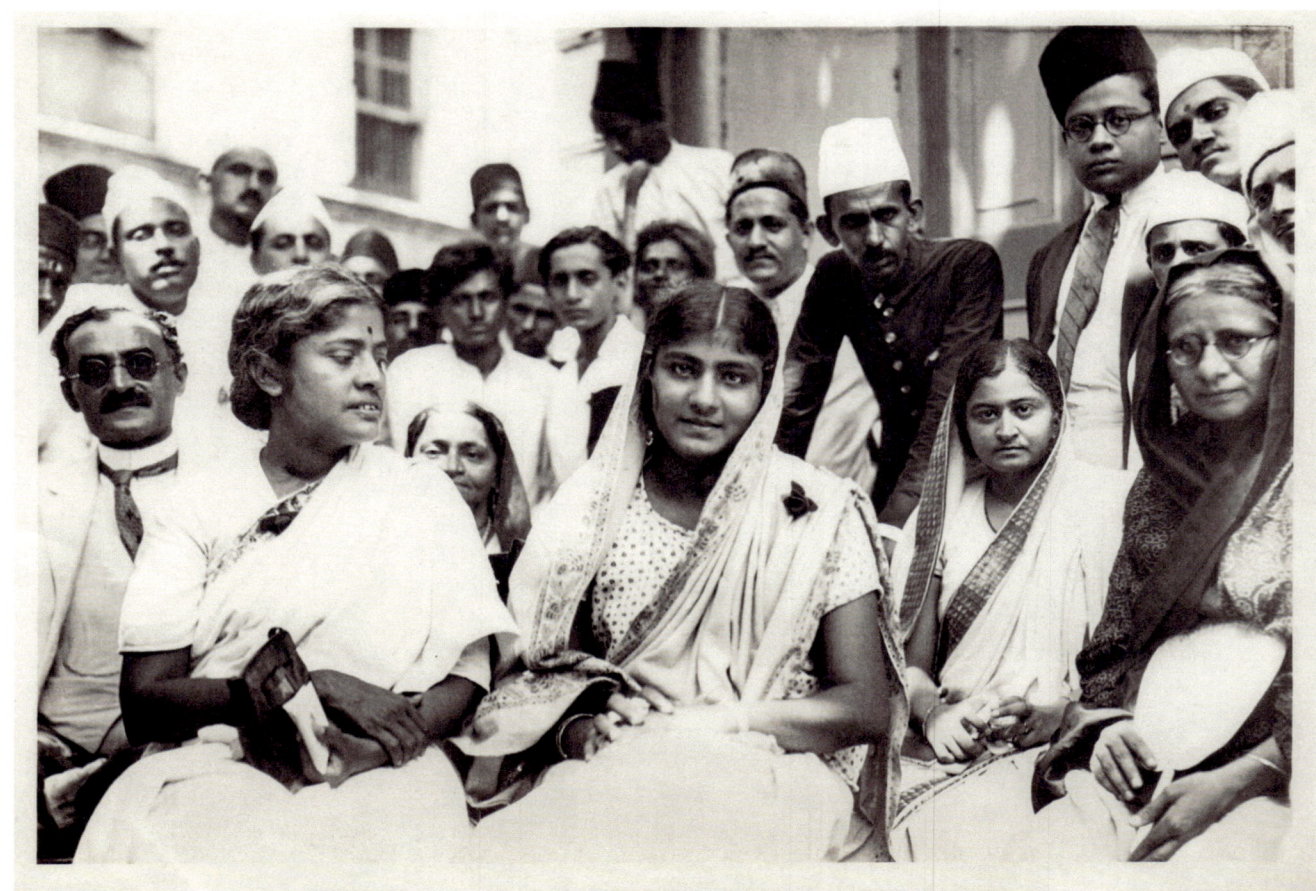

1931, her Congress colleagues gathered around her to say their final goodbyes. Propped up by pillows (Fig. 6.18), an emaciated Ratnaben converses with a visitor as she attempts to peer into the camera. B.G. Kher, who would become premier of Bombay Presidency in 1937, recalls his final meeting with her: "Even a couple of days before her death which she knew was impending, when she was too weak even to sit up, she inquired first whether I had any refreshment. I knew that I was seeing her for the last time but tried to conceal my sadness; and she knew it and was brave."[33]

Ratnaben's death on 31 May 1931 did not signify the end of her contribution to the Congress movement. Soon after her passing, plans were initiated to publish a commemoration volume in her honour. Titled *Mulundna Hindu Veer Mahila athva Ramaniratna Ratnadevi* [The Brave Hindu Lady of Mulund], it was published in late 1932 when the revived Civil Disobedience Movement was at its height. One of the earliest commemoration volumes to be published in Gujarati,[34] the book includes an album of photographs illustrating Ratnaben's life and death, and contains reminiscences and tributes from 29 women and 74 men, many of whom were her colleagues in the Congress.[35] Priced at Rs 2, the book served as a presentation volume within Congress circles.[36]

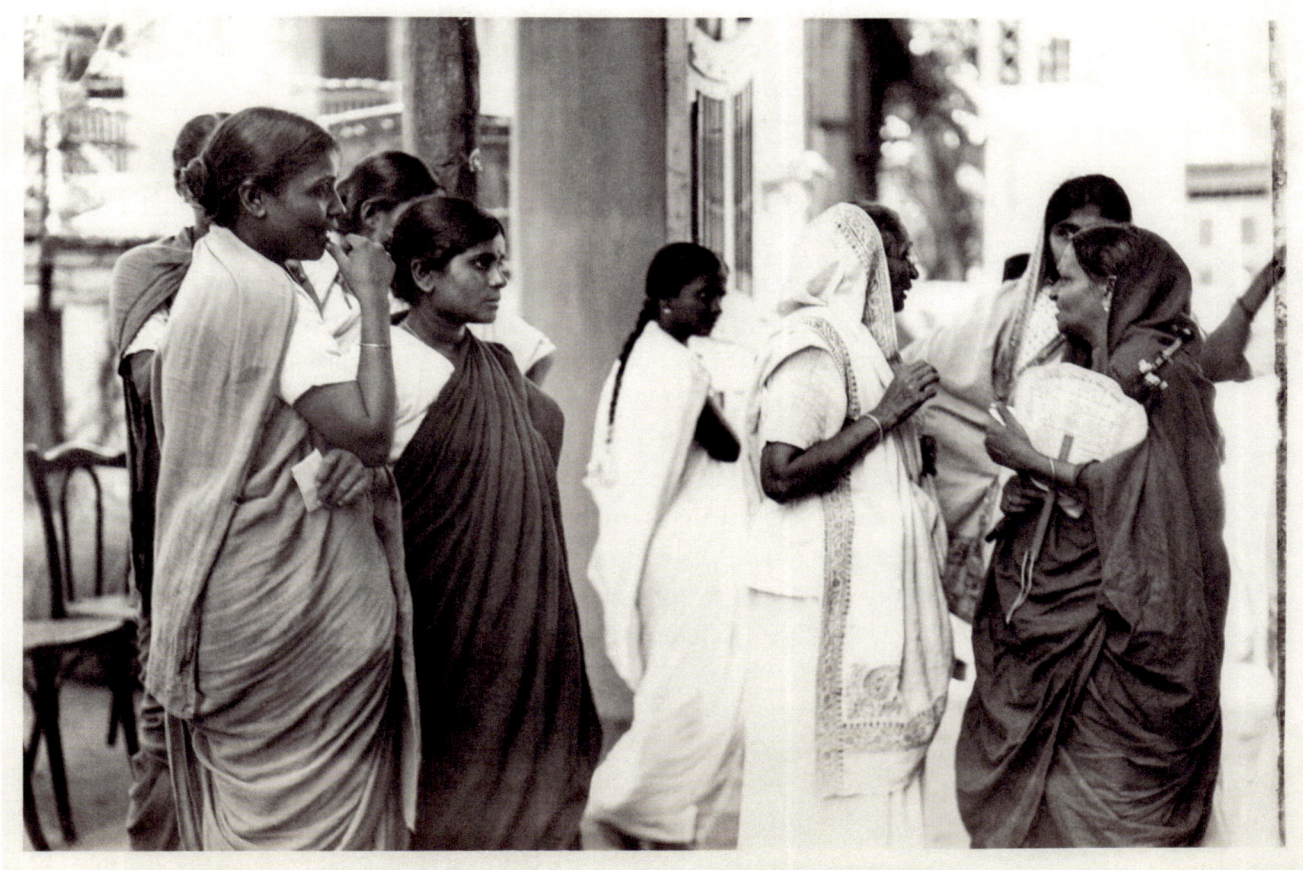

The Civil Disobedience Movement was perhaps the last time Sakinabai Lukmani could actively participate in Congress activities. But the Lukmanis continued to play their part in the civic life of Chembur: while Badruddin Lukmani became the first president of the Chembur Residents Association in 1936,[37] Sakinabai was deeply involved in overseeing the Bhagini Seva Mandal and Bal Vikas Kendra.[38]

After a short internship, Sofia Somji quickly rose to become the president of the Bombay War Council by October 1930. She was arrested at Chowpatty while addressing a public meeting on 20 October 1930 and sentenced to three months imprisonment. While the Congress awaited the outcome of the second session of the Round Table Conference being held in London in September 1931, it overhauled its organizational structure and the Seva Dal became its principal volunteer corps. Kamaladevi Chattopadhyay, with Somji as her assistant, was given the responsibility of organizing its women's wing, the Desh Sevika Dal, its members were aged between 16 and 45 years. A training centre was established in Borivli, in the north-west corner of the Bombay Suburban District, with Somji in charge. After the failure of the Round Table Conference, the Congress intensified its agitations in the city. The Borivli centre was considered a threat to public order and closed down in 1932; Somji was arrested once

Fig. 6.20
"A rush of voters to the poolig [polling] station."
Gelatin Silver Print, 114 x 165 mm
ACP: 98.77.0002 (93b)
The elections were held on 31 May 1931.

again.[39] Taking the name Safia Khan after marriage, she had a long career as a Congresswoman until 1947, when she presumably accompanied her husband, Sadullah Khan, to Pakistan. Reviewing the performance of the Seva Dal in Bombay in 1945, S.K. Patil, a prominent city Congressman, noted, "Under the very able and energetic leadership of Mrs. Safia Khan, the women volunteer organisation in this city has grown into a model which other Provinces can copy to their advantage."[40]

These exceptional suburban Congresswomen also ensured that the Congress was well-positioned to win the provincial elections in these areas. They managed to get a toehold in the Congress hierarchy by contesting the elections held on 31 May 1931 for the Bombay Provincial Congress Committee.[41] In a photograph of candidates standing for the election (Fig. 6.19), a confident-looking Sofia Somji dominates the foreground. She is flanked by other women candidates, including Sakinabai Lukmani (with a fan). Women were also part of the electorate and exercised their franchise in large numbers (Fig. 6.20). Their support continued post-Independence. In 1946, the Congress won all three seats allocated to the Bombay Suburban District constituency, and in the 1952 provincial elections, it managed to win all the four constituencies in the same area. Though they contributed to the creation of pockets of Congress influence which lasted for decades, women were hardly ever nominated as candidates for these elections. Reviewing the situation as it is today, it is evident that their whole-hearted participation in the nationalist movement and in the electoral process notwithstanding, women still tend to be relegated to the margins of India's political power structures.

Notes

1. K.K. Chaudhari (ed.), *Source Material for a History of the Freedom Movement in India,* Vol. XII, Civil Disobedience Movement, October 1930–December 1941 (Bombay: Gazetteers Department, Government of Maharashtra, 1995), p. 60.
2. For more details on the changing contours of suburban Bombay, see B. Arunachalam, 'Geography', in K.K. Chaudhari (ed.), *Maharashtra State Gazetteers: Greater Bombay District*, Vol. 1 (Bombay: Gazetteers Department, Government of Maharashtra, 1986), pp. 1–78.
3. In 1931, when the population of Bombay city was recorded as 1,161,383, the population of the Bombay Suburban District was 179,524. The populations of its municipalities were as follows: Bandra / 43,290; Kurla / 30,311; Vile Parle / 11,290; Ghatkopar-Kirol / 8,168 and Juhu / 1,851. See *Census of India, 1931,* Vol. VIII – Part II, Bombay Presidency, Statistical Tables, compiled by A.H. Dracup and H.T. Sorley (Bombay: Government Central Press, 1933), p. 40. By 1941, the population of these towns had increased substantially: Bandra / 71,789; Kurla / 39,066; Vile Parle-Andheri / 38,493; Ghatkopar-Kirol / 18,176; Mulund / 6,917 and Chembur / 6,198. See *Census of India, 1941*, Vol. III, Bombay Tables, compiled by A.H. Dracup (Delhi: Manager of Publications, 1942), pp. 58–59.
4. Chaudhari (ed.), *Source Material for a History of the Freedom Movement in India,* Vol. XI, Civil Disobedience Movement, April–September 1930 (Bombay: Gazetteers Department, Government of Maharashtra, 1990), p. 4.
5. Chaudhari (ed.), *Source Material,* Vol. XII, p. 249.
6. The name has variant spellings: Sofia/Sophia/Safia and Somji/Somjee. I have used 'Sofia Somji', as appears in the Nursey album.
7. N.V. Thakkar (ed.), *Mulundna Hindu Veer Mahila athva Ramaniratna Ratnadevi* [The Brave Hindu Lady of Mulund or Ramaniratna Ratnadevi] (Vadodara: Hindugaurav Granthmala Karyalaya,

1932), p. 238: tribute by Burjorjee Framjee Bharucha, Bombay.

The translations of Gujarati extracts quoted from this book are by the author.

8. Though the English transliteration of the Gujarati orthography of the family name would be 'Maheshwar', the family preferred to render it as 'Meisheri' or 'Mehisheri' in English.

9. Thakkar, *Mulundna Hindu Veer Mahila*, p.148: tribute by Perinben Captain and Jamnaben Purushottam, Bombay.

10. Thakkar, *Mulundna Hindu Veer Mahila*, p. 201: tribute by B.N. Meisheri, Bombay.

11. Thakkar, *Mulundna Hindu Veer Mahila*, p. 184: tribute by Jethabhai Damji Meisheri, Mulund.

12. Thakkar, *Mulundna Hindu Veer Mahila*, p. 152: tribute by Kamalaben Sanghvi, Ghatkopar.

13. Thakkar, *Mulundna Hindu Veer Mahila*, p. 128: tribute by Savitagauri Gijulal Kamdar, Ghatkopar (one of the Bandra picketers).

14. Thakkar, *Mulundna Hindu Veer Mahila*, p. 336: tribute by S.S. Naik, President, Bombay Suburban District Congress Committee.

15. *The Bombay Chronicle*, 21 October 1930.

16. ibid., 15 December 1913.

17. Salima Tyabji, *The Changing World of a Bombay Muslim Community, 1870–1945* (New Delhi: Oxford University Press, 2023), p. 95.

18. "Emperor v. Sakinabai Lukmani", *All India Reporter,* Bombay Section (1931), p. 72.

19. *The Bombay Chronicle*, 8 July 1930. Sakinabai was 59 years old when she was arrested; it took a month for the newspaper to publish a correction.

20. Chaudhari (ed.), *Source Material*, Vol. XI, p. 277.

21. "Mrs. Lukmani. Sentence Commuted", *The Bombay Chronicle*, 19 July 1930.

22. *The Bombay Chronicle*, 25 July 1930.

23. "Emperor v. Sakinabai Lukmani", p. 74.

24. *The Bombay Chronicle*, 18 September 1930.

25. ibid., 4 October 1930.

26. Thakkar, *Mulundna Hindu Veer Mahila*, p. 329: tribute by S.A. Brelvi, editor of *The Bombay Chronicle.*

27. "A Solemn Ceremony", *Young India*, 2 February 1928.

28. "Mulundma Sudharak Lagna" [A Reformist Wedding in Mulund], *Hindustan ane Prajamitra*, 23 April 1931, quoted in Thakkar, *Mulundna Hindu Veer Mahila*, p. 350.

29. "Safia Somji Engaged", *The Bombay Chronicle*, 27 January 1935.

30. B.R. Nanda, *In Gandhi's Footsteps: The Life and Times of Jamnalal Bajaj* (New Delhi: Oxford University Press, 1990), p. 252.

31. "Mulundma Manohar Mahotsva" [A Grand Event in Mulund], *Hindustan ane Prajamitra*, 24 April 1928, quoted in Thakkar, p. 346.

32. Over a ten-year period from 1948 to 1958, the towns in the erstwhile Bombay Suburban District were gradually subsumed into the Municipal Corporation of Greater Bombay as its boundaries edged northward. This left them shorn of any small-town character, but they still retained the status of suburbs.

33. Thakkar, *Mulundna Hindu Veer Mahila*, p. 330: tribute by B.G. Kher.

34. I could trace only one other Gujarati commemoration volume (*smarak granth*) published before 1932: for Haji Mohammad Allahrakhiya Shivji (1922).

35. The contributors included many whose names have already appeared in this essay; other prominent contributors include K.M. Munshi, A.G. Viegas, N.D. Savarkar, R.H. Chemburkar, D.N. Wandrekar and Swami Anand.

36. The copy of the Ratnaben Meisheri commemoration volume which I consulted was presented to S.A. Brelvi by Virji Gangajar Meisheri in 1933.

37. Aloysius Soares, *Down the Corridors of Time: Recollections and Reflection*, Vol. 1 (Bombay: A. Soares, 1971), p. 318.

38. Yasmeen Lukmani, "The Role Played by the Tyabji Women in the National Movement", in N.B. Mody (ed.), *Women in India's Freedom Struggle* (Bombay: Allied Publishers, 2000), p. 222.

39. Jasleen Dhamija, *Kamaladevi Chattopadhyay* (Delhi: National Book Trust, 2007), p. 35.

40. S.K. Patil, *The Indian National Congress: A Case for its Reorganisation* (Aundh: Aundh Publishing Trust, 1945), p. 53.

41. *The Times of India*, 23 May 1931.

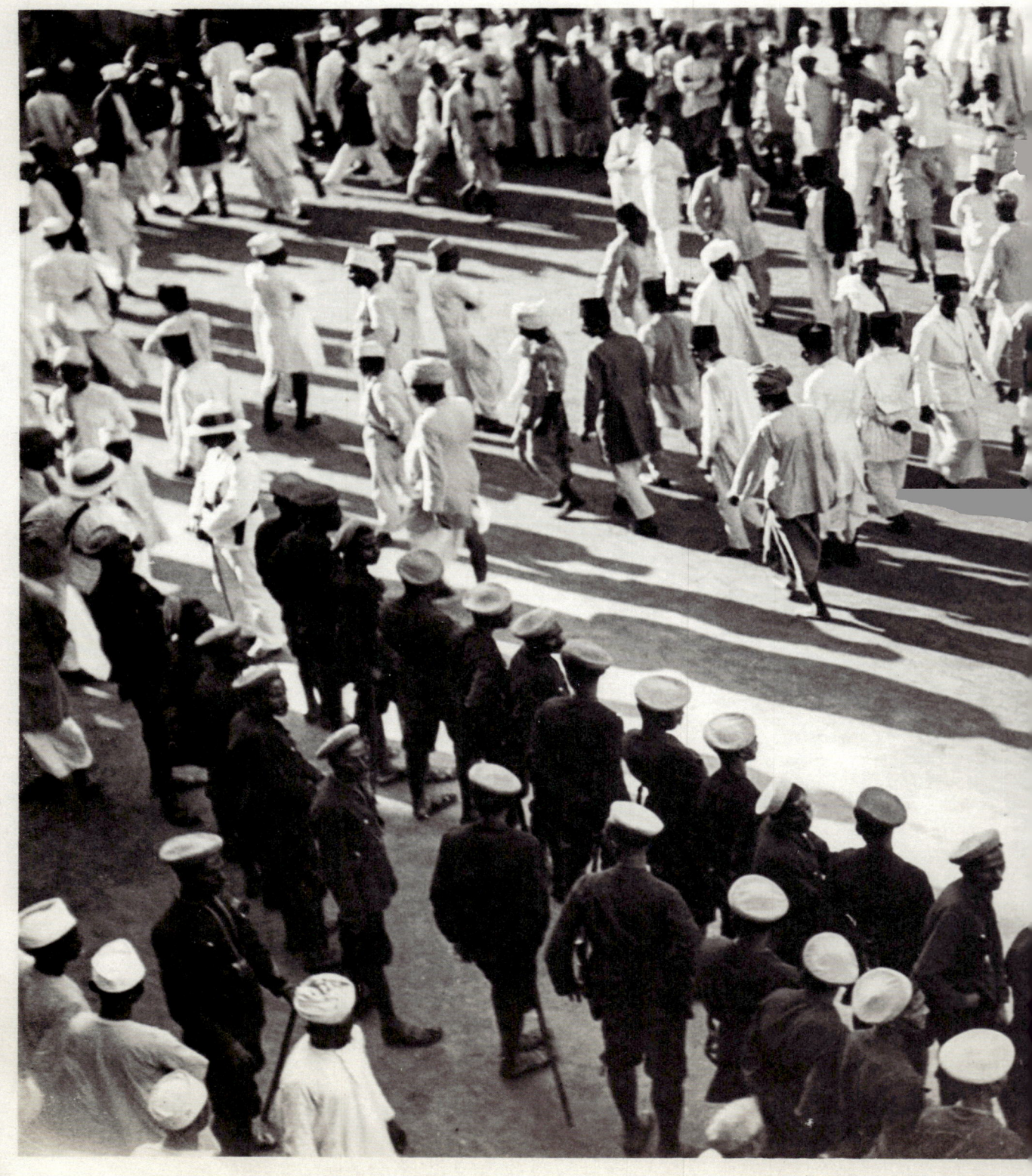

Police ready for the lathi charge .

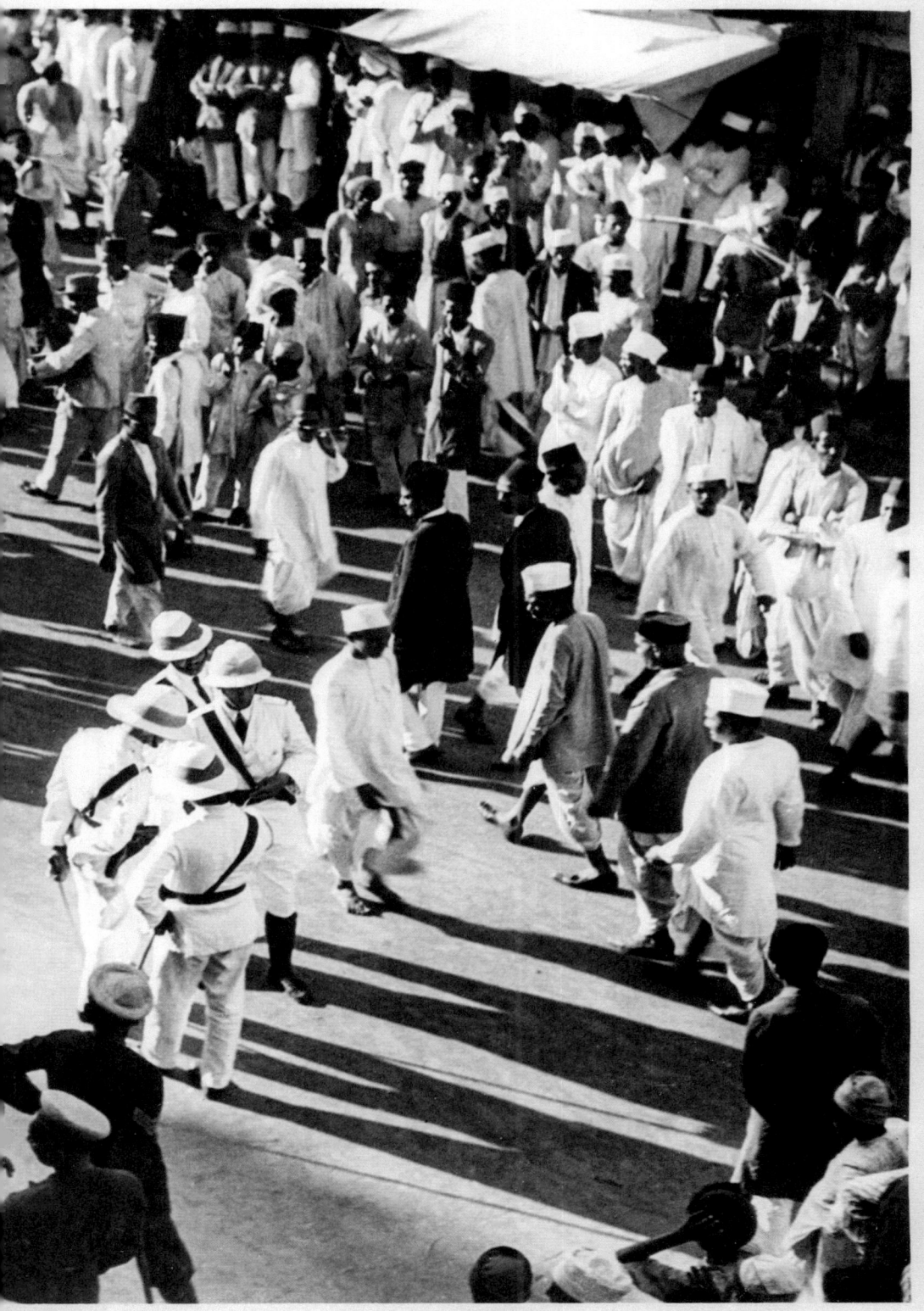

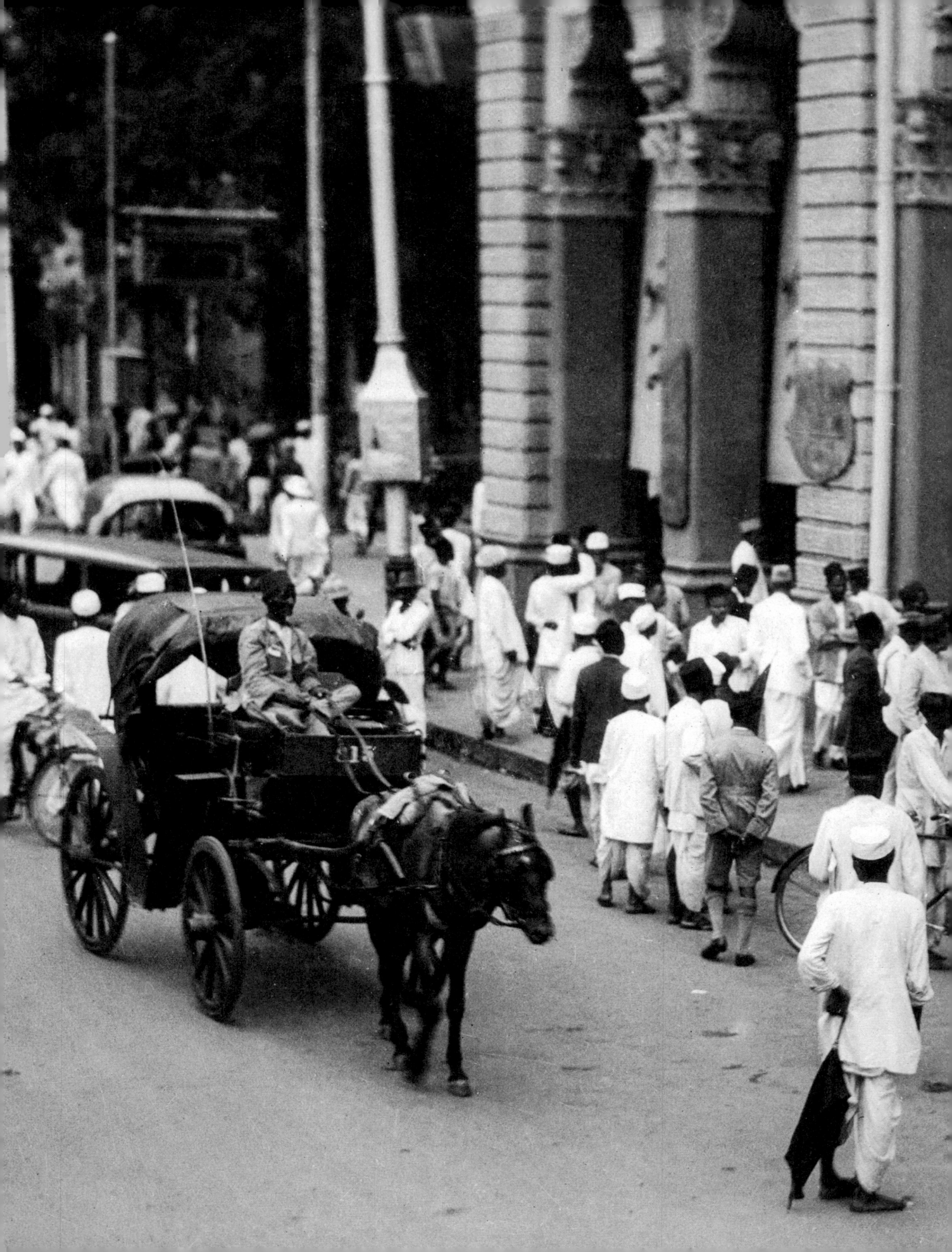

CHAPTER 7

BOYCOTTING WOMEN
THE STREET POLITICS OF
CONSUMER ACTIVISM IN BOMBAY, 1930-31

Abigail McGowan

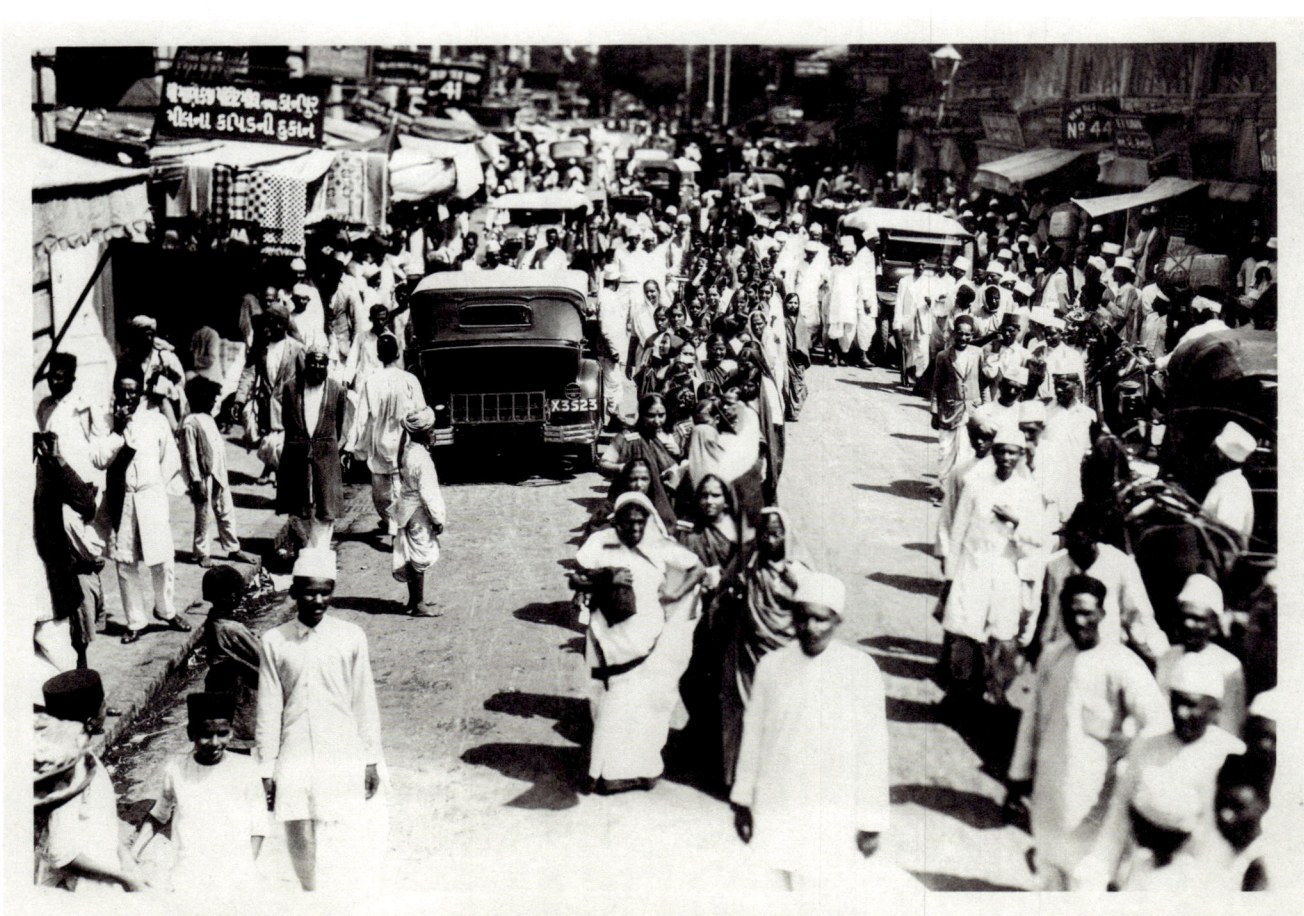

A Boycott procession in the market area.

One of the prominent innovations of the 1930–31 Civil Disobedience Movement—and a striking element of the Nursey album's documentation of that movement—was the prominence of female agency. In Bombay, considered the heart of the movement, women took to the streets in carefully disciplined processions, made speeches, produced and distributed nationalist salt made from seawater, picketed shops, sang nationalist songs, and more (Fig. 7.1). Women were, of course, not just dynamic protagonists of the movement, but also the targets—they were asked to change the goods they used, how they navigated markets and how they moved through public spaces. And, finally, women helped inspire the movement, with police ill-treatment of female nationalist volunteers galvanizing outrage and resistance against the colonial state.[1]

Those multiple roles enacted by women activists—as agents, subjects and rallying points of protest—were a source of creative tension for the Civil Disobedience Movement. As Avrati Bhatnagar and Sumathi Ramaswamy have explored eloquently in their analysis of violence over salt and flags, women took the literal and figurative stage to dramatize injustices and declare new possibilities for the future.[2] There are, however, other elements of tension related to women's activism in 1930-31: namely, the gendered nature of confrontations over boycotts of foreign goods. Within spectacular efforts targeting the core European shopping area of Bombay, protesters, shoppers and the observing crowds drew on social norms of feminine respectability to stage boycott as women's political work.

This analysis will focus in particular on two key streets in the Fort area of South Bombay: Hornby Road and Esplanade Road (Fig. 7.2). Serving as major thoroughfares through the heart of the imperial city, these two streets were also central to the promotion and sale of European goods. Home to the biggest European department stores in the city—Evans Fraser, Whiteaway Laidlaw, and the Army and Navy Stores (Fig. 7.3)—these streets also featured a wide range of smaller shops offering imported goods for Westernized lifestyles: items such as clothing, spectacles, food and provisions, watches, smoking supplies, pianos, silver tea sets and more. Thanks in part to its proximity to the Esplanade Maidan —recently renamed in nationalist parlance as the Azad (Freedom) Maidan—

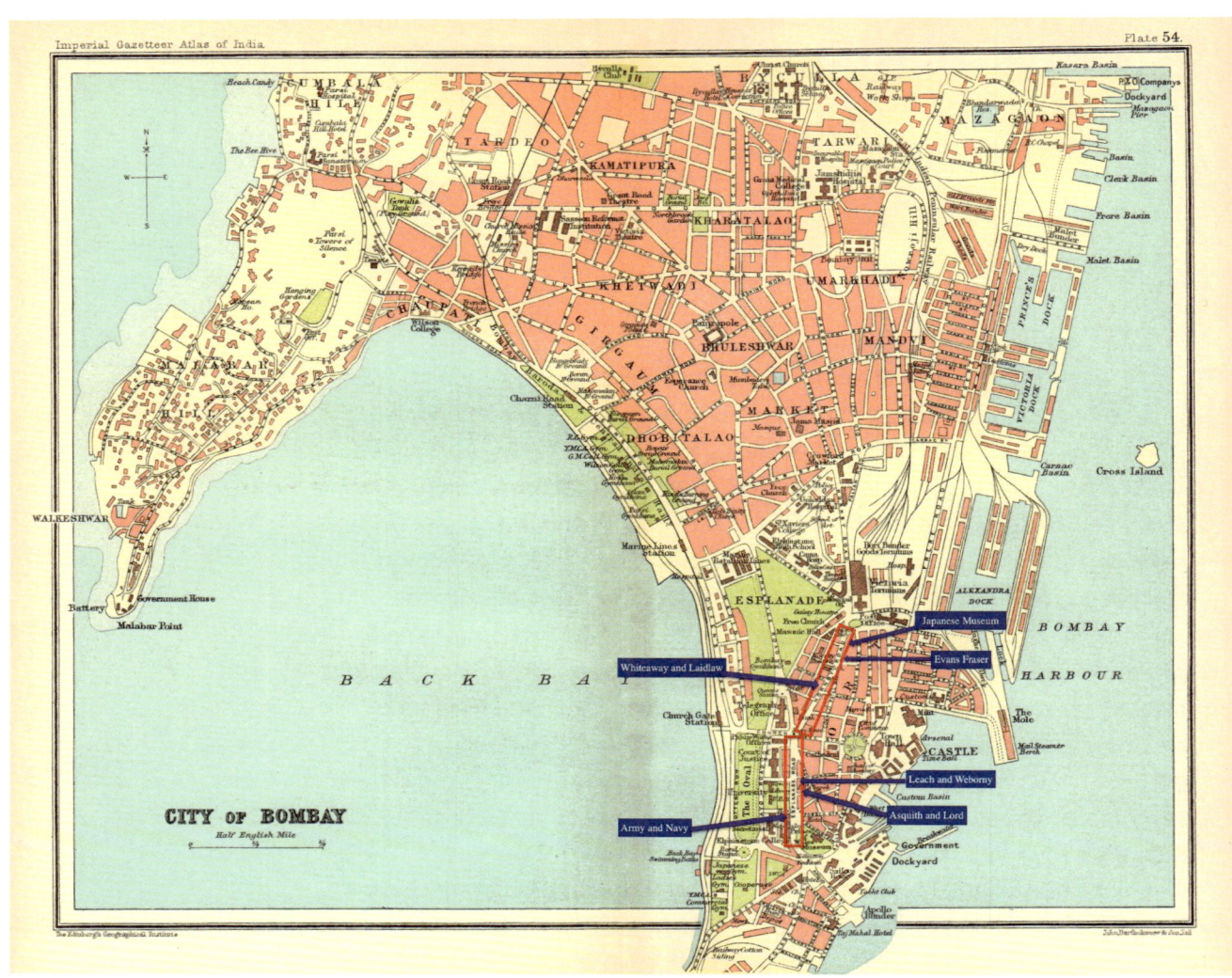

Fig. 7.2
Major European stores on Hornby and Esplanade Roads (outlined in red). Source map: *The Imperial Gazetteer of India,* Vol. XXVI, Atlas, (revised edition), Oxford: Clarendon Press, 1931, plate 54.

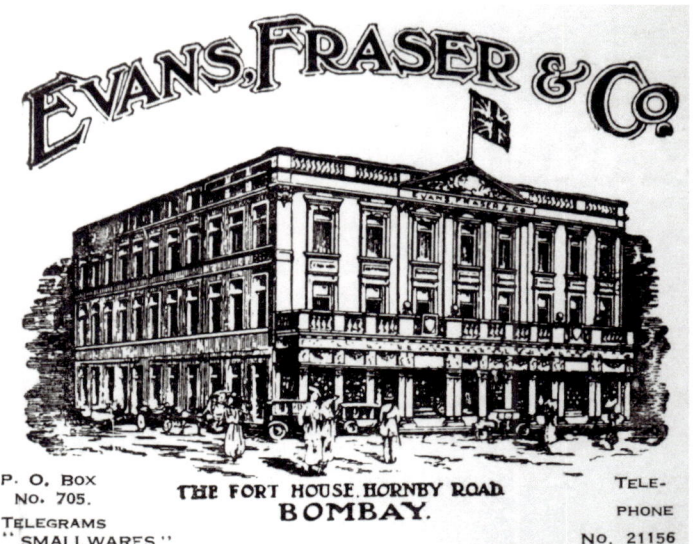

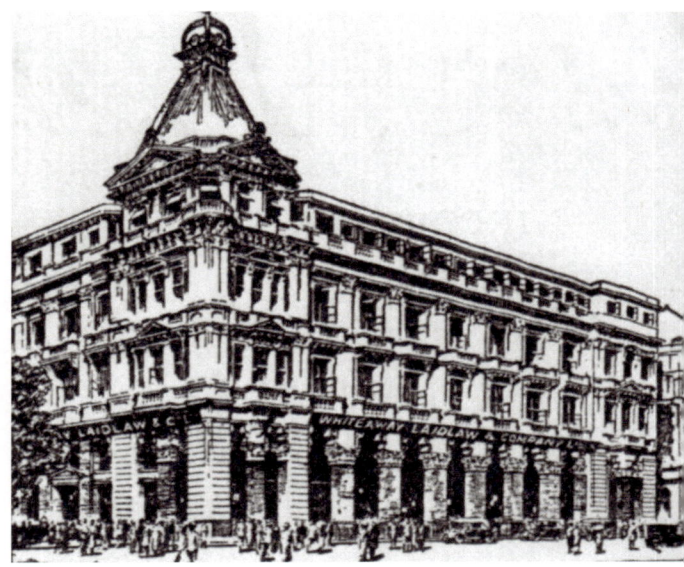

Hornby Road in particular became a major focus of protest mobilities in the city. Everyday picketing activities on Hornby Road, throughout June 1930 for instance, drew crowds in the hundreds or thousands, sparking prominent public confrontations over boycott.[3] On a more spectacular basis, by the time a massive procession on 6 May 1930 made it from Congress House in Girgaum to Flora Fountain (at the intersection of Hornby and Esplanade roads) some 50,000 participants thronged the street (Fig. 7.4).[4] Whether for huge crowds or more modest groups of schoolboys, Hornby Road served as a key final stage of marches headed to giant rallies on the Esplanade Maidan.[5] Dramatizing the confrontations that marked these events, in August 1930 a Congress leader proposed renaming Hornby Road "Lathi Road," given how often the police *lathi*-charged protesters there.[6]

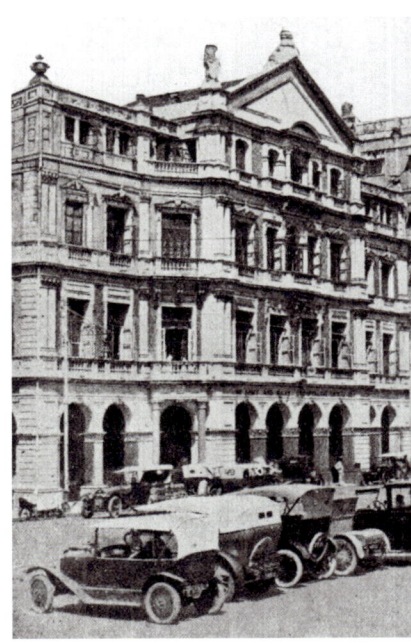

Fig. 7.3
Bombay's major European department stores: Evans Fraser, Whiteaway Laidlaw, and the Army and Navy Stores
Source: *The Times of India Guide to Bombay*, pp. vii, iv; and *Bombay, The Metropolis of the East*, p. 12

The photos in the Nursey album offer compelling evidence in relation to how gender dynamics structured the protest events on Hornby and Esplanade roads. For all we have been told that women were at the heart of boycott movements, early images of boycott events at key stores in the Fort do *not* feature women as central players. Instead, in these photographs boycott appears to be a male experience. Thus, men mill around on the street in front of Whiteaway Laidlaw (Fig. 7.5) or are led off by police after arrest in front of Leach and Weborny (Fig. 7.6). The one exception here is a set of two images in front of Whiteaway featuring local Congress leader Lilavati Munshi (Fig. 7.7, Fig. 7.8). But in these photographs she is interestingly positioned, appearing not as a picketer prepared for arrest herself, but instead as a negotiator, coordinating the details of mass action. Thus in Fig. 7.7, she stands on the footpath, handbag tucked under her arm, adjusting her sari over a very modern short-sleeved sari blouse, bobbed hair uncovered, in the midst of a group of uniformed volunteers and white and native police. All are at ease, leaning on canes and *lathi*s, equally confident in looking at the camera,

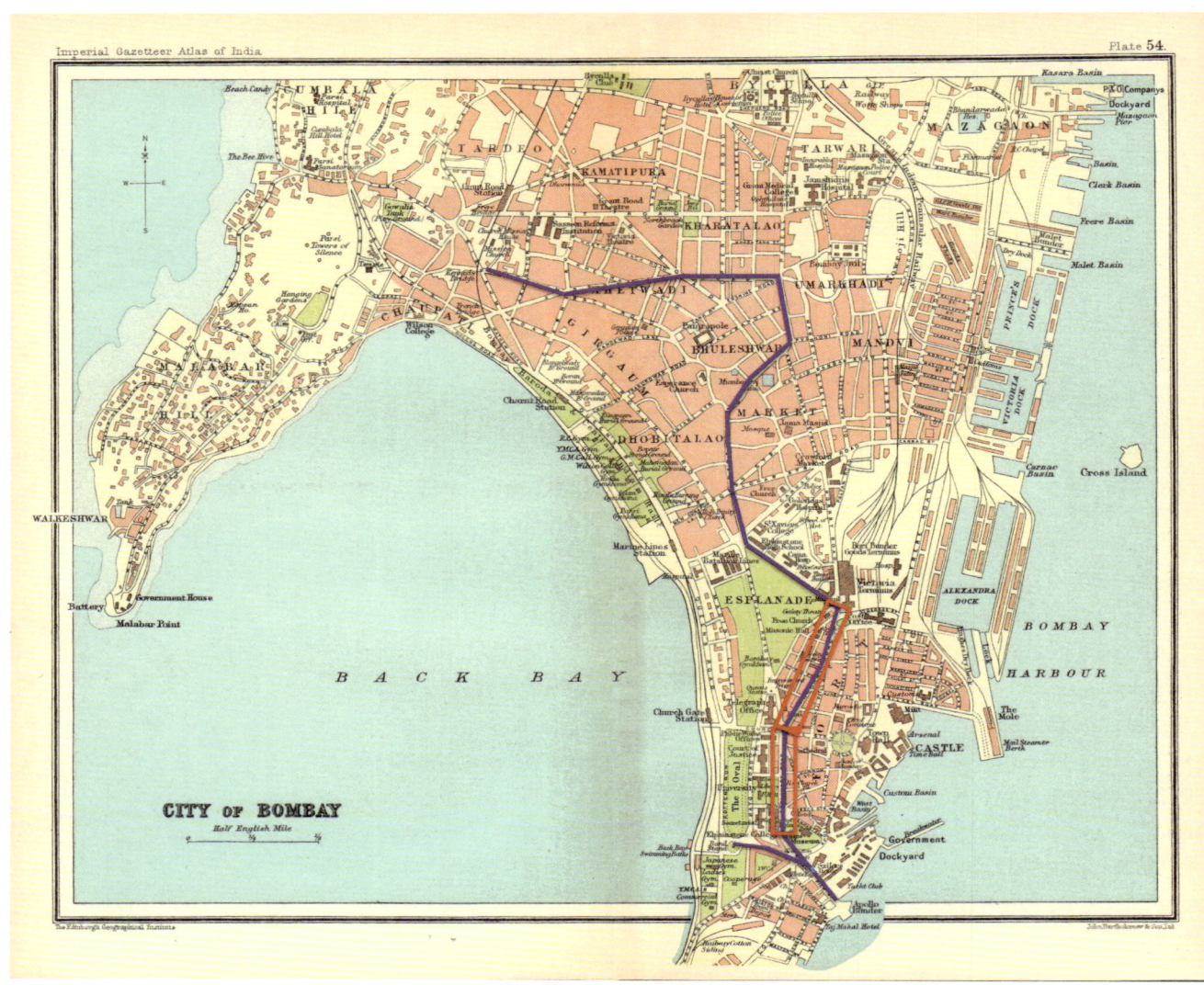

Plate 54.

Fig. 7.4
Procession route
(marked in purple),
6 May 1930. Red boxes
indicate Hornby and
Esplanade Roads.
Source map: *The
Imperial Gazetteer
of India*, Vol. XXVI,
Atlas, (revised
edition), Oxford:
Clarendon Press,
1931, plate 54.

FACING PAGE, ABOVE
Fig. 7.5
"Several lathi
charges were made
during the recent
civil disobedience
movement on the
picketers outside
Messers Whiteways."
1930
Gelatin Silver Print,
114 x 162 mm
ACP: 98.77.0002
(105b)
Protests in front of
Whiteaway Laidlaw,
likely in June 1930.

FACING PAGE, BELOW
Fig. 7.6
"A police officer
arresting a picketer
at Leach and Weberny
[Weborny]." 1930
Gelatin Silver Print,
116 x 160 mm
ACP: 98.77.0002 (46a)
Arrest of picketer
in front of Leach &
Weborny, likely in
June 1930.

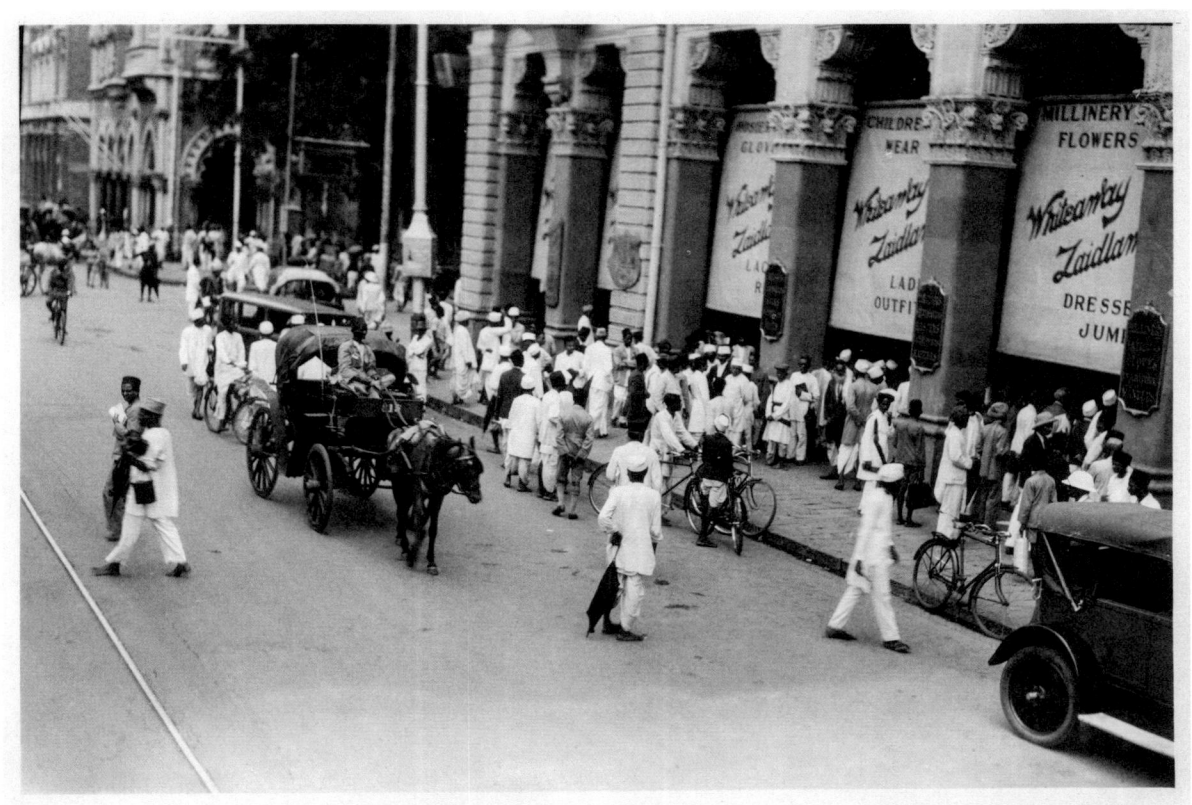

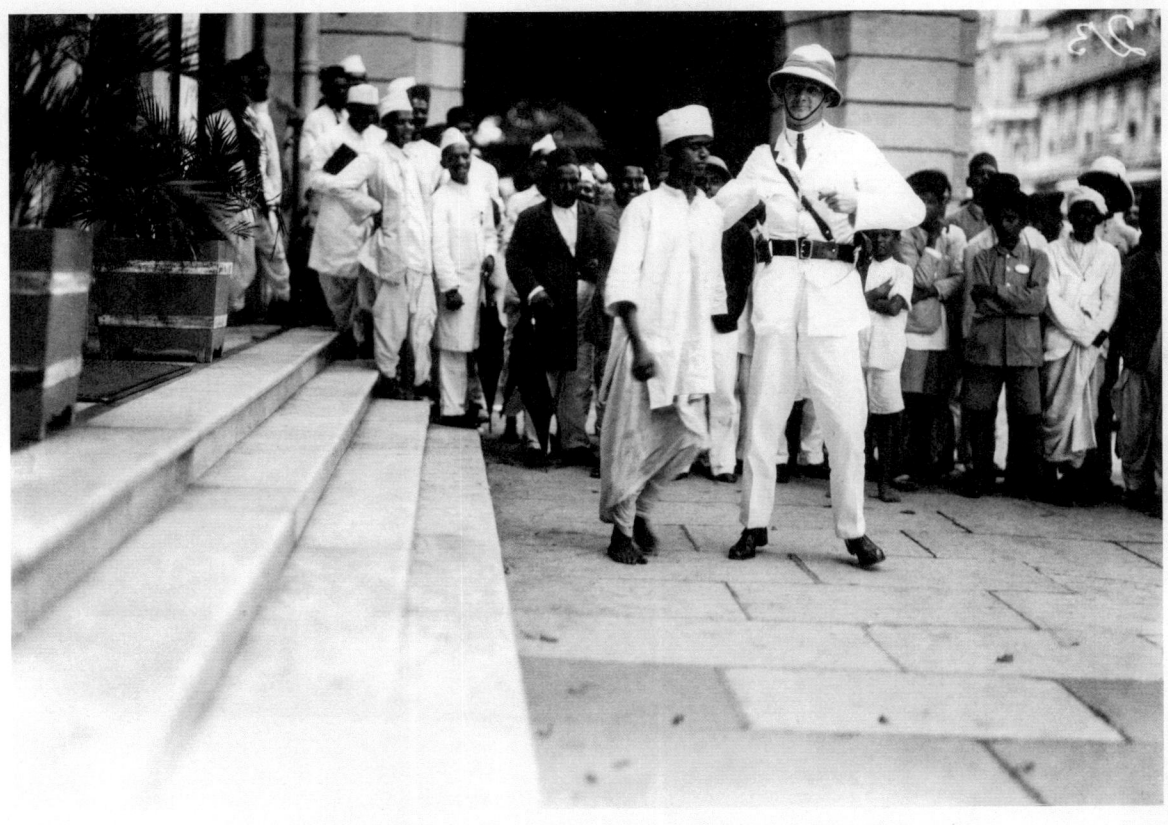

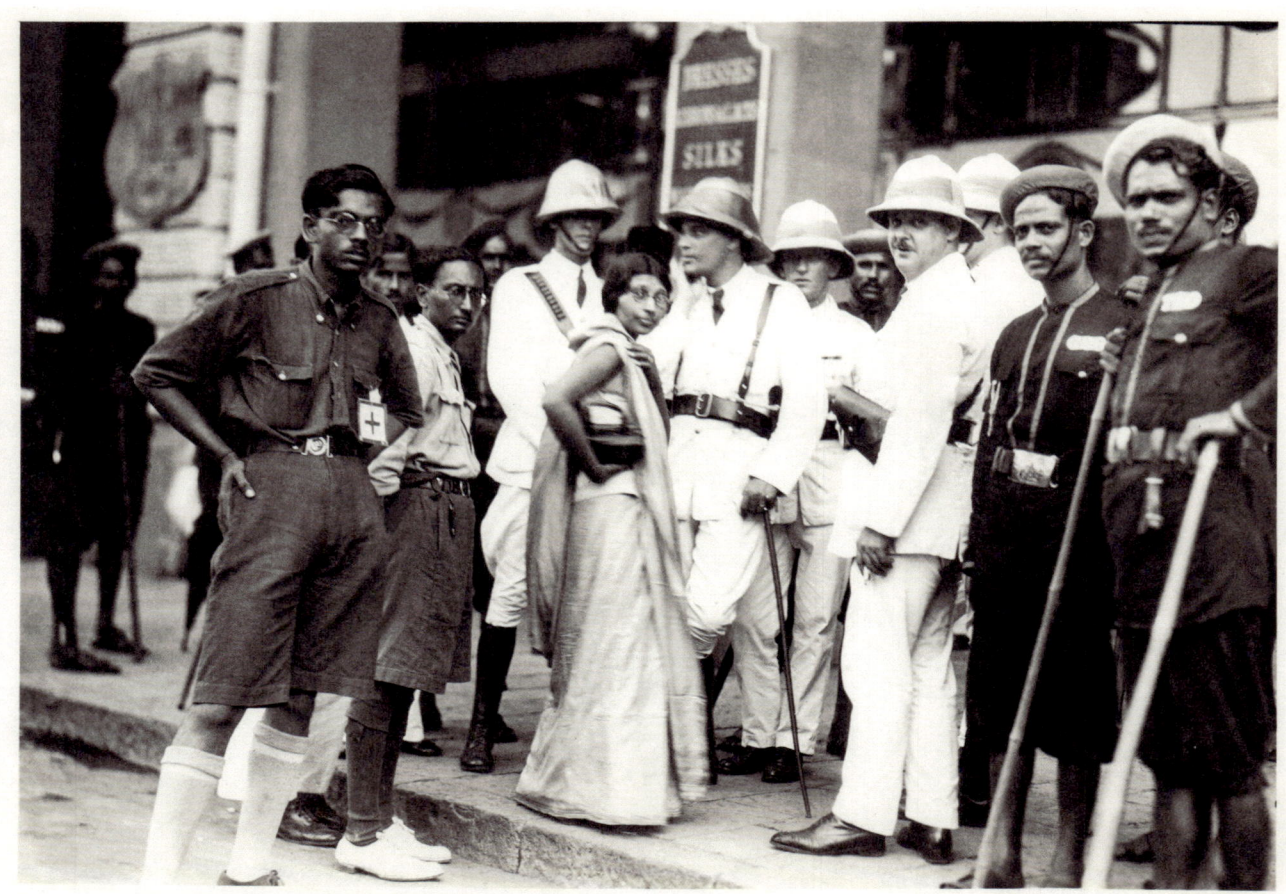

Fig. 7.7
"Whiteaway under police guard. Owing to the picketing activities of the congress [Congress] at Messers Whiteaway Laidlaw Ltd the police commissioner stationed a police pose [posse] to guard the showrooms and entrence [entrance] to the shop from pickeeters [picketers]. Daily several pickets were arrested." 1930 Gelatin Silver Print, 115 x 159 mm ACP: 98.77.0002 (45b) Congress leader Lilavati Munshi, in front of Whiteaway Laidlaw, likely in June 1930.

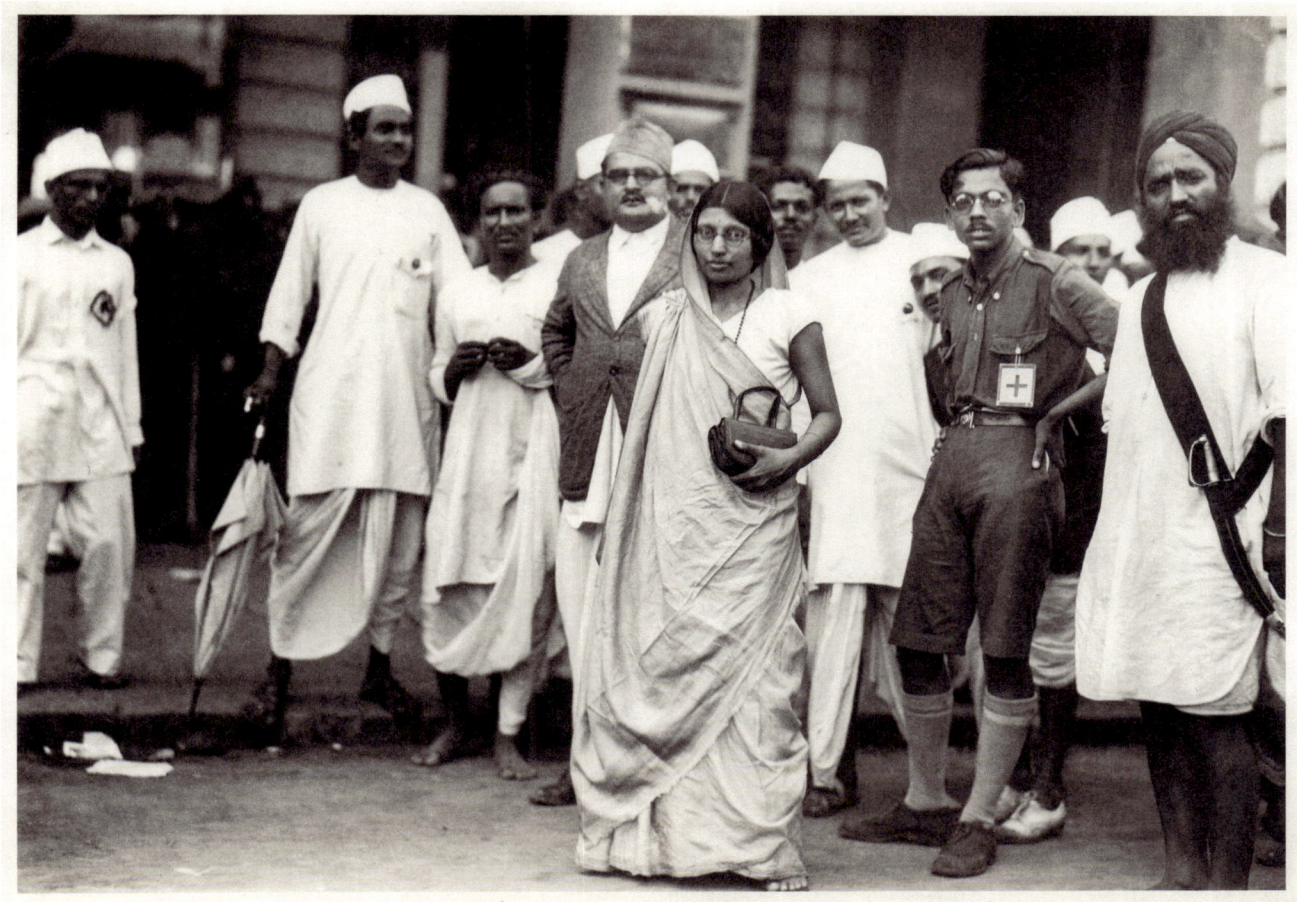

their conversation perhaps interrupted by the photographer. Figure 7.8 frames Munshi in the street, farther from the shop's arcade, standing assuredly in front of and apart from the male volunteers who, while returning the photographer's gaze, appear to be waiting for the next step in the action to unfold.

Lilavati Munshi's presence at Whiteaway Laidlaw speaks to the role that this particular venue and street played in the boycott events of 1930. Whiteaway Laidlaw was among the most publicly contested individual stores in the European shopping area, not only because it was one of the biggest, but also because its white managers actively called in and supported police action against picketers, earning the ire of the crowds.[7] But these photographs from Hornby Road also reveal three other elements. First, they show the variable deployment of women on the streets in boycott actions, a process that changed across different topographies and contexts. Second, these photographs reveal how the boycott tried to redefine the visibility of market relations, moving choices about what to buy or use into public view, subject to monitoring by crowds. Third, the images reveal how concerns about female respectability structured media and public conversations about boycott efforts, defining picketing for supporters and opponents alike. Building on earlier efforts to wean Indians off

Fig. 7.8
"Mrs. Lilavti [Lilavati] Munshi outside Whiteway [Whiteaway] Laidlaw when it was picketed." 1930
Gelatin Silver Print, 113 x 157 mm
ACP: 98.77.0002 (58a)
Congress leader Lilavati Munshi, in front of Whiteaway Laidlaw, likely in June 1930.

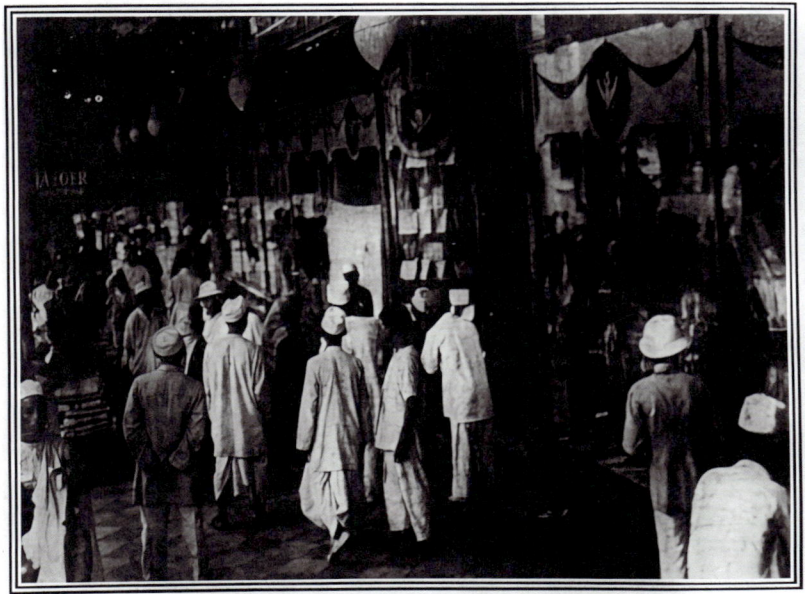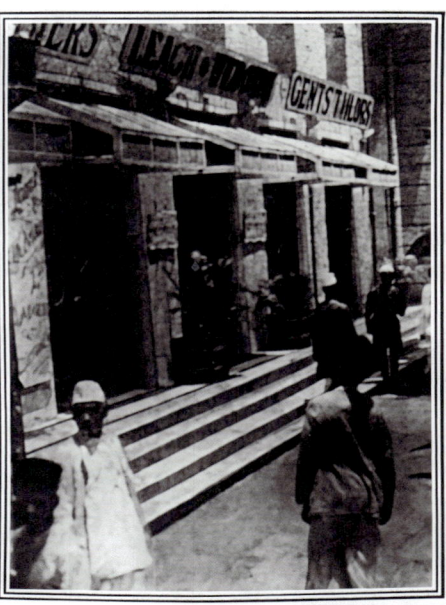

Fig. 7.9
"Picketing of Foreign
Shops in Defiance
of the Viceroy's
Ordinance" at
Whiteaway Laidlaw
(left) and Leach and
Weborny (right).
*The Illustrated
Weekly of India*,
8 June 1930, Late News
Supplement, p. I.

foreign goods (see Chapter Four in this volume), the strategic reinvention of boycott along gendered lines reveals key points of political innovation for the 1930–31 Civil Disobedience Movement.

In its earliest days, Civil Disobedience boycott efforts in the Fort area did not involve women as volunteers at all. Picketing efforts began to target shops selling foreign goods in earnest only in early June 1930, with the arrival of the monsoon forcing a halt to contraband salt production.[8] By mid-June, the Congress was regularly sending volunteers out every day to 10 or so prominent shops on Hornby and Esplanade roads, where they were just as regularly arrested by police (Fig. 7.9).[9] These volunteers were only men, not just in Fort but also in other areas of the city seen as unreceptive to the Congress cause—areas such as Charni Road, Bhendi Bazaar, Falkland Road, Byculla and Parel.[10] Female picketers, meanwhile, were sent to parts of town considered sympathetic to nationalism (see Fig. 4.2).[11] Only in September 1930 were women assigned to picket in the Fort area.[12] After an initial cohort picketed successfully outside the Army and Navy Stores, *desh sevikas* (members of the Desh Sevika Sangh, the volunteer women's auxiliary of the Congress) then regularly took up picketing duties in the area.[13]

It is, of course, worth asking what "success" meant in terms of these picketing efforts. In terms of economic impact, certainly sales were affected. At the April 1931 annual meeting of the Bombay Trades Association, held at its headquarters on Hornby Road itself, Association President L. Leuba complained that 1930 was the worst year for trade in the country on record, due both to the global economic depression and to Civil Disobedience, which was responsible for "practically paralysing" trade for a considerable period.[14] Despite such gloomy assessments, most of the shops in the Fort area targeted for boycott in 1930–31 not only survived but thrived, continuing to provide diverse imported goods to ready consumers into the 1940s. Evans Fraser ran advertisements throughout the period of the Civil Disobedience Movement, declaring itself to be "Bombay's dependable store," perhaps to assure patrons anxious about accessing goods.[15] The Army and Navy Stores, meanwhile, leaned heavily into their catalogue sales, in 1933 advertising free deliveries, often twice daily, on telephone and mail orders within Bombay.[16]

"Successful" picketing can be gauged in ways other than preventing the sale of imported goods. One tactic effectively deployed was to publicize the politics of shopping. Building on earlier boycott efforts during the Non-Cooperation Movement in 1920–22, nationalist volunteers in 1930–31 made collective daily street drama out of their picketing on Hornby and Esplanade roads.[17] These efforts drew together four main groups: nationalist volunteers, police, crowds of onlookers, and shoppers/shopkeepers. Each played a fairly formulaic role, particularly in the early days. In June 1930, Congress leaders sent male volunteers to particular shops on set schedules, often arriving singly or in groups of two, every half an hour (Fig. 7.6). Once picketers took their places outside a shop, the police would swoop in to arrest them and take them away in police vans to be detained, intervening again when the next batch of picketers showed up.[18] All of this was overseen by crowds who gathered on the streets and footpaths, sometimes appearing well before the picketers themselves arrived.[19] These crowds were not just passive onlookers, but active agents in the unfolding action (see Chapter Three in this volume). On 17 June, for instance, it was the 2,000 people assembled to watch picketers at Whiteaway Laidlaw who effectively barricaded the store, denying shoppers entry.[20] Reporting on events of 20 June, The Times of India noted that while the police had no trouble arresting the 25 Congress picketers involved that day, they "had an extremely difficult task in dispersing the crowds that gathered to witness the proceedings," eventually resorting to four separate lathi charges which injured 42 people, eight of them seriously (Fig. 7.11).[21]

The central targets of all these efforts were, of course, shoppers and shopkeepers. Picketers aimed to dissuade consumers from buying foreign goods, using tactics that ranged from persuasion to physical obstruction, heckling and jeering at customers and spitting on shops, to traffic disruption and crowd action. The British-oriented The Times of India complained endlessly about picketers, carefully noting the movement and press of bodies as crowds moved across roads and onto footpaths, impeding access to shops and—as seen in Fig. 7.9— filling porticos, with display windows rendering visible the consumers inside and staging those consumers as witnesses to the drama on the street.[22] A July 1930 letter to the editor complained about the "supreme contempt of law and order" and "intimidation" shown by the Congress in their picketing campaigns, noting

ABOVE

Fig. 7.10

Army & Navy
Stores, Bombay.
Original caption:
"Women pickets in Fort
Shops: Since Friday
women have been posted
to picket shops in the
Fort Area."
*The Illustrated
Weekly of India*, 7
Sept. 1930, Late News
Supplement, p. V.

BELOW

Fig. 7.11

"Armed police
arriving on the scene
of the disturbance
where a large crowd
demonstrated[.] A
lathi charge was
ordered were [where]
several persons were
injured."
Gelatin Silver Print,
113 x 161 mm
ACP: 98.77.0002 (40a)
Police deployed at
Whiteaway Laidlaw,
likely in June 1930.

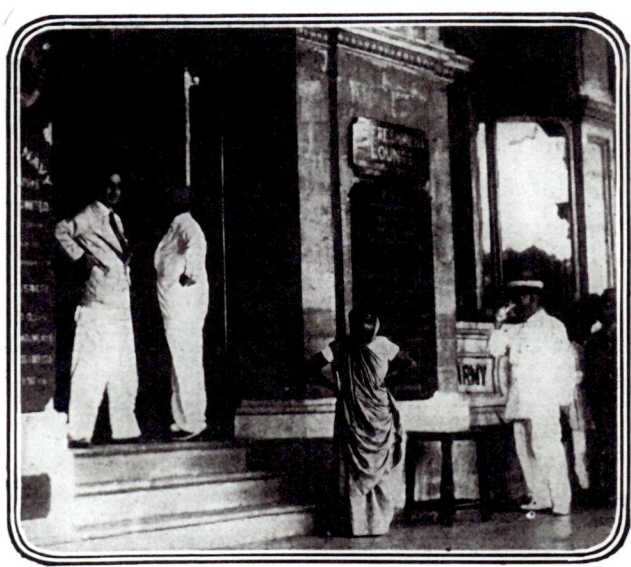

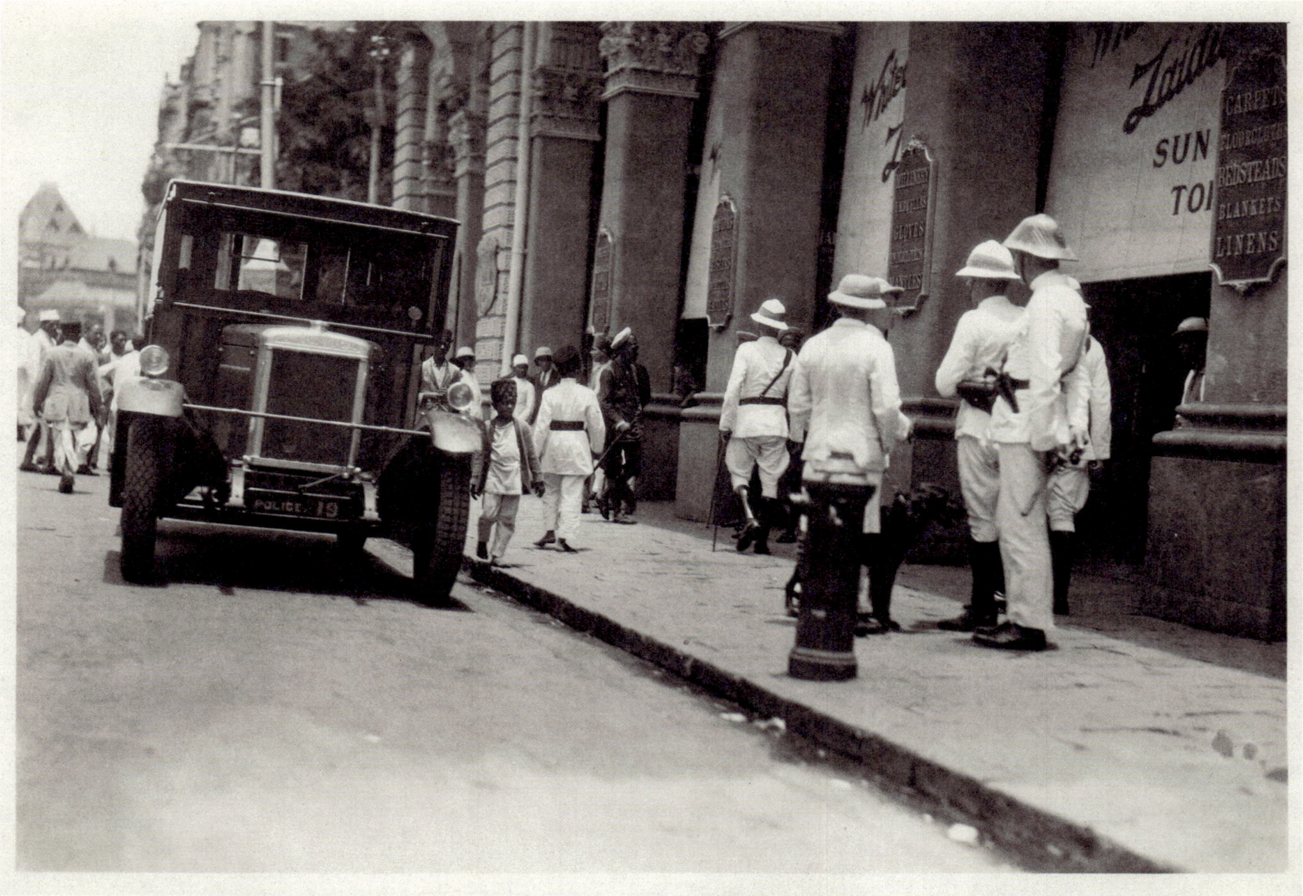

that "a lady at times cannot enter Messrs. Whiteaway and Laidlaw's without being met with insults and jeers," while traffic could be disrupted for hours at a time.[23]

The focus on the aforementioned "lady" harassed at the entrance of Whiteaway Laidlaw is, of course, telling. *The Times of India* regularly articulated its concerns in gendered terms to dramatize picketing as an outrage against privileged minority women, depicting Parsi or European female shoppers as helpless victims of aggression by unruly Hindu and Muslim male volunteers and crowds—bringing to mind the communitarian violence of the Prince of Wales riots in Bombay in 1921.[24] These accounts delineated picketing not primarily as an economic threat to imported goods and large-scale business, but as a moral threat to female safety and to the freedom of a certain kind of entitled cosmopolitan woman to move unimpeded through the city to shop as she saw fit.[25] Describing an incident from December 1930, *The Times of India* reported that a rowdy group of male Hindu and Muslim volunteers had accosted a Parsi lady going to a shop on Hornby Road, demanding to inspect the parcel she carried; "she got frightened and wanted to go back, but the crowd did not allow her to do so," preventing her movement until she was rescued by several Parsi men.[26] In a letter to the editor on 8 June 1930, a Dr. W. Nunan described his own encounter with picketers on Hornby Road, presenting himself as the heroic avenger of beleaguered women frightened by Congress volunteers. Stopping his car to aid a European lady trying to enter a picketed Parsi-owned shop, he first had to brush aside a male volunteer who was "interposing his body between her and the doorway," only to then find that another volunteer had lain down across the steps to prevent entry. Furious "against these insults to a woman," he picked up the second male volunteer and bodily threw him out of the way—an act of violence he described as being "the only one thing to do." Entering the shop, he was "greeted with a chorus of thanks" from five frightened Parsi ladies, who entreated him to stay until their purchases were complete so that he could escort them past the crowd on their way out.[27]

In these media accounts, privileged minority women are the only persecuted shoppers, while Hindu and Muslim men are the only unruly picketers. Fear is felt by a specific kind of woman; insults and abuse are perpetrated by a specific kind of man. This is obviously a selective and highly reductive presentation of complex encounters, ignoring the early presence of women picketers in other parts of the city (including Parsi women on the picket lines), rifts between Hindus and Muslims over boycott efforts, and the fear male and female volunteers alike would have felt in the face of *lathi* charges.[28] My highlighting of this dichotomous rhetoric does not discount the authentic fear women of any race, community and class would have felt—and will always feel—when confronted by a hostile crowd. Rather, I use the media reports to contextualize new ways of reading the two images cited earlier: Lilavati Munshi confidently in charge outside Whiteaway Laidlaw (Fig. 7.7), and the lone woman picketing defiantly outside the Army and Navy Stores in the presence of three white men (Fig. 7.10). These images present a very different dynamic from that dramatized in *The Times of India* reportage, subverting the moral charge of boycott. Neither image frames European men as knights in shining armour, ready to rescue vulnerable European or native "ladies" besieged by hostile opponents. Instead, well-known or anonymous native women appear as leaders or as solitary agents of resistance, challenging their own vulnerability as they confront male onlookers—as evident in Fig. 7.10, where the authoritative stance of the picketing protagonist, shoulders squared and hands on hips, mirrors that of the two white men on the steps.

Indeed, the presence of women picketers upended the gendered dynamics of boycott in complex ways (Fig. 7.12). Even in the hostile reportage of *The Times of India*, women picketers were described in comparatively sympathetic language. Women persuaded and convinced and held discussions with shoppers while men heckled or threatened the latter; women maintained disciplined processions while men stirred crowds to violence.[29] In practice too, women were treated differently. Shop owners offered women picketers seats and treated them with courtesy—not just at nationalist-leaning stores, but even at imperial bastions like the Army and Navy Stores, where women picketing in September 1930 were given chairs on which to rest.[30] *The Times of India* also carried descriptions of crowds defending *female* picketers against rude *male* shoppers, reversing the normative media script of European and Parsi women shoppers being harassed by Hindu and Muslim men.[31]

Deploying women picketers thus was both a sensible allocation of volunteer labour, stretched thin by a rising tide of arrests, and also a strategic intervention to define and shift the politics of boycott. The strategic dimension becomes clear in the decision to finally send women out to Hornby and Esplanade roads in September 1930, months after they had been picketing elsewhere. That choice was made in the face of new, more aggressive measures to halt civil disobedience—measures which included the arrest of local Congress leaders; declaring of the Desh Sevika Sangh and other activist groups illegal; and the confiscation of Congress properties in the city. The deployment of women picketers to the Fort area posed a direct challenge to British administrators anxious to avoid the public outrage that was sure to follow the arrests of women on prominent thoroughfares. Initially, the police chose not to arrest female picketers in the Fort, even as arrests of picketers continued in other parts of the city.[32] When they did move, in November 1930, to finally arrest women in the Fort, the fears of public outrage proved to be well founded, even in a city accustomed to nationalist turbulence. After two female picketers were handled roughly by Englishmen in front of Whiteaway Laidlaw, native volunteers threatened "to pull

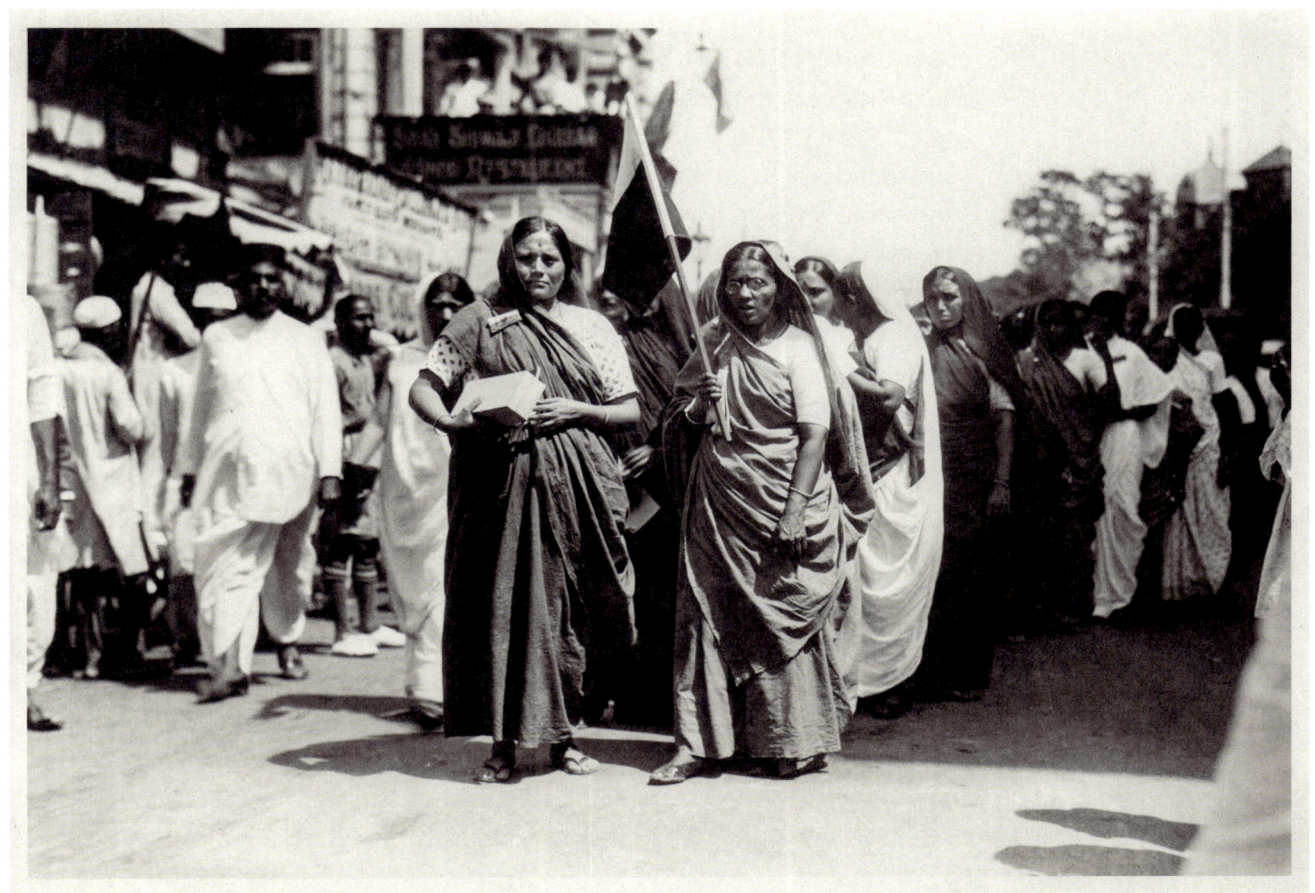

Fig. 7.12
"A boycott procession
in the market area."
c. 1930—1931
Gelatin Silver Print,
114 x 160 mm
ACP: 98.77.0002 (41a)
An example of the
generally disciplined
conduct of women
protesters.

or push any Englishwomen" who entered the store—a threat averted by a stern rebuke from Desh Sevika Sangh leaders.[33] Some shops selling foreign cloth refused to open, thus foreclosing the possibility of picketing and arrest.[34] To try to keep women picketers out of jail, a Bhuleshwar shop owner appeared in a local court in order to argue that the four women under trial had not, in fact, picketed his store at all. Meanwhile native merchants on Charni Road lodged a protest with the magistrate, asking for charges to be dropped as they had "no objection to the peaceful picketing carried on by lady volunteers in front of their shops."[35] Here, roles were reversed, with women picketers—rather than shoppers—eliciting rescue and support, in this case, by Indian men.

Events on Hornby and Esplanade roads staged boycott as a deeply gendered experience, putting respectable female shoppers or female picketers at the mercy of male crowds, with the women's bodily safety to be protected or defended in political contests over the sale of European goods. By shifting boycott efforts in the Fort into women's hands over time, nationalist leaders tactically and successfully deployed deeply embedded social codes and cultural tropes of gender, embracing women's public roles even while calling on men to join street crowds and volunteer on their own account. Mohandas Gandhi may have declared that feminizing picketing efforts was a strategy of non-violence, chosen in order to reduce unrest and ensure an "elevated" and "calmer" atmosphere;[36] but staging boycott as women's political work was also about intensifying the results and repercussions of picketing practices. Whatever Gandhi's goals of non-violence, it was of course both the literal and potential violence surrounding female shoppers and picketers that elicited attention from police, journalists and the public—and the photographer(s) of the Nursey album—with paths blocked, packages opened, abuse hurled and modesty subverted. Shop entrances, windows and steps, nearby footpaths and streets, all provided the stage on which that violence was threatened, enacted, witnessed and documented. As a political practice, organized boycott transformed women into frontline activists, central to the public disruption of colonial commerce at a crucial moment of nationalist upheaval.

Notes

My thanks to my research assistants, Ross Kennon and Lea Greco, for their work gathering materials for this essay. I also thank Sumathi Ramaswamy, Avrati Bhatnagar and Dinyar Patel for their helpful comments on earlier drafts of my text.

1. See, for instance, the rallies held to express outrage at police treatment of women on 26 October 1930. See K.K. Chaudhary (ed.), *Source Material for a History of the Freedom Movement in India*, vol. XII (Bombay: Gazetteers Department, Government of Maharashtra, 1995), pp. 54–56.

2. Avrati Bhatnagar and Sumathi Ramaswamy, "Light Writing on the Lathi Raj: Bombay, 1930–31", *History of Photography*, vol. 45, no. 4 (2021), pp. 304–19. See also Chapters Five and Nine in this volume.

3. See, for instance: "Mob Violence in Bombay", *The Times of India*, 19 June 1930.

4. Chaudhary (ed.), *Source Material for a History of the Freedom Movement in India*, vol. XI, p. 76.

5. ibid., p. 394; also see "Bombay Procession: Indian Prisoners' Day", *The Times of India*, 11 August 1930, p. 7.

6. ibid., p. 402.

7. ibid., pp. 209, 229. Perhaps reflecting the contested nature of this site and the disruption of normal shopping in the area on boycott days, the Nursey album photographs show no Europeans present at the store, aside from police officers.

8. According to one list from September 1930, the specific shops targeted were: Army and Navy Stores; the Japanese Museum; Madame Rose; Asquith and Lord; Hoar and Co.; Leach & Weborny; Whiteaway Laidlaw; Evans Fraser & Co.; Ahmed Essel Ali; Karanjia and Co.; Bhesania and Co; and Madhowdas Raghunathdas. See "Hoisting of Congress Flag on Municipalities", *The Times of India*, 8 September 1930, p. 11.

9. "Negotiations with Government Denied", *The Times of India*, 21 June 1930, p. 9.

10. "Mass Picketing of Foreign Cloth Shops in Bombay", *The Times of India*, 7 August 1930, p. 11.

11. ibid.

12. "Hoisting of Congress Flag".

13. Chaudhary (ed.), *Source Material*, vol. XI, p. 476. See also "Volunteer Stabbed in Bombay: Rowdy Demonstrators", *The Times of India*, 5 December 1930, p. 11.

14. "Signs of Return to Normal Conditions in Commerce", *The Times of India*, 24 April 1931, p. 3.

15. From advertisement for Evans Fraser & Co., *The Times of India*, 28 November 1930, p. 4.

16. *Army and Navy Cooperative Society, Bombay Catalogue* (Bombay: Army and Navy Stores, 1933), p. v.

17. My discussion of this as drama, and of the role of the crowd, draws from Jim Masselos's early study "Audiences, Actors and Congress Dramas: Crowd Events in Bombay City in 1930", *South Asia*, vol. 8, no. 1 (1985), pp. 71–86.

18. "Mob Violence in Bombay".

19. "Picketing of Foreign Cloth Shops in Bombay", *The Times of India*, 20 June 1930, p. 11.

20. "Mob Violence in Bombay".

21. "Negotiations with Government Denied".

22. See, for example, "Picketing of Foreign Cloth Shops in Bombay".

23. 'Equity' [pen name], "Picketing Race Trains", Letter to the Editor, *The Times of India*, 30 July 1930, p. 11.

24. Dinyar Patel, "Beyond Hindu-Muslim Unity: Gandhi, the Parsis and the Prince of Wales Riots of 1921", *Indian Economic and Social History Review*, vol. 55, no. 2 (2018), pp. 234–35.

25. See, for example, "Picketing of Liquor Shops: Bombay 'War Council's' New Move", *The Times of India*, 11 June 1930, p. 11.

26. "Volunteer Stabbed in Bombay".

27. See, for example, W. Nunan, "Street-Life in Bombay: What Picketing Means", Letter to the Editor, *The Times of India*, 10 June 1930, p. 11.

28. For a discussion of communal tensions during the 1930–31 movement, see Prashant Kidambi, "Mill, Market, Mandir, Masjid: The Geographies of Communal Conflict in Colonial Bombay, c. 1929–39", *South Asia*, vol. 46, no. 6 (2023), pp. 1272–93.

29. See, for instance, "Foreign Cloth Boycott: Picketing in City", *The Times of India*, 9 May 1930, p. 11.

30. Chaudhary (ed.), *Source Material*, vol. XI, p. 476.

31. See, for example, "The Sweet Sevikas", Letter to the Editor, *The Times of India*, 18 October 1930, p. 15.

32. Chaudhary (ed.), *Source Material*, vol. XI, pp. 488, 495.

33. See Uma Shanker's two-part audio interview with Mrs Goshiben Captain, 16 May 1970 (Interview Number 122, 110 minutes), archived at the Centre of South Asian Studies, University of Cambridge, https://www.s-asian.cam.ac.uk/archive/audio/collection/g-captain/; digitized typewritten interview transcripts at http://media.s-asian.cam.ac.uk/pdf/122a.pdf (Part 1) and http://media.s-asian.cam.ac.uk/pdf/122b.pdf (Part 2).

34. "Avoiding Arrest of Picketers: Hindu Shopkeepers", *The Times of India*, 8 November 1930, p. 13.

35. "Police Round up Women Pickets in Bombay", *The Times of India*, 5 November 1930, p. 11.

36. "Work of Demobilising Bombay Volunteers", *The Times of India*, 12 March 1931, p. 11.

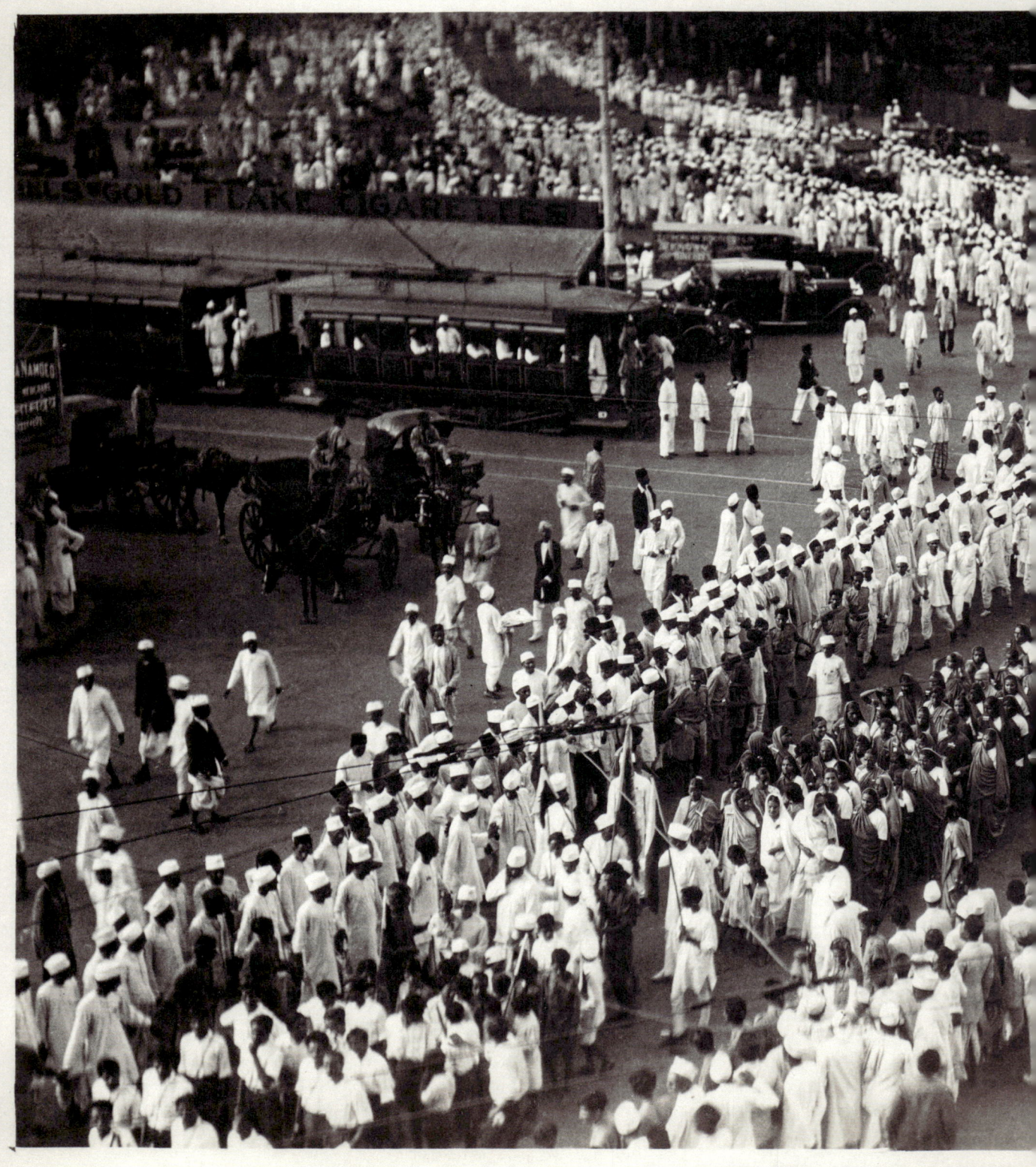

Mr Vithalbhai taken in a procession on hi[s]
arrival from Surat to Bombay.

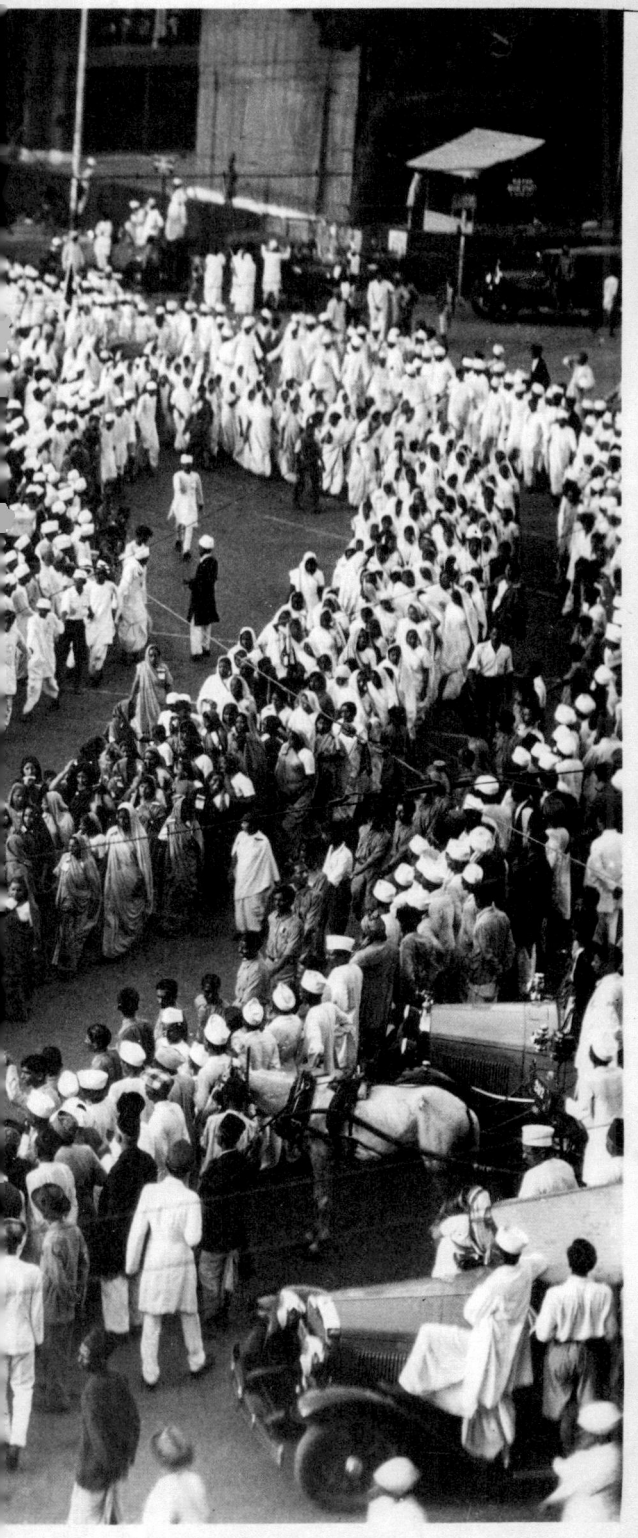

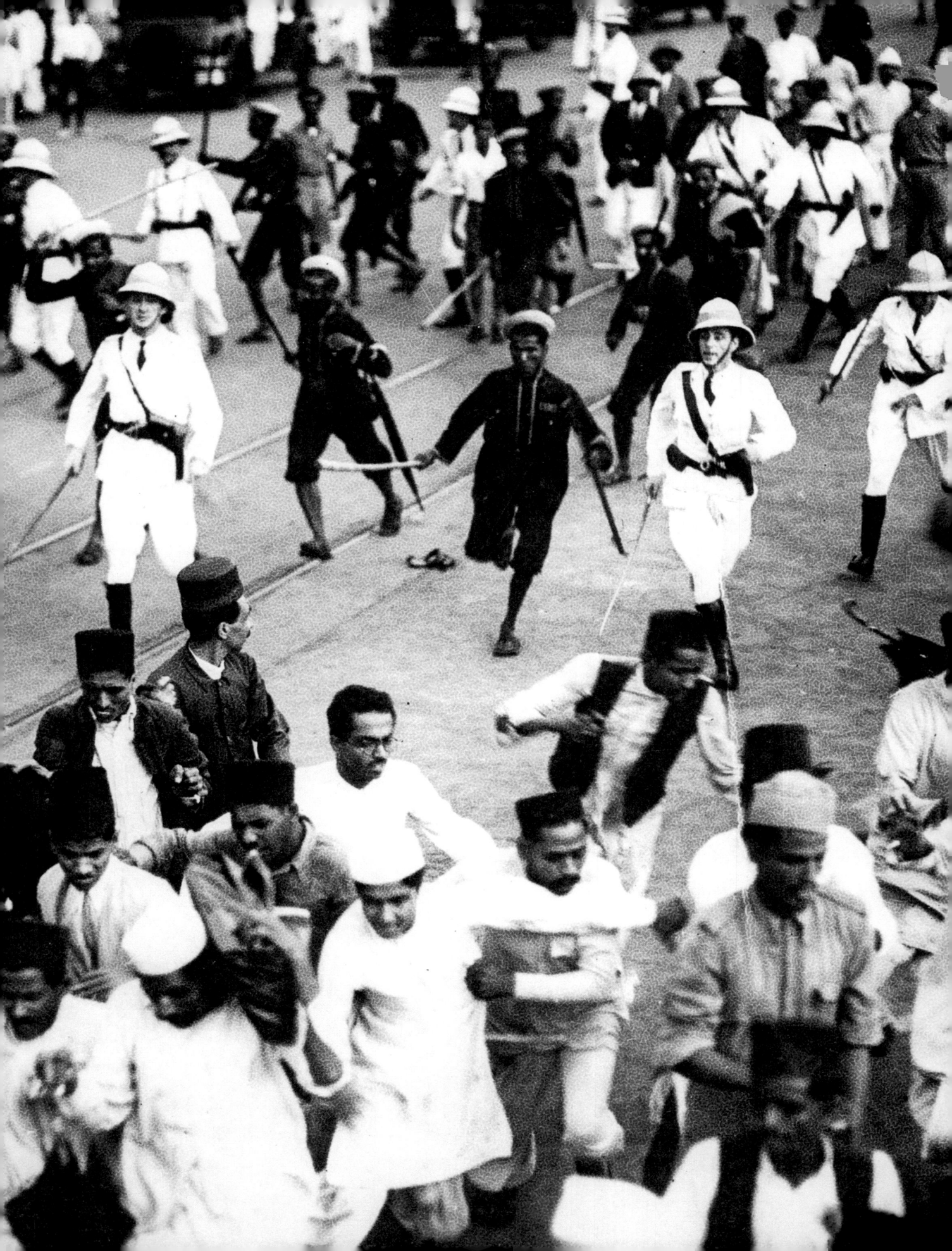

CHAPTER 8

PATROLLING THE STREETS OF DISOBEDIENCE IN BOMBAY

Avrati Bhatnagar

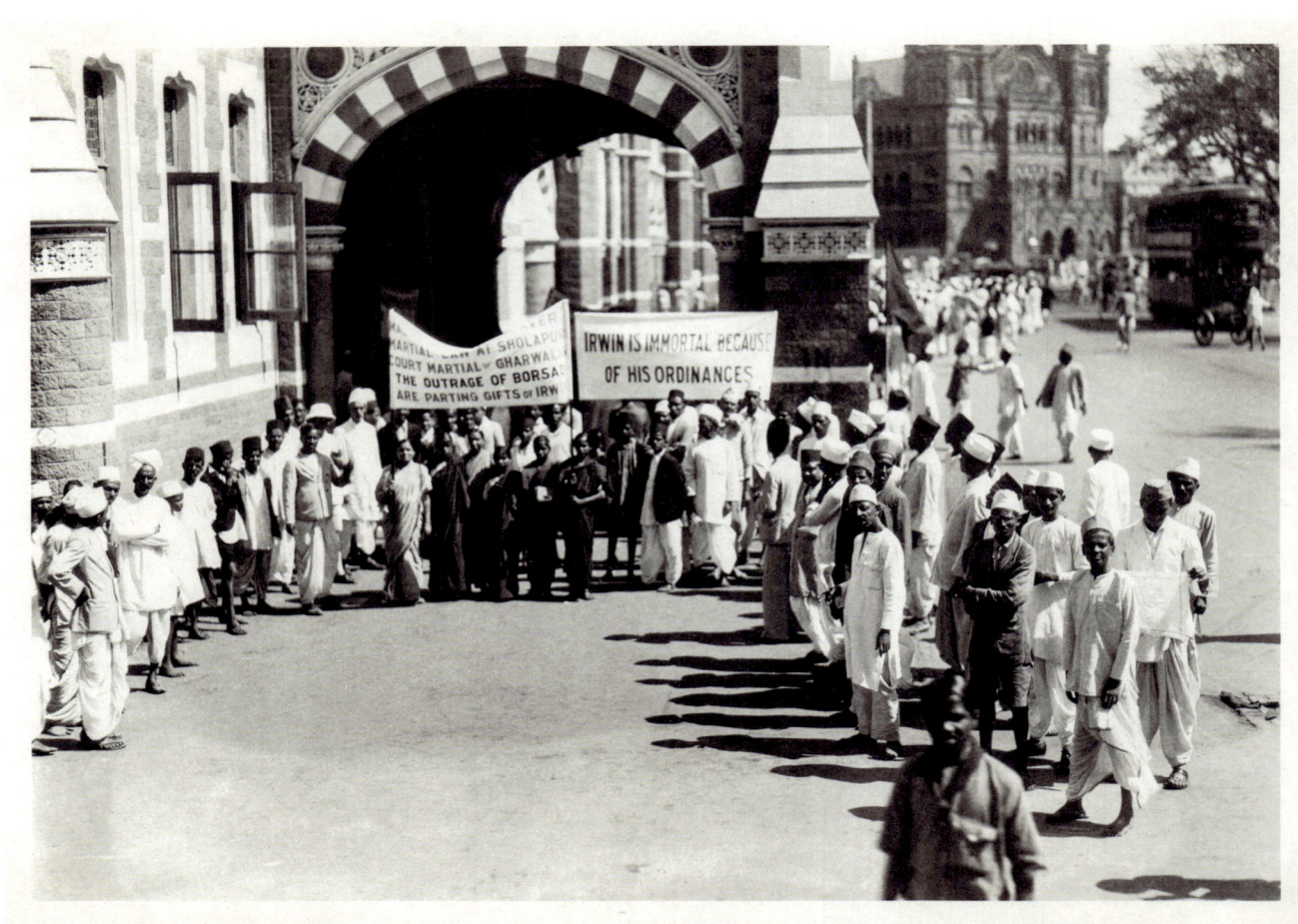

Congress women demonstrate outside the
Corporation hall .

On 23 February 1931, 10 months into the Civil Disobedience Movement that had spread across the breadth of colonial India, hundreds of nationalist volunteers gathered at the gates of the Municipal Corporation Hall in Bombay. Together, they staged a protest against their local representatives who were planning to honour Lord Irwin, the outgoing British Viceroy of India, in a farewell ceremony (Fig. 8.1). In the lead up to this day, organizers of anticolonial action in the city had especially appealed to Bombay women to participate in the demonstration, inviting "our sisters to muster in their thousands."[1] And the women showed up, as they had consistently done so for the past 10 months, eager to serve the nationalist cause. They arrived with raised banners condemning the legacy of tyrannical laws and ordinances left behind by Viceroy Irwin, issued during his tenure.[2] Closely in tow came the men of the Bombay colonial police, to oversee this demonstration and shut it down by force, when instructed to do so.

Part of a series of concerted and carefully planned efforts to exhibit nationalist will and challenge the arbitrary and unjust policies of the colonial state, the events that unfolded on this late February afternoon are well documented in the official record. Yet, textual accounts of both nationalist and colonial organizations, actively involved in shaping the (micro)events that unfolded on this hectic day, hardly register the presence of a photographer (or photographers) at this site. For amidst what inevitably turned into a violent confrontation between anticolonial protesters and the colonial police, a photographer approached a group of women and a handful of constables of the Bombay police with a camera in hand. This encounter between the so-far unidentified photographer(s), the camera and a heterogeneous group of colonial subjects, along with other images from this day, finds its way into the folios of the Nursey album.

In one of these photographs, six women in saris and four men in uniform are symmetrically placed in two rows, in self-conscious contained poses reminiscent of the practice widely prevalent in studio portraiture of this time (Fig. 8.2). The woman at the centre of the image stands with her arms crossed and stares resolutely, even defiantly, at the camera. Another avoids meeting the camera's gaze altogether, instead focusing her attention on her feet while holding hands with her nationalist sisters on either side. Present at the site as representatives

PAGES 198—199
"Mr. Vithalbhai [Patel] taken in a procession on his arrival from Surat to Bombay." c. 1930—1931
Gelatin Silver Print, 114 x 150 mm
ACP: 98.77.0002 (28b)

PAGE 200
"The city police dispersing the Hugh [huge] crowds that had assembled to witness the proceedings on Garwali day."
(Detail, see p. 213)

Fig. 8.1
"Congress women demonstrate outside the Corporation hall." 1931
Gelatin Silver Print, 115 x 160 mm
ACP: 98.77.0002 (84a)

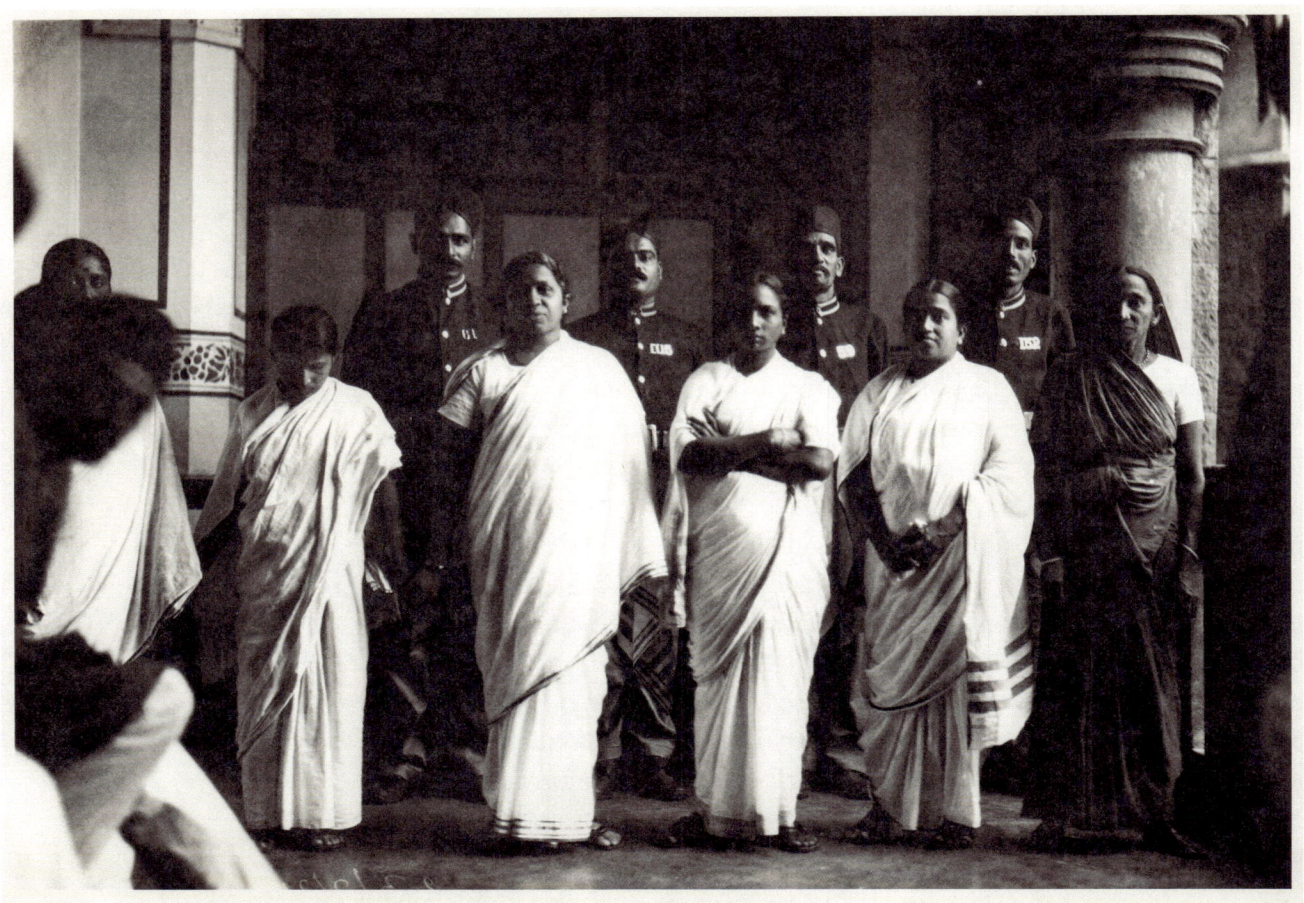

Fig. 8.2
"Women picketing
the Municipal hall
entranc[e]." 1931
Gelatin Silver Print,
114 x 159 mm
ACP: 98.77.0002 (86a)

of colonial authority, one of the police guards (on the extreme right) can barely hide a look of intrigue on his face while his peers strike an attentive pose. Disrupting the photographer's meticulous arrangement, another man enters the photographic frame on the left just when the image is captured and leaves a blurred trace of his presence in the historical archive. The photographer creates an unsettling ambivalence by setting these respective native bodies, opponents and champions of British colonial authority, as a foil to each other within a single frame. Yet, much like the dynamic blur of the man unexpectedly disrupting the frieze-like stasis of this equivocal, edgily compliant "group portrait," the contrast between these two sets of figures was not as stark, nor did it remain fixed, in these years of socio-political upheaval. Such dramatic juxtaposition of nationalist women and colonial policemen in the photographs of the Nursey album presents an opportunity to explore how colonial social relations were reconfigured alongside the (anti)colonial drama that unfolded on the streets of Bombay during the Civil Disobedience Movement.

Indeed, sari-clad female nationalist volunteers (*desh sevikas*) are prominent protagonists of the visual narrative of disobedience assembled in the Nursey album (see Chapters Six and Seven in this volume). But the photographs in this collection equally compel us to turn our attention towards the low-ranked, *lathi*-wielding police constable of native origin. With his back turned away from the camera, we find the native police constable charging towards intractable nationalist volunteers, at times under the supervision of his white colonial officers (Fig. 8.3, Fig. 8.5, see also Fig. 3.2a). From the Wadala salt pans on the outskirts of the city (see Chapter Five in this volume) to the bustling streets of the Bombay bazaar, the policemen on the spot—frequently mounted on horses and identified as "*sowars*" (riders) in the captions to these images—were photographed letting their batons loose on *satyagrahi*s, conducting forced arrests and trying to disperse the masses that gathered to witness civil disobedience in action. In other instances, they can be seen standing guard in anticipation of disobedient activities, ready to reassert colonial law and order (Fig. 8.4). The same *lathi* which would be raised to hit disobedient actors is used by the constables pictured in this image as a means to support their own bodies, likely weary from hours of standing duty.

Evidently, the native police constable played an indispensable role in the day-to-day running of colonial machinery. Indeed, while anticolonial action is often imagined as a struggle between the colonized native and the European

Fig. 8.3
"The mounted sowars who were called out to keep order on the election day making a lathi charge on the crowds." c. 1930–1931 Gelatin Silver Print, 115 x 157 mm
ACP: 98.77.0002 (75a)

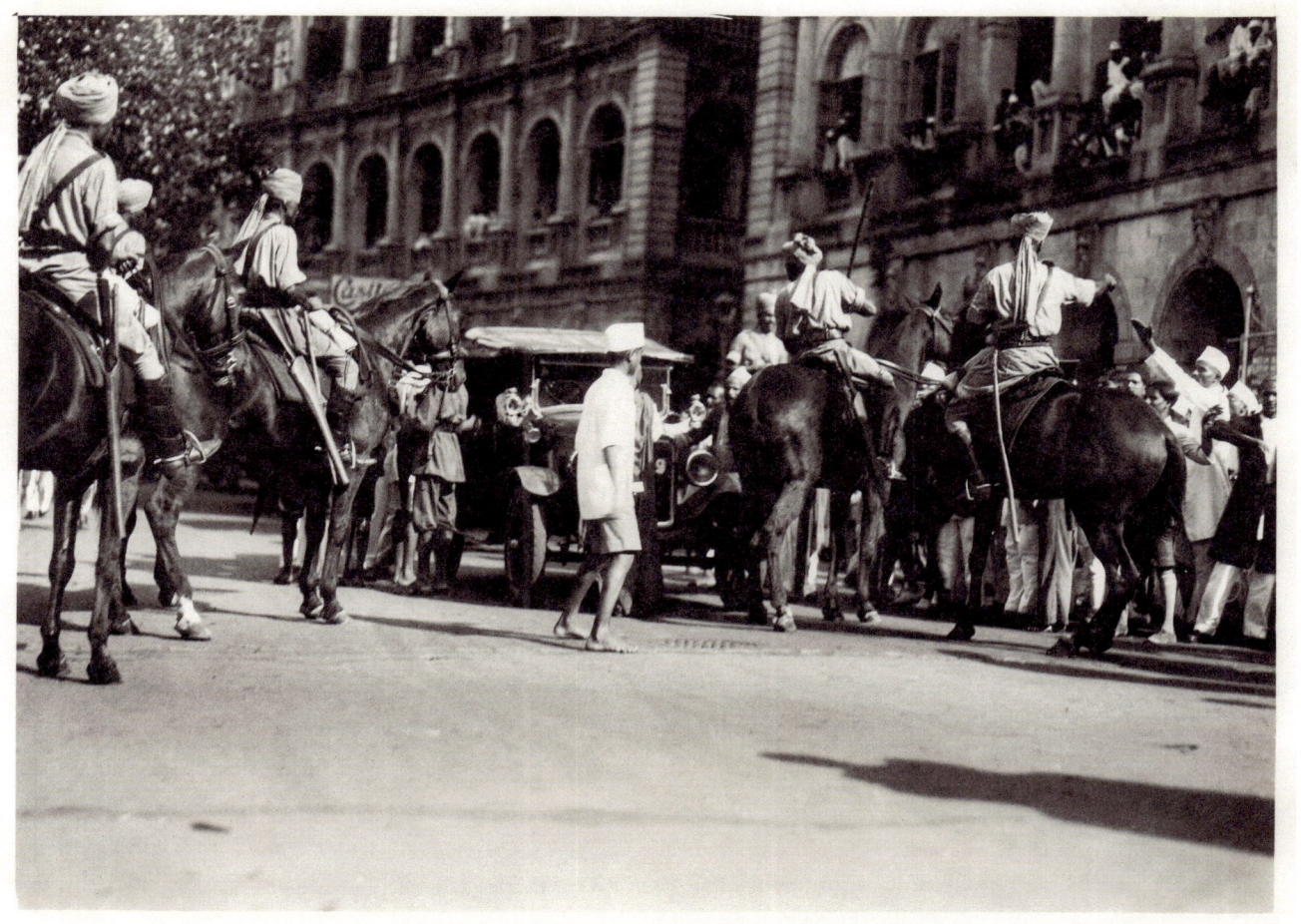

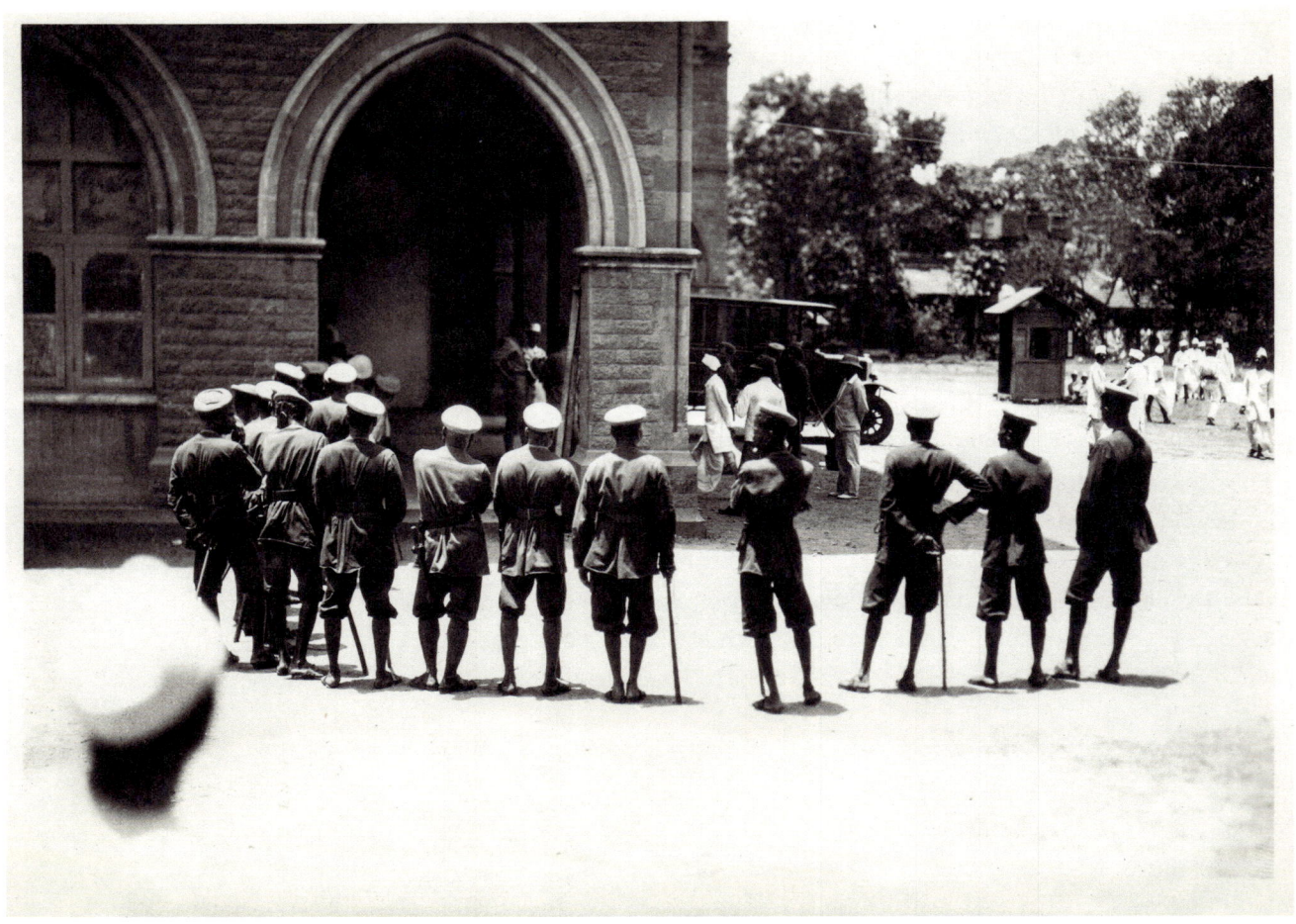

Fig. 8.4
"Police guarding
the entrance to the
Esplanade police
court." c. 1930—1931
Gelatin Silver Print,
115 x 161 mm
ACP: 98.77.0002 (76a)

colonizer, ironically, the most accessible, and visible, figure representing colonial authority during this time of disobedient action was the native figure of the police constable.[3] Like most units of colonial administration in British India, the Bombay police extensively relied on native labour to sustain itself. The white-skinned colonizer may have held on to all positions of any effective authority within the police organization but, ultimately, the British were far too few in numbers. The lowest and largest ranks in the force—that of the police constable—were held by men from a growing working class in the city, most of whom migrated from the hinterland in search of jobs and better financial prospects.[4]

Outfitted in a blue uniform, with a *lathi* in his hand, the native police constable thus assumed the responsibility of upholding colonial law and order on Bombay streets. Yet, he has not received enough attention within the vast scholarship on Indian colonial history, especially in Bombay. This essay engages with a selection of photographs in the Nursey album to show how a layered crisis of social and gender relations came to converge on this ambivalent figure, by the simultaneous ways in which he embodied colonial authority and yet remained in a fraught position as a colonized subject.

A *Lathi* Charge in the Lathi Raj

Violence under colonial rule was an everyday experience, residing "in the very ontology of the empire."[5] This inherent experience manifested in the form of physical violence at moments when an escalation of anticolonial mass action met with organized repression from the colonial state and its baton-bearing representatives. Once their *lathi* was raised on 7 April 1930 at a group of Congress volunteers participating in a bonfire of foreign goods, scenes of brutal *lathi* charges became pervasive in Bombay, and indeed elsewhere in the country. The itinerant documentary photographer, equipped by the interwar years with a portable camera and compact photographic film, regularly captured ongoing clashes between the colonial police and nationalist volunteers; and the *lathi*-charge photo with its visceral appeal became a potent new genre of news photography (see Chapter Three in this volume).

Among many such images in the Nursey album, one photograph archives the aftermath of a brutal attack on volunteers, including members of the Akali Dal, carrying out a *dharna* (non-violent sit-in demonstration) (Fig. 8.5). While the caption testifies to the ferocity of the *lathi* assault, the image itself presents the eerie calm manifesting in the aftermath of such violence, with our eyes repeatedly drawn to the unwavering, unmovable *satyagrahi*s who had flung themselves on the ground. In this remarkable composition, the figure of the centrally positioned white police officer bisects the space horizontally and vertically, creating near-perfect axial symmetry vis-à-vis the upper and lower, and right and left, halves of the frame. The political agitation/action is now under control, enabling the two automobiles to make their indifferent way forward. The large mass of dark-uniformed *lathi*-bearing native constables behind the white officer is mirrored by the smaller huddle of white-clad *satyagrahi*s across from him, and he himself is mirrored by the native constable who, with his back to these resilient protesters, leans on his *lathi* and follows his superior's gaze. The intense, recursive, complex relationship between colonial authority and its obedient native instruments may be symbolically read into the figure of this constable whose shadow falls in a diagonal towards the officer's feet.

Negley Farson, an American correspondent present at this site, produced an evocative eyewitness account of the day that instils a deeper affective register to the photographic record. Describing the police action on protesters in great and gory detail, he recounts being intrigued by how despite possessing the *kirpan* (small dagger worn by devout Sikhs), the Sikh volunteers swore that they would not draw the "sacred sword" to defend themselves amid the "crashing" and "whacking" of police batons—"'Never, never, never!' they cried to the terrific delight of their Hindu brother in Swaraj. 'We will never retreat. We will die!'" Farson quoted. He went on to further note, "I cannot describe it, but such fanaticism made one feel sick! The police felt so, too, and hesitated before hitting

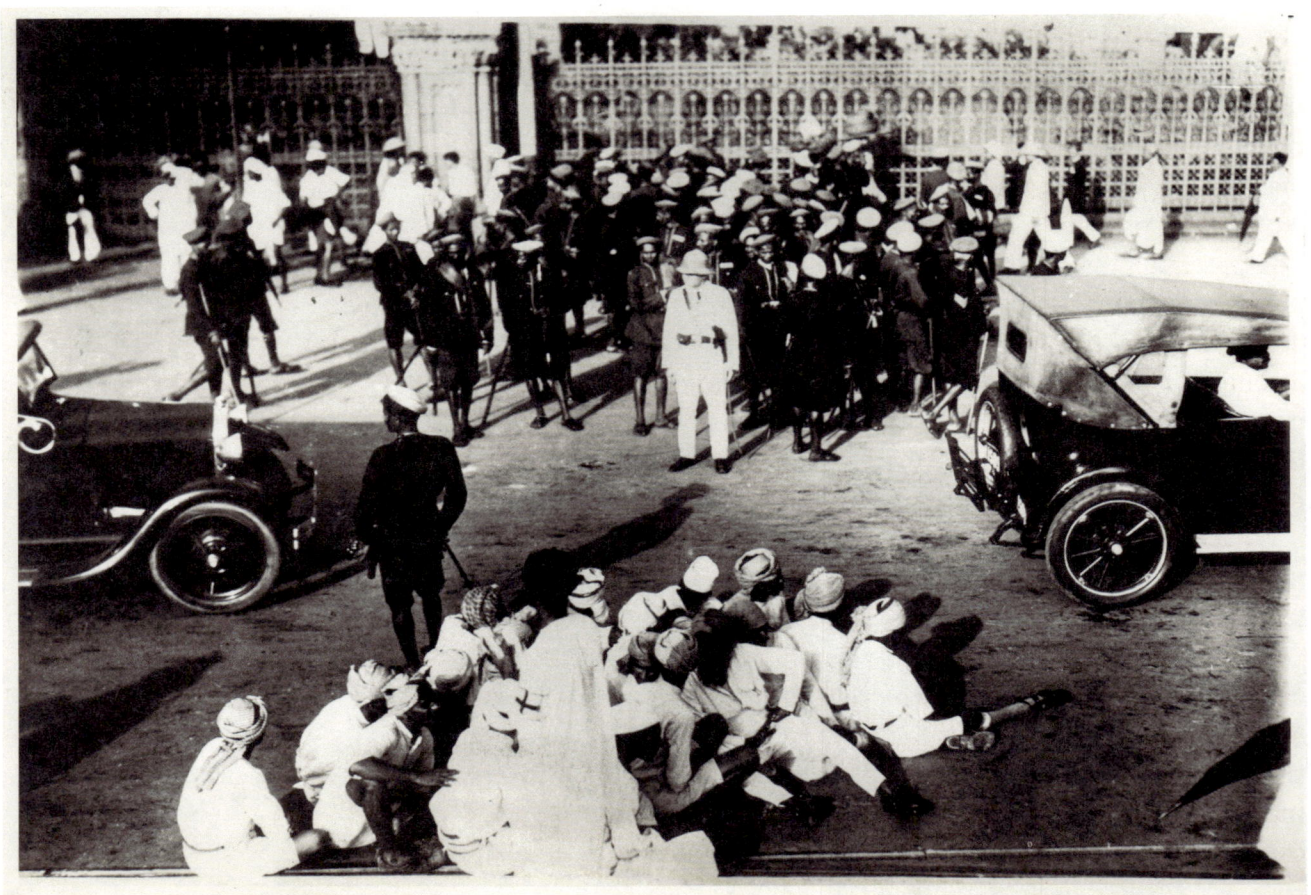

Fig. 8.5
"A batch of brave sikhs [Sikhs] refused to move inspite [in spite] of the lathi blows showered on them. Finally they were lifted from the spot." c. 1930—1931
Gelatin Silver Print, 113 x 160 mm
ACP: 98.77.0002 (64b)

the Sikhs … 'the Sikh are brave men—how can we hit them?' It was not fear but sheer respect."[6]

In light of the abundant visual evidence in this album of vicious police attacks on non-violent protesters, the constables' apparently short-lived hesitation before hitting these "brave men" needs to be analysed further. After all, within the colonial and racialized hierarchy that structured a history of masculinity in colonial India, the Sikhs, along with the Pathans and Gurkhas, were designated a "martial race". In contrast to men from other parts of British India who were characterized as effeminate to underscore the manliness of the English,[7] the martial races were stereotyped as brave, disciplined and proficient at combat. Thus, on one side of this violent encounter stood Bombay's *lathi*-wielding police constable who, despite his "non-martial" ethnicity, by virtue of representing British authority came to embody colonial masculinity in its conspicuously brutal form. On the other side lay "prostate [sic] figures of crumpled [Sikh] men"[8] practising the Gandhian gospel of non-violence (*ahimsa*). The constables' hesitation, thus, is arguably borne out of the moral charge of the latter's resolve to not put up any resistance to the cruel blows of the police *lathi*. Even from within the skewed framework of colonial masculinity, any claims of righteous manly conduct on behalf of the colonial police, and by extension the colonial British government, is thus violently deflated. Moreover, the confrontation between the policemen and nationalist volunteers, both of native origin, acts as a reminder of how despite essentializing conceptions of the native male body under the colonial regime, Indian masculinity was inherently variegated, heterogeneous and hybrid.

The perverse logic of colonial relations violently turned native bodies against each other in this manner across the empire.[9] Photographs from the Nursey album nod to this complex enmeshment of race and colonialism in an image that shows the two opposing positions occupied by native bodies in yet another presentation of dramatic contrasts (Fig. 8.6). Re-invoking a characteristic framing device of our unknown photographer(s), the camera hovers above an outdoor space partitioned by a low metal railing. One half of the scene is maximally occupied by the dense, compressed nationalist crowd; the other half minimally occupied by two native constables and a white officer, the berets and pith helmet contrasting sharply with the turbans, Gandhi caps and traditional headgear of the massed volunteers. Some men are looking up with slight smiles, presumably aware of being framed by the camera; one constable similarly directs his gaze. The radical incompatibilities and incommensurability on view within the bisected photographic space are symbolically accentuated by two very different visual manifestations of the same natural entity (wood)—the thick, solid, gnarled tree trunk, and the sinister, agile, versatile *lathi*.

Similarly, in another image from the album (Fig. 8.7) the subjects stand along diagonal lines which converge at a central point within the photographic space: the raised arm of a constable ready to strike his fellow native with a *lathi*. This is the affective climax of a composition that indeed brings into focus the cruel blows of the *lathi* and brutal police action literally foregrounded as Congress volunteers recede into the background. Our gaze is further triangulated by the figures of the white officers—on the left, one fully visible, holding a baton; a little ahead of him the second, partly obscured by a constable, holding some papers; and on the right, the third merely glimpsed as a pith helmet. However, when we allow our attention to wander beyond what the photographer has framed us into seeing, we simultaneously discover alternative narratives also indexed in the same image via the camera's documentary eye. For example, consider the constable closest to us in the group of policemen on the left, standing above the collapsed body of a volunteer. Instead of putting his *lathi* to its usual purpose, which is to hit the volunteer, this constable appears to be nudging the prone body, perhaps trying to figure out if he remains conscious.

The textual archive testifies that such moments of apprehension, and even exasperation, in the middle of intense police action were not uncommon. On one occasion, for example, while trying to stop a raid on the Wadala salt pans in April

1930 (see Chapter Five in this volume), constables, "tired of beating the innocent *satyagrahis*, disobeyed four orders of their superior, and subsequently retired."[10] A police report confirms this, and notes how the next day when another such salt raid was being carried out, the police administration, anticipating that the constables might refuse to follow orders, did not send them to stop illegal salt-making that morning.[11]

Facing such issues of insubordination in the early weeks of the Civil Disobedience Movement, the colonial administration came up with several measures to secure the loyalty of police personnel of native origin. For one, the Bombay police announced a special monthly allowance to motivate local constables. This monetary award was reserved for those who discharged their duties and continued to participate in the quelling of demonstrations.[12] In addition to financial compensation, the state also rewarded low-ranking constables with certificates issued by the Collector of Salt Revenue in Bombay. Titled, with conceit, "Government Honours for Lathi Wielders," these certificates were specifically handed out to those who had "proved themselves serviceable

Fig. 8.6
"Police guarding the entrance to the Esplanade police court." c. 1930–1931 Gelatin Silver Print, 117 x 161 mm
ACP: 98.77.0002 (95a)

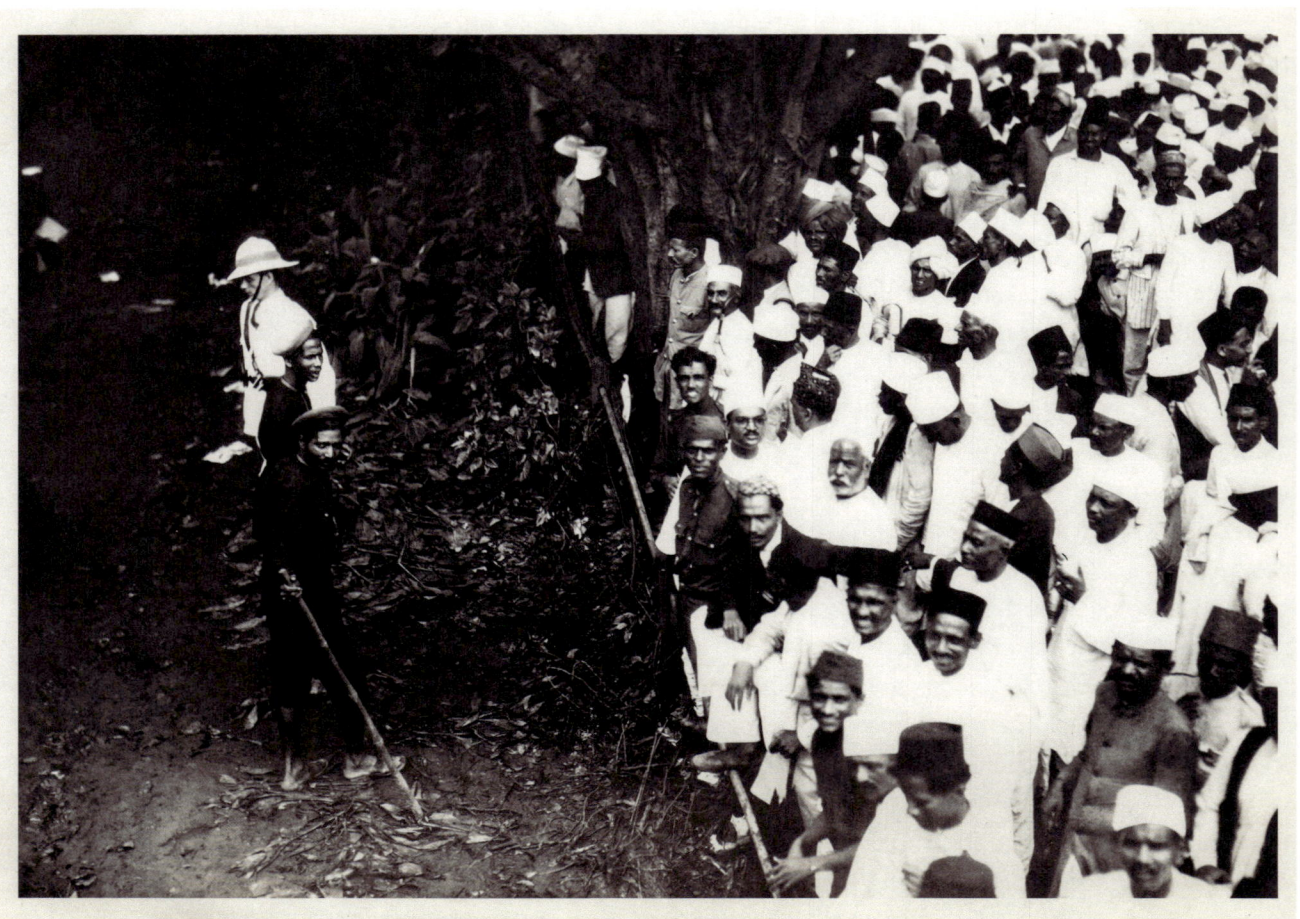

to the Govt. [sic] in assaulting *satyagrahi*s at Wadala and in recognition of the excellent work performed by them."[13] The extent to which these specific programmes were successful cannot exactly be determined. But as these documentary photographs show us, the Lathi Raj and the routine clashes between the police and Congress volunteers continued to prevail.

On the receiving end, practitioners of *ahimsa* deemed their injuries and arrests as glorious (Fig. 8.5, Fig. 8.7). Farson, the American journalist, struck by how nationalist leaders persisted with their non-violent tactics and, in fact, held to them even more tenaciously in the face of certain violent backlash at the demonstration that he witnessed, asked a "bleeding volunteer" if he and his leaders "wanted" to be brutalized in this manner. "Yes, the volunteer cried frantically ... we wanted it! We want to show the whole world what the British are doing to us!"[14] The cruel blows of the *lathi* were, thus, invited through a ritualized form of public opposition developed early in the movement. This included nationalist political festivals which punctuated the city's calendar. Flag salutation days, observed on the last Sunday of every month, were regularly

Fig. 8.7
"An impressive picture showing how cuuely [cruelly] the Volunteers were bitten [beaten]."
c. 1930–1931
Gelatin Silver Print,
114 x 156 mm
ACP: 98.77.0002 (67a)

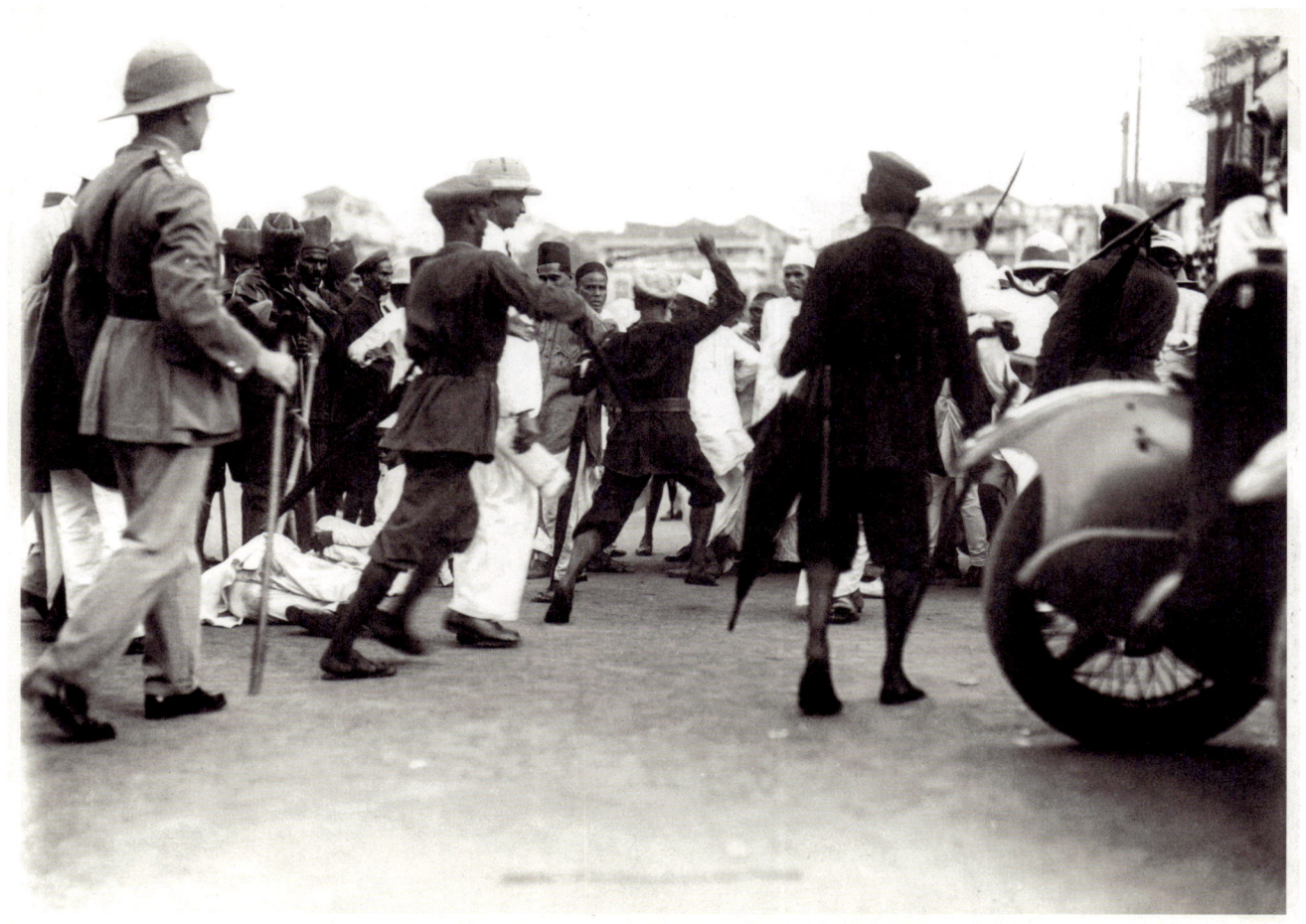

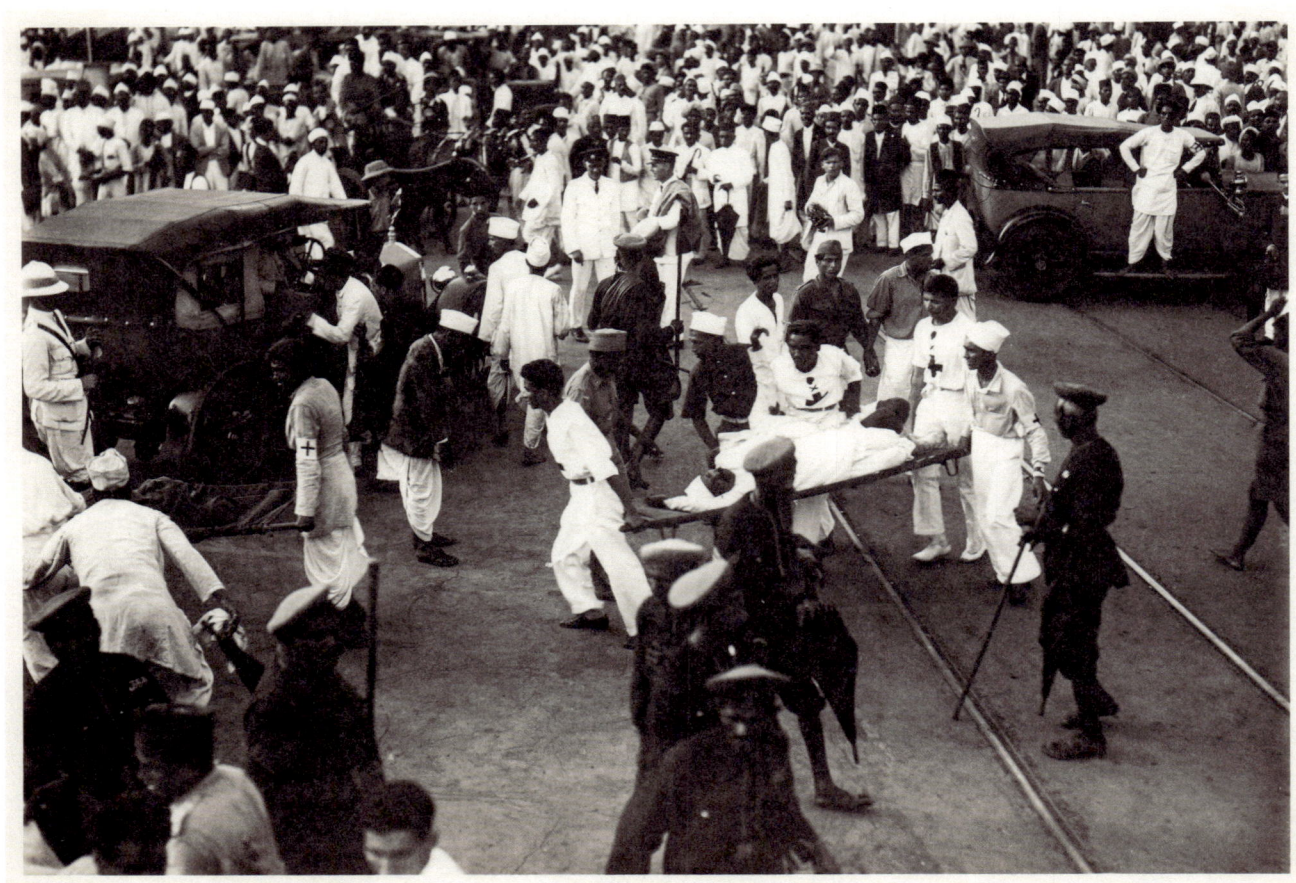

ABOVE
Fig. 8.8
"Ambulance attending
to the Wounded."
c. 1930—1931
Gelatin Silver Print,
114 x 162 mm
ACP: 98.77.0002 (74b)

FACING PAGE, ABOVE
Fig. 8.9
"Month ending 'Flag
Salutation' lathi
[charge] in action."
c. 1930—1931
Gelatin Silver Print,
114 x 158 mm
ACP: 98.77.0002 (58b)

FACING PAGE, BELOW
Fig. 8.10
"The city police
dispersing the Hugh
[huge] crowds that had
assembled to witness
the proceedings on
Garwali [Garhwali]
day." 1930
Gelatin Silver Print,
116 x 159 mm
ACP: 98.77.0002 (65a)
This photograph was
also published in
The Times of India,
14 July 1930.

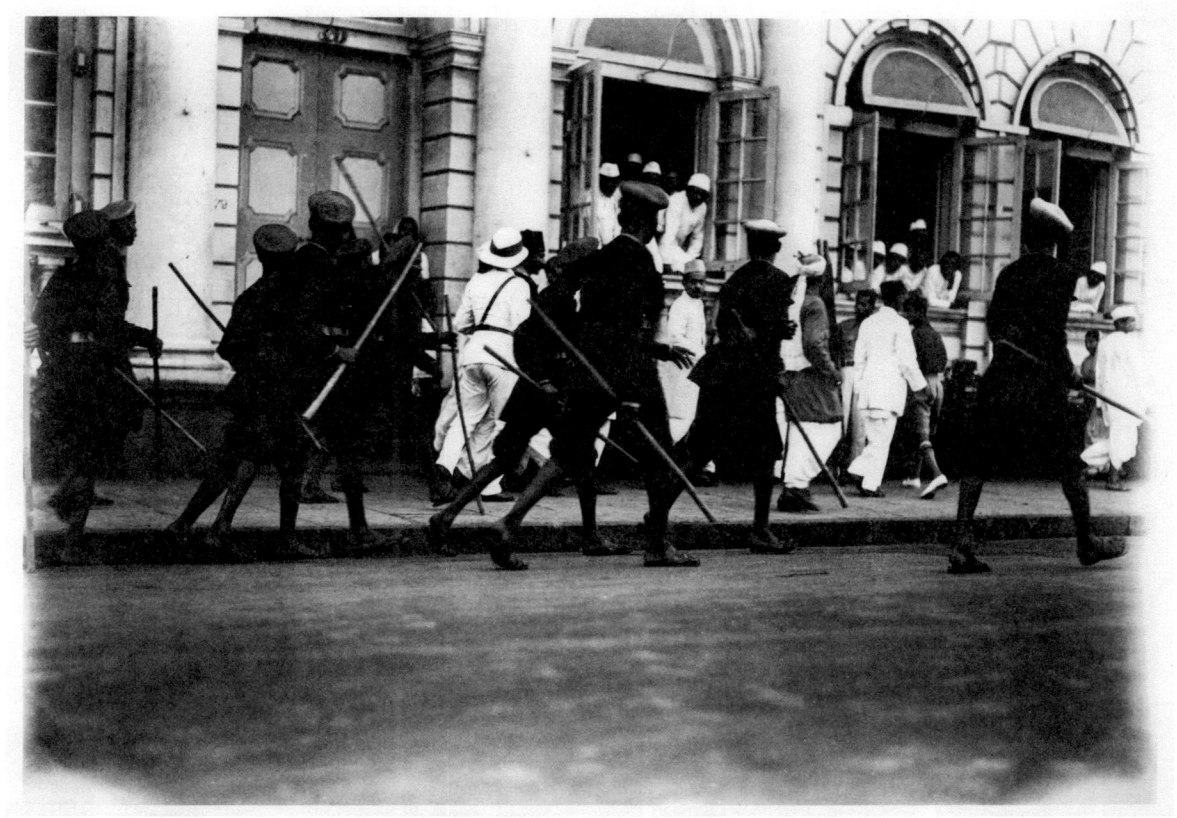

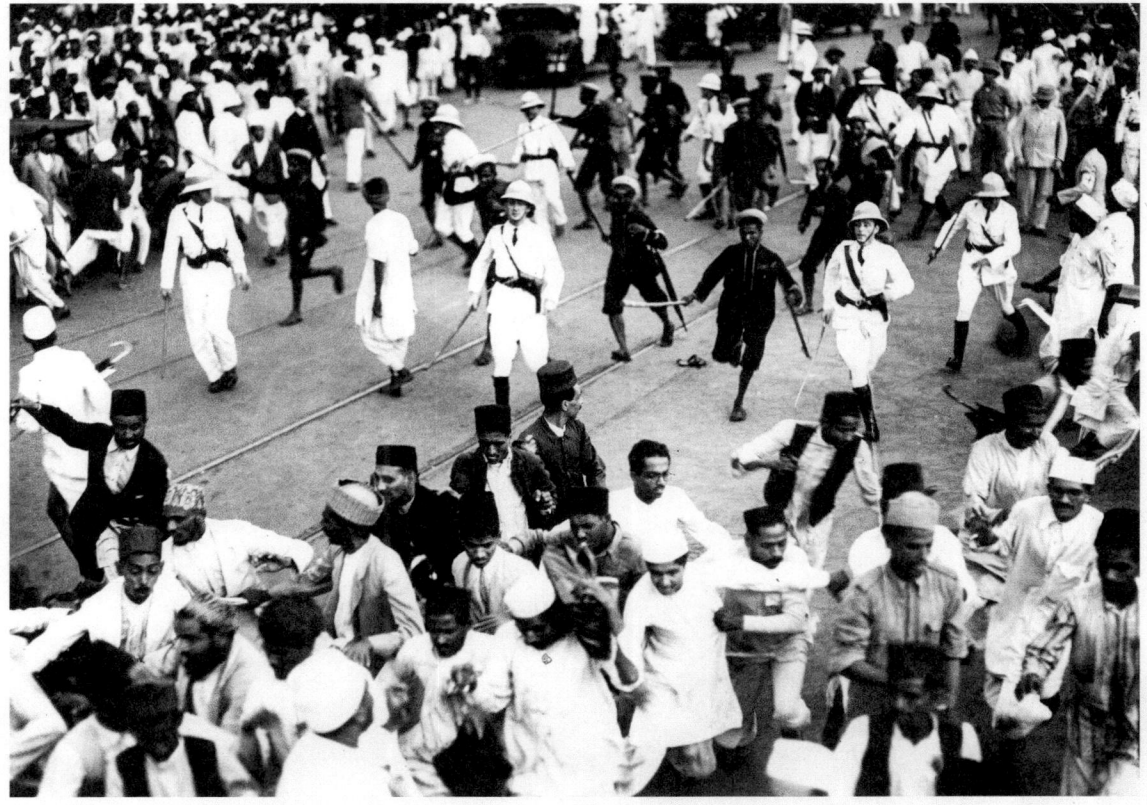

disrupted by police (Fig. 8.9). Other demonstrations such as "Garhwal Day," organized to celebrate the defiance of the Garhwal regiment of the British army, and "Tilak Day," to commemorate the popular western Indian political (and Congress) leader, made headlines for how civil demonstrators showed up on the occasion and were met with brutal police violence (Fig. 8.10, see also Fig. 4.11).

"Boycott the Police"

Beyond such affective—and strategic—displays of passive resistance, Bombay's nationalist public pushed back against the colonial police and their violent methods in rather creative ways. Rallies condemning the Bombay police became commonplace. Led by Bombay women and including a large number of men and some children, one such march carried an effigy of a policeman on the roof of a motor vehicle (Fig. 8.11). Noticeably, this reviled figure had its face whitened, and was dressed in a white uniform, including the pith helmet that referenced officers of the senior ranks, reserved for the British within the hierarchy of the colonial police administration.

The native police constable was also publicly reproached and denounced in more mundane and widespread forms. The city's nationalist leaders called for a social boycott of all those who remained employed by the colonial government, especially in the police administration, after the call for civil disobedience led to an initial slew of resignations.[15] Parchas (handouts or notices) advocating such a boycott were pasted on walls in the market area, and were documented so in the police archives.[16] Records also list several instances when Bombay police constables were refused tea, and even drinking water, at local shops,[17] or faced difficulty in finding chakkis (mills) that would agree to grind grains for use in their households.[18] Even relatives of constables were openly challenged to "approach the police and ask them to stop their lathi raj under the pain of social boycott."[19] In at least one instance, a constable was forced out of his rental home by a nationalist landlord.[20]

Much as Gandhi caps and khadi (homespun) saris became embodied symbols of nationalist identity, the Bombay police constable's blue uniform became an object of rebuke and invited hostility from locals. Instances of "cap-snatching" where young men attempted, sometimes successfully, to grab the cap or turban of the traffic or the police constable on duty, became common.[21] According to a police report from May 1930, for example, a constable patrolling a street in the Gaiwadi neighbourhood was reprimanded by a woman for serving the government and was told "to remove his uniform"; another woman, leaning out of her first-floor balcony "threw dirty water on him, spoiling his uniform."[22]

The deliberate violation of the police uniform humbled colonial authority and also worked to emasculate the native police personnel donning that uniform.

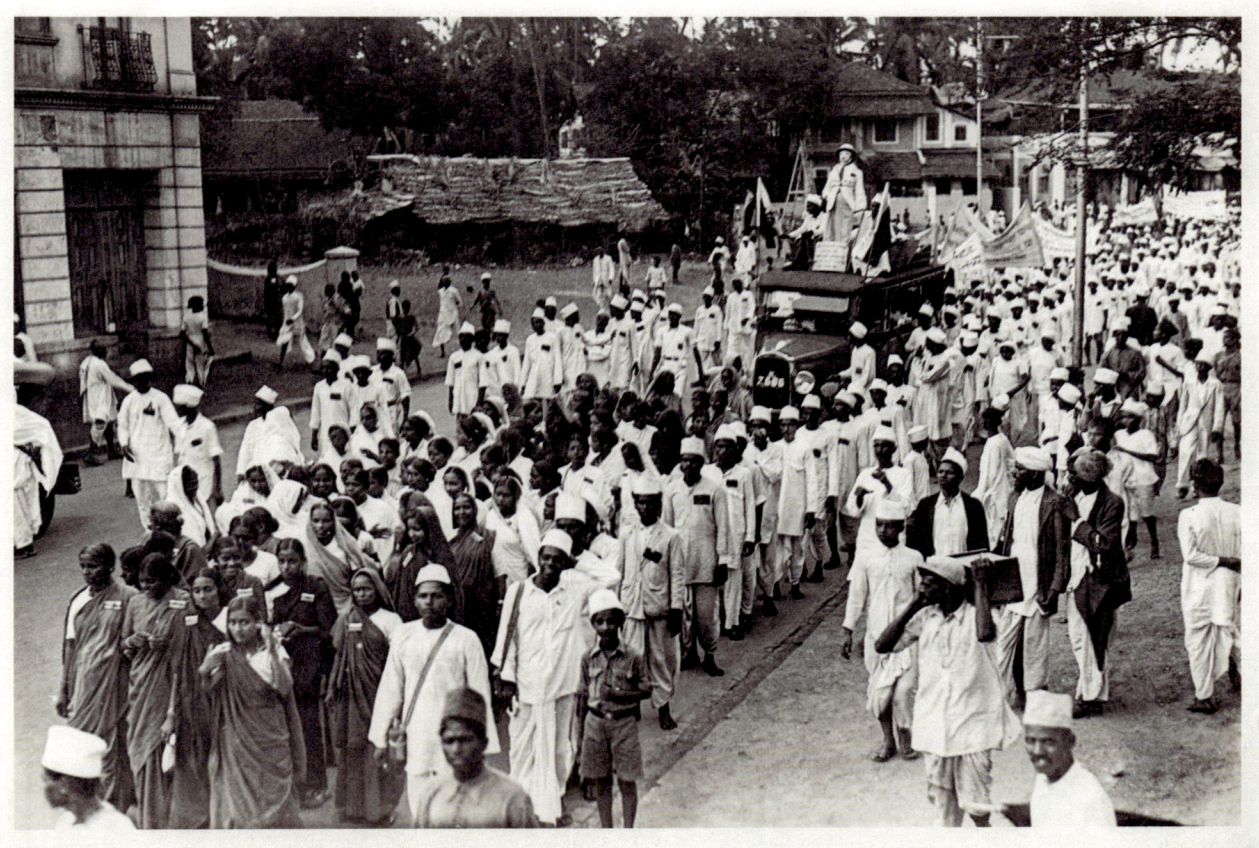

Fig. 8.11
"An effigy of an
police man taken in
procession." 1930
Gelatin Silver Print,
115 x 165 mm
ACP: 98.77.0002 (29b)

Soaked to the skin, abased and disempowered by "disobedient" women, the constable of Gaiwadi would appear as a disgraced reflection of the violent colonial masculinity embodied by him and his *lathi*-wielding associates. When a police case was registered by the officers at his station, the constable claimed he was unable to identify either of these women by any means, although he may have been well aware of their respective house addresses. Was the failure to report these women borne out of the threat of further social boycott and rebuke? Perhaps it was equally informed by a complicated set of responses: sympathy for the women's motives and an acknowledgement of his own complicity with the "wrong" side—a humiliating and emasculating professional hazard that native constables had to bear.

Such was the degree of "harassment" faced by the uniform-wearing constable that it encouraged some extraordinary measures. In one instance the government even withdrew traffic police from isolated corners of the city, and they were replaced by volunteers wearing *khadi* clothes.[23] Quite literally, the authority of the nationalist party was taking over urban spaces as colonial authority retracted. This substitution of the colonial police personnel with the *khadi*-clad bodies prefigures the ways in which the colonial institution of police would eventually be transformed in the postcolonial period, at least in terms of its sartorial emphasis, by adopting the *khadi vardi* (uniform). Nevertheless, the continued legacy of the use of the *lathi* in police violence against civil demonstrators remains very much in place.[24]

Locals also devised creative ways to deter the police from carrying out their regular duties. In one instance they brought the city to a halt by hindering the flow of traffic and public transport (Fig. 8.12). In a deeply symbolic and aesthetically poignant photograph captured from a low angle, the foreground is dominated by cumbersome metal chains strewn across a cordoned-off section of the street, the loose arcs and ellipses of the chains offset by the rigid parallels of the tram tracks. Isolated, the two figures of colonial authority, interlinked, interdependent and mutually bound within their profession, are engaged in removing the chains—the constable, bending low, with his hand; the white officer, upright, with a *lathi*.

In several other instances locals successfully thwarted the police from making arrests for petty crimes on the streets. For example, a sergeant and a constable pursuing a roadside gambler were in turn chased away by a group of about 300 people. In another instance, when a constable arrested six hawkers charged for

Fig. 8.12
"Babu Ganu day hartal organised by the Congre[ss] [with] Chains strewn on the road at Dhobi Talao to stop the traffic."
c. 1930—1931
Gelatin Silver Print, 114 x 155 mm
ACP: 98.77.0002 (59a)

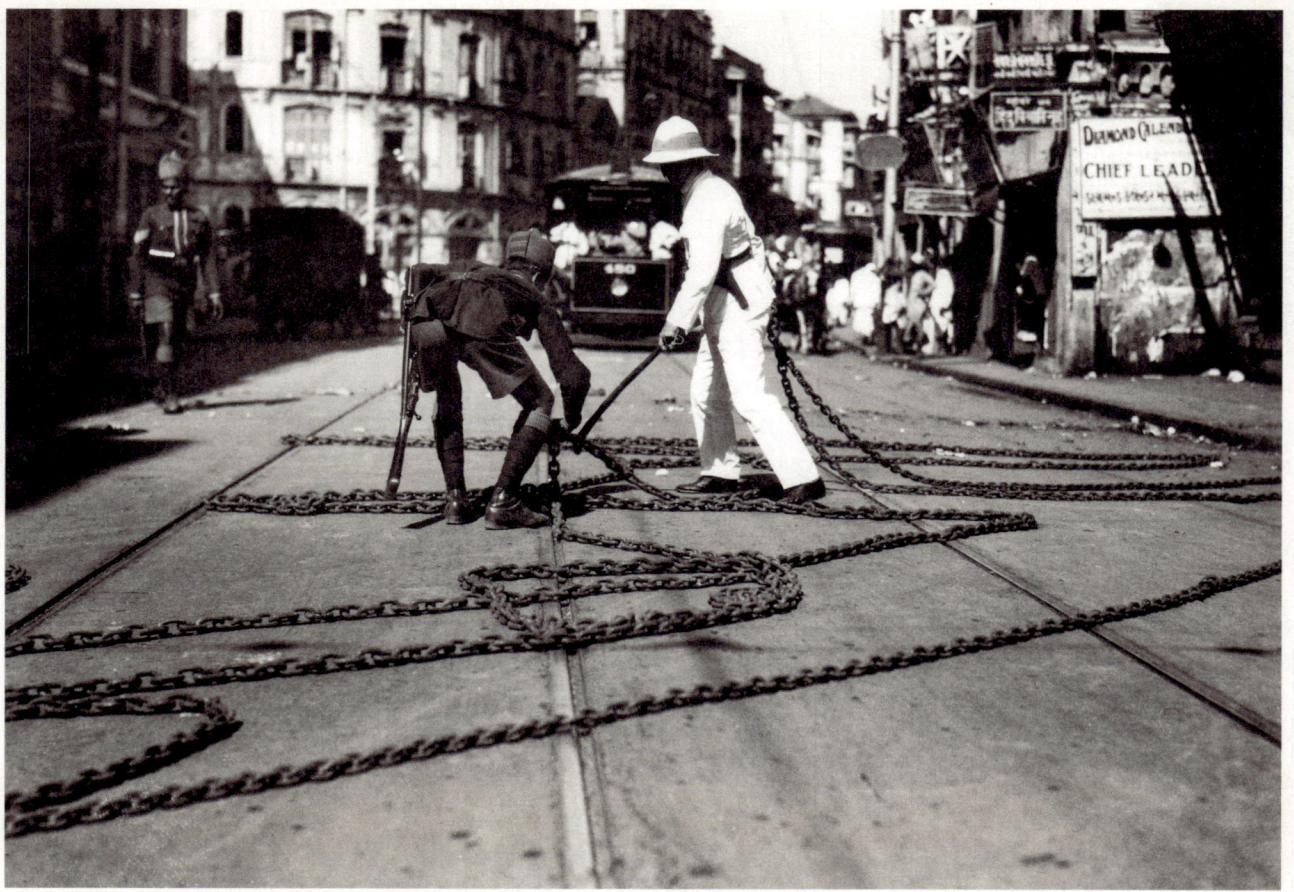

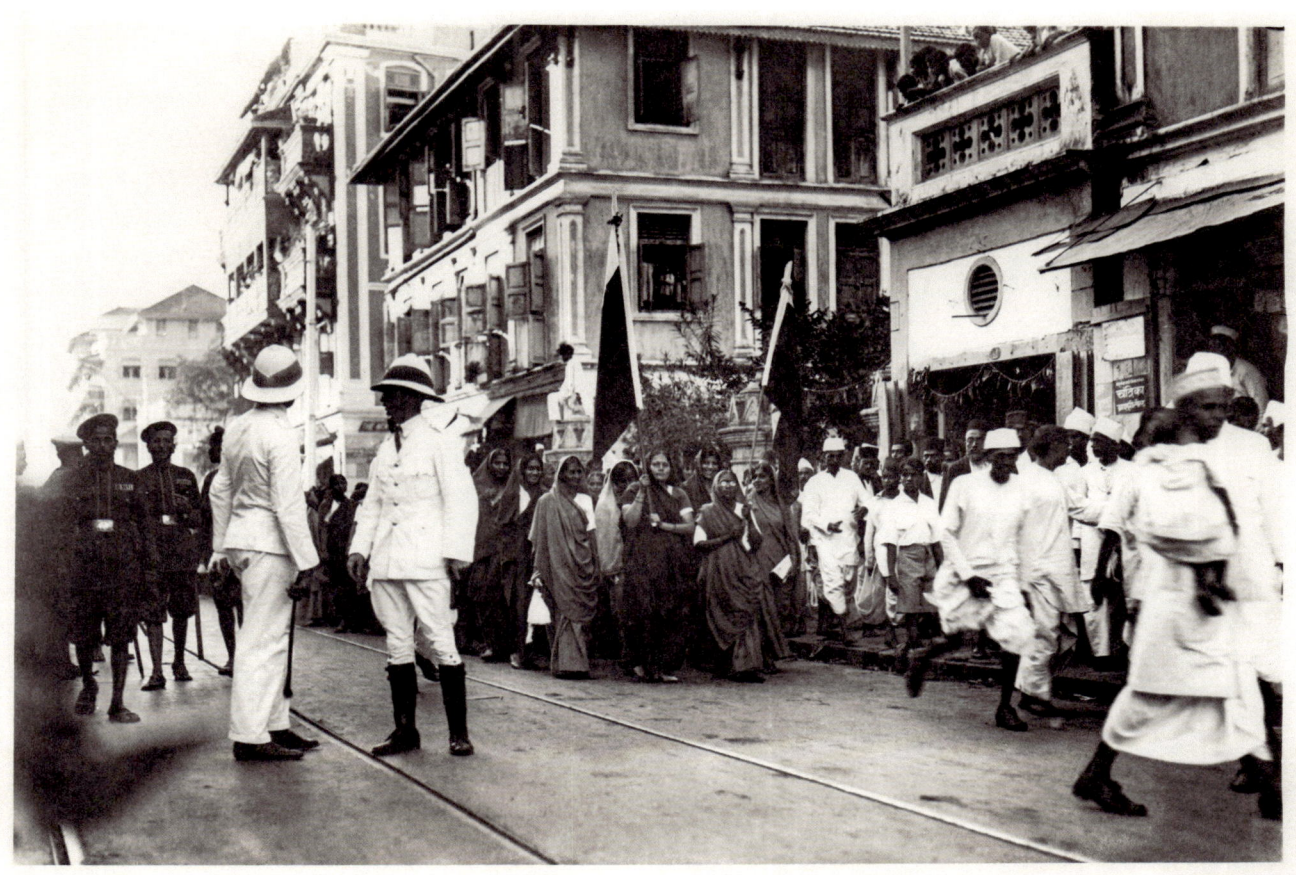

causing obstruction in the Bombay market area, a crowd of 500 people met them on their way to the police station and rescued the hawkers.[25] Such incidents sometimes also led to violence, where both civilians as well as native constables ended up with grave injuries and had to be rushed to hospitals. Leaders of the nationalist party, of course, warned the public and Congress volunteers against the use of violence towards the police, declaring that the "Government was waiting for an opportunity to declare martial law" and that "the moment a constable or police officer was killed, martial law would be put in force."[26]

While native police constables were on the receiving end of public aggression, they were also the target of nationalist propaganda. Volunteers regularly distributed pamphlets in Gujarati and Marathi to police patrols, inviting them to resign from their service and join the movement.[27] At a public meeting attended by around 700 people, the speakers revealed that the police constable's lowly salary of Rs 15 per month was equivalent to the amount higher-ranking white officials lavished on their pets in a week. Thus, the speakers insisted, a boycott of the British government and all government servants was necessary to bring attention to the colonial state's grossly unequal, even humiliating, treatment of Indian workers.

Fig. 8.13
"The Mandvi Congress dictator under arrest when he defied the police order by bringing our [out] a procession which was banned. Here the police are seen giving orders to disperse before making a lathi charge." c. 1930–1931 Gelatin Silver Print, 115 x 165 mm
ACP: 98.77.0002 (77a)

The strategy to thus shame, even coerce, police constables to quit their jobs worked to some degree. Many resigned from the force and even gave anti-government speeches at Congress meetings.[28] According to a statement issued by a constable named Jogeshver Singh Baghel, for example, he resigned on "seeing the manner with which the *Satyagrahi*s were treated."[29] Stories of resignations such as these were particularly celebrated in the nationalist press and extensively circulated to motivate others to follow suit, and to display the wider public's faith in the nationalist movement.

Disobedient Women and Orderly Men

As urban women volunteered for the nationalist programme and claimed a new relationship with their city, they too came in direct confrontation with Bombay's colonial police. These confrontations assumed various forms and were documented by the photographer(s) of the Nursey album. Nationalist women thus shared the frame with the colonial police, offering a window into a new form of gendered political relationship emerging in the city. For example, a recurring motif in the album is of women who continued to lead marches and processions on the streets of Bombay, despite the declaration of any political and anticolonial gatherings as unlawful. The colonial police were often posted near these locations, maintaining a close watch over these disobedient women (Fig. 8.13). Another photographic instance in which women nationalist volunteers were regularly featured alongside Bombay policemen was at the moment of their arrests. As the women were compelled into police vans, the camera captured this unprecedented imagery (Fig. 8.14, see Fig. 6.1). Not only did women step out onto the streets in unprecedented numbers to join mass politics during this movement; they were also sent to prison in record numbers. By documenting them in these risky novel spaces and situations, these photographs testify to the major transformation in women's social and political presence.

In fact, the Bombay police commissioner even noted that although he expected nationalist activities led by women to be "trifling," they were increasingly proving to be a major "nuisance" for colonial authority.[30] In claiming public spaces by means of protests and taking up political responsibilities, nationalist women simultaneously challenged the British colonial state and traditional notions of gendered public conduct that were elemental to Gandhian nationalism's prescriptive ideals of Indian womanhood.

During the Civil Disobedience Movement, Gandhi maintained that the female nationalist volunteer should remain at the forefront of disobedient action because women had an innate (and gendered) proclivity towards practising non-violence. Perceptions of the pacifism of Indian women were thus pitched against and seen as a counterpart to perceptions of the *lathi*-wielding native constable's violent manhood. Yet a closer examination of such confrontations

Fig. 8.14
"Police arresting the women pickets at the Town hall." 1930
Gelatin Silver Print,
114 x 157 mm
ACP: 98.77.0002 (70b)
Also published in
The Times of India,
23 July 1930.

Fig. 8.15
"A tug of war between police and Desh-Sewika's [*desh sevikas*] on the flag salutation day."
c. 1930–1931
Gelatin Silver Print,
115 x 162 mm
ACP: 98.77.0002 (53a)

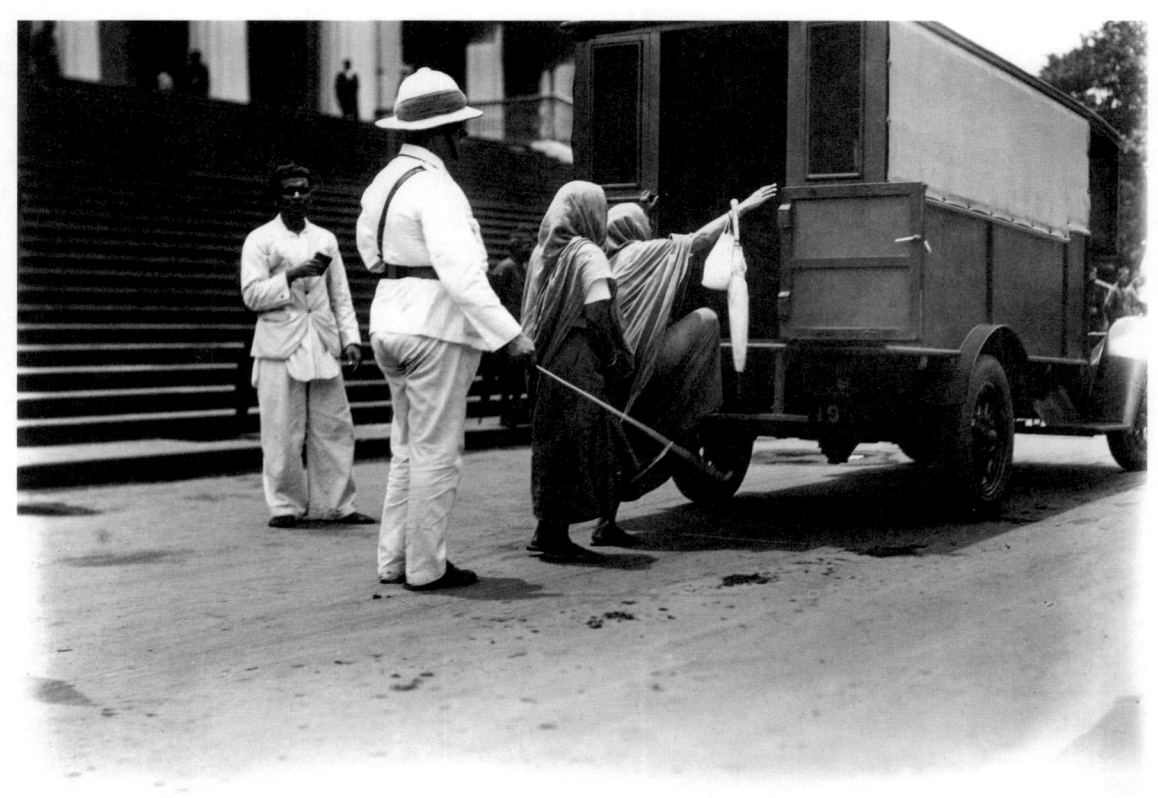

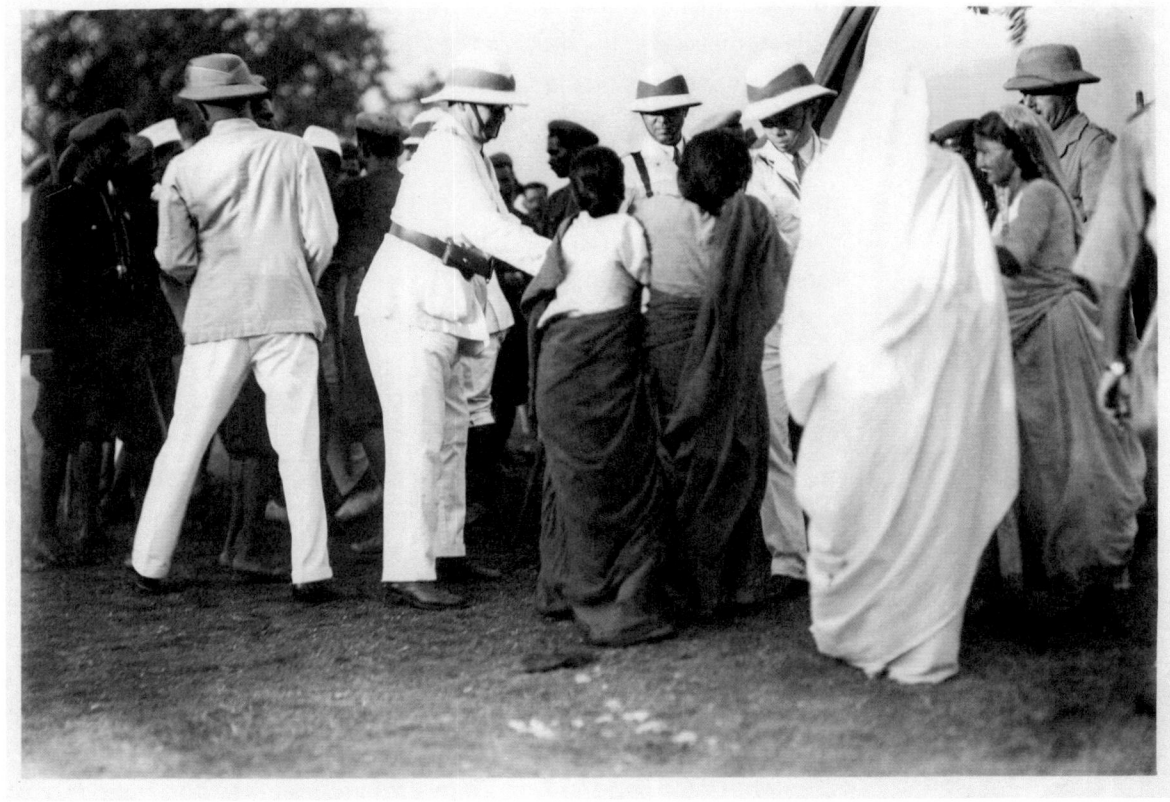

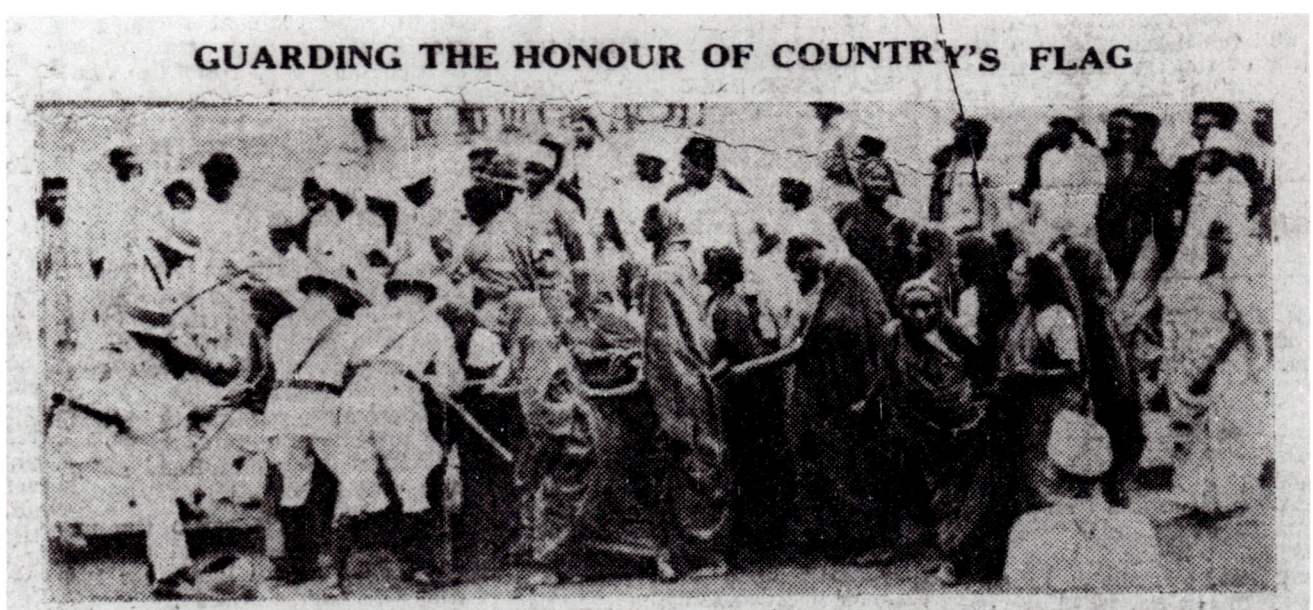

GUARDING THE HONOUR OF COUNTRY'S FLAG

A remarkable snap of a tug-of-war between ladies on one side and Police sergeants on the other for possession of the National tri-colour flag. An incident on Azad Maidan on Friday.

Fig. 8.16
"Guarding the honour of the country's flag." *The Bombay Chronicle*, 6 December 1930.

shows how the idea of a stoic and passive female volunteer was, at best, a myth. On several occasions, the camera found female nationalists engaged in a tug-of-war with police authority over the nationalist flag (Fig. 8.15, Fig. 8.16). Interestingly, the images reveal that while in most instances the native constable often remained at the forefront of *lathi* charges against civil protesters, their white officers took the lead when a physical skirmish broke out with women volunteers. The photographs reveal a hesitation on the part of the native constable—who most likely hailed from the humble end of the class and caste spectrum—in directly confronting the elite and middle-class women who constituted women's nationalist organizations such as the Desh Sevika Sangh (see Chapter Six in this volume).[31] These public encounters are thus thoroughly complicated by overlapping gender, race and class contradictions.

Within this context, let us revisit the protest at the Bombay Municipal Corporation (BMC) Hall in February 1931 that opened this essay (Fig. 8.17). In the aftermath of the demonstration, a member of the Corporation, Dwarkadas, alleged in a newspaper report that as he attempted to enter the picketed gates of the BMC hall, he was "kicked" by a female volunteer; another member similarly complained that he had been made a "victim of the non-violent methods of the fair fighters."[32] While this demonstration was described as particularly "rowdy" and outrageous by popular dailies, we find that at the heart of the outrage and the extensive public discourse generated in response to the violent clashes of the day was the "rowdyism" attributed to women.[33] Some opinions defended the women by arguing that they had been provoked to

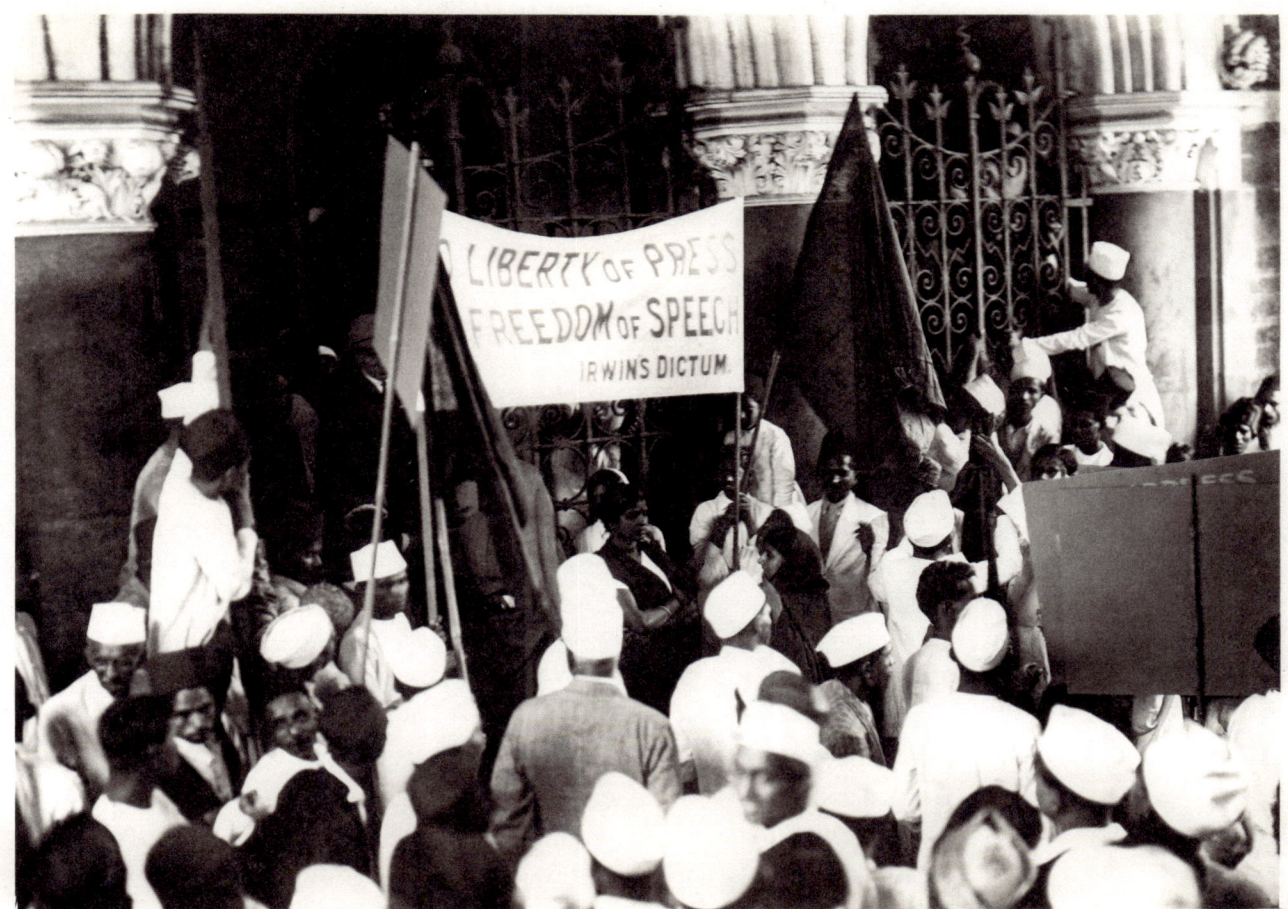

resort to violence, but could not deny that the demonstration had clearly gone outside the scope of non-violent picketing, a foundational premise of Gandhian civil disobedience.

Of course, this was not the first and only instance when volunteers on duty resorted to some form of violence. Male nationalist volunteers, in fact, were known to be aggressive, and at times violent, in how they promoted the nationalist cause in public. This was precisely the reason why Gandhi was convinced that for the Civil Disobedience Movement to succeed, women should be made responsible for street propaganda and dissent. The fact that women were the transgressors, both when it came to the political playbook of passive anticolonial action and prescriptive "womanly" public conduct, generated varied reactions imbued with a moral charge, ranging from condemnation to "raised eyebrows," to editorials lamenting the loss of propriety among Indian women. By resorting to physical aggression and thus behaving like men, these "deviant" nationalist "Gandhian" women audaciously broke away from culturally valorized notions of womanliness and gendered expectations of how women should occupy public spaces, even in the act of political protest.

Fig. 8.17
"Rowdy scenes were witnessed when the Bombay Municipal corporation proposed to give a farewell to Lord Irwin on his retirement from India outside the Municipal Buildings. The Corporation hall was picketed by the Desh Sevikas." 1931 Gelatin Silver Print, 115 x 155 mm
ACP: 98.77.0002 (85a)

Conclusion

The native police constable of Bombay, employed in the British colonial police force, is a hyper-visible but relatively undertheorized historical figure from the late colonial period of the city. While women's role in the history of the nationalist movement has garnered scholarly attention, a comprehensive picture of their acts of disobedience towards the colonial state would remain incomplete without a study of the colonial policeman as their counter figure.

An embodiment of colonial masculinity in its street form, the *lathi*-wielding police constable played a critical role in imperial attempts to violently suppress nationalist dissent. While the ideologies of the colonial state sanctioned such displays of violence to maintain law and authority as a manly act, the visual and textual record testifies how the Bombay constable's regular assault on his compatriots was perceived by the public as brutal, treacherous, and thereby unmanly. As a result, fraught social relations and fluctuating notions of colonial and Indian masculinity came to impinge upon the work of the colonial police administration. The photographer(s) of the Nursey album repeatedly draw our attention to this tension between the "fair fighters" of the nation and the colonial police through dramatic compositions that highlight the stark opposition between the dissidents and the champions of colonial authority. At the same time, the historical archive offers instances where such visual juxtaposition folds into moments that trouble the apparently clear boundaries and borders of colonial relations, both social and gendered.

Notes

Acknowledgements: I am grateful to Sumathi Ramaswamy and Preeti Chopra for their insightful comments on an earlier draft. Additionally, I extend my thanks to Jeehey Kim, Yechen Zhao and the participants of the Photography Network's online Summer Writing Workshop (2023) for their thoughtful engagement with the preliminary ideas that were later developed in this essay.

1. *Bombay Congress Bulletin* [No. unclear], 23 February 1931, All India Congress Committee Papers, Nehru Memorial Museum and Library, New Delhi.

2. As Viceroy of India from 1926–1931, Lord Irwin was responsible for issuing a series of ordinances over the course of the year in 1930, directed towards quelling widespread forms of nationalist dissent. One example of such laws is the infamous Ninth Ordinance promulgated in October 1930. Aimed at suppressing the Civil Disobedience Movement, the Ordinance granted the government broad powers to ban organizations and arrest and detain individuals without trial. It was particularly aimed at suppressing the Indian National Congress and other nationalist organizations that were active at the time. The Ninth Ordinance was widely criticized by the Indian public for violating civil liberties and for its indiscriminate use of detention and repression against political opponents of the colonial government. Many leaders of the Congress and other nationalist organizations were arrested and detained as a result of this law, and nationalist activities were severely curtailed.

3. Mira Rai Waits, "Visualising Order: Photography and the Production of the Colonial Police in India", *History of Photography*, vol. 45, no. 3–4 (2021), pp. 278–91.

4. Sheetal Chhabria, *Making the Modern Slum: The Power of Capital in Colonial Bombay* (Seattle: University of Washington Press, 2019).

5. See Robert McLain, *Gender and Violence in British India: The Road to Amritsar, 1914–1919* (New York: Palgrave Macmillan, 2014), p. 4. A similar argument is put forward in Elizabeth Kolsky, *Colonial Justice in British India: White Violence and the Rule of Law*, Cambridge Studies in Indian History and Society (Cambridge: Cambridge University Press, 2010), p. 17; and Durba Ghosh, *Gentlemanly Terrorists: Political Violence and the Colonial State in India, 1919–1947*, Critical Perspectives on Empire (Cambridge: Cambridge University Press, 2017).

6. *The Bombay Chronicle*, 27 September 1930.

7. Mrinalini Sinha, *Colonial Masculinity: The "Manly Englishman" and the "Effeminate Bengali" in the Late Nineteenth Century* (Manchester: Manchester University Press, 1995).

8. *The Bombay Chronicle*, 27 September 1930.

9. See for example, Caroline Elkins, *Britain's Gulag: The Brutal End of Empire in Kenya* (London: Pimlico, 2005).

10. K.K. Chaudhary (ed.), *Source Material for a History of the Freedom Movement in India*, vol. XI (Mumbai: Maharashtra State Gazetteers Office, 1991), p. 39.

11. ibid., p. 38.

12. *Bombay Congress Bulletin*, No. 92, in Chaudhary (ed.), *Source Material*, p. 387.

13. *Bombay Congress Bulletin*, No. 102, All India Congress Committee Papers, Nehru Memorial Museum and Library, New Delhi.

14. *The Bombay Chronicle*, 27 September 1930.

15. Chaudhary (ed.), *Source Material*, p. 424.

16. ibid., p. 88.

17. ibid.

18. ibid., p. 961.

19. ibid., p. 304.

20. ibid., p. 648.

21. ibid., p. 112.

22. ibid., p. 98.

23. ibid., p. 650.

24. The website Lethal in Disguise, a project of Physicians for Human Rights and the International Network of Civil Liberties Organizations, describes the *lathi* charge as "a deadly holdover from colonial times in India" and remarks that over a century later, "Little has changed about the prevalence of the lathi in policing. Unlike other nations' baton charges, however, the Indian police's extensive use of the tactic is linked with a startling number of deaths," including from blows to the head, and with some of the deaths "attributable to crowd crushing or trampling in the panicked environment that often follows a lathi charge." https://lethalindisguise.org/case-studies/india/

25. Chaudhary (ed.), *Source Material*, p. 169.

26. ibid., p. 277.

27. ibid., p. 733.

28. ibid., p. 998.

29. *The Bombay Chronicle*, 18 June 1930.

30. Extract from minutes of discussion, Commissioner of Police, Bombay, File no. 750 (26) B, Independence and Civil Disobedience Movements, Maharashtra State Archives, Mumbai.

31. Avrati Bhatnagar and Sumathi Ramaswamy, "Light Writing on the Lathi Raj: Bombay, 1930–31", *History of Photography*, vol. 45, no. 3–4 (2021), pp. 304–19. Also see Geraldine Forbes Hancock, *Women in Modern India* (New York: Cambridge University Press, 1999), pp. 132–33.

32. *The Times of India*, 25 February 1931.

33. "'Sevikas' Rowdyism': City Fathers Narrate Their Experience", *The Times of India*, 25 February 1931, p. 1.

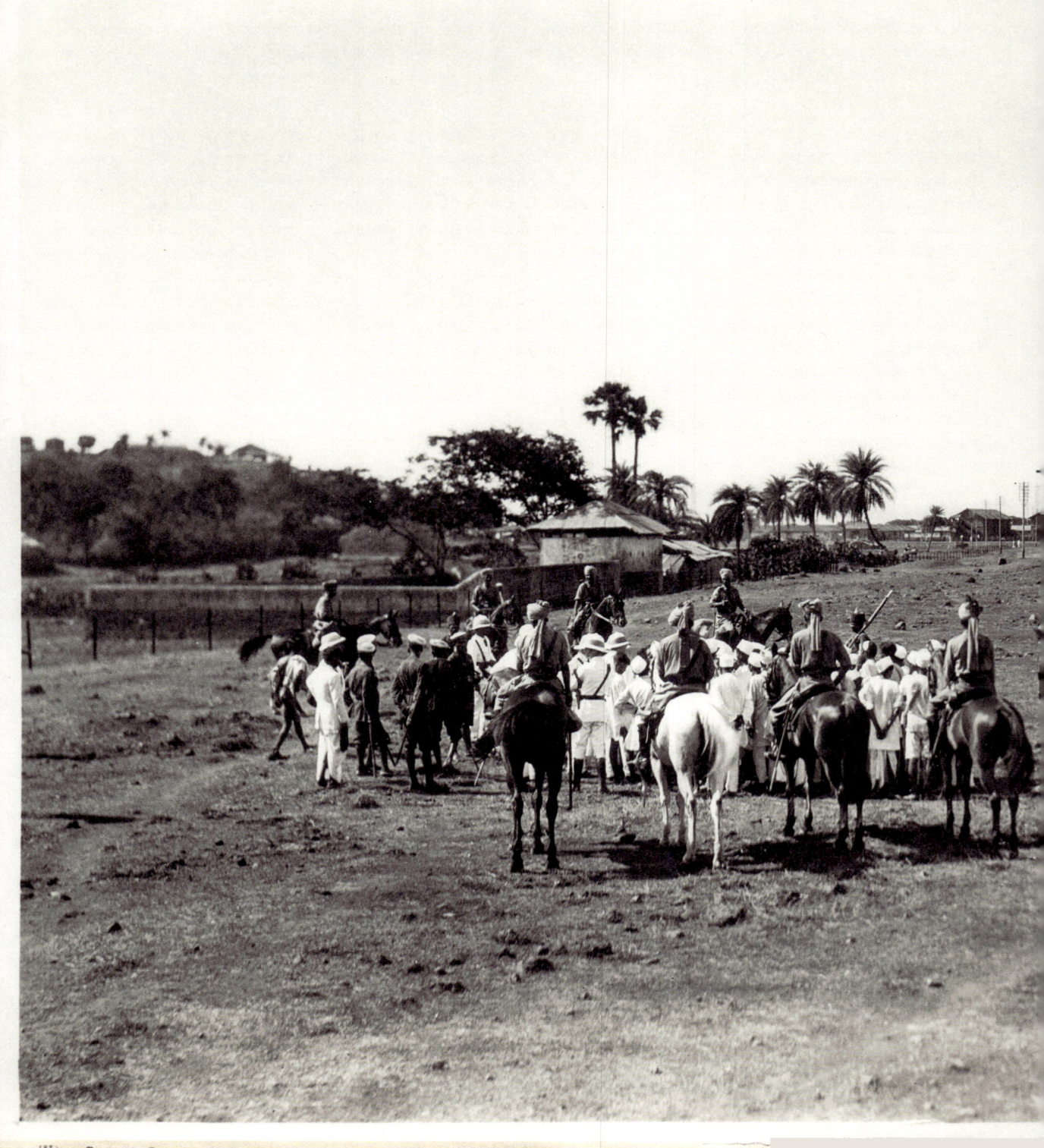

Wholesale arrest of congress volunteers at
Wadhla.Here the police are seen guarding the
arrested members. They were transfered to the
Worli chawls.

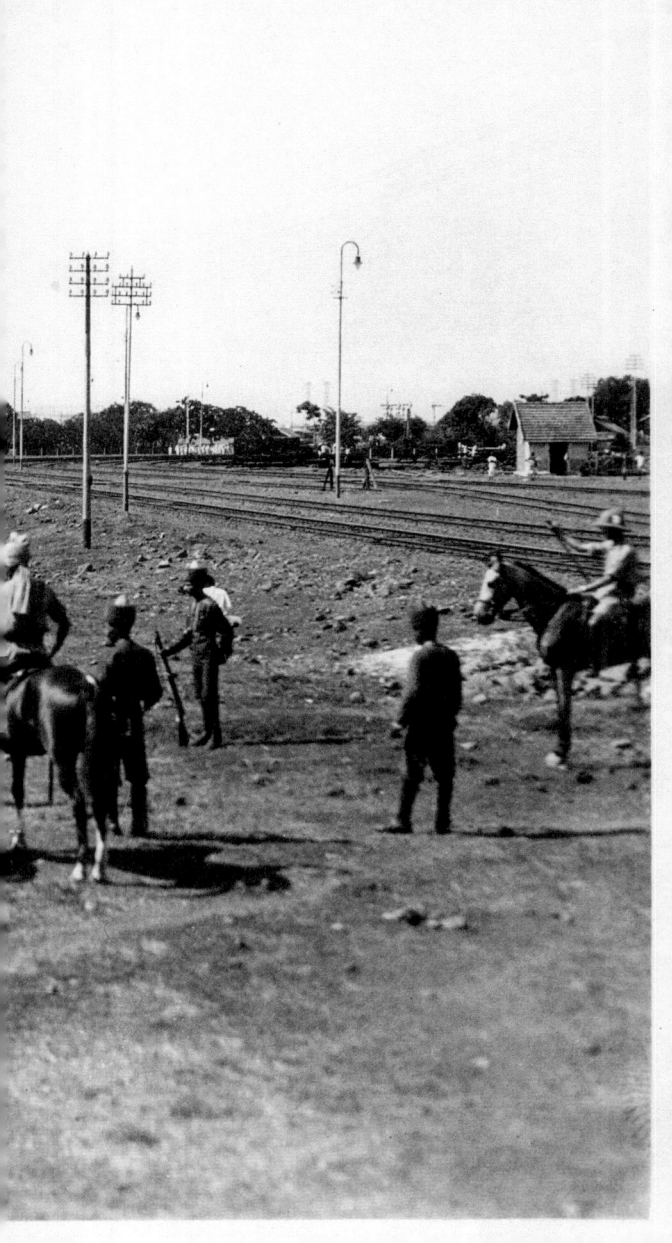

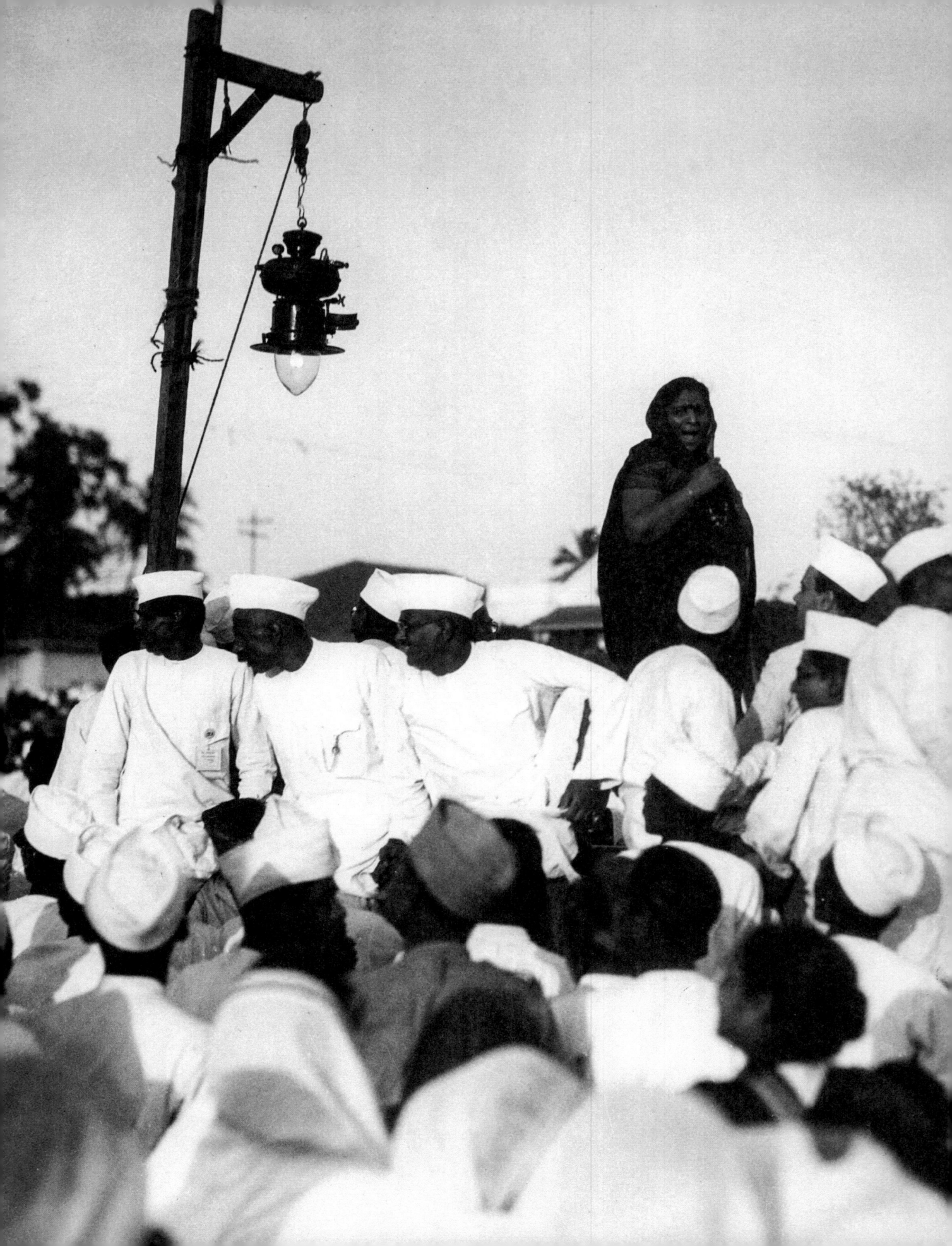

CHAPTER 9

"NOISY" PHOTOGRAPHS
LISTENING TO IMAGES FROM
THE CIVIL DISOBEDIENCE MOVEMENT
IN BOMBAY

Kama Maclean

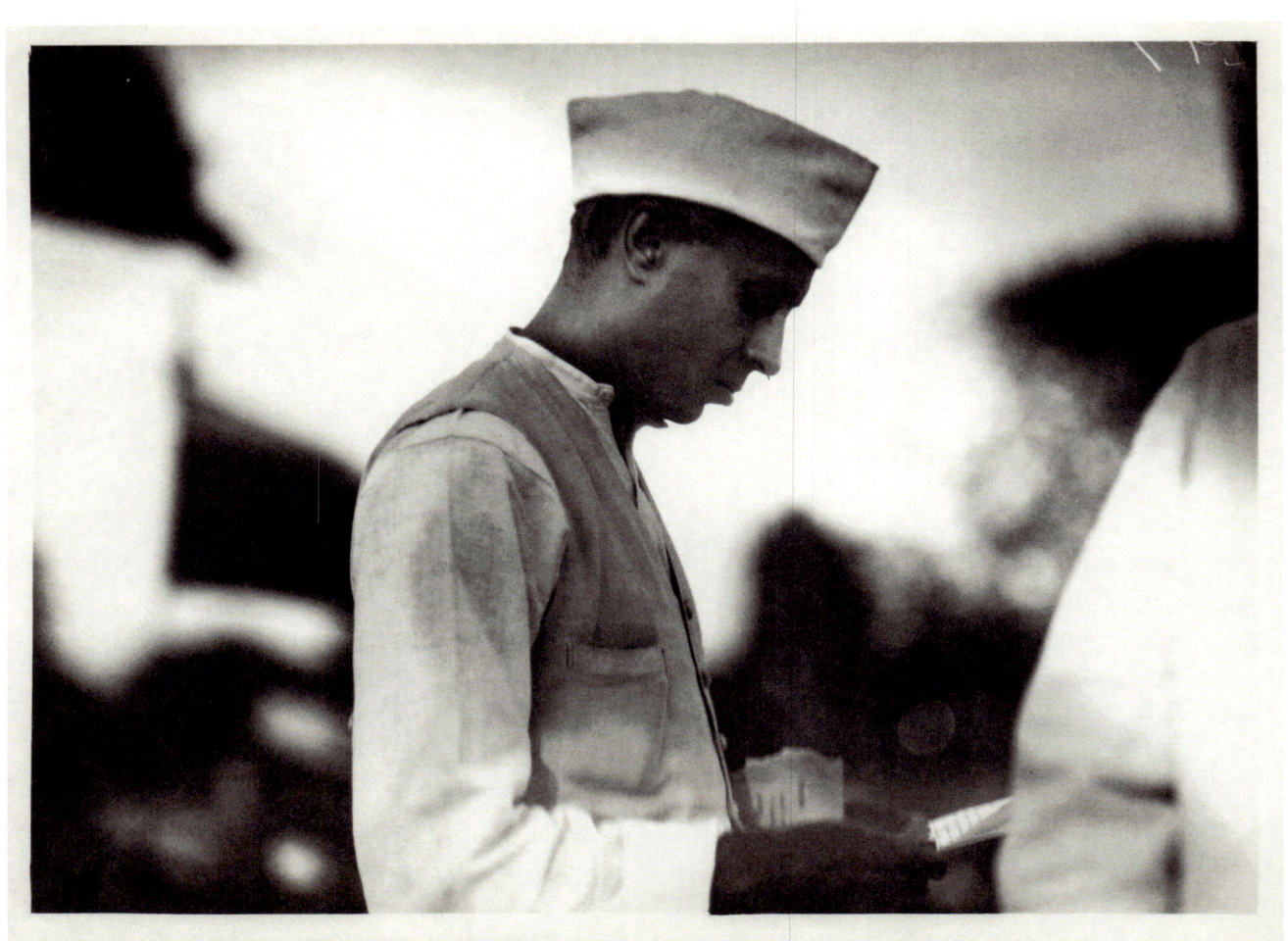

Nehru addressing a meeting.

As a grand colonial capital, Bombay was witness to and participant in a long history of nationalist struggle between Indian claims on public space and colonial counter-attempts to reinscribe "public order" within that frictive space.[1] This struggle is visible in the Nursey album, aligning with scholarship that shows the degree to which central Bombay, "the physical and symbolic centre of the British political and business establishment," became a site of contestation as Congress workers purposefully occupied colonial streets and parks to challenge British rule in India.[2] The regular convergence of crowds on the Esplanade— a colonially-crafted space shaped in the environs of the Fort, originally intended as a security measure to ensure visibility around it—can be read as a collective assertion of sovereignty in the city, as can the widespread adoption of its new name, Azad Maidan (lit., "Freedom Field").[3] The police attempted to prevent gatherings by banning meetings at the site. These bans were contested by the Bombay Satyagraha Committee, which issued a press communiqué stating that using the Azad Maidan was "the inherent right of every citizen," for "purposes of congregation, exercise, drill or such other purposes as are non-violent."[4]

A number of photographs in the Alkazi Collection's Nursey album feature speeches being delivered by Congress leaders to large crowds at key public spaces in Bombay, such as Chowpatty Beach and Azad Maidan. While these photographs reveal a well-known politics of occupying material colonial spaces and remaking them as nationalist, they also invite us to read the struggles as expressed in *sonic* space—by which I mean the acoustic domain that resonated with energetic nationalist speeches, songs and slogans during the Civil Disobedience Movement, which were framed to appeal to "the masses," to make the politics of civil disobedience action meaningful to them. Literacy in British India was relatively low, estimated at around 16% of the population in 1931, although this greatly varied in terms of region, gender and religion.[5] This presented challenges for nationalist mobilization, which were in part overcome by a reliance on vibrant images.[6] However, critical analysis via multi-sensory historical approaches is beginning to demonstrate the extent to which "making noise" was also crucial to effective nationalist messaging.

PAGES 224—225
"Wholesale arrest of congress [Congress] volunteers at Wadhla [Wadala]. Here the police are seen guarding the arrested members. They were transfered [transferred] to the Worli chawls." 1930 Gelatin Silver Print, 115 x 156 mm
ACP: 98.77.0002 (55b)

PAGE 226
"Mrs Sarojini Naidu addressing a meeting." (Detail, see p. 239)

Fig. 9.1
"Nehru addressing a meeting."
c. 1930—1931
Gelatin Silver Print, 116 x 158 mm
ACP: 98.77.0002 (4b)

Retrieving the ways in which anticolonial sounds take up space in the context of the Salt Satyagraha is methodologically challenging. Sound Studies scholars have long grappled with the flows of sound, which is by nature transient and presents a problem for historians with a penchant for hard evidence.[7] However, it is precisely this slippery and fleeting nature of sound that makes seditious speeches, songs and slogans so subversive. Critical attention to the sounds of political mobilization can enable a deeper understanding of the dynamics and "resonance" of nationalist messaging, and the parallel creation of citizens and publics committed to the cause.[8] And one particularly effective way of retrieving it is to listen to images, as Tina Campt proposes, to draw out their often unintended messages and to hear voices otherwise stifled in the historical record.[9]

Sound may not be visible in the straightforward sense, but we can exercise a historical imagination to listen in. Although Campt invites us to listen to quiet resistance in portrait photography taken by the state for purposes of identification and control, my focus here is the Nursey album's noisy photographs, which illuminate how Congress leaders sought to vocally project their messages to increasingly larger crowds, aided by rhetoric, gesture and performance and, eventually, through the use of acoustic technology (microphones and loudspeakers), successfully building and commanding more expansive publics. These oratorical and sonic strategies developed in the course of the Civil Disobedience Movement pictorially unfold before our eyes in the pages of the album, allowing us to re-read the ways in which crowds at Chowpatty Beach and Azad Maidan assert a mode of sovereign subjectivity through the act of listening.

We can imagine the charged sonic atmosphere of 1930s Bombay, of chanting, sloganeering, singing, impassioned oration and the buzz of excited crowds—all this political "noise" intensified by new audio technology (tangled wires, imposing metallic microphone discs, trumpet loudspeakers). These photographs provide a window on diffused articulations of power, as indexed by the revolving possession of the microphone by Congress leaders who were arrested and removed from the field of action. We find references to this sonic turbulence in other sources of the time. In a report tendered to the British parliament, we read of how "gigantic yelling processions passed through the main thoroughfares of the city" of Bombay throughout the movement.[11] A recently discovered film clip comes with a rare audio file of sloganeering and bugles playing.[12] There are newspaper articles and letters to the editor in which European residents complain of the peace being disturbed, and of the anxiety they experience upon hearing the lyrics of songs sung by defiant women protesters: "Break all the oppressive laws of the government, oh daughters of India, awake, the drums are beating!"[13] The relentless sound of nationalism was a regular challenge to British notions of urban order, as evident in complaints about "noisy" *prabhat pheris* (lit., "dawn rounds," processions that moved through neighbourhoods in the early hours singing *bhajan*s or scripture and, in 1931, nationalist songs), which letters to *The Times of India* complained ruined people's sleep, causing fatigue and rendering them less productive.[14]

Congress leaders were acutely aware of the value of noise as a potent tactic and instrument for spreading nationalist news and plans about Civil Disobedience action. Jawaharlal Nehru recommended a means of communicating with the public that was adopted in the lead up to National Week in Bombay (7–13 April 1930):

> In Bombay, the volunteers are doing something which might interest you. They go out in batches, stop at a street corner, blow a bugle, shout out various national cries, which have been previously given to them on a piece of paper, and then one of them delivers a short speech, the notes of which have been previously supplied. The whole thing does not take more than 10 minutes. Then they move onto the next street corner. In this way they have more than 200 street-corner meetings in Bombay. You can imagine the tremendous propaganda value of these meetings, specially when they are practised in poor quarters where newspapers are not often read.[15]

What is striking here is the use of a fixed script to ensure that the same message was disseminated in the same way in different areas of the city. It is difficult to know which text was read on these occasions, but the key point is the emphasis on the reiteration and recursion of a singular message, one that aligned with Gandhi's instructions. Here it is important to consider the extent to which Gandhi's call for Civil Disobedience in 1930 was driven, in part, by his recognition of the need to reassert control over "the escalating radicalization and tacit endorsement of political violence in nationalist circles," which had been evident, even within the Congress in 1929, as a "revolutionary wave" was discernibly shaking the tenet of non-violence.[16] An organized public protest movement with scripted public rhetorical strategies became a significant focus in the early stages of Gandhi's mobilization campaign.

"Noise" in the Nursey Images

The images in the Nursey album are not arranged in strict chronological order, nor are they dated. However, a sequence can be deduced through the events and people depicted in the photographs and the descriptions in the captions, mapped against the known dates of the leading protagonists' arrests and release from prison. By putting the photographs and their captions in conversation with published newspaper accounts of the day, the shifts and developments in oratorical practices become clear. The first few pages of the album include a handsome profile study of Jawaharlal Nehru "addressing a meeting" (Fig. 9.1), reading from a prepared text—the background is out of focus, but it appears to indicate a flag and the silhouette of a crowd. It is not clear that the photograph was taken in Bombay, although Nehru was indeed there in February and spoke at several meetings, including in Congress House, so well attended that they had to be repeated as "overflow meetings."[17] Jawaharlal's reliance on a text to read his speech, as suggested by this photograph, indicates a level of nationalist organization and planning not evident in the later parts of the movement. As prominent Congress leaders were progressively arrested, the "noisy" images gradually began to feature less prominent speakers, including some who were unidentifiable, or at least unrecognized by the collator of the Nursey album. Most of its photographs depict speakers addressing the crowd ex tempore.

The continuing arrests of Congress leaders led to some anxiety in the Bombay Provincial Congress as to who would be left with sufficient influence and skill to coordinate the campaign along constructive lines.[18] The Bombay Provincial Congress Committee therefore elected a "shadow cabinet" of leaders who directed action covertly, while the members of the "War Council" and office-bearers named in the *Congress Bulletin* publicly courted and risked arrest.[19] One of those in the shadow cabinet until late August when he was pushed to the fore was Navin Khandwala, named in *The Bombay Chronicle* as "Captain of the National Militia."[20] Khandwala was a keen photographer, and it is possible that he took at least some of the photographs in the Nursey album. In a 1971 interview, Khandwala named several major political personalities with whom he interacted: national leaders Motilal Nehru, Jawaharlal and Kamala Nehru, Madan Mohan Malaviya, Vallabhbhai Patel and Sarojini Naidu; and local leaders Yusuf Meherally, Kamaladevi Chattopadhyay, K.M. Munshi, Uma Shankar Dixit, Hansaben Mehta and Perin Captain. As a member of the shadow cabinet, Khandwala knew where and when to go to photograph what Jim Masselos famously described as "Congress dramas," which are featured in the album.[21] It also explains the willingness of some Congress workers to pose for the camera, as is evident in several images. Khandwala was undoubtedly a committed observer, a witness and a participant in the events that are captured in the album. Nationalist photographers were active in Bombay during this period, and in alignment with boycott principles they were urged to eschew British-made plates, papers and chemicals in favour of products by German companies such as Hauff and Agfa.[22]

Oratorical Infrastructure: Scripts, Stages and Lighting

As demonstrated by Jawaharlal Nehru's "overflow" public meetings in February, the courtyards and meeting halls of Bombay were inadequate to the task of hosting large public gatherings. Bombay's open spaces were much more amenable to accommodating masses of people. In the first half of National Week, crowds followed processions through the streets of Bombay and congregated at Chowpatty Beach to listen to speeches, take part in flag salutations and collect

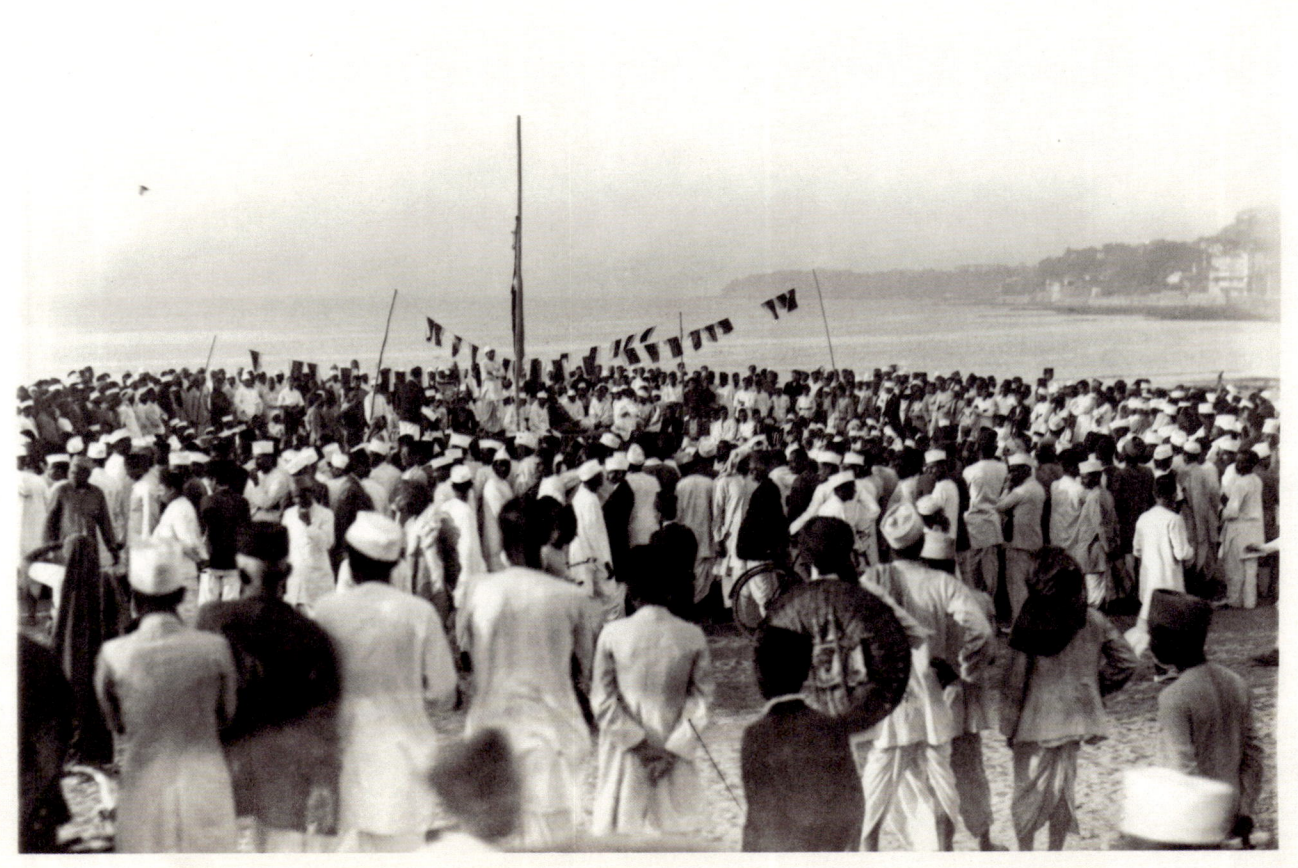

Fig. 9.2
"A meeting on the
chaupatty [Chowpatty]
sands Bombay."
c. 1930—1931
Gelatin Silver Print,
116 x 163 mm
ACP: 98.77.0002 (109a)

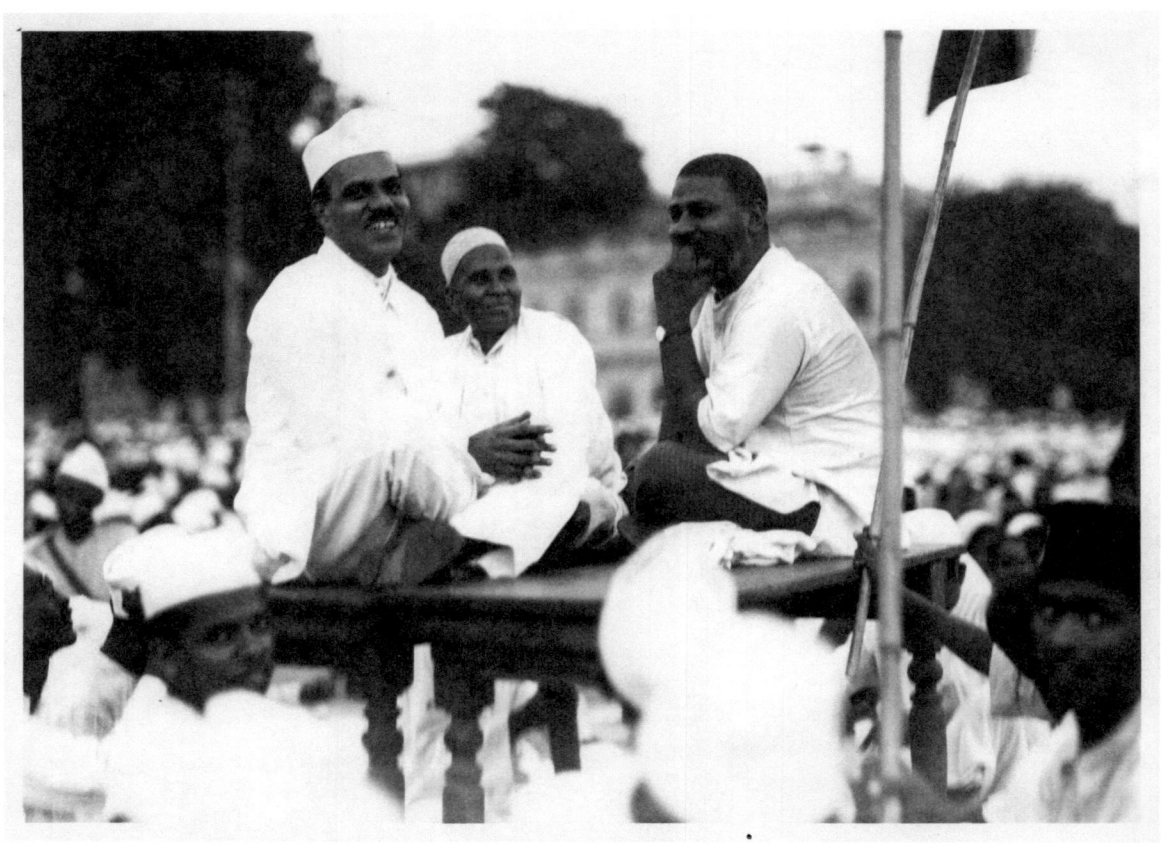

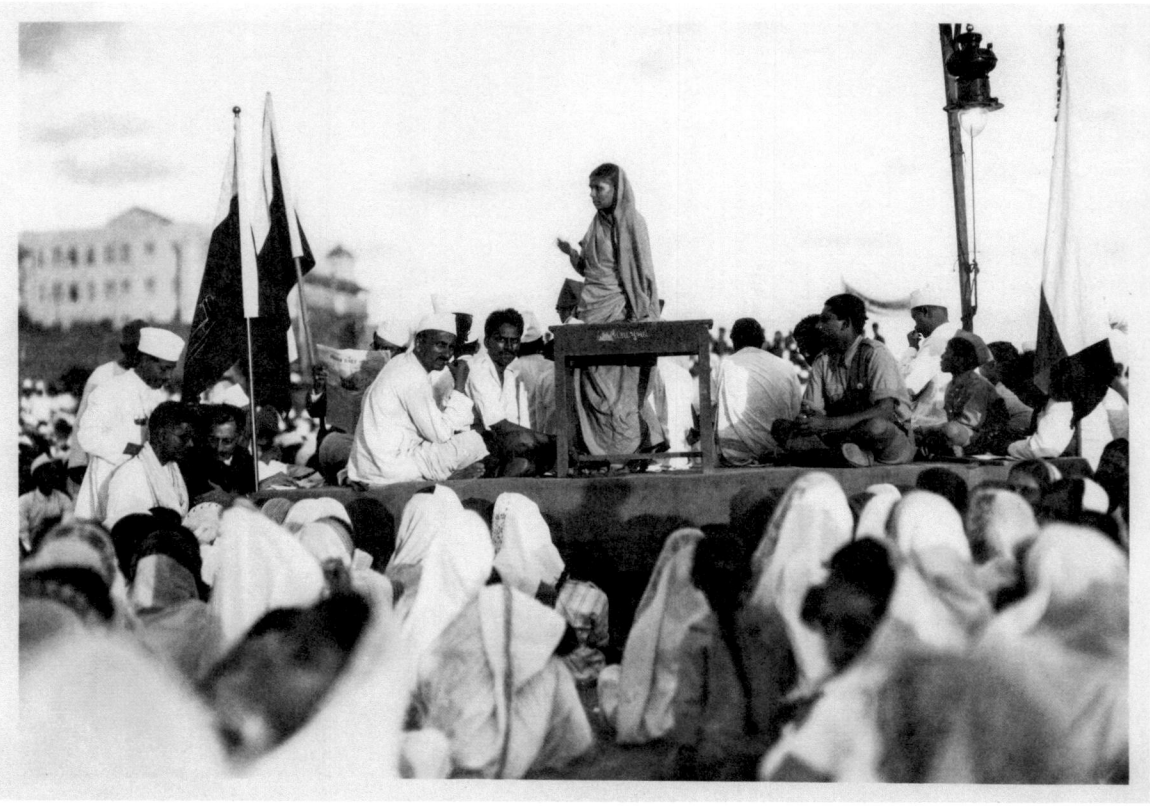

seawater from which to illegally make salt, as part of Gandhi's Salt Satyagraha (Fig. 5.5, Fig. 9.2; see also Chapter Five in this volume). On days of *hartals* (strikes), for example at the meeting called to protest the arrests of the Congress leaders K.F. Nariman and Ali Bahadur Khanon on 8 April 1930, crowds at Chowpatty swelled to "mammoth" proportions.[23] As National Week progressed, the long beach became so densely populated that numerous purpose-built wooden daises were erected in order that speeches could be simultaneously given across the length of the beach.[24]

This concurrent performance naturally had the effect of expanding the visibility of a number of leaders in the Bombay Provincial Congress Committee and ensuring their public recognition. As projecting one's voice to a large crowd was quite tiring,[25] a diverse array of speakers, sometimes not identifiable, took turns to address the public.[26] For example, a principal speaker at Chowpatty on 13 April was Sarojini Naidu, giving a short speech appealing to Muslims to take part in the "non-violent fight that Mr Gandhi was giving to Government," while from another platform unnamed officials of the Bombay Provincial Congress Committee joined "a few Mahomoden and Sikh leaders from upcountry."[27]

In many of the photographs it is clear that the use of what we might call oratorical infrastructure was key to commanding the crowd's attention. In some cases, speakers are identified as "prominent leaders" in the captions not because they are well-known individuals, but because they are standing or sitting on a platform (Fig. 9.3, Fig. 9.4). Newspaper accounts indicate that these platforms, sometimes bare and sometimes draped with a rug or with *khadi*, were purpose-built, presumably at the behest of the Bombay Congress, and most likely dismantled after each event.[28] The platforms vary in their features, are with or without railings, and sometimes decorated with flags or garlanded images of Gandhi and other leaders (Fig. 9.5, Fig. 9.6). These improvised "stages" are an essential element of nationalist infrastructure, raising speakers above the crowd to enable better voice projection and also enable the activist "performers" to be seen from a distance.

Many speakers' platforms were constructed beneath kerosene-fuelled Kitson lamps (Fig. 9.6, Fig. 9.7, Fig. 9.8), their heavy elegant bulbs suspended from a post; it is likely that Congress installed this infrastructure along with the platforms. During the summer campaign these pendulous lamps enabled meetings to be held in the cool of the evening. The lamps testify that some of the Nursey images were taken in the early evening (Fig. 9.9, see also Fig. 4.2), but such gatherings were a challenge to photograph because in 1930 flash photography was costly, and sometimes hazardous as well. Navin Khandwala describes how, when he went to photograph Gandhi during the Salt March in Surat in early April 1930, he attempted to use magnesium flash powder to photograph a "huge meeting" on the banks of the river Tapti, with unfortunate consequences: "Wind blew against

Fig. 9.3
"Another prominent Northern India leader." c. 1930–1931
Gelatin Silver Print, 116 x 156 mm
ACP: 98.77.0002 (26a)

Fig. 9.4
"A meeting on the Azad maidan where many prominent speakers addressed the crowd. Here is a prominent congress [Congress] leader addressing the meeting."
c. 1930–1931
Gelatin Silver Print, 115 x 161 mm
ACP: 98.77.0002 (82b)

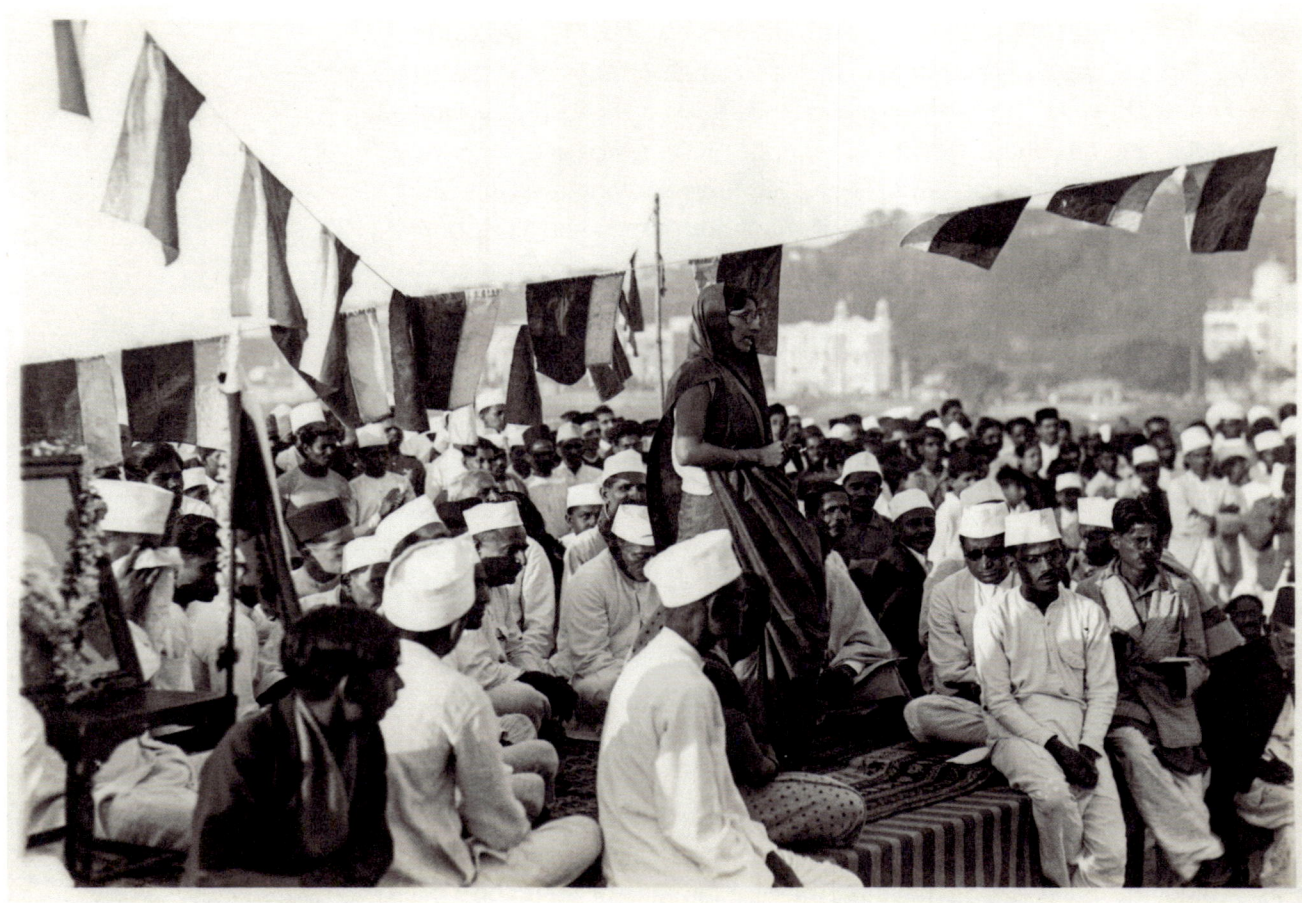

Fig. 9.5
An uncaptioned
photograph of
Lilavati Munshi
speaking from a
platform, festooned
with flags,
c. 1930–1931
Gelatin Silver Print,
118 x 165 mm
ACP: 98.77.0002 (85b)

the camera and the lighted powder burnt a part of my face, including my eye-brows."[29] When he met Gandhi afterwards, the Mahatma asked about the source of the burns and advised him to use a cold pack to relieve the pain.

Oratorical Strategies: Gestures, Rituals and Repetition

The considerable ambient noise of the crowd often drowned voices out, and they often used dramatic gestures and body movement to help the crowd construe meaning at mass gatherings.[30] In a photograph taken at Azad Maidan (Fig. 9.10), Sarojini Naidu clutches her sari *pallu* with one hand, and emphatically stabs the air with a finger as she speaks. Newspapers documenting these speeches reiterate the same themes—boycotting of British goods, and the urging of courageous and fearless public activism—as well as pleas for participation by all communities. Nationalist messaging was driven home at these "noisy" meetings through demonstrative rituals. These often drew on established religious practices, including the ceremonial immersion of idols at the end of major festivals such as Ganesh Chaturthi and Durga Puja: for example, to conclude one meeting in Chowpatty a picture of the Salt Act in the form of a "demon trampling the poor, helpless Indian under his feet" was thrown into the sea.[31]

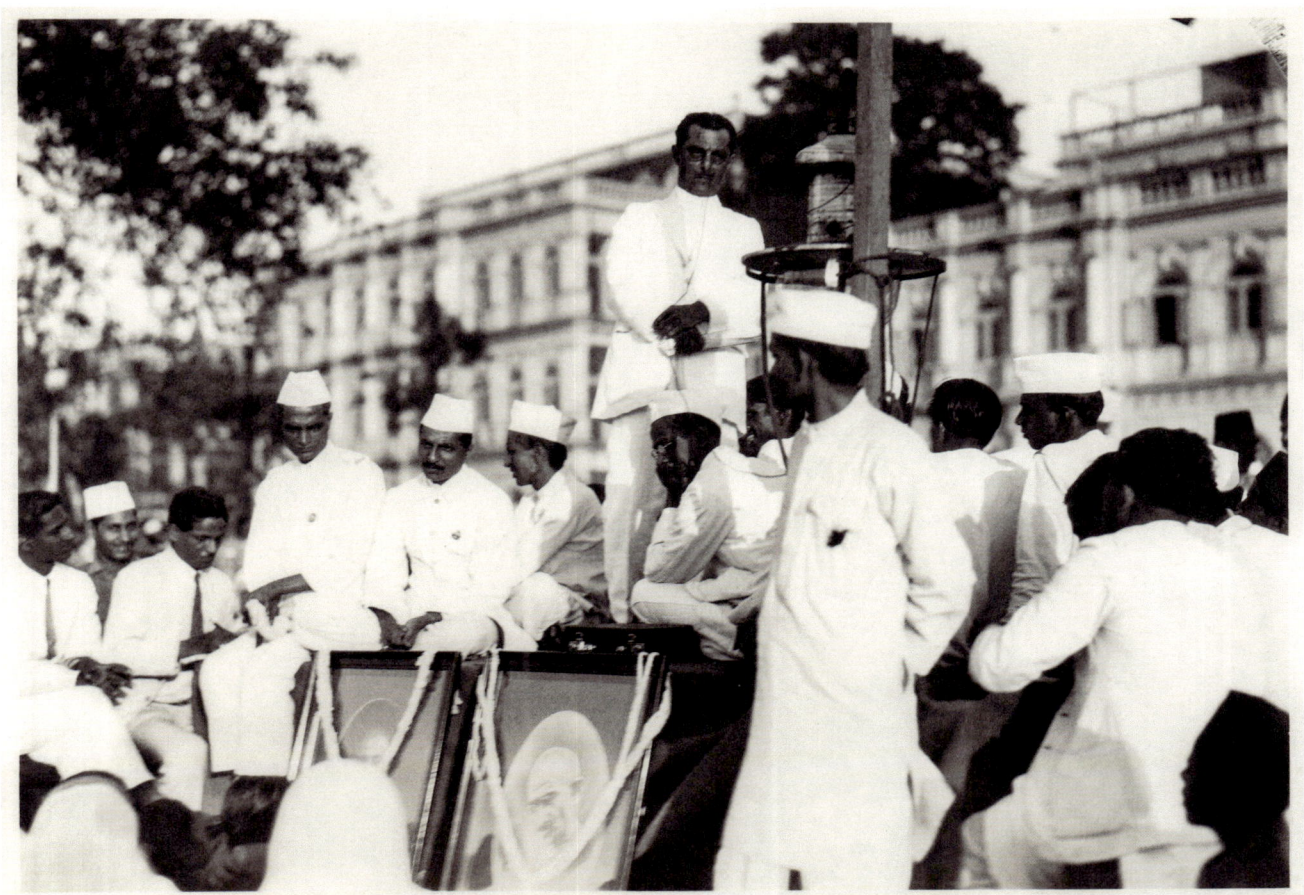

Fig. 9.6
"Mr K.F. Nariman
addressing a meeting
before his arrest."
c. 1930—1931
Gelatin Silver Print,
114 x 155 mm
ACP: 98.77.0002 (38b)

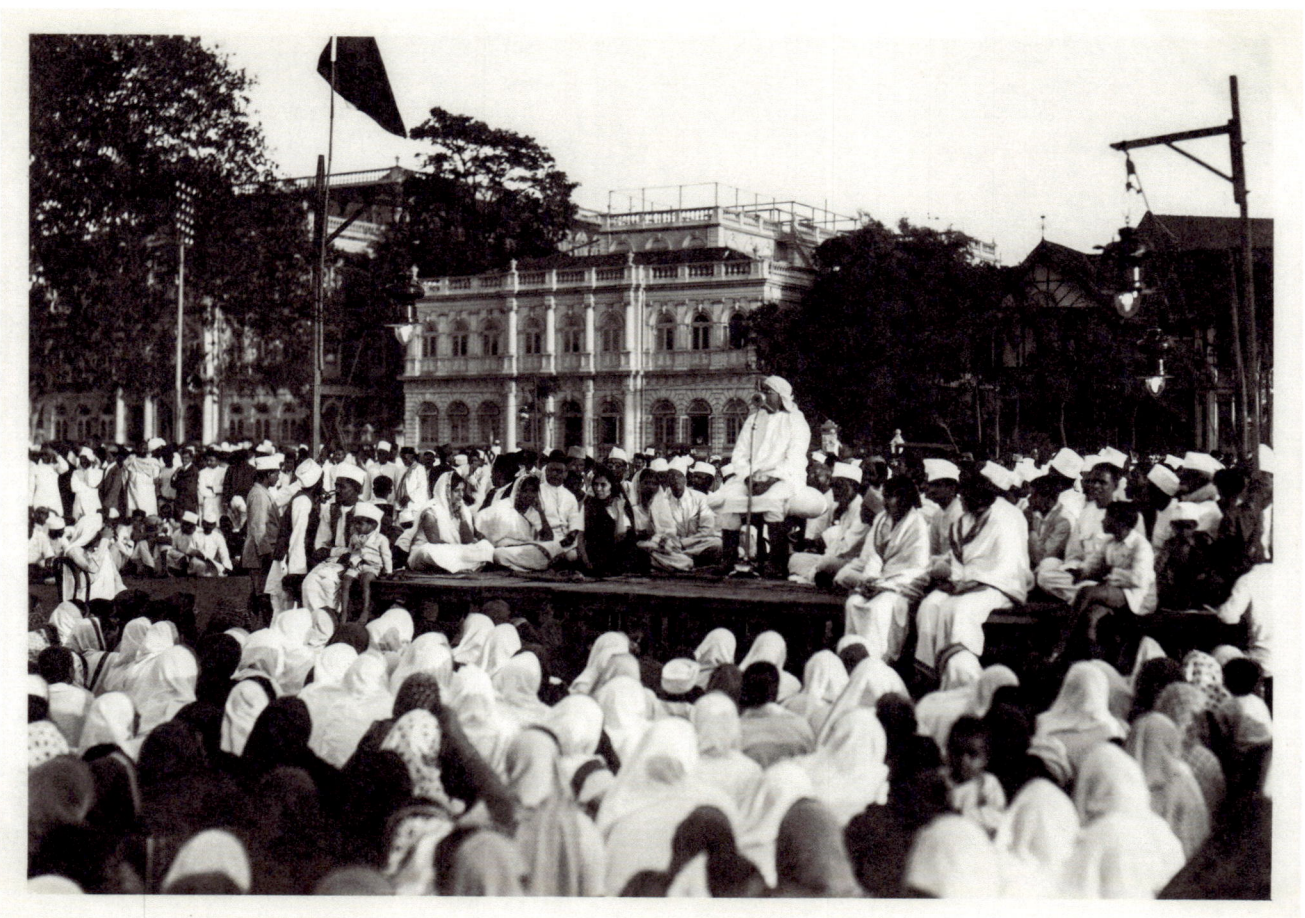

Fig. 9.7
"Ladies meeting on the Esplanade maidan to condemn the Government, of its repressive policy."
c. 1930—1931
Gelatin Silver Print, 115 x 160 mm
ACP: 98.77.0002 (104a)

FACING PAGE, ABOVE
Fig. 9.8
"A view of platformone [platform one] of the Congress meeting."
c. 1930—1931
Gelatin Silver Print, 115 x 160 mm
ACP: 98.77.0002 (112b)

FACING PAGE, BELOW
Fig. 9.9
"Mrs Sarojini Naidu addressing a meeting." 1930
Gelatin Silver Print, 116 x 155 mm
ACP: 98.77.0002 (21b)

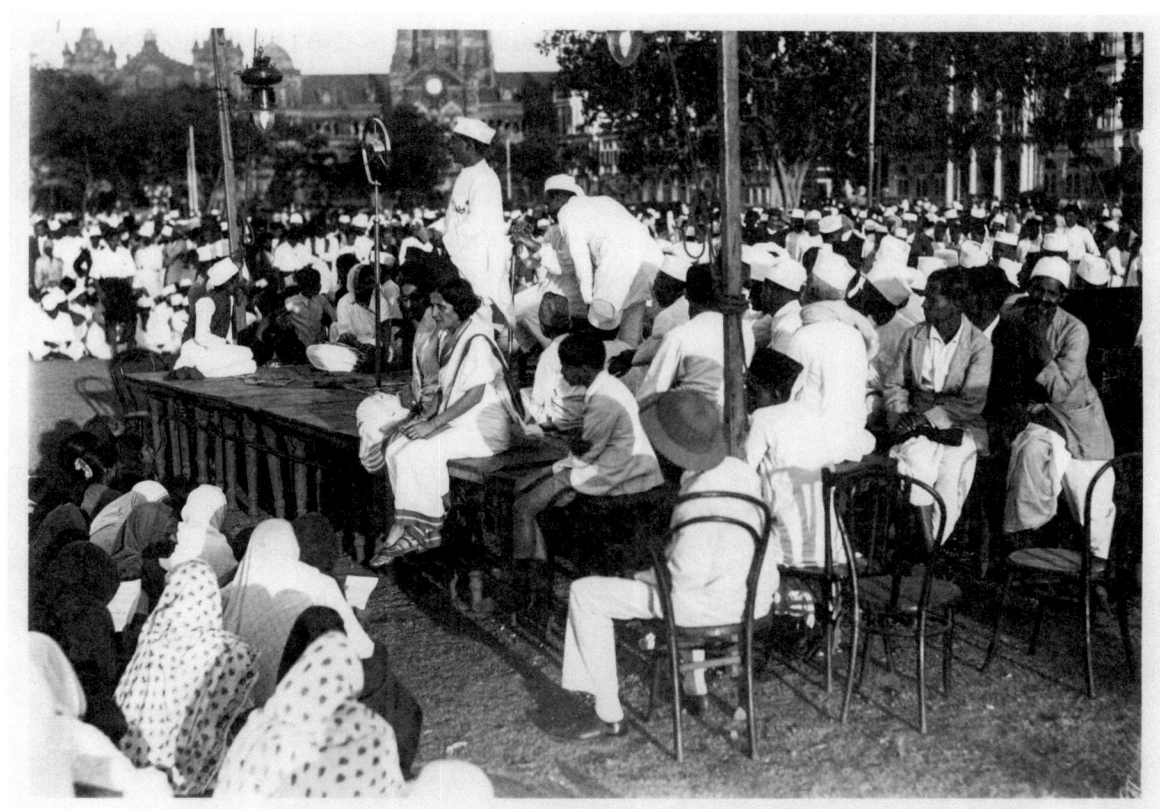

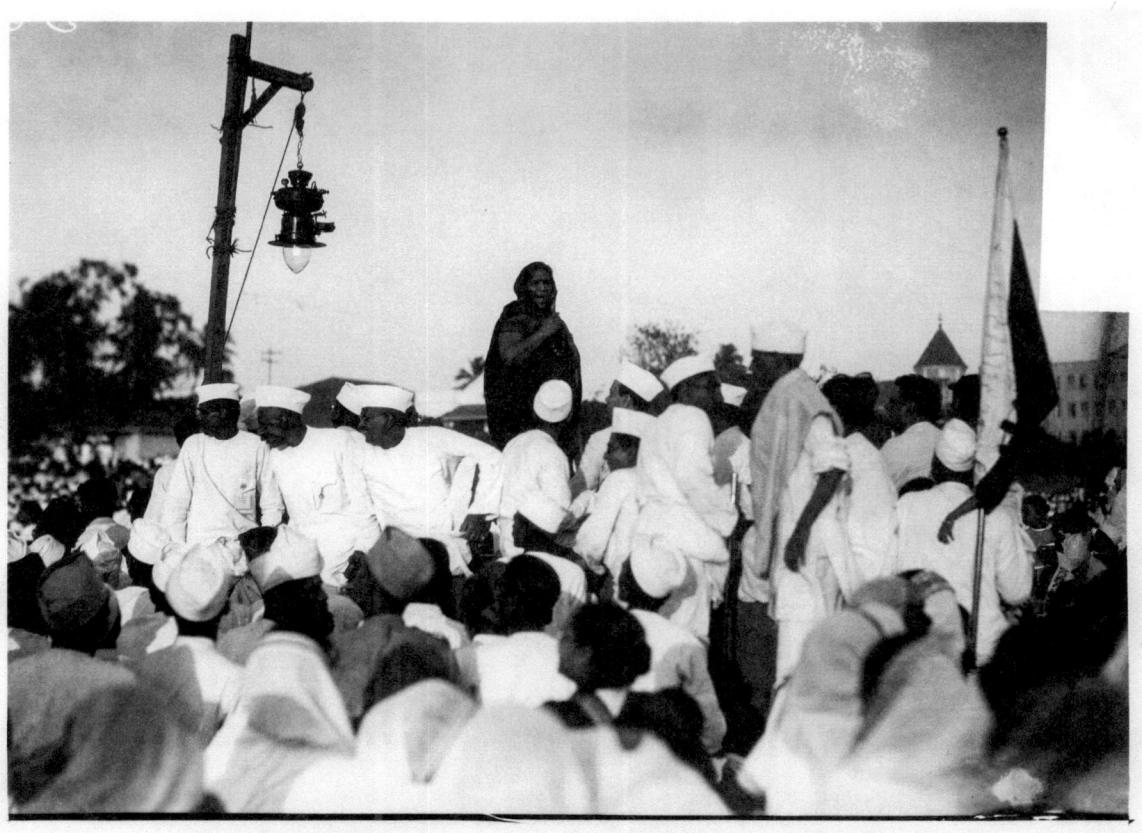

Speakers frequently exhorted the audiences to renounce the use of foreign cloth, with the focus on wearing white *khadi* caps instead of foreign-made black caps; the latter could be immediately surrendered and ceremoniously burned (Fig. 9.11).[32] Crowds were encouraged to formally vow to not use foreign cloth, and to repeat slogans given by the speakers. At a meeting on Chowpatty Beach on 8 April 1930, the "whole audience in once voice repeated 'Down with Foreign Cloth'" at the behest of a speaker.[33] The documentation of collective protest "noise" in nationalist newspapers such as *The Bombay Chronicle* indicates a high level of audience participation: for example, after Abid Ali Jafferbhai appealed to the crowd to either throw themselves into the battle of *satyagraha*, or to remain cowards, the reporter records the response to the speaker's provocation: "(Voices: We are not cowards)."[34] Listeners —and perhaps readers too—were thus goaded into participation in the "noisy" nationalist agenda.

The Loud Crowd

As noted earlier in this essay, Bombay's "noisy" nationalist crowds were not passive, but highly interactive. Many public meetings interspersed speeches

Fig. 9.10
"Mrs Sarojini Naidu addressing a meeting on the Esplanade maidan before her arrest urging the people to join Mahatma in his non-violent fight for freedom."
1930
Gelatin Silver Print, 117 x 158 mm
ACP: 98.77.0002 (21a)

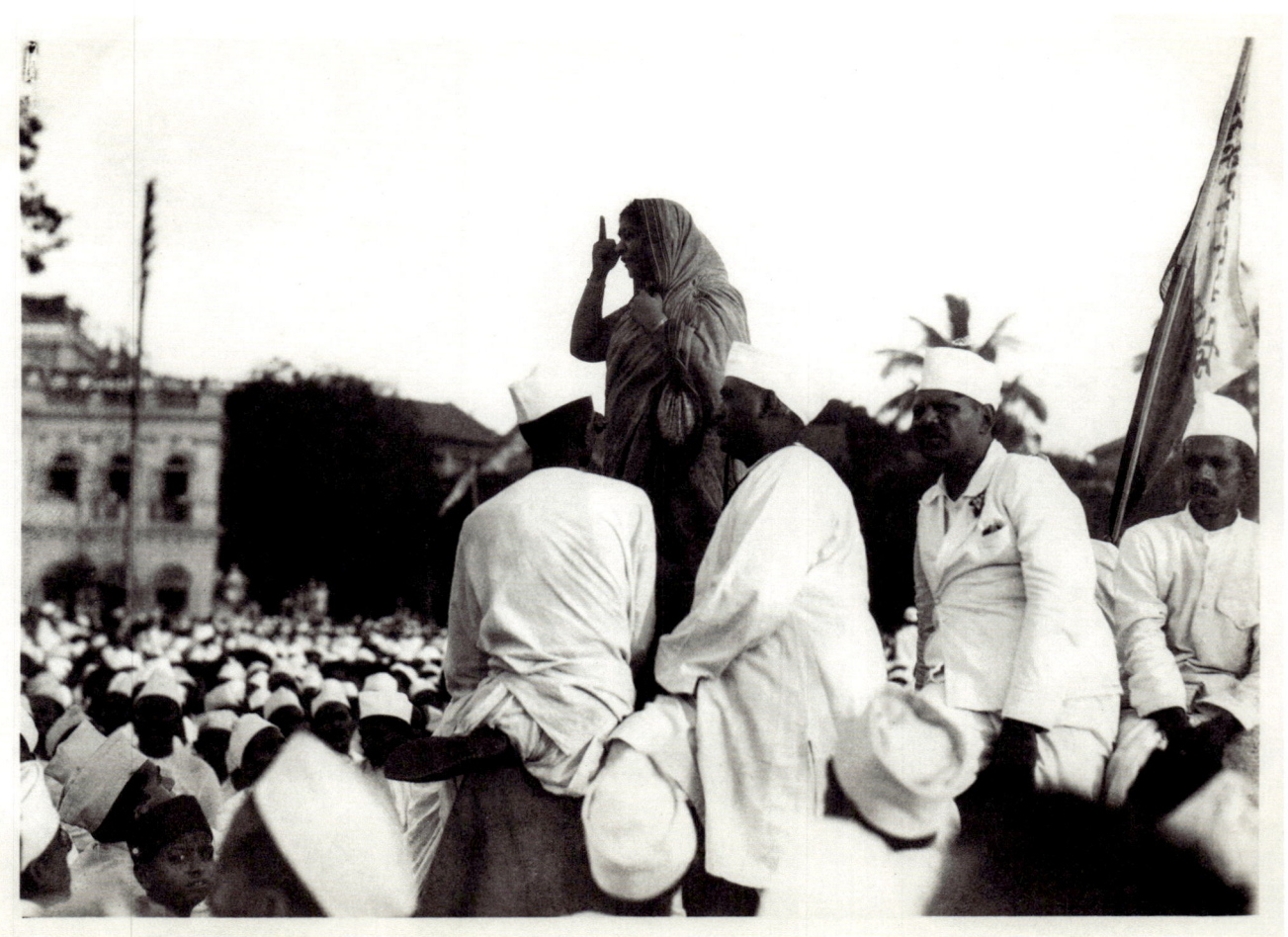

with song, and pamphlets of collected songs were published in this period to enable the popularization of nationalist lyrics.[35] Call-and-response songs enabled quick learning of lyrics and melodies, and added a richly emotive element to mass mobilization. As Gandhi noted in 1928, song-singing was an effective mechanism for "controlling and stopping the noise which is a usual feature of public meetings in this country."[36] On a practical level, songs reduced the load and strain on orators, and also assisted in the select amplification and reiteration of certain messages, based on the choice of some songs over others.

Song-singing also distributed political agency, including to children who could lead the event with their singing, their innocent enthusiasm adding to the political potency of their performance. A photograph of a mass meeting on Chowpatty Beach on 7 April 1930, the first day of National Week, shows a "young Hindu boy" standing on a raised stool (Fig. 6.7) placed on a platform that elevates him to the level of the Kitson lamp; he is singing a "*rashtra gita*" (lit., "national song," as noted in the caption), with Yusuf Meherally and Kamaladevi Chattopadhyay among others seated with their back to him.[37] This group, however, seems distracted

Fig. 9.11
"At a meeting organised by the congress [Congress] committee on the chaupatty [Chowpatty] shore to support the civil disobedience movement, A bon-fire of foreign caps etc was made."
c. 1930—1931
Gelatin Silver Print, 115 x 156 mm
ACP: 98.77.0002 (23a)

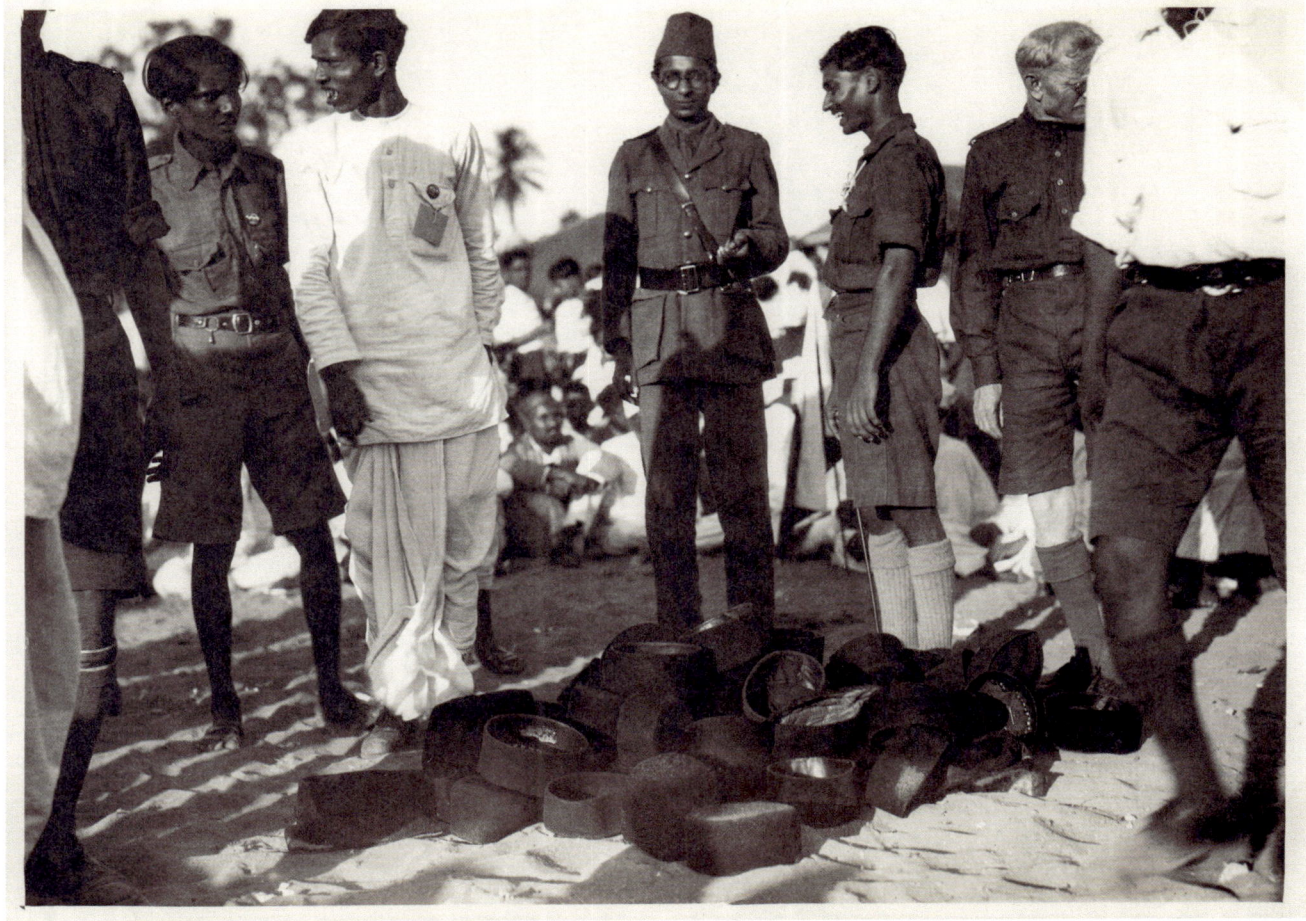

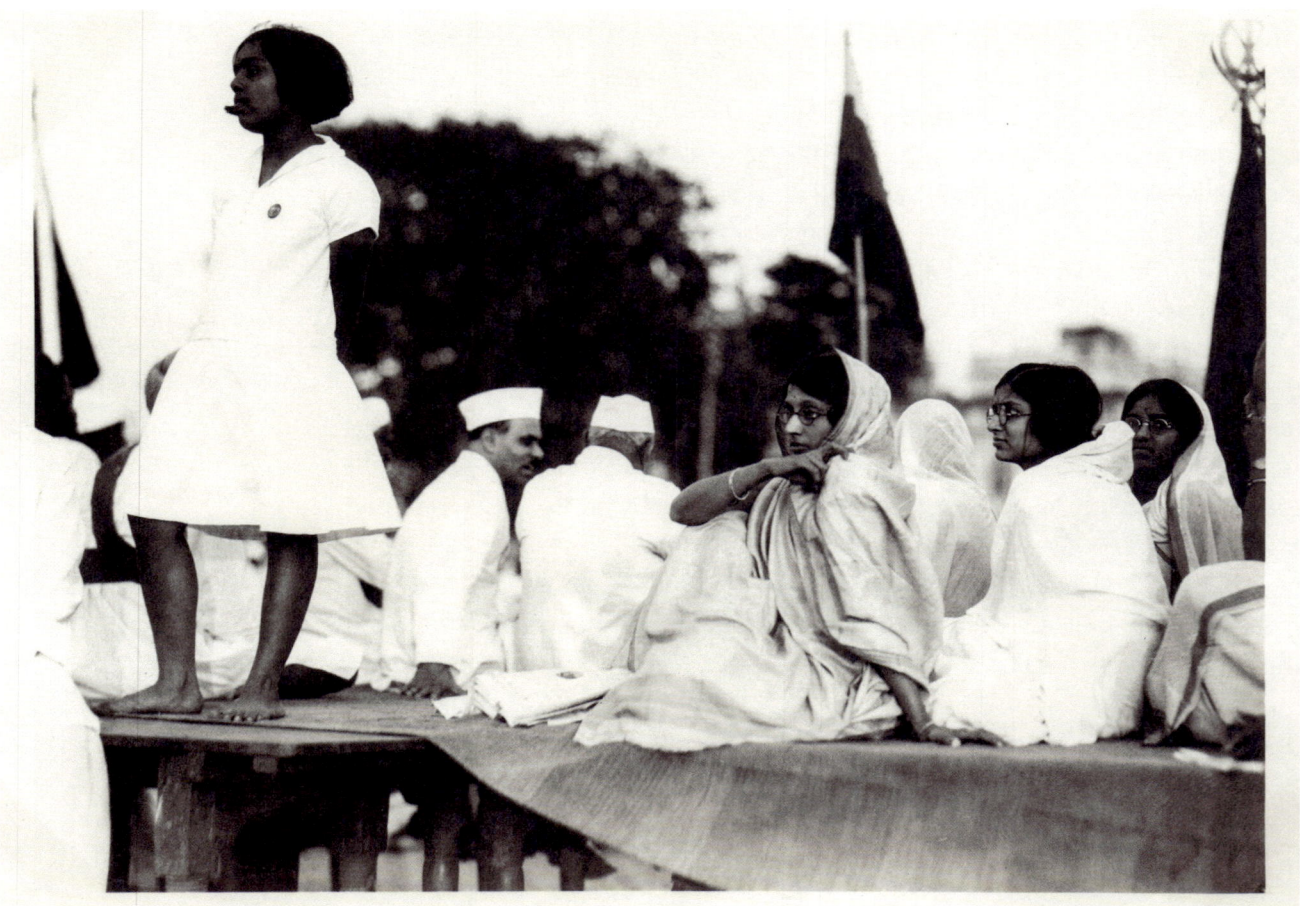

Fig. 9.12
"A young hindu girl
singing the National.
Anthem 'Rastra Gita'
during a meeting on
the Azad maida[n]."
c. 1930—1931
Gelatin Silver Print,
117 x 157 mm
ACP: 98.77.0002 (19b)

and not actively listening to the young singer. A photograph of a "young Hindu girl" singing a "*rashtra gita*" during an Azad Maidan meeting (Fig. 9.12) features Lilavati Munshi and two women seated on the dais listening attentively, while in the background two men facing the other way chat animatedly. In another photograph taken moments later (or perhaps moments earlier), Munshi studies a newspaper, while two men look in her direction (Fig. 9.13). This does not suggest particularly attentive listening. Indeed, in these and in other photographs in the Nursey album, in the visible absence of the police the political gatherings at public spaces of dissent emerge as hospitable, convivial, even sociable, events—as seen in the depiction of an unnamed but "prominent northern India leader" at a Bombay meeting addressing the crowd while immediately behind him on the dais a small group of his colleagues, facing away from him, are engaged in a lively discussion (Fig. 9.14).

In some photographs, the ambience is positively festive. For instance, in an image featuring Sarojini Naidu at Chowpatty Beach (Fig. 9.9) we see the famed "Nightingale of India", centrally positioned, declaiming with gusto. This particularly "noisy" image, (also available through Getty Images, where it is captioned 'India's Joan of Arc, Released after Arrest'), is dated 16 May 1930.

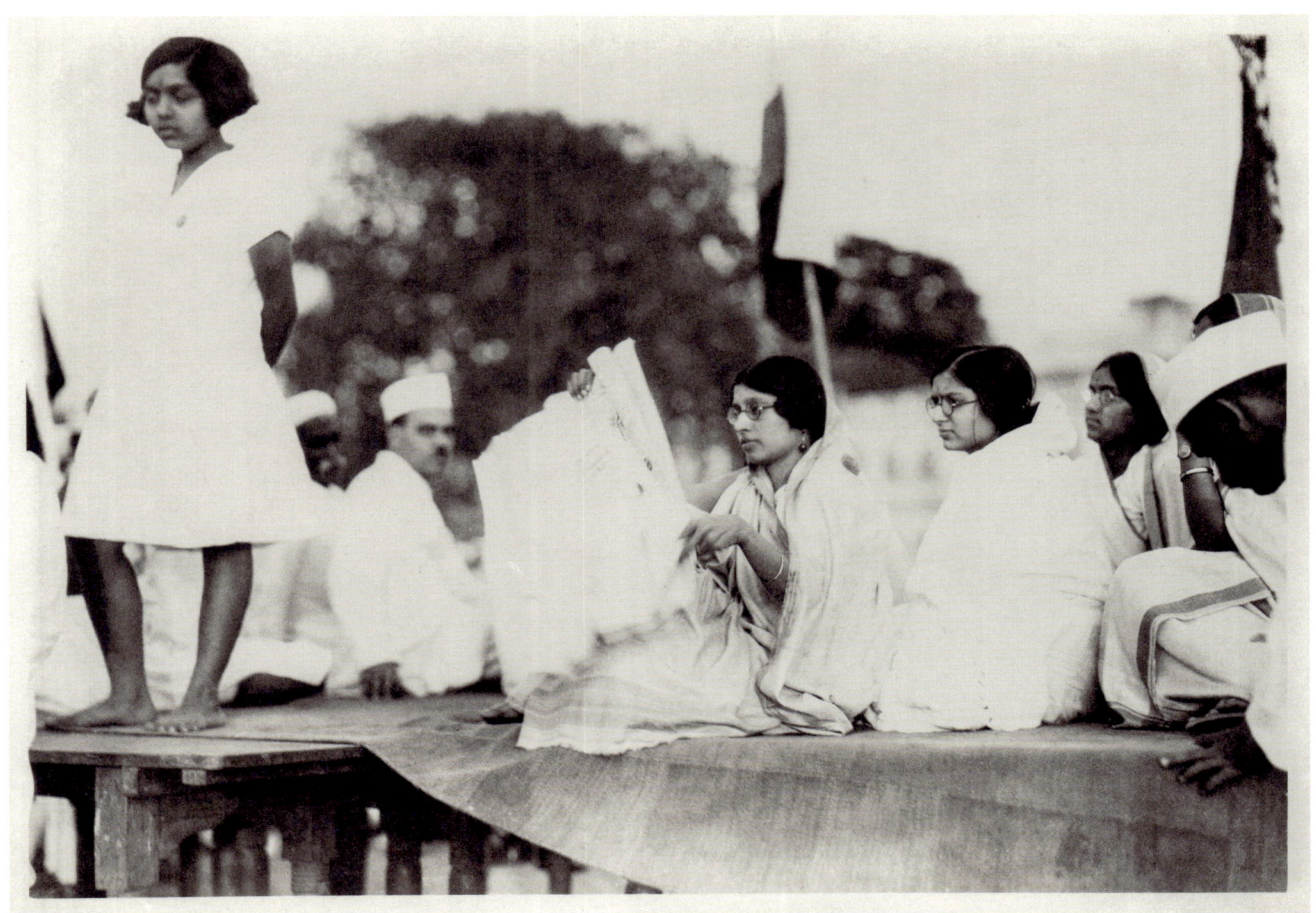

Fig. 9.13
"A Hindu girl singing
National songs on the
Esplanade maidan."
c. 1930—1931
Gelatin Silver Print,
116 x 160 mm
ACP: 98.77.0002 (20a)

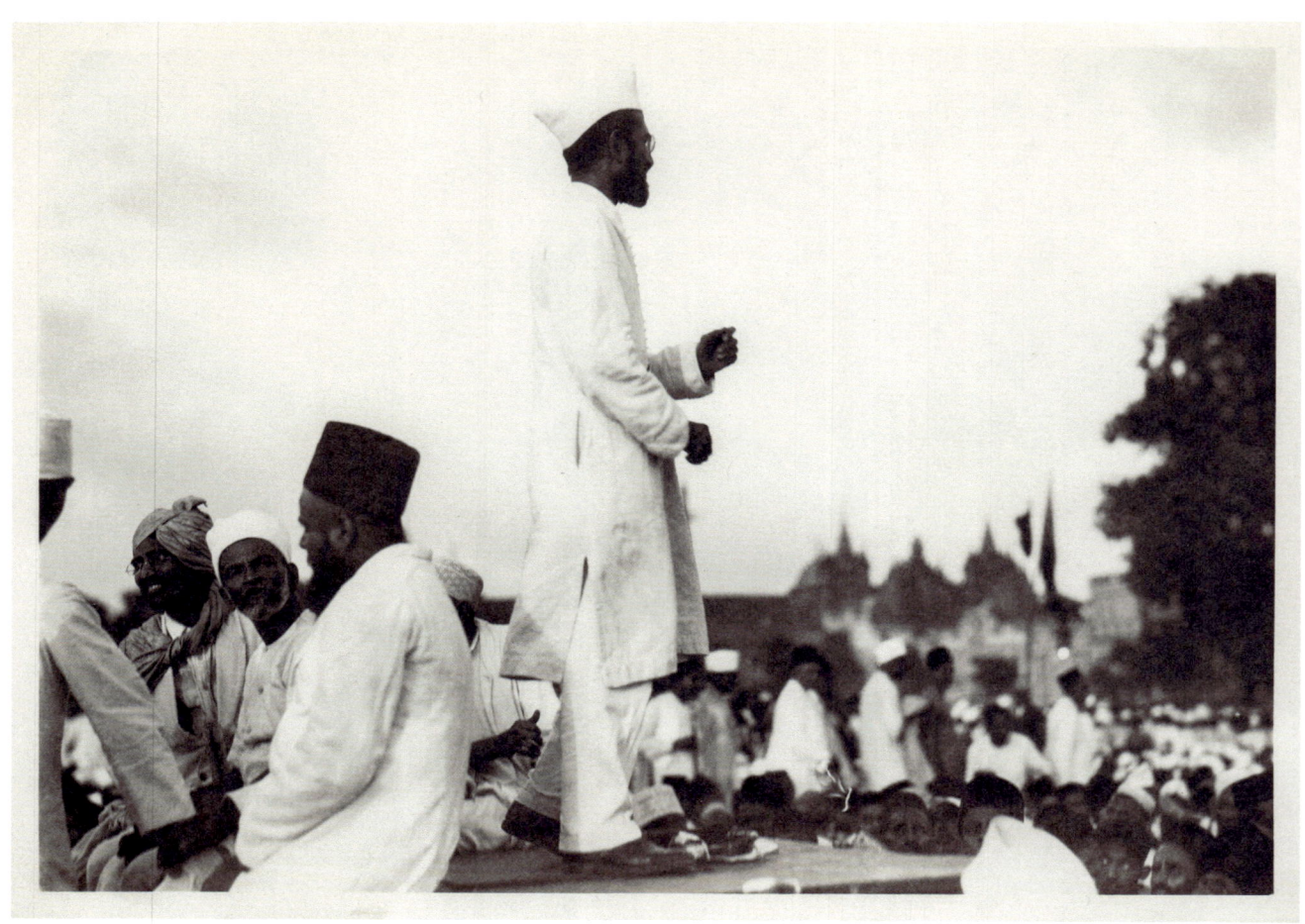

Fig. 9.14
"A prominent Northern
India leader at a
Bombay Meeting."
c. 1930—1931
Gelatin Silver Print,
115 x 160 mm
ACP: 98.77.0002 (23b)

A few of the Gandhi-capped men seated on the dais around Naidu are seemingly diverted by something to the left; seated below the dais, members of the crowd also look away, in different directions. This seems to indicate a form of "active audiencing", not necessarily focused on listening to the speech itself, but the act of being there. Such a response is, I suggest, predicated on the understanding that the noise of large, enthusiastic gatherings can make it very difficult, or even impossible, to hear orators, no matter how impassioned or persuasive their delivery.

The Marvellous Microphone and "Attentive Audiencing"

This presumption changes with the arrival of the public address system, which makes hearing in noisy contexts *theoretically* possible.[38] Microphones and loudspeakers had been used in annual Indian National Congress meetings since 1927; however, the infrastructure was expensive and had to be hired from British companies.[39] In 1929, Nainik Motwane's Chicago Telephone and Radio Company, which was based in Bombay, began to invest in microphones and loudspeakers and to lend them to the Congress to be installed, and then dismantled, for major speeches held at Azad Maidan.[40] The presence and the nationalist sentiments of the entrepreneurial owner of Chicago Radio provided easy access to the expensive equipment, so that the regular use of the public address system became a feature of nationalist events in Bombay ahead of elsewhere in India.[41] By the beginning of 1931, Chicago Radio's microphones and loudspeakers were branded with the company name; and the company's nationalist activities included eventually providing radio equipment during the Quit India Movement (1942–45) to enable Congress Radio, an underground radio station operated by a small group of young activists, that for three months secretly transmitted nationalist messaging, in defiance of the ban on all amateur broadcasting in the British Empire during World War II.[42] Each large public gathering required the infrastructure to be set up, and then dismantled after the event. The technology, with wiring strung about connecting the microphone to loudspeakers, was an elaborate affair, clearly evident in the image of Nariman addressing a meeting at Azad Maidan (Fig. 9.15).

It was during the Bombay visit of prominent lawyer and legislator Vithalbhai Patel, the older brother of Congress leader Sardar Vallabhbhai Patel, on 22 May 1930 that nationalist organizers first used the loudspeaker *in a public space*.[43] Patel used the microphone to explain the resolutions of the Congress Working Committee to the enormous assembled crowd at Azad Maidan. He also talked in detail about the police violence against *satyagrahi*s at the Dharasana Salt Works near Dandi on 21 May[44] and of Sarojini Naidu's arrest there as leader of the demonstrators.[45] "Four loudspeakers were installed at the meeting which worked excellently and the huge concourse of people could hear every word of what Mr Patel said," according to *The Bombay Chronicle*, which added that "Mr Patel spoke in Gujrati

[sic] for one hour and twenty minutes."[46] It is almost certainly this event that is captured in Fig. 9.16, with rapt listeners surrounding Patel, who speaks from the dais, silhouetted against the splendid neo-Gothic facade of the Bombay Municipal Corporation building. Figure 9.17 demonstrates a frontal view of the platform, showing an impressive cross-section of the crowd, a sea of white caps, and on the right, a cluster of four horn loudspeakers, projecting the speech in four directions. Most of the crowd are seated, settled in for a long speech, and focus on hearing Patel's words. The stillness of the crowd in this image is almost audible.

This vast, attentive audience provides an extraordinary contrast to the more active audiences described above—those who shout their responses ("We are not cowards!"); those who are visibly distracted; and those who talk among themselves while the speaker is addressing the crowd. Here it is important to note that the Civil Disobedience Movement coincides with new modes of audience formation in Bombay, with people flocking eagerly to cinemas seeking entertainment and information that was efficiently disseminated through new sound technology, as described by Debashree Mukherjee.[47] The heightened anticolonial political sensibilities of this critical period, when talkie technology

Fig. 9.15
"Nariman addressing a meeting on the Esplanade maidan."
c. 1930–1931
Gelatin Silver Print,
115 x 160 mm
ACP: 98.77.0002 (60b)

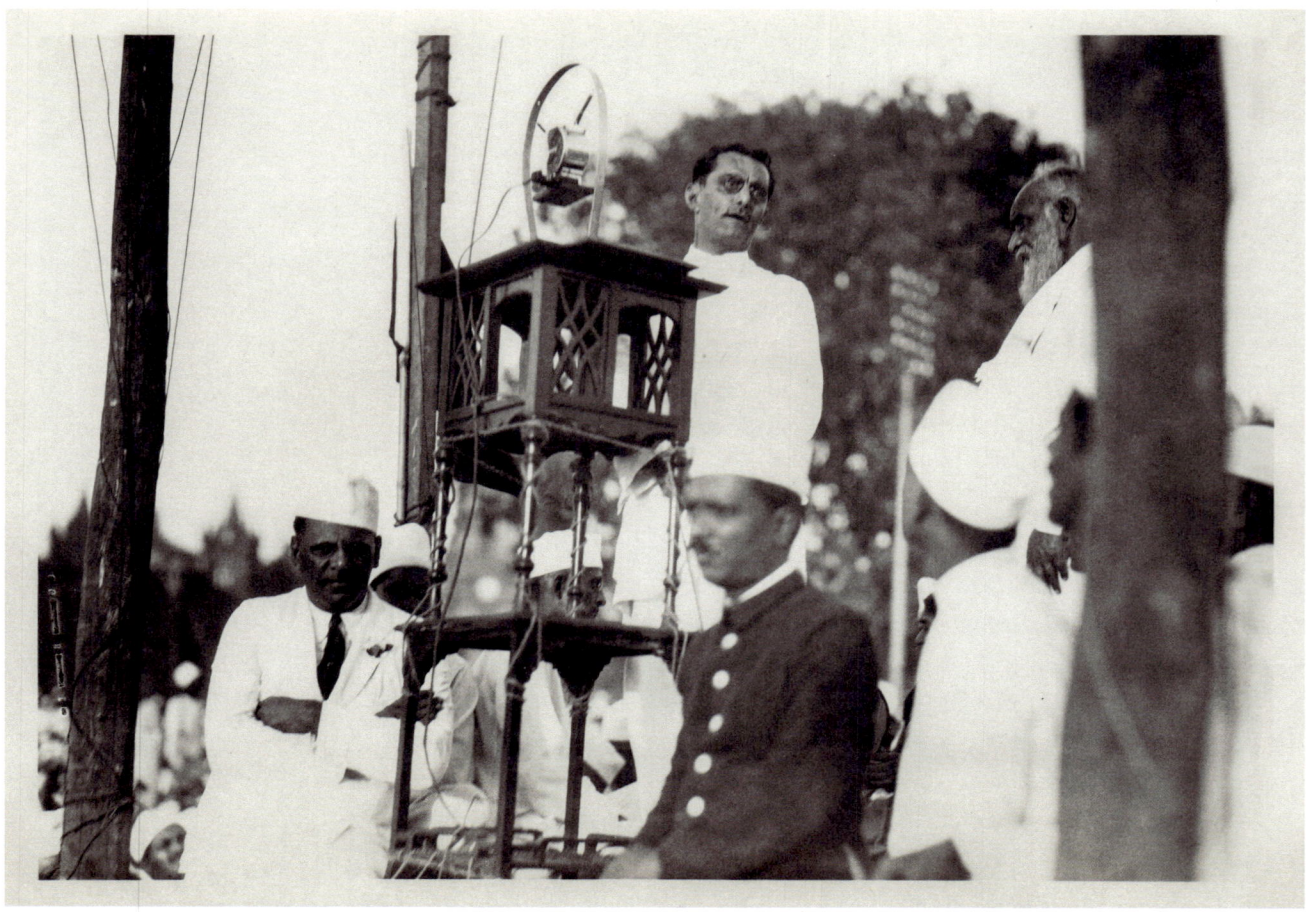

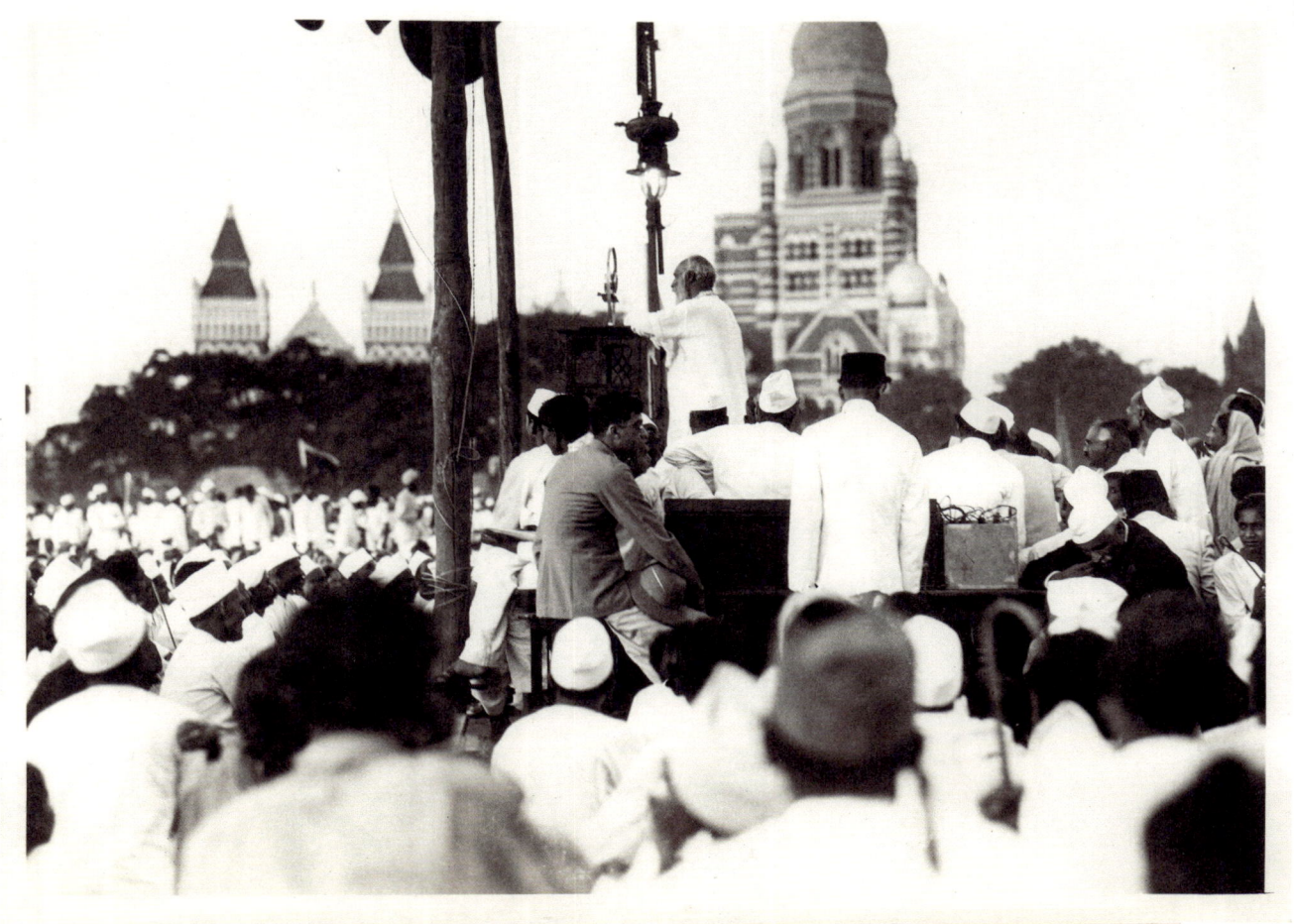

Fig. 9.16
"Mr Vithalbhai
addressing a public
meeting on the
Esplanade maidan."
c. 1930–1931
Gelatin Silver Print,
116 x 157 mm
ACP: 98.77.0002 (38a)

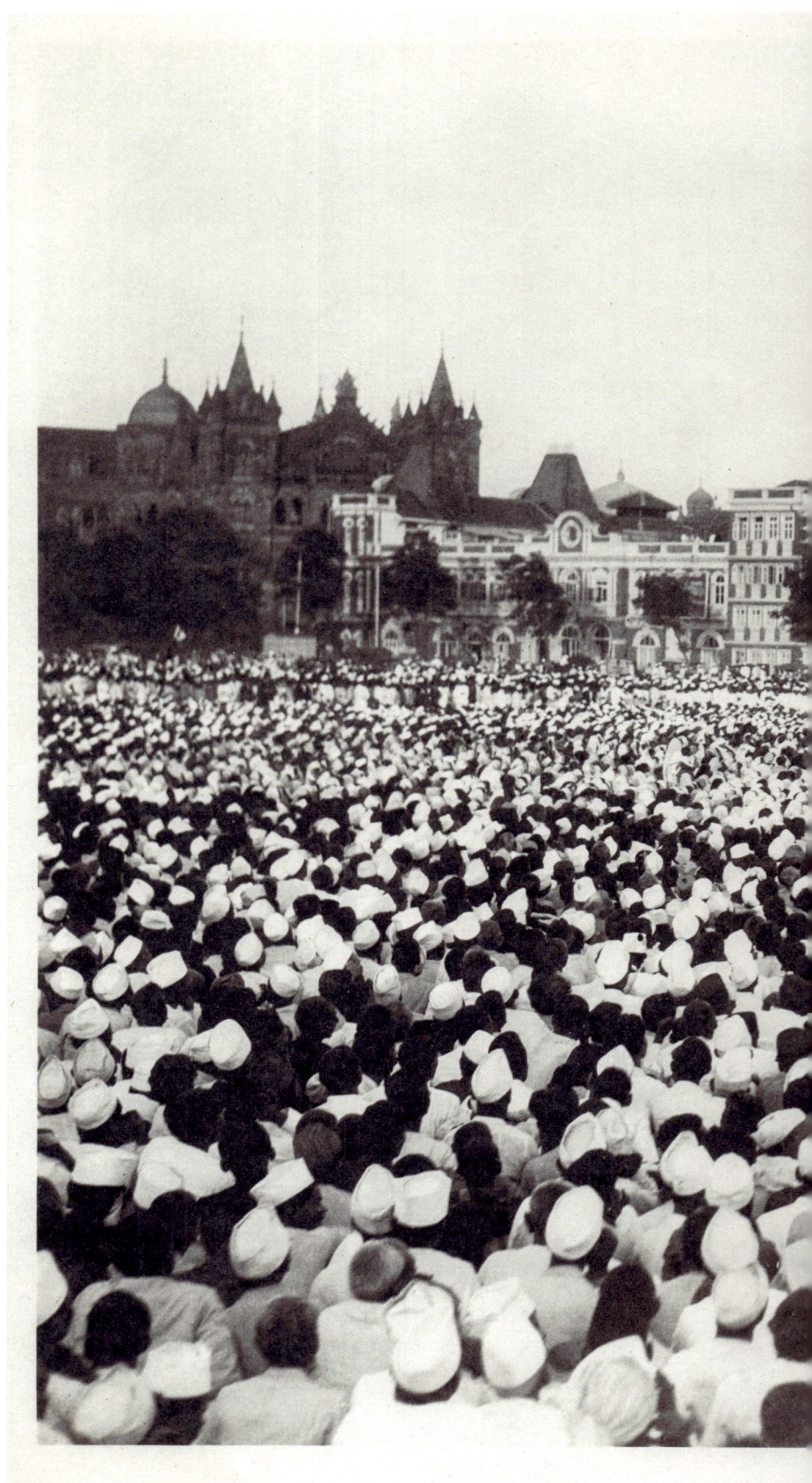

Fig. 9.17
"Thousands had
assembled to hear Mr
Vithalbhai Patel, on
the Esplanade maidan
where he addressed a
hugh [huge] meeting.
His subject was the
importance of the
Congress Working
committee."
c. 1930—1931
Gelatin Silver Print,
116 x 161 mm
ACP: 98.77.0002 (32a)

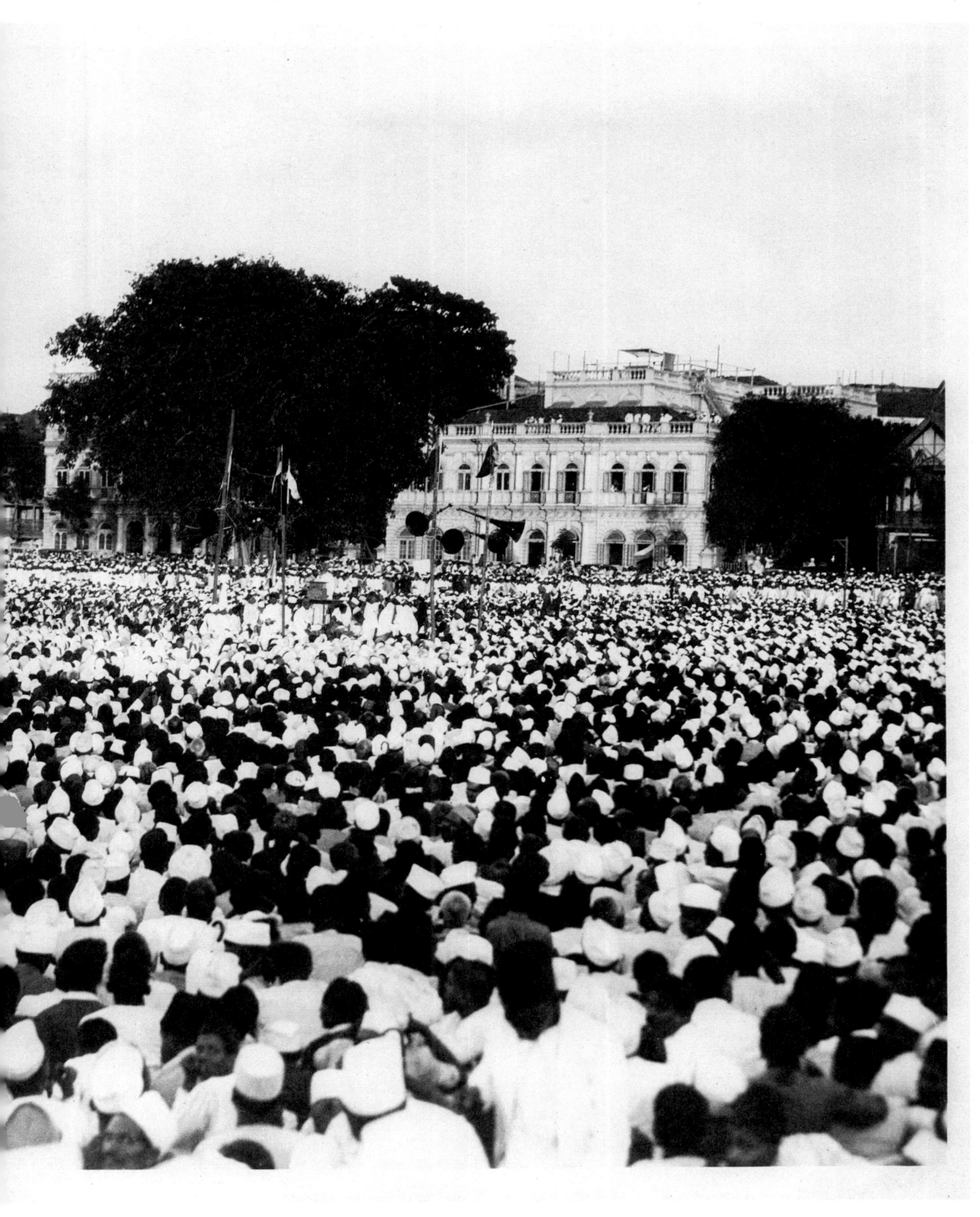

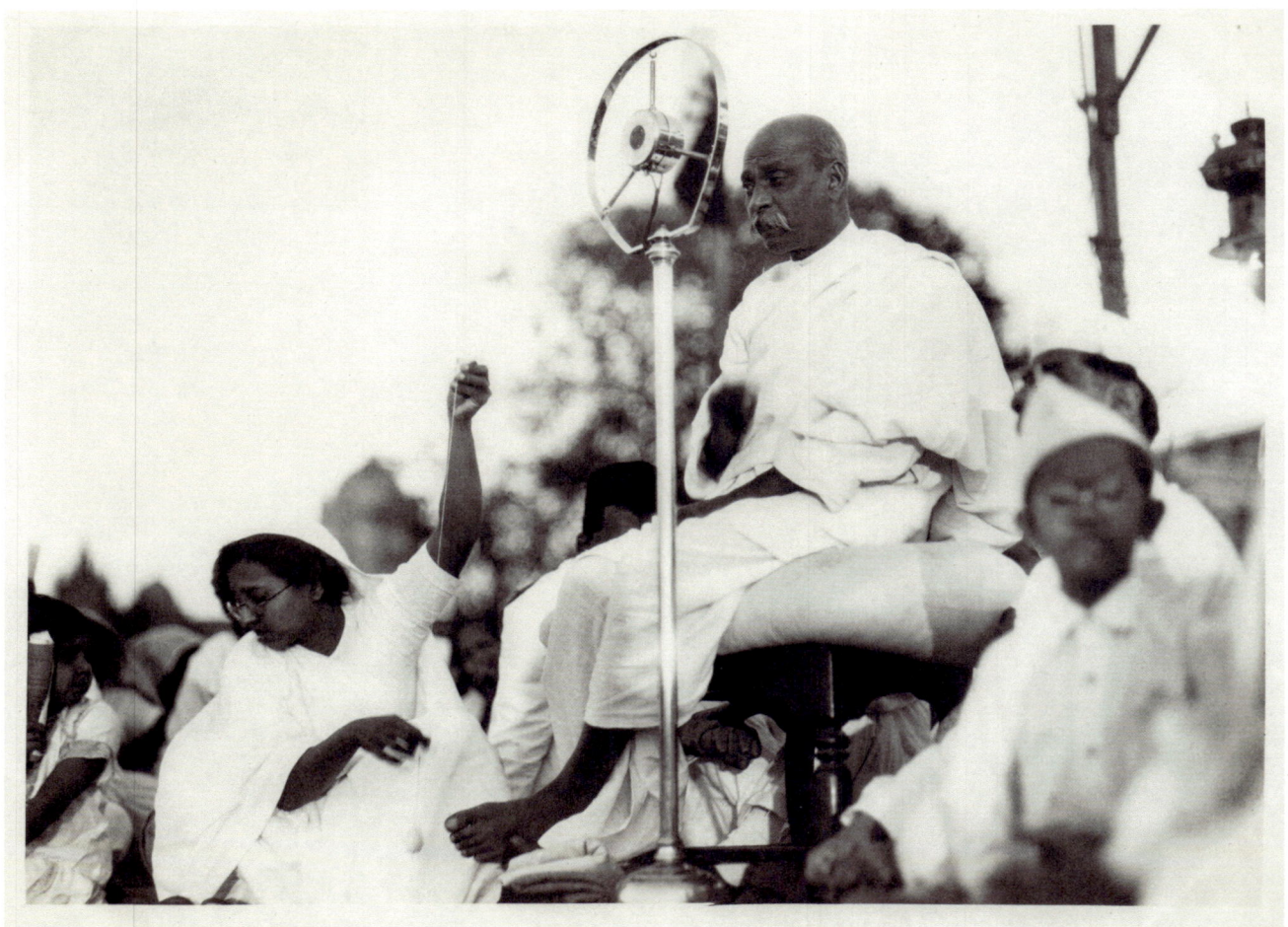

Fig. 9.18
"Mr Vallabhai
[Vallabhbhai] Patel
the President of All
India Congress."
c. 1930—1931
Gelatin Silver Print,
115 x 159 mm
ACP: 98.77.0002 (6b)

began to filter into the film industries, and fired a desire for Indian-made talkie technologies, such as the Chatterjee-Sono-System.[48] Sitting in a movie hall and listening to the soundtrack of a talkie became a new form of collective audiencing, both "active" and "attentive," that is mirrored in crowd responses at large political meetings (see Chapter Three in this volume).

The increasing reliance on the microphone while addressing larger crowds shifted the way leaders *could* speak, shaping their oratorical practices and raising new conditions for the success of speakers' performances. The fixed microphone meant that they were no longer free to move around the dais or to gesticulate freely,[49] as demonstrated by the stiff posture of Vallabhbhai Patel (Fig. 9.18, Fig. 9.19) as well as that of an unidentified speaker before the microphone (Fig. 9.20). Like the occupation of the dais, possession of the microphone increasingly becomes an index of power and leadership, amplifying influential voices. A stunning profile shot of Lilavati Munshi at an Azad Maidan event, speaking into a microphone set far too high for her (Fig. 9.21), indicates, predictably, that despite the active presence of women leaders in the Congress,

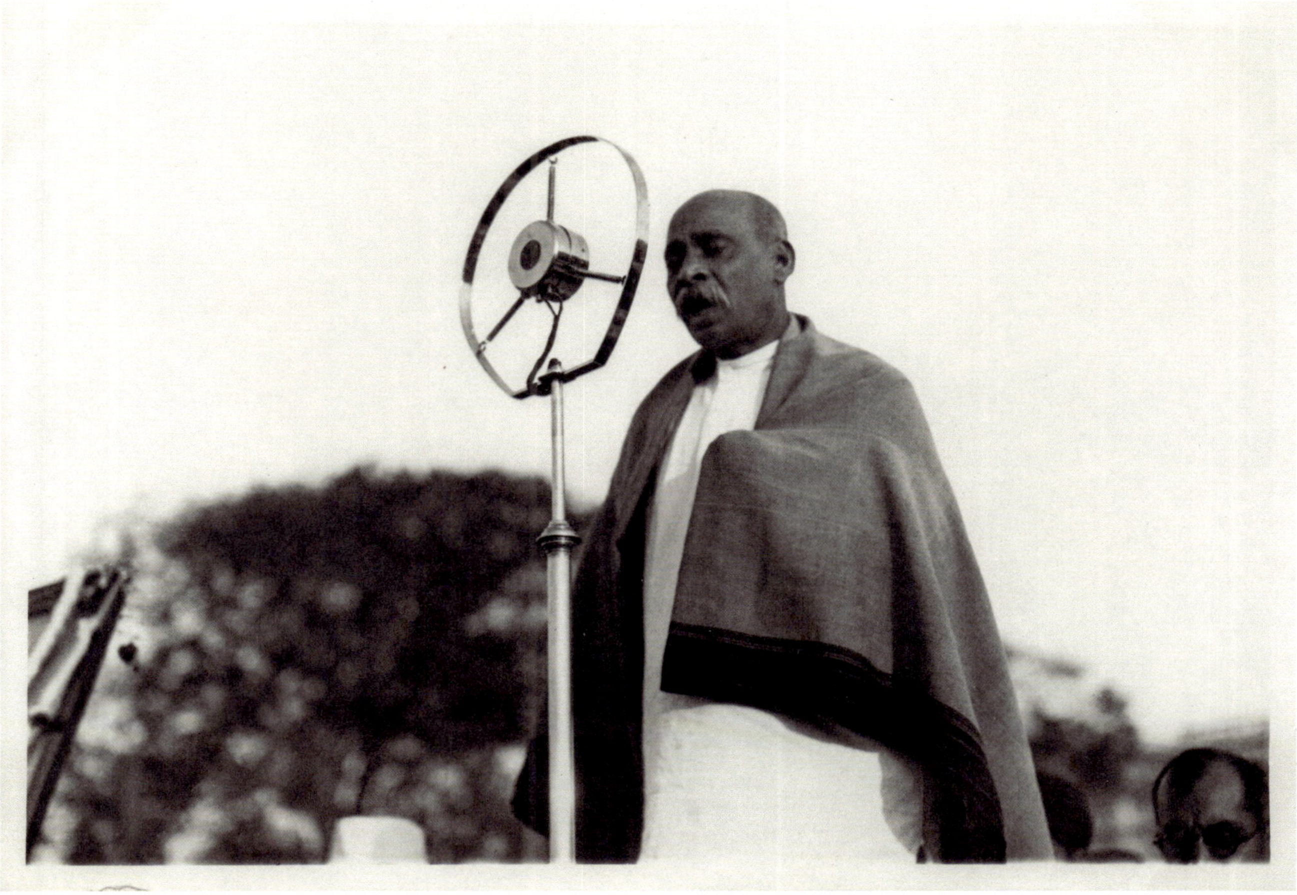

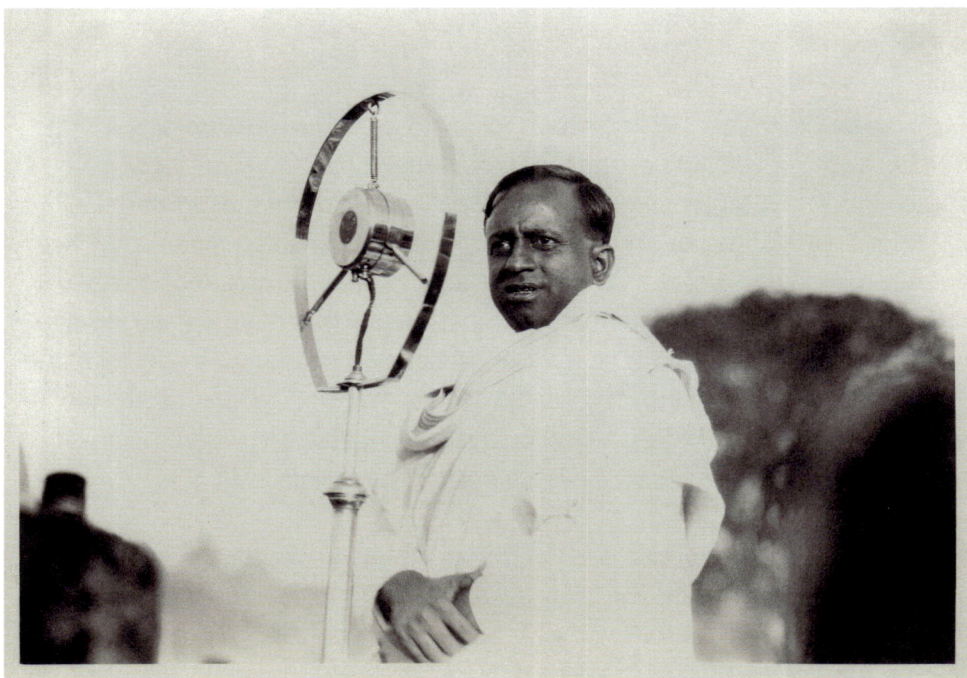

Fig. 9.19
"Sardar Vallabhai
[Vallabhbhai] Patel
the President of all
[All] India Congress
Committee."
c. 1930–1931
Gelatin Silver Print,
114 x 161 mm
ACP: 98.77.0002 (7a)

Fig. 9.20
An uncaptioned
photograph of an
unidentified leader,
speaking into a
microphone,
c. 1930–1931
Gelatin Silver Print,
115 x 160 mm
ACP: 98.77.0002 (8b)

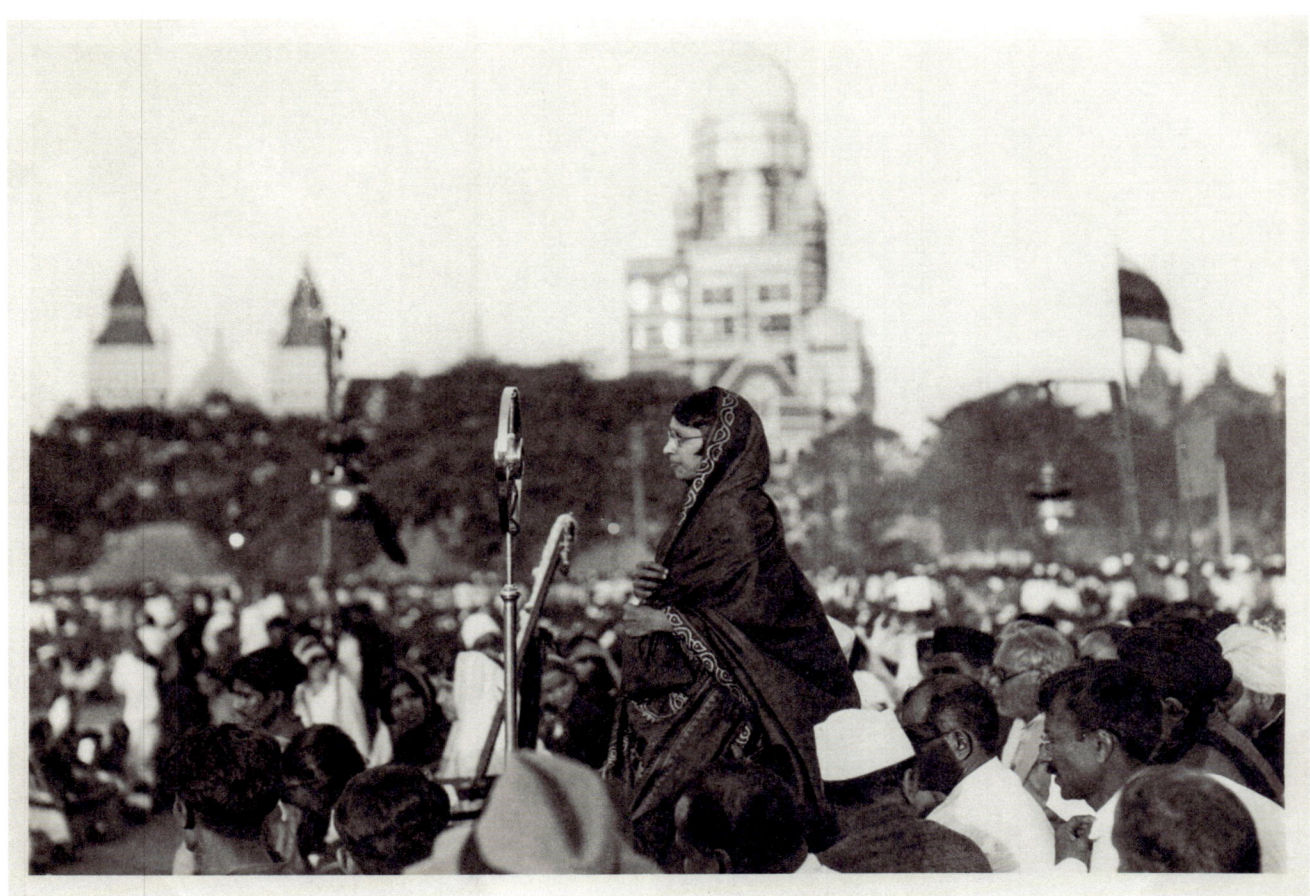

Fig. 9.21
An uncaptioned
photograph of
Lilavati Munshi
addressing a crowd
on the Azad Maidan,
in front of the
BMC building.
c. 1930—1931
Gelatin Silver Print,
114 x 165 mm
ACP: 98.77.0002 (11a)

male speakers continued to dominate nationalist discourse in the public sphere.[50] She is not the only female orator to feature in the Nursery Album, but she is the only woman shown at the microphone.

The new public address systems filled the public space with nationalist sound that frequently extended beyond the immediate vicinity. Unsurprisingly, complaints about "noisy demonstrations" at Azad Maidan were registered in the English-language newspapers.[51] In addition, loudspeakers made speeches audible to assembled crowds *and* to the CID, and soon the presence of the loudspeaker was used in court proceedings to argue that there was no mistake in the allegations of seditious sounds. For instance, a police sub-inspector in the Bombay CID attested to the clarity with which he was able to hear, at a distance, Vallabhbhai Patel addressing a thousand-strong audience in Gujarati inside the Gaya Building, an event for which loudspeakers were installed.[52]

The extraordinary photographs in the Nursey album render simultaneously visible the interdependent aural/oral fields of the Civil Disobedience Movement in Bombay, and provoke the historical imagination to further trace and excavate the sounds of mass protest: the speeches, call-and-response chants, songs, slogans and bugles that gave the call to disobedience, and rent the air, taking up sonic space and making noises that could not be ignored. This unique compilation of "noisy" images offers a fascinating glimpse into the new sound worlds that radically animated anticolonial strategies of dissent and successfully inspired people hoping for systematic change and ready for the challenge of political struggle.

Notes

Acknowledgements: I am indebted to the thoughtful input I received from this volume's contributors/fellow participants in the online Fall 2023 workshop at Duke; and to Sumathi Ramaswamy, Avrati Bhatnagar and Debashree Mukherjee for their critical comments on the first draft of this essay. Thanks are due to Prateek Pankaj for research assistance. Additional thanks to Jim Masselos, Tom Weber, Nikhil Rao and Dinyar Patel for discussions about Gandhi, the Civil Disobedience Movement and Bombay's urban infrastructure.

1. See Prashant Kidambi, "Nationalism and the City in Colonial India: Bombay, c. 1890–1940", *Journal of Urban History*, vol. 38, no. 5 (2012), p. 961; and Jim Masselos, "Audiences, Actors, and Congress Dramas: Crowd Events in Bombay City, 1930", *South Asia: Journal of South Asian Studies*, vol. 8, nos. 1–2 (1985), pp. 71–86.

2. See Robert Rahman Raman, "Civil Disobedience and the City: Congress and the Working Classes in Bombay", in Prashant Kidambi, Manjiri Kamat and Rachel Dwyer (eds.), *Bombay Before Mumbai: Essays in Honour of Jim Masselos* (London: Hurst & Co., 2019), p. 271; and the chapter "Appropriating Urban Space: Social Constructs of Bombay in the Time of the Raj" in Jim Masselos, *The City in Action: Bombay Struggles for Power* (Delhi: Oxford University Press, 2007), p. 285.

3. Kidambi, "Nationalism in the City", p. 959.

4. "Congress Decision to Defy Magistrate's Ban", *The Times of India*, 29 August 1930, p. 3.

5. See Report by J.H. Hutton, *The Census of India*, Vol. 1: India, 1931 (Delhi: Manager of Publication, 1932), p. 324.

6. Kama Maclean, *A Revolutionary History of Interwar India: Violence, Image, Voice and Text* (New York: Oxford University Press, 2015), pp. 20, 52, 57. Also see the author's discussion of this book with host Samee Siddiqui on the New Books Network podcast, 28 May 2021; https://newbooksnetwork.com/a-revo\lutionary-history-of-interwar-india.

7. Mark M. Smith, *A Sensory History Manifesto* (Pennsylvania State University Press, 2021), pp. 22–23.

8. See Isabel Huacuja Alonso, "Radio, Citizenship and 'Sound Standards' of a Newly Independent India", *Public Culture*, vol. 31, no. 1 (2019), pp. 117–44; and Patrick Eisenlohr, "Atmospheric Citizenship: Sonic Movement and Public Religion in Shi'i Mumbai", *Public Culture*, vol. 33, no. 3 (2021), pp. 371–92. Laura Kunreuther points to the surge in critical studies "that explore the affective, sensory, and embodied dimensions of political subjectivity," drawing attention to the political and sonic referents of the Nepali word "awaj," which translates as "noise," "sound" and "voice". Kunreuther writes that *awaj* also denotes "a wide array of phenomena that are not human or discursive at all: natural and mechanical sounds or noises" that can affect us just as much as human vocalization. The polysemic *awaj* and *awaj uthaune* (lit., "to raise voice") combine two registers of articulation: first, vocal sound; and second, sound as a "discursive category related to discussions of power, subjectivity, representation, and agency." See Laura Kunreuther, "Sounds of Democracy: Performance, Protest, and Political Subjectivity", *Cultural Anthropology*, vol. 33, no. 1 (2018), pp. 1–31, at p. 3.

9. Tina Campt, *Listening to Images* (Durham: Duke University Press, 2017). For Kunreuther ("Sounds of Democracy"), the concept of *awaj* ruptures the "ubiquitous discourse of voice used in global human rights organizations, humanitarian discourse, and liberal understandings of the public sphere"– contexts in which disempowered individuals or groups are "presented as voiceless but who might be able to 'gain a voice' through some effort, often with the help of another organization, medium, authority, or knowledge producer." These "global ideas about voice" are indeed relevant to *awaj / awaj uthaune*; however, the concept should rather be read as offering "another global trajectory of voice-one that might provincialize Northern discourses of voice."

10. Campt, *Listening to Images*.

11. Anonymous, "Note by an Observer on the Civil Disobedience Movement in Bombay City", in *India in 1930–31* (New Delhi: Anmol Publications, 1985), p. 661.

12. I am grateful to Murali Ranganathan for sharing with contributors to this volume Fox Movietone's film clip of Bombay on 29 May 1930; https://www.youtube.com/watch?v=gB8sw8OAjuE.

13. *The Times of India*, 11 August 1930, p. 6.

14. *The Times of India*, 14 August 1930, p. 8. See also the chapter "Controlling the Prabhat Pheris", in Masselos, *The City in Action*.

15. "India Tomorrow", 6 April 1930, in *Selected Works of Jawaharlal Nehru*, vol. 4 (Delhi: Orient Longman, 1973), p. 299.

16. Maclean, *A Revolutionary History*, p. 166. As noted in the book's Introduction, "Narratives of the Indian freedom struggle have been predominantly framed as a triumph for the Gandhian ideology of nonviolence [and tend to occlude the significant] political impact of the north Indian revolutionaries-the votaries of violence who coordinated attacks on colonial interests in an attempt to undermine British confidence and expedite decolonisation-on the broader national movement ... Too frequently the revolutionaries' critique of Gandhian nonviolence is presumed to have rhetorically positioned them in perpetual opposition to the Congress as a whole ... While the importance of the revolutionaries has long been cemented in memory and popular culture, an overly rigid violence/nonviolence dichotomy, inferring a strict either/or choice between two opposing strategies to wrest power from the British [who designated the revolutionaries as "terrorists"], has towered over the history of Indian nationalism ... Occasional moments of anticolonial violence are noted, but they are portrayed as deplorable exceptions to nonviolent rule. ... [But] the extraordinary popularity of figures such as Bhagat Singh even during the first wave of civil disobedience in 1930-31 would suggest that support for nonviolence was far from unanimous or unambiguous during those years" (pp. 1, 2, 3). Full text of Introduction uploaded as a preview by the author, available at https://www.researchgate.net/publication/283230424_A_Revolutionary_History_of_Interwar_India_Violence_Image_Voice_and_Text; doi:10.1093/acprof:oso/9780190217150.001.0001

17. "Pt. Jawaharlal Nehru's Call to Youth", *The Bombay Chronicle*, 18 February 1930, p. 1.

18. See the sentiments expressed in a letter from "Nationalist", titled "Appeal to Leaders", *The Bombay Chronicle*, 24 May 1930, p. 4.

19. Navin T. Khandwala interviewed by Uma Shankar, Oral History Interview, 16 May 1971, Transcript 167a, p. 2, Centre for South Asian Studies, Cambridge University.

20. "Police Officer Opens Fire", *The Bombay Chronicle*, 1 September 1930, p. 1.

21. Jim Masselos, "Audiences, Actors, and Congress Dramas: Crowd Events in Bombay City, 1930", *South Asia: Journal of South Asian Studies*, vol. 8, no. 1-2 (1985), pp. 75-95.

22. "Photographers and National Movement", *The Bombay Chronicle*, 24 May 1930, p. 4.

23. A photograph of this "huge public meeting" appeared in *The Bombay Chronicle*, 9 April 1930, p. 12.

24. Masselos, "Audiences, Actors, and Congress Dramas", p. 72.

25. A.R. Venkatachalapathy, "Foreword: Speaking of Barney Bate", in Bernard Bate, *Protestant Textuality and the Tamil Modern: Political Oratory and the Social Imagination in South Asia*, (eds.) E. Annamalai, Francis Cody, Malarvizhi Jayanth and Constantine V. Nakassis (Stanford: Stanford University Press, 2021), xxviii.

26. "Bombay Police Prevent Salt Manufacture", *The Times of India*, 22 April 1930, p. 11.

27. "Salt Making in Bombay", *The Times of India*, 8 April 1930, p. 10.

28. *The Times of India*, 29 March 1930, p. 14.

29. Khandwala interview transcript, p. 1. This aligns with a description of an evening meeting on the Tapti river in Surat on 1 April 1930 (*The Bombay Chronicle*, 1 April 1930, p. 1).

30. Bate, *Protestant Textuality*.

31. "Salt Law Breach in Bombay", *The Times of India*, 14 April 1930, p. 12.

32. See also photographs in *The Bombay Chronicle*, 9 April 1930, p. 7.

33. "Follow Leaders to Jail", ibid., p. 1.

34. ibid.

35. For one such example, see "Swarajya ki Lahar" (The Wave of Self-rule), British Library, PIB 29/51.

36. M.K. Gandhi, Letter to Mulkaraj, enclosure titled "Questions on Education V", 1 July 1928, *Collected Works of Mahatma Gandhi*.

37. *The Bombay Chronicle*, 8 April 1930, p. 1. We can narrow down the date somewhat as the photograph was republished in *The Illustrated Weekly of India*, 20 April 1930, p. 27, with the caption stating that Nariman was arrested shortly after the photograph was taken. Nariman, then the President of the Bombay Provincial Congress Committee, was arrested for leading satyagrahis to break Section 47 of the Salt Act on 7 April 1930.

38. The technology, however, was extremely sensitive and often failed, as I have argued in my essay "Gandhi's Voice: Mass Politics and Public Address in Interwar India", currently under review.

39. ibid.

40. *The Bombay Chronicle*, 20 May 1930.

41. See https://chicago-radio.net/picture-archives/. Motwane's technical expertise was invaluable in the context of the Quit India Movement, where he provided the infrastructure for Congress Radio.

42. See Usha Thakkar, *Congress Radio: Usha Mehta and the Underground Radio Station of 1942* (New Delhi: Penguin, 2021). Helped by young activists Chandrakant Jhaveri, Vithaldas Jhaveri, Nanka Motwane (whose family owned the Chicago Telephone and Radio Company) and amateur radio operator Nariman Printer, Usha Mehta brought Congress Radio into operation; the first broadcast was on 14 August 1942. Mehta, then 22, had long been involved in civil disobedience action-picketing, protests, boycotting British imports, spinning cotton, wearing *khadi*, Gandhi's Salt Satyagraha.

43. As opposed to addressing the public on Congress property, such as Congress

House, or at an annual meeting. *The Bombay Chronicle*, 23 May 1930, p. 7.

44. In his first-hand account of the Dharasana violence, renowned American journalist/war correspondent Webb Miller describes Vithalbhai Patel's mid-morning arrival at the Salt Works on 22 May 1930: "He had been leading the Swaraj movement since Gandhi's arrest [on 6 May], and had just resigned as President of the Indian Legislative Assembly in protest against the British. Scores surrounded him, knelt, and kissed his feet. He was a venerable gentleman of about sixty with white flowing beard and moustache, dressed in the usual undyed, coarse homespun smock. Sitting on the ground under a mango tree, Patel said, 'All hope of reconciling India with the British Empire is lost for ever. I can understand any government's taking people into custody and punishing them for breaches of the law, but I cannot understand how any government that calls itself civilized could deal as savagely and brutally with non-violent, unresisting men as the British have this morning.'" See Webb Miller, *I Found No Peace: Journal of a Foreign Correspondent* (New York: Garden City, 1938), p. 196.

45. The Dharasana *satyagrahi*s, including Gandhi's second son Manilal, welcomed Miller and escorted him to "Mme Naidu", who is vividly delineated: "The famous Indian poetess, stocky, swarthy, strong-featured, bare-legged, dressed in rough, dark homespun robe and sandals, welcomed me. She explained that she was busy martialling her forces for the demonstration against the salt pans and would talk with me more at length later. She was educated in England and spoke English fluently. Mme Naidu called for prayer before the march started and the entire assemblage knelt. She exhorted them, 'Gandhi's body is in gaol but his soul is with you. India's prestige is in your hands. You must not use any violence under any circumstances. You will be beaten but you must not resist; you must not even raise a hand to ward off blows.' Wild, shrill cheers terminated her speech." ibid., p. 192.

46. "Three Stages of Civil Disobedience Campaign", *The Bombay Chronicle*, 23 May 1930, p. 7.

47. Debashree Mukherjee, *Bombay Hustle: Making Movies in a Colonial City* (New York: Columbia University Press, 2020), p. 153.

48. Madhuja Mukherjee, "To Speak or Not to Speak: Publicity, Public Opinion and the Transition to Talkies", in Laura Brueck, Jacob Smith and Neil Verma (eds.), *Indian Sound Cultures, Indian Sound Citizenship* (Ann Arbor: University of Michigan Press, 2020), pp. 282–83.

49. Venkatachalapathy in Bate, *Protestant Textuality*, xxviii.

50. I owe this observation to Meera Ashar, who suggests that the microphone height is calculated on the presumption of a male speaker.

51. "Tuesday Meeting Banned by Police", *The Times of India*, 5 November 1930, p. 9; "Praise of Lawlessness", *The Times of India*, 11 August 1930, p. 6.

52. "Police Inspector's Evidence: Seditious Speeches", *The Times of India*, 18 December 1930.

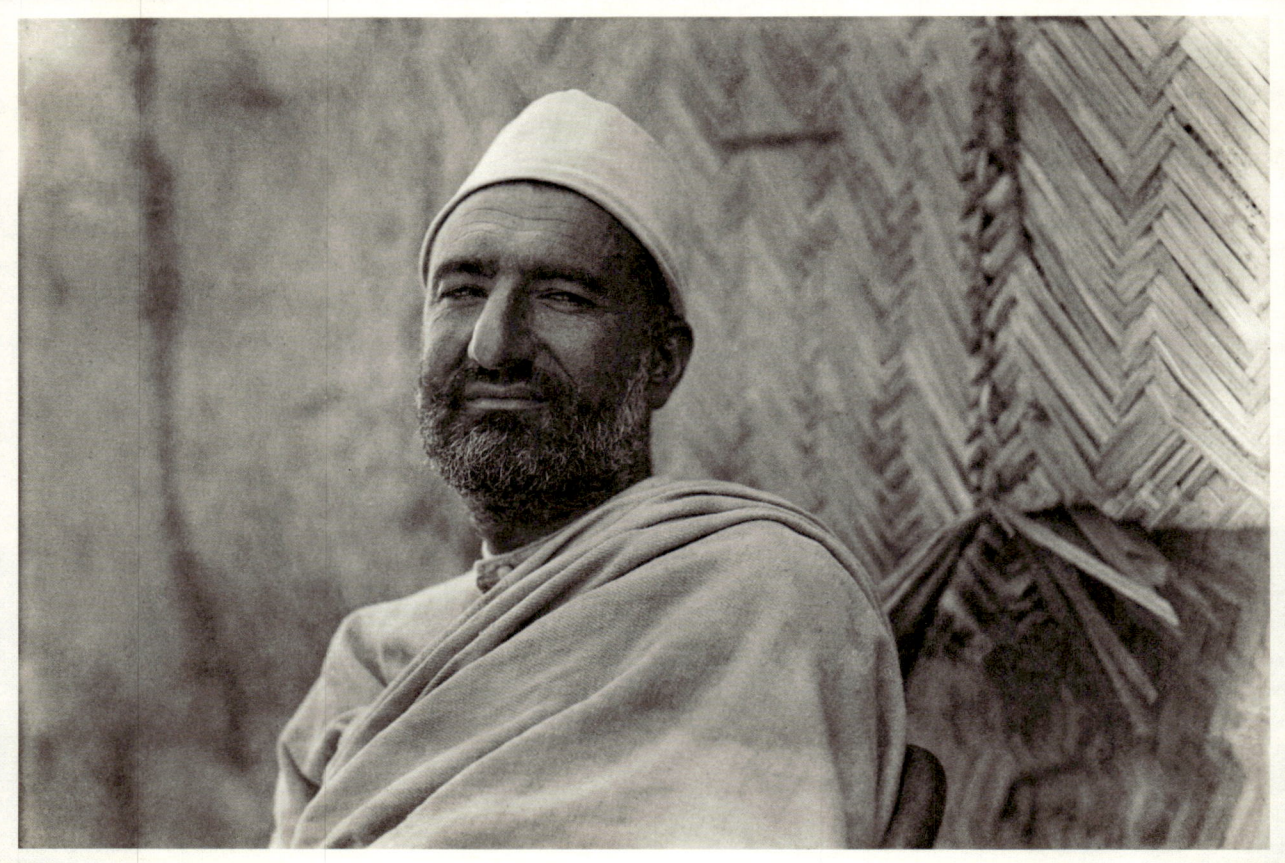

Abdul Ghaffar Khan also known as frontier Gandhi.

"Abdul Ghaffar Khan
also known as frontier
[Frontier] Gandhi."
c. 1930
Gelatin Silver Print,
115 x 165 mm
ACP: 98.77.0002 (1b)

For Further Reading

Ambalal, Anuj, and Rijuta Mehta. *23 Grams of Salt: Retracing Gandhi's March to Dandi*. Ahmedabad: Navajivan, 2020.

Arnold, David. *Police Power and Colonial Rule, Madras, 1859-1947*. Oxford: Oxford University Press, 1986.

Bakshi, S.R. *Gandhi and Salt Satyagraha*. Kaladi: Vishwavidya Publishers, 1981.

Barrie, David G., and Susan Broomhall, eds. *A History of Police and Masculinities, 1700-2010*. Florence: Taylor & Francis Group, 2012.

Blaney, Aileen, and Chinar Shah. *Photography in India: From Archives to Contemporary Practice*. London/New York: Bloomsbury Academic, 2018.

Boehme, Kate. "Princely Urbanism and the Colonial City: Bombay, c. 1860-1940s." *Urban History* 51, no. 1 (December 2022): 1-17.

Brown, Judith. *Gandhi and Civil Disobedience: The Mahatma in Indian Politics*. Cambridge: Cambridge University Press, 1977.

Chandra, Bipan [1966]. *The Rise and Growth of Economic Nationalism in India: Economic Policies of Indian National Leadership, 1880-1905*. New Delhi: People's Publishing House, 2018.

Dharker, Anil. *The Romance of Salt*. New Delhi: Lotus, 2005.

Dwivedi, Sharada, and Rahul Mehrotra. *Bombay: The Cities Within*. Bombay: India Book House, 2001.

Farooqui, Amar. *Opium City: The Making of Early Victorian Bombay*. New Delhi: Three Essays Collective, 2006.

Fernandes, Naresh. *City Adrift: A Short Biography of Bombay*. New Delhi: Aleph Book Company, 2013.

Gaskell, Nathaniel, and Diva Gujral. *Photography in India: A Visual History from the 1850s to the Present*. New York: Prestel, 2018.

Jahanbegloo, Ramin. *Disobedient Indian: Towards a Gandhian Philosophy of Dissent*. New Delhi: Speaking Tiger Books, 2018.

Jain, Jyotindra. *Bombay/Mumbai: Visual Histories of a City*. New Delhi: Centre for Indian Visual Culture, 2013.

Kidambi, Prashant. *The Making of an Indian Metropolis: Colonial Governance and Public Culture in Bombay, 1890-1920*. Hampshire: Ashgate Publishing, 2007.

Kumar, Radha. "Seeing Like a Policeman: Everyday Violence in British India, c. 1900-1950." In *Violence, Colonialism and Empire in the Modern World*, edited by Philip Dwyer and Amanda Nettelbeck. New York: Palgrave Macmillan, 2017.

McGowan, Abigail. "Selling Home: Marketing Home Furnishings in Late Colonial Bombay." In *Bombay Before Mumbai: Essays in Honour of Jim Masselos*, Prashant Kidambi, Manjiri Kamat and Rachel Dwyer, eds.,: 117-45. London: Hurst, 2019.

Moser, Gabrielle. *Projecting Citizenship: Photography and Belonging in the British Empire*. University Park: Penn State University Press, 2019.

Naik, J.V. "Forerunners of Dadabhai Naoroji's Drain Theory." *Economic and Political Weekly* 36, no. 46/47 (November 2001): 4428-32.

Prakash, Gyan. *Mumbai Fables*. Princeton: Princeton University Press, 2010.

Raianu, Mircea. *Tata: The Global Corporation that Built Indian Capitalism*. Cambridge, MA: Harvard University Press, 2021.

Shaikh, Juned. *Outcaste Bombay: City Making and the Politics of the Poor*. Seattle: University of Washington Press, 2021.

Taylor, Miles. "The Ungrudging Indian: The Political Economy of Salt in India, c. 1878-1947." *South Asia: Journal of South Asian Studies* 46, no. 4 (October 2023): 791-805.

Velkar, Aashish. "Swadeshi Capitalism in Colonial Bombay." *The Historical Journal* 64, no. 4 (2021): 1009-34.

Weber, Thomas. *On the Salt March: The Historiography of Gandhi's March to Dandi*. New Delhi: HarperCollins Publishers India, 1997.

Willcock, Sean. "Aesthetic Bodies: Posing on Sites of Violence in India, 1857-1900." *History of Photography* 39, no. 2 (April 2015): 142-59.

INDEX

About the Contributors

Avrati Bhatnagar is an Instructor of History and International Comparative Studies at Duke University. Her current book project, *Disobedient Women in a Consumer City*, presents the gendered history of *swadeshi* and the spread of political consumer culture in early 20th-century India, with special attention on urban market practices and archival images. As an interdisciplinary scholar, Bhatnagar works at the confluence of history and photography studies. Her latest publication, a co-authored article titled "Light Writing on the Lathi Raj: Bombay 1930–31," appears in the *History of Photography* (2021).

Preeti Chopra is Professor of Modern Architecture, Urban History and Visual Studies at the University of Wisconsin-Madison. She specializes in the visual, spatial and cultural landscapes of South Asia and the British Empire. Trained in India and the US as an architect, landscape architect, urban planner and architectural historian, with a research focus on western and southern India, she is the author of *A Joint Enterprise: Indian Elites and the Making of British Bombay* (2011) and is currently working on a second book on colonial Bombay. Chopra has published on a range of subjects, including charity and philanthropy, naming practices, and French colonial urbanism in Pondicherry. A recipient of numerous research grants and fellowships, she was awarded the 2023 Suzanne Deal Booth Rome Prize by the American Academy in Rome.

Kama Maclean holds the Chair of History in the South Asia Institute at the University of Heidelberg, Germany, and is Honorary Visiting Professor in the Department of Humanities and Languages at UNSW, Sydney. She is an interdisciplinary scholar, whose research is informed by historical, visual and cultural studies, as well as religious and performance studies. She is author of *Pilgrimage and Power: The Kumbh Mela in Allahabad* (2008), *A Revolutionary History of Interwar India: Violence, Image, Voice and Text* (2015), and *British India, White Australia: Overseas Indians, Intercolonial Relations and the Empire, 1901–1947* (2020), and many articles in journals and edited collections. She is currently working on a research project, funded by the German Research Council (Deutche Forschungsgemainshcaft, or DFG) on Sonic Aspects of Anticolonialism in Interwar India (Project Number DFG 519791652).

Abigail McGowan is Professor of History at the University of Vermont, USA, where she teaches about South Asia with a particular focus on visual and material culture. Her research focuses on 20th-century India, including her first book on the politics of crafts and craft development (*Crafting the Nation in Colonial India*, 2009), and a new book exploring how changing ideas about home and domestic space shaped the city of Bombay (*Home Improvements*, forthcoming). She co-edited the book, *Towards a History of Consumption in South Asia* (2010) and has published numerous articles on the history of design, domesticity, housing, retail, consumption, and domestic furnishings in India that have appeared in the *Journal of the Society of Architectural Historians, Modern Asian Studies, Journal of Asian Studies, South Asia, Journal of Women's History, and elsewhere*. Guest-editor of a 2022 special issue of *Marg* devoted to writings about Indian textiles, her current research examines the history of mid-century interior design in India through the story of the Bombay firm, Kamdar, Ltd.

Debashree Mukherjee is Associate Professor, Department of Middle Eastern, South Asian, and African Studies (MESAAS), Columbia University, and co-director of the Center for Comparative Media. She is the author of *Bombay Hustle: Making Movies in a Colonial City* (2020), and editor of *Bombay Talkies: An Unseen History of Indian Cinema* (2024).

Her current book project, *Tropical Machines*, develops a media history of South Asian indentured migration and plantation modernity from the 1830s onwards, and has been awarded an ACLS fellowship for 2025–26. Mukherjee edits the peer-reviewed journals *BioScope: South Asian Screen Studies* and *Screen*, and has published in journals such as *Film History, Film Quarterly, Feminist Media Histories, Representations, MUBI Notebook,* and *Modern Asian Studies*.

Dinyar Patel is Associate Professor of History at the S.P. Jain Institute of Management and Research (SPJIMR) in Mumbai. His academic work focuses on the Indian nationalist movement, the city of Bombay/Mumbai, and the Parsi Zoroastrian community. His research has been supported by the National Endowment for the Humanities, the Fulbright Foundation, and the American Institute of Indian Studies. He is the author of *Naoroji: Pioneer of Indian Nationalism* (2020), which was awarded the 2021 Kamaladevi Chattopadhyay New India Foundation Book Prize. He has also co-edited *Dadabhai Naoroji: Selected Private Papers* (2016) and *From Ghalib's Dilli to Lutyens' New Delhi* (2013). Patel has contributed to the *Atlantic, Foreign Affairs, New York Times, Hindu, Indian Express, BBC News* and *Scroll.in*. At the moment, he is working on a book on Indian liberalism and its global connections in the 19th century.

Sumathi Ramaswamy is James B. Duke Distinguished Professor of History at Duke University. She has published on language politics, gender studies, spatial studies and the history of cartography, visual studies and the modern history of art, and more recently, on digital humanities and on the history of philanthropy in modern India. Her most recent works are *Gandhi in the Gallery: The Art of Disobedience* (2020), the digital project *B is for Bapu: Gandhi in the Art of the Child in Modern India* (https://sites.duke.edu/bisforbapu/) and the co-edited volume *Motherland: Pushpamala N.'s Woman and Nation* (2022). She is a contributor to *Another Lens: Photography and the Emergence of Image Culture,* Volume 4 [India Since the 90s series] (2024). Ramaswamy's research has been supported by, among others, the John Simon Guggenheim Foundation, the American Council of Learned Societies, the Alexander von Humboldt Foundation, the National Humanities Center, the US Fulbright Commission and the American Institute of Indian Studies. She is currently working on a project on educational philanthropy in British India.

Murali Ranganathan is an unaffiliated scholar who researches 19th-century South Asia with a special focus on Mumbai and western India, relying largely on non-English resources of this period. His current areas of interest include the history of the book, print history and culture, photography, newspapers and periodicals, public performance and entertainment, and the Bombay Country Trade. Ranganathan has published extensively for academic and general audiences in print and digital media. He edited *The Collected Works of J.V. Naik: Reform and Renaissance in Nineteenth Century Maharashtra* (2016) and J.R.B. Jeejeebhoy's *Bombay Vignettes: Explorations in the History of Bombay* (2018). His other publications include Govind Narayan's *Mumbai: An Urban Biography from 1863* (2008), translated from Marathi, and *The First World War Adventures of Nariman Karkaria* (2022), a memoir in Gujarati that he discovered and translated. His forthcoming publications include *The World of Late Colonial Print,* a history of printing in pre-independence India, and *In Search of the Buddha,* a translation from Hindi of Rahul Sankrityayan's first Tibet travelogue.

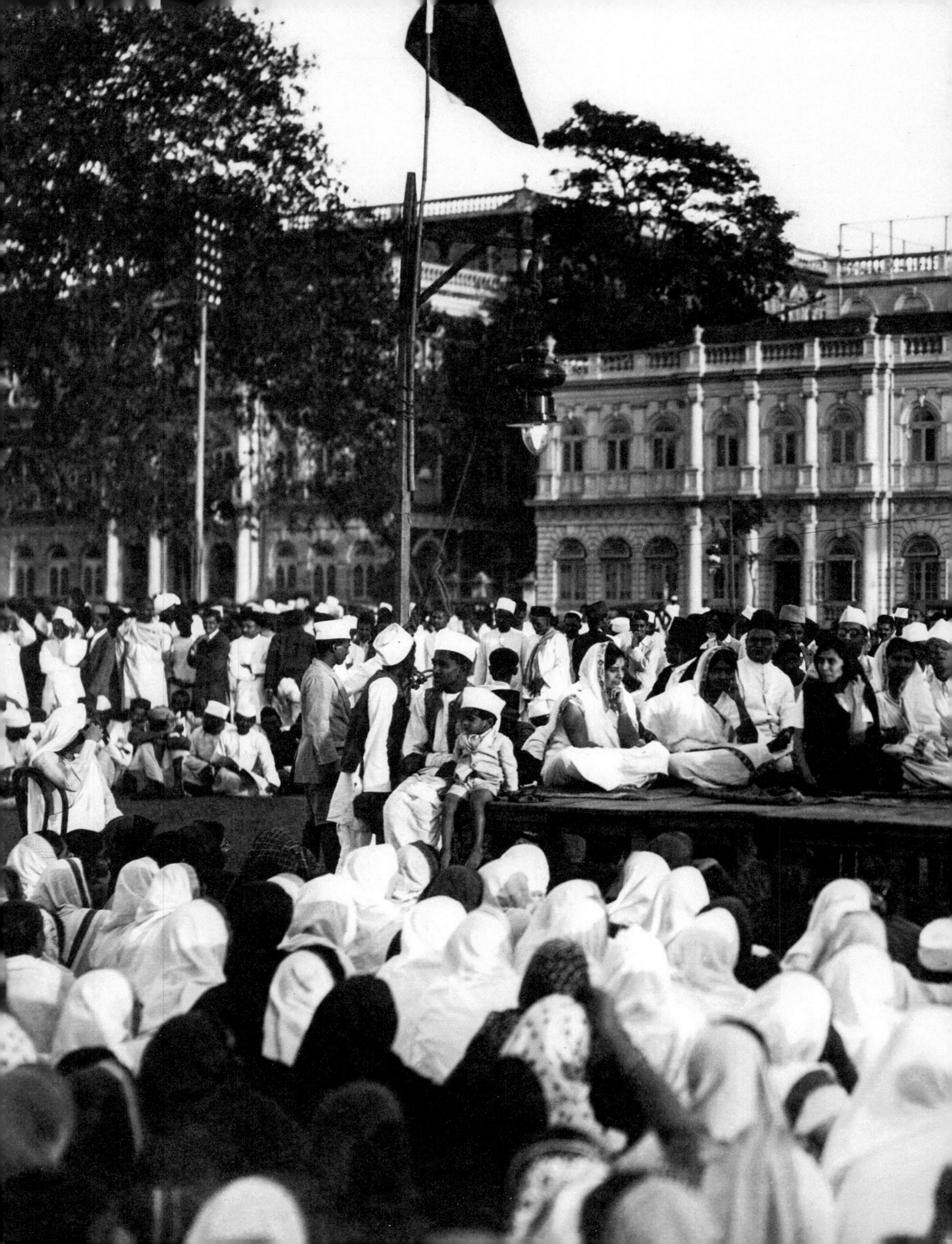